The Treacherous World of Joseph Valachi

The Treacherous World of Joseph Valachi

Thomas Hunt, editor

Informer
November 2024

Informer is published in electronic and print editions, in magazine and book formats. Print magazine (ISSN 1943-7803) and electronic magazine (ISSN 1944-8139) issues are available for preview/purchase through informer.magcloud.com. Print and electronic book formats are available through Amazon.com and Google Play Books.

INFORMER

THE HISTORY OF AMERICAN CRIME AND LAW ENFORCEMENT

November 2024 Issue
Hardcover ISBN 9798340925138,
Paperback ISBN 9798340935007,
Kindle Ebook ASIN B0DJD793GL,
Epub Google GGKEY CF4A036805C.
Publisher / Editor Thomas Hunt
64 N. Main Street, Whiting, VT 05778
informerjournal@gmail.com
860-946-4322

Articles were researched and written by Thomas Hunt, except where noted. Writers granted permission for *Informer* to publish their works in one issue (print and electronic editions) and to use short excerpts in promotional materials. All other rights to original (unedited) works remain with the writers themselves. *Informer* strives to ensure the truthfulness and to document the sources of factual assertions within the works it publishes. Conclusions and expressions of opinion represent the views of the writer only, and *Informer* accepts no responsibility for those views.

CONTENTS

INTRODUCTION

Betrayal

Betrayal ranks among the worst emotional wounds in the human experience. The pain of betrayal probably impacts every person's life to some degree. But in Joseph Valachi's life story, betrayal became a strong and recurring theme.

Valachi must have felt betrayal from the earliest moments of his existence, and he may have been a victim of what has recently become known as "betrayal trauma."[1] (Jennifer Joy Freyd, Ph. D., is credited with developing this concept in the 1990s.)

Valachi's father Dominick - his first role model and the sole provider for a fairly large family - neglected the basic physical and emotional needs and comforts of the household, used limited financial resources to support his own alcohol addiction and was periodically abusive to his wife and their children.[2]

If Valachi was a childhood victim of caregiver betrayal, he could be expected to unconsciously suppress awareness of that betrayal and to remain engaged with the abusive caregiver. Later in life, he could be expected to frequently experience further betrayals, to adopt a distorted view of acceptable family roles, to feel disconnected from his own thoughts and emotions, and to suffer from anxiety, depression, physical ailments and other symptoms.[3]

Valachi had a generally poor relationship with other family members. Of his five siblings – two brothers and three sisters – he recalled getting along only with one sister. His autobiography revealed his deep shame at the poor quality of his boyhood living conditions. His mother, responsible for the housekeeping, reportedly fashioned his bedding by sewing together discarded cement bags (made from layers of brittle paper) and stored collected bits of incompletely burned coal and other collected fuel materials in the room where Valachi slept. The home was perpetually infested with bed bugs. While Valachi made no direct criticism of his mother, he noted that he preferred to sleep in parked wagons in a nearby stable and often was forced to steal in order to feed himself.[4]

When Valachi was a teenager, he went to work beside his father at a city dump. Instead of repairing the relationship between the two, the experience became a new betrayal for Valachi. His father would regularly take his salary in order to pay off bar tabs.[5]

In the mid-1920s, Valachi observed many of his childhood chums making their way into racketeering in association with the Ciro Terranova Mafia organization. He was at that moment unwelcome to join them. When the organization finally reached out to him, it was with the request that he help set up other acquaintances in a rival organization for a gangland attack. Valachi's feelings of abandonment quickly became resentment and rage. He associated himself with the rival group and swore to attack his old pals on sight.[6]

A few years later – despite the fact that the new group sold him out[7] – he followed through on his pledge. The U.S. Mafia divided into warring camps in 1930, and Valachi eagerly joined a rebellion against those early friends and the neighborhood underworld chiefs. He did so though he was aware the odds, based on manpower, wealth, influence, favored the opposition.

Valachi held lifelong grudges against those he felt had turned on him. His own big brother may be included in this category. Late in 1930, Valachi visited his imprisoned-for-life brother Anthony, who went by the name Frank Rocco. He found that his brother irrationally blamed Valachi for his imprisonment. Valachi never visited him again.[8]

He also carried grudges against figures in the Terranova group and a one-time close friend, "Johnny Dee" DeBellis. The offense committed by DeBellis was merely removing himself from a 1931 confrontation between Valachi and his personal neighborhood nemesis, "Crazy Chuck."[9]

Following the surprisingly successful conclusion of the Mafia rebellion, Valachi found that the Mafia's new supreme leader, Salvatore Maranzano, went back on promises of sharing with his loyal followers the vast wealth he suddenly accumulated.[10] Maranzano soon was assassinated, and Valachi moved into another underworld organization, where his immediate superior, Anthony Strollo, consistently undermined Valachi's interests for his own advantage.[11]

During those times when Valachi suffered his greatest betrayals, he acted recklessly and placed himself in great danger. At those moments, he essentially added to his troubles by betraying his own best interests and was saved from destruction merely by good fortune.

In the 1940s, Valachi committed to business and racket partnerships with Frank Luciano, who was widely regarded as unreliable. Following a substantial Valachi investment in a Luciano-run restaurant in the Bronx, Valachi found that Luciano was stealing money from the restaurant to gamble. Though he knew striking another mafioso was a capital offense in the underworld, Valachi delivered a beating. Luciano appeared to acknowledge that he was the wrongdoer in the situation and said they should put the incident behind them, but he secretly brought the offense to higher-ups, and Valachi was tried before a regional Mafia council. Albert Anastasia, showing uncharacteristic patience, took control of the meeting and let Valachi off with a scolding.[12]

When Valachi felt in 1962 that his longtime underworld boss Vito Genovese and fellow mafiosi turned on him within the walls of Atlanta Federal Prison, Valachi did what he knew would make his situation worse: he sought the protection of prison administrators and law enforcement agencies. Then he lashed out at what he assumed was a gang assigned to murder him, knowing that he could not win the confrontation. Wielding a section of pipe, he inflicted a fatal beating on a nearby inmate he identified as a member of the gang. He was then removed from the prison general population. The fact that Valachi was entirely mistaken cost the other inmate his life but managed to save Valachi from an underworld death sentence.[13]

A few years later, new "friends" in the U.S. Department of Justice went back on their promise to Valachi, removing permission for the turncoat mafioso to have his memoirs published. Valachi had hoped that the publication of his autobiography would pay back Genovese and other former underworld associates for turning on him. In addition to the emotional trauma of this betrayal, Valachi was physically banished from comfortable quarters at the District of Columbia Jail to a drafty and cold, prison cell in Milan, Michigan. He responded by attempting to take his own life. Once again, luck was on his side, and he escaped with mere bruises.[14]

Valachi often exhibited his own tendency toward treachery. Though he provided for his wife and their son, he generally was not available to them. His wife, Carmela "Mildred" Reina Valachi, put up with a series of Valachi affairs during their thirty years together.[15]

Underworld informant Vincent Teresa, who was a fellow inmate at La Tuna Federal Prison in Texas during Valachi's final years, recalled that Valachi exhibited a chameleon-like loyalty that varied with his setting:

> He was the type of guy who would knock Genovese when he was with, say, Gambino, and then knock Gambino when he was with Genovese. It was part of his makeup - he couldn't help himself... To the mob, Joe was a *facci due* - two-faced in Italian. No one trusted him in the mob long before he talked.[16]

Joseph Valachi is far better remembered for the final underworld betrayal he committed than for the numerous betrayals he suffered. While certainly not the first mafioso to become a government informant – as is often reported – Valachi was the first member of the Italian-American underworld to go public with his violation of the oath of silence.

Valachi's abandonment of his oath was unequivocal. After decades, in which he had pledged to give his life and had taken many other lives in service to "Cosa Nostra," his treason against the organization was complete. He did not merely break with the organized crime tradition, he sought to eradicate it. Feeling himself abandoned by mob bosses, he decided, "I'm going to destroy them."[17]

His effectiveness as a turncoat was less clear. Few mobsters were convicted of wrongdoing as a direct result of his efforts. Crime bosses and their organization endured through the period of Valachi's celebrity. But Valachi's information forced general acknowledgment of the existence of an interstate and international criminal conspiracy, encouraged additional underworld informants, provided understanding of the membership and methods of the Cosa

Nostra organization and led to its infiltration by law enforcement and its gradual decline.

This issue

The idea of a Valachi-focused *Informer* issue was discussed for some years. The importance of the subject was undeniable.

Valachi is one of just a few primary sources into Castellammarese War-era Mafia history. Valachi's accounts provide a window into early East Harlem gangland history and a soldier-level view of the structure and activities of New York-area crime families between Prohibition and Apalachin. His media celebrity of later years and his inspiration for the U.S. Department of Justice's Witness Protection Program (later "WITSEC") heighten his historical significance.

But we considered whether the quantity and quality of recently discovered Valachi-related data warranted an entire issue. We wondered how much more could reasonably be said of a life story already dealt with in a best-selling biography, a motion picture viewed by millions and many hours of widely broadcast testimony.

Investigation proved that a great deal of the Valachi story remained undocumented by these popular sources, unexamined by many crime historians and unexplained even within an unpublished autobiography that runs more than a thousand pages. Details about his family, his associates, his criminal activities, his career as an informant and his final years were still largely unknown. Other neglected subjects included the impact of Valachi on the FBI, the stresses of bringing the Valachi story to public awareness and the painful process of birthing both *The Valachi Papers* book and *The Valachi Papers* movie.

The timing seemed appropriate for a reexamination of Valachi. This issue goes to press sixty years after Valachi put pen to paper (eventually consuming a vast supply of ink and paper) to record his life story.

Assembling a team of crime historians in areas around the globe – the United States, the United Kingdom, France and New Zealand – *Informer* set to the job of building on Valachi's work, researching and revealing the lesser known aspects of his life and of the lives that touched his.

Often, as we toiled on the enormous project, we drew inspiration from the thought of that Mafia survivor / Mafia traitor who labored in solitude six decades ago in a desperate attempt to communicate his story.

The *Informer* issue now before you is the result of our efforts. While Valachi is surely well known to you, we're certain that you will find a great deal that is new and fascinating in these pages.

Joseph Valachi

Introduction Notes

1 Jennifer Joy Freyd, Ph.D., is credited with developing this concept in the 1990s.

2 Valachi, Joseph, *The Real Thing - Second Government: The Expose and Inside Doings of Cosa Nostra*, unpublished manuscript, Joseph Valachi Personal Papers, John F. Kennedy Presidential Library and Museum, 1964, p. 1; Maas, Peter, *The Valachi Papers*, New York: G.P. Putnam's Sons, 1968, p. 62.

3 Freyd, J.J., "What is a betrayal trauma? What is betrayal trauma theory?" Freyd Dynamics Lab, dynamic.uoregon.edu, 2020; Lovering, Nancy, "What is betrayal trauma, and where can a person seek help?" *Medical News Today*, medicalnewstoday.com, 2023; Gillespie, Claire, "What is betrayal trauma? Definition and recovery," *Health*, health.com, Oct. 9, 2023.

4 Valachi, *The Real Thing*, p. 6f3-6g, 8, 10; Maas, *The Valachi Papers*, p. 63.

5 Valachi, *The Real Thing*, p. 8.

6 Maas, *The Valachi Papers*, p. 72-73

7 Valachi, *The Real Thing*, p. 141.

8 Valachi, *The Real Thing*, p. 296.

9 Valachi, *The Real Thing*, p. 344.

10 Valachi, *The Real Thing*, p. 355, 361.

11 Valachi, *The Real Thing*, p. 338, 416, 446, 460, 463.

12 Valachi, *The Real Thing*, p. 655-660, 665-666.

13 Testimony of Joseph Valachi, *Organized Crime and Illicit Traffic in Narcotics, Part 1*, Hearings before the Permanent Subcommittee on Investigations of the Committee on Government Operations (McClellan Committee), U.S. Senate, 88th Congress, 1st Session, Washington D.C.: U.S. Government Printing Office, 1968, p. 94-104.

14 Hayes, Loy S., "Memo of phone call from Warden Sartwell, Milan," Federal Bureau of Prisons, April 11, 1966, in Carr, Charlie, *New York Police Files on the Mafia*, Hosehead Productions, 2012, p. 570; Maas, *The Valachi Papers*, p. 53-55; Maas v. United States, U.S. Court of Appeals, District of Columbia Circuit, 371 F.2d 348 (D.C. Cir. 1966), decided Nov. 25, 1966.

15 "Valachi's wife loved him not," *Hackensack NJ Northern Valley Record*, Oct. 10, 1963, p. 8; "I never loved him, castoff wife says," *Binghamton NY Press*, Oct. 10, 1963, p. 8.

16 Teresa, Vincent, with Thomas Renner, *My Life in the Mafia*, Garden City NY: Doubleday & Company, 1973, p. 320/

17 Maas, Peter, "Mafia: The inside story," *Saturday Evening Post*, Aug. 10-17, 1963, p. 19.

Growing up Valachi

East Harlem boy becomes Mafia soldier

As the newborn "Giuseppe Vilacio" took his first breath in autumn 1903, his East Harlem community was home to an already substantial and still growing population of first- and second-generation Italian Americans.

While the largest ethnic groups in that region, bounded by Ninety-sixth Street, Fifth Avenue and the Harlem and East rivers, still were Irish- and German-Americans, in this first decade of the 1900s members of those groups were leaving East Harlem's dilapidated tenements as quickly as Italian new-comers were arriving.[1]

The Harlem region more generally experienced an influx of African Americans in the period. Harlem's designated "negro quarter" began in a northwest neighborhood centered on the blocks from West 133rd Street to West 135th Street, between Lenox Avenue (Malcolm X Boulevard today) and Seventh Avenue (Adam Clayton Powell Jr. Boulevard), and very quickly expanded to 140th Street and then outward, despite determined racist opposition.[2] Growth of the community was later fueled by the start of "The Great Migration" of southern-born African Americans into northern and western regions and by a World War I economy that drew additional black southerners into industrial cities of the North. Though the black and white populations lived in fairly close proximity, the communities were largely segregated from each other.[3]

At the time the future "Joseph Valachi" was born in October 1903, Theodore Roosevelt was U.S. President. The first Roosevelt-inspired "teddy bear" toys were being sold. The administration, after failing to negotiate a lease with Colombia for a planned Panama Canal, began backing Panamanian independence from Colombia.[4]

Benjamin B. Odell, former ice business and utility company executive from Newburgh, served as governor of the Empire State. Seth Low, who previously held leadership positions at Columbia University and in the City of Brooklyn, was Gotham's chief executive, just the second mayor since New York City had been enlarged five years earlier through the consolidation of Manhattan and the Bronx with Brooklyn, Queens and Richmond (Staten Island).[5]

The Williamsburg Bridge was nearing completion and would by year's end join Manhattan's Delancey Street with the Williamsburg section of Brooklyn. "Horseless carriages" were not yet a common sight on city streets. The newly formed Ford Motor Company took its very first order for a Model A during the summer of 1903. Its first automobile priced for the masses – the Model T – was five years in the future. The opening of the New York City subway system was still a year away. Orville and Wilbur Wright would achieve powered flight for the first time near the end of 1903.[6]

City residents flocked to Coney Island for their warm-weather recreation and found in 1903 a glitzy, new amusement facility, Luna Park. Theater-goers watched veteran performers The Four Cohans conclude a successful group career with the musical "Running for Office" at Manhattan's Fourteen Street Theater just west of Sixth Avenue. In Manhattan's Washington Heights section, New York's Highlanders, later known as Yankees, completed their first season of professional baseball. That fall, baseball fans followed newspaper reports of action in the first ever World Series between the Pittsburgh Pirates and the Boston Americans, champions of the recently united National and American leagues.[7]

Youth

Domenico "Dominick" and Maria Michaela Casale Villacci (their surname was written a variety of ways before son Joseph settled on the non-Italian spelling of "Valachi"), both reportedly from near Naples in southern Italy, settled in East Harlem late in the 1890s. They had a difficult life. They resided at 325 East 109th Street in June 1900, when Dominick reported for the census that he was a fresco painter who had been out of work for the past five months. According to the census, the couple had been married for four years. Maria Michaela had given birth to three children, but none had survived.[8]

Within ten weeks of the recording of the census information, the Villaccis moved to 337 East 109th Street. On August 23, a son was born. They gave him the name Antonio.[9] Before October 3, 1903, the family moved again, to 239 East 111th Street. That was the moment of their second son's arrival. His name was recorded in birth records as "Giuseppe Vilacio," but he is known to history as Joseph Valachi. For some reason, Valachi came to believe his birth occurred eleven days earlier, and he regularly stated September 22, 1903, was his date of birth.[10]

East Harlem at the time was transforming into a Little Italy community. Pockets of Italian-speaking residents were growing around Second Avenue between 102nd Street and 116th Street. Some of these identified for a time with specific regions of southern Italy and Sicily. One historian has noted an early settlement of immigrants from Bari on East 112th Street, a Neapolitan neighborhood on East 107th Street near the East River, a Calabrian conclave along East 109th Street and a Little Sicily neighborhood on East 100th Street between First and Second avenues. The same region was home to diminishing numbers of Irish and German residents and a community of Eastern European Jews.[11]

The Villaccis resided at 320-322 East 108th Street in 1910. The family had grown to include daughter Filomena, and before the year was out another daughter Madeline arrived. Dominick, no longer waiting for fresco painting opportunities, was working as a street vegetable peddler. The family also took in a boarder in an effort to pay the bills. Young Joseph Valachi by then was already a habitual truant from Public School 83 on East 109th and East 110th streets between Second and Third avenues.[12]

The family existed in squalor. Valachi spent some of his nights sleeping in the back of wagons parked within the infamous Murder Stable nearby, rather than deal with the bed bugs in the makeshift mattresses at home. About 1912, responding to a late night argument between his parents over living expenses, eight-year-old Joseph and his older brother went out and burglarized an East Harlem store. They got away with a quantity of soap bars, which they sold around the neighborhood to raise money for the family bills.[13]

Valachi subsequently became known for collecting discarded items and selling them from carts he assembled himself. The activity gave him his nickname, "Joe Cargo."[14]

Another son, John, was born to Dominick and Maria on May 16, 1914. Within months of John's arrival, Joseph Valachi got into serious trouble at school. He threw a rock at a teacher, supposedly intending just to scare her, and struck her in the eye. For that offense, the eleven-year-old Valachi was sent to the New York Catholic Protectory.[15]

New York Catholic Protectory

The New York Catholic Protectory began in Manhattan in April 1863 as a project of the Society for the Protection of Destitute Roman Catholic Children. It originally took in Catholic children, from age seven to fourteen, who were entrusted to it by parents or guardians, as well as "truant, vicious or homeless" children sent there by city magistrates.

A boys department, occupying a building on Eighty-sixth Street near Fifth Avenue, was run by the Brothers of the Christian Schools. The Sisters of Charity were in charge of a girls department on Eighty-sixth Street and Second Avenue.[85]

Within just a couple of years, the program had outgrown its Manhattan facilities. The former Varian Farm near the Village of West Chester, today the Bronx, was purchased for $40,000 in 1865. The 114-acre property was bounded by East Tremont Avenue, Castle Hill Avenue, Westchester Avenue and White Plains Road. A cornerstone for the new New York Catholic Protectory facility was laid in a ceremony on Sunday, July 23, 1865.[86]

The Protectory expanded its enrollment to include children as young as two and a half years and as old as sixteen. The curriculum was a unique combination of academic, spiritual and practical subjects. "...In addition to providing religious training in the faith and a thorough grounding in elementary or common school subjects, practical training in mechanical or industrial areas was also emphasized." Industrial classes were offered in various fields, like printing, tailoring, carpentry, electrical and farming. The facility also had athletic competitions and music programs.

Over time, the Protectory property grew to 129 acres. It continued its operations in the Bronx through the 1930s. The site was sold in spring 1938 to Metropolitan Life Insurance Company for just over $4 million.

Protectory functions were phased out, and Metropolitan Life soon began construction of the Parkchester housing complex at the site.[87]

In his memoirs, Valachi recalled spending about two years at the Protectory before he was released. Truancy almost immediately caused him to be returned there for another stay. While he did not achieve much in the way of formal learning at the institution, his Protectory years gave him an appreciation of religion and of sports, and they also persuaded him of the practical advantages of gang membership and of blending in with humanity's lowest common denominator.[16]

Following his second release from the Protectory around 1917, Valachi was re-enrolled in Public School 83 but still had no interest in learning. His father was then doing "scow trimming" at a city garbage dump on the East River and had Valachi help out there after school hours. The scow trimmers picked through gathered municipal trash to extract items of value and reduce the volume of the garbage before it was brought out to sea.

"We, the workmen, will sort out rags, bottles, brass, bones, paper or anything that can be used," Valachi said of the filthy work. "You can imagine how the dust and ashes got in our lungs."

Soon, Valachi was assigned to carry the bushels of sorted garbage over a wobbly plank between the dock and the garbage scow. When he turned fifteen, he obtained his working papers and left school for good. His days at the dumps began at five o'clock in the morning. For a brief time, he piloted scows for the O'Brien Brothers, holders of a city contract. "I was a captain on a scow," he remembered. "I told them I was twenty one."[17]

Valachi worked his difficult job for about a year. He found it an entirely unrewarding experience. The small pay he received for his labor was generally taken by his father to pay off a bar tab.[18]

Embarrassment over his continued poverty and lack of prospects was at least partly responsible for young Valachi avoiding any meaningful relationships with women. "I was ashamed," he later wrote.[19] Though he ruled out relationships, he was a regular visitor to houses of prostitution: "If I wanted to play, I knew where to go without getting married."[20]

Minute Men

To boost his income, he began running around with a smash-and-grab burglary gang that gathered at Harlem's East 107th Street. Burglaries were committed by throwing a milk can or other large, heavy object through a store window and taking whatever valuables were within reach before the police could respond.

With experience, the gang learned that stores equipped with popular Holmes burglar alarms could be easy targets. Using electricity and telephone lines, break-ins at Holmes-protected locations were communicated to a central office, which dispatched the police. According to Valachi, it took police at least five minutes to reach the scene of the break-in at a Holmes-protected establishment. "It took us only a minute to rob a store."[21]

The gang used automobiles to make speedy getaways, and Valachi became the trusted driver. He honed his skills through practice, research and some mechanical modifications.[22]

After regularly escaping pursuits, Valachi's gang became known to the police. Valachi recalled, "They started to call us Minute Men."[23]

Valachi's brother Anthony and, later, his brother John involved themselves in similar criminal activity. However, the brothers largely avoided working together.

Teenage Joseph Valachi lived through some momentous historical events, but he seemed not to notice most of them. He certainly took notice of U.S. participation in Europe's Great War. He was just fifteen when he and some friends attempted to join the Army. Their lies about their ages were discovered when they were identified by a city truant officer, who knew the boys well. Valachi saw the Army as a possible route of escape from his East Harlem existence: "Maybe if they had accepted me, things might have been different." The war was long over by the time he reached adulthood.[24]

Valachi was in his seventeenth year when the 1920s arrived along with great social change. The Prohibition Era formally began on January 17, 1920. A constitutional amendment guaranteeing women the right to vote was ratified in August 1920.[25]

At almost the same moment, the "New Negro" movement began to take hold in American cities. The African-American community in Harlem and elsewhere began to embrace and promote its unique culture, while it demanded an end to segregation and to racial inequality in social, political and economic spheres.

Government resorted to extreme measures to combat radical political thought – anarchism, socialism, communism – which had been growing in popularity around the world and had gained adherents in U.S., particularly in immigrant communities Beginning in January 1920, agents of the federal Department of Justice began their constitutionally questionable "Palmer Raids" – wholesale arrests and deportations of suspected radicals.[26]

None of these were a distraction for Valachi, who continued to trudge his way through life as a barely literate burglar.

By 1921, Valachi had been picked up for suspicion of burglary a number of times and released for lack of evidence. On November 10, 1921, as Valachi and four accomplices prepared to rob a fur store in Jersey City, New Jersey, their car got a flat tire. While they worked to repair the flat, police happened along. One of the would-be burglars had a handgun and did not want to be caught with it. As police approached, he dropped it to the ground and kicked it away. The police saw the weapon and arrested the whole group.

For this arrest, Valachi gave authorities a false name, borrowing the identification of an uncle, "Anthony Sorge." Valachi called that uncle to bail him out. The uncle did so but made it clear, "this will be the first and the last time."[27]

Valachi recalled that the matter came to trial after about a year and resulted in a hung jury. Records indicate that he was put on probation and fined $100 in October 1922 for possession of a concealed weapon.[28]

Anthony Valachi

Antonio Villacci was born August 23, 1900, to Italian immigrants Domenico and Maria Villacci of 337 East 109th Street. His career as a burglar apparently began sometime before age eleven, when he introduced his eight-year-old brother Joseph to the criminal activity.[88]

The elder Valachi brother was serving time at a correctional facility on Hart Island in Long Island Sound on September 12, 1918, when he filed his Great War draft registration. He gave the name "Tony Peter

Valachi" and stated his home address was then 320 East 108th Street. The eighteen-year-old was described vaguely as medium height, medium build, with brown eyes and black hair.[89]

Early in 1920, Anthony Valachi was sentenced by Judge Charles Cooper Nott Jr. to a year and a half in prison for third degree attempted burglary. He entered Sing Sing Prison on January 19 but was transferred to other state prisons. He was paroled from Great Meadow Prison in Comstock, New York, on January 17, 1921.[90]

Just four months later, he was again convicted of third degree burglary. The sentence from Judge Alfred J. Talley was three and a half years. He was received at Sing Sing Prison on May 26. He apparently served at least some of his term at Auburn State Prison. An Auburn document suggests he also had half a year of his earlier parole-ended term to serve. As he entered the facility, he was given a precise description. He was five feet, five and a half inches in height and weighed 142 pounds.[91]

Following his May 1924 release, Tony Valachi adopted a new name, Frank Rocco. The reason he selected this name is unknown. But the different moniker did little to change his behavior patterns or their outcomes.

On December 24, 1924, he was brought again before Judge Nott on a burglary charge. He was convicted and sentenced to two and a half years. He again passed through the gates of Sing Sing on December 30, 1924. At the prison, he stated that he had been working as a chauffeur and had a home address of 2104 Second Avenue. The name "Frank Rocco" appeared on his prison record. It also appeared in the New York State Census for the Ossining, New York, facility in 1925.[92]

The conduct of "Frank Rocco" was not the best during this prison term. Before he was released, from Great Meadow Prison in April 1927, a report by prison officials noted his various punishments while incarcerated. "This man has caused considerable trouble right along," the report said. It stated that he regularly shirked his work, stalled, loitered and insisted on seeing the doctor. On several occasions, he was observed entering the cell blocks or other buildings when he should have been in the prison yard.[93]

Frank Rocco was arrested and held at Bronx County Jail in May 1928. As a fourth-time offender, punishable by a life prison sentence, he was not eligible for bail and remained in the lockup for months before his case came to trial. His brother Joseph Valachi insisted that this arrest was for a robbery Rocco could not have committed. Valachi said

Rocco came out to visit him at Sing Sing Prison on the same day the crime was committed thirty miles away in New York City. When brought to trial, a Sing Sing Prison guard revealed the visitor records and saved Rocco his fourth adult conviction.[94]

In 1928, the Valachi brothers attempted a burglary together, bringing a reluctant Nick Paduano along. They entered the cellar of a New Jersey store and cut a hole into the floor of the store at a spot chosen by Rocco. When the hole was punched through, Valachi took a look and found that it came up in the center of the store in line with the front door. Feeling that any activities inside the store would surely be seen from outside, Valachi urged his brother to call off the job. Rocco still wanted to go ahead and did not relent until Valachi offered him $150. "I knew now why he always got caught red-handed in stores," Valachi later wrote.[95]

Rocco tried to work with Valachi on a job in February 1929, but Valachi saw the store and decided it was a "death trap." He refused to do it and advised his brother to stay away from it. He later learned that Rocco went ahead with some other pals and were caught trying to rob the store.

Knowing that a fourth conviction would mean a life sentence, Valachi sent word to Rocco to do what he could to postpone a hearing on the charges. Rocco answered that he knew what he was doing and insisted on a hearing. After an arraignment, Rocco was transferred to the Tombs prison in lower Manhattan. Valachi visited his brother there.

> He said that he thought that he had them beat. Now he tells me that the D.A. wants to give him a plea to petty larceny, which meant that he would get three years in the pen, but he refused and he went to trial. I got a lawyer for him and fought his appeal, which he lost, and he ended up by receiving life.[96]

Newspapers reported in April 1929 on the conviction of Rocco. According to some press accounts, Rocco and an accomplice managed to extract a single box of stockings, valued at $1, from the dry goods store of Leonard Gioscia, 2129 Third Avenue, before they were caught by patrol officers. Other press reports stated, however, that Rocco did not steal a box of stockings but merely a bunch of empty boxes, which he believed contained stockings.

Judge Joseph F. Mulqueen informed Rocco that he could have forty eight hours before sentence was passed, but Rocco waived the waiting period. Judge Mulqueen then stated that he was compelled to sentence Rocco to spend the rest of his life behind bars.[97]

Rocco's accomplice, eighteen-year-old Joseph Marcoroni, was judged "mental defective" and was "committed to the reformatory for feeble-minded in Napanoch."[98]

Frank Rocco, also known as Anthony Valachi, was twenty eight when he was received at Sing Sing Prison on April 23, 1929. He was soon transferred to Clinton State Prison at Dannemora.[99] Joseph Valachi went to visit him there in November 1930.[100] It was an unpleasant visit:

> Already you could see he wasn't right in the head... All he talked about was how I was to blame for all his troubles. I don't know why.[101]

In the 1940 U.S. Census, Frank Rocco, thirty eight, showed up as an inmate of the Dannemora State Hospital for the Criminally Insane. The census noted that he lived at the same institution five years earlier. Rocco, forty eight, was still an inmate there at the time of the 1950 Census.[102]

When Joseph Valachi was given a psychiatric evaluation following his murder of a fellow inmate at Atlanta Federal Prison in 1962, Dr. Harry Lipton noted that Valachi's brother was still held at the Dannemora facility.[103] Valachi believed he was still living at Dannemora a couple of years after that, as Valachi penned his 1964 autobiography. "...To this day, he is still there. He is at Box A, Dannemora, New York, under the name of Frank Rocco... Box A is the bug house. He is there since he was arrested in 1928, until now it is thirty six years."[104]

The death of Frank Rocco / Anthony Valachi is not noted in available records, and the Central New York Psychiatric Center of the state Office of Mental Health has refused access to the information.[105]

Additional burglary and robbery arrests and discharges occurred during 1922 and 1923. In the early summer of 1923, Joseph Valachi and the Minute Men went into the Mount Hope section of the Bronx to burglarize a silk store at Tremont Avenue and 177th Street. Police arrived soon after a milk can went through the store window. Shots were fired as the gang made a dramatic escape down the Grand Concourse. Valachi suffered an arm wound. One of his associates took a bullet to the chest, but it did not penetrate deeply enough to be life-threatening. For the moment, it seemed the gang got away, but police identified the car and managed some good looks at gang members.[29]

Valachi identified himself as Charles Charbano when he was picked up by police for grand larceny of an automobile in August of 1923. According to his story, the car had been entrusted to him by a friend, who simply forgot to provide the ownership papers. The charge was reduced to disorderly conduct, and Valachi/Charbano was sentenced to an easy ten-day term in the workhouse.[30]

But, while looking into the stolen automobile matter, police identified Valachi as a suspect in the interrupted burglary on Tremont Avenue. As he was released from the workhouse, he was charged with attempted burglary of a store. It took weeks for the matter to be brought into court, and he was held at Bronx County Jail during that time. He pleaded guilty, but was then held additional weeks before sentencing.

When he was bought in for sentencing late in October. his attorney advised him to adopt a tough gangster manner in front of the judge. The attorney reasoned that Valachi was better off with what appeared to be a stricter sentence. He would be eligible for release from the state penitentiary within about nine months, because the penitentiary could release him early on parole and would give him an allowance for time already served. If he appeared to be no more than a misguided young man, he could be sent to Elmira Reformatory for a year and a half, without a time served allowance or possibility of parole.

Valachi played the gangster role well enough. On October 23, 1923, Judge Culkin sentenced him to between fifteen and thirty months in prison. That sentence would make him eligible for parole after serving eleven months and twenty days, and Valachi was credited for about two months of jail time.[31]

Joseph Valachi, then twenty, became inmate 75260 at Sing Sing Prison on October 26, 1923.[32] Valachi's relatively brief stay in the prison was not an entirely negative experience. He found a number of fellow inmates from his East Harlem neighborhood, did productive work on a prison construction project and received gift packages from his associates back home. But the prison term also reinforced the idea that membership in some sort of a gang was critical to survival. "Everybody was mobbed up," Valachi remembered. "There wasn't much trouble, but if there were, you had to be with someone, or you had to be just a punk and stay to yourself."[33]

Mobs

Valachi noticed differences in his East Harlem neighborhood following his August 19, 1924, parole from Sing Sing. His former gang buddies from 107th Street were gathering at a new spot, a pool room and cafe on East 116th Street near First Avenue. The gang was under the influence of regional Mafia boss Ciro "the Artichoke King" Terranova and his organization. At night, gangsters of different backgrounds drank together at Joe's Restaurant on 116th Street.[34]

Prohibition Era jazz clubs were opening throughout the area, in a period that became known as the Harlem Renaissance. The clubs, which generally featured African-American performers entertaining whites-only audiences in white-owned venues, drew into Harlem top entertainers and entertainment-starved New Yorkers. They also were a magnet for profit-driven hoodlums, including Lower East Side Jewish racketeers Jacob "Augie" Orgen, Louis "Lepke" Buchalter and Jacob "Gurrah" Shapiro, as well as West Side Irish-American gang leader Owen Madden.

Valachi recalled that top men in the rackets regularly met at 116th Street and Lenox Avenue. At that location, the popular Vienna Restaurant did business over a bowling alley. Both businesses remained open all night.[35]

Valachi's social life in this period included time spent at night clubs and taxi-dance halls, which featured paid female dance partners. He recalled visits to a taxi-dance place at West 125th Street between Lenox and Seventh avenues he knew as "Dream Land dance hall." He also visited Tangoland - recalling its name as "Tangle Land" – on Eighty-sixth Street and Lexington Avenue, the enormously popular Cotton Club at 142nd Street and Lenox, the Ritz and the Alamo cabarets at 125th Street and Lenox and the Pelham Heath Inn cabaret at 1500 Pelham Parkway in the Bronx.[36]

"If people from downtown wanted to have a real good time, they would have to come to Harlem," Valachi wrote.[37]

Valachi was generally excluded from the activities of his now-mobbed-up buddies, and he gathered together a new burglary gang. They began using less obvious methods to access targeted businesses, jimmying locks or cutting through floors, ceilings or walls from adjacent quarters.

On one occasion late in 1924, Mafia-connected acquaintances Dominick "the Gap" Petrelli and Joey Rao asked Valachi to drive for a burglary at a factory, 174th Street and St. Nicholas Avenue in the Washington Heights section of Manhattan. He agreed to do the job. Soon after his associates began trying to open the factory door, they told Valachi their tool broke and they needed to return to East Harlem to get a replacement. As Valachi started to drive away, police opened fire. He later learned that about sixty shots were fired. He only heard the first one, which struck him in the head.

The group succeeded in getting away from police. Valachi regained his senses in time to hear his associates discuss dumping his body somewhere. "I ain't dead," he muttered. In an effort to get him medical attention, his burglar buddies left him on 114th Street near the East River and fired some shots into the air before driving away. They believed police would respond to the sound of shooting and find the wounded Valachi, thinking him a casualty of an incident at that location. But police never showed up. The group returned an hour later, finding Valachi where they left him. They picked up their wounded driver and brought him to a doctor who did secret work for crime figures. Valachi's recovery from the wound took months.[38]

While still not fully recovered, Valachi went back to "work." In March 1925, another job done with Petrelli turned out badly. The target was a factory warehouse filled with silk shirts. There was so much there to steal that the gang, including Petrelli, Rao and Joseph "Pip the Blind" Gagliano, felt they should bring two cars. Valachi drove a 1921 Packard and Gagliano drove his own 1923 Lincoln. After the group gained access to the warehouse, they noticed a watchman in a nearby phone booth and charged at him. The watchman told them he had already telephone for police. The group fled, but left behind Valachi's Packard because it refused to start.

The next day, a Valachi friend and Valachi's sister went back to the neighborhood of the warehouse to try to retrieve the Packard. Police were watching the vehicle and followed the two back to where Valachi was staying. Officers woke Valachi from a nap and arrested him on a robbery charge. He was able to post bail and get back out onto the streets, though his Packard had been seized.[39]

Later in 1925, there was some friction between the Terranova-linked "Italian mob" and a rival group of gangsters that Valachi knew as the "Irish mob" (though few of the members actually were Irish Americans). Valachi had friends in both gangs. One night, he found himself surrounded by Terranova men, including "Big Dick" Amato and Joseph Rao.[40] Valachi was accused of driving for the Irish mob when its members went to Italian mob headquarters at 116th Street and First Avenue and caused a panic by shooting up the place. Valachi denied that. Rao offered him the chance to prove himself by setting up the Irish mob for a counterattack.

Valachi said he would consider it, and went out to find the Irish mob. Valachi was so enraged by the suggestion that he should betray friends who trusted him that he offered to join up with the Irish mob. He then made an angry telephone call to Rao, declaring himself an enemy of the Italian mob.[41]

A largely inconsequential conflict erupted between the rival mobs. It ended with a truce just as Valachi was sentenced to three years in prison for third-degree burglary. He was also forced to serve the remainder of the earlier sentence, for which he had been paroled. (At trial, the judge wondered how he managed to be released on bail rather than immediately returned to Sing Sing as a parole violator. Valachi had no idea.) He reentered Sing Sing on April 9, 1925.[42]

John Valachi

Joseph Valachi's "kid brother" was born May 16, 1914. It appears John followed in the footsteps of both of his older brothers, leaving school early and trying to make a career of burglary.

While still a youngster, John appears to have been treated as an errand boy by Joseph. In Joseph Valachi's autobiography, he shares just a few memories of his little brother, and two of those were merely of sending John to do something for him.[106]

The three brothers generally had a poor relationship. Joseph Valachi recalled, "I never got along with the older one, and neither did I get along with the young one."[107]

John left school at age fourteen. The family patriarch, Dominick Valachi, passed away the following year.[108]

John seems to have avoided serious trouble with the law until November 1935, when he was sentenced to between two and a half years and five years in prison after being convicted of attempted burglary.

For prison records, he stated that he had not worked for seven months. His last employer was his brother Joseph. Asked what caused his criminal activity, he stated that he "needed money."[109]

John left prison on December 22, 1938, but was again locked up on May 23, 1940, likely for violating the terms of his parole. He still was an inmate of Auburn State Prison in May 1941, when he registered for the World War II draft. The draft registration stated that he was twenty seven years old, five feet seven inches tall, 135 pounds, with brown eyes, black hair and a dark complexion.[110]

In the summer of 1946, John was out of prison and living at 2318 Third Avenue in East Harlem. On the morning of July 24, he was found dead in the street in front of his home. An autopsy determined that death was caused by "contusions and hemorrhages into neck and structures of larynx; laryngeal edema and shock." The certificate of death contains a note saying that the circumstances of his death were "undetermined, pending investigation."[111]

When writing his autobiography, Joseph Valachi blamed the police for his little brother's death:

> I find out later that they, the bulls, lock the kid up for something and the kid promised them some money and they let him go. But the kid did not pay the money, and when they caught up with him they gave him a beating but did not mean to kill him. One of the big dogs hit him a rap, and the kid fell and broke his collar bone. Then they took him out of the 126th Street police station and put him on the street and made it appear as though he got hit by a car.[112]

He told a similar story to biographer Peter Maas:

> My kid brother, Johnny, was a drifter, and I couldn't do a thing with him. He was found dead in the street, and the cops claimed it was a hit-and-run accident. I heard that they pulled him in for questioning and worked him over too much.[113]

Education

The return to Sing Sing after such a short time away was like a reunion. "The same boys were there that I used to eat with my first time," Valachi recalled, "...and they told me that I was welcome to go back with them again."[43] In prison, Valachi picked up his studies. He attended classes and became better able to read and to express himself in written form.[44]

He also acquired education of a different sort. He became close to prisoner Alessandro Vollero. About fifteen years older than Valachi, Vollero was a former Brooklyn Neapolitan gang boss who had tangled with the Terranova Mafia and had set up the murder of Ciro Terranova's brother.[45]

Vollero warned Valachi to steer clear of Sicilians like the Terranovas. "You can hang out with a Sicilian twenty years, and if you get in a fight with one of his own kind, he will go against you."[46]

Valachi learned more about underworld treachery when Ludwig "Dutch" Augustine, a member of East Harlem's Irish mob, was sent to Sing Sing at the end of 1925.[47] Augustine revealed to Valachi that the truce between the Irish mob and the Italian mob had been achieved only through the agreement that Valachi and Frank LaPuma, another Italian-American gangster who sided with the Irish mob, would be murdered.

Augustine told Valachi that LaPuma had been shot to death in June, while sitting on the front stoop of a building on East 105th Street. According to Augustine, the truce terms were agreed to by Irish mob leader Nick Caputo, and LaPuma was executed by John "Bum" Rogers. "Dutch" noted that Rogers received $100 from Ciro Terranova for eliminating LaPuma.[48]

Early in 1926, an attempt was made on Valachi's life inside the walls of Sing Sing. A fellow inmate stabbed him in the left side. The wound required thirty eight stitches. His assailant was transferred out to Clinton State Prison at Dannemora.[49]

Valachi grew worried that Terranova assassins would soon get to him and finish the job. He was greatly reassured when his Mafia-connected friend Dominick "the Gap" Petrelli became an inmate at Sing Sing. When Valachi shared his concerns, Petrelli told him, "Don't worry about nothing, because I heard them talking on the outside and they know that you got a bum rap." He advised that when Valachi was released he just "play dumb and keep it to yourself."[50]

Valachi was freed from Sing Sing on June 15, 1928. Before he left the prison, Vollero suggested that he leave East Harlem and head to a safer area like Long Island or out to Chicago, where he could join up with successful Neapolitan gangster Al Capone. Valachi promised, "I will keep in mind what you told me."[51] Valachi actually didn't seriously consider a move to join Capone. Many years later, when questioned about it, he said, "I don't know... I guess I wanted to stay in New York."[52]

As he went back to the streets, he felt better able to make his way:

> ...I came home with an education... I didn't learn much, but I can read something and know what I'm reading. Before I went in, I couldn't read the streets in the Bronx... But [most] of all, the education I'm talking about is what they call an education of worldy-wise, and also a study of human nature.[53]

Changing world

Once again, Valachi emerged from prison to find many changes. While he was behind bars, the entire world seemed to shrink, as Charles Lindbergh made the first solo transatlantic flight, taking off from New York on May 20, 1927, and landing in Paris thirty three and a half hours later. The new medium of television was launched with a successful demonstration in San Francisco on September 7, 1927. A month later, the movie industry was forever changed with the release of the first feature-length (partial) "talkie," *The Jazz Singer*.[54]

There was no hint that years of economic growth and social upheaval were nearing an end. That the Twenties would suddenly stop "Roaring," with a catastrophic stock market crash in autumn 1929 and the beginning of the Great Depression, was unimaginable.[55]

At the moment of Valachi's release, New York City was the sports capital of the U.S. The New York Giants football team, which had not existed when he entered prison, were the reigning champions of the National Football league. Baseball's New York Yankees, Valachi's favorite team, were well on their way to achieving a third consecutive American League pennant and a second consecutive (and third overall) World Series title. On the day Valachi left prison, Babe Ruth, who set a league record with sixty homers the previous season, cracked his twenty fourth homer of the season (in a rare loss to the St. Louis Browns). The New York Rangers, in just their second year in the National Hockey League, would begin a championship season of their own in the fall.[56]

Gotham was flexing its political muscles as well. Just two weeks after Valachi's release, New York Governor Alfred E. Smith, raised in an Irish-Italian-German-American household on Manhattan's Lower East Side, became the first Roman Catholic to be a major party nominee in a U.S. Presidential election.[57]

Significant changes were occurring in the Italian-American underworld, and Valachi, not yet a Mafia member, did not become aware of them for some time. A powerful new Mafia crime family had formed in Manhattan and Brooklyn around Giuseppe "Joe the Boss" Masseria. Ciro Terranova commanded a Harlem arm of the organization. Linked through their relationships with Terranova, Masseria became an ally of Dutch Schultz, who ran bootlegging and numbers gambling operations based in Harlem and the Bronx.

In October 1928, about four months after Valachi returned to East Harlem, reigning Mafia boss of bosses Salvatore D'Aquila was murdered in Manhattan. Masseria became the new boss of bosses, supreme arbiter of inter-family disputes within the American Mafia network. Giuseppe Morello, Terranova's half-brother and the pre-D'Aquila boss of bosses, became Masseria's top adviser. Masseria even brought Chicago gang boss Capone into his organization, making Capone his lieutenant and encouraging him to fight against Chicago's uncooperative local Mafia boss Joseph Aiello.[58]

Four other Mafia crime families were based in New York City at that time. D'Aquila's large organization, which had interests in the Bronx and on Long Island, had been taken over by Masseria ally Manfredi "Al" Mineo. A Bronx-based crime family with interests in East Harlem was led by Gaetano Reina. A family made up largely of mafiosi from Castellammare del Golfo, Sicily, and based in Williamsburg, Brooklyn, was led by Nicola Schiro. And a smaller Brooklyn-headquartered unit had Giuseppe Profaci as its boss.

All of this was beyond Valachi's awareness. He was busy with burglaries. Each week, he and his associates committed several break-ins and earned about $1,500 a week from sale of the loot to a "fence" named Fat West. After splitting the proceeds with members of his small gang, he had enough money to pay rent on some rooms on Second Avenue for himself and the rest of his family.[59]

Then about twenty five years of age, Valachi began spending much of his leisure time at the Rainbow Gardens, an all-night taxi-dance hall at 125th Street and Lexington Avenue that boasted many female "dance instructors." He became friendly with many of the women employed at the hall, and formed an especially close bond with a woman he knew as "May."[60]

In the early stages of their relationship, May had a serious boyfriend. Valachi often danced with her at the Rainbow Gardens, and he would think of her when he out on a heist. If he robbed dresses from a store, he would select one out of the loot to give her as a present. When May broke up with her boyfriend, she and Valachi talked about becoming a couple. But Valachi was insecure about his ability to provide for her.[61]

Valachi made it a point to try to repair his relationship with the Mafia organization that had ordered his murder. He contacted an old friend, Frank Livorsi. Livorsi worked for Terranova as a chauffeur and bodyguard. He put in a word for Valachi with Terranova and went back to Valachi with good news:

"You mind your business and everybody else will mind theirs. There are no hard feelings. What's over is over."[62]

Valachi's pal Dominick Petrelli was released from Sing Sing early in 1929. Keenly aware of the recent upheaval in the Mafia, Petrelli expressed an eagerness to bring Valachi into the organization, but said that would need to wait.[63] At the same time, Frank Livorsi also spoke to Valachi about the same thing. Valachi understood that Petrelli and Livorsi were from rival racketeering organizations. He also understood that, despite Livorsi's assurance that there were "no hard feelings," he would never really be welcome in an organization led by Terranova and "Big Dick" Amato. (And Valachi himself still held a grudge over how he was treated by the Italian mob.)

Valachi admitted to Livorsi that he felt he would soon be offered membership in a rival outfit: "It may be with people that you don't like." If and when that happened, he promised to signal Livorsi.[64]

Filomena, Maddalena, Antonetta

Joseph Valachi had three sisters who survived to adulthood. They were Filomena "Fanny," born February 6, 1907; Maddalena "Lena," born August 17, 1910; and Antonetta "Anna" or "Nettie," born Feb. 22, 1917.[114]

Fanny married Michael Siano and, in June 1927 gave birth to Fiore Siano.[115] As Fiore grew up, he followed his uncle Joseph into Cosa Nostra rackets and assisted with mob murders. Fiore Siano disappeared in the spring of 1964.[116]

Lena was apparently the only sibling who developed a close bond with Joseph Valachi. In his autobiography, Valachi recalled that, when neighborhood nemesis "Crazy Chuck" was threatening to kill him, Lena directly confronted Chuck and caused him to back down.[117]

Near the end of 1934, Lena married plumber Frank Rizzo in a civil ceremony. They were married in a religious ceremony at East Harlem's Our Lady Queen of Angels Church the following June.[118] Lena was just thirty eight when she died at Montefiore Hospital in the Bronx in December 1948.[119]

Nettie married East Harlem butcher Carmine Alfano at Our Lady of Mount Carmel Church on East 116th Street. Her wedding occurred on April 15, 1935, sandwiched between the two ceremonies of her older sister Lena.[120]

Straightened out

Valachi's father Dominick died at Harlem Hospital on August 16, 1929. He was fifty two. The cause of death was determined to be "chronic myocarditis and generalized arteriosclerosis" (heart inflammation and hardening of the arteries).[65]

Valachi, however, was certain that his father died from alcoholism, and he partly blamed himself. The night before, as he went out, he gave his father $10 to buy some wine. When he returned with "Gap" Petrelli, they found Dominick passed out on the floor. They moved him to a bed and left again. Valachi came home to find Dominick unresponsive and in precisely the same position he left him. He ran out to get a police officer and an ambulance.[66]

Valachi noticed that his father had been drinking milk as well as wine, and he felt the combination led to his condition. A doctor arrived from Harlem Hospital and told Valachi that Dominick was in a coma. Under questioning from Valachi, the doctor reportedly acknowledged that the wine and milk may have helped bring on the problem, but he emphasized that it appeared Dominick had been abusing himself with alcohol for a very long time.

Dominick was brought to the hospital and soon passed away. The wake for Valachi's father was held in the Valachi home on Second Avenue. It was attended by all of Valachi's friends and associates, including May.[67] Soon after this, Valachi and May decided to move in together. They found an apartment in the Van Nest section of the Bronx, just east of Bronx Park.[68]

Valachi noticed that friends of Petrelli took an interest in him later in 1929. During encounters, they asked him questions, such as what did he think about Terranova and his aide "Muskie" Castaldo. Later on, they were concerned about how many members Valachi had in his burglary gang.

Girolamo "Bobby Doyle" Santuccio wanted to know if Valachi could assemble six or seven men. Valachi said he probably could get a dozen. Santuccio and Gaetano "Tommy" Lucchese tried to convince Valachi that he should not be doing burglaries, but they were vague on what he might be doing instead.

At one point, these new acquaintances asked Valachi if he could be counted on to shoot someone if he was instructed to do so: "I said will they shoot someone for me? They said yes. Then I will shoot someone for you."[69]

Valachi had a final conversation about the mob with Livorsi, and asked him what to do about the obvious interest by Petrelli's friends. "Think for yourself," Livorsi said. "I tried to get you with us. They are stalling me, and you go right ahead."[70]

In a subsequent encounter with Santuccio, Valachi was specifically asked about his feelings for Frank Livorsi. Valachi found the questioning unnerving and complained about it to Petrelli. "Gap" assured Valachi that Santuccio was "all right." He said, "Listen, they got to ask you questions… They are thinking about asking you about Frank… He is with the people we intend to have trouble with… I think they want to take care of him."

Valachi exploded at the thought of turning on Livorsi: "I don't want anything to do with this mob… How would you like for someone to ask me to take you?"

Petrelli said he would see to it that Valachi was not asked to act against Livorsi. He made Valachi promise not to breathe a word of the conversation to Livorsi.[71] Petrelli and Santuccio began treating Valachi as a member of their Bronx-based organization, though there had been no formal induction.

Rebellion

A steep eight-year climb in New York Stock Exchange values was suddenly reversed at the end of October 1929. "Black Thursday," October 24, saw an 11 percent dip in the market, followed by some recovery. But "Black Monday" on the twenty eighth brought a 13 percent plummet, and "Black Tuesday" delivered another 12 percent decline.

That was just the start of a market crash and subsequent economic downturn that would erase more than 80 percent of stock values by the summer of 1932. The staggering and growing losses to personal and corporate wealth strained and broke the banking system; prompted factory and farm foreclosures; depressed purchasing, prices and productivity; and led to massive unemployment. There were widespread rumors and reports – mostly false – of Wall Street speculators, their fortunes lost, throwing their lives away by jumping from the windows of New York skyscrapers.[72]

The Roaring Twenties decade of postwar celebration was over.

Joseph Valachi, twenty six, seemed not to notice the market crash or any of the catastrophes that followed. The New York-area underworld was entering a violent period that would become known as the Castellammarese War. Valachi would be an important participant in that conflict, and it would be the start of his thirty year career as a "cosa nostra" soldier and racketeer.

In the spring of 1930, Petrelli brought Valachi to a Midtown Manhattan bar on Seventh Avenue and introduced him to Bonaventura "Joe" Pinzolo. Valachi later recalled Pinzolo as a "greaseball." He had a large handlebar mustache and smelled of garlic.

Pinzolo was accompanied by eight or ten other men. As Valachi was known to be friendly with many of the women at the Rainbow Gardens, he was asked to invite some women down to the bar. Valachi made a show of telephoning the Rainbow Gardens, but he did not intend to ask any of his friends to associate with Pinzolo and made up an excuse about the women being too busy at work to leave.

Valachi pulled Petrelli aside and gave his negative impression of Pinzolo. Petrelli whispered, "You're going to drive him home. He's our new boss."

"Holy smokes!" Valachi said. "I'm sure going to take off."

"Shut up," whispered Petrelli. "He is going to die."

Valachi stuck around until about two the next morning and then drove Pinzolo to a downtown hotel. The two men said nothing to each other during the drive and merely exchanged pleasantries as they parted.[73]

It was August 1930, when Valachi heard about some mob big shot being murdered in an office on East 116th Street. "His name was Peter Morello, the 'Clutching Hand.' He was the half-brother of Ciro Terranova… I didn't think anything of it." Valachi noticed that his mob friends in East Harlem were avoiding conversation of that killing.[74]

Later in August, Valachi, his pals "Nickie" and "Solly" and other men were brought to an upstate New York farm owned by Tommaso Gagliano. There they practiced firing shotguns, rifles and handguns. That event was followed by a two-week vacation for the group at a resort hotel in the Catskills. Valachi brought May along.[75]

They returned to the city in early September. Valachi soon heard that Joe Pinzolo was recently murdered.

Petrelli associate Stefano "Steve" Rannelli informed Valachi that top underworld boss Joe Masseria had called a large meeting on Staten Island to determine who was responsible for the recent murders of Morello and Pinzolo. Rannelli explained that their organization was secretly fighting Masseria's sprawling organization. "'Joe the Boss' killed our boss," he said. "Then he put this guy Joe Pinzolo in his place without us having anything to say about it. So we killed him. Now, they are calling a meet. They figure that whoever don't show up is guilty."[76]

The boss killed by Masseria was Gaetano Reina of the Bronx. After some conflict with Reina – possibly sparked by ongoing tension between the Reina group and Ciro Terranova-Dutch Schultz alliance – Masseria simply had Reina murdered. The Bronx boss was gunned down February 26, 1930, outside the apartment building of his mistress at 1521 Sheridan Avenue.[77] Ignoring Reina's top lieutenants, Tommaso Gagliano and Gaetano Lucchese, Masseria installed Pinzolo as crime family leader. Gagliano and Lucchese then began quietly organizing opposition.

Valachi, Paduano and Shillitani were told not to go to the Staten Island meeting. They were not yet known to be part of the Bronx rebel organization, and that secret was deemed an asset. Petrelli admitted to Valachi that the group was vastly outnumbered in the fight against Masseria: "We are about eight or nine. They are an army."[78]

Valachi later learned that the army included New York crime figures Salvatore "Charlie Luciano" Lucania, Vito Genovese, Giuseppe "Joe Adonis" Doto, Ciro Terranova, Guarino "Willie Moore" Moretti, as well as Chicago gang boss Al Capone.[79]

Masseria apparently gleaned nothing useful from the Staten Island meeting. But soon after the meeting, the Gagliano-Lucchese group found that it had allies. While the Reina loyalists knew they were responsible for the killing of Pinzolo, they also knew they were not responsible for the earlier killing of Giuseppe Morello. Eventually, through member Steve Rannelli, they became aware of another rebel group.[80]

This second group, mostly made up of mafiosi from Castellammare del Golfo, Sicily, had broken away from the Williamsburg, Brooklyn, organization of Nicola Schiro after "Joe the Boss" Masseria ousted Schiro, murdered Castellammarese Mafia leader Vito Bonventre in July 1930 and installed Masseria ally Joseph Parrino as boss. The Castellammaresi were led in the New York area by Salvatore Maranzano and received support from Mafia bosses Stefano Magaddino in Buffalo and Joe Aiello in Chicago.[81]

As the two anti-Masseria factions merged, they decided to cooperate on the assassination of a close Masseria aide named Stefano Ferrigno, who lived in the Alhambra Apartments complex at 750-760 Pelham Parkway in the Bronx.[82]

Valachi was assigned to take part in the hit, providing support and serving as driver for the gunmen. This assignment brought him in contact with Joseph Profaci, Vincent "Doc" D'Anna, Sebastiano "Buster" Domingo, Nick Capuzzi and Joe "Palisades" Rosato. Before it was over, it brought him dangerously close to "Joe the Boss" Masseria himself.[83]

After a stakeout lasting two months, the group succeeded in assassinating both Manfredi Mineo and Stefano Ferrigno in the Alhambra Apartments courtyard on November 5, 1930. Valachi was rewarded for his performance by meeting Salvatore Maranzano and by receiving a formal induction into Maranzano's Mafia organization.[84]

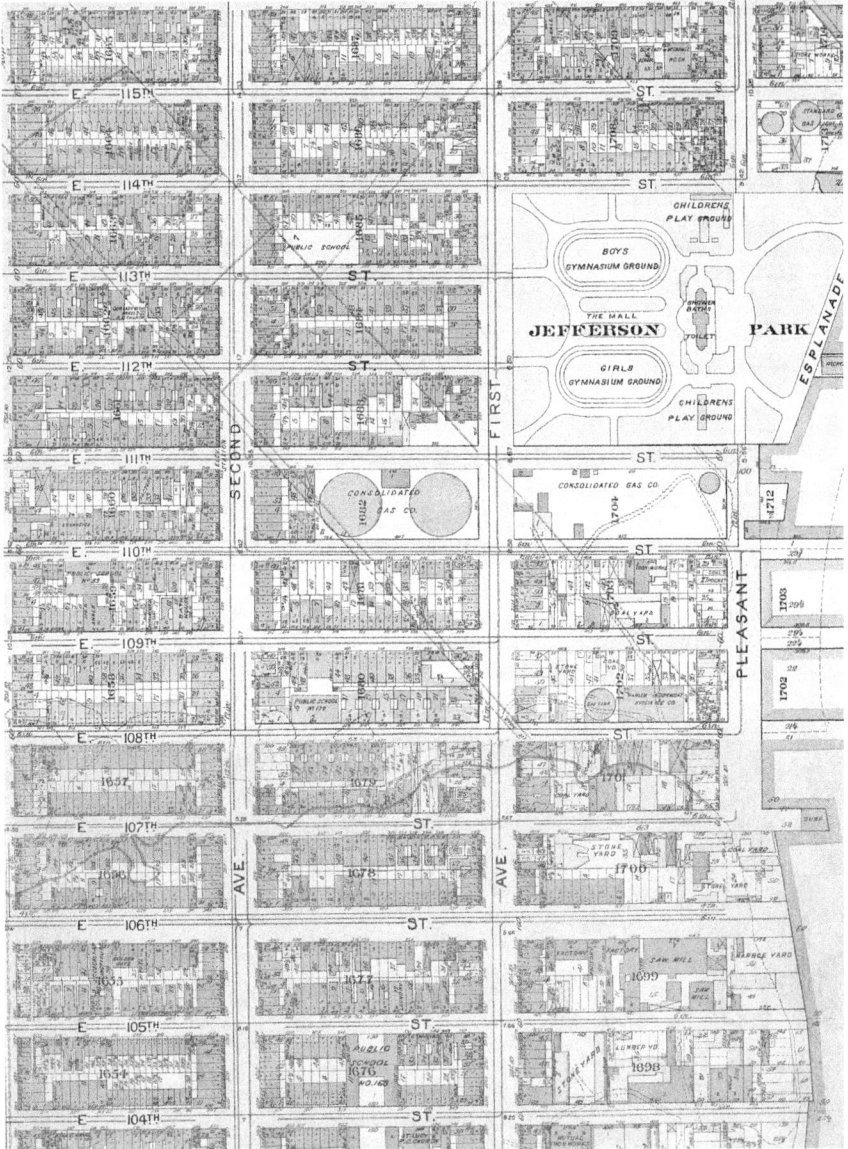

Valachi's East Harlem neighborhood (1911)

Valachi birth certificate

Harlem's First Avenue, c1908. (italianharlem.com)

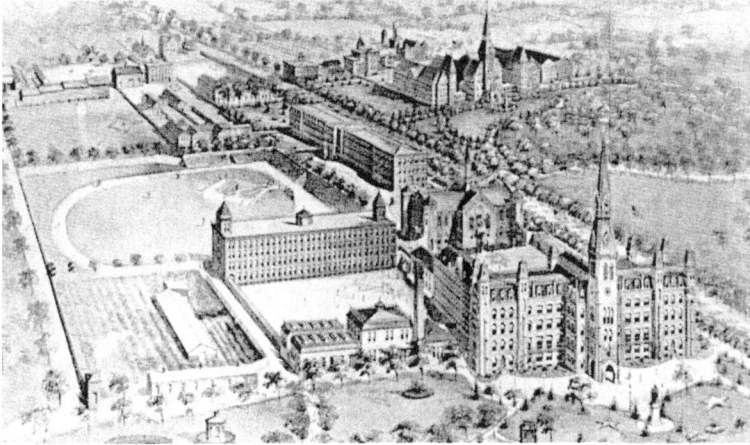

New York Catholic Protectory

TAKE FIVE ARMED MEN IN AN AUTO

A quintet of what the police of the Central avenue station designated as "real tough birds" were arrested at six o'clock this morning by Sergeant Winter, Detective Flannery and Patrolman Hughes while driving an automobile in Central avenue, Jersey City. The car, which was in charge of Fred Russo, of 561 Palisade avenue, was proceeding along at a leisurely rate of speed conforming to all the laws of propriety and society, but the occupants looked anything like assets to good society and were held up to give an account of themselves.

Besides Russo in the car were Dominick Puccelli, of 2076 First avenue; Charles Chisingo, of 405 East 106th street; Joseph Tilligrino, of 400

Young Joseph Valachi (left), 1921 arrest report in Hudson Observer (right).

Ciro Terranova (left), Frank Amato (right)

John Valachi 1946 death certificate.

Dannemora State Hospital

Feature 1 Notes

Newspaper abbreviations: *BC – Brooklyn Citizen; BDE – Brooklyn Daily Eagle; BSU – Brooklyn Standard Union; BT – Brooklyn Times; NYDN – New York Daily News; NYHT – New York Herald Tribune; NYT – New York Times; NYTR – New York Tribune.*

1 Cordasco, Francesco, and Rocco G. Galatioto, "Ethnic displacement in the interstitial community: The East Harlem (New York City) experience," *Kansas Journal of Sociology*, Vol. 6, No. 1, Spring 1970; Meyer, Gerald, "Italian Harlem: America's largest and most Italian Little Italy," Our Lady of Mount Carmel Shrine of East Harlem, mountcarmelofeastharlem.com; "New York's new East Side explored," *NYT*, Oct. 9, 1904, p. 32. Cordasco and Galatioto report that there was a period of overall population decline, suggesting that the Irish and German exodus at one point exceeded new Italian arrivals. The *Times* estimated that 40,000 Italian Americans lived in a congested area north of 108th Street in October 1904.

2 "More rioting feared in Harlem's negro colony," *BSU*, July 5, 1907, p. 4; "Fight plan to move training school," *NYT*, Nov. 25, 1908, p. 5; "$20,000 to keep negroes out," *NYT*, Dec. 8, 1910, p. 2; "To hold Watt Block for white persons," *NYTR*, Aug. 24, 1913, part 8, p. 1. Much of the opposition to expansion of the African-American neighborhood was organized by a the "Property Owners' Protective Association of Harlem," which reportedly feared a drop in property values.

3 "The Negro's peril," *NYT*, Dec. 6, 1904, p. 8; "How Harlem became black," Black New York, eportfolios.macaulay.cuny,edu; "Black capital: Harlem in the 1920s," New York State Museum, nysm.nysed.gov; "Fight plan to move training school." Between 1910 and 1930, the African American population of Harlem grew from 50,000 to more than 200,000.

4 George, Alice, "The Teddy Bear was once seen as a dangerous influence on young children," *Smithsonian Magazine*, smithsonianmag.com, December 2023; "Building the Panama Canal, 1903-1914," Office of the Historian, U.S. Department of State, history.state.gov.

5 "Benjamin B. Odell, Jr.," Visit the Empire State Plaza & New York State Capitol, empirestateplaza.ny.gov; "Seth Low," Columbia University Archives, library.columbia.edu; Golliher, Daniel, "1898: The birth of New York City," Maximum New York, maximumnewyork.com, July 2, 2023.

6 "History of the Williamsburg Bridge in New York City," NYC Moments, nycmoments.nyc, modified May 4, 2022; "Company timeline: 1903," Ford, corporate.ford.com; "The Model T," Ford, corporate.ford.com; Hazelwood, Madeleine, "Contemplating and commemorating rapid transit in New York City," Museum of the City of New York, mcny.org, April 24, 2017; "Wright brothers," *History*, history.com, modified June 13, 2023.

7 "About: Our history," Luna Park, lunaparknyc.com; "Crowds at the beaches start season merrily," *BT*, June 1, 1903, p.2; "Royal Arcanum picnic draws many thousands," *BC*, July 2, 1903, p. 5; "'Running for Office,'" *NYT*, April 28, 1903, p. 5; "New York Yankees team history 7 encyclopedia," *Baseball Reference*, baseball-reference.com; "1903 World Series," *Baseball Almanac*, baseball-almanac.com. The "Highlanders" name was not noted in local coverage of the team during 1903, but it appeared regularly in the press in 1904. The terms "Washington Heights," "Highlanders" and "Hilltop Park" all relate to the relative elevation of the area.

8 United States Census of 1900, New York State, New York County, Enumeration District 920. It is uncertain how Maria arrived at the total number of deceased children. It seems unlikely that these pregnancies were all carried to term in such a short time.

9 Antonio Villacci Certificate and Record of Birth, Borough of Manhattan, certificate no. 34174, City of New York Bureau of Records, Aug. 23, 1900, reported Aug. 30, 1900, received Sept. 5, 1900.

10 Gioseppo Vilacio Certificate and Record of Birth, Borough of Manhattan, certificate no. 44544, City of New York Department of Health, Oct. 3, 1903, received Oct. 16, 1903 (Thank you to crime historian Justin Cascio for locating this document); Molloy, James T., "Crime conditions in the New York Division," FBI Report of New York Office, file no. CR 62-9-34-811, NARA no. 124-10348-10069, Nov. 27, 1963; Testimony of Joseph Valachi, *Organized Crime and Illicit Traffic in Narcotics*, Part 1, Hearings before the Permanent Subcommittee on Investigations of the Committee on Government Operations (McClellan Committee), U.S. Senate, 88th Congress, 1st Session, Washington D.C.: U.S. Government Printing Office, 1968, p. 78.

11 Meyer, Gerald, "Italian Harlem: America's largest and most Italian Little Italy," Our Lady of Mount Carmel Shrine of East Harlem, mountcarmelofeastharlem.com.

12 United States Census of 1910, New York State, New York County, Ward 12, Enumeration District 339; Madeline Rizzo, New York City Index to Death Certificates, Dec. 22, 1948; Madeline Rizzo Certificate

of Death, Borough of Manhattan, certificate no. 12664, Bureau of Records Department of Health, Dec. 22, 1948, filed Dec. 26, 1948; "Valachi dies in jail; bared mob secrets," *NYDN*, April 4, 1971, p. 3.

13 Valachi, Joseph, *The Real Thing: Second Government - The Expose and Inside Doings of Cosa Nostra*, unpublished manuscript, John F. Kennedy Presidential Library and Museum, 1964, p. 1, 10; Maas, Peter, *The Valachi Papers*, New York: G.P. Putnam's Sons, 1968, p. 61-63.

14 Valachi, *The Real Thing*, p. 3.

15 John Valachi Certificate of Death, Borough of Manhattan, certificate no. 16981, Bureau of Records Department of Health, July 24, 1946, filed Aug. 5, 1946; Valachi, *The Real Thing*, p. 4; Maas, *The Valachi Papers*, p. 63-64.

16 Valachi, *The Real Thing*, p. 4-6c.

17 Valachi, *The Real Thing*, p. 7; Testimony of Joseph Valachi, Sept. 27, 1963, McClellan Committee, p. 79.

18 Valachi, *The Real Thing*, p. 8; Maas, *The Valachi Papers*, p. 63-64.

19 Valachi, *The Real Thing*, p. 6k, 24.

20 Valachi, *The Real Thing*, p. 6k.

21 Valachi, *The Real Thing*, p. 44-45.

22 Valachi, *The Real Thing*, p. 33, 36, 47.

23 Valachi, *The Real Thing*, p. 47.

24 Valachi, *The Real Thing*, p. 6k-6l.

25 "18th Amendment to the U.S. Constitution," Research Guides, Library of Congress, guides.loc.gov; "The Eighteenth and Twenty-First Amendments: Prohibition in America," Jack Miller Center, jackmiller-center.org, Nov. 25, 2020; "Milestone documents: 19th Amendment to the U.S. Constitution: Woman's Right to Vote (1920)," National Archives, archives.gov; "Woman suffrage and the 19th Amendment," Educator Resources, National Archives and Records Administration, archives.gov.

26 Editors, "The New Negro – What is he?" *Messenger*, New York, NY, August 1920, p. 73-74, HathiTrust Digital Library, hathitrust.org; "Famous Cases and Criminals: Palmer Raids," FBI, fbi.gov. Though 1920 developments in Prohibition and Women's Suffrage were historically significant, they may not have seemed particularly exciting to many at the time, as alcohol prohibition had already existed for years through Wartime Prohibition and women in New York had attained voting rights in 1917.

27 Valachi, *The Real Thing*, p. 19-20; Joseph Valachi, Prisoner's Criminal Record, New York Police Department, no. 58468, in Carr, Charlie, *New York Police Files on the Mafia*, Hosehead Productions, 2012, p. 567; Joseph Valachi, FBI record no. 544, in Carr, Charlie, *New York Police Files on the Mafia*, Hosehead Productions, 2012, p. 569.

28 Valachi, *The Real Thing*, p. 20-21; Joseph Valachi Classification Study, register no. 82811-A, U.S. Department of Justice Bureau of Prisons, 1960, p. 2-4; Joseph Valachi, Prisoner's Criminal Record, p. 567, 569.

29 Valachi, *The Real Thing*, p. 62-64.

30 Valachi, *The Real Thing*, p. 66-67; Joseph Valachi Classification Study, register no. 82811-A, U.S. Department of Justice Bureau of Prisons, 1960, p. 4; "Valachi, 'syndicate' informant, began his crime career in 1918," *NYT*, Tues. Aug. 6, 1963, p. 25; Joseph Valachi, Prisoner's Criminal Record, p. 567; Joseph Valachi, FBI record no. 544.

31 Valachi, *The Real Thing*, p. 67-70; Joseph Valachi Classification Study, register no. 82811-A, U.S. Department of Justice Bureau of Prisons, 1960, p. 4; Joseph Valachi, Prisoner's Criminal Record.

32 Sing Sing Prison Receiving Blotter, inmate no. 75260, received Oct 26, 1923.

33 Valachi, *The Real Thing*, p. 71-75.

34 Valachi, *The Real Thing*, p. 81.

35 Valachi, *The Real Thing*, p. 40, 82, 508; Maas, *The Valachi Papers*, p. 69.

36 Valachi, *The Real Thing*, p. 40-41, 83-84a.

37 Valachi, *The Real Thing*, p. 84a.

38 Valachi, *The Real Thing*, p. 98-103; Maas, *The Valachi Papers*, p. 70-71.

39 Valachi, *The Real Thing*, p. 104-105.

40 Valachi initially reported that Amato was accompanied by Vincent Rao. But he may have gotten his Rao's crossed for a moment. He later clearly stated that he considered Joey Rao, who was known to be a close associate of Amato and a lieutenant of Terranova, responsible for his difficulties with the Italian mob.

41 Valachi, *The Real Thing*, p. 112-116; Maas, *The Valachi Papers*, p. 72-73.

42 Sing Sing Prison Receiving Blotter, inmate no. 77100, received April 9, 1925; Joseph Valachi Classifica-

tion Study, register no. 82811-A, U.S. Department of Justice Bureau of Prisons, 1960, p. 2; Joseph Valachi, FBI record no. 544; Valachi, *The Real Thing*, p. 136.

43 Valachi, *The Real Thing*, p. 136.

44 Valachi, *The Real Thing*, p. 161-162.

45 Valachi, *The Real Thing*, p. 146. Vollero was initially convicted of the first degree murders of Nicholas Terranova and Charles Ubriaco and faced the death penalty. On appeal, he won a new trial. Rather than take his chances with another jury, he opted for a deal, pleading guilty to second-degree murder and avoiding the electric chair.

46 Valachi, *The Real Thing*, p. 146-147.

47 Ludwig Augustine, no. 77952, Sing Sing Prison Receiving Blotter, Dec. 30, 1925. Augustine was given concurrent sentences of 20 years and 10 years for first degree robbery and first degree grand larceny and a suspended sentence for second degree assault.

48 Valachi, *The Real Thing*, p. 141.

49 Valachi, *The Real Thing*, p. 148-149.

50 Valachi, *The Real Thing*, p. 149-150.

51 Valachi, *The Real Thing*, p. 158.

52 Testimony of Joseph Valachi, Oct. 2, 1963, *Organized Crime and Illicit Traffic in Narcotics*, Part 1, Hearings before the Permanent Subcommittee on Investigations of the Committee on Government Operations (McClellan Committee), U.S. Senate, 88th Congress, 1st Session, Washington D.C.: U.S. Government Printing Office, 1963, p. 209.

53 Valachi, *The Real Thing*, p. 161-162.

54 "Charles Lindbergh biography," Charles Lindbergh: An American aviator, charleslindbergh.com, Spirit of St. Louis 2 Project, 2014; "Who invented television: history of TV," TCL, tcl.com, June 28, 2023; "The Jazz Singer (1927)," IMDB, imdb.com; McGowan, Andrew, "The first sound film was NOT The Jazz Singer," *Collider*, collider.com, April 3, 2023.

55 Richardson, Gary, "The Great Depression: 1929-1941," Federal Reserve History, federalreservehistory.org, Nov. 22, 2013.

56 Zeiler, Millie, "History Of The New York Giants NFL Football," Classic New York History, classic-newyorkhistory.com; "Yankees history," MLB, mlb.com; "New Brownies beat Yankees early in year," *BDE*, June 16, 1928, p. 14; "Rangers history," New York Rangers, nhl.com.

57 "Smith nominee; Robinson likely mate," *BDE*, June 29, 1928, p. 1; "Demos break camp as Smith sounds Wet battle cry," *Austin TX American*, June 30, 1928, p. 1.

58 Gentile, Nick, with Felice Chilante, *Vita di Capomafia*, Rome: Crescenzi Allendorf, 1993, p. 87; Flynn, James P., "La Cosa Nostra...," FBI report from New York Office, file no. CR 92-914-58, NARA no. 124-10337-10014, July 1, 1963, p. 12; Salvatore D'Aquila Certificate of Death, Manhattan Borough, certificate no. 25482, Department of Health of the City of New York Bureau of Records, Oct. 10, 1928, filed Oct. 11, 1928; Valachi, *The Real Thing*, p. 280-282; Bonanno, Joseph, with Sergio Lalli, *A Man of Honor: The Autobiography of Joseph Bonanno*, New York: Simon and Schuster, 1983, p. 98-101; Maas, *The Valachi Papers*, p. 142; "Reveal millionaire as real head of new 'numbers' banking combination," *New York Age*, Aug. 20, 1932, p. 1.

59 Valachi, *The Real Thing*, p. 185, 263; Maas, *The Valachi Papers*, p. 78-79.

60 Valachi, *The Real Thing*, p. 176, 206.

61 Valachi, *The Real Thing*, p. 224.

62 Maas, *The Valachi Papers*, p. 78; Valachi, *The Real Thing*, p. 228, 266.

63 Valachi, *The Real Thing*, p. 224; Maas, *The Valachi Papers*, p. 79.

64 Valachi, *The Real Thing*, p. 230.

65 Domenico Villacci Standard Certificate of Death, Borough of Manhattan, register no. 20678, Department of Health of the City of New York Bureau of Records, Aug. 16, 1929.

66 Valachi, *The Real Thing*, p. 262-263; Maas, *The Valachi Papers*, p. 79-80; Lipton, Dr. Harry R., "Neuropsychiatric report, Name: Valachi, Joseph," July 11, 1962, attached to SAC Atlanta, "La Cosa Nostra, AR - Conspiracy," FBI Airtel to Director, file no. 92-6054-419, NARA no. 124-10286-10381, Sept. 3, 1963, p. 2.

67 Valachi, *The Real Thing*, p. 264-265.

68 Valachi, *The Real Thing*, p. 227-228.

69 Valachi, *The Real Thing*, p. 242, 250.

70 Valachi, *The Real Thing*, p. 252.

71 Valachi, *The Real Thing*, p. 266-267.

72 Richardson, Gary, Alejandro Komia, Michael Gou and Daniel Park, "Stock Market Crash of 1929," Federal Reserve History, federalreservehistory.org; Kramer, Leslie, "The Stock Market Crash of 1929 and the Great Depression," Investopedia, investopedia.com, Feb. 27, 2024; Klein, Christopher, "1929 Stock Market Crash: Did panicked investors really jump from windows?" *History*, history.com, March 7, 2019.

73 Valachi, *The Real Thing*, p. 271-273.

74 Valachi, *The Real Thing*, p. 275; Joseph Morello Certificate of Death, Borough of Manhattan, registered no. 19631, Department of Health of the City of New York Bureau of Records, Aug. 15, 1930; "Harlem racket gang murders two in raid," *NYT*, Aug. 16, 1930, p. 1. The victim was Giuseppe (not Peter) Morello, 63.

75 Valachi, *The Real Thing*, p. 276-277, 304.

76 Valachi, *The Real Thing*, p. 280; Bonaventura Pinzolo Certificate of Death, Manhattan Borough, registered no. 20943, Department of Health of the City of New York Bureau of Records, Sept. 5, 1930; Cassidy, Tom, "Mystery man slain on B'way," *NYDN*, Sept. 6, 1930, p. 3.

77 Gaetano Reena Certificate of Death, Borough of Bronx, registered no. 1800, Department of Health of the City of New York Bureau of Records, Feb. 26, 1930, filed Feb. 27, 1930; "Wealthy ice dealer slain in doorway," *NYT*, Feb. 27, 1930, p. 3. Reina's organization, which likely split off from the Morello-Terranova family during the 1920s reign of boss of bosses Salvatore D'Aquila, had a history of encouraging opposition to the Terranova-Schultz combination. It had been supportive of Valachi and other members of the "Irish mob" in the mid-1920s and appears to have had a later relationship with the Coll gang, which broke away from and fought against Schultz in the late 1920s and early 1930s. At the time of his murder, Reina had recently moved his mistress into the large apartment complex on Sheridan Avenue. The same complex happened to be the home of top Schultz aide Abe "Bo" Weinberg.

78 Valachi, *The Real Thing*, p. 281.

79 Valachi, *The Real Thing*, p. 291.

80 Valachi, *The Real Thing*, p. 322.

81 Vito Bonventre Certificate of Death, Borough of Brooklyn, registered no. 14800, Department of Health of the City of New York Bureau of Records, July 15, 1930, filed July 16, 1930.

82 Valachi, *The Real Thing*, p. 283, 320-322.

83 Valachi, *The Real Thing*, p. 285, 288, 292-293.

84 Valachi, *The Real Thing*, p. 295, 303-304.

85 Munch, Janet Butler, "At home in the Bronx: Children at the New York Catholic Protectory (1865-1938)," City University of New York Academic Works, CUNY Lehman College, academicworks.cuny.edu, 2015; *The Catholic Church in the United States of America*, Vol. II, The Religious Communities of Woman, New York: Catholic Editing Company, 1914, p. 60; "The new protectory for destitute Catholic children," *NYT*, July 24, 1865.

86 "The new protectory for destitute Catholic children"; Munch, "At home in the Bronx."

87 Munch, "At home in the Bronx."

88 Antonio Villacci Certificate and Record of Birth, Borough of Manhattan, certificate no. 34174, City of New York Bureau of Records, Aug. 23, 1900, reported Aug. 30, 1900, received Sept. 5, 1900; Valachi, *The Real Thing*, p. 1-2.

89 Tony Peter Valachi World War I Draft Registration, Harts Island NY, Sept. 12, 1918. At the time, Hart Island held a workhouse for delinquent boys. The offense that caused Anthony Valachi to be sent there is undocumented.

90 Anthony Valachi, Sing Sing Prison Receiving Blotter, inmate no. 70849, received Jan. 19, 1920; Anthony Valachi, Auburn Prison Release Record, inmate no. 5181, Jan. 19, 1920; Great Meadow Prison Parole Register 1911-1929, New York, p. 161.

91 Anthony Valachi, Sing Sing Prison Receiving Blotter, inmate no. 72533, received May 26, 1921; Names of Convicts Received during Month of September 1923, Auburn Prison, New York; Anthony Valachi, Sing Sing Prison Receiving Blotter, inmate no. 72533, received May 26, 1921; Auburn Prison Records, Indefinite and Definite Sentences, 1921-1929, Ancestry.com; Names of Convicts Received during Month of September 1923, Auburn Prison, New York.

92 Frank Rocco, Sing Sing Prison Receiving Blotter, inmate no. 76657, received Dec. 30, 1924; New York State Census of 1925, Clinton County, Dannemora, Clinton Prison, Assembly District 1, Election District 3.

93 Hunt, Warden William, Principal Keeper George F. Seibert, Physician Harley Heath, Report to governor on Definite Sentences, Great Meadow Prison, Feb. 2, 1927.

94 Valachi, *The Real Thing*, p. 169-170.

95 Valachi, *The Real Thing*, p. 170.

96 Valachi, *The Real Thing*, p. 171-172.

97 "Gets life after $1 theft," *NYT*, April 20, 1929, p. 25; "Man is given life term in $1 theft," *Beacon NY News*, April 20, 1929, p. 2; "4th offender gets life stealing empty boxes," *NYHT*, April 20, 1929, p. 2; "Fourth offender gets life term for stealing boxes," *Buffalo Courier*, April 21, 1929, p. 2; "Stole empty boxes, gets life sentence," *BDE*, April 20, 1929, p. 14; Frank Rocco, Sing Sing Prison Receiving Blotter, inmate no. 81933, received April 23, 1929.

98 "Gets life after $1 theft."

99 Frank Rocco, Sing Sing Prison Receiving Blotter, inmate no. 81933, received April 23, 1929; United States Census of 1930, New York State, Clinton County, Dannemora Village, Clinton State Prison, Enumeration District 10-16.

100 Valachi, *The Real Thing*, p. 173.

101 Maas, *The Valachi Papers*, p. 92.

102 United States Census of 1940, New York State, Clinton County, Dannemora Village, Dannemora State Hospital for Criminal Insane, Enumeration District 10-19; United States Census of 1950, New York State, Clinton County, Dannemora Village, Dannemora State Hospital for the Criminal Insane, Enumeration District 10-23.

103 Lipton, Dr. Harry R., "Neuropsychiatric report, Name: Valachi, Joseph," July 11, 1962, attached to SAC Atlanta, "La Cosa Nostra, AR - Conspiracy," FBI Airtel to Director, file no. 92-6054-419, NARA no. 124-10286-10381, Sept. 3, 1963, p. 2.

104 Valachi, *The Real Thing*, p. 174.

105 Access to any information in patient files held in state archives, including a date of death from decades in the past, is "indefinitely restricted" under the New York State Mental Hygiene Law unless access is specifically permitted by the New York State Office of Mental Health (OMH). A request for access to merely the archived but unreleased historic death date of Anthony Villaccio, alias Anthony Valachi, alias Frank Rocco (who appears in U.S. Census records for 1940 and 1950 as a patient at the Dannemora State Hospital), was denied by OMH in June 2024. OMH provided several justifications for denying access to this basic detail: "No patient could be identified with the name(s) given"; "The information requested is not part of the clinical record maintained…"; "We have been unable to determine that there is a demonstrable need for the requested information." The first two justifications appear to have been selected randomly, as our request did not relate either to an existing patient or to a clinical record. Given the final justification, that data gathered by a government entity need only be released upon demonstration of what that entity judges to be a "need" (precisely opposite the principles of a free and open government), it is a wonder that the office bothered to give any other reason.

106 Valachi, *The Real Thing*, p. 261, 364.

107 Valachi, *The Real Thing*, p. 6f3.

108 John Valachi, inmate no. 91127, Sing Sing Prison Receiving Blotter, received Nov. 8, 1935.

109 John Valachi, inmate no. 91127, Sing Sing Prison Receiving Blotter, received Nov. 8, 1935.

110 Names of convicts discharged from Auburn Prison during the month of December 1938; Names of convicts received at Auburn Prison during the month of May 1940; John Valachi World War II Draft Registration Card, serial no. 3671, order no. 289A, Local Board no. 52, Auburn, New York, May 14, 1941.

111 John Valachi Certificate of Death, Borough of Manhattan, certificate no. 16981, Bureau of Records Department of Health, July 24, 1946, filed Aug. 5, 1946.

112 Valachi, *The Real Thing*, p. 649.

113 Maas, *The Valachi Papers*, p. 62.

114 Filomena Villagi Certificate and Record of Birth, Borough of Manhattan, certificate no. 8873, Feb. 6, 1907; Filomena Siano, 059-52-1458, Social Security Death Index, death date July 1972; Madeline Rizzo Certificate of Death, Borough of Manhattan, certificate no. 12664, Bureau of Records Department of Health, Dec. 22, 1948, filed Dec. 26, 1948; Antonetta Valachi, New York City Birth Index, Manhattan Borough, certificate no. 10369, Feb. 22, 1917.

115 Fiore F. Siano, certificate no. 21593, Births Reported in 1927 - Borough of Manhattan, June 22, 1927

116 Miller, Assistant Attorney General Herbert, Department of Justice Memorandum forwarded to New York County District Attorney on July 22, 1963, p. 17, enclosed within Evans, C.A., "La Cosa Nostra," FBI memorandum to Mr. Belmont, file no. 92-6054-406, NARA no. 124-10220-10111, Aug. 13, 1964; Maas, The Valachi Papers, p. 224;

117 Valachi, *The Real Thing*, p. 346-347.

118 Frank Rizzo and Madeline Valachi Certificate and Record of Marriage, Borough of Manhattan, certificate no. 3310, City of New York, State of New York, Dec. 26, 1934; Frank Rizzo and Madeline Valachi

Certificate and Record of Marriage, Borough of Manhattan, certificate no. 12683, City of New York Department of Health, June 9, 1935.

119 Madeline Rizzo Certificate of Death, Borough of Manhattan, certificate no. 12664, Bureau of Records Department of Health, Dec. 22, 1948, filed Dec. 26, 1948.

120 Carmine C. Alfano and Antoinette Valachi Certificate and Record of Marriage, certificate no. 7325, City of New York, State of New York, April 14, 1935, received April 17, 1935.

FEATURE 2

The 'Murder Stables'

By Jon Black

A menacing maze of run-down structures played a significant role in the East Harlem childhood of Joseph Valachi. The structures, built and rebuilt over time from discarded building debris, packing crates and old sheet iron, stood at the corner of First Avenue and East 108th Street. They included junk and rag collection shops, wagon storage and other business uses. At the heart of the ramshackle complex was a boarding stable infamous for criminal activity. Due to its presence, the cluster of shacks acquired an evil reputation and became collectively known as the "Murder Stables."

A 1918 study of the East Harlem property showed that it yielded little income to its landlords and that its nest of decrepit structures had become a neighborhood liability: "The low frame buildings are unsightly and dangerous and should be [razed]. They are a menace to the new law tenements to the west of them."[1] In truth, the property already had been a threat to area residents and nearby structures for many years.

The story of the Murder Stables began about 1898, when the John Cullen

& Thomas Dwyer stone and granite company occupied the land and erected some buildings and stables needed for its work. The stone works were shut down in the early 1900s. The Cullen & Dwyer enterprise was scaled back to a single contracting business office in the neighborhood. Ownership of the former stone works property eventually passed to Cullen's daughters.

The area became the scene of robberies, violence and occasional fires in the period of 1905 to 1909.[2] In addition to being frequented by unsavory characters, the nature of the known businesses – a blending of rag and junk storage with furnace-dependent blacksmithing operations within deteriorating timber shacks – was itself a hazard.

When an April 1909 fire damaged the property, swarms of rats fled a burning junk shop and six adjoining rag-filled shacks into the surrounding neighborhood. At that moment, the proprietor of the destroyed junk shop was Pasqua Musone,[3] a stocky Neapolitan woman who would become a notorious figure in East Harlem.

Harlem's Hetty Green

Pasqua Musone made the journey to the United States in 1892 at the age of thirty six. She likely traveled from the town of Marcianise, Campania, twenty miles north of Naples.[4] Three years later, her eighteen-year-old daughter Concetta married Michelle Lasco, also originally from Marcianise. Lasco ran a blacksmith shop on East 107th Street, next to what was still the Cullen & Dwyer stone yard.[5]

Pasqua began building a property portfolio by about 1904. Together with her son-in-law, she purchased property on First Avenue consisting of a one-story timber frame building and an adjacent vacant lot.[6] The purchases were conveniently located just south of 345 East 109th Street, where she lived with her husband Pietro Sollazzo and two of her children from an earlier marriage to Domenico Lener. Pietro Sollazzo worked at a fish store located on Pasqua's First Avenue property. Son Tomasso Lener left home in 1907 after his marriage at St. Lucy's Church on East 104th Street.[7]

By April 1909, Pasqua was also owner of the junk shops connected to the East 108th Street stables. In June, she spent $1,000 extending and remodeling an adjacent property at 2097 First Avenue. The old stone structure there housed the three-hundred-seat Elena Cinematograph theater and the upstairs office of Cullen & Dwyer. Pasqua and her husband Pietro managed the theater. By August, the family moved into rooms above the auditorium.[8]

Pasqua became known as "The Hetty Green of Harlem" for her wealth and thrifty business manner. (The real Henrietta "Hetty" Green was a rich and miserly New York City businesswoman of the era.) Pasqua was said to walk the same route each day, making personal inspections of her Harlem properties. She did not trust anyone else to manage them.[9]

Pasqua's daughter Nicolina Lener married Gaetano Napolitano on August 24, 1909. Her husband, who emigrated from Campania in 1897, ran a butcher shop in the Bronx. The pair were wed in a civil ceremony, witnessed by Nicolina's stepfather. Their choice of a civil wedding upset Pasqua. She prevented the pair from living together until they could be wed in a religious ceremony and until Napolitano could prove his financial worth.[10]

Two days after the wedding, Pasqua gifted her First Avenue real estate to her daughter. Gaetano Napolitano soon ended the relationship with Nicolina. The press speculated that quarrels with his mother-in-law caused him to leave. Eight months later, census records listed him as single.[11]

Young Valachi

Around this time, a seven-year-old Joe Valachi lived with his family in a tenement house just to the west of the stables complex. With his home infested with bed bugs, Valachi often sneaked out to sleep in wagons kept at the stables. He later recalled his encounters with Pasqua:

> …When she caught us sleeping in those vans believe me she would wake us up by hitting us on top of our heads with a broom handle. I hated her so much, in fact all of us hated her. I used to see her sitting down in front of the stable and I used to pray that someone would kill her.[12]

Pasqua's stables became so notorious in the region, that Valachi's potential employers reportedly turned him away when he revealed his home address: "They would snap back and say no we don't need anyone."[13]

Troubled properties

A January 30, 1910, fire at the stables caused about $1,500 worth of damage. As the loss was reported under Pasqua's name, it revealed her owner-

ship or at least part-ownership of the livery business, as well as the surrounding junk shops.

Her theater also faced problems at the time. It was in violation of fire regulations and was the scene of dangerous incidents. A major fire was narrowly
averted when police spotted two men fleeing from the building and prevented
an arson blaze. They found the stage had been doused in kerosene, but managed to quickly extinguish flames before serious damage could be done.[14] A
week later, as the theater was hosting a vaudeville show for around two-hun-
dred patrons, a small explosive device was tossed through a window. Panicked
cries of "Black Hand!" caused a stampede for the exits that left several people
seriously injured. The police dismissed the incident as a practical joke, finding
the device to be little more than a firecracker.[15]

Pasqua continued her property investments and began to purchase land outside of Harlem. In October, she acquired a plot located next to an old marble
quarry in the town of Eastchester.[16]

She had more troubles in July 1911. The First Avenue fish store where her
husband worked was auctioned under foreclosure, likely the result of a recent
court judgment against her. The court found that she and a man named Aniello
Prisco were in default on a debt.[17]

Prisco, born in 1880, had sailed from Naples in 1905. He joined a cousin
living close to Pasqua and eventually settled at 2133 First Avenue. He acquired
a reputation as a violent criminal and won the nickname "*Zoppo*" (lame) after
a gunfight with "Scar-faced Charlie" Pandolfi shattered his leg and left him
with a permanent limp. He was linked with frequent blackmail crimes in the
East Harlem neighborhood. A week after his court judgment with Pasqua, he
was caught with a concealed weapon and sentenced to six months in prison.[18]

In September 1911, three goats were stolen from a grain store adjacent to
the stables. The animals were taken by nineteen-year-old Generoso "Joe
Chuck" Nazzaro, who had emigrated from Avellino to New York in 1901. He
lived opposite the store on First Avenue and worked as a bodyguard for Giosue
Gallucci, a Neapolitan crime boss based on East 109th Street. The goats had
belonged to the store's owner, Antonio Gerosa, an experienced grain dealer
who would later incorporate a feed company with Angelo Gagliano and Fortunato Lo Monte (future leader of the Morello Mafia faction in East Harlem).
Gerosa worked at the store with his wife Concetta. They were aided by their

son Lorenzo, who later went on to serve two terms as comptroller of New York City and also ran for city mayor.[19]

'Chick' Monaco

Following the string of business troubles, Pasqua and her family moved back to East 109th Street. Daughter Nicolina Lener had previously been romantically involved with a criminal named Frank "Chick" Monaco. Born in the U.S., his parents had arrived from Campania in the 1880s and settled in Harlem close to the stables. He was described as the last of a triumvirate that held the district in terror and was said to have been a "former lieutenant of Paul Kelly in Harlem." According to the police, Nicolina and Monaco frequently quarreled. Nicolina lodged complaints against Monaco on several occasions, but the police took no action in the domestic problems.[20]

On October 6, 1911, Monaco, who recently completed his parole from Elmira reformatory, killed an acquaintance of Nicolina named Michael Barbaro – a notorious horse thief who lived on the same block as the stables.[21]

After posting $5,000 bail, Monaco went to Nicolina's home on East 109th Street and was killed there in a brutal and sustained attack in which he suffered eighteen stab wounds. Nicolina later walked to the East 104th Street police station and calmly confessed to the murder. Police escorted her back to her residence, which was found in a wild state of disorder with Monaco's body lying on the floor. Nicolina was charged with homicide and awaited the coroner's inquest.[22]

Nicolina's defense was reported in the following day's papers. She claimed she had been assaulted by Monaco several months earlier. He took her to Westchester, supposedly to locate her estranged husband, but he instead held her captive in a remote building for several days. She claimed she escaped and made her way back to Harlem. She said she killed Monaco when he tried to steal her family's savings.[23]

The authorities doubted her story. After performing an autopsy on Monaco, the coroner's physician revealed his own skepticism:

> I cannot see how it was possible for this girl to find the strength to make the prolonged fight evidenced by the man's condition … in my opinion, no woman of her slight strength could carry through such a ferocious attack.

An inspection of her clothing showed light marking, but somebody involved in such a fight should have been heavily blood stained.[24] Her claim that she acted alone was also doubted. Monaco's body was found pinned under a four-hundred-pound safe that she could not have moved by herself. In addition, a witness who passed the apartment before the murder recalled seeing four hats placed on a table, but later they had all vanished.

The police thought Nicolina was shielding the real killers. They suspected she had lured Monaco to her apartment where he was murdered in revenge for shooting Barbaro. Despite the discrepancies, the coroner's jury acquitted Nicolina.[25]

Pasqua's end

Pasqua and her family moved to 335 East 108th Street, directly across from the stable's entrance. (Joseph Valachi lived in this building during the 1930s.) Five relatives kept the apartment under close guard. They were warned that Monaco's murder would be avenged, and the family seldom ventured outside. Pasqua hoped to attend Harlem's Thanksgiving celebrations, but friends advised her it would be too dangerous. Her isolation resulted in paranoia. She often awakened at night, thinking someone had broken into her home.[26]

In December 1911, the U.S. Secret Service learned that the Terranova brothers had opened a blacksmith shop "in a shanty in 107th Street near 1st Avenue."[27] It was likely located in the same yard as Pasqua's stables. The Terranova brothers – Nicolo, Vincenzo and Ciro – were half-brothers of Giuseppe Morello, recently incarcerated "boss-of-bosses" of the U.S. Mafia.

Pasqua felt her death was inevitable. She told her daughter she expected they would both be killed. On March 9, 1912, she transferred ownership of her land in Eastchester to her son Tomasso.[28] Eleven days later she ventured outdoors. She made her way over to the stables, reassured by the knowledge that her husband was already on the premises.

Nicolina was keeping watch from her apartment window when she spotted two men following her mother. It was too late to warn her. The men shot Pasqua, killing her instantly, and made their escape toward Second Avenue.[29]

A large crowd of excited locals assembled at the stables before being dispersed by the arrival of police. Joseph Valachi was among those who managed to get into the structure at that time. Apparently, he felt no sorrow over Pasqua's death:

She was laying on the floor. I made it my business to get in there somehow and I just spit on her and said it's about time. I guess everybody was happy as she was a very mean woman.[30]

Nicolina and her stepfather were taken to the East 104th Street police station. A distraught Nicolina described the two killers to the police, who recognized them as close associates of the late Frank Monaco. Twenty-five detectives were sent out in search of the killers.[31]

Investigation

Two days later the police arrested Luigi Lazzazara, a middle-aged horse dealer and part-owner of the stables. Nicolina had implicated him in the murder, and other witnesses had seen him open the stable's doors to aid the killers' escape. He was eventually released due to lack of evidence.[32] He was later placed on trial for horse theft and his stables put under surveillance on the suspicion it was sheltering stolen horses.[33]

Horse theft had become so widespread that insurance companies stopped offering policies. It was estimated that five horses and wagons, each worth around $800, were stolen every day in New York. The horses were disguised by trimming their manes and tails and concealing distinctive marks with dye. Wagons were chopped, reconfigured and repainted.[34] During a meeting of the Horse Owners' Protective Association in 1913, an organizer charged that the "Lazzazarro Gang" was a top criminal organization and accused it of performing murder, blackmail, arson and poisoning of rival horse businesses.[35]

The next suspect arrested was Aniello "Zoppo" Prisco, recently released from prison. He was picked up on June 18, 1912, due to his resemblance to one of the men described by Nicolina. The case against him was dismissed in September after several key witnesses failed to appear. Nicolina had fled to Italy for her safety.[36] Pasqua's murder remained unsolved.

According to Valachi's recollection, Pasqua had committed the murder of Monaco in revenge for an assault on Nicolina. A Monaco associate then took revenge on Pasqua after he was released from prison. Valachi's version of events points to Prisco as the killer, as he had been in prison at the time of Monaco's death and was released shortly before Pasqua's murder.[37]

Prisco

Valachi's memoirs contain details of several other Harlem shootings from his childhood. One account covered the 1912 killing of Antonio "Sharkey" Zaracca (or Zaccaro), a gangster who was known to shake down Harlem's cart merchants, including Valachi's own father.[38]

Zaracca, hiding since a shootout with a man known as "Coney Island" Joe, was tracked down on September 2 and killed in a café on East 109th Street. "Coney Island" Joe and his fellow gunmen managed to escape the area before the police arrived.[39] A month later, Prisco was arrested on East 108th Street as a suspect. He was once again discharged due to lack of evidence.[40]

The deputy police commissioner received new information connecting Prisco to Pasqua's killing. Anonymous tips indicated that he was hired to commit the murder by Giosue Gallucci. The informants claimed that Gallucci had been angered by Pasqua's apparent readiness to pass information to the police following the death of Monaco.[41]

At around midnight on December 15, Prisco walked into Gallucci's bakery on East 109th Street. Soon after his arrival, he was fatally shot by Gallucci's nephew John Russomano. Russomano later confessed to killing Prisco. He claimed the shooting was done in self-defense after Prisco had attempted to rob his uncle at gunpoint. Russomano escaped a homicide charge five days later when his action was was deemed justifiable homicide.[42]

Buonomo

Two months after Prisco's assassination, his allies retaliated. On February 18, 1913, Russomano was wounded and his bodyguard Tony Vivolo was killed in an ambush outside 329 East 109th Street.[43]

Gallucci exacted revenge on those connected with the attack. Charles Marone, suspected of being one of the gunmen, was later killed in a saloon. Nicolo DelGaudio, whose name was linked to the attack, was later shot down after returning from a trip to Naples and reportedly demanding money from Gallucci. Another victim was Amedio Buonomo, an associate of Prisco. He was described as a man of importance in Harlem's Little Italy, and a "leader of a coterie of men."[44]

Buonomo was born in 1884 to Generoso and Grazia Morano Buonomo. He arrived in Boston from Pratola Serra, Campania, in 1895.[45] He appeared briefly in the New York papers two months after Monaco's 1911 murder, when he was shot in a fight in Harlem's Thomas Jefferson Park. Twenty men, including some who traveled from Philadelphia, met in the park for a pre-arranged fight. Some witnesses said the battle was a vendetta, while others said it was a fight over a girl. (One of those injured was a notorious character known as "Tough Louie" Brindisi, who formerly ran a saloon on Water Street in Bridgeport, Connecticut.) Buonomo was taken to the hospital, where he gave his address as Westchester Avenue in a then-undeveloped part of the Bronx.[46]

Buonomo purchased a chain mail vest for his personal protection on the streets. On April 5, 1913, he left home without his armor and was gunned down on East 113th Street close to Thomas Jefferson Park. Five days later, his impressive funeral procession made its way from his home on Madison Avenue. Headed by a forty-two-piece band, it included more than a hundred carriages and was guarded by a similar number of detectives.

The police arrested "Diamond Joe Pepe" Viserti as a suspect in the Buonomo killing. A friend of the Terranova brothers, Viserti later made his fortune in bootlegging. Joe Valachi recalled visiting Viserti's restaurant and dance hall, the "Zoo Casino" at 681 East Fordham Road in the Bronx. He claimed he once saw a Viserti vendetta victim bound in the dance hall's basement.[47]

Police counted six "mysterious street murders," and ten shootings as part of the recent East Harlem feud. The press identified the warring groups as the "Russomanno-Gallucci" and the "Prisco-Buonomo" factions. The tit-for-tat conflict continued when Joe DeMarco, was wounded on April 14. DeMarco was an ally of the Terranova brothers and ran a feed store attached to the stables. Two days later, Pietro Martino was shot while entering his home on East 117th Street. He had been suspected of hiring the men who killed Buonomo. Two weeks later, Gallucci's faction was credited with the shooting of three people outside the Elena theater once managed by Pasqua Musone.[48]

Vice Ring

Prisco's death triggered a wide-ranging investigation that eventually revealed a city-wide vice ring and ensnared Gallucci.[49] Both factions in the gang war had connections to the city's vice trade. Buonomo's brother, "Chicago Joe," was part of a "white slave" gang. He was sentenced to death in 1912 for killing a woman he had trafficked from New York to Chicago, where he was said to be a friend of vice-king Jim Colosimo of the Chicago mob. Gallucci was also linked the trade and was referred to as "King of the White Slavers." He ran a brothel close to his bakery on East 109th Street.[50]

City prosecutors learned that the ring leaders were also involved in policy gambling. In the summer of 1913, twenty-five detectives raided policy shops in East Harlem and lower Manhattan's Little Italy. Among the forty arrests were Gallucci and his nephew Russomano, who were both held for carrying concealed weapons. Gallucci was released on $10,000 bail, while Russomano was convicted and sentenced to three to six years in Sing Sing prison.[51]

Other policy men arrested around this time included Anthony Celantano, described as even more powerful than Gallucci. Born in 1869 in Muro Lucano, Italy, he controlled the policy racket near his home on Kenmare Street. The local gang there was said to include Oreste "Harry Shields" Shilitano, a relative of Valachi's close companion "Sally Shields" Shilitano.[52] Celantano was later stabbed during a robbery by a group that included Silvio Tagliagambe (who was involved in a 1922 shootout with rising Mafia power Giuseppe Masseria). Celantano survived the attack and continued running policy rackets, he later paid a Mafia organization for the privilege of running its game.[53]

Last Vendettas

Two years after the death of Pasqua Musone, the stables were still managed by her old business partner Luigi Lazzazara. Although he had been arrested in connection with her murder, he had managed to escape conviction. He finally met his end on February 19, 1914. He was making his way past 2106 First Avenue, when he was stabbed to death by Angelo Lasco, a brother of Pasqua's son-in-law. The police found Lasco nearby, drunk and bloodstained. A detective overheard him muttering to himself, "Now, I've made a mess of this thing."[54]

The war had left Gallucci and his allies with a number of dangerous enemies:

Andrea Ricci was a partner of Prisco but had been in jail for horse theft at the time of his friend's murder. He left Harlem and became a leader in Brooklyn's Navy Street Gang and was later initiated into the Camorra.[55]

John Mancini, who stole horses with Ricci, later became an inducted member of the Coney Island Camorra group.[56]

Pellegrino Morano had previously been a friend of Gallucci and was an uncle to the late Amedio Buonomo. He lived on East 116th Street and ran a liquor store near Buonomo's coffee shop. He was forced to leave Harlem. He later led the Camorra group in Coney Island and demanded retaliation against the Terranovas for the murder of his nephew.[57]

Alessandro Vollero, a boss in the Navy Street Gang, sought retribution for the killing of Nicolo DelGaudio, his "fellow townsman" from Gragnano, Campania. Another Navy Street leader from Gragnano was Leopoldo Lauritano. He married Delgaudio's widow, who had sworn a vendetta against her husband's killers.[58]

Andrew Rege, who stole horses with Pasqua's old business partner Luigi Lazzazara, relocated from Harlem to Brooklyn. He aided the Navy Street Gang with the killing of a Gallucci associate.[59]

Joe "Chuck" Nazzaro, a Gallucci bodyguard, turned his allegiance after being arrested alongside his employer for carrying a concealed weapon and receiving no help with bail.[60]

Gallucci was assassinated in May 1915 in his son's East 109th Street café. One of the gunmen was Andrea Ricci, Prisco's old partner and then boss of the Navy Street Gang. Gallucci had been betrayed by his own allies and bodyguard who assisted the Brooklyn gang with its first killing. It was primarily an effort to gain control over his criminal empire, but many of those involved also sought revenge for the deaths of their associates.

Valachi later recalled Gallucci's funeral, describing it as "one of the biggest of all the ones I saw around this time." The procession was comprised of one hundred and fifty carriages, and the roofs, fire escapes and doorways along its route were teeming with curious onlookers.[61]

Most of the key figures involved in the war were dead or incarcerated. The Brooklyn Camorra, which had conspired with the Terranova brothers to assassinate Gallucci, continued the relationship and began work on expanding its gambling operations in the city.

Other killings

Not all the shootings and murders that occurred in the vicinity of the stables were connected to the Gallucci feud. In 1914, Giuseppe Gandolfo, who had run a wagon business on the premises since 1910, was shot for reasons unknown.[62] Fortunato and Gaetano Lo Monte, who ran a feed store on the corner, were both killed in a Mafia war with "Toto" D'Aquila. Their store then passed to Fortunato's brother-in-law, Frank Badolato, who had run the Ignatz Florio Co-operative with mafioso Giuseppe Morello.[63]

Ippolito Greco, who ran the stables in 1915, was gunned down outside the premises. He had been connected to the killing of poultry merchant Barnet Baff, a case that featured the sensational term "Murder Stables" in its head-lines. The car used in the killing of Barnet Baff was said to have belonged to "Scar-faced Charlie" Pandolfi, the same man who had shattered Prisco's leg in a gunfight.[64]

Calabrian Carmelo Mollico, who ran a cafe opposite the stables at 335 East 108th Street, was killed in May 1915. He had bought the business from Joe "Chuck" Nazzaro, who was arrested for the Mollico murder.[65]

End of the stables

The old stables site was eventually converted into an automobile garage. The owner leased the property to John Rumore, a Morello gang associate who ran an undertaker business nearby.[66]

The term "murder stables" lingered in the press for decades to come. In 1939, the *New York Sun* used the term in a light-hearted Saturday quiz, asking readers to name the location of the infamous shacks.

The entire city block was demolished and remodeled in 1961 as part of the Franklin Plaza project.[67]

Pasqua Musone (left), Nicolina Lener (right)

Aniello Prisco (left), Frank Monaco (right)

TWO SHOT DOWN IN HARLEM FEUD

Most Hated Man in Little Italy and Son Dying, Victims of Black Hand.

Giosue Gallucci, said to be the most feared and most hated man in all of Harlem's Little Italy, was shot and mortally wounded last night while in his son's coffee house at 326 East 109th Street. His son, Lucca, proprietor of the place, was also shot. Both were

Giosue Gallucci (left), NY Tribune of May 18, 1915 (right).

Corner of East 108th and First Avenue. (UMC Digital Galleries, gcah.org)

"Murder stable." (New York Herald, 1917)

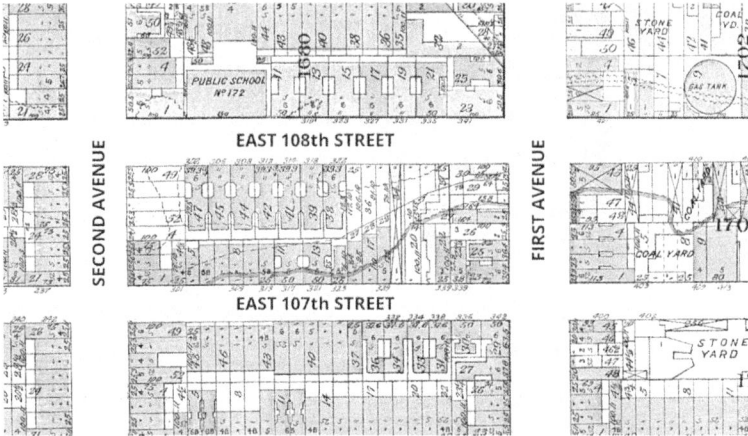

Neighborhood surrounding the "Murder Stables" in 1911.

Feature 2 Notes

1 *New York Times* (*NYT*), Oct 17, 1901; *NY Tribune*, Mar 15, 1910; *Block sketches of New York City*, Clara Byrnes, New York: Radbridge Co Inc, 144 Pearl St., 1918; New York City Record Office, Annual record of assessed valuation of real estate in the city of New York, New York, 1906–1916.

2 *Evening Telegram*, June 12, 1905. p. 2; *Boston Globe*, Sep 27, 1905; *NY Sun*, Sep 28, 1905; *Tribune*, Jan 8, 1906; *NYT*, Jan 8, 1906; *Sun*, Jan 8, 1906, p. 12.

3 *NY Herald*, Apr 26, 1909, p. 6.

4 Ship: *Hindoustan*, July 6, 1892. New York, U.S., Arriving Passenger and Crew Lists; New York Marriage certificate, Manhattan #14403 (Tomasso Lener); New York State Population Census 1905, New York County, A.D. 33, E.D. 05.

5 New York Marriage certificate, Manhattan #17498 (Concetta Lenere); *Trow's New York City Directory*, 1897-1898, p 825; NYT, Mar 9, 1898, p. 10; U.S. Passport Applications, Michele Lasco #7469, 1 1920.

6 *Real Estate Record and Builders' Guide*, New York: F. W. Dodge Corp. Vol. 73, March 12, 1904, p. 567 (2113 – 2115 First Av.). Lasco previously leased the property for his wagon business in 1899 (*Trow's New York City Directory*, 1899-1900; *Real Estate Record and Builders' Guide*, Vol. 64, 1899, p. 893). The neighboring land of 2117 First Ave. was briefly acquired at some point later, shown when Pasqua leased the property (*Real Estate Record and Builders' Guide*, Vol. 76, Sept 2, 1905, p. 383).

7 New York State Population Census, 1905, New York County, A.D. 33, E.D. 05; Pietro Sollazzo was listed as Pietro Spinelli in the 1905 census. Hunt, Thomas, "Spinelli's killing sparked Murder Stable legends," The American Mafia, mafiahistory.us, revised 08 Dec 2021; NYT, Oct 30, 1911, p. 20; New York Marriage certificate, Manhattan #14403 (Tomasso Lener).

8 *Herald*, Apr 26, 1909, p. 6; *Real Estate Record and Builders' Guide*, New York: F. W. Dodge Corp. V. 83, June 19, 1909, p. 1250; *Block sketches of New York City*, Clara Byrnes, New York: Radbridge Co Inc, 144 Pearl St., 1918; *Herald*, Mar 22, 1912; New York Marriage certificate, Manhattan #17326 (Nicolina Lener); United States Census of 1910, New York State, New York County, W 12, ED 339; *NY Tribune*, Mar 15, 1910, p. 1.

9 *NY Daily Tribune*, Mar 21, 1912, p. 2.

10 New York Marriage certificate, Manhattan #17326 (Nicolina Lener); 1910 United States Federal Census, New York, Bronx, AD 32, ED 1469; New York Marriage certificate, Manhattan #14403 (Tomasso Lener); *NYT*, Mar 21, 1912. p. 1.

11 *Sun*, Oct 30, 1911, p. 2; *Sun*, Mar 21, 1912, p. 3; *NYT*, Oct 30, 1911, p. 20; *Real Estate Record and Builders' Guide*, New York: F. W. Dodge Corp. v. 84, Jul-Dec 1909 Index, p. 460. The conveyance was likely made as a gift. It requested a mortgage around 70% lower than the property's estimated value (New York City Record Office, Annual record of assessed valuation of real estate in the city of New York, 1906 – 1911).

12 Valachi, Joseph, *The Real Thing: Second Government - The Expose and Inside Doings of Cosa Nostra*, unpublished manuscript, John F. Kennedy Presidential Library and Museum, 1964, p. 10-11.

13 Valachi, *The Real Thing*, p. 10-11; 1910 United States Federal Census, New York, Manhattan, Ward 12, ED 0339.

14 *Herald*, Feb 1, 1910, p. 14; Entertainment license granted to Aristide Carbone, *The City Record: Official Journal*, New York: V.37, Oct 6, 1909, p. 1; *The City Record: Official Journal*, New York: V.38, Jan 5, 1910, p. 87; *Herald*, March 9, 1910, p. 8.

15 *Herald*, Mar 15, 1910, p. 4; *York Dramatic Mirror*, Mar 26, 1910, p. 8; *Tribune*, Mar 15, 1910, p. 1.

16 New York Land Records, 1630-1975, Westchester, Grantor index (Eastchester) 1898-1931; *Daily Argus*, Oct 5, 1910.

17 *Real Estate Record and Builders' Guide*, New York: F. W. Dodge Corp. V.88. Jul 8, 1911, p. 22 & Jul 15, 1911, p. 60; *Real Estate Record and Builders' Guide*, New York: F. W. Dodge Corp. V.88, Jul 8, 1911, p. 37; *NYT*, Jul 6, 1911, p. 17 c7.

18 Ship: *La Gascogne*, 2 Jul 1905, New York, U.S., Arriving Passenger and Crew Lists (including Castle Garden and Ellis Island), 1820-1957; *Evening World*, Dec 16, 1912; *NY Press*, Dec 16, 1912; New York Death Certificate, Manhattan #35154; *Evening World*, Dec 16, 1912; *NYT*, Dec 17, 1912.

19 *Evening World*, Sep 21, 1911; NYC Magistrates Court Docket, Sep 21, 1911; Ship manifest for *Archimede*, Feb 23, 1901; Marriage Certificate, Manhattan #29333; United States Census of 1910, New York State, New York County, W 12, ED 286; Gerosa & Lo Monte Company Inc., Certificate of

Incorporation, Jan 11, 1913; "New York's No. 2 Official Recalls Youth in Vineland," *Vineland Times Journal*, May 4, 1957.

20 United States Census of 1910, New York State, New York County, W 12, ED 286; New York State Population Census, 1905, New York County; *Evening World*, Oct 30, 1911; *Sun*, May 24, 1909; *NYT*, Oct 30, 1911, p. 20.

21 *Evening World*, Oct 30, 1911, Oct 31, 1911; *Sun*, May 24, 1909; 1910 United States Federal Census, Elmira, Chemung, W 7, ED 28.

22 *NYT*, Oct 30, 1911; *Evening World*, Oct 30, 1911; *NY Call*, Oct 30, 1911; *Sun*, Oct 30, 1911.

23 *NYT*, Oct 30, 1911; *Evening World*, Oct 30, 1911; *Call*, Oct 30, 1911; *Sun*, Oct 30, 1911.

24 *NYT*, Oct 30, 1911; *Evening World*, Oct 30, 1911; *Call*, Oct 30, 1911; *Sun*, Oct 30, 1911; *Herald*, Oct 31, 1911; *Evening World*, Oct 31, 1911; New York Marriage certificate, Manhattan #17326 (Nicolina Lener).

25 *Herald*, Oct 31, 1911; *Evening World*, Oct 31, 1911; *NYT*, Mar 21, 1912.

26 *Press*, Mar 21, 1912, p. 1, 3; *Herald*, Mar 22, 1912.

27 U.S. National Archives and Records Administration, RG 87, Daily Reports of United States Secret Service Agents, William Flynn, Vol. 33, Dec 12, 1911.

28 *Press*, Mar 21, 1912, p. 3; New York Land Records, 1630-1975, Westchester, Grantor index (Eastchester) 1898-1931.

29 *Herald*, Mar 21, 1912; *Press*, Mar 21, 1912, p. 1.

30 Valachi, *The Real Thing*, p. 11.

31 *Herald*, Mar 21, 22, 1912.

32 *New York City Directory*, 1911; *Herald*, Mar 24, 1912; *Sun*, Mar 23, 1912; *Tribune*, Feb 20, 1914, p. 1.

33 *Tribune*, Feb 20, 1914, p. 1; NY Court of General Sessions, 1912, #91763, The People v. Andrew Rege and Luigi Lazzazzara.

34 *NYT*, Apr 23, 1911, p. 9.

35 *NYT*, Apr 7, 1913, p. 2.

36 *Evening Telegram*, Oct 3, 1912, p. 9; *Evening World*, Oct 3, 1912, p. 13; *Wausau Daily Herald*, Dec 23, 1912; The People of The State of New York v. Aniello Prisco, #89082 (Docket), Aug 9, 1912.

37 Valachi, *The Real Thing*, p. 11.

38 Valachi, *The Real Thing*, p. 11.

39 *Herald*, Sep 3, 1912; *Tribune*, Sep 3, 1912, p. 2.

40 *Call*, Oct 4, 1912, p. 3; *Brooklyn Daily Eagle*, Dec 16, 1912, p. 4.

41 *Evening Telegram*, Oct 3, 1912, p. 9; NYMA, DA Record of Cases, #95249, The People v. John Russomano (Memo in reference to the character of the defendant).

42 *Sun*, Dec 17, 1912, p. 16; *Tribune*, Dec 17, 1912, p. 16; *Evening News*, Dec 17, 1912; *Wausau Daily Herald*, Dec 23, 1912; United States Census of 1910, New York State, New York County, W 12, ED 327; *Herald*, Dec 20, 1912, p. 8.

43 *Evening World*, Feb 18, 1913, p. 9; NYMA, DA Record of Cases, #95249, The People v. John Russomano (Memo in reference to the character of the defendant).

44 *Herald*, Dec 6, 1913, p. 7; *Tribune*, Oct 20, 1914; Court of Appeals, The People of the State of New York against Alessandrio Vollero, Case on Appeal, Vol 1, (1918) 226/587 PT1, p. 473; *Evening World*, Apr 11, 1913, p. 10; *Herald*, Apr 11, 1913, p. 20.

45 Ship: *Tartar Prince*, Mar 26, 1900, New York, U.S., Arriving Passenger and Crew Lists (including Castle Garden and Ellis Island), 1820-1957.

46 *Utica Herald Dispatch*, Dec 19, 1911, p. 1; *Bridgeport Evening Farmer*, Dec 23, 1911, p. 1; *Sun*, Dec 19, 1911, p. 1.

47 *Herald*, Apr 6, 10, 11, 1913; *Evening World*. Apr 11, 1913, p. 10; *Sun*, Apr 30, 1913, p. 5; *Evening World*, Apr 29, 1913; Marriage Certificate, Manhattan #21340; Valachi, *The Real Thing*, p. 11-12.

48 *Sun*, Apr 19, 1913; *Herald*, Apr 17, 1913; *Sun*, Apr 19, 1913; *Herald*, Jul 21, 1916, p.1; *NYT*, Apr 27, 1913; *Fort Wayne Journal-Gazette*, Dec 12, 1915.

49 *Times Democrat*, Aug 2, 1913, p. 3.

50 *Berkshire Evening Eagle*, Oct 29, 1912, p. 3; *Tribune*, Oct 24, 1912, p. 2; U.S. National Archives and Records Administration, RG 87, Daily Reports of United States Secret Service Agents, William Flynn, Vol. 29, Mar 8, 1910; *Tribune*, May 23, 1915.

51 *Times Democrat*, Aug 2, 1913, p. 3; *Evening World*, Jul 26, 1913; *Herald*, May 18, 1915, p. 7; Sing Sing Prison Admission Registers, 1865-1939, #64408; Court of General Sessions for New York County, The People of the State of New York against John Russomanno, Mar 20, 1914.

52 *Press*, Jul 7, 1913, p. 3; U.S. Passport Applications, Antonio Celetano #41656, 1921; Washington Post, Mar 4, 1917; Van't Riet, Critchley, Turner, "A lifetime tangling with the law: Salvatore 'Sally Shields' Shillitani," *Informer*, April 2013.

53 *Evening World*, Feb 12, 1914; Court of Appeals, The People of the State of New York against Angelo Giordano, Record on Appeal, Court of General Sessions, 231/633 PT1, People's exhibit #1 (Statement of Leopoldo Lauritano, Mar 27, 1918).

54 *NYT*, Feb 20, 1914; *Tribune*, Feb 20, 1914; *Herald*, Feb 20, 1914; Ship: *Citta Di Milano*, Dec 10, 1902, New York, U.S., Arriving Passenger and Crew Lists (including Castle Garden and Ellis Island), 1820-1957; World War I Draft Registration Cards, 1917-1918, Angelo Lasco #A2122.

55 *Brooklyn Daily Times*, Nov 14, 1917. p. 1; Court of Appeals. The People of the State of New York against Angelo Giordano, Record on Appeal, Court of General Sessions, 231/633 PT1, People's exhibit #1 (Statement of Leopoldo Lauritano, Mar 27, 1918).

56 Court of Appeals, The People of the State of New York against Alessandrio Vollero, Case on Appeal, Vol 1 (1918), 226/587 PT1.

57 New York Court of Appeals, 1921, Vol 107, People vs Pellegrino Morano, p. 733, Folio 2198; United States Census of 1910, New York State, New York County, W 12, ED 323; *Trow's New York City Directory*, Aug 1910, p. 1029; Critchley, David (2009) *The Origin of Organized Crime in America: The New York City Mafia, 1891 – 1931*, New York: Routledge, p. 111, 113; *Herald*, Apr 10, 1913, p. 1.

58 *Brooklyn Daily Standard Union*, Mar 8, 1918, p. 9; New York marriage certificate, Manhattan #123324; *Standard Union*, Oct 12, 1916, p.3

59 NY Court of General Sessions, 1912, #91763, The People vs. Andrew Rege and Luigi Lazzazzara; *Evening World*, Nov 17, 1916, p. 19.

60 *Evening World*, May 29, 1915; *Herald*, Mar 18, 1917.

61 Court of Appeals, The People of the State of New York against Angelo Giordano, Record on Appeal, Court of General Sessions, 231/633 PT1, People's exhibit #1 (Statement of Leopoldo Lauritano, Mar 27, 1918); Critchley. *The Origin of Organized Crime in America*, p. 111; *Barre Daily Times*, May 18, 1915; Valachi, *The Real Thing*, p. 17.

62 *Tribune*, Apr 10, 1914. p. 2; *Polk's (Trow's) New York Copartnership and Corporation Directory*, boroughs of Manhattan and Bronx, 1910, p. 310.

63 Warner, Santino, Van't Riet, "Early New York Mafia: An Alternative Theory," *Informer*, May 2014; *R.L. Polk & Co.'s Trow General Directory of New York City*, 1916. p. 211; The Ignatz Florio Co-Operative Association Among Corleonesi, Certificate of Incorporation, 1902.

64 *Herald*, Oct 8, 1915, p. 1; *Tribune*, Oct 28, 1919, p. 22.

65 *Evening World*, May 29, 1915; *Herald*, Mar 18, 1917.

66 *Brooklyn Daily Eagle*, Dec 17, 1922, p. 42; *Sun*, Aug 2, 1924, p. 16.

67 *Sun*, Nov 11, 1939, p. 14; New York City Zoning and Land Use Map, zola.planning,nyc.gov.

Mafia minor leaguers

East Harlem gangsters became 'mobbed up'

By Thibaut Maïquès

Pushed by poverty and peers, by about 1920 young Joseph Valachi was engaged in gang crime. He was excluded as many of his contemporaries graduated into regional racketeering. The pressure of the underworld conflict known as the Castellammarese War caused a Mafia organization to induct Valachi late in 1930.

Young Valachi (Villacci) grew up on East 108th Street in Harlem. His father, Dominick, had settled there in 1899 after emigrating from the mainland Italian community of Cervinara, about twenty miles from Naples. It appears that Dominick may have been joined in New York City by one sibling. A Nicholas Villacci lived on 108th Street, was a boxer in 1904 and later became a member of the carpenter's union committee. Dominick did not follow the same path; Joseph Valachi described his father as a violent alcoholic constantly in need of money. The family lived in a squalid ground-floor apartment, which allowed passersby to see everything that happened inside.

Joe Valachi disliked school. He preferred roaming the city rather than attending classes. At eleven years old, he showed aggressive tendencies and injured a teacher. That led to his placement in a religious reformatory in the Bronx. A few years later, he dropped out of school entirely and went to work, initially hiding his job from his father to avoid having his money taken. He later worked alongside his father at a city garbage dump. Dominick took almost all of Joe's pay.

Joe Valachi began stealing with other young men as a means of providing for himself.

His criminal career began to take shape in 1921 when he was eighteen and a member of a burglary gang on 107th Street. The gang of seven or eight members included Charles "Charley Bullets" Albero, Angelo "Charley 4 Cents" Salerno, Frank "Big Dick" Amato, the Corleonese Giovanni "Al Brown" Schillaci, Joseph "Pip The Blind" Gagliano and a certain Joseph Pellegrino (who was later deported). Valachi, a lover of cars, was the gang's driver.

The gang became known as "Minute Men" because of the speed of their burglaries. A garbage can was typically used to smash a store window, and the goods inside were quickly looted. The gang committed about a hundred burglaries in New York between 1919 and 1923.

In the spring of 1923, during a robbery on 117th Street, the gang found itself surrounded by police cars. Valachi managed to escape with his associates in the car, but the vehicle was recognized shortly after. Since Joe owned the car, he was arrested and convicted of attempted burglary. On October 26, 1923, he was sentenced to nine months in Sing Sing prison.

During his prison term, he met Camorrista Alessandro Vollero. The former Brooklyn Neapolitan gang boss became Valachi's mentor, explaining to him Neapolitan traditions and urging him to "beware of the Sicilians." Vollero's Camorra had been in conflict with the Mafia organization of the Terranova brothers, originally from Corleone, Sicily.

However, there had been a Neapolitan associate of the Terranova organization. He was Giuseppe Viserti, originally from Sarno in the Salerno region, south of Naples. Sarno was also the hometown of Angelo Salerno. Known as "Diamond Joe Peppe" because he always wore extravagant jewelry with his fine suits, Viserti had been a killer for Giosue Gallucci, a Neapolitan boss on East 107th Street. He was believed responsible for the murders of rival Amadio Buonomo, as well as police informant Jerry Maida. During the early stages of Prohibition, Viserti was actively involved with Vincenzo Terranova in bootlegging rackets.

Viserti lived for a time on the same street as Valachi. Valachi was friendly with a nephew of Viserti and came to know "Joe Peppe." Around 1920, Viserti showed Valachi a corpse hanging in the basement of his Bronx business. In October of the following year, Viserti was killed in a Manhattan cafe.

Joe Valachi was paroled after serving nine months in prison. When he went to see his old gang, he discovered they had relocated to 116th Street, near the headquarters of the Terranova brothers, and had found a new driver to replace him. He decided to pull together his own gang and went back to burglaries.

Valachi narrowly escaped death during one job. As he drove away from the scene, a policeman shot him in the head. His associates thought he was dead and left him on the street. When they passed by again later, they saw that Valachi was still alive and took him to a doctor. After several months of rehabilitation, he resumed his burglaries and partnered with Dominick "The Gap" Petrelli. Valachi came to regard Petrelli as one of his best friends. Petrelli came from Abruzzo, an uncommon region for mafiosi. His criminal record began when he was fourteen.

Gang conflict in Harlem

Valachi also made new connections, including some young Irish-American hoodlums from Harlem. They worked together on some crimes. The Irish gang had a reputation for brutality. During one warehouse burglary, Valachi found his Irish lookouts lined up and robbed passersby. Valachi felt his life would be short if he stayed with them. He was soon drawn into a territorial war between the local Italian gang and a gang referred to as Irish, though it also included German, Jewish and Italian members. Mobster Joseph Rao (a close associate of Terranova with his uncle Anthony "Big Tee" Buzzone) confronted Valachi and demanded that he set up the Irish for an attack. Valachi refused, and he was considered a traitor by many of his former Italian friends.

An April 1925 robbery conviction returned Valachi to Sing Sing for a term that included a few months from his previous conviction. Valachi described it like a family reunion. Early in 1926, Valachi learned from a fellow inmate that Ciro Terranova's gang had put a contract on his head in exchange for peace with the Irish. A similar arrangement had resulted in the murder of Francesco LaPuma months before.

Valachi thought himself safe at that moment, but an attempt soon was made on his life in the prison. A young Pietro LaTempa, who entered prison a month before Valachi, approached an unwary Valachi and stabbed him in the left side. Seriously wounded but still conscious, Valachi tried to catch LaTempa but collapsed. Valachi was treated for his wound at Sing Sing's hospital. LaTempa was transferred to another prison to avoid further conflict. (LaTempa later became an associate of the same crime family as Valachi and continued carrying out murders for the organization, only to be killed himself in 1945 because he was suspected of planning to testify against Vito Genovese.)

In December 1926, Valachi's friend Dominick Petrelli joined him in prison, while bloodshed continued back in Harlem. Dominick Albero, brother of Charles Albero, was found murdered. A true "tough guy," with a record of fourteen arrests and a term in Sing Sing, Dominick Albero was known as the "King of Tire Thieves." It was said that he once escaped law enforcement officers who fired 150 shots at his car to stop him. Near the middle of December, five gangsters kidnapped Dominick Albero, killed him and then tossed his body from the car at 108th Street and Park Avenue.

Joseph Valachi was released from Sing Sing in June 1928, concerned by the Terranova death sentence against him. He approached his friend Frank Livorsi, a Terranova aide, who told him that everything was fine. Valachi went back to what he knew best – burglary. He found that his former associates on 116th Street had moved on to "gangsterism."

The 116th Street Crew would become known as the most powerful crew of the future Genovese Crime Family. Decades later, Valachi would testify about the activities of the organization, but immediately after his release from prison he was largely unaware of its rackets.

Artichoke racket

He understood that Ciro Terranova was the "Artichoke King" in New York because he bought all the artichokes shipped into the city. Valachi did not yet know that Terranova used members of the 116th Street Crew for this racket, especially Neapolitan associate Giuseppe "Muskie" Castaldo. Castaldo was originally from Brusciano, near Naples. He became an in-law of 116th Street Crew member Angelo "Charley Four Cents" Salerno, when Salerno married Castaldo's sister Josephina. According to Federal Bureau of Narcotics records,

Salerno also was the brother-in-law of Charles "Charlie Bullets" Albero, whose parents were from Sarno (like Salerno and Viserti).

Close cooperation between Terranova and Castaldo was evident on January 17, 1924, when a company certificate was filed at the county clerk's office, identifying Castaldo and Ciro Morello (that is, Terranova) as the owners of "J. Castaldo & Co." Castaldo's address was on 106th Street, and Ciro's was 338 East 116th Street (the same address where he suffered a stroke in 1938). The company bought a portion of the artichokes from wholesalers who transported them from California. The company soon assembled a near-monopoly over artichokes in Harlem. Authorities took serious interest, noting Terranova had a long criminal record. Terranova later claimed he retired from the business in 1927, but he remained secretly active. Castaldo eventually was arrested for not complying with tax laws. Soon after, he closed the company and, along with associates, established the renowned "Union Pacific Produce Company."

Terranova was thus very close to local Neapolitan gangsters. He also worked with Calabrian gangsters, most notably through Harlem mafioso Francesco "Casino" Cucola. During the reign of Frank Costello, also Calabrian, Cucola reportedly reached the rank of capodecina, and Angelo Salerno became his personal bodyguard. Cucola appeared as a witness at the wedding of Lorenzo "Buddy" Salerno, Angelo's cousin. (It's important to note that Anthony "Fat Tony" Salerno had no blood relation to Angelo, as he was Sicilian, with parents from San Fratello.)

Castaldo's Union Pacific Produce Company forced businesses in the Bronx and Harlem region to ignore competing artichoke wholesalers. If a business did not comply, its office windows would be smashed, its staff would be assaulted and its goods would be plundered. When regional wholesalers found themselves without clients, Union Pacific Produce would step in and offer to redistribute their artichokes. Castaldo and associates reportedly bought artichoke crates for $2 each and resold them at three times that amount.

Angelo Salerno and his brothers were heavily involved in the racket. Official associates included Paul DiGeorge (a pseudonym for mobster Harry Bonsignore), Neapolitan Colombo Christopher and Francesco "Casino" Cucola. It was also noted that some members of the Camorra from Brooklyn, including the Migliaccio family and Giuseppe "Garibaldi" Conte, were involved in artichoke rackets.

Union Pacific Produce made nearly half a million dollars in profit annually, and the 116th Street Crew formed around this lucrative racket. Castaldo's business continued until 1935, when Mayor Fiorello La Guardia moved aggressively to break up the monopoly. In December of that year, he banned the sale of all artichokes for a time and appointed former detective Michael Fiaschetti to police mob activity in produce markets. By early 1936, Union Pacific Produce was shut down, and several associates were sentenced to a year in prison.

Different course

While the friends of his youth were making their way into the Terranova organization, Valachi took a different course. His pal Dominick Petrelli was close to the respected Mafia leader Tommaso Gagliano, a Terranova rival. Petrelli introduced Valachi to Gagliano.

At that time, Valachi was still just a petty burglar, associated with Salvatore "Sally Shields" Shillitani and Nicholas Padovano.

The Shillitani family was influential: Salvatore's father, Michele, had a reputation in Lower Manhattan's Little Italy and owned a large property on Mulberry Street. Salvatore had a cousin with the same name, known as "Sammy," and together they committed thefts. Additionally, Oreste Shillitani, the cousin's brother, had been executed in the electric chair in 1916. He had a criminal record dating back to 1909 but was sentenced to death after killing a police officer and injuring two others. Sally and Sammy Shields had also been at Sing Sing from 1926 to 1930 for theft and assault.

Little is known about Padovano except that he was arrested for multiple thefts, participated in the 1930-31 Castellammarese War, and was inducted into the Mafia at the end of the conflict. He was killed in 1932 by a police officer, while he was attempting to assassinate Benedetto Bellini with Shillitani on Gagliano's orders.

When Valachi met Gagliano in 1930, he was informed that there was tension between Mafia crime families. Gagliano mentioned Ciro Terranova, knowing that Valachi didn't like him and considered him responsible for the prison stabbing incident.

As the bloody Castellammarese War broke out that year, Gagliano and his men joined Salvatore Maranzano in a fight against reigning Mafia boss of bosses Giuseppe "Joe the Boss" Masseria. Terranova's organization was aligned with Masseria. Valachi, Shillitani and Padovano became active associates of the Gagliano group and were eventually welcomed as members of that Mafia faction.

Maranzano was victorious in the war in spring 1931, and Valachi became part of the new boss of bosses' personal guard. By late summer, Valachi found himself in a difficult position, as Maranzano was assassinated. Fearing he would be targeted due to his support of Maranzano, Valachi hid for a time. When he emerged, he received invitations to join two different crime families. One was the organization led Tommaso Gagliano, in which Tommy Lucchese served as underboss. The other was commanded by Salvatore "Charlie Luciano" Lucania and his underboss Vito Genovese.

Genovese, a Neapolitan, had connections to the Brooklyn Camorra organization once led by Alessandro Vollero (whom Valachi had seen in prison). A prison document shows Genovese was a visitor to the Camorrist Tony Paretti, who was sentenced to death after the murder of Nicolo Terranova, Ciro Terranova's brother. The visitor list also included Carmine "Tuddy the Lion" Franzese (father of John Franzese), as well as Frank Amato and John Volpe from Pittsburgh.

Valachi chose the Luciano-Genovese organization. Though Ciro Terranova and his men were also incorporated into that crime family, Valachi was not placed in their crew. He was assigned, along with his friend Girolamo Santuccio, to a crew captained by Anthony "Tony Bender" Strollo. Valachi later regretted this decision, finding that Strollo and Genovese were the cause of many of his problems.

Shortly after becoming a Luciano Crime Family member, Valachi was called upon to square things between an old friend and a former enemy. Alessandro Vollero was released from Sing Sing in 1933. Concerned over a possible vendetta related to his war against the Terranovas, Vollero asked Valachi to ensure his protection against any reprisals.

> *Thibaut Maïquès, who often uses the pen name of "Harry Horowitz," studies early Mafia history of the U.S. and Sicily. He publishes a blog on Mafia history entitled, "La Fratellanza" (the Brotherhood), and is active on social media platforms, such as Instagram, Facebook and Pinterest.*

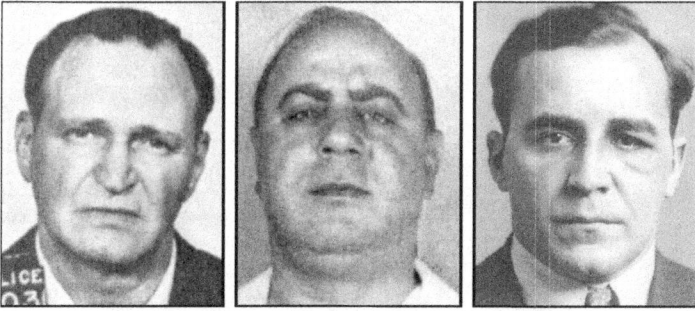

Charles Albero (left), Angelo Salerno (center), Joey Rao (right).

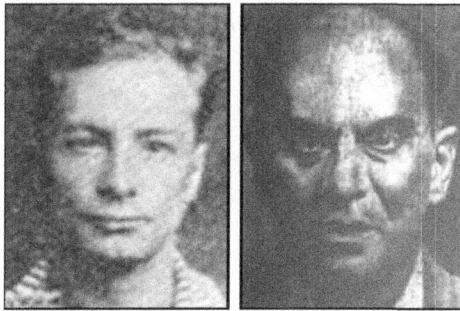

Pete LaTempa (left), Giuseppe Castaldo (right)

ARREST FOR MURDER

ORESTO SHILLITONI

Oreste Shillitani

Union Pacific Produce.

Feature 3 Sources

The Valachi Papers by Peter Maas.

Nicholas Villacci: Passport application on Ancestry (father matches that of Dominick); New York NY *National Police Gazette*, 1904; *New York Daily News*, May 30, 1923.

Minutemen Gang and Irish Gang: *The Valachi Papers*, p. 65-76; *Organized Crime and Illicit Traffic in Narcotics*, p. 136-144.

Giuseppe "Diamond Joe Peppe" Viserti: WWI Draft Registration (born March 1891 in Sarno); Murder of Jerry Maida, *Brooklyn Daily Eagle*, April 29, 1913; Murder of Amadio Buonomo, *Evening World*, April 11, 1913; Sing Sing Register, 1914; Death of Viserti, *Daily News*, Oct. 14, 1921.

Attempted Prison Murder and Death of LaTempa: *The Valachi Papers*, p. 77-78; Sing Sing Admission Register for LaTempa, March 25, 1925; Findagrave Memorial for Peter LaTempa, 1906-1945; Testimony of Ernest Rupolo on LaTempa, *Daily News*, Sept. 24, 1949.

Dominick Albero: New York Death Index (1898/1926), father Aniello; Car Chase, *Daily News*, May 06, 1922; Sing Sing Register, June 16, 1922; Death, *Commercial Appeal*, Dec. 12, 1926.

Angelo "Charley Four Cents" Salerno: FBN files (born 1902, died in 1987, brother-in-law of Albero); Marriage index between Giuseppina Salerno and Giuseppe Castaldo; Father, Ferdinando (1859-1937) from Sarno; Brother, Gaetano "Bobby Lyons" and Anthony; Cousin, Lawrence "Buddy" (1908-1983); Marriage index between Lawrence Salerno and Carmela Pecoraro (Neapolitan families).

Union Pacific Produce Company: Arrest of the Salerno brothers and Castaldo, *Brooklyn Daily Eagle*, July 16, 1932; LaGuardia against the rackets, *Times Union*, Dec. 21, 1935; Details on the Union Produce Company, *New York Post,* Dec. 27-28, 1935.

The Robbers' Gang: Death Index of Salvatore "Sally Shields" Shillitani (1906-1990), father Michele; Death Index of Salvatore "Sammy Shields" Shillitani (1899-2000); Sing Sing Register of Oreste "The Paper Box King" Shillitani (1891-1916); Death Index of Nicholas Padovano (1908-1932); Shooting of Oreste Shillitani, *Times Union*, June 22, 1916; Murder of Nicholas Padovano, *Daily News*, Jan. 29, 1932.

FEATURE 4

Mystery victims

Two killed due to underworld deal were not identified by Valachi

Two rebel groups in the New York area joined forces against the reigning Mafia boss of bosses in 1930. But before they did so, they needed to prove commitment to their shared cause by murdering two men. Valachi described the arrangement in his autobiography but did not identify the victims.

In his autobiography, Joseph Valachi described the joining of the Tommaso Gagliano and Salvatore Maranzano forces in secret opposition to U.S. Mafia supreme arbiter Giuseppe "Joe the Boss" Masseria. Valachi's friend "Buster" – Sebastiano Domingo – told him that the two anti-Masseria forces accidentally became aware of each other in the late summer of 1930. The two groups both had been outwardly obedient, following Masseria-orchestrated murders of key group leaders, while they covertly plotted counterattacks against "Joe the Boss."[1]

Maranzano's group was made up of mafiosi originally from Castellammare del Golfo, Sicily, who had quietly split off from a Brooklyn crime family. The members were enraged by Masseria-approved killings of fellow Castellam-maresi, including Gaspare Milazzo (killed June 1, 1930, in Detroit[2]) and Vito Bonventre (killed July 15, 1930, in Brooklyn[3]). Maranzano helped to spread the rumor that "Joe the Boss" intended to kill off all mafiosi from Castellam-mare.[4]

Gagliano's group consisted of insurgents within the Bronx-based crime family formerly led by Gaetano Reina. "Joe the Boss" had Reina killed on February 26, 1930.[5] Bypassing Reina's top lieutenants, Gagliano and Gaetano "Tommy Brown" Lucchese, Masseria inserted Bonaventura "Joe" Pinzolo as leader of the former Reina family.[6]

Maranzano's men were first to strike back against Masseria. Domingo informed Valachi that he was personally responsible for the Maranzano-ordered assassination of top Masseria aide Giuseppe Morello in East Harlem on August 15, 1930.[7] No one outside of Maranzano's small rebel group knew who was responsible for taking out Morello.

Nineteen days later, Sept. 3, 1930, Pinzolo was murdered at a Manhattan office building. Only a tight circle around Gagliano knew that Gagliano under-ling Girolamo "Bobby Doyle" Santuccio was responsible for Pinzolo's death.[8]

Let's make a deal

The Gagliano group was certain that none of its members was responsible for Morello's murder, Domingo told Valachi, "so you guys figured that there is someone else doing this, and they made it their business to find out who is doing it."

A Gagliano soldier named Stefano Rannelli was acquainted with Maran-zano and learned that he was organizing armed opposition to Masseria. Some early consideration was given to joining forces against Masseria. But they decided that they first would prove their commitment by each group mur-dering one Masseria loyalist named by the other group. Domingo told Gagliano associate Valachi of the arrangement:

> They made a deal between them, after all they've got to be sure of one another. So your people [Gagliano's group] gave us a name for us to kill, and the old man [Maranzano] gave Tom Gagliano a name for you guys to kill. And, when that was done, we got together, and now we are working as a team and we are all one.[9]

Either Domingo did not reveal or Valachi did not recall the names of the two Masseria-aligned victims murdered as a result of this conspiracy. Author Peter Maas avoided the issue in his book, *The Valachi Papers*, by skipping ahead to a cooperative venture in which the two groups targeted Masseria supporter Stefano Ferrigno in the Bronx. In Valachi's own text, however, the two test murders clearly were placed before the move against Ferrigno.

Valachi noted that the Maranzano and Gagliano groups already were working together on the planned ambush of Ferrigno on October 24, 1930. At that time, the combined force learned of the fatal shooting of Chicago Mafia boss Joseph Aiello, a Castellammarese ally, by Masseria's Windy City lieutenant Al Capone.[10]

The two killings committed as part of the Maranzano-Gagliano deal can therefore be bracketed on a calendar between the September 3 murder of Pinzolo and the October 24 murder of Aiello. Given that some time was consumed by the groups identifying, carefully contacting and negotiating with each other, the later part of that period appears more probable.

Mafia historian David Critchley reviewed the possibilities in his 2009 book, *The Origin of Organized Crime in America*. Critchley considered several candidates for the two unnamed victims and determined that Giovanni Anselmo and Ruggiero "Roger" Consiglio were most likely done in by the deal.[11] Those two men, both natives of the Palermo area of Sicily and both linked to the Brooklyn wing of Masseria's Mafia organization, were killed about ten days apart in October 1930.

Consiglio

Consiglio was born March 2, 1883, and entered the United States from Canada in the early 1900s. He married Leonora "Nora" Giglio in Brooklyn on August 21, 1910. At the time of his 1919 naturalization petition Consiglio reported working as an importer. He also was known to involve himself in real estate and building construction. He made a series of trips across the Atlantic between 1920 and 1930. His final one ended with his return to Brooklyn on September 23, 1930.[12]

Home about two weeks, on Wednesday, October 8, he and his brother Arthur traveled around the Bath Beach section of Brooklyn in separate cars. Arthur later explained – probably falsely – that they were visiting Roger's contacts in the hope of acquiring new clients for Arthur's insurance business. In the late afternoon, as they decided to return home for dinner, a tire on Roger's car went flat. Both brothers parked on Eighty-sixth Street near Seventeenth Avenue, across from Milton Green's service station. At about six o'clock, the brothers were standing at the street and Green was working on the tire, when another car pulled up behind them. Two gunmen emerged, fired at the Consiglio brothers and then fled. Arthur was wounded in the shoulder, apparently by accident. Roger was dead of multiple wounds to the face and head.[13]

In Roger Consiglio's pocket, police found an address book. Listed inside were some names familiar to the authorities, including Anthony "Li'l Augie Pisano" Carfano, Albert Anastasia, Giuseppe Florina and Ciro Terranova. Police knew Carfano and Terranova to be lieutenants of Giuseppe Masseria. Asked about the list, Arthur Consiglio claimed it was a list of attendees at the recent wedding of his son.

Both of the Consiglio brothers had arrest records. Roger had been picked up four times on charges of assault, confidence work, grand larceny and robbery. He had never been convicted. Arthur once served a six-month prison sentence for illegal possession of a firearm.[14]

Detectives theorized that Consiglio had been murdered for attempting to muscle in on a racket supplying grapes to the Italian-American neighborhoods for home wine-making.[15] For a time, police suspected Ignazio "the Wolf" Lupo, a Brooklyn-based Mafia boss from an earlier era, of involvement in the Consiglio murder. Lupo was arrested and charged in the case, but later released due to a lack of evidence.[16]

Anselmo

Giovanni Anselmo was born December 8, 1881. He arrived in the United States on May 28, 1911, aboard the *S.S. Rochambeau*, from Le Havre, France. For his 1918 military draft registration, he stated that he worked as a grocer at 119 Thirty-second Street in Brooklyn and lived just around the corner at 885 Third Avenue. He noted that his left eye was artificial.[17]

On November 8, 1918, a few Brooklyn boys were playing in a vacant lot on Forty-fifth Street between Eighth and Ninth avenues and discovered the body of a dead man inside a barrel discarded there. The body exhibited dozens of stab wounds, including a cut across the throat.

Authorities identified the victim as Gaspare Candello, of 2828 West Seventeenth Street on Coney Island, collector for the Governale Brothers tomato paste company.[18]

One month later, police arrested John, Angelo and Antonio Governale, along with wine seller Joseph "the Clutching Hand" Piraino and grocer John Pennino. After questioning, the five men were released.

Piraino was again arrested in connection with the Candello "barrel murder" on January 23, 1919. Also arrested at that time were grocers Giovanni Anselmo and Anthony Dabbene. The three men were charged with first-degree murder and were scheduled for separate trials.

According to an early police version of the killing, Candello was viewed by a Mafia gang as a traitor and an informant and a key reason that gang member Antonio Sansone had been charged in connection with a September 1918 East Harlem murder. (Sansone reportedly hid at Candello's home after committing that murder.) As punishment for betraying the organization, Anselmo allegedly lured Candello, with promise of payment for a debt, to the wine cellar operated by Piraino at 355 Hicks Street.[19] Piraino and Dabbene were waiting and attacked Candello as he arrived.[20]

Dabbene did not live long enough to be tried for for murder. He passed away in Manhattan's Bellevue Hospital on February 27, 1919, survived by a wife and three minor children.[21] Piraino was brought to trial and acquitted.[22] (Ultimately, underworld enemies caught up with Piraino. He was shot to death in front of 151 Sackett Street in Brooklyn on March 27, 1930.[23])

When Anselmo was brought to trial in April 1919 for complicity in the barrel murder, prosecutors abandoned the Mafia discipline angle and accused Anselmo of participating in the killing because of business disagreements with Candello. The trial jury could not reach a decision in the case, and Anselmo was retried in May. An Anselmo alibi defense – that he was sick in bed at the time Candello was murdered – helped secure a second hung jury. The indictment against Anselmo was dismissed in December of 1920.[24]

(The Palermo-born Sansone attempted to take full responsibility for the Candello barrel murder in May 1919. At that time, Sansone had been convicted of the East Harlem murder and was being sentenced to die in the electric chair. As the judge passed sentence, Sansone confessed to killing Candello and offered to provide information on other killings he had been involved in.[25] Newspapers speculated that Sansone was attempting to bargain for his life. It seems more likely that, understanding he could be executed only once, it cost him nothing to take law enforcement heat off underworld associates.)

In the autumn of 1930, Giovanni Anselmo was working as a produce dealer, specializing in wine grapes. He and two business partners sold their produce from a market at 182 Avenue U near West Sixth Street in the Gravesend section of Brooklyn. At the time, Anselmo lived about one block from that market at 201 Avenue T.

Near dinnertime on Saturday, October 18, Anselmo was stacking crates of grapes outside the market, when an automobile drove up. A gunman jumped out and fired four times at Anselmo, who ran into the street. Three slugs struck him in the midsection. The fourth was fired into his head through his artificial eye. The gunman climbed back into the auto, and it sped away.

Critically wounded, Anselmo made it to a drugstore on the opposite side of Avenue U. He received some emergency treatment there and was then moved to Coney Island Hospital. As he passed in and out of consciousness, detectives tried to question him about the gunman who attacked him. Anselmo communicated that he did not know the gunman and could not imagine why anyone would want to shoot him. He died at eleven o'clock the following morning.[26]

The *New York Daily News* offered one possible motive for the murder of Anselmo. In addition to selling grapes, according to the newspaper, Anselmo sold liquor, and he had been dramatically undercutting the prices of his competitors.[27]

Ruggiero Consiglio

Feature 4 Notes

1 Valachi, Joseph, *The Real Thing: Second Government - The Expose and Inside Doings of Cosa Nostra*, unpublished manuscript, 1964, JFK Presidential Library and Museum, p. 320-322.

2 Gaspari Milazzo death certificate, Michigan Department of Health Division of Vital Statistics, Reg. No. 7571, June 1, 1930.

3 Vito Bonventre Certificate of Death, Borough of Brooklyn, registered no. 14800, Department of Health of the City of New York Bureau of Records, July 15, 1930.

4 Valachi, *The Real Thing*, p. 321.

5 Gaetano Reena Certificate of Death, Borough of Bronx, registered no. 1800, Department of Health of the City of New York Bureau of Records, Feb. 26, 1930; Valachi, *The Real Thing*, p. 321.

6 Bonanno, Joseph, with Sergio Lalli, *A Man of Honor: The Autobiography of Joseph Bonanno*, New York: Simon and Schuster, 1983, p. 106.

7 Maas, Peter, *The Valachi Papers*, New York: G.P. Putnam's Sons, 1968, p. 87-88; Valachi, *The Real Thing*, p. 321-322; Joseph Morello Certificate of Death, Borough of Manhattan, registered no. 19631, Department of Health of the City of New York Bureau of Records, Aug. 15, 1930.

8 "Castellammarese War of La Cosa Nostra," FBI report 92-6054-551, NARA no. 124-10277-10302, Nov. 20, 1963, p. 1; Bonanno, *A Man of Honor*, p. 116; Valachi, *The Real Thing*, p. 280-282, 321.

9 Valachi, *The Real Thing*, p. 322.

10 Maas, *The Valachi Papers*, p. 89; Valachi, *The Real Thing*, p. 291.

11 Critchley, David, *The Origin of Organized Crime in America: The New York City Mafia, 1891-1931*, New York: Routledge, 2009, p. 182.

12 Ruggiero Consiglio Petition for Naturalization, no. 90816, Supreme Court of the State of New York, Aug. 28, 1919, certificate no. 1222517 issued Dec. 4, 1919; Ruggiero Consiglio passport application, no. 4424, U.S. State Department, March 24, 1920; Rugiero Consiglio and Leonora Giglio Certificate and Record of Marriage, Borough of Brooklyn, certificate no. 7751, City of New York Department of Health, Aug. 21, 1910; Passenger manifest of *S.S. Canopic*, departed Naples on Aug. 6, 1920, arrived Boston MA on Aug. 20, 1920; Passenger manifest of *S.S. Mauretania*, departed Cherbourg on Oct. 24, 1925, arrived New York on Oct. 30, 1925; Passenger manifest of *S.S. Conte Grande*, departed Naples on July 27, 1929, arrived New York on Aug. 5, 1929; Passenger manifest of *S.S. Augustus*, departed Naples on Sept. 13, 1930, arrived New York on Sept. 23, 1930.

13 Rogers Consiglio Certificate of Death, Borough of Brooklyn, registered no. 19749, Department of Health of the City of New York Bureau of Records, Oct. 8, 1930, filed Oct. 10, 1930; "Contractor slain by Bath Beach gang," *New York Times*, Oct. 9, 1930, p. 29; "Gangsters here slay two more," *Brooklyn Citizen*, Oct. 9, 1930, p. 1; "Boro gangster killers elude police," *Brooklyn Standard Union*, Sports Final, Oct. 9, 1930, p. 1; "Slayers trap brothers replacing flat tire at garage in Bensonhurst," *Brooklyn Standard Union*, Late News, Oct. 9, 1930, p. 1.

14 "Contractor, back in country 10 days is ambushed and killed," *Brooklyn Home Talk-The Star*, Oct. 10, 1930, p. 1; "Boro gangster killers elude police"; "Slayers trap brothers replacing flat tire at garage in Bensonhurst"; "Schwartz believes outside gunmen killed Consiglio and left body near home," *Pough-keepsie NY Eagle-News*, Feb. 9, 1933, p. 1.

15 Monroe, Gates, "Gang gun deaths laid to grape racket feud," *New York Daily News*, Oct. 12, 1930, p. B4.

16 Seery, John J., letter to B.F. Bates, July 21, 1936, Ignazio Lupo Prison File, #2883, Atlanta Federal Prison, NARA; "Only two crimes reported in 24 hours as police seize 84 suspects in city round-up," *New York Times*, Aug. 28, 1931, p. 1; "Brooklyn police seize 33 as unrelenting crusade puts crooks to flight," *Brooklyn Standard Union*, Aug. 28, 1931, p. 1; "'Lupo the Wolf' is freed in murder; lack of evidence," *Brooklyn Daily Eagle*, Aug. 31, 1931, p. 10.

17 Giovanni Anselmo World War I Draft Registration Card, serial no. 664, order no. 3367, Local Board no. 37, Brooklyn, NY, Sept. 12, 1918; Giovanni Anselmo Declaration of Intention, no. 56208, U.S. District Court for the Eastern District of New York, April 5, 1922.

18 "Barrel murder arrests made," *Brooklyn Daily Times*, Dec. 3, 1918, p. 1; "Hoboken slayer and sweetheart held without bail," *New York Evening World*, Dec. 3, 1918, p. 12; "Murder jury out 19 hours," *Brooklyn Citizen*, May 15, 1919.

19 Antonino Dabbene had an earlier link to 355 Hicks Street. That was the location of Dabbene's grocery at the time of his Sept. 12, 1918, World War I draft registration.

20 "Woman's tip leads to three arrests for barrel murder," *Brooklyn Daily Eagle*, Jan. 24, 1919, p. 2; "Say prisoners are murderers," *Brooklyn Daily Times*, Jan. 24, 1919, p. 1; "Sansone, sentenced to die, confesses to many murders," *Brooklyn Daily Eagle*, May 29, 1919.

21 Antonio Dabbene, New York City Extracted Death Index, certificate no. 8552, Feb. 27, 1919; Petition of Rose Dabbene for Letters of Administration for Antonio Dabbene, Kings County Surrogate's Court, decree March 10, 1919.

22 "Anzelmo absolved of barrel murder," *Brooklyn Daily Eagle*, Dec. 6, 1920, p. 16.

23 Giuseppi Piraino Certificate of Death, Borough of Brooklyn, registered no. 7070, Department of Health of the City of New York, March 27, 1930.

24 "Murder jury out 19 hours," *Brooklyn Citizen*, May 15, 1919, p. 1; "Disagree in barrel murder," *New York Sun*, May 16, 1919, p. 8; "'Barrel murder' jury again unable to agree," *Brooklyn Daily Times*, May 16, 1919, p. 6; "Murder indictment must stand, says Justice Cropsey," *Brooklyn Daily Times*, Nov. 26, 1919, p. 3; "Anzelmo absolved of barrel murder," *Brooklyn Daily Eagle*, Dec. 6, 1920, p. 16.

25 "Sansone, sentenced to die, confesses to many murders"; Antonio Sansone, no. 70186, Sing Sing Prison Receiving Blotter, received May 29, 1919.

26 "Gunman shoots merchant," *Brooklyn Daily Eagle*, Oct. 18, 1930, p. 25; "Gunmen fell grape man at Coney Island," *Brooklyn Standard Union*, Oct. 18, 1930, p. 1; "Police character wounded in shop," *Brooklyn Daily Times*, Oct. 18, 1930, p. 36; John Anselmo Certificate of Death, Borough of Brooklyn, registered no. 20418, Department of Health of the City of New York, Oct. 18, 1930, filed Oct. 20, 1930; "Merchant dies hiding identity of assailants," *Brooklyn Citizen*, Oct. 19, 1930, p. 2.

27 "$6 alkie peddler shot by gang, dies," *New York Daily News*, Oct. 19, 1930, p. 28.

FEATURE 5

How a mafioso is 'made'

Comparing underworld induction ceremonies of different times and places

By J. Michael Niotta, PhD

By the time Joe Valachi bared all in front of television cameras for Arkansas Senator John L. McClellan and his subcommittee in October of 1963, the agencies working "Italian crimes" in America already had a fair amount of intel on the Mafia, including versions of the criminal society's induction ceremony.

More than a decade and a half earlier, on April 21, 1947, an agent of the Federal Bureau of Narcotics (FBN) received a very simplistic historical view: "The Mafia is originally traced to a Sicilian organization known as the *Fratellanza* (brotherhood) which subsequently was known as the Mafia. This was a secret society." Its members show "absolute obedience to the chief," provide "reciprocal aid in case of any need whatsoever," and understand "an offense received by one of the members must be considered an offense to the entire association and must be avenged at any cost." Though confidential, by 1959 this report had made its way over to the San Bernardino County Sheriff's Office in southern California.

Americans actually caught a startling glimpse of this foreign criminal threat decades earlier – way back in the 1870s! In late summer 1877, the *Sacramento Daily Union* printed the following description: "In Sicily the Mafia is the spontaneous organization of those whose trade is crime." But the reporter with the *Daily Union* didn't view the entity as "a sect or secret society." Instead, he insisted its presence was well-known. "Every one of the 360 communities of Sicily has its Mafia, of which the character varies according to local tendencies and interests."

Within another year or two, outsiders were referring to some of these groups by their proper titles.

On May 25, 1879, the *Detroit Free Press* published "How to become a *Fratuzzi*." A week later, the *Chicago Tribune* ran a similar story. By the coming of the 1880s, Jules Verne and his lesser contemporaries were penning weekly serials about the Mafia – often spelling the term with two Fs. Surprisingly, this early coverage relayed very intimate details, including the induction ceremony.

> A secret society of malefactors called *Fratuzzi* has recently been broken up at Palermo. It was duly organized under one Chief, with subdivisions of labor, a Council of Directors, and its own physician, notary, Councillors, and apothecary. An oath bound the members to mutual defense and succor, and all infringement of the rules were punished with death. The rites of admission were horrible. The finger of the candidate was punctured, and with the blood issuing from the wound the image of some saint was sprinkled, and the image was then burned, and the ashes were scattered to the winds. The neophyte was afterwards conducted to a ball wherein was placed a crucifix. The candidate was stationed opposite. A pistol was put in his hand, and he was required to fire at the crucifix. It is supposed that the man who shoots at the image of the crucified Redeemer will have no scruple in killing his father, son, or brother at the will of the Society, and, after this proof of his courage, the candidate is dubbed *Fratuzzi*, and made a full member of the craft.
> - *"Fratuzzi," Chicago Tribune*, May 31, 1879.

More recent research into the Mafia has focused on genealogy, delving into birth, death, marriage and baptismal records to establish relational roots and reveal a sprawling web connecting this thing of theirs across state lines and continental gaps. Analysis has uncovered a history of relationships between well-known mafiosi and wealthy landowners on the island of Sicily, and has even linked some of these influential individuals to their criminal counterparts on the other side of the globe in major American cities like New York and Los Angeles. The gangs of old maintained their strength through blood, friendship and matrimony. And coming over to the new world, this practice did not diminish. Nor did the practice of certain societal rituals.

Crime historian Richard Warner wrote that "The Mafia was, with its ceremony that included a Catholic prayer card, a religion unto itself, almost a Satanic inverse of Catholicism. Its oath of omertà was sacred."

Since the press's unveiling of the secret induction ceremonies of fraternal *coschi* of Sicily in the late 1870s, a handful of members have come forward – "rats" telling all with the hopes of leniency from the courts and government protection from the fraternal brothers they betrayed. Some of these turncoats even scored book deals, either dictating their life stories to crime writers or jotting their own private memoirs for a profit. Nicola Gentile's still untranslated *Vita di Capomafia* and Ovid Demaris's biography on Jimmy Fratianno, *The Last Mafioso*, are prime examples.

Surprisingly, the accounts which have surfaced over the last fifty years don't stray all that far from the earlier depictions. The more recent iterations still mention the prick of a finger, drops of blood falling over the image of a saint or skull, or the burning of an offering in one's hands while an oath is spoken. But it does appear that time and setting have made a mark, slightly altering, or perhaps diluting, this ritual.

Discussing his own initiation during these televised hearings, Valachi revealed that he sat with thirty-five other men, among them some of the top brass and emerging leaders of the American Mafia – individuals like Tommaso Gagliano, Joseph Profaci, Joe Bonanno and Tommy Lucchese. It was in the New York area, 1930, and boss Salvatore Maranzano led the proceedings, mouthing a chant in Sicilian for the initiates to repeat. Valachi also disclosed what might just be a newer inclusion to these near-religious rites: "There was a gun and a knife on the table." This statement was later echoed by West Coast mafioso Jimmy "the Weasel" Fratianno.

Aside from the gun and the knife, the recollections aren't all that different.

And so, either the induction ceremony remained fairly similar among fraternities (on other continents and on other coasts), or Joe Valachi and Jimmy Fratianno were avid readers of the very old books and newspapers that told of it.

Clarifying, John Dickie's *Cosa Nostra* stated the initiation ritual in Sicily during the 1870s "was virtually identical to the one that men of honour still undergo today." Providing a backstory, he described a memorandum sent in 1875 which "provoked the Minister [of the Interior] into asking for a report from the Chief of Police of Palermo." In this document, the chief indicated "any man of honour due to be initiated would be led into the presence of a group of bosses and underbosses." The would-be mafioso would then receive a prick in the arm or hand and be told "to smear blood from the wound on to a sacred image." Afterward, he would give the chant of loyalty as the image burned, "thus symbolizing the annihilation of all traitors."

Richard Warner felt "the *Fratuzzi* of Bagheria took sacrilegiousness to an extreme." In his explanation, he described a portion of the ritual which may have been omitted after the jump to America. "Before the initiate's ceremony was completed, he was taken before a wall painting of Christ, given a pistol, and told to fire a shot at the image of Jesus without shaking." Those who completed this task were said to be unafraid and could be counted on to kill their own father or brother upon request. Though the expectation of new initiates remained the same, this specific act does not appear in any of the accounts offered by American mafiosi.

Discussing the ritual in Sicily, Mafia genealogist Justin Cascio analyzed a popular figure. "When the pioneering labor organizer Bernardino Verro joined the Mafia in the spring of 1893, he was inducted through a ritual involving his own blood, and the burning image of a skull."

Verro, a leader in the peasant movement in Sicily, joined with the notion that membership might help him advocate for the people. Perhaps for this reason, Cascio felt it "likely that Verro was fooled by an insincere ritual, and was never seriously inducted" into the *Fratuzzi*. As support, Cascio offered the theory of author Henner Hess, who believed "the original Sicilian Mafia never used initiation rituals, as it would have been clear to all who was a member and who was not." Given the stature of those in attendance at Verro's initiation (Bernardo Terranova and Luciano Gagliano to name just two) and the fact that boss Giuseppe Battaglia presided over the ceremony, it is doubtful his induction was a sham.

Jimmy Fratianno's account of his 1947 acceptance into the Los Angeles *"Brugad"* is retold by author Ovid Demaris in *The Last Mafioso*. "Early that evening, he was brought to a winery on South Figueroa Street and now he waited in a small, dimly lit room for the final act to be played out." Fratianno's story rings similar to Valachi's, with family boss Jack Dragna filling Salvatore Maranzano's role and some fifty "made" men gathered all around. Fratianno divulged that four others were brought into the organization that same night, including the boss's nephew.

Valachi also experienced a group initiation. According to Lennert van't Riet and David Critchley, "Valachi made the trip upstate with Frank "Chick 99" Callace, Salvatore "Sally Shields" Shillitani and Nick Paduano. The last two were also to be 'made' that day."

"After five minutes I was the first one to be called," Valachi divulged, saying, "I went in the room and they were all standing by their chair and I walked to the right of the room. I was directed to sit next to Mr. Maranzano, and on the table there was a gun and a knife." Then Maranzano "said some words in Italian." Roughly translated, the words he was told to repeat meant, "You live by the gun and the knife and you die by the gun and the knife."

Elaborating, Fratianno had this to say about the oath: "The way Jack Dragna said it to me, you're joining this thing of ours, you know, an honored society, and you've to be brave and loyal. You come in alive and you go out dead. That's what the gun and knife are all about." You see, "the gun and knife are the instruments by which you live and die," because "this thing of ours, Cosa Nostra, comes before anything else, your wife and kids, your country, even God. When you're called, you got to come even if your mother's dying."

After Joe Valachi repeated Salvatore Maranzano's words, the boss gave him a piece of paper – one which likely contained the image of a saint. "He said that he will burn it and I shall push it back and forth and I shall say as I do it, this is the way I shall burn if I ever expose this cosa nostra."

Next they moved to a bond of blood. "The last thing that was done before you were made a member was to draw a little blood from your shooting finger." A pin or needle was used. "He pricks your finger" – "the Godfather" – and "a little blood comes out... to express the blood relation. It's supposed to be like brothers." And after "it was all over, everyone stood by their chairs and held hands again [then] something was said in Italian."

The same events occurred in Los Angeles.

In Jimmy Fratianno's case, Johnny Roselli – who by then had been a soldier in the Los Angeles family's ranks for roughly two decades (and a very influential one at that) – "greeted the initiates at the door." When the moment arrived, he announced, "It's time," then "led them to Dragna," where the "incanting in Sicilian" hit their ears. "Everybody join hands," the boss instructed. Obeying, Fratianno reached out and did his best to understand the "confusing mixture of Sicilian and Italian." Like Valachi, Fratianno observed "a dagger and a revolver lying crossed on the table." And Fratianno was also asked "to raise the index finger of his right hand." Then came the prick and "a small bubble of blood."

Immediately after experiencing this end of the ritual back in 1893, Bernardino Verro exchanged "a fraternal kiss with each of the mafiosi in turn," an act directly in line with Jimmy Fratianno's account more than half a century later. When Jack Dragna kissed him on each cheek, Fratianno "moved from man to man, kissing and shaking hands." Although Valachi failed to mention this aspect of his own ceremony, he did let on that kissing was fairly standard; at least under the brief reign of Salvatore Maranzano. "The old man said hello and I went over and kissed him on both cheeks as those days we used to kiss when we met."

Informer editor Tom Hunt pointed out that Joe Valachi was made during a turbulent time – amid the bloodshed of the Castellammarese War – and intimated this urgency may have impacted the usual protocols. "Maranzano explained that membership had rules. Since they were in a time of war, he abbreviated the rules to just two: Never have a relationship with another member's wife, and never provide information to the authorities."

Highlighting the importance of these two rules, Maranzano felt it necessary to instruct Valachi on these points despite the impending threat and the expressed need for brevity: Never go to the cops and never mess around with another member's wife! Jack Dragna laid down these very same rules (and a few others) for Jimmy Fratianno during the second half of the following decade. And years later, Fratianno had the opportunity to do the same. Imparting the lessons he had been taught, he warned a new initiate don't "become a snitch"… "you can't violate the wife or family of another member and you can't deal in dope. If you do any of them things, the penalty's death."

Unfortunately, each of these rules that Jack Dragna conveyed to members in Los Angeles – what can be called the romantic moral code of the Mafia –

dissolved when he passed in 1956. Dragna's replacement, lawyer Frank DeSimone, wasted no time in becoming intimate with the wife of Dragna's underboss. When Momo Adamo found out about the affair, the shame drove him to shoot his wife in the head then take his own life. Jack Dragna had been dead for less than four months!

To further illustrate the level of decay, within a handful of years at least three members who'd been loyal to the former "don" began to cooperate with the feds. Jimmy Fratianno, Frank Bompensiero and Salvatore "Dago Louie" Piscopo all became informants during the 1960s. Moving forward, Carmen Milano, the brother of later Los Angeles leader Peter J. Milano, would be added to the list. And it appears the boss himself strayed from the original code too: Milano wore a narcotics rap on his record for trafficking in heroin.

The *Fratuzzi* executed Bernardino Verro for betraying their trust. It happened in 1915, the year after he assumed office as mayor of Corleone, Sicily. Fratianno and Valachi, who were also marked for death for breaking the vow of *omertà*, managed to escape this avenging hand.

Fratianno, who entered witness protection in the late 1970s, toured the country testifying against his former brothers and even helped author two bestsellers about the Mafia. Despite this, he didn't pass until the summer of 1993, dying of natural causes under an alias.

Though not hidden like Fratianno, Valachi also lived out the remainder of his days outside the Mafia's reach. He passed away in prison on April 3, 1971.

It appears Nicola Gentile and Dago Louie Piscopo remained untouched for other reasons. Although the organization had opportunity, it let nature take its course instead. Perhaps the pair were doomed to live out the remainder of their existence in fear, exile and shame.

Journalist Ed Valin pointed out that Piscopo, who was blind and alone after the death of his wife, passed a few days before turning eighty four. Although reports are "sketchy at best, and [the] information is conflicting," the general consensus on Gentile's passing (as offered by crime author Christian Cippolini) is that he was a pitiful old man who relied on the kindness of neighbors for survival.

Similar to the decline in adherence to the Mafia code, the art of ceremony seems also to have been impacted. In the summer of 1976, with the leadership of the L.A. *"Brugad"* in prison and Jimmy Fratianno serving as an acting underboss beneath acting boss Louie Tom Dragna, the pair did their best to induct new initiate Mike "Rizzi" Rizzitello. "Well, how're we going to do this?" Jimmy asked, hearing Louie's suggestion of having Frank Bompensiero "say the words," seeing as "He can do it in Sicilian."

Speaking to the watered down induction Rizzi was about to receive, Fratianno offered the following apology: "I'm sorry, Mike, you're going to get a quickie deal. It's kind of like a kid going to college four years and getting his diploma in the mail instead of going to graduation."

When Bompensiero asked where they should do it, Fratianno shrugged, mouthing "Let's do it in the car, find some deserted spot and park. We don't have a gun and knife, but I brought a pin."

In Senate testimony, Valachi describes Mafia initiation.

Jimmy Fratianno surrounded by security during court appearance.
(Niotta Collection)

Feature 5 Sources

Cascio, Justin. "Born This Day: Bernardino Verro." Patreon.com, July 3, 2022.

—. "Labor and the Mafia." Mafia Genealogy. May 9, 2016. Retrieved from mafiagenealogy.com/2016/05/09/labor-and-the-mafia/

—. "The First Great Wars." Mafia Genealogy. February 20, 2017. Retrieved from mafiagenealogy.com/2017/02/20/the-first-great-wars/

Chicago Tribune. *"Fratuzzi."* May 31, 1879.

Cipollini, Christian. "Nicola Gentile – Meet the Mafia's Most Elusive Yet Revealing Historical Figure," The Writers of Wrongs, February 22, 2017.

Demaris, Ovid. *The Last Mafioso: The Treacherous World of Jimmy Fratianno.* Crown Publishing Group, 1980.

Detroit Free Press. "How To Become A *Fratuzzi.*" May 25, 1879.

Dickie, John. *Cosa Nostra: A History of the Sicilian Mafia.* New York: Palgrave Macmillan, 2004.

Gentile, Nicola, and Felice Chilanti. *Vita Di Capomafia.* Rome: Editori Riuniti, 1963.

Hess, H. *Mafia & Mafiosi: Origin, Power and Myth.* NYU Press, 1998.

Hunt, Thomas. "What was revealed about Maranzano by those who actually knew him?" *Informer*, August, 2019.

Maas, Peter. *The Valachi Papers: The First Inside Account of Life in the Cosa Nostra.* New York: G. P. Putnam's Sons, 1968.

Niotta, J. Michael. *Beneath the Hollywood Mafia Mask: The Rise of Los Angeles Godfather Jack I. Dragna.* Unpublished manuscript, 2024.

Sacramento Daily Union. "The Mafia." July 28, 1877.

Valin, Edmond. "Salvatore Piscopo: The man who betrayed Johnny Roselli," Rat Trap, The American Mafia, 2018.

Van't Riet, L., and Critchley, D. "Mafia, moonshine and murder," *Informer*, August, 2019.

Verne, Jules. "Sandorf's Revenge," *Coffeyville Weekly Journal*, June 26, 1886, 4.

Warner, Richard. "Strength is what matters: The ethics of Nick Gentile," *Informer*, October, 2020.

Zuckerman, Michael J. *Vengeance is Mine: Jimmy "the Weasel" Fratianno Tells How He Brought the Kiss of Death to the Mafia.* London: Macmillan Publishing, 1987.

FEATURE 6

'Little Apples'; big lie

We weren't told the truth about Valachi's early Mafia murder contract

By Patrick Downey

Having survived both the Castellammarese War and the purge of Salvatore Maranzano's faithful that followed, by the fall of 1932, Joe Valachi was settling into Mafia life. As a new member of a crew run by Anthony Strollo, aka Tony Bender, he became safely entrenched in the Mafia organization headed by Charlie "Lucky" Luciano (Salvatore Lucania) and his underboss Vito Genovese. Through *The Valachi Papers*, we learn that Joe received his first Luciano Crime Family murder contract via Bender that autumn. The victim was twenty-one-year-old hoodlum Michael Reggione, nicknamed Little Apples, who hung around a coffee shop on East 109th Street.

Michael was the youngest of nine children, including seven brothers. The majority of the brothers became criminals. According to Bender's explanation to Valachi, two of the brothers had messed with Luciano and Genovese in the early days and had been killed as a result. Now that they were top dogs, the mob kingpin and his underboss were afraid that young Michael Reggione might attempt to avenge his brothers. In a preemptive move, they wanted Little Apples hit.

For assistance, Valachi called on his pals Petey Muggins and "Johnny D" DeBellis to act as trigger men. To set the kid up, Valachi started hanging out at the East Harlem coffee shop that Reggione frequented and struck up conversations with him. Over the course of several days, he developed a rapport with the young hoodlum.

On November 25, 1932, four days shy of Reggione's twenty-second birthday, Valachi made his move. While chatting with Little Apples at the coffee shop, he suggested that they attend a crap game over on 110th Street. The two men walked to a tenement, and Valachi fell behind as Little Apples entered the building. Hiding inside were Petey Muggins and Johnny D, who fired a few rounds into the victim's head. Valachi turned on his heels and walked off.

Valachi and his confederates got away. Luciano and Genovese didn't have to worry about Michael "Little Apples" Reggione avenging his brothers. The assignment was successful all the way around. Only, the motive behind the killing was all a lie. Perhaps Tony Bender didn't realize he wasn't telling Valachi the truth. It could be that Bender's bosses had lied to him.

The fact of the matter was that none of Reggione's brothers had been killed by Luciano and Genovese by that time. In fact, none of Reggione's brothers had been killed at all – not by Luciano, Genovese or anyone else. All were still alive at the time of Little Apples' demise. He was the first of the Reggione brothers to meet an untimely death.

So why the hit?

Newspaper articles pointed out that he had been paroled from Elmira Prison shortly before his murder. However, according to his prison file, he was paroled to the city on May 26, 1931, due to overcrowding. Reports of the murder also stated that his usual address was downtown at 125 Thompson Street, and not the 109th Street neighborhood where Valachi befriended him. For some reason, it appeared he wasn't comfortable in the old neighborhood and was staying away. Why?

Neighborhood

Petey Muggins (real name Peter Leone), one of those who put the fatal bullets into Little Apples' head, was familiar with Thompson Street. He confided in Valachi that the previous March 16, on behalf of Vito Genovese, he participated in another murder across the street from where Little Apples lived. The victims were Gerard Vernotico and Luigi Lanza.

Both men were crooks, but they weren't killed for any underworld transgressions against Genovese. Vernotico's crime was that he was married to the woman that Vito coveted and wanted to marry. Lanza was most likely in the wrong place at the wrong time. Each man was found bludgeoned and strangled with sashcord. Their bodies were left on the roof of 124 Thompson Street.

Vito Genovese and Vernotico's widow, Anna Petillo Vernotico, were married fourteen days later.

Another curious address from Thompson Street was number 174. It was where Little Apples' older brother Louis lived. He was arrested at the location a month or so before the Vernotico murder. Called "Fat Elevator," Louis was part of a counterfeiting ring that was busted in early 1932. Just across the street at 175 Thompson was the Greenwich Village residence of Vito Genovese, who himself had been arrested for counterfeiting some years earlier.

Was Genovese somehow involved in the Reggione ring as well? Did Genovese actually want Louis Reggione hit, was unable to get him because he was in jail, and went after his younger brother Michael instead?

Although none of Little Apples' brothers were killed before him, three would follow him to an early grave.

Reggiones

James Reggione, about thirteen years older than Little Apples, was a career criminal with a record that included both drugs and robbery. He was arrested in 1914 on a narcotics charge and sent to the Tombs. Inside the prison was a block of cells designated especially for drug addicts, and after Reggione was incarcerated, authorities noticed that the addicts were getting a steady supply of drugs from the inside.

James' brother John came to visit him every day. After one visit, a guard noticed that John walked out wearing black shoes, which struck the guard as odd since he was wearing tan ones when he entered. When John arrived the following day, detectives took his shoes and found that the heels had been hollowed out and that he was transporting both cocaine and heroin into the jail. On each visit he would simply exchange shoes with his brother. John was arrested and joined James in prison.

More arrests came for the brothers over the years. James was arrested again in 1922 for holding up a card game on Thompson Street. That same year saw two of his brothers arrested: John was taken into custody for his part in a burglary and Pasquale, aka Patsy Chip Chip, was picked up on a drug charge.

James was arrested again in 1926 for another card game robbery, He was convicted and sentenced to fifteen years in Sing Sing. He was serving this sentence when Michael "Little Apples" Reggione was slain.

In 1930, another brother, Thomas, was sent away for from twenty to forty years for his part in a fatal nightclub robbery.

Murders

After serving about eight years for the card game robbery, James was paroled in December of 1934. Five months later, on May 23, 1935, he visited his sister in Lower Manhattan and asked his twelve-year-old niece to take a walk with him. When arriving at a specific building, James asked her to go inside and ask for a certain person. She was told the person wasn't there. They continued their walk, and while passing a vacant lot, a man stepped out from behind a sign and opened fire on him.

Pushing his niece aside, James grappled with the gunman, but collapsed dead after being shot three times. Chances are James knew he was on the spot and had his niece with him in the hope a gunman wouldn't attempt anything while a child was present.

Five years later in April 1940, Louis "Fat Elevator" Reggione was released from prison after serving eight years for his counterfeiting offense. On August 26, he was walking with another brother, Joseph, in Little Italy when two men, who had been following them, opened fire on the duo. Five bullets found their mark in Fat Elevator and he dropped into the gutter dead. When questioned about the murder, a sister declared, "It's a vendetta, somebody has sworn to kill us all. Oh, God, who's going to be next?"

The next was Pasquale, aka Patsy Chip Chip. His violent death wasn't the result of mafia gunmen however, he was brought down by police bullets in 1950 following an armed robbery.

Unanswered questions

So, what was it that the Reggione brothers did to deserve their fate? Since Little Apples originally lived directly across the street from where Vernotico and Lanza were killed, did his murder have something to do with the double killing? And then James and Louis were the "insurance" hits to avoid retribution?

Or was Louis somehow involved with Vito in counterfeiting? And, in turn, Little Apples was killed as a result, followed by James and then Louis himself?

Did Genovese feed information to the authorities that resulted in Louis being arrested and thought he had better have Little Apples hit in case he wanted revenge?

Were the brothers still involved in narcotics and somehow crossed Luciano? When James was killed, Luciano and Genovese were still at their height, but when Louis was bumped off, Luciano was serving a long sentence in state prison and Genovese was in Italy. So, why bother?

Why the brothers were killed may never be known, but one motive that can be scratched off the list is the one that Tony Bender gave to Valachi back in 1932.

Michael, James and Louis Reggione (left to right).

CERTIFICATE OF DEATH

No. 124 Thompson St.

Character of premises, whether tenement, private, hotel, hospital or other place, etc. **Tenement**

(If institution, state name)

Registered No. **6707**

2 FULL NAME **Girard Vernotico**

3 SEX	4 COLOR OR RACE	5 SINGLE, MARRIED, WIDOWED or DIVORCED (Write the word)	15 DATE OF DEATH
Male	White	Divorced	March 16, 1932 (Month) (Day) (Year)

5A WIFE HUSBAND OF

6 DATE OF BIRTH (Month) (Day) (Year)

7 AGE 28 yrs. mos. ds. If LESS than 1 day, hrs. or min.?

8 OCCUPATION (a) Trade, Profession or particular kind of work **Carpenter**
(b) General nature of industry, business or establishment in which employed (or employer)
(c) No. years so occupied

9 BIRTHPLACE (State or country) **United States**

(A) How long in U.S. (if of foreign birth) **Life**
(B) How long resident in City of New York

10 NAME OF FATHER **Louis**

11 BIRTHPLACE OF FATHER (State or country) **Italy**

16 I hereby certify that the foregoing particulars (Nos. 1 to 15 inclusive) are correct as near as the same can be ascertained, and I further certify that I have this 17 day of March 1932, taken charge of the body of deceased found at City Mortuary and that I have investigated the essential facts concerning the circumstances of the death.

17 I further certify that I have viewed said body and from autopsy and evidence, that he died on the 16 day of March 1932, at —— M., and that the chief and determining cause of his death was Asphyxia by Strangulation Fracture about neck

CERTIFICATE OF DEATH 25435

No. 340 East 110 St.

Character of premises, whether tenement, private, Hotel, hospital or other place, etc. **Hallway of Tenement**

(If institution, state name)

Registered No. **25435**

2 PRINT FULL NAME **Michael Reggione**

3 SEX	4 COLOR OR RACE	5 SINGLE, MARRIED, WIDOWED or DIVORCED (Write the word)	15 DATE OF DEATH
Male	White	Married	November 25, 1932 (Month) (Day) (Year)

5A WIFE HUSBAND OF

6 DATE OF BIRTH (Month) (Day) (Year)

7 AGE 22 yrs. mos. ds. If LESS than 1 day, hrs. or min.?

8 OCCUPATION (a) Trade, Profession or particular kind of work **Laborer**
(b) General nature of industry, business or establishment in which employed (or employer)
(c) No. years so occupied

9 BIRTHPLACE (State or country) **United States**

(A) How long in U.S. (if of foreign birth) **Life**
(B) How long resident in City of New York

10 NAME OF FATHER **John**

11 BIRTHPLACE OF FATHER (State or country) **Italy**

16 I hereby certify that the foregoing particulars (Nos. 1 to 15 inclusive) are correct as near as the same can be ascertained, and I further certify that I have this 26 day of November 1932, taken charge of the body of deceased found at City Mortuary and that I have investigated the essential facts concerning the circumstances of the death.

17 I further certify that I have viewed said body and from autopsy and evidence, that he died on the 25 day of November 1932, at 9:30 M., and that the chief and determining cause of his death was Bullet Wounds of Left Chest, Left Side of Neck, Lower jaw and Hemorrhage

Though separated by six miles and eight months, the murders of Gerard Vernotico (top) and Michael Reggione may have been linked.

Feature 6 Sources

Girard Vernotico Death Certificate, #6707, Borough of Manhattan, March 17, 1932.

James Reggione Death Certificate #12312, Borough of Manhattan, May 23, 1935.

Louis Reggione Death Certificate #18020, Borough of Manhattan, Aug. 26, 1940.

Michael Reggione Death Certificate, #25436, Borough of Manhattan, Nov. 25, 1932.

Michael Reggione prison dossier, New York State Archives.

Peter Maas, *The Valachi Papers*, New York: G.P. Putnam's Sons, 1968.

Sing Sing Prison Receiving Blotter (Ancestry.com) pages for #73914 John Reggione, #74247 James Reggione, #75793 Louis Reggione, #75155 Pasquale Reggione, #78587 James Reggione, #70352 James Reggione, #102552 Pasquale Reggione, #76832 Joseph Reggione, #83521 Thomas Reggione.

Vito Genovese and Anna Vernotico Marriage Certificate, #7209, NYC Municipal Archives, March 30, 1932.

"Smuggles drug to cell in heel," *New York Tribune*, July 30, 1914.

"Fiddler seized in $30,000 safe cracking series," *New York Tribune*, March 24, 1922.

"Robbery is explained." *New York Tribune*, April 4, 1922.

"Patsy Chip Chip, gangster caught," *New York Daily News*, Oct. 10, 1927.

"US jury indicts 8 as counterfeiters," *Times Union*, June 20, 1930.

"Holdup repays youth with 20 years in prison," *New York Daily News*, Oct. 8, 1930.

"Capture $24,000 synthetic cash and 6 persons," *New York Daily News*, Feb. 6, 1932.

"7 counterfeit ring members held on bail," *Brooklyn Citizen*, March 3, 1932.

"Missing counterfeit suspect convicted in his absence," *Brooklyn Daily Eagle*, April 12, 1932.

"Patsy, a mug, dies hero, saving niece," *New York Daily News*, March 24, 1935. (Paper erroneously labeled James as "Patsy Chip Chip.")

"One Reggione saved by rain, brother slain," *New York Daily News*, Aug. 27, 1940.

"Cop corners bandit in hall, kills him," *New York Daily News*, Feb. 23, 1950.

Killing of off-duty officer linked to Valachi kin

By Thomas Hunt with Ellen Poulsen

The killing of off-duty New York Police Officer Alfred Loreto in the summer of 1950 occurred in a Bronx neighborhood familiar to Joseph Valachi and may have resulted from the criminal ventures of Valachi's brother-in-law Giacomo "Jack" Reina.

On Friday evening, July 21, 1950, Ralph Sgueglia (sometimes written "Squeglia") locked up his butcher shop, 754 Morris Park Avenue in the Bronx, made a few deliveries and drove to his home about a mile away. It was near seven-forty-five when he arrived at 1841 Hering Avenue and found a car parked in his short driveway. Sgueglia beeped the horn of his 1949 Buick. His wife Mary emerged from the home's front door. She told him the car belonged to a visiting relative, and she went back inside to get someone to move the vehicle.

When she left, two men rushed to Sgueglia's car. They opened its front doors and shoved their way into the bench seat on either side of him. They began physically abusing Sgueglia. One of the men took control of the car and drove away.

The activity caught the attention of neighbor Alfred Loreto at 1870 Hering Avenue. The forty-six-year-old, off-duty New York City police officer was outside loading up his car for a two-week family vacation trip to York Harbor, Maine. Loreto shouted to his son and then climbed into his green Dodge and went after Sgueglia's Buick.

The Buick traveled down the block and turned right onto Morris Park Avenue. It moved southwest on Morris Park just a short distance before veering off and smashing into a utility pole at the corner of Morris Park and Yates Avenue. Loreto pulled up behind it.

The two men who took control of Sgueglia's Buick rushed over to Loreto's car. One of them wrestled briefly with Loreto, while the other ran off on foot. Gunshots were fired, and the man who wrestled with Loreto also ran away.

Officer Loreto, a seventeen-year-veteran of the police force, soon died there of a bullet wound through his chest. He was survived by his wife of twenty-five years Thelma Gunther Loreto, their twenty-year-old son Alfred Jr. and Officer Loreto's four brothers.

Police arrived at the scene, finding Sgueglia bleeding and bruised and Loreto dying. No murder weapon was found at the scene. Officers were directed by witnesses toward the fleeing suspects. They arrested John Corbo, thirty two, of 3467 DeKalb Avenue, Bronx, and Rudolph Santobello, twenty one, of 4366 Wickham Avenue, Bronx.

As he was treated at Fordham Hospital for his injuries, Sgueglia told investigators that he had about $1,000 in his possession when the two men forced their way into his car. He said the men told him, "We're old friends of yours; we're butchers, too," and then they laughed. When the man identified as Santobello started driving down Hering Avenue, the man identified as Corbo repeatedly struck Sgueglia with a pistol. Santobello then began asking, impatiently, "Shall I shoot him? Shall I shoot him now?" Sgueglia told police he was able to grab the steering wheel and force the car to crash. He recalled hearing shots as he lost consciousness. He said he awakened in an ambulance.

Both Corbo and Santobello were brought to the aging station house of the Forty-third Precinct, 1415 Williamsbridge Road, and taken upstairs to the detective offices. There they were given the "third degree." Both were interrogated and beaten. Santobello reportedly absorbed far greater punishment.

Corbo was nearby and saw and heard much of what happened to Santobello. When detectives turned their attention to Corbo, they found him cooperative.

Just after midnight, Corbo provided a statement to an assistant district attorney, admitting that he and Santobello had forced their way into Sgueglia's car. He further admitted that he struck Sgueglia with a pistol. For this statement, he claimed to know nothing about Officer Loreto, Loreto's green Dodge or any shooting.

New York City Mayor William O'Dwyer appeared at the police station at about twelve-thirty Saturday morning to find that a substantial crowd of reporters had gathered there. O'Dwyer, widely blamed for an ongoing police corruption scandal and dealing with fresh questions following the recent suicide of a Brooklyn precinct captain, took the opportunity to express his resentment against the press. Newspapers, he claimed, had improperly linked the captain's tragic end with a Brooklyn grand jury's investigation of police corruption.

Minutes later, the assistant district attorney took a statement from Santobello. The young suspect denied having a gun. He acknowledged hearing shots fired as he ran from the Sgueglia automobile.

Additional interrogation followed. By five-thirty in the morning, Corbo had more to say. He agreed to help officers locate a handgun that he dropped while fleeing from the scene. The handgun was recovered before seven o'clock. It was found in some brush on a vacant lot at Van Nest and Tomlinson avenues.

After nine that morning, the assistant district attorney took additional statements from Corbo and Santobello. In questioning the suspects, the assistant district attorney made an effort to have them admit that they approached Loreto's green Dodge with the idea of stealing it to make a getaway. Under such a scenario, the unintended killing of the police officer could be charged as first-degree murder, as it would have occurred during the commission of a felony – the attempted theft of the car. Neither of the suspects clearly indicated an intent to steal the Dodge, but both gave positive-sounding answers to the prosecutor's questions.

According to a published report, Corbo claimed that he did not intend any harm to Loreto: "The gun in my hand went off," Corbo told the assistant district attorney. "I didn't fire it intentionally." In this statement, Corbo appears also to have provided information about other persons involved in the Sgueglia matter, but that data was kept from the press for a time.

Corbo and Santobello were brought before a magistrate in the early afternoon to be arraigned for homicide. Bruises and swelling around Santobello's eyes and cheeks were apparent. Additional bruising was later noted on his chest, back, arms and legs, and a doctor reported evidence of a broken rib.

More than five thousand police officers and four hundred firefighters participated in the inspector's funeral given to Officer Loreto on Tuesday, July 25. Mayor O'Dwyer, city council President Vincent R. Impellitteri, Police Commissioner William P. O'Brien, Chief Inspector August W. Flath and Chief of Detectives William T. Whalen were among the attendees.

The cortège, said to be the largest ever assembled for an officer killed in the line of duty, moved along Rhinelander Avenue to Saint Clare of Assisi Roman Catholic Church at the corner with Paulding Avenue. Following a funeral Mass celebrated by the Rev. Francis Cagnina, parish pastor, and a sermon delivered by Monsignor Joseph A. McCaffrey, the police department chaplain, the solemn procession continued on Rhinelander Avenue to Williamsbridge Road, then along Williamsbridge to Pierce Avenue. At that point, the march was halted, and the hearse and cars of mourners proceeded southeast on Williamsbridge and East Tremont avenues to Saint Raymond's Cemetery.

Others charged

Authorities revealed information about additional suspects in the case on Monday, July 31, as Edward De Lalla was placed under arrest. De Lalla, twenty-six, worked as a driver for a private garbage collection company.

Assistant District Attorney Walter X. Stanton told the press that De Lalla and another man, still at large, were working with Corbo and Santobello on the planned robbery of Sgueglia. De Lalla and the other accomplice followed the Sgueglia vehicle during the robbery attempt, intending to transport the robbers away after they obtained money from Sgueglia. The criminal plot was upset by the presence of Loreto, and the De Lalla car drove off without Corbo and Santobello.

De Lalla's defense attorney, Abraham J. Gellinoff, quickly admitted that his client knew the other suspects in the case and had met with them for coffee sometime before the July 21 shooting of Loreto. He insisted, however, that De Lalla was at home at the time of that shooting.

According to press reports, Stanton identified the still missing conspirator as Jack "Lefty" Rena.

On August 3, a Bronx County grand jury indicted Corbo and Santobello for the first degree murder of Officer Loreto. De Lalla was arraigned in Bronx Magistrate's Court on kidnapping and robbery charges, related to the alleged attempt to steal from Sgueglia. Bail was set at $10,000, and De Lalla was held for a scheduled August 17 hearing. Police continued to search for the missing "Rena."

Four days later, Giacomo "Jack" Reina surrendered to police. The press described him as a Bronx butcher and provided different Bronx addresses for him, including 1848 Hone Avenue and 2010 Lurting Avenue. He explained that he had been away on vacation and did not know he was wanted by authorities until his return. He was arraigned on assault, kidnapping and robbery charges and held in $15,000 bail.

Giacomo Thomas "Jack" Reina was the brother of Carmela "Mildred" Reina, who in summer of 1932 became Mrs. Joseph Valachi. Their father, Gaetano Reina, had been one of five Mafia bosses based in New York City until his assassination in February 1930. The killing was a cause of the Mafia's 1930-31 Castellammarese War. When that war concluded, Reina's former organization was under the command of Thomas Gagliano and Thomas Lucchese. Giacomo Reina married Phyllis Verona in New Jersey in 1941. They set up their home in Kearny, New Jersey. He was believed to be an active member of the Gagliano-Lucchese organization.

The district attorney's office in mid-August pursued additional charges against the group of suspects. In August 17, a grand jury indicted Corbo, Santobello, De Lalla and Reina for kidnapping and robbing Sgueglia. At the end of the month, Santobello was also charged with violating terms of an earlier release. He reportedly had been placed on probation in the spring of 1950.

Trial

Corbo and Santobello went to trial in May 1951 for the murder of Officer Loreto. At trial, Corbo testified that he and Santobello went to Sgueglia to collect on a gambling debt owed to Reina. Sgueglia invited them into his car, Corbo said, so that his wife would not overhear their conversation. Corbo claimed that Sgueglia then drew a handgun on them and that he pulled the weapon away from Sgueglia and struck Sgueglia on the head with it, as Santobello drove the car away and crashed into a utility pole. Corbo said he believed the car following them contained friends. After the crash, he went to that car: "As I opened the door, somebody grabbed my arm and pulled me into the car. The gun went off. When he let go, I realized I was in the wrong car and I ran."

Corbo also testified that he was beaten by police following his arrest. He said he was struck repeatedly with a rubber hose and that two of his teeth were knocked out when detectives hit him in the face with handcuffs.

Santobello's testimony supported much of Corbo's. But Santobello insisted that he was already a block away from Loreto's car at the time the police officer was shot.

On Thursday, May 31, 1951, the jury convicted both defendants of first-degree murder but recommended mercy, advising that they be sentenced to life in prison rather than death in the electric chair. The verdict followed just over five hours of deliberation.

Acceding to the jury's mercy recommendation, Bronx County Judge Samuel Joseph sentenced the cop-killers to life in prison on June 22, 1951. Warrants related to the additional charges of robbery and kidnapping were filed with Sing Sing Prison, allowing for further prosecution if the two were ever granted parole.

It appears that Reina and De Lalla were never brought to trial on charges related to the Sgueglia matter.

Reina involvement

Giacomo Reina's involvement in the events of July 21, 1950, was tracked by Bronx historian Thomas Vasti, a retired police officer. A Vasti article on the killing of Officer Loreto was published close to the fiftieth anniversary of the crime, July 20, 2000, by the *Bronx Times Reporter*.

According to Vasti, Corbo and Santobello were dropped off across the street from the Sgueglia home by Reina and De Lalla, who were using a borrowed, light blue, late model Mercury automobile. The Mercury was owned by Eugene Pinello of 1725 Paulding Avenue in the Bronx and was loaned that day to Carmela "Mildred" Reina Valachi (Giacomo Reina's sister and Joseph Valachi's wife), then resident of 2010 Lurting Avenue.

(Vasti reported that the 1848 Hone Avenue address belonged to other Giacomo Reina in-laws.)

Giacomo Reina visited the Valachi home that evening, Vasti reported. Reina apparently departed from the Valachi place in Pinello's light blue Mercury and then used the car to set up the robbery of Sgueglia. The Mercury followed as Corbo and Santobello drove off with Sgueglia in Sgueglia's car. It approached the scene of the Sgueglia car crash but, "when [the driver] saw the shooting come down he apparently kept right on going, leaving his confederates to fend for themselves."

No other published accounts of the incident mention the light blue Mercury, Eugene Pinello or Carmela Valachi. Vasti explained that those details were drawn from witness statements contained in police reports.

Vasti's placement of Valachi in the 2010 Lurting Avenue address was not a match for other sources. Census records from April 13, 1950, show Joseph and Mildred Valachi and their teenage son Donald living at 165 East Mosholu Parkway (very close to the longtime Reina family home at 3183 Rochambeau Avenue), several miles from the Lurting Avenue address. The Valachis soon moved to a private home at 45 Shawnee Avenue in Yonkers, New York. It is possible that they lived briefly at Lurting Avenue in between.

In his July 2000 article, Vasti claimed that Mayor O'Dwyer interfered with investigation of the Loreto killing and "would cause the investigation to grind to a halt." Support for the claim is lacking. Detectives had extensively questioned (and had repeatedly beaten) the suspects before O'Dwyer arrived early in the morning of July 22. Confessions were obtained overnight and early the next day that would lead to the convictions of both suspects involved in the events that led to the death of Officer Loreto. If O'Dwyer intended to hold back the investigation, that was not evident. It seemed from published reports that he viewed Loreto's selfless actions as exoneration for his entire police department, then facing corruption accusations.

Vasti vaguely suggested impropriety in connection with the dismissal of charges against De Lalla and Reina. He further noted that legal appeals resulted in the release of both convicted cop-killers Corbo and Santobello. And Vasti suggested that the "definite organized crime link through the Reina family" was not explored.

Prison for Reina

Giacomo Reina was soon sent to prison on another matter. A federal jury convicted him in March 1956 of heroin smuggling. His brother-in-law Joseph

Valachi was also convicted, along with three other codefendants, of operating a ring that moved about $100 million worth of heroin into the United States beginning in 1950.

On April 24, 1956, Judge Alexander Bicks sentenced the conspirators. The judge noted that he "received a very touching letter" from Reina's daughter, asking for leniency. In court, Bicks addressed Reina: "She seems to be a fine, good, decent girl, and I want to ask you a question. Suppose someone introduced your daughter to the use of heroin. What would you want the court to do to that person?"

After considering the question for a moment, Reina answered, "Just what you are going to do to me here."

Bicks sentenced Reina and his codefendants to five years in prison.

Reina was still in prison when he was summoned to testify before a grand jury investigating Mafia involvement in narcotics trafficking. Though granted immunity from prosecution, Reina refused to answer questions. That caused him to be convicted of criminal contempt and sentenced to additional time behind bars.

Cop-killers' appeals

The physical and emotional trauma suffered by Corbo during his questioning by police became the basis of his legal appeal. Statements admitting guilt were obtained through coercion, his attorneys argued. It also was argued that having a defendant assist in the search for a murder weapon while under coercion violated protections against illegal search and seizure.

Appeals failed in state court, as judges determined that there was ample evidence of guilt aside from any statements that may have resulted from coercion. In the early autumn of 1959, however, the U.S. Court of Appeals for the Second Circuit sided with Corbo and ordered him released.

The Bronx district attorney immediately had him rearrested and scheduled a new trial. In February 1961, Corbo was convicted of second-degree murder. In March, he was sentenced to serve from thirty years to life in prison for the offense. With credit for the nearly ten years he already served, he would become eligible for parole after about ten years more.

When a U.S. Supreme Court ruling on illegal searches was applied to Santobello's case in the mid-1960s, he won his release, having served fourteen years of his life sentence.

Santobello became a tavern owner in the Bronx. He also reportedly became an important member of the Genovese Crime Family. In the late 1960s, he was arrested by Officer Frank Serpico for engaging in policy gambling. Santobello's conviction in that case led to a second successful legal appeal.

Santobello argued that he pleaded guilty to a charge of promoting illegal gambling in exchange for a promise of leniency by the prosecutor. Before sentencing, the prosecutor in the case changed and no leniency was offered. Late in 1971, the U.S. Supreme Court ruled that prosecutors are bound by the promises of their predecessors, and Santobello was once again freed.

In the early 1990s, the FBI moved against crap games and bookmaking operations at Santobello businesses at several Bronx locations. Late in 1994, he was convicted of conducting bookmaking and loansharking operations from his Club Arthur on Arthur Avenue. He was sentenced to seven years in prison. He was released in June 2000. He died in spring 2013.

Loreto remembered

A city park was opened in the location where the Loreto murder weapon was found. South of Morris Park Avenue and between Haight and Tomlinson avenues, the 2.18-acre park was dedicated to the memory of Officer Alfred Loreto.

Bronze plaques describing Loreto's heroism and noting the sacrifices of other New York Police Department officers slain in the line of duty were placed at the site on the thirty-fifth anniversary of his death. One plaque bears a biblical quote from the Gospel of John: "Greater love than this no man hath, that a man lay down his life for his friends."

Officer Loreto

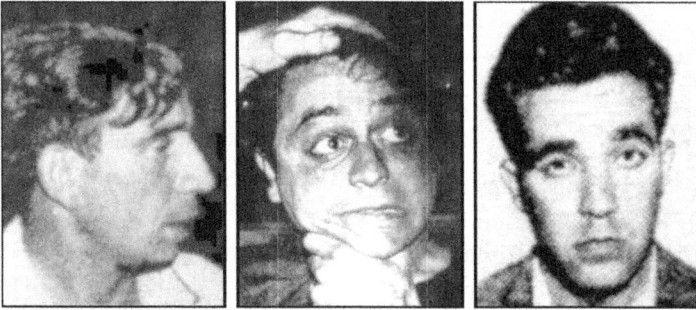

John Corbo (left), Rudolph Santobello (center), Giacomo Reina.

Feature 7 Sources

Newspaper abbreviations: *BDE – Brooklyn Daily Eagle; NYDN – New York Daily News; NYP – New York Post; NYT – New York Times; RD – White Plains NY Reporter Dispatch.*

"2 Loreto killers start life terms," NYP, June 24, 1951, p. 3.

"2 men indicted in policeman slaying," Albany NY Times Union, Aug. 4, 1950, p. 13.

"4 extra indictments filed in Loreto killing," NYP, Aug. 18, 1950, p. 4.

"4 men indicted in fatal kidnap," NYDN, Aug. 18, 1950, p. 23.

"5 convicted in dope ring," Binghamton Press, March 22, 1956, p. 13.

"5,000 police honor slain patrolman," NYT, July 26, 1950, p. 50.

"7-man high court splits on liberal-conservative lines in criminal rulings," NYT, Dec. 21, 1971, p. 25.

"Accused vows he'd left when cop was slain," NYDN, May 26, 1951, p. 12.

Alfredo Loreto and Thelma Gunther Certificate and Record of Marriage, Borough of Manhattan, certificate no. 20605, City of New York Department of Health, July 1, 1925.

"Age of 1 saves Loreto killer from hot seat," NYDN, June 23, 1951, p. 18.

Austin, Vincent D., "Slayer Corbo, a round won, now seeking quick release," NYP, Feb. 24, 1961, p. 24.

"Butcher surrenders in Loreto murder," BDE, Aug. 8, 1950, p. 3.

Capeci, Jerry, "Gang Land: Serpico gets the last laugh," NYDN, Jan. 10, 1995, p. 12.

Clark, Robert E., "High court to review verdict against FHA," Washington DC Evening Star, Dec. 19, 1960, p. 1.

"Conviction of slayers upheld," Troy NY Times Record, Dec. 3, 1954, p. 1.

"Cop admits he socked Loreto killing suspect," NYDN, May 15, 1951, p. 18.

"Corbo gets thirty years to life term," NYP, March 28, 1961, p. 39.

"DA hammers story of Loreto 'accident,'" NYP, May 23, 1951, p. 5.

Desmond, James, "Loreto killers guilty but may escape chair," NYDN, June 1, 1951, p. 6.

Dillon, Edward, "3d man yields in cop killing; 4th is hunted," NYDN, Aug. 1, 1950, p. 14.

Dillon, Edward, "5,000 cops march for slain mate," NYDN, July 26, 1950, p. 2.

Gaetano Reena Certificate of Death, Borough of Bronx, registered no. 1800, Department of Health of the City of New York Bureau of Records, Feb. 26, 1930, filed Feb. 27, 1930.

Giacomo Thomas Reina World War II Draft Registration Card, serial no. 2906, order no. 120B, special panel Local Board 503, Elmira, NY, Local Board no. 35, Kearny, NJ, April 27, 1943.

Golding, Bruce, "2 receive coercion charges," RD, Feb. 1, 1996, p. 7.

"He tells jury killing of cop was accident," NYDN, May 23, 1951, p. 31.

"Indict two owners of raided, shut bar," NYDN, Dec. 2, 1970, p. 3.

Joseph Valachi Presentence Report, Judge Matthew T. Abruzzo, United States District Court for the Eastern District of New York, indictment no. 45869, sentence date Feb. 19, 1960.

"Jury convicts 2 of murder," RD, June 1, 1951, p. 30.

Kivel, Martin, and Charles McHarry, "O'D. flies in, willing to testify," NYDN, Oct. 10, 1950, p. 3.

Kleinknecht, William, "Insider singing a Mafia medley to FBI," NYDN, March 31, 1994, p. 12.

Kline, Sidney, "5 guilty in huge dope operation," NYDN, March 22, 1956, p. 3.

"Life sentence given pair for slaying of cop," Oswego NY Palladium-Times, June 22, 1951, p. 1.

"Loreto jurors hear 9 more," NYDN, Aug. 16, 1950.

"Loreto Playground," NYC Parks, nycgovparks.org.

"Loreto roundup's No. 4 held in bail," NYDN, Aug. 9, 1950, p. 28.

Maas, Peter, Serpico: The Cop Who Defied the System, New York: Viking Press, 1973, p. 221-224.

Mulligan, Arthur, "Fired by accident, pleads killer of cop who balked kidnapers," NYDN, July 23, 1950, p. 4.

"Nationwide drive under way against Maffia, dope traffic," Buffalo Evening News, Jan. 16, 1959, p. 10.

"Pair indicted in cop killing," NYDN, Aug. 4, 1950, p. 6.

"Patrolman Alfred Loreto," Officer Down Memorial Page, odmp.org.

"Patrolman slain in chase of thugs," NYT, July 22, 1950, p. 30.

Patterson, Neal, "Getting what's coming, dope figure admits," NYDN, April 25, 1956, p. 20.

"Plan hero's rites for slain officer," BDE, July 22, 1950, p. 1.

"Police hero will get inspector's funeral," BDE, July 24, 1950, p. 3.

"Puts 2 at cop death scene," NYDN, May 12, 1951, p. 21.

Rosenblum, Constance, "A Bronx state of mind," NYT, July 8, 2012, Section RE, p. 4.

Rudolph Santobello, New York City Birth Index, Bronx County, certificate no. 14521, Oct. 9, 1926.

Rudolph Santobello, Social Security Death Index, 054-20-0998, April 22, 2013.

"Slain cop will have inspector's funeral," NYDN, July 24, 1950, p. 12.

Sgueglia Family, United States Census of 1950, New York State, Bronx County, Enumeration District 3-1438.

Spagnoli, Gene, and James Desmond, "Cop slain as he traps kidnapers; 2 seized," NYDN, July 22, 1950, p. 3.

Storino, Pascal Jr., "Lineage of the NYPD's 43rd Precinct & a brief history of policing in the Bronx," The History of Policing in the City of New York, nypdhistory.com, June 10, 2016.

"Suspect arraigned as parole violator," NYDN, Sept. 1, 1950, p. 6.

"Suspect no. 4 yields, booked in cop killing," NYDN, Aug. 8, 1950, p. 6.

"Suspect surrenders in New York case," Poughkeepsie Journal, Aug. 1, 1950, p. 11.

"Thousands attend rites for hero cop," BDE, July 25, 1950, p. 1.

United States of America ex rel. Joseph Corbo, relator-appellant, v. J. Edwin La Vallee, warden, Clinton Prison, and the People of the State of New York, appellees (Corbo v. La Vallee), 270 F.2d 513 (2d Cir. 1959), argued June 1, 1959, decided Sept. 29, 1959.

Valachi family, United States Census of 1950, New York State, Bronx County, Enumeration District 3-2019.

Vasti, Tom, email to Ellen Poulsen, Aug. 23, 2024.

Vasti, Tom, "The supreme sacrifice," Bronx Times Reporter, July 20, 2000, p. 10.

"Wanted man surrenders," Tarrytown NY Daily News, Aug. 1, 1950, p. 9.

FEATURE 8

Valachi and women

Through his teen years and early adulthood, Valachi avoided serious romantic entanglements, feeling shame over his poor living conditions and the crimes he was committing in an effort to remedy them.[1] Around his mid-twenties, he began to more highly value his bonds with women. While fidelity was never his strong suit, he formed a series of meaningful connections with women.

Joseph Valachi's first serious romantic relationship was with a taxi-dancer he knew as "May." They apparently met at a dance hall. Their romance developed after an extended period of platonic friendship. Then they lived together in an apartment in the Van Nest section of the Bronx for roughly six weeks. Their overall relationship apparently lasted from late in 1928 to early in 1931. May was discussed several times in the Valachi autobiography during that time and then simply disappeared.

Her exit occurred at the height of the Castellammarese War between New York mobs. May had expressed concern about Valachi's involvement in the conflict. Her last mention in the autobiography coincided with a threat rival gangsters made to her mother. They reportedly promised to kill May and her mother if May continued to date Valachi.[2]

Valachi did not explain how he met Carmela "Mildred" Reina. (He did not reveal very much about any of the the women in his life.) Mildred was the daughter of Mafia boss Gaetano Reina, who was murdered by rivals on February 26, 1930, in the Bronx.[3] She and Valachi possibly knew each other from childhood.

Carmela "Mildred" Reina was born October 12, 1906, when her family lived at 228 East 107th Street in East Harlem. Within a few years, the family moved across the street to 225 East 107th Street. The Reinas remained there through the time of the New York State Census in June 1925, when Mildred was twenty two and working as a bookkeeper. Soon after that, the family relocated to 3183 Rochambeau Avenue in the Bronx.[4] Valachi was raised in the same East Harlem neighborhood and reportedly changed addresses many times. None of his known pre-1930 homes – 325 East 109th, 337 East 109th, 239 East 111th, 320 East 108th, 327 East 109th, 2104 Second Avenue, 335 East 108th – was a close match to a Reina address.[5] On the few occasions that Valachi bothered to show up for school, he may have seen Mildred there.

It appears likely that Valachi encountered Mildred's brother Giacomo "Jack" Reina, two years her junior, during the Castellammarese War. Both Joseph Valachi and Giacomo Reina would have sided with the forces of Reina's top lieutenants, Tommaso Gagliano and Gaetano Lucchese, during that conflict.

A strong connection between Valachi and some member or members of the Reina household must have existed in September 1931, when Valachi's superior Salvatore Maranzano was assassinated. Fearing that he also would be targeted by anti-Maranzano forces, Valachi went into hiding. One of the places he briefly secreted himself was the attic of the Reina home in the Bronx. No explanation has been offered for the Reinas putting themselves at risk for Valachi.[6]

Valachi told author Peter Maas that Mildred Reina had "heard a lot" about Valachi through a mutual acquaintance, "Charlie Scoop."

After just a few days, Valachi was assured by gangland contacts that no one was gunning for him. He was invited into a Mafia organization run by Gagliano and also into another run by Salvatore "Charlie Luciano" Lucania and Vito Genovese. As some of his old friends were welcome in the Lucania family but not the Gagliano family, Valachi went with Lucania.[7]

Valachi learned through the wife of underworld colleague Girolamo

"Bobby Doyle" Santuccio that Mildred Reina was interested in him. He reportedly dated Mildred for a time, though her mother, her brother Giacomo and her uncles all opposed the relationship. Late in 1931, Valachi and Mildred considered eloping. When brother Giacomo managed to convince Mildred that Valachi had lost his interest in her, she reportedly attempted suicide by swallowing iodine. When she recovered, Valachi asked Vito Genovese to intercede on his behalf with the Reina family. The result reportedly was a family commitment to the relationship, providing an engagement was not announced for six months.[8]

Joseph Valachi and Mildred Reina were married in a civil ceremony before the deputy city clerk at the Manhattan Municipal Building on July 22, 1932. It is not certain that the Reina family knew of this marriage. (The couple may have decided to elope, and this may be what Genovese explained to the Reinas.) Mildred at that time reported an address of 175 Thompson Street in Manhattan's Greenwich Village, a considerable distance from her family's Bronx home. Vito Genovese served as Valachi's best man, and Genovese's recent bride, Anna Petillo Vernotico Genovese, was the matron of honor.[9]

About two months later, the couple had a church wedding and a lavish reception at the Palm Gardens on Fifty-second Street near Broadway. Genovese could not be present for that ceremony. Crime family lieutenant Anthony "Tony Bender" Strollo stood in for him as best man and is seen in the Valachi wedding photo. Valachi recalled that the use of the hall cost $1,000 (equivalent to more than $23,000 today).[10] The event featured two bands, thousands of sandwiches, $500 worth of Italian cookies and pastries, as well as wine and whiskey (during Prohibition).[11]

There was no honeymoon vacation after the wedding. The newlyweds settled into their first apartment at 3029 Briggs Avenue in the Bronx. About 1935, they moved to 29 East Mosholu Parkway North in the Bronx, closer to the Reina family home at Rochambeau Avenue.[12] One winter in the mid-1930s, Valachi took Mildred on vacation to Florida. "I wanted to make up for not going away after the wedding," he recalled. Valachi's friend Dominick "the Gap" Petrelli and his wife came along. During a visit to a Florida racetrack, Mildred placed a bet on a longshot and won, turning a $2 bet into $300.[13]

A son, Dominic "Donald" John Valachi, was born to the couple in May 1936.[14] Valachi blamed the arrival of their child for starting a rupture in his relationship with his wife:

I brought my wife everywhere I went before we got the kid, and
then it was hard on me staying home. I will be thinking too much.
So, I made myself busy, and I will go here and there.[15]

Over time, Valachi began to feel that other crime family members were
attempting to interfere with his marriage. He noted that Santuccio criticized his
in-laws when speaking to him, and he assumed that Santuccio was similarly
criticizing him when speaking to the Reinas.[16] He blamed Strollo and Santuccio for creating a rumor that Valachi had been responsible for murdering
Mildred's father, Gaetano Reina, back in 1930. Valachi speculated that they
hoped to make him more vulnerable by removing the protection of the Reina
family.[17]

But Valachi also did a fair share to damage his marriage. While trying not
to think "too much," he spent his nights carousing and was often in the company of other women. In the 1940s, he set up a mistress, named Laura, in an
apartment.[18]

Mildred was not entirely unaware of any of this misbehavior – Valachi was
certain that Santuccio was reporting to her. Knowing of her own father's similar behavior – Gaetano Reina was killed while in the company of his mistress[19] – she may have been tolerant to the idea of extramarital affairs.

The Valachi family moved a couple of times within the same neighborhood
during the early 1940s, first to 3204 Rochambeau Avenue and then to 165 East
Mosholu Parkway.

After 1950, Valachi began a long-term extramarital relationship with
young, blonde Carol Jacobs of 1005 Esplanade Avenue in the Bronx. Sus-
pecting Valachi involvement in narcotics racketeering, agents of the Federal
Bureau of Narcotics kept him under surveillance and noted that he spent more
time with Carol Jacobs than with his family.[20]

Valachi was then a secret owner of the popular Lido Restaurant, 1362
Castle Hill Avenue in the Bronx. (A photograph of Valachi with Carol Jacobs
at the Lido is sometimes misrepresented as Valachi and wife Mildred.) The
affair continued through 1955, when the New York State Liquor Authority
revoked Lido's liquor license due to its undisclosed relationship with Valachi.[21]

Journalist Jack Anderson years later discovered that Valachi had written
love poems to Carol Jacobs, who, according to Anderson, was about thirty
years younger than Valachi and entered their relationship when she was just a

teenager. According to Anderson, "[Valachi's poems] made up in passion what they lacked in rhyme."[22]

Miss Jacobs became Mrs. Gildo Cuccuru from 1952 until 1959, when she and Gildo Cuccuru of the Bronx were divorced. The relationship with Valachi ran through the same period. (Records suggest that Gildo was a minor hoodlum. In the later 1950s, he served prison time for causing the death of a cafeteria manager.)[23]

While Valachi was spending his time with Carol Jacobs, Mildred and Donald were getting comfortable in a recently constructed home he purchased at 45 Shawnee Avenue in a quiet residential section of Yonkers, New York.[24]

Mildred stood by Valachi through affairs, criminal rackets, murders, drug deals, imprisonments. She even toughed it out in February 1960 when Valachi quickly sold the family's Yonkers home at below market value and moved her and son Donald into a cheaper Bronx residence, at 3976 Hill Avenue, in order to finance his flight from narcotics charges.[25] But, when he became a government informant in 1962, the relationship was finished. Following Valachi's 1963 televised testimony before a Senate subcommittee, Mildred brought her marriage grievances to the press.

After more than thirty years with Valachi, she told a reporter from the *New York Mirror* that she never loved him. She said her husband was always chasing after other women. "He was always playing around with them – girl after girl..." She said that an affair about five years earlier – this was likely the relationship with Carol Jacobs – convinced her that her marriage was over. "As Mrs. Valachi, I have been dead since," she said. "I am now Mildred Reina."

The marriage had been continued merely for convenience: "He was always a good provider. We always ate well and I was always dressed well. But I never loved him."[26]

Valachi was then in protective federal custody and also serving a life sentence for the slaying of a fellow inmate in Atlanta Federal Prison - a man he incorrectly believed Mafia bosses had sent to kill him. He would soon begin writing his autobiography. In that lengthy manuscript, he had little to say about Mildred. But his few words were words of praise. She was a "saint" and "a good soul." In one spot, he wrote, "There isn't a woman on Earth that is better than her." In another, he wrote, "If I lose her I do not care to live any more."[27]

Valachi did live just a bit more after losing Mildred. And there would be one last love affair in the handful of years he had left. It is uncertain if he ever personally met Marie K. Jackson, the Niagara Falls, New York, woman with whom he corresponded from his prison quarters. Jackson reportedly received many letters from Valachi. There is evidence that she received at least one poem.

With his wife refusing communication from him, Valachi named Jackson his executor and the primary beneficiary of his estate. Following his death, when Valachi's wife and son refused to claim his remains, Jackson had the body transported to Niagara Falls and buried there.[28]

Valachi-Reina wedding ceremony of September 1932, with Anthony Strollo substituting for best man Vito Genovese.

Mildred Valachi in 1963.

Carol Jacobs with Valachi.

Feature 8 Notes

1 Valachi, Joseph, *The Real Thing: Second Government - The Expose and Inside Doings of Cosa Nostra*, unpublished manuscript, John F. Kennedy Presidential Library and Museum, 1964, p. 6k.

2 Valachi, *The Real Thing*, p. 207, 224-229, 238, 240, 252-253, 265, 277, 285, 296, 311-312, 334. Maas, Peter, *The Valachi Papers*, New York: G.P. Putnam's Sons, 1968, p. 80.

3 Gaetano Reena Certificate of Death, Borough of Bronx, registered no. 1800, Department of Health of the City of New York Bureau of Records, Feb. 26, 1930, filed Feb. 27, 1930.

4 Carmela Reina Certificate and Record of Birth, Borough of Manhattan, certificate no. 50689, City of New York Bureau of Records, Oct. 12, 1906; United States Census of 1910, New York State, New York County, Ward 12, Enumeration District 338; United States Census of 1920, New York State, New York County, Ward 18, Enumeration District 1269; New York State Census of 1925, New York County, Assembly District 18, Election District 23; U.S. Census of 1930, New York State, Bronx County, Enumeration District 3-679.

5 Antonio Villacci Certificate and Record of Birth, Borough of Manhattan, certificate no. 34174, City of New York Bureau of Records, Aug. 23, 1900, reported Aug. 30, 1900, received Sept. 5, 1900; Gioseppo Vilacio Certificate and Record of Birth, Borough of Manhattan, certificate no. 44544, City of New York Department of Health, Oct. 3, 1903, received Oct. 16, 1903; United States Census of 1910, New York State, New York County, Ward 12, Enumeration District 339; Anthony Valachi, Sing Sing Prison Receiving Blotter, inmate no. 70849, received Jan. 19, 1920; Names of Convicts Received during Month of September 1923, Auburn Prison, New York; Anthony Valachi, Sing Sing Prison Receiving Blotter, inmate no. 72533, received May 26, 1921; Sing Sing Prison Receiving Blotter, inmate no. 75260, received Oct 26, 1923; Sing Sing Prison Receiving Blotter, inmate no. 77100, received April 9, 1925; Frank Rocco, Sing Sing Prison Receiving Blotter, inmate no. 81933, received April 23, 1929.

6 Maas, *The Valachi Papers*, p. 112, 121.

7 Maas, *The Valachi Papers*, p. 121; Valachi, *The Real Thing*, p. 367-368, 370.

8 Maas, *The Valachi Papers*, p. 122-124.

9 Joseph Valachi and Mildred Reina Certificate and Record of Marriage, certificate no. 15917, City of New York, July 22, 1932; Joseph Valachi Presentence Report, Judge Matthew T. Abruzzo, United States District Court for the Eastern District of New York, indictment no. 45869, sentence date Feb. 19, 1960.

10 CPI Inflation Calculator, U.S. Bureau of Labor Statistics, data.bls.gov.

11 Joseph Valachi Presentence Report, sentence date Feb. 19, 1960; Maas, *The Valachi Papers*, p. 124-125. Valachi recalled that wedding attendees included Tom Gagliano, Tommy Lucchese, Albert Anastasia, Vincent Mangano, Carlo Gambino, Mike Miranda, Girolamo Santuccio and other mafiosi. Not attending but sending gifts, according to Valachi, were Salvatore "Charlie Luciano" Lucania, Joseph Bonanno, Joseph Profaci, Joe Adonis, Frank Costello and Willie Moretti.

12 Maas, *The Valachi Papers*, p. 125; John Valachi, inmate no. 91127, Sing Sing Prison Receiving Blotter, received Nov. 8, 1935; United States Census of 1940, New York State, Bronx County, Assembly District 8, Enumeration District 31272. Maas reported that their first apartment was on Briggs Avenue. John Valachi stated for prison records that his brother's address in spring 1935 was 3029 Briggs Avenue. Joseph Valachi stated the Mosholu Parkway address for the 1940 Census and said he lived at that address in 1935.

13 Valachi, *The Real Thing*, p. 399.

14 Dominic John Valachi, 077-30-9494, Social Security Applications and Claims Index, Ancestry.com.

15 Valachi, *The Real Thing*, p. 521. The claim that he brought Mildred everywhere he went before the birth of their son was blatantly false.

16 Valachi, *The Real Thing*, p. 445.

17 Valachi, *The Real Thing*, p. 446.

18 Maas, *The Valachi Papers*, p. 169-170.

19 "Wealthy ice dealer slain in doorway," *New York Times*, Feb. 27, 1930, p. 3; Jarrell, Sanford, "Police save rival from wife's fury," *New York Daily News*, Feb. 27, 1930, p. 2.

20 Joseph Valachi Presentence Report, sentence date Feb. 19, 1960.

21 Maas, *The Valachi Papers*, p. 251.

22 Anderson, Jack, "'Washington Merry-Go-Round: Irish Mafia' irks cabinet," *Buffalo Courier Express*, Sept. 8, 1963, p. 24; Anderson, Jack, "The underworld of killer Joe Valachi," *Parade*, March 21, 1965, p. 4;

    Anderson, Jack, "Washington Merry-Go-Round: Curious exception," *Zanesville OH Times Recorder*, Feb. 18, 1966, p. 4.

23 Gildo Cuccuru and Carol Jacob, New York City Marriage License Index, Borough of Bronx, license no. 5426, 1952; Bronx County NY Divorce and Civil Case Records, 1914-1995, Ancestry.com; Smee. Jack, "Brawler hurls bowl, kills cafeteria boss," *New York Daily News*, Nov. 21, 1954, p. 3; Wantuch, Howard, and Henry Lee, " Ex-con shoots benefactor in store," *New York Daily News*, Jan. 19, 1958, p. c3; Spagnola, Eugene, "4 payroll bandits at large, 4 in jail," *New York Daily News*, Sept. 2, 1960, p. 5.

24 Kline, Sidney, "5 guilty in huge dope operation," *New York Daily News*, March 22, 1956, p. 3; "1 drug case conviction upset, another upheld," *Yonkers Herald Statesman*, March 23, 1957, p. 6; Tangel, Joseph L., "Activities of top hoodlums in the New York Field Division," FBI report from New York office, file no. CR 62-9-34-367, NARA no. 124-90103-10093, Sept. 14, 1959, p. 35; "45 Shawnee Avenue, Yonkers, NY 10710," Zillow, zillow.com.

25 SAC Atlanta, "Joseph Valachi, aka; John Joseph Saupp, aka - victim," FBI Report to Director, file no. 70-35395-9, July 23, 1962, p. 69; Valachi, *The Real Thing*, p. 963; Maas, *The Valachi Papers*, p. 259. Valachi expressed regret over his haste in selling the Yonkers house, because his need for cash forced him to sell for $10,000 less than the home was worth and because the move "really hurt my family."

26 "Valachi's wife loved him not," *Hackensack NJ Northern Valley Record*, Oct. 10, 1963, p. 8.

27 Valachi, *The Real Thing*, p. 446, 992.

28 Farrell, Cecil, "'Mystery woman' arranged for burial of Joe Valachi," *Naples FL Daily News*, April 1, 1973, p. 9. According to Farrell, on Memorial Day 1971, someone matching Marie Jackson's description submitted a poem, written on U.S. Department of Justice letterhead, for publication in the *Niagara Falls Gazette*.

FEATURE 9

Valachi and 'the French Connection'

By Fabien Rossat

On December 27, 1961, Joseph Valachi, a member of the Genovese Crime Family, and ten codefendants were convicted of importing into the United States $150 million worth of heroin. Sentenced to twenty years for this affair, it was the end of Valachi's long racketeering career. A few months later, he would become the first penitent to publicly testify to the existence of Cosa Nostra in the U.S. While Valachi had been an important link in the drug operation, that link was near one end of a vast chain – a multinational trafficking network that the general public would later know (thanks to Director William Friedkin's 1971 film) as *The French Connection*.

First steps into drugs

The first narcotics case against Valachi went to trial in March 1956.[1]

Valachi and four accomplices were charged with participating in a ring that had smuggled $100 million worth of heroin into the United States since 1950. The accomplices were Pasquale Moccio, Pasquale Pagano, Lawrence Quarterio and Giacomo Reina. Reina was Valachi's brother-in-law and a member of the Lucchese Crime Family.[2]

The group was accused of having purchased large quantities of morphine base in order to have it refined in a laboratory near Paris. As Valachi later recounted, through Peter Maas in *The Valachi Papers*, his friend Salvatore "Sally Shields" Shillitani introduced him to an experienced French contact.[3] (For more on Shillitani, see *Informer's* issue of April 2013.[4])

Valachi said he didn't recall the contact's full name, only his first name, "Dominique." Author Peter Maas surmised that this was probably Dominique Reissent. Born in Marseilles (not Corsica, as stated by Maas) on July 6, 1896, Reissent was active in drug trafficking since the 1940s. Reissent operated from Paris and acted as a "middle man" in the import of morphine base from Turkey into France.

The morphine base was transformed by a team of chemists in a laboratory – probably that of Marius Ansaldi, which was dismantled in 1953. The product then was smuggled into America. The U.S. Federal Bureau of Narcotics (FBN) eventually pieced together the major figures in the narcotics ring, connecting Giacomo Reina and Salvatore Shillitani to both Reissent and Ansaldi.[5]

Though the details of Reissent's early career are unclear, about a decade later his name featured prominently alongside Corso-Marseillais underworld boss Jean-Baptiste Croce. Reissent at that time was described as an importer of morphine base, but it seems he was never convicted for this role. He died on October 22, 1979.[6]

Valachi and his codefendants were convicted on March 21, 1956. They were sentenced the following month. All received five-year prison terms. Each also was assessed a $10,000 fine, except Quarterio, whose fine was $5,000.[7]

Valachi briefly entered Atlanta Federal Prison but was then released on bail, pending a legal appeal, which he financed by selling his interest in the successful Lido Restaurant on Castle Hill Avenue in the Bronx. About a year later, the verdict against him was reversed when the U.S. Circuit Court of Appeals in New York determined that the statute of limitations had expired on two acts committed by Valachi.[8]

As he stated through *The Valachi Papers*, the American Cosa Nostra had a policy against involvement in narcotics at that time (which obviously was widely ignored). To cover himself in the event of a problem, Valachi had brought his underworld superior, caporegime Anthony "Tony Bender" Strollo, into his drug scheme.[9]

This became a problem for Valachi, as Strollo brought in more men from his crew, causing the profits to be further divided. Among the men Strollo included in the operation were Vincent Mauro and Frank "Frankie the Bug" Caruso. (When brought to trial in 1956, Valachi learned that some of these partners actually received no portion of the proceeds and were used merely to increase Strollo's share.[10])

The Canadians take the stage

Toward the end of the 1950s, Mauro and John Angelo "Pops" Papalia worked to set up their own heroin distribution network.

Born in 1924 in Hamilton, Ontario, Canada, Papalia became one of the more influential Buffalo Crime Family members operating in Ontario. Papalia acquired some experience in the field of narcotics: He was sentenced in 1949 to two years in prison and a $300 fine for possession of narcotics.[11] Upon his release from prison, he went to Montreal and worked for a time under the wing of Carmine Galante, before Galante was expelled from Canada in 1955.[12]

In an office secretly bugged by the FBI, Buffalo crime boss Stefano Magaddino once explained to two underlings that he had helped set up a heroin pipeline passing through Ontario, Canada. In addition to Mauro and Papalia, the network was said to have involved Giuseppe Rugnetta, consigliere of the Philadelphia Crime Family and leader of that organization's Calabrian faction. (Rugnetta was never prosecuted for any involvement in the racket.)[13]

To be successful, the network required a reliable source of supply. One of Magaddino's men in Ontario had precisely the right contacts. He was Alberto Agueci.

Born in Salemi, Sicily, on July 27, 1920, Agueci emigrated to Canada in 1950 after being refused entry to the U.S. When he arrived in Canada, he held a letter of recommendation from a travel agent in Windsor. It was signed by Rosario Mancino, a Palermo mafioso well known to authorities on both sides of the Atlantic for his involvement in drug trafficking. In Toronto, Agueci co-owned a bakery with an individual named Benedetto Zizzo.[14]

Benedetto Zizzo was a significant underworld character. His brother happened to be the boss of the Salemi underworld organization or cosca. Salvatore "Don Turiddu" Zizzo, born January 18, 1910, in Partanna, Sicily, had been a heavyweight in heroin trafficking for some time and began using his Toronto-based brother Benedetto in the operation in the 1950s. According to the FBN, their organization was "capable of financing and organizing large shipments of heroin to the United States."[15]

The method used to ship the heroin was quite classic. With the help of travel agent Salvatore Valenti, transatlantic travelers were recruited to take along an additional piece of luggage in exchange for a sum of money. The luggage had a double bottom which concealed its illicit cargo. The traveler, perhaps a little naive, did not suspect the contents of the suitcase. Upon arrival in America, he handed it over to an intermediary who then passed it on to an American mafioso.

Giuseppe Palmeri, leader in the Santa Ninfa cosca in the province of Trapani, also was heavily involved in the scheme and worked under the supervision of Salvatore Zizzo. This was also true of mafiosi such as brothers Salvatore and Ugo Caneba, residents of Rome but originally from Palermo, Sicily, and brothers Serafino and Giuseppe Mancuso from Alcamo in Trapani. The Mancusos also had links in the United States and in France, having lived there for a time.[16]

The French source for heroin shipped to Trapanese and Canadian/American middle men was Antoine "Le Vieux" ("the Elder") Cordoliani. Born on February 22, 1890 in Brando, Corsica, Cordoliani led a vast drug trafficking network and was considered by the French Sûreté Nationale police and the FBN as one of key figures in the global drug trade. He was one of the main suppliers of morphine base for traffickers in France and Italy.[17]

Among his clients in France were the Aranci brothers (considered by the FBN as an element in one of the four largest networks of the time). In Italy, he dealt with Carmelo Caruana and Giovanni Mira, two mafiosi of Siculiana, province of Agrigento.

Benedetto Zizzo was also in contact with Leonardo Caruana, the brother of Carmelo. Giovanni Mira worked with Settimo Accardi, a member of the Genovese Family on the run since 1955 and active between his hometown of Vita, Trapani province, and Toronto, Canada. Magaddino reportedly assessed a five kilogram heroin penalty (equivalent to $100,000 on the wholesale market of the day) against Accardi because he was working in Magaddino's Ontario territory without permission.[18]

Cordoliani supervised several laboratories for transforming morphine base into heroin. He put the legendary chemist Joseph Césari in charge of operations. Césari had the reputation of being the best chemist of the "French Connection" and had the nickname "Mr. 98%," acquired due to the purity he was able to give the final product.[19]

(Talented chemists ran in the family. Joseph Césari was the half-brother of Dominique Albertini, who earlier served as main chemist of the "French Connection." Albertini had a large address book and was connected to a good number of mafiosi in Italy, the U.S. and Canada.)

These drug trafficking operations were largely unhindered by law enforcement until October 21, 1960, when two smugglers were arrested.

Valachi and friends

Valachi's own problems with narcotics authorities began a bit earlier than that. He was indicted for drug trafficking in June 1959, after one of his accomplices, John Freeman, denounced him. Freeman's son had been caught offering to sell 3 kilos of heroin to an undercover FBN agent in Brooklyn. Learning that FBN agents were after him, Valachi went into hiding and could not be located at the time of his indictment.[20]

Valachi was arrested on November 19, 1959, while waiting for a call from associate and codefendant Ralph Wagner at a Thomaston, Connecticut, pay telephone booth. At arraignment, as he attempted to arrange release on bail, Valachi explained to the judge that he had been unaware of the narcotics case against him. He was at the phone booth, he claimed, because he had recently heard he was wanted by police and hoped to learn the reason. He was released on bail of $25,000. As his February 1960 trial date approached, Valachi decided to jump bail.[21]

Underworld associates Vincent Mauro and Frank Caruso put Valachi in contact with Albert Agueci. Valachi and Agueci met at "Maggie's Bar" on Manhattan's Lexington Avenue near Fifty-seventh Street to work out the travel plans. Agueci sent Valachi to Buffalo, where they met again, and he then took Valachi to the house of an Italian family in Toronto, where Valachi holed up for a few weeks.[22]

Valachi received communication from Strollo, who assured him the case was fixed and Valachi would only serve five years in prison following a guilty plea. Just before surrendering, Valachi got the feeling that he was facing a far harsher sentence and considered running again. He tried without success to acquire phony travel papers to Brazil from contact Salvatore Rinaldo in Mount Vernon, New York. In a subsequent meeting with his bail bondsman Al Newman, Valachi was persuaded to turn himself in.[23]

Wagner had failed to appear for trial in early March and was labeled a fugitive. He was apprehended March 10 at a cafe near the docks in Houston, Texas.[24]

Valachi pleaded guilty in May 1960 to a single count of conspiracy to violate narcotics laws. In June, Valachi received the lengthy sentence he feared: fifteen years in federal prison and a $10,000 fine.[25] But that was just the beginning for him.

Arrests lead to turncoats

Agents of the Federal Bureau of Narcotics received a tip in autumn 1960 that a drug transaction was to take place upon the arrival at North River Pier 84, West Forty-fourth Street in Manhattan, of the Italian ocean liner Saturnia from Palermo.

At nine-thirty, Friday morning, October 21, 1960, an individual under surveillance, Salvatore Rinaldo, was spotted leaving Pier 84 with a crate and three trunks. He was joined by one accomplice Matteo Palmeri, who helped him load the luggage into a panel truck. The two men then drove separately on the New York Thruway toward Yonkers. When they exited the highway near the Cross County Center and continued eastward toward Mount Vernon, New York, they were halted and arrested by by a law enforcement team including federal narcotics agents, Westchester County sheriff's deputies and Mount Vernon police.

Beneath a double-bottom in the crate, agents found ten plastic bags, each containing a kilo of heroin (the crate mostly contained stuffed animals and other toys). A search of Rinaldo's home in Mount Vernon also was productive. Authorities found more than $20,000 in cash and a quantity of drugs there.

As agents moved against Rinaldo, they also took into custody his wife Grace and his brother-in-law Dominick Cesario. Cesario was arrested in a store that he and Rinaldo had recently rented and which had been under police surveillance. Cesario was later released.

According to authorities, the luggage was brought across the Atlantic by the Torrente family. Pietro and Anna Torrente and their two children, Vita, eight years old, and Vincenzo, four, were on their way to visit family in California. Travel agent Salvatore Valenti arranged for them to take the additional luggage. The family, having in all likelihood been fooled by the racketeers, were not charged with any wrongdoing.[26]

Rinaldo and Palmeri were indicted for felonious possession of narcotics with intent to sell and with conspiracy to illegally sell narcotics.[27] The two men soon agreed to confess in exchange for reduced sentences. They reportedly told everything they knew to the prosecutor at White Plains, New York. They explained that they were part of a vast network of drug traffickers who since 1951 had brought 451 kilos – about 1,000 pounds – of drugs into the U.S.[28]

Additional arrests

Following the Westchester County arrests, American, Italian, French and Canadian police agencies launched a coordinated operation and carried out raids on both sides of the Atlantic.

The first to be arrested in Italy were the French Antoine Joseph Panza and Mafia leader Giuseppe Palmeri. They were taken into custody at Rome's Termini train station as Palmeri handed Panza a suitcase containing $60,100 in U.S. currency. Brothers Salvatore and Ugo Caneba (wrongly described by Rinaldo as being the leaders of the network) were picked up a few days later in Milan, Italy.[29]

In the early morning hours of Wednesday, May 17, 1961, police around New York City made seventeen arrests of narcotics trafficking suspects. Among those arrested were Vincent Mauro, forty five, of 155 East Fifty-seventh Street in Manhattan, and Frank Caruso, fifty, of 1569 Eighty-first Street in Brooklyn. Officials believed Mauro and Caruso were among the top leaders of the narcotics ring. The others arrested were Salvatore Maneri, Joseph Mogavero, Luigi LoBue, Charles DiPalermo, William Henry "Shorty" Holmes, Edouard Giribone (sometimes referred to as "Robert Angelo Guippone"), Filippo Cottone, Frank Giorgio Tarabella, Anthony Porcelli, Arnold Joseph Barbeto, Charles Tandler, Matthew Palmeri, Charles Schiffman, Michael Maiello and Vincent John Scirghio.[30]

A New York federal grand jury returned indictments in two narcotics cases five days later. In the larger case, targeting a ring that smuggled heroin into the

U.S. through Italy and Canada, a total of thirty counts of wrongdoing were charged against twenty defendants, including many of those arrested on May 17. Mauro was named in ten of the counts. Caruso was named in sixteen of them. Federal authorities made no secret of the fact that the case against the narcotics traffickers grew out of the October 21, 1960, arrests of Rinaldo and Palmeri.[31]

Also named as defendants in the case were Italian-Canadians Alberto and Vito Agueci, Rocco Eugenio Scopelliti and John Papalia. The Aguecis and Scopelliti were quickly extradited from Canada to the U.S. to face the narcotics charges. Papalia's situation was complicated. He recently had been convicted of the vicious beating of Max Bluestein, a Toronto gambling czar, and Canadian authorities decided he must conclude his eighteen-month sentence before he could be surrendered to the U.S.[32]

In August of 1961, Valachi was taken from Atlanta Federal Prison to New York City as one of the accused in the sprawling narcotics case.[33]

Disappearing defendants

As is often the case in this type of affair, a sort of "cleaning" took place within the underworld to eliminate what was deemed to be "weak links" – existing or potential informants. The first to be eliminated was William Henry "Shorty" Holmes, described by Assistant District Attorney Thomas Facelle as the sole African-American defendant in a "huge Mafia operation."

The lifeless body of Holmes, thirty eight, a resident of Teaneck, New Jersey, was found by a milkman on busy Bruckner Boulevard in the Bronx on the morning of August 10, 1961. Holmes had two bullet wounds in the back of his head. There was evidence that he had been bludgeoned before he was shot. Authorities determined that he was killed in a different location and then dumped along the Bronx highway. Theft was ruled out as a motive, when $18 and a set of car keys were found in his pockets. Holmes had posted $10,000 bail to acquire his freedom while awaiting trial in the narcotics case.[34]

On September 18, Vincent Mauro, Frank Caruso and Salvatore Maneri (linked with the Lucchese Crime Family), failed to appear in court for a scheduled hearing. Each had posted significant bond amounts, which were forfeited. Bail had originally been set at $250,000 each for Mauro and Caruso but was later lowered to $50,000. Maneri, a resident of Palermo, Sicily, had to put up $10,000 plus an "immigrant bond" of $5,000.[35] While on the run, Mauro,

Caruso and Maneri reportedly were aided and financed by Henry Rubino, a New York businessman linked with Salvatore "Charlie Luciano" Lucania in Italy and the Genovese Crime Family in New York.[36]

Another "cleaning" murder followed in autumn. The victim was a "bigger fish," Alberto Agueci.

According to Valachi, Agueci had difficulty coping with confinement at the Federal House of Detention on Manhattan's West Street and blamed Buffalo region Mafia boss Stefano Magaddino for not taking adequate care of his family. Alberto Agueci asked his wife to raise enough money to bail out both Agueci brothers. Agueci made the dangerous suggestion that, if Magaddino did not help get him out of prison, Agueci would reveal Magaddino's involvement in the narcotics ring.[37]

Agueci's wife sold the family home and posted his $20,000 bail. (There apparently was not enough money to free brother Vito.) Alberto Agueci was released from prison in September and returned to Toronto for what was expected to be a brief stay.[38] Agueci missed the start of trial in October, at that moment increasing to four the number of fugitives connected with the case.[39]

Defendant Arnold J. Barbeto of the Bronx reportedly attempted suicide in early November, while the trial was under way. The court found that he was incompetent to stand trial at that time, and he was removed from the list of defendants.[40]

On Thanksgiving morning, November 23, 1961, a murdered male body was found by two hunters in a field at Penfield, New York, east of Rochester. The body was in a very bad state. It took two days for authorities to identify it as that of Alberto Agueci. According to initial findings, Agueci had been strangled with a plastic clothesline, his hands tied with wire behind his back and his ankles also bound. It was later established that Agueci was violently beaten and tortured for several days, then finally doused with gasoline and set on fire.[41]

Mrs. Agueci explained to investigators that her husband left their Toronto home on October 9 to go to New York for trial. Investigators found evidence that Agueci boarded a plane at Malton International Airport (later named Toronto Pearson International Airport), but they were uncertain of his flight and destination.

Sources indicated that shortly before his murder Agueci went to Buffalo to confront Stefano Magaddino. The threat that Agueci might reveal Buffalo

Mafia leaders' interests in the narcotics operation led Magaddino and his aide Federico Randaccio to arrange the murder of Agueci.[42]

(The murder of Alberto Agueci caused turmoil within the Buffalo Crime Family. Vito became determined to avenge his brother. Vito attempted to send messages out of the Federal House of Detention in Manhattan through David Petillo, a soldier of the Genovese Crime Family, but Petillo refused the role of messenger.[43] In spring of 1962, Vito tipped narcotics agents that Magaddino was behind the affair which led to the arrest of the Agueci brothers. Vito also confirmed that Alberto had threatened to expose Magaddino's involvement if the boss did not come to their aid.[44] On February 19, 1964, the FBI learned of a meeting in Niagara Falls, New York, that included mafiosi Stefano Magaddino, Peter A. Magaddino, Peter J. Magaddino, Federico Randaccio, Daniel Sansanese and Sam Rangatore. The group decided that Sansanese and John Camilleri would accompany an unidentified gunman to Toronto in order to eliminate Alberto Agueci's wife, who they feared would go to police and expose activities of the regional crime family. The hit was later canceled.[45])

As the narcotics case reached its conclusion, only eleven of the original twenty defendants remained. On December 27, 1961, all eleven were convicted on all counts. They continued to be held at the Federal House of Detention as they awaited sentencing in February.[46]

U.S. trials

The New York narcotics case was based in large part on the testimony of Rinaldo, and Valachi insisted that he was falsely accused. He told biographer Maas that he had nothing to do with narcotics after 1956 and was uninvolved in any of the offenses described in the May 1961 indictment. According to Valachi, Rinaldo "just moved the dates around to fit me in."[47]

It is reasonable to question Valachi's claim, as Rinaldo recalled specific incidents involving him, including an April 1960 conversation in which John Papalia and Albert Agueci spoke with Rinaldo about Valachi. It is telling that Valachi had no quarrel with Rinaldo testimony about any of the others involved in the case.[48]

Matthew Palmeri's testimony also was damaging to the accused narcotics traffickers, particularly the Canadian defendants. He explained that he was brought into the ring in October 1958 by Alberto Agueci, who asked him to help pick up deliveries of "diamonds" from Europe at Pier 84. A month after that initial meeting, Palmeri was contacted by Luigi LoBue, another of the defendants, who supervised Palmeri's role in the operation. Numerous trips were made to the pier between 1958 and 1960. Over time, Palmeri learned that the precious cargo was heroin not diamonds. Palmeri stated that in 1960, Alberto Agueci asked him to meet Rocco Scopelliti at Pier 84 and help him load a trunk into his bakery truck. The truck was driven to Palmeri's bakery in Brooklyn. Another individual joined them there. When the trunk was opened, Palmeri observed the men taking ten plastic bags filled with white powder out of it. For his work, Palmeri said he was paid a total of just $300.[49]

While the New York defendants were waiting to hear their sentences, Mauro, Caruso and Maneri were located.

According to FBN Commissioner Henry Giordano, police were tipped off by a Canadian tourist, who recognized the individuals from newspaper photos. The tourist observed them in Nassau, Bahamas, "spending lavishly." Authorities were able to track the racketeers to Kingston, Jamaica; Caracas, Venezuela; Nice, France; London, England; and to Spain. On January 22, 1962, Caruso was apprehended in Barcelona. The next day, Mauro was picked up in Barcelona, and Maneri was arrested on the Spanish Mediterranean island of Majorca.[50]

New York federal Judge William B. Herlands on February 13 imposed sentences totaling 175 years to the eleven convicted traffickers. Charles Schiffman received the longest sentence of twenty five years. Joseph Valachi and Edouard Giribone were sentenced to twenty years. Valachi's new term was to be served concurrently with his previous fifteen-year penalty.

Charles Tandler, Anthony Porcelli, Michael Maiello, Vito Agueci and Luigi LoBue, each received fifteen-year terms, Rocco Scopelliti got ten years, and Filippo Cottone got five years. Palmeri was sentenced with the group, technically receiving a twenty-year term. However, the sentences for Palmeri and Rinaldo were reduced to eleven years each, due to their cooperation.[51]

In March 1962, the Canadian government surprisingly commuted the remainder of John Papalia's assault sentence and quickly extradited him to the U.S. to face narcotics charges in New York.[52] He was brought to trial along with Mauro, Caruso and Maneri in early March, 1963. Following jury selection and before the government began presenting its case, the four men pleaded guilty to conspiring to smuggle heroin into the U.S. over a ten-year period. A week later, Mauro, Caruso and Maneri were sentenced to fifteen years in prison for their narcotics violations, with concurrent sentences of five years for bail-jumping. Papalia got ten years in prison.[53]

(Joseph Valachi avoided prosecution in yet another related narcotics case late in 1963. Lucchese Crime Family lieutenant Carmine LoCascio; his top aide, Genovese Crime Family member Rosario Mogavero; and nine other men were tried in New York federal court on charges of narcotics conspiracy in December 1963. LoCascio and Mogavero were sentenced on January 20, 1964, to fifteen years in prison and $20,000 fines. Valachi initially had been named a defendant in that case, but he was deleted from the case following his public testimony before the Senate's McClellan Committee in early autumn 1963.[54])

Italy trial

On the other side of the Atlantic, the process was more complex. A trial opened in Italy in February 1967. Of the more than thirty named defendants in the case (including accused traffickers in Italy, France, Canada and the U.S.), just seven appeared in court.

Two others refused to appear: Salvatore Caneba, believed to be the leader of the group, was hospitalized; Vincenzo Di Trapani, was in a nursing home.

Other big fish like Salvatore Zizzo managed to escape indictment.

Salvatore Rinaldo once again testified for the prosecution, accusing all defendants present of being important cogs in the drug trafficking machine. The defendants fiercely denied the accusation.[55]

One of the accused was more talkative than the others. He was Alberto Marazziti. He explained to the judge that he was brought into the trafficking racket by Angelo DiCosimo. DiCosimo introduced him to Giuseppe Provenzano and Gerlando Ferruggia, saying they could help him earn millions.

Marazziti explained that a laboratory on the coast of Marseilles, hidden in the house of a police officer, was capable of manufacturing 30 kilos of pure heroin in twenty four hours. He said that Provenzano and Ferrugia once visited his office in Rome with Edouard Giribone and Antoine Cordoliani to complete a transaction for 10 kilos of heroin and that they had sent him to San Remo to complete a sale for $18 million dollars. Marazziti claimed that he was not aware at the time that the large transactions involved drugs. The judge was skeptical of the claim.[56]

In late May of 1967, the Italian court took the extraordinary step of relocating from Rome, Italy, to the Italian consulate in Manhattan. This was done to satisfy a requirement that all defendants be given the opportunity to appear. But it also allowed the court to hear from New York-based FBN agent Frank Selvaggi. Agent Selvaggi stated that Stefano Magaddino and Federico Randaccio were among the most important figures in the drug smuggling operation. The agent read a lengthy statement from Vito Agueci, which further accused Magaddino and Randaccio of the murder of his brother. Agueci went on to describe a heroin importing deal proposed to him in Toronto by a Mafia member. The Agueci hometown of Salemi, Sicily, where Salvatore Zizzo reigned as local boss, figured in the arrangements. Vito Agueci said the agreement was to be finalized in Salemi, after which Magaddino was expected to approve the cooperation of his Italian-Canadian underlings with the Sicilian drug racketeers. On instructions from his brother, Vito Agueci subsequently traveled to Salemi to purchase 15 kilos of heroin, worth $35,000, and have the drugs transported to the U.S. Vito also revealed that he had been sponsored by Federico Randaccio when inducted into the Buffalo Mafia in 1960.[57]

The Agueci statement detailed the arrangements behind the smuggling operation but could only be dealt with as hearsay in court.[58]

On November 1, 1967, following six hours of deliberation, the Italian court found thirty one defendants guilty. Among those who were present at trial, Ugo Caneba, Salvatore Caneba and Vincenzo Renna were sentenced to ten years in prison, Salvatore Valenti and Vincenzo Di Trapani were sentenced to nine years, Giuseppe Mancuso to four years, Serafino Mancuso to three years, Alberto Marazziti to five years and Gerlando Ferruggia to two years.

Others sentenced by the court included Giuseppe Palmeri and Giuseppe Provenzano, who each received eleven years; Salvatore Valenti, nine years; Antoine Panza, six years; Angelo Di Cosimo and Domenico Farina, three years.

French citizens Antoine Cordoliani and Joseph Césari were sentenced to ten years each, and Jean-Baptiste Piersanti was sentenced to three years.

Césari had been arrested with five accomplices on October 8, 1964, in a villa near Marseilles that served as a laboratory for refining morphine base into heroin. Authorities seized 105 kilos of heroin and 68 kilos of morphine base. When tried by French authorities, Césari was convicted and sentenced to seven years.[59] As France would not extradite prisoners who faced a heavier sentence abroad than imposed at home, Césari remained imprisoned in France.

Two of the accused, Franco Tarabella and Vito Di Prima, were acquitted by the Italian court.[60]

Fabien Rossat publishes on online blog, entitled Une Histoire de Crime Organisé (A Story of Organized Crime) and he moderates "The Early History of the American Mafia" and "The Canadian Mafia Archives" groups on Facebook. This is his first article in Informer. The original article was written in French and translated into English with the assistance of Google Translate.

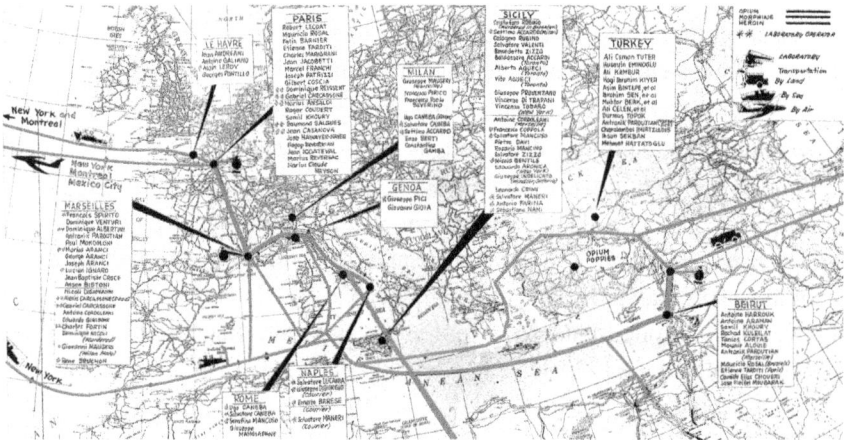

McClellan Committee map shows narcotics trafficking routes across Europe, Middle East and North Africa.

Frank Caruso (left), Vincent Mauro (center), Salvatore Maneri.

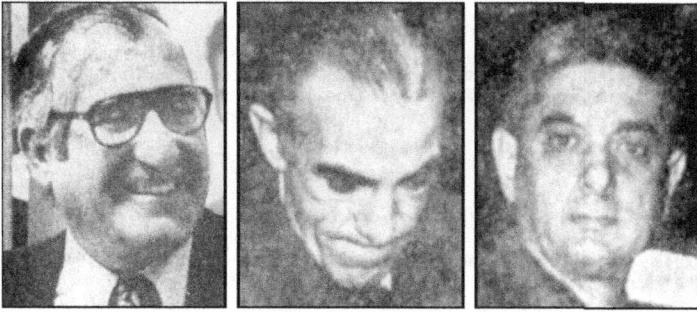

John Papalia (left), Salvatore Rinaldo (center), Matteo Palmeri.

Torch Victim Identified as Dope Figure

By LOUIS REGNER and TOM RYAN

With the identity of a man found slain in Penfield now known, Monroe County sheriff's investigators last night began delving into the workings of an international narcotics ring to find his slayers.

Albert George Agueci, 39, of Toronto, who jumped $20,000 bail to avoid prosecution in a $150 million narcotics smuggling case in New York City, was the victim.

Rochester NY Democrat and Chronicle of Nov. 26, 1961 (left), Carmine Locascio (right).

Feature 9 Notes

1 Valachi told biographer Peter Maas that his earliest involvement in narcotics dated from around 1952. Valachi recalled that his friends Frank Livorsi and Dominick "Gap" Petrelli invited him to join them in a narcotics venture in the 1940s, but he refused. See Maas, Peter, *The Valachi Papers*, New York: G.P. Putnam's Sons, 1968, p. 185, 233.

2 Kline, Sidney, "5 guilty in huge dope operation," *New York Daily News*, March 22, 1956, p. 3; "5 convicted in dope ring," *Binghamton Press*, March 22, 1956, p. 13.

3 Maas, *The Valachi Papers*, p. 234.

4 Van't Riet, Lennert, David Critchley and Steve Turner, "A lifetime of tangling with the law: Salvatore 'Sally Shields' Shillitani," *Informer*, April 2013, p. 29-52.

5 Appendix, *Organized Crime and Illicit Traffic in Narcotics*, Part 4, Hearings before the Permanent Sub-committee on Investigations of the Committee on Government Operations, U.S. Senate, 88th Congress, 1st and 2nd Sessions, Washington D.C.: U.S. Government Printing Office, 1964, p. 952, 959.

6 Fichier des personnes décédées (File of deceased persons), data.gouv.fr.

7 Kline, "5 guilty in huge dope operation"; Patterson, Neal, "Getting what's coming, dope figure admits," *New York Daily News*, April 25, 1956, p. 20.

8 Patterson, "Getting what's coming, dope figure admits"; Maas, *The Valachi Papers*, p. 57, 251; Joseph Valachi Classification Study, register no. 82811-A, U.S. Department of Justice Bureau of Prisons, 1960, p. 4; SA, "Joseph Valachi, aka Anthony Sorge...," FBI report from Atlanta Office, file no. 70-35395-5, June 28, 1962, p. 27; "1 drug case conviction upset, another upheld," *Yonkers Herald Statesman*, March 23, 1957, p. 6.

9 Maas, *The Valachi Papers*, p. 234-236.

10 Maas, *The Valachi Papers*, p. 237.

11 "See 'something suspicious' but client given 2 years," *Toronto Daily Star*, May 27, 1949, p. 2.

12 Edwards, Peter, "Clock was ticking for Johnny Pops," *Toronto Star*, June 7, 1997, p. 1; Adams, Claude, "Galante operated here in wide-open era," *Montreal Star*, March 26, 1977, p. 18; Rowe, Trevor, "Galante no stranger to city's underworld," *Montreal Star*, July 13, 1979, p. 1.

13 SAC Buffalo, "Steve Magaddino, aka AR," FBI memorandum to Director, file no. 9206054-1st nr 1038, NARA no. 124-10204-10421, March 31, 1965, p. 10.

14 Charbonneau, Jean-Pierre, *The Canadian Connection*, Ottawa: Optimum Publishing Company Limited, 1976, p. 156.

15 U.S. Bureau of Narcotics, "Salvatore Zizzo," list no. 246, International List: Persons known to be or suspected of being engaged in illicit trafficking in narcotic drugs, Washington D.C., revised March 1965.

16 U.S. Bureau of Narcotics, "Salvatore Caneba," list no. 038, "Ugo Caneba," list no. 039, "Giuseppe Mancuso," list no. 145, "Serafino Mancuso," list no. 146, International List. Salvatore Caneba and the Mancuso brothers had been deported from the U.S.

17 U.S. Bureau of Narcotics, "Antoine Cordoliani," list no. 053, International List.

18 Blickman, Tom, "The Rothschilds of the Mafia on Aruba," Crime and Globalization Project, Amsterdam: Transnational Institute, 1997, p. 23, 26; "Two Buffalo area men tied to Mafia drug smuggling," *Buffalo Evening News*, June 1, 1967, p. 16.

19 Collins, Larry, and Dominique Lapierre, "The French Connection – in real life," *New York Times Magazine*, Feb. 6, 1972, p. 14.

20 "Drug suspect freed on bail," *Hartford Courant*, Nov. 21, 1969, p. 1; Maas, *The Valachi Papers*, p. 255.

21 Valachi, Joseph, *The Real Thing: Second Government - The Expose and Inside Doings of Cosa Nostra*, unpublished manuscript, John F. Kennedy Presidential Library and Museum, 1964, p. 947, 950, 952, 965; "Drug suspect freed on bail."

22 Maas, *The Valachi Papers*, p. 258; Valachi, *The Real Thing*, p. 966-973.

23 Maas, *The Valachi Papers*, p. 273-277; "Drug suspect freed on bail"; Andrews, Leon F. Jr., "La Causa Nostra, Buffalo Division," FBI report of Buffalo Office, file no. 92-6054-296, NARA no. 124-10200-10453, June 14, 1963.

24 "FBI seizes bail-jumping dope figure," *Battle Creek MI Enquirer*, March 11, 1960, p. 3.

25 SA, "Joseph Valachi, aka Anthony Sorge..."; Maas, *The Valachi Papers*, p. 260-261. Valachi asserted that Strollo lied to him about the penalty being limited to no more than five years in prison. Valachi did

not consider that his own repeated attempts to avoid prosecution figured into the judge's imposition of a harsher penalty.

26 Regan, Con, "$5.5 million in dope seized in county," *White Plains NY Reporter Dispatch*, Oct. 22, 1960, p. 1; *New York Daily News*, Oct. 22, 1961.

27 "Indictments rise in county dope seizure," *New Rochelle NY Standard-Star*, March 3, 1961, p. 2.

28 *La Stampa*, Feb. 16, 1967; Hoffman, Milton, "County kept secret, and Valachi is alive," *White Plains NY Reporter Dispatch*, Sept. 27, 1963, p. 1; Hoffman, Milton, "Top county dope raid netted $5,750,000 in heroin," *White Plains NY Reporter Dispatch*, July 24, 1967, p. 1.

29 U.S. Treasury Department Bureau of Narcotics, *Traffic in Opium and Other Dangerous Drugs*, Washington D.C.: U.S. Government Printing Office, 1962, p. 29; Riesel, Victor, "Italy tired of U.S. unloading its criminals," *Massillon OH Evening Independent*, July 31, 1961, p. 4; *Corriere della Serra*, Feb. 2, 1967; "Mafia drug ring chieftains jailed for 10 years," *Toronto Daily Star*, Nov. 1, 1967, p. 24.

30 Lancellotti, John R., "Giant narcotics ring smashed," *White Plains NY Reporter Dispatch*, May 17, 1961, p. 1; Federici, William, and Henry Lee, "$1,000 race bets tip $50 million dope ring," *New York Daily News*, May 18, 1961, p. 3.

31 U.S. Treasury Department Bureau of Narcotics, *Traffic in Opium...*, p. 30; "Narcotics indictments," *New York Times*, May 23, 1961, p. 42; "24 indicted in dope cases," *White Plains NY Reporter Dispatch*, May 23, 1961, p. 12.

32 "U.S., Canada map law enforcement," *Port Chester NY Daily Item*, June 1, 1961, p. 16; "'Murder, etc.' cuts suspects to 14," *Windsor Ontario Star*, Oct. 5, 1961, p. 1; U.S. Treasury Department Bureau of Narcotics, *Traffic in Opium...*, p. 30.

33 Maas, *The Valachi Papers*, p. 262-263.

34 "Narcotic ring suspect found slain in street," *New York Daily News*, Aug. 10, 1961, p. 14; U.S. Treasury Department Bureau of Narcotics, *Traffic in Opium...*, p. 30; "Body of member of narcotics ring found in street," *Buffalo Evening News*, Aug. 9, 1961, p. 1.

35 U.S. Treasury Department Bureau of Narcotics, *Traffic in Opium...*, p. 30; "County getting photos of 3 in dope search," *White Plains NY Reporter Dispatch*, Sept. 20, 1961, p. 12; "County gets photos of 3 in dope search," *Port Chester NY Daily Item*, Sept. 20, 1961, p. 41.

36 Healy, Paul, "Lucky link trapped dope trio," *New York Daily News*, Feb. 3, 1962, p. 2; "N.Y. dope conspiracy linked to Luciano," *White Plains NY Reporter Dispatch*, Feb. 3, 1962, p. 1.

37 Maas, *The Valachi Papers*, p. 262-263.

38 U.S. Treasury Department Bureau of Narcotics, *Traffic in Opium...*, p. 30.

39 U.S. Treasury Department Bureau of Narcotics, *Traffic in Opium...*, p. 30.

40 "Court denies mistrial plea in dope case," *White Plains NY Reporter Dispatch*, Nov. 28, 1961, p. 8; Allsbrook, Raleigh, "Westchester-linked narcotics case loses two defendants by murder," *Mount Vernon NY Argus*, Nov. 29, 1961, p. 1.

41 Regner, Louis, and Tom Ryan, "Torch victim identified as dope figure," *Rochester Democrat and Chronicle*, Nov. 26, 1961; U.S. Treasury Department Bureau of Narcotics, *Traffic in Opium...*, p. 30; "Gangland killed Agueci afraid he's sing – RCMP," *Toronto Daily Star*, Nov. 27, 1961, p. 1; "Dope trial fugitive found slain, burned," *New York Daily News*, Nov. 26, 1961, p. 3; "Man found dead at Rochester was dope-ring figure," *Buffalo Evening News*, Nov. 25, 1961, p. 1.

42 Andrews, Leon F. Jr., "La Causa Nostra, Buffalo Division," NARA no. 124-10200-10453; Andrews, Leon F. Jr., "La Cosa Nostra Buffalo Division," FBI report of Buffalo Office, file no. 92-6054-700, NARA no. 124-10223-10427, July 27, 1964, p. 15; SAC Buffalo, "Frederico Gabriel Randaccio," FBI Air-Tel to SAC New York, file no. 92-61-529A, NARA no. 124-10346-10207, Feb. 16, 1962, p. 3.

43 Andrews, Leon F. Jr., "La Causa Nostra, Buffalo Division," NARA no. 124-10200-10453, p. 23.

44 SAC Buffalo, "Fred G. Randaccio, aka- AR," FBI Teletype to Director, file no. 92-174-350, NARA no. 124-10335-10039, May 18, 1962.

45 Andrews, Leon F. Jr., "La Cosa Nostra Buffalo Division," NARA no. 124-10223-10427, p. 15.

46 U.S. Treasury Department Bureau of Narcotics, *Traffic in Opium...*, p. 30-31; "All 11 convicted in narcotics plot," *New York Times*, Dec. 28, 1961, p. 11; Maas, *The Valachi Papers*, p. 264.

47 Maas, *The Valachi Papers*, p. 264.

48 "Order extradition of Papalia to U.S.," *Toronto Daily Star*, July 7, 1961, p. 27.

49 "Testifies Toronto man key in $150 million drug ring," *Toronto Daily Star*, Nov. 9, 1961, p. 1; "B'klyn bakery qas hdq. for heroin gang," *New York Daily News*, Nov. 9, 1961, p. B5.

50 "Dope bail jumpers seized in Span," *New York Daily News*, Jan. 24, 1962, p. 6; Healy, Paul, "Link to Lucky trapped trio in dope bail jump," *New York Daily News*, Feb. 3, 1962, p. 2; U.S. Treasury Department Bureau of Narcotics, *Traffic in Opium...*, p. 31.

51 "11 get long terms in narcotics case," *New York Times*, Wed. Feb. 14, 1962, p. 42; "11 men jailed in drug case," *Hamilton Ontario Spectator*, Feb. 14, 1962, p. 1; U.S. Treasury Department Bureau of Narcotics, *Traffic in Opium...*, p. 31; Maas, *The Valachi Papers*, p. 264.

52 Thomas, Gwyn, "Whisked to U.S. Papalia fights," *Toronto Daily Star*, March 16, 1962, p. 24.

53 "Changes plea to guilty, Papalia dope trial ends," *Hamilton Ontario Spectator*, March 5, 1963, p. 7; "Four plead guilty to dope charge," *White Plains NY Reporter Dispatch*, March 6, 1963, p. 39; "Heroin plot brings long prison stays," *Yonkers NY Herald Statesman*, March 13, 1963, p. 58.

54 Kline, Sidney, "Court hurls book at 11 in dope plot," *New York Daily News*, Jan. 21, 1964, p. 3.

55 *La Stampa*, Feb. 2, 1967.

56 *La Stampa*, Feb. 4, 1967.

57 "Italian court here hears of Mafia method," *New York Daily News*, June 1, 1967, p. 7; "Papalia in drugs court comedy of 'Justice Italian Style,'" *Toronto Daily Star*, June 1, 1967, p. 21; "Two Buffalo area men tied to Mafia drug smuggling," *Buffalo Evening News*, June 1, 1967, p. 39; "Mafia in our midst," *Buffalo Evening News*, June 2, 1967, p. 28.

58 "Two Buffalo area men tied to Mafia drug smuggling."

59 Sapin, Louis, and Pierre Galante, *La Grand Filière: Croissance, déferlement et débâcle de la French Connection*, Robert Laffont, 1979, p. 20.

60 "Sintesi delle conclusionne cui era pervenuto nel corso della V Legislature il Comitato per le Iindigiani sui casi ai singoli Mafiosi, sul traffico di stupefacenti e sul legame tra fenomeno mafioso e gangsterismo Americano," p. 12-13.

FEATURE 10

Murder by mistake

Saupp was fatally beaten because he physically resembled a mobster

Though reportedly involved in thirty-three homicides, Valachi generally denied committing killings with his own hands.[1] The one murder he admitted to performing himself, the vicious beating death of prison inmate John Joseph Saupp, was said to be the result of a mistake.

Valachi was serving time in Atlanta Federal Penitentiary following drug trafficking convictions, when he and other Mafia-member inmates had a dramatic falling out. Also held in Atlanta on similar charges was Vito Genovese, boss of the New York-based Genovese Crime Family in which Valachi was a member/soldier. Around May 1962, Genovese concluded that Valachi had cooperated with federal narcotics investigators, and he ordered henchmen within the prison to murder Valachi.[2]

Valachi quickly perceived the threat and did what he could to make the job of his assigned assassins a difficult one. He stayed awake at night, trying to anticipate moves against him. Fearing poison, he largely avoided eating. He stayed away from groups, despite invitations and provocations. And he refused to go into the showers.[3] Days dragged on, then weeks.

He attempted, without noticeable result, to get word to his longtime family friend Tommy Lucchese, a Mafia boss in New York. Briefly, he had himself admitted to the prison hospital. On June 16, Inmate 82811, seeing no better options, asked to be put "in the hole" – solitary confinement.

Solitary

From there he tried to request help from federal authorities. He asked the prison's chief parole officer, whose name he recalled as "Mr. Squire," to get in touch with George Gaffney of the Federal Bureau of Narcotics. The FBN's district supervisor in New York, Gaffney had tangled with Valachi in the past and had tried to persuade Valachi to become a government informant, reportedly promising security and comfort in exchange for cooperation.

> ...[Gaffney] told me that if I join on the side of the Government he would give me a arm chair for the rest of my life... if I change my mind I could call him as the offer that he gave me was always good.[4]

As Valachi sat in solitary – exhausted, hungry and fearful – he was preparing to take Gaffney up on his offer. He believed that a good number of fellow inmates were plotting with Genovese against him. These included mafiosi Vito Agueci, Joseph "Joe Beck" DiPalermo, John "Johnny Dio" Dioguardi and "Trigger Mike" Coppola, as well as non-member Genovese associate Ralph Wagner.[5]

Valachi soon added prison administrators to the list of those he suspected of conspiring against him. A June 17 letter he sent to his wife, asking her to reach out to Lucchese, was returned to him without explanation by prison Associate Warden Marion Jesse Elliott.[6] Valachi learned that the parole officer, "Mr. Squire," did not send any communication to Gaffney, later claiming that the circumstances did not merit it:

> I advised Valachi that [Gaffney] would hardly make a trip to Atlanta without further information as to what he wanted to talk to him about. Valachi refused to elaborate or to state any reasons... I did not take any further action on the matter, as I did not feel that

[Gaffney] would be interested in making the trip to Atlanta without additional information to support the request for the interview.[7]

After two days in solitary, during which he caught up on lost sleep and ate a small amount, Valachi was brought to the office of the associate warden. Inmate Ralph Wagner, assuming the role of a Valachi friend but regarded by Valachi as a Genovese minion, was reportedly present for the meeting.

Elliott questioned Valachi on his reasons for wanting solitary confinement. When Valachi hesitated, Elliott obliquely referred to Valachi's earlier stated wish to speak with Gaffney: "Mr. Elliott asked me if I said anything to the Chief Parole Officer." That was enough to convince Valachi that Mr. Squire had not kept secret the request to communicate with the FBN agent. Valachi made an excuse, "I told him that when I came in the [hole] that I was in bad shape, and I really did not know what I was doing," and then he clammed up. He indicated he wanted to remain in solitary. As an explanation, he said only that a life was at stake.

Back to general population

Elliott ordered Valachi returned to his normal cell, one that was shared with Genovese, Wagner and others. Valachi assumed he did so out of some allegiance to Genovese. However, the associate warden may have believed either there was no real reason for Valachi to remain in solitary or the threat awaiting Valachi might convince him to provide a detailed statement.

The unspoken dangers awaiting Valachi were on both of their minds as they parted: "All [Elliott] said to me was if anyone wants to kill [me], get in touch with him. I told him OK I'll call you when I'm dead."[8]

Valachi knew that he had confirmed the suspicions of his underworld colleagues merely by hiding out in solitary. "...Putting myself in the [hole] is just like as if I was on the outside and I ran to a police station."[9] If anyone needed any additional evidence of his betrayal, they'd soon get it when news of his failed attempt to contact Gaffney circulated through the prison.[10]

He made a last attempt to reconcile with Genovese. They discussed Vito Agueci. Valachi believed Agueci was a "rat" and had given information to federal investigators.[11] To cover up his own treachery, Valachi figured, Agueci went to Genovese and convinced him Valachi was a "rat." Genovese appeared to take Valachi's side and encouraged him to confront Agueci. Valachi agreed to do so, but he was certain that Genovese simply sought to have his two problems eliminate each other.[12]

Valachi felt that his time was running out, and he could see no way of getting out of his predicament. He decided on the night of June 21 that he would not wait for his enemies to strike; he would move against them first:

> I am getting bitterer and bitterer as I think about it. I can't go back in the hole, as between the mob and Mr. Elliott it is all one. I'll do some damage and then I'll burn in the Electric Chair. I must defend myself at any cost. I ran to the officer and I got into a worse jam.
>
> ...If anyone can tell me that I had any other choice, I would like to know. If I go to Mr. Elliott I'm ruined... I went to him and he turned me loose. If I keep my mouth shut, I have already been branded and I would never be able to live through it. Mr. Squire had sent out word that I wanted to get in touch with Washington.
>
> All of this stuff was going through my mind so I figured that in the morning I would go and hang out near the construction [site on prison grounds] and the first one that I would see I would get. Over and over all this was going through my mind. Then whatever happens let it happen but I want to give them the surprise of their lives...[13]

The attack

On Friday morning, June 22, 1962, Valachi's cellmates went outside to the prison recreation yard. Valachi made it a point to say goodbye to Vito Genovese, and he remained in the cell for a while after Genovese and the others had left. At about fifteen minutes after seven, Valachi went out to the yard. He walked back and forth across the grounds a couple of times, as if announcing his presence. Then he moved off to a construction area about fifty yards behind the baseball field's grandstand. His pacing continued there, but across a much smaller distance. He was sure he saw other inmates watching his movements from the area of the grandstand. He was unable to identify them.[14]

At close to eight o'clock, another inmate walked by. Valachi saw the man from behind. He was short, slender, balding, wearing eyeglasses. Valachi was certain that it was "Joe Beck" DiPalermo. He recalled that the man said, "Hello, Joe," as he walked by Valachi, though other witnesses reported that nothing at all was spoken.[15]

Valachi glanced at the construction debris around him on the ground and grabbed the first thing he could find that resembled a weapon. It was a piece of three-quarter-inch galvanized water pipe with a brass faucet attached to the end. It was two feet and four inches in length. He quickly moved toward the small man from behind and swung the pipe at the right side of his head.[16]

The pipe struck the man in the area of the right temple. He was knocked unconscious and collapsed to the ground. Valachi delivered additional blows to the head and face of his victim. A witness recalled that Valachi "appeared to be in a rage and was taking full arm swings when delivering these blows."[17]

Valachi saw the men near the grandstand move toward him. He prepared to engage them and advanced in their direction. When they backed away, he returned to his fallen victim. Other inmates gathered in the area and shouted at Valachi, but none did anything to stop him.[18]

Eventually, Valachi moved a short distance away toward the construction office. A prison guard ran to him there and told Valachi repeatedly to drop the bloody pipe. Noting the growing crowd, Valachi said, "I may need it." The guard called for a stretcher for the victim, and asked Valachi why he beat the man so badly. "I just went crazy," Valachi answered.[19]

The rage was gone from him, and Valachi accompanied the guard to the Assistant Wardens Building. On the way, he asked the guard if the man he struck was dead. "Just about," the guard said. Valachi responded, "Good."[20]

Valachi was taken inside to the office of Associate Warden Elliott. When he saw Elliott, he remarked, "They are carrying a guy to the hospital and it ain't me. Surprised?" Elliott asked what happened, and Valachi responded with a bitter crack: "I told him that I had no time to call him."

Elliott left the office and returned fifteen minutes later with two photographs. He showed one to Valachi and asked, "Do you know him?" Valachi thought the photo was of DiPalermo, but he wasn't sure. He said he did not know the man. Elliott showed the second photo, and Valachi was sure he knew that one. He said it was DiPalermo. Valachi didn't understand what Elliott was getting at, but the associate warden quickly made it clear: "The first guy that I showed you is the guy you hit. But you made a mistake. You meant to hit Joe Beck."[21]

Valachi immediately blamed Elliott and Squire for mishandling his situation. Elliott appeared to accept some responsibility and acknowledged that news of the request for Gaffney had leaked. He tried to assure Valachi that the victim of his attack would recover and Valachi would not face capital murder charges. Valachi was locked into solitary until the following night.[22]

The victim

John Joseph Saupp, Inmate 78776, was carried into the prison hospital with "multiple fractures of facial bones, depressed fractures of temple bones." An employee there noted "that Saupp's head was a mass of blood and that his features were not discernible." He was unconscious but alive. His breathing was labored. Blood clots were found to be blocking both nostrils, and pieces of a broken dental plate were partly obstructing his airway. The hospital staff removed the blockages. Several transfusions were performed in an effort to compensate for blood loss.[23]

Arrangements were made for an Atlanta neurosurgeon to visit the penitentiary the following day and operate on Saupp in the hope that his life could be saved.[24]

Like Valachi, Saupp had been engaged in criminal activity for decades and had been frequently in and out of prisons.

Born in Pittsburgh in 1910,[25] Saupp served in the U.S. Army as a young adult. He reportedly enlisted on June 20, 1927, and the 1930 Census found him stationed at Fort Howard in Baltimore County, Maryland. In summer 1931, he reenlisted. His first documented legal trouble occurred in November 1932, when Washington, D.C., police arrested him for he offense of "joy riding."[26]

In 1935, he was arrested in Rockford, Illinois, for stealing an automobile. He was convicted and sentenced to between one and twenty years in the Illinois State Prison at Joliet – a sentence that would haunt him for much of his life.

On the way to Joliet, it was learned that he was wanted as a deserter from the Army. He was held for a time in Sycamore, Illinois, while that charge was investigated. He entered the state prison on June 15, 1935. He was paroled at the end of July 1936, and dishonorably discharged from the Army the following month.[27]

Apparently unconcerned with parole restrictions, he traveled to Marshfield, Wisconsin, in 1940, using the assumed name of John Schaefer. Under that name, he appeared at Cory Motor Company and expressed an interest in a new car. He claimed he needed to show it to his wife before he committed to purchasing it, and drove away in the "borrowed" automobile. The vehicle was later discovered about 120 miles away outside of Fond du Lac, Wisconsin. Saupp was found in that community, arrested and transported back to Marshfield.

He faced two charges there. On the complaint of Cory Motor Company's owner, he was charged with driving a car without the owner's consent. He pleaded not guilty to that charge. He also was cited for driving without a license. To that, he pleaded guilty. He was sentenced to just $5 plus court costs or a fifteen-day stay in the Wood County Jail. Saupp did not pay the fine, and he became a short-term resident of the jail. While there, the local authorities shared his fingerprints with the FBI and soon received word that their prisoner was wanted for violation of his Illinois parole.[28]

On September 4, 1940, Saupp was returned to Joliet as a parole violator. The following year, he registered for the World War II draft while an inmate. He was again released on parole in December 1941.[29]

Saupp's tendency to drive off in cars he did not own got him in trouble again in February 1942. At that time, he was accused of breaking federal law by driving a stolen vehicle across state lines. Following an arrest in Ohio, he was taken to Pittsburgh for trial. He was convicted and sentenced to five years at Atlanta Federal Prison.[30]

While serving that sentence, he was named a draft delinquent. Apparently, draft registration rules mattered no more to him than parole rules, and he had neglected to keep the his draft board informed of his location.[31]

Saupp was released from Atlanta in October of 1946. Almost immediately, he reentered Illinois State Prison, once again for violating the terms of his parole. It appears he stepped out of prison in 1949 and went to work for a feed business.

At that time, he asked for state permission to leave Illinois in order to visit his mother, then in Ohio. Permission was granted. But, before Saupp left Illinois, he secretly wrote out a few business checks, signing the name of his feed company boss. He also pocketed a full month's pay and $100 for expenses that were generously provided by the employer, emotionally touched by Saupp's trip to his mother. An Illinois newspaper, learning how Saupp took advantage of his boss's compassion, labeled Saupp "the lousiest ingrate on record."[32]

A Chillicothe, Ohio, arrest for attempt to defraud went on his rap sheet in February 1951, and it appears that efforts were made in 1951 and 1953 to return him yet again to Joliet.[33]

Early in 1957, the final items were added to his long arrest record. Saupp was charged with forgery, securities counterfeiting and theft from the mails in the Cleveland, Ohio, area. As the case received some regional publicity, dozens of residents of Pittsburgh's North Side identified Saupp as the man who had stolen government checks from their mail as well.[34]

Saupp was convicted in Cleveland Federal Court on May 17, 1957. He received three consecutive five-year prison sentences, and reentered Atlanta Federal Prison on May 29, 1957. He had some friends in the facility, but he had no known connections with the Genovese clique and no known interactions with Valachi. One friend recalled that Saupp was "a fun loving man who liked to joke."[35]

While Saupp's fifteen-year prison term was not set to expire until May 16, 1972, a full "good time" allowance could have caused the sentence to expire on June 12, 1967. Saupp's earliest possible parole date was May 16, 1962. Had he been a better candidate for parole, he might have been let out a month before the unfortunate meeting with Valachi in the recreation yard.[36]

Emergency surgery

The surgery on Saturday, June 23, was no simple matter. To access the severe wounds, an incision was made across Saupp's scalp, and the skin on the top front of his head was pulled down onto his face. Extensively damaged tissue and bone was removed from the wounded regions, particularly around the eye sockets, which had been smashed into multiple pieces, and around the shattered sinuses of the lower forehead and the upper nose.

Swelling brain matter, freed by Valachi-inflicted tears in the protective dura membrane, was pushing out through many of the wounds. It was first noted oozing from a two-inch, compound depressed skull fracture in the left temple. It was subsequently seen making its way out of the wounds of the eye sockets. "...The only thing one could do was to suck away the brain as it oozed out," the surgeon's report stated. "At one stage decompression was fairly good but again the brain would take advantage of all possible room that had been made."

The surgeon also had to deal with a great deal of arterial bleeding. That ultimately was controlled through the use of silver "clips."

Saupp was not given much chance for recovery. "Patient tolerated that procedure none too well but was in very poor condition before we began, having required four bottles of blood previously and requiring nine bottles during the procedure," the surgeon stated. "The procedure itself was a troublesome one because of excessive bleeding. Prognosis for life here is poor because of the fact that there is no way of controlling the cerebral edema [swelling] which doubtless will continue. There are also possibly other clots scattered about the brain where it was thrown about inside the skull due to the terrific forces involved."[37]

Later in the day, a hospital employee reported that Saupp's blood pressure was dropping, and his breathing was becoming irregular.[38]

Murder charge

Valachi was brought back to Associate Warden Elliott's office on Saturday evening. An FBI agent was present. Because the assault against Saupp occurred on the grounds of a federal institution, the incident was within federal jurisdiction and was investigated by the FBI.

Elliott asked Valachi to tell the story behind his attack on Saupp. Valachi, suspicious of both Elliott and the man identified as an FBI agent, initially claimed he didn't remember anything. Elliott made some effort to win Valachi's trust. The associate warden said he understood that there was conflict between Valachi and DiPalermo and that Valachi confused Saupp with DiPalermo. Elliott said, "I make a mistake myself between these two guys."

Elliott tried to assure Valachi that there still was a chance he would not be charged with capital murder and face likely execution. He reportedly said Saupp was still alive and if he managed to survive for at least seventy two hours after the attack, Valachi would not be charged with first degree murder.

Valachi was skeptical both of Elliott's report of Saupp's condition and Elliott's view of the law. He believed Saupp basically had been dead from the moment of the attack but was being kept technically alive by authorities as a means of pressuring Valachi. He initially refused to make any statement in front of federal agents.[39]

Sunday morning, Valachi's legal situation abruptly changed. John Joseph Saupp, after lingering near death for nearly forty five and a half hours, succumbed to his wounds and passed away. A hospital employee reported, "In spite of blood replacement and other measures, all vital activity ceased and the patient was pronounced dead at 5:24 a.m., June 24, 1962."[40]

When Valachi saw Elliott on Monday, the associate warden promised that Valachi would "burn."[41]

Federal agents and prison officials questioned Valachi several times over a four-day period. Each time, he admitted assaulting Saupp, but he offered different reasons for doing so: he attacked Saupp by mistake; he attacked Saupp because he openly accused Valachi of being a "rat"; some poorly defined group was poised to murder him but "I got one of them first."[42]

A federal grand jury at Atlanta on June 26 indicted Valachi for committing first degree murder on a government reservation. The indictment charged that Valachi killed Saupp "with premeditation."[43]

Federal marshals transported Valachi into Atlanta Federal Court on Wednesday, June 27. He was arraigned before Judge Boyd Sloan and pleaded not guilty. A trial date was set for July 23. Valachi expressed a preference for a New York attorney rather than a court-appointed attorney. Judge Sloan ordered the prison to allow him a long-distance phone call to New York to arrange representation.[44] It was a rare opportunity for Valachi to speak with someone he knew outside of the prison, as his letter home had been returned to him and his one attempt to speak with a known federal agent leaked inside the prison but was not mentioned outside of it.

Avoiding execution

During continuing discussions with Elliott, Valachi picked up on a possible excuse for his attack on Saupp. Elliott suggested that Saupp may have spread the rumor that Valachi informed on two inmates planning an escape. Branded a "rat" and finding his life in jeopardy from the prison population as a result, Valachi may have taken action against the man he viewed as the cause of his problems. Elliott later told the FBI about the discussions:

> I had received information on Thursday, June 14th that [two prisoners – one known to Valachi] were intending to attempt an escape through the rear gate in the counter balance box of a mobile crane ("cherry picker"). I had locked these two men up over the week-end of June 15th... It was on June 16th that Valachi turned himself in to [the Assistant Wardens Building]. I may have given Valachi the idea of using this as a motive by questioning him as to whether or not this was the reason he had been branded.[45]

Valachi interpreted these discussions differently. He believed Elliott was presenting a plan for having the charge against him reduced to manslaughter. According to Valachi's recollection, Elliott knew that forcing him against his will from solitary into the general population was improper and directly led to the killing of Saupp. By helping reduce the charge to manslaughter, Elliott hoped Valachi would keep quiet about the associate warden's mistake. Elliott had a statement prepared explaining that Valachi blamed Saupp for branding him a "rat":

> "I'll call the FBI and you sign in front of them." I asked him what would be the charge. He said he will tell the D.A. to bring it down to manslaughter. So he pulled out a statement – something about escape – and I signed it and I went upstairs.[46]

The statement, turned over to FBI agents on Thursday, June 28, specifically referred to the "cherry picker" escape scheme:

> I certainly did not tell anyone of the escape plot. In some manner unknown to me John Saupp began spreading the word among inmates that I was the person who tipped off the penitentiary officials... On Thursday, June 21st, 1962, I found out for sure that John Saupp was the one who was spreading the false rumors. I did not mean to hit him as hard as I did.

The statement described the Valachi attack against Saupp. Following the initial strike of the pipe against the right side of Saupp's head, the statement said, "He fell to the ground and I guess I went crazy for I hit him several more times on the head."[47]

Valachi's signed statement did not cause his charge to be reduced. Assistant U.S. Attorney J. Robert Sparks of the Northern District of Georgia announced that he intended to seek the death penalty against Valachi.[48]

In early July, Valachi received a letter from the New York attorney he contacted. The letter claimed the attorney had been contacted by an acting warden at the prison who advised him not to take Valachi's case. (Valachi did not recall the acting warden's name but said "he looked like Al Capone.") The attorney then traveled to Atlanta to meet with Valachi but told him he was refusing the case because it was too far from his usual practice. Valachi then requested court-appointed representation.[49] (The FBI later learned that the attorney was accompanied on the trip to Atlanta by a crime figure "who came to find out whether Valachi had done any talking."[50])

Two defense attorneys were assigned. They advised Valachi to do what he could to avoid going to trial. They were certain that he would be convicted of first degree murder. The judge then would be legally compelled to sentence him to death. For a while, however, Valachi was adamant that he wanted a public trial. He wanted to air his grievances against the mafiosi who turned on him and against the prison officials he saw as their allies. "I want to stand trial and I don't care if I burn because I want to blast all of Atlanta," he later wrote.[51]

The court ordered a psychiatric evaluation of Valachi. Atlanta psychiatrist Dr. Harry R. Lipton interviewed Valachi on July 9 and 10. The second interview occurred following a prison visit to Valachi by his wife. (Valachi reportedly believed that Mildred Reina Valachi had been followed to Atlanta by a crime syndicate member concerned that her husband was cooperating with authorities.[52]) That interview was cut short when Dr. Lipton used words that matched an earlier comment made by Elliott. Angered by the apparent connection between the associate warden and the psychiatrist, Valachi stormed out.[53]

Dr. Lipton filed his report on July 11. The report explained Valachi's personal and family history, recalling that his brother was serving a life sentence in a New York institution for the criminally insane, two sisters had been in mental hospitals in New York and a grandmother had been in a mental hospital in Italy. His father's alcoholism also was mentioned. Valachi's criminal history was described in some detail, including the incident in which he was shot in the head by a police officer.

At the time of the attack on Saupp, the report said, Valachi felt he had been accused of "squealing," was skipping meals and stopped bathing. He was suffering from frequent dizziness. Dr. Lipton said Valachi did not specifically recall striking Saupp with the pipe.

Dr. Lipton concluded that Valachi had some issues but was mentally able to stand trial for murder:

> Subject is suffering from a paranoid state and generalized and cerebral arteriosclerosis. Whether his paranoid state and ideas of being branded and called an informer by other inmates have any basis in fact this physician does not know. At the present time he is considered to be not psychotic. He understands the proceedings against

him; he is able to intelligently advise with counsel, assist in his own defense, and stand trial.[54]

But Valachi did not stand trial.

In the middle of July, as Vito Genovese was quietly reassigned from Atlanta to Leavenworth Prison (a move that would not be publicly acknowledged until more than a year had passed),[55] Valachi's attorneys began pressuring him to make a deal and avoid the electric chair. At one point, the attorneys threatened to quit the case if he would not authorize them to pursue a deal with the prosecutor.[56]

At about the same moment, Robert Morgenthau, the U.S. attorney for the Southern District of New York, became aware of the Valachi matter and involved himself. His reason for doing so has not been explained, but possibly the New York attorney who had declined to represent Valachi communicated to him that Valachi was ready to become an informant. Morgenthau contacted the Federal Bureau of Narcotics. Agent Frank Selvagi, who had dealt with Valachi before, was sent to Atlanta.[57]

On Tuesday, July 17, Valachi was taken out of the prison to meet with his attorneys and with Selvagi. A federal marshal told Valachi that he would not be returning to the prison, as it was well known by the inmates that he was giving information to the FBN. During their meeting, Selvagi offered to take Valachi to a New York prison as a government informant if he would plead guilty to a second degree murder charge.

Valachi agreed to the deal. Judge Sloan immediately sentenced him to life in prison. The same day, he was flown out of Atlanta to New York. He became an inmate at the Westchester County Jail, where FBN typically held its informants. He was given a private cell in the jail's hospital wing.[58]

In Westchester, Valachi began his life sentence for his brutal and misguided attack against John Joseph Saupp, and he began his new career as a government informant into the workings of organized crime in the United States.

Atlanta Federal Prison

DiPalermo (left), Saupp (right).

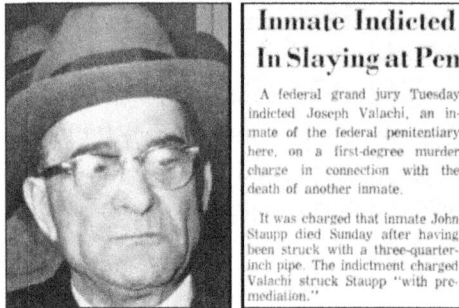

Inmate Indicted In Slaying at Pen

A federal grand jury Tuesday indicted Joseph Valachi, an inmate of the federal penitentiary here, on a first-degree murder charge in connection with the death of another inmate.

It was charged that Inmate John Staupp died Sunday after having been struck with a three-quarter-inch pipe. The indictment charged Valachi struck Staupp "with premediation."

Vito Genovese (left), Atlanta Constitution of June 27, 1962 (right).

Feature 10 Notes

1 Testimony of Joseph Valachi, Oct. 9, 1963, *Organized Crime and Illicit Traffic in Narcotics*, Part 1, Hearings before the Permanent Subcommittee on Investigations of the Committee on Government Operations (McClellan Committee), U.S. Senate, 88th Congress, 1st Session, Washington D.C.: U.S. Government Printing Office, 1968, p. 356, 359; Maas, Peter, *The Valachi Papers*, New York: G.P. Putnam's Sons, 1968, p. 50. Valachi claimed he was typically involved in plotting or in driving.

2 Valachi, Joseph, *The Real Thing: Second Government - The Expose and Inside Doings of Cosa Nostra*, unpublished manuscript, John F. Kennedy Presidential Library and Museum, 1964, p. 1093; Maas, *The Valachi Papers*, p. 28; Maas, Peter, "Mafia: The inside story," *Saturday Evening Post*, Aug. 10-17, 1963, p. 19; Testimony of Joseph Valachi, McClellan Committee, p. 94; "Underworld informer: Joseph Michael Valachi," *New York Times*, Sept. 27, 1963, p. 14

3 Maas, *The Valachi Papers*, p. 26-27, 267-268; Testimony of Valachi, McClellan Committee, p. 102.

4 Valachi, *The Real Thing*, p. 1062, 1104. Two separate references to the "armchair" offer are joined here.

5 Valachi, *Real Thing*, p. 1062-1063, 1100-1104, 1106, 1112; Maas, *The Valachi Papers*, p. 29-30, 267-268.

6 SAC Atlanta, "Joseph Valachi, aka; John Joseph Saupp, aka - victim," FBI Report to Director, file no. 70-35395-9, July 23, 1962, p. 74; Maas, *The Valachi Papers*, p. 30. Deleted from the FBI report were the name of the prison official, the name of letter's intended recipient and the content of the letter. However, the situation is identical with a portion of the Maas book.

7 SA, "Joseph Valachi, aka Anthony Sorge...," FBI report from Atlanta Office, file no. 70-35395-5, June 28, 1962; Valachi, *The Real Thing*, p. 1101-1102; Maas, *The Valachi Papers*, p. 29-30. The FBI report quoted does not identify Squire as the speaker or Gaffney as a subject, but details of the report precisely match more revealing Valachi recollections in the other sources.

8 Valachi, *The Real Thing*, p. 1104-1105.

9 Valachi, *The Real Thing*, p. 1104.

10 Valachi, *The Real Thing*, p. 1112.

11 The FBN asserted that Vito Agueci had not been an informant by this time. He later became one.

12 Valachi, *The Real Thing*, p. 1113-1114.

13 Valachi, *The Real Thing*, p. 1113, 1120.

14 Valachi, *The Real Thing*, p. 1122; Maas, *The Valachi Papers*, p. 30.

15 Valachi, *The Real Thing*, p. 1122; Maas, *The Valachi Papers*, p. 30; SA, "Joseph Valachi, aka.; John Joseph Saupp, aka. - victim," FBI report of Atlanta office, file no. 70-35395-9, July 6, 1962, p. 41.

16 Valachi, *The Real Thing*, p. 1122; SAC Atlanta, "Joseph Valachi; John Joseph Saupp - victim," FBI Memorandum, file no. 70-35395-4, June 26, 1962.

17 "Joseph Valachi, aka Anthony Sorge...," June 28, 1962, p. 3; "Joseph Valachi, aka.; John Joseph Saupp, aka. - victim," July 6, 1962, p. 41. The July 6 FBI report, which seems based on a statement from Associate Warden Marion Elliott (the source was deleted), states that Valachi dropped the pipe after the first strike. After his victim moved, he picked it up and delivered more blows.

18 "Joseph Valachi, aka Anthony Sorge...," June 28, 1962, p. 4, 8.

19 "Joseph Valachi, aka Anthony Sorge...," June 28, 1962, p. 8, 11.

20 "Joseph Valachi, aka Anthony Sorge...," June 28, 1962, p. 12.

21 Valachi, *The Real Thing*, p. 1123.

22 Valachi, *The Real Thing*, p. 1123.

23 SAC Atlanta, "Joseph Valachi. John Joseph Saupp - victim." FBI Teletype to Director, file no. 70-35395-1, June 22, 1962; "Joseph Valachi, aka; John Joseph Saupp, aka - victim," July 23, 1962, p. 51, 54.

24 "Joseph Valachi; John Joseph Saupp - victim," June 26, 1962.

25 "Joseph Valachi, aka Anthony Sorge...," June 28, 1962, p. 28; John Joseph Saupp World War II Draft Registration Card, serial no. 1887, order no. 1572A, Local Board No. 1, Belvidere IL, 1941. The FBI listed his date of birth as February 10, but Saupp reported a birth date of February 1 on his draft registration.

26 "Joseph Valachi, aka Anthony Sorge...," June 28, 1962, p. 29, 33; United States Census of 1930, Maryland, Baltimore County, Fort Howard, Election District 15, Enumeration District 3-70;

27 "Joseph Valachi, aka Anthony Sorge...," June 28, 1962, p. 29, 33.

28 "Joseph Valachi, aka Anthony Sorge...," June 28, 1962, p. 29, 30; "FBI identifies John J. Saupp," *Marshfield WI News-Herald*, Aug. 28, 1940, p. 1.

29 "Joseph Valachi, aka Anthony Sorge...," June 28, 1962, p. 30; John Joseph Saupp World War II Draft Registration Card; "Five Winnebago men to go free," *Belvidere Daily Republican*, Dec. 2, 1941, p. 3.

30 "Joseph Valachi, aka Anthony Sorge...," June 28, 1962, p. 30.

31 "Last warning given draft delinquents," *Belvidere IL Daily Republican*, Jan. 8, 1943, p. 8.

32 "Round about," *DeKalb IL Daily Chronicle*, May 3, 1949, p. 9; "Joseph Valachi, aka Anthony Sorge...," June 28, 1962, p. 31.

33 "Joseph Valachi, aka Anthony Sorge...," June 28, 1962, p. 31.

34 "Check-thief suspect held," *Pittsburgh Post-Gazette*, March 1, 1957, p. 14; "Joseph Valachi, aka Anthony Sorge...," June 28, 1962, p. 31.

35 "Joseph Valachi, aka Anthony Sorge...," June 28, 1962, p. 15, 28, 32.

36 "Joseph Valachi, aka Anthony Sorge...," June 28, 1962, p. 28, 32.

37 "Joseph Valachi, aka; John Joseph Saupp, aka - victim," July 23, 1962, p. 61-62.

38 "Joseph Valachi, aka; John Joseph Saupp, aka - victim," July 23, 1962, p. 56.

39 Valachi, *The Real Thing*, p. 1123-1124.

40 "Joseph Valachi, aka; John Joseph Saupp, aka - victim," July 23, 1962, p. 56; "Joseph Valachi, aka.; John Joseph Saupp, aka. - victim," July 6, 1962, p. 41; Maas, *The Valachi Papers*, p. 32.

41 Valachi, *The Real Thing*, p. 1125.

42 "Joseph Valachi, aka Anthony Sorge...," June 28, 1962, p. 7.

43 SAC Atlanta, "Joseph Valachi; John Joseph Saupp - victim," FBI Airtel to Director, file no. 70-35395-3, June 27, 1962; "Joseph Valachi, aka Anthony Sorge...," June 28, 1962; "Prison death true bill voted," *Atlanta Journal*, June 26, 1962, p. 2; "Inmate indicted in slaying at Pen," *Atlanta Constitution*, June 27, 1962, p. 14.

44 "Joseph Valachi; John Joseph Saupp - victim," June 27, 1962; "Joseph Valachi, aka Anthony Sorge...," June 28, 1962.

45 SA, "Joseph Valachi; John Joseph Saupp - victim," FBI report from Atlanta Office, file no. 70-35395-9, July 13, 1962, p. 42. The name of the official submitting this information to the FBI was deleted, but circumstances indicate it was Associate Warden Marion Elliott.

46 Valachi, *The Real Thing*, p. 1131.

47 "Joseph Valachi, aka.; John Joseph Saup, aka. - victim," July 13, 1962, p. 38-40.

48 Maas, *The Valachi Papers*, p. 33.

49 Valachi, *The Real Thing*, p. 1126-1127.

50 Treadwell, SA George H., "Joseph Valachi; John Joseph Saupp - victim," FBI report of Atlanta office, Bureau File no. 70-35395, Jan. 31, 1963.

51 Valachi, *The Real Thing*, p. 1134-1135.

52 Treadwell, SA George H., "Joseph Valachi; John Joseph Saupp - victim," FBI report of Atlanta office, Bureau File no. 70-35395, Jan. 31, 1963.

53 SAC Atlanta, "La Cosa Nostra, AR - Conspiracy," FBI Airtel to Director, file no. 92-6054-419, NARA no. 124-10286-10381, Sept. 3, 1963, p. 2; Valachi, *The Real Thing*, p. 1136-1137; Lipton, Dr. Harry R., "Neuropsychiatric report, Name: Valachi, Joseph," July 11, 1962, attached to SAC Atlanta, "La Cosa Nostra, AR - Conspiracy," FBI Airtel to Director, file no. 92-6054-419, NARA no. 124-10286-10381, Sept. 3, 1963, p. 2. Valachi did not recall specifically what was said: "He asked me the question that [Elliott] asked me." According to Lipton, "When advised that this physician would like to discuss with him further the trouble he had had a couple of weeks ago, he became quite agitated."

54 Lipton, Dr. Harry R., "Neuropsychiatric report, Name: Valachi, Joseph," July 11, 1962, attached to SAC Atlanta, "La Cosa Nostra, AR - Conspiracy," FBI Airtel to Director, file no. 92-6054-419, NARA no. 124-10286-10381, Sept. 3, 1963, p. 2. The evaluation mentioned a USPHS Classification Test, which was given to arriving prisoners. Valachi scored 85 on the test, indicating borderline or low-average I.Q.

55 Valachi, *The Real Thing*, p. 1134; "Genovese prison changed to break up mob clique," *Montgomery AL Advertiser*, Sept. 28, 1963, p. 13.

56 Valachi, *The Real Thing*, p. 1139.

57 Maas, *The Valachi Papers*, p. 33; Valachi, *The Real Thing*, p. 1142-1144.

58 Valachi, *The Real Thing*, p. 1142-1144; SAC Atlanta, "Joseph Valachi, aka; John Joseph Saupp, aka - victim," FBI Radio to Director and SAC Baltimore, file no. 70-35395-11, July 17, 1962, p. 110; Maas, *The Valachi Papers*, p. 33-34; "Inmate gets life in prison death," *Atlanta Journal*, July 18, 1962, p. 27; "U.S. convict gets life for killing," *Atlanta Constitution*, July 19, 1962, p. 19.

FEATURE 11

Was Valachi insane?

Joseph Valachi's rationality and emotional stability were questioned by a number of sources on a number of occasions. Some issues were raised by Valachi's history, actions and comments; some by the underworld colleagues he publicly betrayed; some by a critical press.

Valachi's mental fitness became a legal issue after he beat to death fellow Atlanta Prison inmate John Joseph Saupp in June 1962. Immediately following the incident, a prison guard asked him why he brutally beat Saupp, and Valachi responded, "I just went crazy."[1]

When interviewed by FBI agents investigating the crime at the federal facility, Valachi claimed that he didn't remember what happened.[2] He later admitted responsibility for the attack but cited a number of conflicting reasons for it.[3]

There was additional cause to question Valachi's mental faculties. At the time, believing his underworld colleagues were planning to kill him, Valachi was refusing food, avoiding sleep and had withdrawn from people and activities.[4]

Valachi was arraigned June 27 on a first-degree murder charge before Judge Boyd Sloan of Atlanta Federal Court. The judge ordered a psychiatric evaluation to gauge Valachi's competence to stand trial, and Dr. Harry R. Lipton, an Atlanta psychiatrist affiliated with the U.S. Public Health Service, was called in to perform it. Lipton examined Valachi's records and interviewed him twice, on July 9 and 10. On July 11, he filed his report:

Neuropsychiatric report

Name: Valachi, Joseph   Date: July 11, 1962

Subject is a short, rather heavy-set white-haired, fifty-nine year old, white male. He was examined at this office July 9, 1962. He was amiable in manner, appeared to be under much tension, and his mood was characterized by moderate anxiety and depression, Speech was relevant and coherent; there was hesitancy and emotional blocking of speech in discussing his present difficulty.

He related he was born September 20 or 22nd, 1903 of immigrant parents. His father died in 1931 at fifty-two years of age, he believes of alcoholism. His mother died about nineteen years ago of diabetes; she was in her seventies. He was the second of four siblings. He stated that his brother went under the name of 'Frank Rocco.' He has been a patient for many years in the Hospital for the Criminally Insane at Dannemora, New York. He went to see him one time, quite a few years ago; it depressed him for some months and he never went back. he stated a sister, Fannie Siano, was in a mental hospital for a year. His other sister, Antonia Alfano, had been a patient in a mental hospital, too. A grandmother had been a patient in a mental hospital in Italy.

He related he was born in Harlem, New York. He attended P.S. 83; he left in the seventh grade at fifteen years of age and got working papers. He stated that for quite a few years he was in the dress business. For the past several years he had been in the juke box machine business. He married in 1932. He has a son, Donald, age twenty-seven. Donald is married and the father of three children and lives in the Bronx.

He related he was shot in the head about 1924. He has little memory for a period of about six months. He was shot by a policeman while riding in a car with another man; he believed he had been taken to a private doctor. Six days later he was put in a Catholic hospital; from there he was transferred to Community hospital. He related he was ill with rheumatism about 1931; he went down to about ninety pounds in weight and was under treatment in a hospital for some weeks. He stated he was cut across the left chest while in Sing-Sing prison in the late 20's; the wound required thirty-eight stitches to close and he was hospitalized therefor. He did not know who cut him; he was in charge of a dormitory at Sing-Sing and had chased out some of the inmates when they were not supposed to be there. He stated he accidentally struck himself on the left hand with an ax during the late 30's. He related he drank heavily for a period of about nine years. It was affecting his health; his doctors instructed him to stop drinking and he complied. He stated that for several years he has been on a diet and had taken medications for diabetes. For a number of years he has been troubled with frequent dizziness.

He related he was first sentenced to Sing-Sing for nine months when he was about eighteen for attempted burglary. He was returned the same year and served three additional years on another attempted burglary charge. He stated he had not been convicted of an offense, except the current one, since 1928. He stated that although he had been mixed up with drug addicts, he had never used narcotic drugs.

Regarding his present sentence, he stated he was convicted to serve fifteen years in June, 1960 for conspiracy in connection with narcotics. He stated that, all-in-all, nineteen other men were involved. Two out on bail were found dead and never got to be tried; some went away; eleven of them actually went to trial. He stated that he himself plead guilty and was given a fifteen year sentence. Early this year he was tried on another narcotic charge. He plead not guilty but was found guilty. He was given a twenty year sentence, to run concurrent with his present sentence.

Regarding his present predicament he inquired as to whether this physician knew about it. He was advised that this physician had read about it in the newspapers. Although hesitant to discuss what had happened between him and 'Johnny,' the deceased, he stated that Johnny had accused him; he had said that he had 'ratted out two guys.' He stated that he really did not want any trouble. He had gone to the Associate Warden on the Saturday before and had himself locked up on his own request. He got out on a Wednesday; this was a couple of weeks ago. He got himself locked up as the rumor was over the institution that he had 'squealed' and several inmates had accused him and pointed him out. He felt his life was in danger and that he needed protection. He was so afraid he had been skipping meals and had stopped bathing for about a week. He stated that actually he was 'in bad shape' when he got himself locked up; it would be hard for anyone to understand how it felt to be accused. He was in great torment because of having been 'branded a rat and marked bad,'; actually the whole thing was beyond his control. For twenty-seven months in the Atlanta Penitentiary he had minded his own business and gotten along all right.

Regarding what actually happened, he could not give much of an account; all he knew what that he was sweating like a pig; he found a pipe lying on the floor on the yard one morning, a couple of days after he was released from the Associate Warden's Building. He remembered picking up the pipe but did not remember striking Johnny. He had heard Johnny had been admitted to the hospital and Johnny had died. He stated he was now quartered in the Associate Warden's Building, upstairs; he was satisfied there. He was having trouble with frequent dizziness and a pulling pain in the right side of the back of his neck. His wife was coming to Atlanta that day and was to visit him.

No hallucinatory experience or suicidal thoughts or tendencies could be elicited. He was approximately oriented; he believed this was about the 5th of 6th of July, 1962. He appreciated that the examiner was a physician and psychiatrist. Comprehension and memory showed no gross defects. Whether his ideas in reference to having been 'called and branded a rat' were delusions or had an actual basis in fact, this examiner could not determine.

Neurological examination revealed some swaying in the Romberg position, a coarse tremor of both upper extremities and moderate sclerosis of the radial and brachial vessels. Blood pressure was 188/96. There was a scar about six inches long over the lateral aspect of the left chest and a scar about two inches in length over the left hand. There were two depressed areas in the right parieto-occipital region of the skull, about one centimeter in diameter; these were considered to be either the result of bullet or trephine surgery.

Subject was seen again in the Associate Warden's Building July 10. He was initially amiable in manner and related he had had a nice visit from his wife earlier in the day. When advised that this physician would like to discuss with him further the trouble he had had a couple of weeks ago, he became quite agitated. He got out of his chair, stating, 'Don't bother me. You make me nervous. Come back in a few days.' Upon this, he walked out of the office, terminating the interview.

Perusal of his central file and his medical records indicate no psychiatric treatment contacts at the Atlanta Penitentiary; upon admission he scored 85 on the U.S.P.H.S. Classification Test. The hospital records reveal he had visited the hospital on eleven occasions during the past three months and had asked for and obtained laxatives on sick line.

Subject is suffering from a paranoid state and generalized and cerebral arteriosclerosis. Whether his paranoid state and ideas of being branded and called an informer by other inmates have any basis in fact this physician does not know. At the present time he is considered to be not psychotic. He understands the proceedings against him; he is able to intelligently advise with counsel, assist in his own defense, and stand trial.

Diagnoses:　　(1) Paranoid State.
　　　　　　　(2) Generalized and Cerebral Arteriosclerosis.

Respectfully,
Harry R. Lipton, M.D.
490 Peachtree Street, N.E., Suite 243
Atlanta 8, Georgia[5]

Insane informant?

In July 1962, Valachi pleaded guilty to a second-degree murder charge and became a government informant, first for the Treasury Department's Federal Bureau of Narcotics and then for the Justice Department's Federal Bureau of Investigation. He talked for months to special agents of the FBI, providing them details on the members, hierarchy and activities of an Italian-American organized crime network he called, "Cosa Nostra."

Newspaper and magazine articles describing Valachi's revelations were published beginning in early August 1963. Almost immediately, new questions surfaced about Valachi's mental health.

On August 27, Leonard J. Murphy and J. Bayard Brunt, journalists with the *Philadelphia Bulletin* newspaper, visited Atlanta Federal Prison Warden David Maull Heritage. They requested information on Valachi for an article they were working on. Specifically, they wanted to know about Valachi's mental condition while he was an inmate in Atlanta.

The warden provided them with no information other than public reports of Valachi's second-degree murder conviction. Heritage then told the FBI about the inquiry. The warden stated his belief that the reporters intended to write an article "to discredit information furnished by Valachi."

FBI noted that Murphy and Brunt had contacted its own Atlanta field office on August 26 and again on August 27 in an effort to interview Special Agent George H. Treadwell about Valachi.

On August 30, the FBI's Philadelphia office learned from a friendly staffer on the *Bulletin*, Henry W. "Hank" Messaros that Murphy was generally a "desk man" at the newspaper but Brunt was an investigative reporter known to be "a bulldog." Messaros advised, "Watch everything you tell him and be careful what you tell him."

Messaros told FBI that the *Bulletin* "had received a tip to the effect that Joseph Valachi's information as furnished was 'phony' and that Valachi 'did not know what he was talking about.'" The FBI concluded that Murphy and Brunt were sent to Atlanta "to verify this allegation and would publish articles discrediting Valachi, if such information was furnished them."[6]

Counting up the 'crazies'

While Joseph Valachi was never judged mentally incompetent, it is clear from his autobiography, *The Real Thing*, that the issue of losing one's mind was frequently on his mind.

In that lengthy document, the specific word "insane" appeared only three times. In each use, it referred to a mental health facility: "insane hospital" or "insane asylum."

Valachi more often used the phrase "blowing his top" (and other forms of that phrase) to refer to irrational explosions of rage or frustration. He used this or similar wording a total of thirty times. On seventeen occasions, he was referring to his own fits of rage. He used the phrase twelve times to refer to the outbursts of others. He used it once to describe a group tantrum thrown by Valachi and others.

He wrote of "going nuts" or "being nuts" six times, and half of those mentions related to himself.

Valachi was quite fond of the word "crazy." He used it a total of eighty two times. It was used five times as part of a nickname ("Crazy Chuck"). Sixty two times, it was used in discussions of other people. (It seems he particularly enjoyed asking other people if they were crazy.)

He used it in connection with himself fourteen times. Once, it was used in relation to a group that included Valachi.

Despite these warnings, Murphy and Brunt succeeded in learning about Dr.

Lipton's report on Valachi. On September 14, the *Philadelphia Bulletin* ran an article reporting, inaccurately, that Lipton found Valachi mentally ill immediately before the federal government began using him as an informant. The article stated that Valachi was in a "paranoid state" characterized by "delusions of persecution." It also revealed the history of mental illness in Valachi's family. The *Bulletin* article was quickly shared in other newspapers.[7]

Undermining a witness, 1963

The source of the tip that triggered the *Bulletin* investigation is uncertain. That it was provided by an underworld source seeking to undermine Valachi's credibility before his planned testimony before the Senate's McClellan Committee is a possibility.

FBI listening devices in the period picked up organized crime figures discussing Valachi and the information he gave federal agents. On September 19, New England boss Raymond Patriarca was overheard telling aide Henry Tameleo that Valachi was "nuts." Perhaps building his tale from the reprintings of the Murphy-Brunt story, Patriarca said Valachi had been treated by a psychiatrist who determined he was insane. The New England boss asserted that Valachi's pending testimony would not get far. Patriarca expected that the testimony would be halted once evidence of Valachi's mental problems was brought to light.[8]

Valachi's televised appearances before the McClellan Committee occurred between September 27 and October 9. On October 4, another listening device picked up a conversation between Genovese Crime Family lieutenant "Gentleman John" Masiello and an underworld colleague. Both expressed the hope that Valachi "cracks up because then everything can be charged off to his insanity."[9]

On October 7, FBI overheard a conversation between Buffalo Crime Boss Stefano Magaddino and his underworld soldier Salvatore "Sam" Rangatore. Magaddino asserted that Valachi could have no knowledge of any Italian criminal society. He claimed that Valachi was not really an Italian and that "Valachi" was not an Italian name. Rangatore said Valachi's testimony was "a fairy tale."[10]

One day after Valachi completed his testimony, an informant told the FBI that Genovese Crime Family big shots Gerardo Catena and Thomas "Ryan" Eboli had made arrangements to pay Valachi's wife Mildred Reina Valachi

$10,000 to grant press interviews in which she indicated that Valachi was a habitual liar and often had extramarital affairs. The informant said this was done "to detract from Valachi's testimony."[11]

In fact, a *New York Mirror* interview with Mildred Valachi appeared in newspapers the same day. In it, Mildred reported that her husband was always chasing other women. "Women! He was always playing around with them – girl after girl…" She claimed he went off with another woman about five years earlier. "That ended our marriage in my eyes," she said. "As Mrs. Valachi, I have been dead since. I am now Mildred Reina."

Mildred said she had not seen her husband for years and received no money from him. She recalled that he had been "a good provider" but said, "I never loved him."[12]

An FBI device heard Stefano Magaddino celebrating the *Mirror's* interview: "Valachi's wife told newspaper reporters that Valachi was a woman chaser, and that Valachi's father was a lunatic."[13]

Undermining a witness, 1968

Though the Department of Justice and the McClellan Committee had used Valachi revelations to publicize the fight against organized crime, Valachi information was not used in an organized crime trial until the spring of 1968.

In April, Carmine "the Snake" Persico and four codefendants went to trial in Brooklyn federal court on a charge of hijacking, and Valachi was brought in as a key government witness.

Before Valachi could deliver testimony in the case, concerns were expressed about his mental competence. On April 22, Persico's defense attorney Maurice Edelbaum called for a mental examination, charging that Valachi was a "borderline moron" with an IQ of 85. The court permitted attorneys to question Valachi without the presence of the Persico jury for four hours on April 23.

Valachi fielded questions about incidents and dates, largely without trouble. He was unable, however, to recall the name of "John Joseph Saupp," the man he murdered in prison.[14]

During the questioning, it came out that Valachi had attempted suicide in April 1966, shortly after he was transferred to a federal prison in Milan, Michigan. "I was feeling miserable," he said. "There was a thirty-mile-an-hour draft through my cell, and I was cold and upset."

The defense questioned him about his brother in Dannemora. He was then asked about his grandmother being treated in a mental hospital in Italy, something Dr. Lipton reported back in 1962. Valachi angrily replied, "I don't know anything about a grandmother in Italy!"[15]

After being judged a competent witness, Valachi testified to conversations he had with Persico while they were held in the Federal House of Detention in Manhattan back in 1960. Persico complained that his then-boss Joseph Profaci had demanded a large share of the proceeds from a $50,000 hijacking job Persico performed. Valachi agreed with Persico that the demand was unjust.[16]

Persico and three of his codefendants were convicted on May 9, 1968.[17]

Lipton's troubles

Harry Robert Lipton, the doctor who conducted a psychiatric evaluation of Joseph Valachi in the summer of 1962, was well regarded in mental health circles but battled his own emotional problems at home.

Lipton reportedly was born Harry Liphchitz in Hamilton, Ontario, Canada, in 1909.[18] He entered the U.S. at Detroit as teenager Harry Lipton in July 1926 and began his naturalization process in 1928. He received bachelor's and master's degrees from Wayne State University in Detroit. By 1940, he was working as a medical professional with the U.S. Public Health Service, stationed at the Federal Correctional Institution on Terminal Island in Los Angeles Harbor.[19]

By 1948, he had relocated to Atlanta, Georgia, where he wore many hats. In addition to continuing his work with the Public Health Service, he had a private psychiatric practice and served as an instructor in psychiatry at the Emory University School of Medicine and other colleges. In that year, his article, "An analysis of thirty-one individuals examined while awaiting trial in federal court," was published in the *Journal of Criminal Law and Criminology*.[20]

Two years later, the same journal published his detailed article describing the psychopathic personality. A census record from 1950 indicates that Lipton was then married and living with wife Marjorie at an apartment on Peachtree Memorial Drive NW in Atlanta.[21] They soon had a daughter together.

Lipton and his wife divorced in 1954. Their daughter remained with Marjorie.[22] On February 21, 1966, Lipton married Marlene Schoeter Tener, an engineering graduate of the University of Munich who had designed an airport terminal and a hospital addition in New York City and also worked as a license real estate agent. Marlene had also been married previously and had a young son, Tommy, by that relationship. The new family resided at 3920 Parian Ridge Drive NW, where they hired a maid, Odessa Barrow, in November 1966.[23]

The relationship quickly turned rocky. Before they could celebrate their first anniversary, their marriage had effectively ended. Late in January 1967, Lipton moved his belongings out of the house, and he filed a new will. Around February 10, Lipton reportedly took the last of his clothes out of the house. Oddly, he still appeared to sleep at the house every night.[24]

Odessa Barrow ordinarily lived in a terrace apartment at the Lipton residence, but she was away on Thursday night, February 23. On Friday morning, she showed up as usual to take care of Marlene's young son and get him ready for school. She noticed a number of unusual things. She heard a loud bang, like a door being slammed shut. The telephone rang several times, with no one answering it (Barrow was instructed by her employers not to answer the phone). Dr. Lipton did not show up for his breakfast or leave for work at seven-fifteen as he usually did.

Barrow got Tommy ready for school. At eight o'clock, he was picked up outside the home by a teacher. Barrow explained that she had concerns and asked the teacher to telephone the house when she reached the school. Again the phone rang without being answered. Barrow telephoned the police at nine.

Police found thirty-two-year-old Marlene Tener Lipton dead in her bed, with one bullet wound behind her left ear and another in her mouth. The body of Dr. Harry Lipton, fifty-seven, was found in a chair near the bed, clad in pajamas and dead of an apparently self-inflicted bullet wound to the mouth. A .38-caliber pistol rested on his lap.[25]

According to the police, Lipton had suddenly moved his clothes back into the home on Thursday. Possibly they had been working to mend their relationship. Lipton apparently had brought his wife a dozen roses on the occasion of their anniversary. Police noted the flowers in a vase in the living room.[26]

"NEUROPSYCHIATRIC REPORT"

"Name: VALACHI, Joseph   "Date: July 11, 1962

"Subject is a short, rather heavy-set, white-haired, fifty-nine year old, white male. He was examined at this office July 9, 1962. He was amiable in manner, appeared to be under much tension, and his mood was characterized by moderate anxiety and depression. Speech was relevant and coherent; there was hesitancy and emotional blocking of speech in discussing his present difficulty.

"He related he was born September 20 or 22nd, 1903 of immigrant parents. His father died in 1931 at fifty-two years of age, he believes of alcoholism. His mother died about nineteen years ago of diabetes; she was in her seventies. He was the second of four siblings. He stated that his brother went under the name of "Frank Rocco." He has been a patient for many years in the Hospital for the Criminally Insane at Dannemora, New York. He went to see him one time, quite a few years ago; it depressed him for some months and he never went back. He stated a sister, Fannie Sfano, was in a mental hospital for a year. His other sister, Antonia Alfano, had been a patient in a mental hospital, too. A grandmother had been a patient in a mental hospital in Italy.

"He related he was born in Harlem, New York. He attended P.S. 83; he left in the seventh grade at fifteen years of age and got working papers. He stated that for quite a few years he was in the dress business. For the past several years he had been in the juke box machine business. He married in 1932. He has a son, Donald, age twenty-seven. Donald is married and the father of three children and lives in the Bronx.

"He related he was shot in the head about 1924. He has little memory for a period of about six months. He was shot by a policeman while riding in a car with another man; he believed he had been taken to a private doctor. Six days later he was put in a Catholic hospital; from there he was transferred to Community Hospital. He related he was ill with rheumatism about 1931; he went down to about ninety pounds in weight and was under treatment in a hospital for some weeks. He stated he was cut across the left chest while in Sing-Sing

COPIES DESTROYED
    JUN 8 1978   ENCLOSURE 92 6054 419

Dr. Lipton's report on Valachi included in an FBI document.

Valachi A Mental Case

PHILADELPHIA (AP) — A psychiatrist found Joseph Valachi mentally ill just a week before the federal government took the long-term convict under its protective wing as the outstanding authority on organized crime in

Warden Heritage (left), newspaper report from Sept. 15, 1963 (right).

Dr. Lipton, Psychiatrist, Kills Wife and Self in Home Here

An Atlanta psychiatrist evidently shot and killed his attractive wife Friday and fatally wounded himself in the couple's palatial home at 3920 Parian Ridge Drive NW, police said.

Mrs. Marlene Teper Lipton, 32, was found in a bed in the master bedroom. Lt. J. E. Helms said she had a bullet wound behind the left ear and another in the mouth.

Her husband, Dr. Harry H. Lipton, 57, was sitting in a chair near the bed clad in pajamas, a 38-caliber pistol in his lap with his right hand resting near the gun, Helms related. Dr.

Continued on Page 5, Column 4

ANNIVERSARY ROSES STOOD IN LIVING ROOM VASE
Bodies of Dr. and Mrs. Harry Lipton Were in Bedroom

Atlanta Constitution, Feb. 25, 1967.

Feature 11 Notes

1 SA, "Joseph Valachi, aka Anthony Sorge...," FBI report from Atlanta Office, file no. 70-35395-5, June 28, 1962, p. 8, 11.

2 Valachi, Joseph, *The Real Thing: Second Government - The Expose and Inside Doings of Cosa Nostra*, unpublished manuscript, John F. Kennedy Presidential Library and Museum, 1964, p. 1123-1124.

3 SA, "Joseph Valachi, aka Anthony Sorge...," p. 7.

4 Maas, Peter, *The Valachi Papers*, New York: G.P. Putnam's Sons, 1968, p. 26-27, 267-268; Testimony of Joseph Valachi, *Organized Crime and Illicit Traffic in Narcotics*, Part 1, Hearings before the Permanent Subcommittee on Investigations of the Committee on Government Operations, U.S. Senate, 88th Congress, 1st Session, Washington D.C.: U.S. Government Printing Office, 1968, p. 102.

5 Lipton, Dr. Harry R., "Neuropsychiatric report, Name: Valachi, Joseph," July 11, 1962, attached to SAC Atlanta, "La Cosa Nostra, AR - Conspiracy," FBI Airtel to Director, file no. 92-6054-419, NARA no. 124-10286-10381, Sept. 3, 1963, p. 2.

6 SAC Philadelphia, "La Cosa Nostra; AR - Conspiracy," FBI Airtel to Director, file no. 92-6054-420, NARA no. 124-10286-10383, Aug. 30, 1963.

7 "Paper claims Valachi onetime mentally ill," *Allentown PA Sunday Call-Chronicle*, Sept. 15, 1962, p. A-10; "Valachi a mental case," *Virginian-Pilot*, Sept. 15, 1963, p. A-10.

8 SAC Boston, "La Cosa Nostra, AR - Conspiracy," FBI Airtel to Director, file no. 92-6054-440, NARA no. 124-10215-10244, Sept. 20, 1963.

9 Select Committee on Assassinations, *Investigation of the Assassination of President John F. Kennedy*, Vol. V, Hearings before the Select Committee on Assassinations, U.S. House of Representatives, 95th Congress, 2nd Session, Washington D.C.: U.S. Government Printing Office, 1979, p. 450.

10 Jenkins, SA Francis B., "Steve Magaddino AR," FBI Memorandum, file no. 92-61-1039, NARA no. 124-10346-10310, Jan. 15, 1964, p. 5.

11 Molloy, James T., "Crime conditions in the New York Division," FBI report of New York Office, file no. 62-9-34-811, NARA no. 124-10348-10069, Nov. 27, 1963, p. 6.

12 "Valachi's wife loved him not," *Hackensack NJ Northern Valley Record*, Oct. 10, 1963, p. 8.

13 Jenkins, SA Francis B., "Steve Magaddino, AR," FBI Memorandum to SAC Buffalo, file no. ELSUR 92-61-1051, NARA no., 124-10346-10316, Jan. 24, 1964, p. 4-5.

14 Renner, Tom, and John Cummings, "Hood told of 'tax,' Valachi testifies," *Newsday*, April 24, 1968, p. 4.

15 Walsh, Robert, and Henry Lee, "Valachi testifies about 3 hijack suspects," *New York Daily News*, April 24, 1968, p. 3.

16 Renner and Cummings, "Hood told of 'tax,' Valachi testifies"; Walsh and Lee, "Valachi testifies..."

17 "Persico is guilty in hijacking case," *New York Times*, May 10, 1968, p. 80.

18 Some sources place his birth in October 1910.

19 Harry Lipschitz Declaration of Intention, no. 80353, U.S. District Court for the Eastern District of Michigan, Feb. 27, 1928; United States Census of 1940, California, Los Angeles County, Terminal Island, Federal Correctional Inst., Enumeration District 60-1268; Harry Robert Lipton World War II Draft Registration Card, serial no. 3223, Local Board no. 273, Los Angeles CA, Oct. 16, 1940.

20 Lipton, Harry R., "An Analysis of Thirty-One Individuals Examined While Awaiting Trial in Federal Court," *Journal of Criminal Law and Criminology*, Vol. 38, No. 6, Northwestern University Pritzker School of Law, March-April 1948.

21 Lipton, Harry R., "The Psychopath," *Journal of Criminal Law and Criminology*, Vol. 40, No. 5, Northwestern University Pritzker School of Law, 1949-1950; United States Census of 1950, Georgia, Fulton County, Enumeration District 60-107A.

22 "Dr. Lipton, psychiatrist, kills wife and self in home here," *Atlanta Constitition*, Feb. 25, 1967, p. 1.

23 "Dr. Lipton, psychiatrist, kills wife and self in home here"; Lundy, Walker, "Psychiatrist and wife found dead in bedroom," *Atlanta Journal*, Feb. 24, 1967, p. 1; Shannon, Margaret, "Lipton stepson plans to sue estate in mother's death," *Atlanta Journal*, Sept. 29, 1967, p. 4.

24 Lundy, Walker, "Psychiatrist and wife found dead in bedroom"; "Dr. Lipton, psychiatrist, kills wife and self in home here."

25 Lundy, Walker, "Psychiatrist and wife found dead in bedroom"; "Dr. Lipton, psychiatrist, kills wife and self in home here."

26 Lundy, Walker, "Psychiatrist and wife found dead in bedroom."

FEATURE 12

Valachi and the FBI rechristened the Mafia

The Federal Bureau of Investigation hesitated to join U.S. law enforcement's battle against the Mafia underworld network. The Bureau refused even to recognize the existence of the secret criminal society until circumstances left it no option. FBI did not fully engage organized crime until, with Joseph Valachi's televised assistance, it had rebranded the syndicate.[1]

A long history

The term "Mafia" was in use in American media at least as far back as the 1870s. Early reports defined it as a "long-standing secret organization" based in Sicily. In a short time, the organization became viewed as a sort of support system for Sicilian brigands. By the late 1880s, newspapers reported that elements of the Mafia had sprung up within the United States and that they were involved in theft, extortion and murder.[2]

Broad coverage given to the 1890 killing of New Orleans Police Chief David Hennessy by Mafia assassins and to the lynching murders of eleven

Mafia suspects in that case ensured that the term "Mafia" was in use in every section of the country.[3] Public and private enforcement agencies from coast to coast came to recognize the Mafia as an interstate and international threat to order. These agencies included the Pinkerton National Detective Agency, the U.S. Treasury Department's Secret Service, the U.S. Postal Inspection Service and the municipal police departments of major American cities.[4] Later, the Federal Bureau of Narcotics, born within the Treasury Department in 1930 and led for many years by Harry Anslinger, worked to expose a Mafia network that operated throughout the United States and across the Atlantic in Europe.[5]

Federal legislators recognized the Mafia threat in the early 1950s. Beginning with its Second Interim Report in February 1951, the U.S Senate's Special Committee to Investigate Organized Crime in Interstate Commerce (Kefauver Committee) acknowledged the existence of "a crime syndicate known as the Mafia, operating Nation-wide under centralized direction and control."[6]

Six months later, in its final report, the Kefauver Committee echoed the Bureau of Narcotics position: "World-wide in scope, the Mafia is believed to derive the major source of its income from the distribution and smuggling of narcotics."[7]

FBI's early investigations

Despite growing evidence and what must have been considerable external and internal pressure, the J. Edgar Hoover-led Federal Bureau of Investigation continued to resist the notion of a Mafia crime syndicate.

William F. Roemer, Jr., began his training as an FBI special agent in September of 1950. He later wrote of those days, "The word Mafia was never mentioned. The words organized crime were never mentioned. There simply was no reason in the FBI in 1950 to discuss such nebulous topics."[8]

Bureau agents in and around Chicago eventually found the existence of an interstate criminal conspiracy undeniable. A short-term operation codenamed "CAPGA" (for "Capone Gang") which was focused on what was considered a reactivation of the Chicago organization previously led by Al Capone, began in 1946. While FBI official Cartha D. DeLoach remembered CAPGA as "the first major initiative against racketeering," involving agents across the country in an effort to "investigate organized crime and … gather information on all known criminals,"[9] others viewed the operation as a relatively minor matter. Roemer indicated that it "lasted just a few months in 1946."[10]

Responding to requests from the Bureau's New York office, Hoover initiated a limited Top Hoodlum Program in 1953. In that program, FBI field offices were asked to designate the major racketeers in their districts and open intelligence files on them. Gathered information was funneled to Washington, D.C., for processing.[11] (Disagreeing with other sources, DeLoach placed the start of the Top Hoodlum Program around the middle of 1957. He claimed the Bureau used the program to "identify and track the movements of every mob leader in the United States."[12] If that was the initial purpose of the Top Hoodlum Program, it was very poorly executed.)

The Eisenhower Administration's Department of Justice created an Organized Crime and Racketeering Section in 1954. The section was assigned to coordinate federal efforts against organized crime. But there was little to coordinate.[13] Hoover proved able to resist this pressure as well, and FBI was taken entirely by surprise in November 1957, when New York State Police found dozens of known Italian-American gang leaders from across the country assembled at a single private residence in Apalachin, New York.

Response to Apalachin

The revelation reportedly stunned Hoover. DeLoach admitted that, until Apalachin in 1957, "J. Edgar Hoover had insisted that there was no such thing as... a network of interrelated mobs that coordinated activities and maintained a kind of corporate discipline. He believed the gangs were local, and he expected local authorities to take care of the problem." DeLoach explained Hoover's reluctance to engage organized crime as a function of the Bureau director's arrogance:

> His profound contempt for the criminal mind, combined with his enormous faith in the agency he had created, persuaded him that no such complex national criminal organization could exist without him knowing about it. He didn't know about it; ergo, it didn't exist.[14]

The embarrassment of Apalachin caused Hoover to step up the Top Hoodlum Program, requiring that each FBI field office assemble a list of leading crime figures in its jurisdiction and closely monitor the activities of each, employing physical and (entirely illegal) electronic surveillance.[15] In addition, Charles Peck, a top FBI crime researcher, was instructed to prepare detailed reports on the Mafia in the United States and in Sicily.[16]

Yet these catch-up efforts remained internal matters, hidden even from FBI's parent agency, the Department of Justice. The Bureau remained largely uncooperative in a growing federal effort to understand and combat organized crime. Following Apalachin, when the Justice Department reassigned William Hundley from Internal Security (anti-Communism) to punch up the Organized Crime Section, he found that his previously good relationship with FBI suddenly soured: "It was like night and day."[17] He recalled, "It was like pulling teeth to get anything done in this field at all… you couldn't find an agent."[18]

Charles Peck turned in his report in fall of 1958. The report revealed the existence of a criminal Mafia network across the United States dominated by Italian-American racketeers, as well as connections between that network and the much older Sicilian Mafia. Hoover reportedly responded to the report by calling it "baloney" and suppressing it.[19]

At roughly the same moment, agents of FBI's New York office questioned local crime figure Joseph Valachi and his underworld superior Anthony "Tony Bender" Strollo. The statements of both men supported Hoover's old view of organized crime. Valachi said "there is no Mafia and no organization in the United States composed of criminals of Italian extraction. He said the only organization called the Mafia that he had ever heard of was the organization that existed many years ago in Sicily." Strollo "claimed that the Mafia was a fantasy created by newspapers."[20]

New views, new challenges

Eventually, Bureau eavesdropping on "top hoodlums" produced an overwhelming body of evidence revealing links among Mafia crime families and the existence of a national underworld administration known as "the Commission." According to longtime Hoover aide Courtney A. Evans, "…We had definite, believable information concerning the existence of a hoodlum organization, headed up by the 'Commission' as early as September, 1959."[21] Electronic surveillance of Chicago boss Sam Giancana indicated that the Apalachin gathering had been a meeting of the Commission.[22]

As President John F. Kennedy was inaugurated on January 20, 1961, the FBI already had completely changed its internal stance on organized crime.

Through just a few years, its catch-up efforts had succeeded, and FBI's understanding of the U.S. underworld already rivaled – perhaps exceeded – that of the anti-Mafia veteran Bureau of Narcotics. But there was no simple way of revealing these things. J. Edgar Hoover, who had publicly insisted that criminal gangs were organized on a purely local level, remained at the helm of the FBI. The Bureau could not simply reverse itself without humiliating its own director. It also could not explain its epiphany without revealing its program of extensive illegal eavesdropping.

A few days after the new U.S. attorney general, Robert Kennedy, moved into his office, the FBI sent him a memorandum advising of the existence of the Mafia Commission. The Bureau had begun using the terms "Crime Commission" and "Criminal Commission" to refer somewhat broadly to a national network of organized crime bosses. The memorandum apparently concealed the illegal source of the FBI's information.

Hoover aide Courtney Allen Evans, acting as a liaison to the Kennedy Department of Justice, reportedly mentioned to the attorney general in May and August of 1961 the use in organized crime investigation of "microphone surveillances" requiring "trespass." Evans informed the FBI that Kennedy raised no objection. (This was later cited as Kennedy approval of illegal wiretapping.)[23]

In September, a "live informant" from New York spoke to FBI agents about organized crime using a term that sounded like "causa nostra." The term matched up well with another, "cosa nostra," that had been overheard on electronic surveillance. The FBI translated the terms as "our cause" and "our thing." Though it seemed the terms were common colloquialisms, the FBI began using them in reports as capitalized proper nouns to refer to Italian elements in organized crime.[24] Perhaps more important sounding, "Causa Nostra" was the first to be widely used. The feminine article "La" was eventually attached to it.

The new terminology provided a bit of cover for the FBI's recent about-face on the subject of organized crime. Rather than admit that it was the last to acknowledge the existence of the Mafia, it could trumpet that it was the first to discover "La Causa Nostra."

In a January 1962 announcement in the FBI *Law Enforcement Bulletin*, Hoover stated colorfully and somewhat vaguely that his Bureau had successfully penetrated "the innermost sanctums of the criminal deity."[25] The FBI director still hesitated to acknowledge that Italian-American criminals ruled those "inner sanctums." He specifically stated, "No single individual or coalition of racketeers dominates organized crime across the nation."[26]

The new term was picked up by FBI eavesdropping on Philadelphia racketeers in the summer of 1962. At that time, agents decided that La Causa Nostra was a synonym for what had been known as Mafia and applied not only to a national criminal organization within the United States but also to affiliated organizations outside the U.S.[27]

Bureau documents were updated in summer of 1962 to substitute "La Causa Nostra" for "Criminal Commission."[28] But the changes were made slowly, and "Criminal Commission" continued to appear in FBI report subject lines.

On September 10, 1962, the New York FBI office reported to Washington that a new informant "stated that 'Causa Nostra,' which he translated as 'Our Thing,' is the name usd by members of the organized criminal element to refer to their overall criminal organization."[29] (The Bureau would eventually realize that the term and its translation were not in agreement.)

The new informant was Joseph Valachi.

Informant

Immediately after accepting a July 17, 1962, plea deal on a prison murder charge, Valachi was transported from Atlanta Federal Penitentiary to Westchester County Jail in New York State. He was interrogated there by agents of the Federal Bureau of Narcotics for a time. Valachi's information on narcotics trafficking was limited, and the data he revealed about other organized crime activities was outside of the FBN jurisdiction.

When FBI learned of his cooperation, it demanded access first to interrogation documents and then to Valachi himself. The Justice Department granted that access, and eventually Valachi was fully turned over from FBN to FBI control.[30] New York-based special agents pumped all the information they could out of their new informant.

The New York office released a summary of intelligence gathered on Italian-American organized crime early in January 1963. Twelve days later, Hoover responded with one bit of criticism, instructing that the title of the report be changed from the old "Criminal Commission" to the new "La Causa Nostra."[31]

Armed with new data and a new label for organized crime, Hoover was ready to crow about Bureau achievements in organized crime investigation. A substantial article under his byline was prepared by February 28, 1963. The article summarized what FBI had discovered in recent years. While buttressed by the information provided by Valachi, the article did not reveal Valachi's identity, as FBI sources and methods were considered secret.

The article defined organized crime as an association of criminal gangs, "organized along nationality or ethnic lines" and operating in different areas. "Largest and probably the best organized mob is referred to by its members as 'La Causa Nostra' or 'La Cosa Nostra.' Generally they translate this as 'Our Thing,' 'Our Organization,' 'Our Cause' or 'Our Deal.' It is composed of a number of 'families' and is governed by a 'Commission.'"[32]

Entitled, "The Organized Underworld," the article was designed to establish FBI as the lead agency in U.S. law enforcement's fight against organized crime. After reviewing the article, Hoover aide Alan H. Belmont noted that it would rehabilitate the Bureau's image:

> By the very publication of the article the Bureau will be taking a positive step to lay at rest innuendos which have from time to time appeared in the press that the Bureau has done nothing effective with regard to bigtime crime.[33]

Hoover intended to have the article published in *Reader's Digest*. He submitted the article to the Department of Justice for its review and approval. Edwin O. Guthman, Justice's special assistant for public information, objected to a couple of aspects. First, the discussion of the Italian-American underworld he felt was phrased in a way that communicated the FBI had been aware of it forever. Second, Guthman thought Attorney General Robert Kennedy was deserving of some mention and credit.[34] The article was put on hold. The Justice Department had its own plans for revealing Mafia discoveries.

Hoover seems to have been genuinely fond of the name "La Causa Nostra," but agents in New York, New Jersey and northern California were clearly hearing their local racketeers refer to "Cosa Nostra" rather than "Causa Nostra." These were interpreted for a time as the result of regional preferences in terms instead of merely differences in pronunciation.

Another synonym was introduced when the New York office became aware early in summer 1963 of the autobiography of longtime mafioso Nicola Gentile. Gentile referred to his organization as the "*Onorata Società*" or "Honored Society."[35] Scrambling to accommodate the new terms, the New York office in early July issued an updated summary report with the title, "Changed: La Cosa Nostra aka a Cosa Nostra, Cosa Nostra, La Causa Nostra, a Causa Nostra, Causa Nostra, Onorata Societa."[36]

Unmasking

The Justice Department decided that it would be best to announce the government's new knowledge of organized crime by introducing the human source of its data to the public. After hearing some objections from FBI, the department assisted Peter Maas and Miriam Ottenberg in researching articles on informant Joseph Valachi to be published in the *Saturday Evening Post* and the *Washington Star*.[37]

Justice mulled whether to make Valachi available for a public hearing before the U.S. Senate's Permanent Subcommittee on Investigations, chaired by Arkansas Democrat John L. McClellan (McClellan Committee). FBI was opposed. Initially, Attorney General Kennedy also had misgivings. William George Hundley of the department's Criminal Division was very much in favor of a public appearance and had begun preparing Valachi for the possibility. At the time, Valachi was motivated by vengeance toward former Mafia superiors and saw publicity as his best weapon.[38]

FBI administrators began to perceive benefits to a public appearance by Valachi. It would give publicity to FBI advances, while also providing a source for Bureau information that did not rest upon illegal surveillance.

The Bureau refused, however, to have FBI special agents accompany Valachi at any hearings. Courtney Evans observed:

> While we would gain from the intimate tie-in with Valachi and, in effect, be publicly displayed as experts on organized crime and La Cosa Nostra, the drawbacks outweigh the advantages. It would be setting a precedent of agent testimony; the agent would be open to questions requiring answers from Bureau files; and the agent could be asked what the Bureau is doing about this information.

For once, Hoover was happy to cede the stage. He wrote a bitter-sounding note at the end of Evans' memo: "I concur. Mr. Hundley + the Head of Narcotics Bureau are experts according to A.G. Since J.V. received only fleeting mention. H."[39]

The Justice Department only learned in September – days before Valachi's scheduled appearances – that the McClellan Committee planned to televise the hearings. "I suppose we should have anticipated that," Hundley once remarked. "You know, these senators like nothing better than to get on national television and get it back home. Well, they made a big production out of it."[40]

Under the glare of television lights, Joseph Valachi began his McClellan Committee testimony about ten-thirty Friday morning, September 27, 1963. The nation watched. Early in his testimony, Valachi stated that he became a member of a criminal organization back in 1930. McClellan asked, "What is the name of it?" Valachi responded, "Cosa Nostra."[41]

He did not say, "La Cosa Nostra," but the televised statement was enough to give a new name to American organized crime – a name that put Hoover's FBI immediately at the head of the war against the mob.

Hoover: organized crime expert

Early in 1966, as the federal government considered department budget requests, J. Edgar Hoover appeared before a subcommittee of the House Committee on Appropriations. He delivered testimony focused on FBI successes against La Cosa Nostra.

Near the start of his statement, the Bureau director defined the criminal society and suggested, despite the long struggles of other law enforcement agencies, that it had been entirely secret until recently unearthed by the FBI:

> La Cosa Nostra is the largest organization of the criminal underworld in this country, very closely organized and strictly disciplined. They have committed almost every crime under the sun from murder, torture, and kidnaping... La Cosa Nostra is a criminal fraternity whose membership is Italian, either by birth or national origin, and it has been found to control major racket activities in many of our larger metropolitan areas, often working in concert with criminals representing other ethnic backgrounds. It operates on a nationwide basis, with international implications, and until recent years it carried on its activities with almost complete secrecy. It functions as a criminal cartel, adhering to its own body of "law" and "justice" and, in so doing, thwarts and usurps the authority of legally constituted judicial bodies.

Hoover offered nothing in the way of credit to Valachi or any other source outside of his agency. When specifically asked by Representative John J. Rooney if the facts contained in his remarks had been known to the FBI before Valachi became an informant, Hoover responded, "I would say all the Valachi information was known to the Bureau or had been obtained from informants of the Bureau."

Questioned about Valachi's contribution to criminal prosecutions, the Bureau director stated, "There has been no person convicted as a direct result of any information furnished by Valachi."[42]

BINGHAMTON PRESS

Rain Again

Friday Evening, November 15, 1957   THE TRIPLE CITIES NEWSPAPER   Vol. 79—185 34 Pages 5 Cents

★ ★ ★
Read It in The Press
Hear It Over WINR

Top U.S. Hoods Are Run Out of Area
After 'Sick Call' on Barbara

Genovese Among 65
In Apalachin Roundup

By WOODIE FITCHETTE and STEVE HAMBALEK
Binghamton Press Writers

New York State Police in November 1957 documented a gathering of top hoodlums from around the country at Apalachin, New York.

William Roemer (left), Courtney Evans (center), J. Edgar Hoover.

Feature 12 Notes

1 Edmond Valin tackled elements of this subject in "How 'Mafia' became 'La Cosa Nostra,'" back in the June 2015 issue of *Informer*.

2 "The Sicilian Mafia," *New York Times*, Nov. 2, 1874; "The Mafia," *New York Times*, May 27, 1877; "The Capi-Mafia in Palermo," *New York Times*, Nov. 25, 1877; "Italians in New York," *Buffalo Evening News*, Aug. 9, 1888, p. 7; "Secret tribunals among us," *Brooklyn Citizen*, Sept. 11, 1888, p. 4; "It is 'the Mafia' now," *New York Evening World*, Oct. 22, 1888, p. 1; "Assassins banded," *Philadelphia Times*, Oct. 23, 1888, p. 1.

3 "Mafia murderers slain," *Chicago Sunday Tribune*, March 15, 1891, p. 1; "Eleven Italians lynched," *New York Tribune*, March 15, 1891, p. 1; "Vengeance!," *Salt Lake City Herald*, March 15, 1891, p. 1.

4 The Pinkertons were involved in the investigation of the 1890 Hennessy assassination. In the early 1900s, the agency took a lead role in uncovering a Calabrian underworld organization linked with the death of a public official in western Pennsylvania. The Secret Service was regularly exploring the intersection of Mafia membership and counterfeiting gangs by the 1890s. Before 1910, the Postal Inspection Service with help from the Pinkertons moved to dismantle a vast regional Mafia extortion operation.

5 "Narcotics enforcement in the 1930s," DEA Museum, 2021, museum.dea.gov. The online DEA Museum article boasts that Anslinger worked to bring Mafia drug traffickers to justice "long before the FBI even acknowledged that the mob existed..."

6 U.S. Senate Special Committee to Investigate Organized Crime in Interstate Commerce (Kefauver Committee), *Second Interim Report*, U.S. Senate, 82nd Congress, 1st Session, Washington D.C.: U.S. Government Printing Office, 1951, p. 11.

7 Kefauver Committee, *Final Report*, U.S. Senate, 82nd Congress, 1st Session, Washington D.C.: U.S. Government Printing Office, 1951, p. 28.

8 Roemer, William F. Jr., *Roemer: Man Against the Mob*, New York: Donald I. Fine, Inc., 1989, p. 12.

9 DeLoach, Cartha D., *Hoover's FBI: The Inside Story by Hoover's Trusted Lieutenant*, Washington, D. C. : Regnery Publishing, 1995, p. 303.

10 Roemer, p. 24; Newton, Michael, *The FBI Encyclopedia*, Jefferson NC: McFarland, 2003. Supporting this view, FBI reports of October 1946 speak of the CAPGA investigation in the past tense.

11 Gage, Beverly, *G-Man: J. Edgar Hoover and the Making of the American Century*, New York: Viking, 2022, p. 486; "Turning point: Using intel to stop the mob, Part 2," FBI, archives.fbi.gov, Aug. 9, 2007.

12 DeLoach, *Hoover's FBI*, p. 306.

13 House Select Committee on Assassinations (HSCA), *Investigation of the Assassination of President John F. Kennedy*, Volume IX: Staff and Consultant's Reports on Organized Crime, Select Committee on Assassinations, U.S. House of Representatives, 95th Congress, 2nd Session, Washington D.C.: U.S. Government Printing Office, 1979, p. 6-7.

14 DeLoach, *Hoover's FBI*, p. 302-303.

15 Ungar, Stanford J., *FBI: An Uncensored Look Behind the Walls*, Boston: Little, Brown and Company, 1976, p. 393-394; HSCA, Volume IX, p. 10; Director FBI, "Top Hoodlum Program - Anti-Racketeering," FBI memorandum to SAC New York, Nov. 27, 1957.

16 HSCA, Volume IX, p. 10; Schlesinger, Arthur M. Jr., *Robert Kennedy and His Times*, Volume I, Boston: Houghton Mifflin Company, 1978, p. 275

17 William G. Hundley, recorded interview by James A. Oesterle, Feb. 22, 1971, Robert F. Kennedy Library Oral History Project of the John F. Kennedy Library, p. 63-64.

18 Schlesinger, p. 275-276.

19 Ungar, FBI, p. 393; Schlesinger, p. 275.

20 Tangel, Joseph L., "Activities of top hoodlums in the New York Field Division," FBI report from New York office, file no. CR 62-9-34-367, NARA no. 124-90103-10093, Sept. 14, 1959, p. 34-35.

21 Evans, C.A., "The *Washington Star* feature article dealing with La Cosa Nostra by Miriam Ottenberg," FBI Memorandum to Mr. Belmont, file no. 82-6-54-375, 376, NARA no. 124-10220-10072, July 31, 1963.

22 HSCA, Volume IX, p. 11.

23 Evans, "The *Washington Star* feature..."; Gage, p. 492.

24 Molloy, James T., "Crime conditions in the New York Division," FBI report of New York Office, file no. 62-

9-34-811, NARA no. 124-10348-10069, Nov. 27, 1963, p. 147A; Evans, Courtney, FBI Memorandum to Al Belmont, Aug. 12, 1963, contained in HSCA, Volume IX, p. 19-20. In the Italian language, it is customary for possessive pronouns to precede nouns, as in "nostra cosa."

25 HSCA, Volume IX; Hoover, John Edgar, Proposed introduction to September 1963 FBI Law Enforcement Bulletin, attached to Jones, M.A., "'La Cosa Nostra' publicity concerning," FBI Memorandum to Mr. DeLoach, file no. 92-6054-395, NARA no. 124-10220-10096, Aug. 8, 1963. The January 1962 bulletin could not be located, but Hoover quoted himself in a summer 1962 document.

26 Blakey, G. Robert, "Organized crime in the United States: A review of the public record," prepared for Northwest Policy Standards Center, Bellevue, Washington, 1987, Department of Justice Office of Justice Programs, ojp.gov, p. 32; Cressey, Donald R., *Theft of the Nation: The Structure and Operations of Organized Crime in America*, New York: Harper & Row, 1969, p. 10; Gentry, Curt, *J. Edgar Hoover: The Man and the Secrets*, New York: W.W. Norton & Company, 1991, p. 327; Ungar, FBI, p. 392.

27 Verica, Joseph A., "Angelo Bruno, aka Angelo Bruno Annaloro (True Name), Ange, Russo," FBI Report of Philadelphia Office, file no. 92-2717-641, NARA no. 124-10222-10224, July 28, 1962, p. Cover N, 462.

28 HSCA, Volume IX, p. 12.

29 Collins, Patrick J. Jr., "Nickolas Forlano aka Jiggs, Jigs," FBI Report from New York Office, file no. 92-6384-4, NARA no. 124-10291-10390, Dec. 26, 1962, p. 10.

30 SAC Atlanta, "Joseph Valachi, aka; John Joseph Saupp, aka - victim," FBI Radio to Director and SAC Baltimore, file no. 70-35395-11, July 17, 1962, p. 110; Maas, Peter, *The Valachi Papers*, New York: G.P. Putnam's Sons, 1968, p. 33-34; Hundley interview, p. 48-49; Edwin O. Guthman Oral History Interview - JFK #1, Feb. 21, 1968, John F. Kennedy Presidential Library and Museum, jfklibrary.org, p. 18.

31 HSCA, Volume IX, p. 15, 19.

32 Hoover, John Edgar, "The Organized Underworld," Feb. 28, 1963, enclosed with DeLoach, C.D., "La Causa Nostra, publicity concerning," FBI Memorandum, file no. 92-6054-386, NARA no. 124-10220-10084, Aug. 6, 1963.

33 Belmont, A.H., "La Cosa Nostra," FBI note, file no. 92-6054-385, NARA no. 124-10220-10081, Aug. 6, 1963, response to Evans, C.A., "Proposed article regarding organized crime," FBI Memorandum, Feb. 28, 1963.

34 Guthman interview, p. 18; Navasky, Victor, *Kennedy Justice*, New York: Atheneum, 1971, p. 31-32.

35 Flynn, James P., "Changed: La Cosa Nostra aka a Cosa Nostra, Cosa Nostra, La Causa Nostra, a Causa Nostra, Causa Nostra, Onorata Societa," FBI report of New York Office, file no. 92-914-58, NARA no. 124-10337-10014, July 1, 1963, p. 8.

36 HSCA, Volume IX, p. 19; Flynn, "Changed: La Cosa Nostra...," p. 1.

37 Navasky, *Kennedy Justice*, p. 31-32; Evans, C.A., "La Causa Nostra, Criminal Intelligence Matters," FBI Memorandum to Mr. Belmont, file no. 92-6054-227, NARA no. 124-10284-10232, May 1, 1963; Evans, C.A., "Informant Joseph Valachi," FBI Memorandum to Mr. Belmont, file no. 92-6054-267, NARA no. 124-10284-10277, May 22, 1963; DeLoach, C.D., "The *Washington Star* feature article dealing with La Cosa Nostra by Miriam Ottenberg," FBI Memorandum to Mr. Mohr, file no. 82-6-54-375, 376, NARA no. 124-10220-10072, July 31, 1963.

38 Hundley interview, p. 50, 55; Evans, C.A., "La Causa Nostra, Criminal Intelligence Matters," FBI Memorandum to Mr. Belmont, file no. 92-6054-227, NARA no. 124-10284-10232, May 1, 1963.

39 Evans, C.A., "Joseph Valachi Testimony Before Mc Clellan Committee," FBI Memorandum to Mr. Belmont, file no. 92-6054-1st nr 385, NARA no. 124-10220-10082, Aug. 7, 1963.

40 Hundley interview , p. 51.

41 Testimony of Joseph Valachi, Sept. 27, 1963, *Organized Crime and Illicit Traffic in Narcotics*, Part 1, Hearings before the Permanent Subcommittee on Investigations of the Committee on Government Operations, U.S. Senate, 88th Congress, 1st Session, Washington D.C.: U.S. Government Printing Office, 1968, p. 80.

42 *Departments of State, Justice, Commerce, the Judiciary, and Related Agencies Appropriations for 1967*, Hearings Before a Subcommittee of the Committee on Appropriations - Department of Justice, Feb. 10, 1966, U.S. House of Representatives, 89th Congress, 2nd Session, Washington D.C.: U.S. Government Printing Office, 1966, p. 272, 275. By this time, Valachi testimony had not resulted in any convictions. However, two years later, Valachi testimony played a large role in the conviction of New York mafioso Carmine Persico Jr.

FEATURE 13

DOJ vs FBI

Government agencies squabbled over the release of Valachi's information

The Federal Bureau of Investigation and its parent Department of Justice had very different ideas of what to do with informant Joseph Valachi and the organized-crime data he provided. In a feud that lasted a year, each agency worked to block and undermine the other and eventually made its own secret publicity arrangements.

While the FBI, led by Director J. Edgar Hoover, technically was a unit within the government's Department of Justice, it historically did things its own way and resisted DOJ control. Hoover's long-term and largely self-assigned priority had been battling domestic Communism.[1]

Beginning in the late 1950s, the Eisenhower Administration and the U.S. Senate's Select Committee on Improper Activities in the Labor or Management Field had strongly nudged Hoover in the direction of investigating organized crime. Senator John L. McClellan of Arkansas was the chairman of the select committee (one of the legislative panels to be known by the name,

"McClellan Committee"). Senator John F. Kennedy of Massachusetts was a member, and Kennedy's younger brother Robert F. Kennedy was the committee's chief counsel.

Without publicly acknowledging it, the FBI did take some important steps to recover from a severe intelligence gap, which had been exposed following the 1957 discovery of dozens of U.S. hoodlums in convention in Apalachin, New York. FBI quickly expanded its Top Hoodlum Program in all field offices, documenting the activities of racketeers and their connections to each other, and it conducted extensive and illegal electronic eavesdropping. There was still some foot-dragging when it came to wholeheartedly joining a war on organized crime. William G. Hundley saw that in 1958, when he was moved from the Eisenhower DOJ's Internal Security Division to the new Organized Crime Division:

> I was amazed when I went from Internal Security over to Organized Crime. It was like night and day... I was so used to [FBI] doing everything, overdoing it, you know. And then you get into a new field, which I thought was more of a problem, they wouldn't do anything in those days.[2]

The earlier nudges finally became an order in January 1961, with the inauguration of John F. Kennedy as the thirty-fifth President of the United States and the appointment of Robert F. Kennedy as attorney general, chief of the Department of Justice. The Kennedys were not content with letting Hoover and the Bureau continue doing as they pleased.[3] In the mind of the new attorney general, after decades of FBI surveillance and infiltration, domestic Communism was no reason for concern. He said, "It couldn't be more feeble and less of a threat, and besides its membership consists largely of FBI agents."[4]

Hundley recalled a bit of change in Hoover's direction: "The only one I ever saw try to move him [Hoover] was Kennedy, and he had some success – just some."[5]

The new administration pushed anti-crime legislation through Congress. The new laws, effective in September, 1961, specifically authorized FBI to combat interstate aspects of racketeering. Hoover had never required such authorization to pursue matters of interest to him. But it was thought that the laws at least provided FBI with "face-saving rationalization for past inactivity."[6]

The acquisition of Valachi as an informant in summer of 1962 permitted the FBI to flesh out its intelligence and provide a more legitimate source for data previously acquired through legally questionable means. With Valachi and great quantities of information in hand, the FBI was finally ready, early in 1963, to announce its commitment to the fight against organized crime. But there was a problem.

Hoover's article

The Kennedy Administration insisted that all the Bureau's press releases be approved by Edwin O. Guthman, the Justice Department's new special assistant for public information.[7] Unlike previous department press secretaries, who gave "perfunctory clearance," Guthman took his oversight duties seriously:

> ...As long as I was going to put my initials on something and I was taking the responsibility, then I was going to exercise that responsibility... I think I learned afterwards that I made [FBI] very unhappy, but they never expressed it in that sense until after President Kennedy died.[8]

By February 18, 1963, the FBI had crafted an article, under J. Edgar Hoover's byline, that explained the nature of U.S. organized crime as the cooperation of various criminal mobs and revealed the structure and activities of the "largest and probably the best organized mob," a nationwide crime syndicate reportedly named "La Cosa Nostra." Without revealing specific sources of information, the article titled, "The organized underworld," described the underworld "crime family" hierarchy (boss, underboss, counselor, captains and soldiers), its internal rules, its member induction ceremonies and its dispute-resolution mechanism, called the Commission.

The article broke dramatically with Hoover's previous statements on organized crime and its significance as a threat to the country:

> Without a doubt, the organized underworld is as great a threat to our democratic principles and our system of law and order as is communism. In some areas of our society, the underworld has accomplished far greater penetration than the communists. This is true because many Americans who would not do anything to aid

communism unthinkingly cooperate with and help support organized crime each day.

The article concluded by imploring Americans to starve the criminal entity
of its financial support by refusing to do business with racketeers and to report
information about criminal activities.[9]

Hoover intended to have the article published in *Reader's Digest*, which
had preliminarily accepted it, but Edwin Guthman halted the plan. He felt FBI
was backhandedly acknowledging the existence of the powerful, nationwide
Mafia/Cosa Nostra criminal organization, while claiming long-term leadership
in the war against it:

> ...The implication of it was that the FBI had known this for a long
> time... The basis of my argument was that if we were going to dis-
> close this Cosa Nostra, if we were going to reveal the existence of
> the informant and so forth, that we would get full publicity and full
> credit for it, and the public would know fully what was involved
> and not just sneak it out like this. And I felt that the attorney gen-
> eral should get the credit; at least he should have some of the
> credit.[10]

Much later, Guthman concluded that Hoover wanted the article published
as written so that it would counteract criticism that the Bureau had been slow
to recognize the existence of organized crime. Hoover hoped to be able to say,
"The FBI knew all along."[11]

While DOJ did not entirely suppress publication of the Hoover article, the
edits it insisted upon made the article unpalatable to the FBI.

DOJ-endorsed Maas article

The Justice Department was working on its own to publicize not only the
information obtained from turncoat mafioso Joseph Valachi but also the specific identity of the informant.

DOJ provided Valachi-related reports to Peter Maas, a journalist working
for the *Saturday Evening Post* magazine. Late in April 1963, Edwin Guthman
met with FBI's Justice Department liaison Courtney Allen Evans to discuss a
planned Maas article on Valachi. Guthman hoped to obtain FBI approval to
arrange a personal interview of Valachi by Maas.

Guthman argued that Maas would "get a better feeling for the story" if he could converse with Valachi. Guthman claimed he had complete control over the final product, would have FBI review it before publication and would alter any portion the FBI considered a problem.

Evans explained the FBI's desire to keep informant identities secret but agreed to bring the question back to the Bureau. In an April 30 memorandum to Alan H. Belmont of the FBI, Evans stated, "We should not have any part of this. Obviously, the Department can go around us and make Valachi available to Maas, since Valachi is in custody of the Bureau of Prisons."

FBI made its opposition clear, and in May the attorney general decided that Maas would not personally interview Valachi for the *Saturday Evening Post* article. Hoover and the FBI were clearly incensed by the DOJ's sharing of files with Maas and saw it as a political maneuver. Hoover scribbled a complaint at the bottom of a May 22 FBI memorandum: "I never saw so much skulduggery – the sanctity of Dept files including Bureau reports is a thing of the past."[12]

Galleys for the Maas article were sent to FBI for review in July 1963. The article, scheduled for publication in early August, was focused on Valachi as an informant-source of data about "La Cosa Nostra." The Bureau recommended some edits. A memo from Evans to Belmont stated, "Director [Hoover] personally supervised this matter and definitely his name should appear in so far as FBI receiving credit."

Evans also stressed that, if Valachi must be revealed as an informant, he should be described as one of a number of sources developed by FBI. Evans took issue as well with Valachi statements regarding an Albert Anastasia-ordered murder of Frederick Tenuto. FBI had no information confirming the murder of Tenuto and still had Tenuto on its "Ten Most Wanted Fugitives" list.[13]

A couple of days later, Hoover aide Cartha D. DeLoach in a memo to colleague John P. Mohr reiterated FBI concerns about revealing Valachi's identity: "...the article as written is, in effect, a death warrant for Valachi in that the underworld will certainly attempt to shut him up."

J. Edgar Hoover added, in a note between paragraphs, "It is a disgraceful effort to get headlines."

The next paragraph of the DeLoach memo noted that the FBI would be getting its share of those headlines. DeLoach stated his certainty that FBI would receive credit for developing information on organized crime. The Bureau had used direct and back-channel pressure to secure that credit:

This has been accomplished partly through repeated meetings with Guthman and Bill Hundley as well as the fine work of Special Agent William Stapleton of this Division in talking to Joe Culligan, Publisher of the *Saturday Evening Post*, a personal friend.[14]

Courtney Allen Evans

The liaison between the FBI and the Robert Kennedy Justice Department, Courtney Allen Evans was a longtime devoted aide to Director J. Edgar Hoover. He was born November 12, 1914, to Charles and Frances Gregory Evans in Wright County, Missouri. Evans went to college at the University of Michigan. He served as one of the editors of the school's daily newspaper. He married Betty Ulrich of Detroit on December 21, 1935, nearly a year before beginning law school at Detroit College of Law.[28]

Evans' applied for appointment to the FBI in September 1940. When evaluated by the Bureau in November, he was living with his wife and a three-month-old child at 14022 LaSalle Boulevard in Detroit. He worked in an accounting position. He was said to have a neat appearance and a self-confident manner. Though he had no investigative experience, he was familiar with federal procedures and was thought to possibly have executive ability.[29] The FBI welcomed Evans as a special agent in December 1940. After five years, he was brought to headquarters in Washington, D.C. In the late 1950s, he became a key Hoover aide, as the director sought to cover over earlier denials of the existence of organized crime. In 1960, Evans was made assistant director of the Special Investigation Division. He brought his accounting and law background to investigations of embezzlement, bankruptcy and organized crime.[30]

His liaison position with DOJ began in January 1961. One of his earlier projects was to explain to the new attorney general that the Bureau had been gaining information on organized crime through a program of illegal wiretaps. Evans was able to document that the explanation was given, though Kennedy and his aides later insisted they hadn't heard of it.[31]

Evans announced in December 1964 that he would retire at the end of the month. He had served with the Bureau for twenty four years. Following his retirement, Evans moved to Naples, Florida, He was a resident there at the time of his death on December 11, 2009.[32]

Rush to publish

By the end of July 1963, FBI was reviewing a draft article by Miriam Ottenberg of the *Washington Star* newspaper. The Justice Department also had shared information with Ottenberg about Valachi's underworld revelations. At the time, *Saturday Evening Post* was previewing its upcoming Valachi article, and other periodicals around the country were scrambling to get related articles into print.[15]

Courtney Evans sought corrections in the Ottenberg article. He took issue with a statement that federal authorities had no knowledge of La Cosa Nostra, its hierarchy or its dispute-resolving representative Commission before Valachi became an informant. According to Evans, the FBI knew about the organization and its Commission as early as September of 1959, years before Valachi started talking.[16]

On August 1, the *Chicago Sun-Times* published an article by reporter Sandy Smith revealing information Valachi provided to the FBI. The *Sun-Times* article stunned the *Washington Star* and caused the *Star* to more quickly publish its Ottenberg piece.[17] Unlike the Maas and Ottenberg articles, the *Sun-Times* report had not been authorized by or reviewed by the Department of Justice.

DeLoach later recalled that FBI quietly leaked information for the *Sun-Times* article. Frustrated by DOJ control of the narrative, DeLoach and Hoover decided on their response during a telephone discussion earlier that summer:

> I already had an answer – a strategy that had worked under similar circumstances in the past.
> "I suggest we leak the matter to an experienced reporter like Sandy Smith of the *Chicago Sun-Times*. That should stop them in their tracks."
> "A good idea," Hoover said, "but be careful how you manage it."
> Obviously he didn't want Kennedy or Guthman to find out where the leak came from – or, rather, to be able to prove we were responsible. They would know who had tipped off Smith. But that's the way you played the game in Washington. Each agency had its favorites among the press corps and cultivated their friendship by feeding them information. Sandy Smith was not in the Kennedy camp.[18]

Smith, known to be a very close ally of Hoover's Bureau, had flown to

Washington, had checked into a hotel under an assumed name and had telephoned DeLoach. The Hoover aide had then supplied the data for an FBI-friendly account of La Cosa Nostra revelations.[19]

Ottenberg's article appeared in the *Star's* issue of Sunday, August 4. The report revealed Valachi's work as an informant, previewed his appearance before the McClellan Committee and credited him for a breakthrough in organized crime research, though it did so in terms that must have been acceptable to the Bureau:

> He has verified uncorroborated information previously developed by the FBI as to the existence of a secret, nationwide organization that dominates a network of mobs in more than a dozen American cities.[20]

Newspapers across the country and into Canada picked up the DOJ-backed Ottenberg report and ran their own versions of it. For its widely circulated account, the *New York Times* obtained independent confirmation of the Valachi-related details from sources within the Department of Justice.[21]

Miriam Ottenberg

Miram Ottenberg was a longtime investigative reporter for the *Washington Evening Star*, an author and a Pulitzer Prize winner.

She was born Oct. 7, 1914, in the District of Columbia to Louis and Nettie Podell Ottenberg. Her father was an attorney. Her mother was a social worker. She received a bachelor's degree in journalism in 1935 from the University of Wisconsin-Madison. She worked for a time as a copywriter for a Chicago advertising agency and as a reporter in Akron, Ohio, before returning to D.C. and joining the reporting staff at the *Star*, the first female news reporter for that publication.

Ottenberg specialized in police crime reporting through the 1940s. She was honored for her efforts with a 1958 tribute party thrown by D.C. police, jurists and officials.[33]

She won her Pulitzer Prize in 1960 for a series of *Star* articles that revealed unscrupulous practices among dealers of used cars.[34] In 1962, she wrote *The Federal Investigators*, a book detailing agents' battles against gangsters, spies and traitors. Attorney General Robert F. Kennedy wrote the foreword for that book.[35]

About a decade after publication of her report on Joseph Valachi,

Ottenberg experienced symptoms of multiple sclerosis, including vision problems. She retired from the newspaper in 1975 and wrote a book on coping with M.S. entitled *The Pursuit of Hope.*

She was diagnosed with cancer in 1980 and planned to document that experience in another book. Ottenberg was inducted into the Washington Hall of Fame of the Society of Professional Journalists in 1981. She lost her fight with cancer on November 9, 1982.[36]

Bureau response

Maas's *Saturday Evening Post* article, complete with crime scene photographs, portraits of leading Mafia figures (including one of Valachi) and an introductory sidebar by Attorney General Robert Kennedy, was released at roughly the same moment.[22]

In his introduction to the subject, Kennedy wrote that the turning of Valachi "represents the biggest intelligence breakthrough yet in combating organized crime and racketeering in the United States." Kennedy credited FBI for its work but portrayed the Bureau as just one part of a group effort to expose the crime network: "It is the result of exceptional teamwork among the FBI, the Federal Bureau of Narcotics and the Organized Crime and Racketeering Section of the Justice Department. Without such coordination the information from Valachi would have been largely wasted."[23]

Hoover anticipated that the Maas article would "undoubtedly provoke considerable public reaction." He instructed the staff at FBI to answer all inquiries relating to the story with "No comment."[24]

Hoover's aides immediately returned to discussing the DOJ-rejected *Reader's Digest* article, "The organized underworld." An old Courtney Evans memo from February 28, 1963, began making the rounds again. In that memo, Evans stated that the Hoover article "will have a tremendous impact upon the American public and will drive home to the public and to law enforcement officials the major role which the FBI is playing in the drive against organized crime." On August 6, Alan Belmont supported Evans' earlier position and recommended editing the article for *Reader's Digest* to focus more clearly on La Cosa Nostra. Belmont indicated that the purpose, in addition to "letting it be known that the FBI developed this information even before Valachi," would be in spreading Hoover's recommendations for actions to be taken against organized crime.[25]

Two days later, discussion of the Hoover article continued. Instead of *Reader's Digest*, the article was proposed for publication in *Parade*, a magazine section circulated with Sunday newspapers across the country. According to a memo by M.A. Jones, the article was important for two reasons:

> First it shows that we were fully aware of "La Cosa Nostra" long before Joseph Valachi talked. Second it shows that we were also cognizant of the fact "La Cosa Nostra" is not the only group in the organized underworld.

Jones noted that the article described the threat of organized crime and offered suggestions for public action in opposing it. In an attached note, Belmont offered a plan to explain – plausibly but fraudulently – the timing of the article's publication:

> ...we can take the position that we were not going to write an article, preferring to work investigatively in a quiet manner until evidence was developed for prosecution; however, we have been asked so many questions, following the *Saturday Evening Post* article, that we prepared this article...[26]

The article submission to *Parade* magazine was approved by Hoover with some edits that shortened the piece, focused it on La Cosa Nostra and noted the recent publicity given to the criminal organization. The article appeared in *Parade's* September 15, 1963, issue under the headline, "The inside story of organized crime & how you can help smash it."

The article was accompanied only by a photograph of FBI Director J. Edgar Hoover. It made no mention of informant Joseph Valachi or of Attorney General Robert Kennedy.

It did not acknowledge the contributions of the Federal Bureau of Narcotics nor of any part of the Department of Justice outside of FBI.[27]

February 28, 1963

THE ORGANIZED UNDERWORLD

by

John Edgar Hoover, Director
Federal Bureau of Investigation
United States Department of Justice

"In other action by the court yesterday, John Doe was fined $105 and placed on probation for 6 months following his plea of guilty to a charge of operating a lottery."

Hoover's planned article for Reader's Digest.

By Miriam Ottenberg

Star Staff Writer

For the first time in the Federal war on organized crime, a figure once fairly high in the mob hierarchy is telling all he knows about crime in America.

His existence--the information he's spilling to Federal agents--has been shrouded in a blanket of secrecy until this moment.

Justice Department officials, who have been keeping

A draft of Ottenberg's article.

THE SATURDAY EVENING
POST

Crime in America

Mafia: The inside story

For decades this criminal society managed to keep its secrets. But now a member has talked, identifying the men who rule big-time crime.

By PETER MAAS

Maas's article in Saturday Evening Post.

Miriam Ottenberg (left), Robert Kennedy and J. Edgar Hoover (right).

Hoover's article in Parade magazine.

Feature 13 Notes

1 William G. Hundley, recorded interview by James A. Oesterle, Feb. 22, 1971, Robert F. Kennedy Library Oral History Project of the John F. Kennedy Library, p. 63.

2 Hundley recorded interview, p. 63.

3 House Select Committee on Assassinations (HSCA), *Investigation of the Assassination of President John F. Kennedy*, Volume IX: Staff and Consultant's Reports on Organized Crime, Select Committee on Assassinations, U.S. House of Representatives, 95th Congress, 2nd Session, Washington D.C.: U.S. Government Printing Office, 1979, p. 11-12.

4 Schlesinger, Arthur M. Jr., *Robert Kennedy and His Times, Volume I*, Boston: Houghton Mifflin Company, 1978, p. 273.

5 Hundley recorded interview, p. 63.

6 Navasky, Victor, *Kennedy Justice*, New York: Atheneum, 1971, p. 14-15.

7 Guthman, Edwin, *We Band of Brothers*, New York: Harper and Row, 1971; "Edwin O. Guthman Personal Papers," John F. Kennedy Presidential Library and Museum, jfklibrary.org.

8 Edwin O. Guthman Oral History Interview - JFK #1, Feb. 21, 1968, John F. Kennedy Presidential Library and Museum, jfklibrary.org, p. 15-18.

9 Belmont, A.H., "La Cosa Nostra," FBI note, file no. 92-6054-385, NARA no. 124-10220-10081, Aug. 6, 1963, response to Evans, C.A., "Proposed article regarding organized crime," FBI Memorandum, Feb. 28, 1963; Hoover, John Edgar, "The Organized Underworld," Feb. 28, 1963, enclosed with DeLoach, C.D., "La Causa Nostra, publicity concerning," FBI Memorandum, file no. 92-6054-386, NARA no. 124-10220-10084, Aug. 6, 1963.

10 Guthman Interview, p. 18-19.

11 Navasky, *Kennedy Justice*, p. 31-32.

12 Evans, C.A., "Informant Joseph Valachi," FBI Memorandum to Mr. Belmont, file no. 92-6054-267, NARA no. 124-10284-10277, May 22, 1963.

13 Evans, C.A., "The *Saturday Evening Post* feature article dealing with La Causa Nostra," FBI Memorandum to Mr. Belmont, file no. 92-6054-3rd NR 359, Nara no. 124-10278-10270, July 15, 1963.

14 DeLoach, C.D., "*Saturday Evening Post* feature article dealing with La Causa Nostra," FBI Memorandum to Mr. Mohr, file no. 92-6054-5th NR 359, NARA no. 124-10278-10272, July 17, 1963.

15 DeLoach, C.D., "The *Washington Star* feature article dealing with La Cosa Nostra by Miriam Ottenberg," FBI Memorandum to Mr. Mohr, file no. 82-6-54-375, 376, NARA no. 124-10220-10072, July 31, 1963.

16 Evans, "The *Washington Star* feature article dealing with La Cosa Nostra by Miriam Ottenberg," July 31, 1963.

17 "U.S. mobster gives vital data to FBI," *Montreal Star* (*New York Times* Service), Aug. 5, 1963, p. 1.

18 DeLoach, Cartha D., *Hoover's FBI: The Inside Story by Hoover's Trusted Lieutenant*, Washington, D. C. : Regnery Publishing, 1995, p. 314-315. In DeLoach's recollection, very little time passed between the rejection of Hoover's planned Reader's Digest article and Hoover's approval of the leak to Sandy Smith.

19 "Sandy Smith," *Chicago Tribune*, Dec. 12, 2005; DeLoach, *Hoover's FBI*, p. 314-315. (Peter Maas seemed to attribute this leak of information to the Federal Bureau of Narcotics rather than the FBI. See: Maas, Peter, *The Valachi Papers*, New York: G.P. Putnam's Sons, 1968, p. 46.)

20 "Secret crime society reported identified," *Richmond VA Times-Dispatch*, Aug. 4, 1963, p. 18; "U.S. gets secrets of crime network from gang figure," *New York Times*, Aug. 5, 1963, p. 1.

21 "U.S. gets secrets of crime network from gang figure"; "U.S. mobster gives vital data to FBI."

22 Maas, Peter, "Mafia: The inside story," *Saturday Evening Post*, Aug. 10-17, Issue no. 28, 1963, Philadelphia: Curtis Publishing Company. The periodical was available days before its stated publication date. The article headline interestingly used the older term, "Mafia," rather than the "La Cosa Nostra" name preferred by FBI.

23 Kennedy, Attorney General Robert F., "What it means," *Saturday Evening Post*, Aug. 10-17, 1963, p. 20.

24 Director FBI, "La Cosa Nostra AR - Conspiracy," FBI airtel to SAC New York, file no. 92-6054-386, NARA no. 124-10220-10084, Aug. 1, 1963.

25 Belmont, A.H., "La Cosa Nostra," FBI note, file no. 92-6054-385, NARA no. 124-10220-10081, Aug. 6, 1963, response to Evans, C.A., "Proposed article regarding organized crime," FBI Memorandum, Feb. 28, 1963.

26 Jones, M.A., "Proposed article regarding organized crime," FBI memorandum to Mr. DeLoach, file no. 92-6054-396, NARA no. 124-10220-10097, Aug. 8, 1963.

27 Hoover, J. Edgar, "The inside story of organized crime & how you can help smash it," *Parade*, Sept. 15, 1963, p. 4.

28 "Courtney Allen Evans," FBI Records: The Vault, vault.fbi.gov; Bugas, SAC John S., "Report of interview with applicant Courtney A. Evans for appointment as Special Agent," FBI report of Detroit office, Nov. 7, 1940; Courtney A. Evans and Betty Ulrich Marriage License, no. 468622, Wayne County, Michigan, Dec. 5, 1935, ceremony Dec. 21, 1935.

29 Hoover, John Edgar, Letter to Courtney A. Evans, Sept. 11, 1940; Bugas, "Report of interview with applicant Courtney A. Evans for appointment as Special Agent."

30 Courtney Allen Evans FBI file, Part 1 of 9, vault.fbi.gov; Hoover, John Edgar, "Memorandum for Mr. Tolson," FBI memorandum, file no. 67-80001-1346, March 28, 1952; Evans, C.A., "The *Washington Star* feature article dealing with La Cosa Nostra by Miriam Ottenberg," FBI Memorandum to Mr. Belmont, file no. 82-6-54-375, 376, NARA no. 124-10220-10072, July 31, 1963.

31 Evans, "The *Washington Star* feature article dealing with La Cosa Nostra by Miriam Ottenberg," July 31, 1963; Gage, Beverly, *G-Man: J. Edgar Hoover and the Making of the American Century*, New York: Viking, 2022, p. 492.

32 "C.A. Evans, F.B.I. aide, to retire," *New York Times*, Dec. 12, 1964, p. 16; Courtney A. Evans, 374-09-3185, Social Security Death Index, Dec. 11, 2009.

33 Carper, Elsie, "Reporter Miriam Ottenberg of the *Washington Star* dies," *Washington Post*, Nov. 10, 1982; "Miriam Ottenberg Papers, 1931, 1982," Wisconsin Historical Society, digicoll.library.wisc.edu.

34 "Miriam Ottenberg of The *Evening Star*, Washington, DC," The Pulitzer Prizes, 1960, pulitzer.org.

35 Ottenberg, Miriam, *The Federal Investigators*, Englewood Cliffs, NJ: Prentice-Hall, 1962.

36 "Reporter Miriam Ottenberg of the *Washington Star* dies"; "Miriam Ottenberg Papers, 1931, 1982."

FEATURE 14

Testimony was 'a mixed bag'

Televised appearances amounted to something less than a law enforcement triumph

The televised testimony of Mafia turncoat Joseph Valachi in the early autumn of 1963 certainly was a media spectacle. However, it was not universally regarded as a turning point in law enforcement's war against organized crime.

Valachi appeared before the Permanent Subcommittee on Investigations, of the U.S. Senate's Committee on Government Operations, on September 27 and on October 1, 2, 8 and 9. The subcommittee was led by Senator John L. McClellan, Democrat from Arkansas, and was generally known as "the McClellan Committee."[1]

William G. Hundley, leader of the U.S. Department of Justice (DOJ) Organized Crime Division and overseer of the government's handling of informant Valachi, was left with a largely negative view of Valachi's appearances. Interviewed about seven years after the spectacle, Hundley remarked, "I suppose you'd have to say, on balance, that the highly publicized hearings were – I don't know – perhaps more of a disaster than they were a success." Hundley elaborated on that assessment:

> I just don't think they accomplished as much as we would if... They seemed to really have a divisive effect, the highly publicized hearings about the Cosa Nostra and the Mafia. Valachi seemed to bring out all types of groups that felt very strongly about this, that this was just an attempt to publicize anti-Italian sentiment in the country, and that the function of the Justice Department was to bring cases. If Valachi had evidence to present in court, that's what we should have done; we should not have paraded him before a national television audience just to kick around a lot of people.[2]

Hundley noted that Valachi "was not the most articulate fellow in the world" and was not particularly well educated on matters outside of New York City:

> I used to sit next to Valachi. I was sort of like his counsel up there. And as each senator would get the mike... he wanted to cleanse his area back home and I remember I guess it was Senator Curtis... he got the mike and he started asking him some questions about Nebraska. He said to him, "What is the extent of Mafia influence in Omaha?" Lo and behold, Valachi said, "I want to talk to Mr. Hundley. I want to talk to my lawyer about that." So, you know, everybody thought this was a big deal. He leaned over to me, and what he said was, he says, "Where the hell is Omaha?" ...So, I said, "Well, we'll talk about that in executive session." So everybody thought there was something real big going on in Omaha. That was just one example.[3]

With regard to advancing the Kennedy Administration's war against organized crime, Hundley felt that much of that had already been achieved by the autumn of 1963, and the Valachi testimony, "didn't do any harm. Valachi at best was... It was a mixed bag." In Hundley's view, the television "hoopla" and the public's reaction to it were negatives. "I mean that doesn't help." It appeared that the government, failing to make successful criminal cases against organized crime figures, was using Valachi in an exercise of character assassination:

You get a guy like that and you make cases... and you bring them in courts of law where you have all the protections of the defense counsel, the Constitution, the judge. I mean that's the way to do it, not just tear some guy to ribbons before some televised national audience.[4]

Hundley viewed Valachi as an informed and generally honest witness: "He was a very truthful fellow." Though Hundley believed Valachi bent the truth in a single area:

The only thing, in my judgment, that Valachi ever fudged on was his own physical participation in the murders. He always used to take the position that he was the getaway guy... that he used to drive the getaway car. Quite frankly, I never quite swallowed that. I think he actually was the boom-boom guy.[5]

In the estimation of Peter Maas, who authored *The Valachi Papers*, the televised appearances "had not gone very well. There was still considerable controversy over whether an organization like the Cosa Nostra really existed." Maas characterized the testimony as "a disaster." He felt that the "circuslike atmosphere" of the televised hearings flustered Valachi and kept him from telling a coherent story.[6]

'We wanted... to go public'

The Kennedy Justice Department became aware of Valachi when he began cooperating with the Treasury Department's Federal Bureau of Narcotics (FBN) in the summer of 1962. Believing that he was branded a traitor and condemned to death by his Mafia boss, Vito Genovese, Valachi decided that he would get even with Genovese by revealing what he knew of Genovese's criminal activities and the Mafia network Valachi called "Cosa Nostra." The FBN moved him from Atlanta Federal Prison to Westchester County Jail in New York State, where it typically held its informants, and repeatedly interviewed him.[7]

It became apparent that Valachi's knowledge of international narcotics trafficking was fairly limited. But his discussions of criminal activities went beyond narcotics into other criminal endeavors, such as loan sharking, gambling, labor racketeering, murder, and they exposed a vast, hierarchical criminal conspiracy within the United States. Agents of the Federal Bureau of

Investigation, armed with knowledge obtained through recent illegal surveillance and hungry for a human source of data, learned that Valachi was revealing information on these subjects and demanded access to him.

"They really made a strong pitch that they wanted Valachi," recalled Hundley. The DOJ asked FBN Commissioner Henry L. Giordano to provide reports of his agents' interviews with Valachi. When those arrived, Hundley reviewed them and shared them with the FBI. Director J. Edgar Hoover's Bureau became intensely interested and "pressured" Hundley to turn Valachi over to FBI control. After an uncomfortable tug-of-war period, the FBN phased out its interviews, and the FBI began pumping Valachi for information.[8]

Special Agent James P. Flynn of the New York office led the Bureau effort. Flynn became a constant Valachi visitor, first at Westchester County Jail and later at Fort Monmouth, New Jersey, after Valachi was moved into the secure military stockade there.[9] According to Hundley, Special Agent Flynn connected with Valachi on a personal level:

> He knew exactly when to be tough and when to baby him along. If Valachi was sick, for instance, he was the one who would bring him his medicine. If Valachi went into one of his depressions, he would always come up with the right thing to snap him out of it. Every so often he would bring some of the delicacies – cheese and spiced sausage – that Valachi liked. These may sound like small things, but they made all the difference. Flynn practically lived with him for eight months, and Valachi wound up thinking he was the only friend he had - and quite frankly, Valachi was right.[10]

The FBI was content to have Valachi secretly verify and flesh out intelligence gleaned from its listening devices about the criminal network it called, "La Cosa Nostra." However, the DOJ began to consider a more public use of the underworld informer. The department leaders believed that bringing Valachi's cooperation out in the open could awaken the American public to the threat of the criminal network, rattle underworld bosses and perhaps result in additional turncoats.

"We wanted Valachi to go public," according to DOJ Press Secretary Edwin Guthman. "We thought it would help in the fight against organized crime, that it would shake up the mob to know that one of their guys was talking, and we thought it was good public relations."

Hoover's FBI did not support the idea. It was Bureau policy to tightly control information relating to its own activities and to protect the secrecy of its sources of information. But FBI did not directly oppose it. After extended discussions that included William Hundley of the DOJ and Hoover aides Cartha D. "Deke" DeLoach and Courtney A. Evans, the FBI appeared to consent.[11] Yet the Bureau and its director continued sniping.

Preparing to testify

In March 1963, Hundley discussed with Attorney General Robert Kennedy the idea of making Valachi available to testify before the McClellan Committee. Kennedy reportedly was not enthusiastic.[12] According to Peter Maas, Kennedy was won over by the possibility that Valachi testimony could advance anti-racketeering legislation, win court approvals for government wiretapping and shine a withering light on the nation's racketeers.[13]

Courtney Evans reported on Kennedy's concerns in a memorandum to the FBI. Kennedy was unhappy, according to Evans, that Senator McClellan would "get the glory" of publicly questioning a live Mafia informant. Evans believed that Kennedy was motivated "strictly by political considerations" in arranging the Senate testimony and also in cooperating with Peter Maas in a planned Valachi-related article for the *Saturday Evening Post*. Evans charged that the attorney general was intent on "exploiting this whole situation for their own [the Kennedy Administration's] benefit." In response to the Evans memorandum, J. Edgar Hoover handwrote a note bemoaning the loss of Bureau secrecy: "...I never saw so much skulduggery - the sanctity of Dept files including Bureau reports is a thing of the past."[14]

Hundley saw the matter in a different light. Learning that Valachi was cooperating with the FBI and the DOJ, the McClellan Committee decided it wanted Valachi for a public hearing, "We didn't have much choice." Hundley explained to the attorney general, "We can't hold them off forever. They can go ahead and subpoena him up there."[15]

Additional conversations were taking place at the time between the DOJ and Valachi. By the start of May 1963, Hundley had promised Valachi, whose desire for revenge against Genovese required publicity, that his story would be widely released through public testimony and a series of articles.[16]

In summer, Valachi was moved from the New Jersey military base to the unoccupied top floor of the District of Columbia Jail.[17] (The floor held the district's death chamber, electric chair and related rooms, all unused since the 1957 execution of Robert E. Carter, convicted of the 1953 murder of off-duty Police Officer George W. Cassels.[18]) Valachi was given use of a suite of rooms, including a sitting area and a kitchen.[19]

Justice Department officials, FBI officials and representatives of the McClellan Committee met in August to discuss preliminary arrangements for Valachi's testimony. The FBI continued to view the testimony as a negative development.

Some thought was given to the possibility of having Special Agent Flynn appear alongside Valachi to bolster his testimony. Courtney Evans, in a memorandum to FBI superiors, pointed out that an appearance by a Bureau agent would ensure that FBI was properly credited for its role in investigating organized crime. If FBI refused, the McClellan Committee might turn to other law enforcement professionals – perhaps agents of the FBN, which had already received a great deal of press for its efforts against Mafia narcotics traffickers.

Alan H. Belmont of the FBI recommended against any agent appearing with Valachi:

> While we would gain from the intimate tie-in with Valachi and, in effect, be publicly displayed as experts on organized crime and La Cosa Nostra, the drawbacks outweigh the advantages. It would be setting a precedent of agent testimony; the agent would be open to questions requiring answers from Bureau files; and the agent could be asked what the Bureau is doing about this information.

Hoover, expressing himself in another handwritten note, sided with Belmont.[20]

By September, according to Hundley, the investigators working with the McClellan Committee "kind of took over." They visited with Valachi to prepare him for his public appearance. The Justice Department was not consulted on some significant matters, Hundley said, including the decision to televise the testimony:

> We didn't know in Justice that they were going to be televised hearings or anything like that. I suppose we should have anticipated that. You know, these senators like nothing better than to get on national television and get it back home. Well, they made a big production out of it.[21]

On the eve of Valachi's first appearance, Hoover took issue with a newspaper preview article. A sentence in the article stated that Robert Kennedy stressed that all Valachi revelations had been cleared by Hoover. On a copy of the article, Hoover drew a line to that sentence and wrote, "This is absolutely incorrect. I never cleared anything + in fact opposed the release of information from Valachi + the disclosure of his identity."[22]

September 27, 1963

The McClellan Committee hearings opened in the caucus room of the Old Senate Office Building with an introduction at ten-fifteen on Friday morning, September 27. Present were Chairman John L. McClellan and Senators Karl E. Mundt, Republican from South Dakota; Edmund S. Muskie, Democrat from Maine; Thomas J. McIntyre, Democrat from New Hampshire; Daniel B. Brewster, Democrat from Maryland; Carl T. Curtis, Republican from Nebraska; Jacob K. Javits, Republican from New York. (Senator Henry M. Jackson, Democrat from Washington, did not attend the session.)

Also at the hearing were General Counsel Jerome S. Adlerman; Chief Counsel Donald F. O'Donnell; Minority Chief Counsel Philip W. Morgan; assistant counsels LaVern J. Duffy, Paul E. Kamerick, Harold Ranstad and Arthur G. Kaplan; investigator Alphonse Calabrese; Chief Clerk Ruth Y. Watt and Federal Bureau of Narcotics representatives Eugene J. Marshall and Martin Pera. Thanks to network television, many Americans felt that they, too, had seats inside the hearing room.[23]

Valachi appeared to have prepared a sequential telling of his life story, but he very quickly got caught up responding to various questions from the senators.

During the morning session, he spoke about growing up in East Harlem, New York, his brief public school education, his few early attempts at legitimate employment and his criminal record. He stated that he became a member of a criminal organization, known to him as "Cosa Nostra," in 1930.

He explained the hierarchy within each Cosa Nostra unit or "family," including a boss at the top, supported by an underboss and a group of lieutenants, also known as caporegimes, with the bulk of each family comprised of soldiers assigned to the lieutenants. Valachi noted that a "boss of all bosses" once ruled over all U.S. family leaders but that system had been replaced by a representative Commission. Grievances between members were resolved through trials conducted by regional councils, he said.

He spoke in some detail about the process of becoming a Cosa Nostra member and his initial reluctance to join in the 1920s, a result of a warning he received in Sing Sing Prison from Alessandro Vollero, an old Camorra leader who battled Sicilian-American mafiosi in the 1910s.[24]

Valachi quickly skipped from that account to a description of the events that led Vito Genovese to brand him a "rat" in spring 1962. He spoke of Genovese's apparent responsibility for the disappearance of underworld lieutenant Anthony "Tony Bender" Strollo. Genovese's power, he said, extended beyond his own large crime family and into the similarly numerous Gambino Crime Family. He suggested that Genovese regularly rationalized killings of crime family members by accusing them of betrayal.

Genovese and Valachi had known each other for decades, and Genovese had been best man at Valachi's wedding. When the two men were both serving narcotics conspiracy sentences at Atlanta Federal Prison, Genovese began to view Valachi with concern. At one point, Genovese spoke to Valachi about the danger of allowing a bad apple to remain in a barrel of apples. "It has to be removed," the underworld boss said. When Genovese suddenly kissed Valachi, Valachi got the message that Genovese considered him the bad apple.[25]

Valachi described what he viewed as attempts on his life and told of seeking the protection of solitary confinement. When he returned to the general population, Valachi was convinced that he soon would be killed. He suspected that other Cosa Nostra member inmates Charlie Barcelona, Joseph "Joe Beck" DiPalermo, John Dioguardi, Mike Coppola and Peter LaPlaca were plotting to kill him.

"You honestly believed they were under orders from Genovese to kill you there in prison?" asked McClellan.

"Yes," Valachi answered. "A hundred percent, senator."

On June 22, 1962, Valachi saw a man he believed was DiPalermo come near him in the prison recreation yard. He grabbed a piece of pipe from a nearby construction site and severely beat the man. It turned out his victim was not DiPalermo and not at all connected with the Genovese group.

Asked if he thought he would be safe if he ever was returned to a prison general population, Valachi responded, "If they got at me I wouldn't be in there five minutes, senator."[26]

In the afternoon session of his first day of testimony, Valachi tried to explain the reason he decided to break his underworld oath and cooperate with the Department of Justice and the McClellan Committee:

> The main answer to that is very simple. Number one, it is to destroy them... I was hoping that you or Congress... would come up with some law so as to make it a penalty or felony or whatever you may want to call it, to belong to this organization... If you senators make such a law, so it would be a crime just to belong to it, I will be a happy man.

During the afternoon session, the subcommittee also heard testimony from Sergeant Ralph Salerno of the New York City Police Department's Intelligence Unit and from William Hundley of the DOJ. Both of those sources corroborated the information that had been provided by Valachi.[27]

When the panel's attention returned to Valachi, the informant told in some detail about his early criminal ventures of the 1920s: burglaries performed as part of the "Minute Men" gang, associations with the 107th Street Gang and an organization Valachi knew as the "Irish Mob."[28]

October 1, 1963

Valachi returned Tuesday morning, October 1, sat in front of a full panel of senators and picked up where he left off. He began that day's testimony with a description of a conflict between the "Irish Mob," which had that label despite having only about two Irish Americans in its membership, and an Italian-American gang headquartered at 116th Street and First Avenue. The Italian group was a feeder gang for a Mafia organization run by Ciro "Artichoke King" Terranova. Crime figures such as Willie "Moore" Moretti, Vincent Rao[29], Frank Livorsi and Frank "Big Dick" Amato were connected with it.

Some of Valachi's former pals in that Italian Mob tried to convince him to doublecross other pals in the Irish Mob. The request to turn on friends enraged Valachi, and he declared himself opposed to the Italian Mob. According to Valachi, "I wasn't even sticking up for the Irish guys; I was sticking to my own principles."

A short time later, when Valachi was serving time in Sing Sing Prison, Valachi learned that the two groups settled their differences on the condition that Valachi and Frank LaPuma, another Italian gangster who sided with the Irish Mob, both be killed.

After Valachi's release from prison in 1928, Frank Livorsi helped him smooth things out with the Terranova underworld network. The underworld death sentence against him was dropped, but Valachi still held a grudge against Terranova and his organization.[30]

Valachi friend Dominick "the Gap" Petrelli soon tried to get him into the Mafia. Valachi balked until Petrelli and and Girolamo "Bobby Doyle" Santuccio assured him that his Neapolitan family background would not be held against him and that the organization he was invited into was not the Terranova group but a rival group.

Valachi's account of events around 1930 was interrupted by senators' questions about more recent occurrences. He fielded distracting questions about Vito Genovese investments with Meyer Lansky in gambling casinos and about underworld rumors relating to the death of Murder, Inc., informant Abe Reles. Valachi admitted he had little knowledge of underworld influence in casinos. He said he heard other mobsters assert that police were responsible for throwing Reles out a hotel window to his death.[31]

McClellan Committee Assistant Counsel LaVern J. Duffy helped bring the focus back to 1930 by introducing a chart showing group alliances and leadership changes during a 1930-1931 gangland conflict known as the Castellammarese War. In that war, a dissident faction led by Salvatore Maranzano and Tom Gagliano fought against the establishment of Giuseppe "Joe the Boss" Masseria and his allies. Petrelli and Santuccio initially brought Valachi into the Gagliano family, but all Masseria opposition eventually merged under the leadership of Maranzano.[32]

Valachi described a number of events in the war, including the murders of Masseria allies Al Mineo and Steve Ferrigno. Valachi explained that he occupied an apartment in the Bronx complex where Ferrigno lived, personally witnessed the arrival of Giuseppe Masseria for a meeting at the Ferrigno apartment and drove the getaway car for those who later murdered Ferrigno and Mineo in the courtyard of the complex.[33]

Near the end of the morning session, Sergeant Salerno was brought back to provide police data supporting the events described by Valachi.[34]

The hearings were recessed from twelve-fifteen to about two-thirty, when Valachi returned to his discussion of the Castellammarese War. Shortly after the killings of Mineo and Ferrigno, Valachi said, he and a few other young hoodlums were brought about ninety miles upstate from New York City to be formally inducted into the rebel wing of Cosa Nostra.

Valachi told of being led to a table surrounded by men. A gun and a knife were on the table, and Maranzano stood at its head. Maranzano explained that as a "made" member of the organization, you "lived by the gun and by the knife and you die by the gun and by the knife." Holding a burning piece of paper in his cupped hands, Valachi repeated an oath in Sicilian, a language largely unfamiliar to him. He indicated that the words translated to, "This is the way I burn if I expose this organization." After a selection process, Joseph Bonanno was designated as Valachi's underworld mentor or "godfather." A needle was used to draw blood from Valachi's trigger finger. Basic organizational rules of secrecy and obedience were explained to him.[35]

Valachi described later events in the war against Masseria's forces, including the murder of Masseria lieutenant Joseph "Baker" Catania on February 3, 1931. Sergeant Salerno again confirmed the details in Valachi's account.[36]

The day's testimony concluded with Valachi telling of Masseria's top men turning against their boss and setting him up for assassination at a Coney Island restaurant in the spring of 1931.[37] The hearings recessed at three-thirty.

October 2, 1963

The committee hearings, with all members in attendance except Javits, got off to a bad start on Wednesday, October 2.

During the previous day's testimony, Valachi discussed Girolamo "Bobby Doyle" Santuccio and explained that Santuccio moved from New York to Connecticut, where he continued involvement in rackets. Valachi incorrectly referred to Stamford, Connecticut, as Santuccio's base of operations. That led Connecticut Senator Abraham Ribicoff to protest. As the hearings opened, a statement from Ribicoff was read into the record. According to Ribicoff, only one Robert "Bobby" Doyle resided in Stamford at that time, and he had a sterling reputation:

> ...In all fairness to an innocent man in Stamford, the record should be clear so that his friends and neighbors and employers will have no doubt that the Robert Doyle of Stamford, the only Robert Doyle

in Stamford, is not the man identified by the witness yesterday before this committee.

Valachi corrected his earlier statement: "I thought I said Hartford, Connecticut... I meant Hartford, Connecticut."

Though the record was corrected, an innocent person's reputation had been harmed, and there was suddenly reason to question Valachi's accuracy as a witness. To resolve this second problem, the McClellan Committee called Lieutenant John Roach, leader of the Vice Division in the Hartford Police Department, to testify. Roach said he knew "Bobby Doyle" Santuccio. "He hangs around the streets of Hartford and he has no visible means of support." The lieutenant's description of the Hartford Santuccio was a match for Valachi's description. Sergeant Salerno came on to introduce the criminal record of Santuccio and corroborate the physical descriptions provided by the others.[38]

Valachi was then occupied for some time with questions about his travels and about the activities of Cosa Nostra in various areas of the country. Senator Carl T. Curtis, Republican of Nebraska, asked about the Omaha area. Valachi was forced to admit, "Senator, I never heard of Omaha." He later made a similar admission about Des Moines, Iowa.[39]

He was then asked about why he did not move to Chicago and join the Capone organization. Alessandro Vollero, who warned Valachi about Sicilian gangsters, had offered to recommend Valachi to Capone. "I don't know," Valachi responded. "Not for any reason; I just didn't bother... I guess I wanted to stay in New York, senator."[40]

Valachi finally returned to his narrative, describing the assassination of Masseria by his own men, the accession of Salvatore Maranzano to the position of boss of bosses and the reorganization of Cosa Nostra families in New York and other regions. Valachi became a member of Maranzano's personal guard. Following his victory, Maranzano held a celebratory banquet over the course of several days, in which many thousands of dollars were given to him by underworld bosses of different regions. Valachi estimated that $115,000 was collected. Maranzano claimed that the money would be used to support the soldiers who aided his cause. "I never got a nickel out of that," Valachi said.[41]

Senator Mundt cut in: "Did you ever approach anybody and say, 'How come? Where is my share of the $115,000?'"

"You'd like to do that," Valachi admitted, "but you don't do it... But it ain't actually fear... you figure maybe he has something in mind, maybe next week... You hate to make yourself believe that he is not going to give you anything."[42]

The one time Valachi expressed a difference of opinion with Maranzano it was over Maranzano's order that his men not bring weapons to his new offices on Park Avenue. The new boss of bosses had heard that authorities were preparing to raid the place, and he did not want to take a chance at weapons being discovered there.

In a private meeting at Maranzano's Brooklyn home, Valachi objected to the rule, feeling it left Maranzano vulnerable. Maranzano insisted that it was necessary. At that moment, the boss also revealed that a new gangland war might soon erupt, as he found it impossible to work with some of the younger organization leaders. like Capone, Salvatore "Charlie Lucky Luciano" Lucania and Vito Genovese. Maranzano planned a final meeting at the office with Lucania and Genovese the following day. Valachi anticipated a problem and tried without success to talk Maranzano out of attending the meeting.[43] Valachi was drawn away to Brooklyn the next day. Maranzano was murdered that afternoon at his office by Lucania-allied gunmen posing as law enforcement agents.[44]

After a lunch recess, Valachi testified that several Maranzano loyalists were murdered at about the same time as their boss. Sergeant Salerno corroborated the murder details for Maranzano and Bronx gangster James "Jimmy Marino" LePore.[45]

During the afternoon session, Valachi's storytelling became difficult to follow, as he tried to sort out the events following the Maranzano assassination. He told of some Maranzano followers, most notably Valachi's pal "Buster," who wanted to avenge Maranzano's murder. After a period of uncertainty, Valachi was welcomed into the organization led by Lucania and Genovese. Eventually, he learned that Lucania and Genovese moved against Maranzano out of self-defense, because Maranzano had hired Vincent "Mad Dog" Coll to kill them. Years later, Sam "Red" Levine, who had become a friend of Valachi, admitted that he was one of the gunmen sent by Lucania to kill Maranzano.[46]

Valachi spoke about dispute resolution measures put in place after Maranzano's death. Regional matters were handled by a council, he said, and more serious difficulties were adjudicated by a national Commission.[47]

Responding to various questions, Valachi said he knew Raymond Patriarca of New England from many years earlier, he described qualifications for Cosa Nostra membership and the dues charged of members by their bosses.[48] The hearings were recessed at five minutes after three and scheduled to resume six days later.

October 8, 1963

When the hearings reopened at ten-thirty on Tuesday, October 8, Joseph Valachi did not resume his narrative. Instead, he served a supporting role, as the senators (except absent Senator Curtis) listened to John F. Shanley, deputy chief inspector for the Central Investigations Bureau of the New York Police Department, explain membership charts of New York crime families.

Valachi revealed the names of the leaders of the five Cosa Nostra organizations in the New York area. He said Vito Genovese, then in prison, remained boss of his crime family, with Jerry Catena serving as his underboss. Carlo Gambino led another large organization, with Joe Biondo his underboss. Another organization was controlled by Tommy Lucchese, with Steve LaSalle under him. Joseph Bonanno was boss of a fourth crime family. Valachi said he was unsure of the underboss in that group. The final organization had been run by Joseph Profaci until his death in 1962. Valachi said he heard that Profaci's brother-in-law Joseph Magliocco had succeeded him.[49]

Shanley provided details on the personal lives and criminal records of many of the figures found in the charts. Valachi fleshed out the accounts by discussing certain individuals he was familiar with. He also explained the basics of the loan sharking racket, the wartime black market sale of gasoline ration stamps, his experiences in horse racing and the then-current internal friction in the Magliocco Crime Family.[50]

Valachi told of the recent "commercialization" of Cosa Nostra by former crime family underboss Frank Scalise. According to Valachi, Scalise allowed businessmen to become members of his crime family if they made financial contributions. Some paid as much as $40,000 to be included on the member rolls. Valachi noted that "in the old days, a man had to prove himself to get in.

The paid members, he said, were unproven and unreliable, though "they felt they were equal to the tough guys."[51]

At forty minutes after four o'clock, the day's hearings were recessed until the morning of October 9.

October 9, 1963

Valachi's final day of testimony was Wednesday, October 9. All senators except Brewster were present to hear the former mobster respond to questions and describe a number of gangland murders.

Discussion first focused on the committee's primary legislative concern, the criminal trafficking of narcotics. Valachi indicated that the crime family he belonged to had a rule between 1948 and 1957 prohibiting involvement in narcotics. He said that restriction was imposed by Frank Costello, who preceded Vito Genovese as boss. He said the ban was expanded to all crime families after 1957.

Valachi understood that the Chicago organization paid members to give up handling narcotics. If Chicago mobsters were found to be involved with narcotics, "They would pay with their lives."

The rules against drug trafficking apparently did little to prevent Cosa Nostra soldiers, even bosses, from taking part in extremely profitable narcotics racketeering. Valachi said he knew that at least two New York bosses, Vito Genovese and Albert Anastasia, had conspired with others to handle narcotics.[52]

Valachi then discussed the murder of longtime underworld leader "Willie Moore" Moretti. According to Valachi, Vito Genovese began plotting against Moretti back in 1949. As a powerful ally of then-boss Costello, Moretti was an obstacle to Genovese's ambition. Genovese frequently made comments about Moretti deteriorating mentally (a result of advanced syphilis) and being unable to control what he said. Cosa Nostra bosses began to see Moretti as a liability. Valachi said a death sentence against Moretti was approved by the Commission. No one was specifically assigned to commit the murder. Valachi believed that Johnny "Roberts" Robilotto, a member of Anastasia's organization (later the Gambino Crime Family) was one of the men who fatally shot Moretti at Joe's Restaurant, Cliffside Park, New Jersey, in 1951.[53]

The basic details of Valachi's account were confirmed for the committee by New Jersey Assistant Attorney General John J. Bergin and New Jersey State

Police Captain John A. Fitzsimmons.[54] Bergin noted that Valachi was questioned by police following the Moretti murder and denied knowing suspects
Robilotto and Joseph Licalsi. As that was mentioned, Valachi told the committee that he lied to police on that occasion.[55]

Valachi expressed his belief that Genovese conspired against Anastasia
with Anastasia's own lieutenants Carlo Gambino and Joseph Biondo. They
arranged the murder of Anastasia in 1957. Carlo Gambino succeeded Anastasia as boss and was faced with opposition from Anastasia loyalists, such as
Robilotto and Armand "Tommy" Rava. Valachi said both Robilotto and Rava
were murdered. Sergeant Salerno confirmed that Robilotto was shot to death in
Brooklyn in 1958, but he said the New York Police had no information on
what happened to Rava: "In the case of Armand Rava, there is no official
record of a homicide or even of him being a missing person." Salerno said he
knew Rava attended the Apalachin convention in 1957 and there were reports
suggesting he was seen in Florida in 1959. But he vanished after that. "We pre-
sume that he is dead," said Salerno.

Valachi next provided a detailed account of his participation in the murder
of Eugene Giannini, suspected informant for the Federal Bureau of Narcotics.
Valachi had been friendly with Giannini and had loaned him money. When he
learned from his lieutenant Anthony "Tony Bender" Strollo that Giannini had
been sentenced to death as an informer, he said, "There goes my couple of
thousand that he owes me."

Strollo complained that his men were having a difficult time locating Giannini. Valachi said he would handle it: "I volunteered because I figured now
they are looking for excuses." Valachi arranged a couple of meetings with
Giannini and found that he was followed both times by federal agents. Giannini was nervous and confided in Valachi, "I feel like I am going to be killed."
Valachi learned that Giannini was connected with a crap game near 112th
Street between Second and Third avenues in East Harlem. Giannini worked
outside, meeting potential gamblers, determining their suitability for the game
and sending the approved gamblers to the game location. Valachi arranged for
his nephew Fiore Siano and brothers Joseph and Pasquale Pagano to "hit"
Giannini where he worked and escape through a building to a car waiting on
111th Street.

Sergeant Salerno confirmed that Eugene Giannini had been killed by shotgun blasts to his head and that Giannini had been an informant for the FBN.

Near the conclusion of Valachi's appearance, Senator Carl T. Curtis challenged him on one aspect of his testimony:

> Now, in every murder that you have described, you have always been absent at the time the gun was fired, or at least you didn't fire it... Is that because you have a convenient memory, or are you withholding something from the committee that might incriminate you, or is there some other reason?

Valachi responded that he was often involved in hits as a driver, an important and dangerous role. Others were specialists with firearms, and he was a specialist behind the steering wheel. He also noted that there was no legal or underworld distinction between the gunman and the driver involved in a murder:

> What difference does it make who fires the gun and who drives the car? We are both guilty. How can you get out of that? The opposite mob ain't going to leave me alone because I drove the car, neither is the law going to leave me alone. I didn't think I had to explain that. I took it for granted.[56]

One Valachi revelation could not be confirmed by law enforcement officers and has remained a mystery. Committee General Counsel Adlerman asked Valachi about the succession of crime family bosses that led to Vito Genovese. Adlerman suggested that Frank Costello took over the organization after Salvatore "Charlie Luciano" Lucania was deported to Italy. Valachi corrected him:

> He [Costello] had been there after Che Gusae. There was a Che Gusae there for one year after Charlie went away. He died. Frank [Costello] was put there as acting boss.

Adlerman did not ask for more information on the "Che Gusae" or his brief reign.[57]

As the day's testimony approached its end, Valachi indicated that he had been asked to participate in a Genovese-planned hit against Frank Costello (he refused to provide details in open session). He offered some information on the

Gallo-Profaci War, which he said was initially sparked by abusive taxation of members by late crime boss Giuseppe Profaci. And he indicated that the Apalachin convention had been called at the request of Genovese to justify the 1957 assassination of Anastasia and to remove from the Cosa Nostra rolls hundreds of undeserving members.[58]

Chairman McClellan closed the final day of Valachi testimony at four-thirty-five, indicating that the committee might call Valachi back for additional testimony at a later date.

Early slot machine opposition forgotten

In tellings of his life story, Valachi timed New York City government opposition to the Mafia's slot machine racket to coincide with the arrival of the Fiorello La Guardia Administration in 1934.

La Guardia made a public spectacle of his slot machine fight, but efforts to outlaw and remove the machines actually dated back to the 1920s. A federal court issued a permanent injunction against police interference with the gaming devices in 1924. Mayor Joseph V. McKee, who replaced resigning Mayor Jimmy Walker in 1932, initiated a city-wide police drive against slot machines, in defiance of the court.

(Sources: Maas, Peter, *The Valachi Papers*, New York: G.P. Putnam's Sons, 1968, p. 128; "Permanent injunction given Triangle Novelty Company to protect slot machines," *Brooklyn Citizen*, Jan. 14, 1924, p. 1; "McKee hears help pleas of jobless today," *Brooklyn Daily Eagle*, Sept. 10, 1932, p. 1.)

Valachi is sworn in before McClellan Committee testimony.

Sen. John McClellan (left), Valachi consults with Hundley (right).

Valachi testifies.

Crime family charts line a wall of the hearing room. (Library of Congress)

Valachi with a chart.

Feature 14 Notes

1 Testimony of Joseph Valachi, *Organized Crime and Illicit Traffic in Narcotics*, Part 1 (McClellan Hearings), Hearings before the Permanent Subcommittee on Investigations of the Committee on Government Operations, U.S. Senate, 88th Congress, 1st Session, Washington, D.C.: U.S. Government Printing Office, 1963.

2 William G. Hundley, recorded interview by James A. Oesterle, Feb. 22, 1971, Robert F. Kennedy Library Oral History Project of the John F. Kennedy Library, p. 51.

3 Hundley recorded interview, p. 51-52.

4 Hundley recorded interview, p. 54.

5 Hundley recorded interview, p. 53.

6 Maas, Peter, *The Valachi Papers*, New York: G.P. Putnam's Sons, 1968, p. 12, 46.

7 Hundley recorded interview, p. 48-49; Edwin O. Guthman Oral History Interview - JFK #1, Feb. 21, 1968, John F. Kennedy Presidential Library and Museum, jfklibrary.org, p. 18; Valachi, Joseph, *The Real Thing: Second Government - The Expose and Inside Doings of Cosa Nostra*, unpublished manuscript, John F. Kennedy Presidential Library and Museum, 1964, p. 1146.

8 Hundley recorded interview, p. 48-49; Guthman Interview, p. 18; Maas, *The Valachi Papers*, p. 34-36; Valachi, *The Real Thing*, p. 1158-1162, 1172-1174.

9 Valachi, *The Real Thing*, p. 1179; Maas, *The Valachi Papers*, p. 37.

10 Maas, *The Valachi Papers*, p. 37.

11 Navasky, Victor, *Kennedy Justice*, New York: Atheneum, 1971, p. 31.

12 Evans, C.A., "Joseph Valachi, Anti-Racketeering," FBI Memorandum to Mr. Belmont, file no. 92-6054-1st NR 217, NARA no. 124-10284-10221, March 29, 1963.

13 Maas, *The Valachi Papers*, p. 45. According to Hundley, the administration's anti-crime legislative agenda was already achieved before Valachi's testimony.

14 Evans, C.A., "Informant Joseph Valachi," FBI Memorandum to Mr. Belmont, file no. 92-6054-267, NARA no. 124-10284-10277, May 22, 1963.

15 Hundley recorded interview, p. 50, 55.

16 Evans, C.A., "La Causa Nostra, Criminal Intelligence Matters," FBI Memorandum to Mr. Belmont, file no. 92-6054-227, NARA no. 124-10284-10232, May 1, 1963.

17 Hundley recorded interview, p. 50; Maas, *The Valachi Papers*, p. 46, 48, 50-51.

18 Walsh, Robert, "On this date in 1957 – Robert Eugene 'Bobby' Carter, last man executed in Washington D.C.," CrimeScribe, crimescribe.com, April 26, 2020; "Man electrocuted for slaying policeman," *Salisbury MD Times*, April 27, 1957, p. 1.

19 Maas, *The Valachi Papers*, p. 46, 48; Hundley recorded interview, p. 50.

20 Evans, C.A., "Joseph Valachi Testimony Before Mc Clellan Committee," FBI Memorandum to Mr. Belmont, file no. 92-6054-1st nr 385, NARA no. 124-10220-10082, Aug. 7, 1963.

21 Hundley recorded interview, p. 51.

22 FBI file no. 92-6054-484, NARA no. 124-10215-10291, Sept. 26, 1963.

23 Valachi Testimony, Sept. 27, 1963, McClellan Hearings, p. 78-144.

24 Valachi Testimony, Sept. 27, 1963, McClellan Hearings, p. 78-84.

25 Valachi Testimony, Sept. 27, 1963, McClellan Hearings, p. 84-95.

26 Valachi Testimony, Sept. 27, 1963, McClellan Hearings, p. 96-107, 114.

27 Testimony of Sgt. Ralph Salerno and William George Hundley, Sept. 27, 1963, McClellan Hearings, p. 121-136.

28 Valachi Testimony, Sept. 27, 1963, McClellan Hearings, p. 119-144.

29 Valachi may have been referring to Joseph Rao.

30 Valachi Testimony, Oct. 1, 1963, McClellan Hearings, p. 145-155.

31 Valachi Testimony, Oct. 1, 1963, McClellan Hearings, p. 156-160.

32 Testimony of Lavern J. Duffy and Joseph Valachi, Oct. 1, 1963, McClellan Hearings, p. 161-164.

33 Valachi Testimony, Oct. 1, 1963, McClellan Hearings, p. 165-173.

34 Testimony of Sgt. Ralph Salerno, Oct. 1, 1963, McClellan Hearings, p. 174-178.

35 Valachi Testimony, Oct. 1, 1963, McClellan Hearings, p. 180-185.

36 Testimony of Joseph Valachi and Sgt. Ralph Salerno, Oct. 1, 1963, McClellan Hearings, p. 188-192.

37 Valachi Testimony, Oct. 1, 1963, McClellan Hearings, p. 198-199.

38 Testimony of Joseph Valachi, Lt. John Roach and Sgt. Ralph Salerno, Oct. 2, 1963, McClellan Hearings, p. 201-205.

39 Valachi Testimony, Oct. 2, 1963, McClellan Hearings, p. 205-207.

40 Valachi Testimony, Oct. 2, 1963, McClellan Hearings, p. 209.

41 Valachi Testimony, Oct. 2, 1963, McClellan Hearings, p. 210-218.

42 Valachi Testimony, Oct. 2, 1963, McClellan Hearings, p. 216-220.

43 Valachi Testimony, Oct. 2, 1963, McClellan Hearings, p. 220-222.

44 Valachi Testimony, Oct. 2, 1963, McClellan Hearings, p. 222-224.

45 Testimony of Joseph Valachi and Sgt. Ralph Salerno, Oct. 2, 1963, McClellan Hearings, p. 232-233.

46 Valachi Testimony, Oct. 2, 1963, McClellan Hearings, p. 227-229, 230-231, 233.

47 Valachi Testimony, Oct. 2, 1963, McClellan Hearings, p. 236-237.

48 Valachi Testimony, Oct. 2, 1963, McClellan Hearings, p. 234-235, 238-241.

49 Testimony of Joseph Valachi and John F. Shanley, McClellan Hearings, p. 246-247.

50 Valachi Testimony, Oct. 8, 1963, McClellan Hearings, p. 267-268, 289-291, 306, 309-310.

51 Valachi Testimony, Oct. 8, 1963, McClellan Hearings, p. 297-298, 300-301.

52 Valachi Testimony, Oct. 9, 1963, McClellan Hearings, p. 319-322.

53 Valachi Testimony, Oct. 9, 1963, McClellan Hearings p. 324-325.

54 Testimony of John J. Bergin, Oct. 9, 1963, McClellan Hearings, p. 327, 329-330.

55 Testimony of John J. Bergin, Oct. 9, 1963, McClellan Hearings, p. 332.

56 Valachi Testimony, Oct. 9, 1963, McClellan Hearings, p. 356, 359.

57 Valachi Testimony, Oct. 9, 1963, McClellan Hearings, p. 364.

58 Valachi Testimony, Oct. 9, 1963, McClellan Hearings, p. 364, 368-370, 388-389.

BRIEF BIOS

Minor characters in the Valachi epic

By Thomas Hunt and Steve Turner

Joseph Valachi came into contact with many interesting people, on both sides of the law, during his lifetime. He discussed dozens in his autobiography and in interviews with author Peter Maas, which became the foundation of *The Valachi Papers*. Though minor characters in the Valachi life story, many are deserving of the special attention of crime historians. In this section, we look at a number of these individuals, providing a summary of what Valachi had to say about them, as well as the data we have been able to assemble from historical records.[1]

(Readers are advised that some important crime figures who were quite close to Valachi – such as Sebastiano "Buster" Domingo, Salvatore Maranzano, Dominick "the Gap" Petrelli, Steve Rannelli, Girolamo "Bobby Doyle" Santuccio, Salvatore "Sally Shields" Shillitani – do not have dedicated biographies in these pages, as they have been subjects of substantial articles in earlier issues of *Informer*.[2])

Abruzzo, Judge Matthew Thomas

> *I go in front of the judge, which was Judge Abruzzo, and he says, "Well Joe is safe now. I am glad that he walked in by himself. I did not believe it."*[3]

Fairly early in his autobiography, Valachi described a 1930s racetrack encounter with Mafia leader Vincent Mangano. During their conversation, Mangano revealed that the Mafia in Brooklyn "made a judge or they were going to make a judge. He told me that the judge was Italian and that his name was Abruzzo." Mangano suggested that Abruzzo could be helpful if Valachi was ever in trouble in Brooklyn.[4]

Judge Abruzzo was again mentioned much later in Valachi's book. He was the Brooklyn federal judge who presided over the narcotics case against Valachi in 1959-1960.

Learning of the arrest of a narcotics accomplice, Valachi went into hiding in spring 1959. Narcotics agents arrested him in Connecticut in November 1959 and brought him to Brooklyn for arraignment. He pleaded guilty on January 11, 1960, to a single count of violating narcotics laws and was released to await sentence after posting a $25,000 bond. The law called for a prison sentence of between five and twenty years for a first offense.[5]

As he prepared to sentence Valachi, Judge Abruzzo ordered a detailed report on Valachi's personal, family and criminal history.[6]

Valachi did not appear for his scheduled sentencing hearing on February 19. Fearing a lengthy prison sentence, Valachi had fled to Toronto. He returned to New York only after he was assured by his Mafia superior Anthony Strollo that a deal was in place in which he would receive just a five-year sentence. After some additional delay, he surrendered to authorities on March 28. Valachi later recalled Judge Abruzzo's surprise at his voluntary return.

At sentencing, there was no mention of any deal for a five-year sentence. Judge Abruzzo sentenced Valachi to fifteen years in federal prison and a $10,000 fine.[7]

Matthew Thomas Abruzzo was born to Leonard and Giacoma Randazzo Abruzzo in Brooklyn on April 30, 1889. He began his law practice in New York in 1910. By 1917, he had a private law practice on Fulton Street in Downtown Brooklyn and he resided a few miles away on Eastern Parkway in the residential Brooklyn neighborhood of Crown Heights. During the Great War, he claimed exemption from military service due to his support of a number of dependents, including his father, wife Jane Miller Abruzzo, step-daughter and nephews.[8]

In 1931, he crusaded against the portrayal in plays and movies of Italian Americans as gangsters. He spoke at the April 1931 Atlantic City, New Jersey, convention of the Federation of Italian-American Democratic Organizations of New York, stating that the theatrical presentations were unfair to 6 million Americans of Italian descent:

> Italians engaged in gangster and gunman pursuits represent an infinitesimal portion of the aggregate of their race in this country. It is unfair to cast that majority, working and striving to be real Americans, and bringing up their children to be real Americans, to have the average opinion of the Italian American based on stage and screen portrayals.[9]

Five years later, Abruzzo was appointed by President Franklin Roosevelt to the federal bench in the newly formed Eastern District of New York.[10]

Abruzzo continued as a Brooklyn federal judge until his retirement in 1966, but even then remained available for occasional duty as a senior judge. During his career he heard a wide variety of cases. The *New York Times* noted that early in his term he presided over cases against accused Nazi spies and later heard spy cases against Soviet spies, draft evasion cases ranged from World War II to the Vietnam War. And he presided over prosecutions of tax evasion, stock manipulation and fraud.[11]

He passed away May 28, 1971, after suffering a heart attack at the home of his son, Matthew Jr., in Potomac, Maryland. Following a funeral Mass at St. James Cathedral in Brooklyn, he was interred at Holy Cross Cemetery.[12]

Amato, Frank "Big Dick"

*Now Dick was Ciro Morello's right hand man and I took a
ride at 116th Street and I went and see if they were still
there. Sure enough they were. Dick was laying on the floor
with his head on the curbstone and his arms straight out,
and the other guy was in a store...*[13]

Frank "Big Dick" Amato was well known to Joseph Valachi, who blamed Amato
and Joseph Rao for circulating a rumor that Valachi in 1924 had served as
driver for an Irish Mob attack against a Terranova-aligned street gang.[14] During
the 1930-1931 Castellammarese War, Valachi and the Terranova men were
on opposing sides. At the height of the war, in December of 1930, learning that
Amato and Rao had been seen at the Pompeii Restaurant, Valachi and his
friend Salvatore "Solly Shields" Shillitani drove over to launch an early morning attack. They found Rao getting into a car outside the restaurant. A jittery
Shillitani had trouble firing his shotgun. Valachi fired four shots from a handgun. He believed one bullet wounded Rao in the buttocks.[15]

Amato survived through the end of the war. But he was killed when a new
gangland conflict erupted. Valachi felt no regret when he heard that the Coll
gang had caught up with Amato outside of the Parody Dance Hall on the
night of May 28, 1931. He made it a point to rush over to the scene. "I had
trouble with Dick, so I can't say that I was sorry, but I did order a hundred dollar[s' worth of] flowers for him," Valachi later wrote.[16]

Amato was born November 6, 1902, in New York City. He was the second
child born to Faro and Antonetta Lima Amato (her name was also recorded as
Marianna and Lena), immigrants from Italy. Faro was a native of Corleone,

Sicily, born there on March 17, 1871. He entered the U.S. through New Orleans in 1891, and was a resident of 2079 Second Avenue, between 107th and 108th streets in East Harlem, at the time of Frank's birth.[17]

Faro Amato died in a gangland shooting in Southern California when Frank was just three years old. At the time, Faro and his family were living at 2336 LeGrande Street (later made part of East Eighth Street) in Los Angeles, California, part of a growing colony of Corleonesi there. He worked with his cousin Luca Sabella at a lumber yard. Sabella had recently moved west from Louisiana.[18]

On Tuesday night, April 17, 1906, Faro Amato and Luca Sabella spent some time at the 1811 Sacramento Street home of Tony Streva. Late that night, the two visitors left Streva's home on foot. Near the corner of Enterprise and Wilson streets, gunmen stepped from the shadows and opened fire. Two shots struck Amato, who fell to the ground with a moan. Sabella was wounded in the right arm near the elbow and ran off. Area residents rushed to the scene and brought Amato to the Receiving Hospital. Before losing consciousness, he made a brief statement: "I have no enemies here that I know." Faro succumbed to his wounds by about one o'clock Wednesday morning.[19]

Early in the police investigation of the shootings, there were reports that the gunmen were African Americans. The neighborhood was then about evenly divided between Italian-American and African-American residents, and there was some history of conflict between the two groups. By Thursday, April 19, authorities were convinced that Amato and Sabella were members of a secret Italian criminal society – Mafia or "the Black Hand" – and had been attacked by other Italian gangsters.[20]

After Faro's death, the Amato family returned to East Harlem. When the Irish Mob attack against Italian gangsters occurred, Frank was living with his mother and older brother Edward at 225 East 107th Street, not far from his birthplace.[21] By then, Frank "Big Dick" Amato, a young adult, was involved in a street gang closely affiliated with Terranova's Mafia organization. The 1930 U.S. Census found him at the same address, with his mother and brother. He claimed to be working as a clerk in a clothing office.[22]

During the Mafia's 1930-1931 Castellammarese War, Frank Amato was targeted by underworld organizations struggling against the allied forces of Terranova and Dutch Schultz in East Harlem and the Bronx. Valachi and his associate Salvatore Shillitani were sent out to murder Amato and Joseph Rao late in 1930. Their attempt was a failure.[23] Immediately after the war concluded in spring 1931, another group opposed the the Terranova-Schultz alliance – the organization of brothers Peter and Vincent "Mad Dog" Coll – reportedly had better luck.

Joseph Rao was sitting in his car, parked outside the Parody Dance Hall, 164 East 116th Street between Lexington and Third avenues, on Thursday night, May 28, 1931. Twenty-eight-year-old Frank Amato and associate Dominick "Louis Slats" Bologna, thirty seven, of the Bronx, were standing outside the car chatting with Rao.[24]

Rao and Amato were established racketeers and key men in the Terranova organization. Bologna reportedly involved himself in bootlegging, but he was not at all in the same underworld league as Amato and Rao.

He was born September 10, 1893, in New York City to Vincenzo and Catherine Erichetta Bologna, immigrants from Naples. He noted no employment on his World War I draft registration in 1917. In 1919, he was working as a waiter, and applied for a passport to visit Cuba on "business." He may already have been in Cuba at the time of his application – he asked to have the passport delivered to the American consul at Havana. He was working as a clerk when he married Grace Gasparina in June 1923. He and Grace went to live with Bologna's parents. The 1925 state census showed Dominick, by then a tobacco salesman, and his wife residing with his parents at 2713 Cruger Avenue near Allerton Avenue in the Bronx. In 1930, with mother Catherine deceased and father Vincenzo retired, the family lived at 4318 Byron Avenue in the Bronx.[25] That was the home address of "Louis Slats" at the time of his murder. While some reporting suggested that Bologna was a Rao lieutenant and had a police record, no details of his alleged crimes were provided.[26]

At about nine-forty-five, a dark-colored sedan pulled up to the Parody Dance Hall. A man emerged and opened fire on the Rao group. Additional shots were fired by others inside the dark sedan. As hundreds on the street ran for cover, the gunman returned to the sedan and it sped away.[27]

When the shooting began, Amato attempted to duck behind an automobile as a slug tore through his throat and spinal cord. He fell dead at the curb.[28]

Bologna was shot through his back. He remained alive long enough to stagger into the Alpi restaurant, 156 East 116th Street. Terrified diners heard him call for a doctor as he collapsed onto the floor. He died there of bullet damage to his right lung, bronchus and pulmonary artery.[29]

Police arrived to find the two dead gangsters. Rao could not be located. His car was still parked. There were some bloodstains that indicated the driver was wounded in the attack. His hat and wallet were found on the floor of the vehicle.[30]

After disposing of some early theories – that Rao, Amato and Bologna were targeted for interfering with the rackets of Terranova and Schultz or they were casualties of a new war between the forces of Terranova and Schultz – the press decided that the Colls were responsible.[31] This conclusion appeared to be confirmed two days later, when Peter Coll was fatally shot while driving his car on St. Nicholas Avenue in Manhattan.[32]

Frank Amato received an elaborate gangland funeral on Tuesday, June 2. Underworld associates provided many large floral offerings that were loaded into open cars and carried in a procession along East 107th Street. Amato was buried at St. Raymond's Cemetery in the Bronx.[33]

Amato's funeral procession. (NY Daily News)

Augustine, Ludwig "Dutchman"

...By the Dutchman I don't mean Dutch Schultz, this was a different Dutchman. I don't remember his name. He had more guts than all of 116th [Street]. In fact they all had guts, too much.[34]

Joseph Valachi first met this "different Dutchman" around 1924. The Italian gangsters Valachi grew up with had come together in a gang headquartered at East 116th Street and First Avenue and affiliated with a Mafia organization headed by Ciro Terranova. Its opposition was an organization known as "the Irish Mob," though the membership by that time included a mix of ethnicities and only a few Irish-American toughs. Valachi had been friendly with members of both groups. However, when the Italian gang instructed Valachi to use his friendly connections to help set up the Irish Mob for an attack, Valachi went over to the other side.

Valachi's friend Mike introduced him to the mob's leaders, including "the Dutchman" (this nickname, probably derived from "*Deutsche*," was applied to a number of gangsters with Germanic names), and members Frank LaPuma, Steve Foley and Pete Hessler.[35]

Another Irish Mob leader Nick Caputo eventually reached a peace deal with the Italian gang in a meeting at the Pompeii Restaurant.[36] It took Valachi some time to learn that the Italians agreed to peace only after Caputo agreed to allow the murders of Valachi and LaPuma.

Valachi was in Sing Sing Prison early in 1926, when he discovered the Dutchman was a new inmate there. The Dutchman explained to him that Terranova had insisted that Valachi and LaPuma be sacrificed in order to have peace. LaPuma had been murdered the previous June. Dutchman said that their former pal "Bum" was responsible. Valachi had been protected to a degree by his incarceration. The Dutchman was soon transferred from Sing Sing to Clinton State Prison at Dannemora and played no further role in the Valachi story.[37]

Ludwig "the Dutchman" Augustine was born Ludwig Augenstein at 326 Tenth Avenue in New York City on January 18, 1899. His parents were William and Mary Weidner Augenstein, both immigrants from Baden in southwestern Germany. William worked as a cook in a restaurant.[38]

Ludwig Augustine spent much of his life in various institutions. By age eleven, he was an inmate of the New York Juvenile Asylum in the Town of Greenburgh in Westchester County. (The Juvenile Asylum had been founded within Manhattan's Washington Heights neighborhood in the 1850s to provide residential care for Manhattan orphans and juvenile delinquents. In 1901, it relocated to a 277-acre campus in the Village of Dobbs-Ferry within Green-burgh.[39]) Though listed as a resident of that institution at the time of the United States Census in April 1910, he also was listed as living with his family at 1950 Second Avenue in East Harlem when the census taker arrived there three days later.[40]

Augustine was found to be a habitual truant in 1912. He was sentenced to another two years and six months in the juvenile asylum. He could not have been out of the juvenile asylum very long when, in 1915, he was convicted of felony assault in New York and was sentenced to a term in the workhouse at Hart Island off the coast of the Bronx in Long Island Sound.[41]

He was back on the street briefly early in 1916. On Saturday afternoon, February 12, 1916, the seventeen-year-old Augustine was crossing Man-hattan's Fifth Avenue at Forty-seventh Street, when he felt something sharp strike him in the back and hip and he fell. He was taken to the Flower Homeo-pathic Hospital with bullet wounds. Augustine told police there had been no audible gunshots, but he recalled hearing someone nearby say, "You're the guy we want, and now we've got you."[42]

In the same year, Augustine was sentenced to five years at Elmira Prison for third degree burglary. He followed an early release with a June 1918 con-viction for first-degree attempted robbery. He was sentenced to six years in prison for that offense.[43]

The 1920 U.S. Census found him an inmate of Clinton State Prison. It appears he was an inmate also of Auburn Prison and Sing Sing Prison before being released late in 1921.[44]

Augustine, with Frank LaPuma, John J. "Bum" Rodgers and Raymond Fallon, in early March, 1925, robbed Irene Wadsworth and escort George Giasiello of $738 of payroll cash belonging to H. and D.R. Wadsworth & Company of Valley Stream, Long Island. The gangsters got away in an auto-mobile, but its license plate number was noted. Police were able to track the vehicle and over time they assembled a case against the robbers.[45]

Ludwig Augustine showed up at Mount Sinai Hospital just after midday Tuesday, April 7, 1925. He required treatment for a gunshot wound to his left leg. Police investigated and arrested Augustine, then reporting an address of 2050 Third Avenue, for assault and robbery. Francis Zentgraft, messenger for the Mechanics and Metals National Bank had earlier been surrounded by three bandits, struck by a blackjack and robbed of a leather bag containing canceled checks. When Zentgraft resisted, one of the robbers fired a handgun in his direction but succeeded only in wounding one of his accomplices. The three robbers fled in an automobile.[46]

Augustine was assumed to have been the unlucky bandit in the Zentgraft incident. And it did not take long for investigators to connect Augustine and friends to the earlier Wadsworth robbery. In October 1925, he was sufficiently recovered from his his leg wound to be arraigned in Manhattan on the Zent-graft assault/robbery. That charge was dismissed by the magistrate, but Nassau County officials took charge of him and brought him to the Nassau County Jail for the earlier Valley Stream robbery.[47]

LaPuma and "Bum" Rodgers were out of reach of the law. LaPuma had been murdered. Rodgers, likely the same "Bum" who Augustine said was responsible for killing LaPuma, had been convicted of robbery and sentenced to fifteen years but escaped from a train on his way to Auburn Prison. The last of the robbers, Fallon, turned state's evidence and became the key witness in the case against Augustine.

Augustine was convicted of the Wadsworth robbery on December 22, 1925. Two days later the Nassau County judge sentenced him to twenty years for first degree robbery and a concurrent ten years for first degree grand larceny. Sentence was suspended on an assault conviction.[48] Augustine entered Sing Sing on December 30, apparently still suffering with the leg wound.[49] He was transferred to Dannemora in February 1926, then to Auburn Prison late in 1928 and to Eastern Correctional Facility at Napanoch in New York's Ulster County in March 1931. Records indicate he was again in Sing Sing in 1939 and then in Great Meadow Prison in Comstock, New York, a year later.[50]

It appears he went to live with his younger brother Edward in the Bronx following his release from prison. Ludwig Augustine's World War II draft registration indicates he lived with Edward at 948 Leggett Avenue in the Bronx and worked for United Fruit Company at New York City's Pier 3. The 1950 Census found him living with Edward and Edward's family at 665 Casanova Avenue in the Bronx.[51]

Records show that Ludwig Augustine died at Ronkonkoma, Suffolk County, on September 25, 1972.[52]

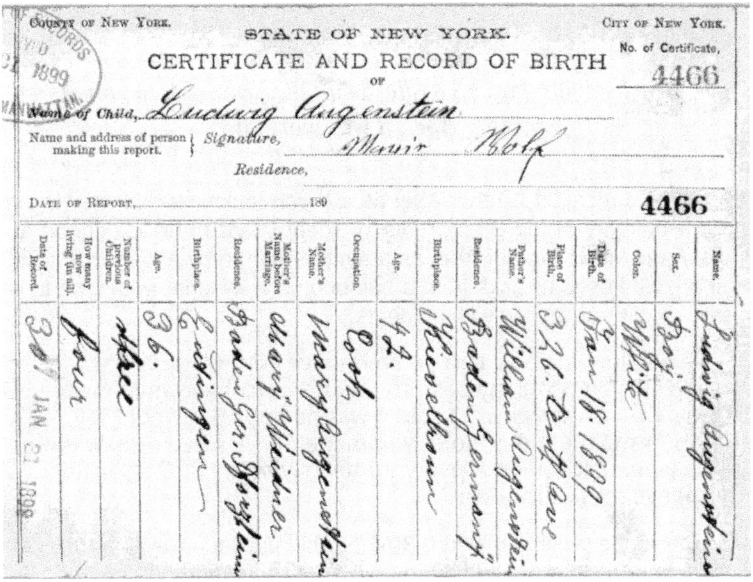

COUNTY OF NEW YORK. STATE OF NEW YORK. CITY OF NEW YORK.

CERTIFICATE AND RECORD OF BIRTH OF

No. of Certificate, 4466

Name of Child, Ludwig Augenstein

Name and address of person making this report. Signature, Maurir Wolf

Residence,

DATE OF REPORT, ...189

4466

Field	Entry
Name.	Ludwig Augenstein
Sex.	Boy
Color.	White
Date of Birth.	Jan 18. 1899
Place of Birth.	326. East 5 Ave
Father's Name.	William Augenstein
Residence.	Baden Germany
Birthplace.	Kieselbronn
Age.	42.
Occupation.	Cook
Mother's Name.	Mary Augenstein
Mother's Name before Marriage.	Mary Weidner
Residence.	Baden Ger. Pforzheim
Birthplace.	Eisingen
Age.	36.
Number of previous Children.	three
How many now living (in all).	four
Date of Record.	301 JAN 21 1899

Ludwig Augenstein birth certificate.

Brother Abel

> ...The kids felt that, no matter what the price was to spit at
> brother Abel, it was worth it.[53]

Joseph Valachi recalled Brother Abel as a harsh taskmaster at the New York Catholic Protectory in the Bronx. Valachi spent years of his childhood at the protectory and knew Brother Abel as an impossible to please instructor in the tailor shop, who used whacks from a bamboo stick wrapped with tape to communicate his dissatisfaction with students.

> He would give you a certain amount of buttonholes to make, and I would do all my best, so that he won't have anything to say. But no matter what I did it was no good. He would say, "Show me the buttonholes you made." Well, when he saw them he would hit you on top of your head with the tape stick, and believe me it hurt awful.[54]

Valachi was in the protectory when Brother Abel passed away. The boys of the institution were assembled to pay their last respects, and one by one viewed the Brother in his coffin. "When it was my turn," Valachi wrote, "I almost fainted when I saw all the spit on Brother Abel's chest. So, I spit at him too."

The entire school was put on "penance" for two weeks for disrespecting the Brother. According to Valachi, their time in the recreation yard was spent in line with their hands on their heads and the same position was held for two hours every night before bed.[55]

An Irish immigrant, Brother Abel began as a teacher at the protectory back around 1868. A few years later, he was assigned to supervise the protectory's highly regarded boys' band. His duties relative to the band appeared to be less musical than disciplinary. When the band traveled for performances, it was said to be under his guardianship.[56]

Brother Abel died January 19, 1917, after a short illness. The *New York Times* reported that he had been at the protectory for "a great number of years." The *Brooklyn Standard Union* stated that he had been at the institution for forty nine years. Neither newspaper took a guess at the Brother's age. Valachi said he was close to eighty.[57]

A High Mass of Requiem was offered for Brother Abel at the protectory's chapel on Monday, January 22. He was buried in the protectory's cemetery.[58]

Callace, Frank "Chic 99"

> *Now I knew an old timer at 108th St, his name was "99." I don't know why, but that is what they called him. I knew him a lot of years since I was a kid.*[59]

"Chic 99" or "99" was not much older than Valachi, but Valachi repeatedly referred to him as an "old timer." Valachi was fond of the term, using it twenty three times in his autobiography. It was often used to refer to people who were more senior in age, but Valachi also may have used it to refer to Italian Americans who were born in Italy and later settled in the U.S.[60]

Valachi apparently teased Chic 99 about his birth in Sicily and called him "a hatchet man." Chic 99 was wise to the Mafia tradition long before Valachi and hinted to him: "...He [Chic 99] will tell me how someday I'm going to find out what it is all about..."[61]

Chic 99 was present when Valachi received his education in the form of a Mafia induction ceremony. Following the Castellammarese War murders of Al Mineo and Steve Ferrigno, in which Valachi acted as assistant and driver, Valachi disappeared from his East Harlem neighborhood for a few days. He then returned as if nothing happened. Walking one night in November 1930 along Lexington Avenue near 110th Street, a car pulled up alongside him. Chic 99 was driving and urged Valachi to get in. "He said, 'You don't know how lucky you are.'" Chic 99 told him that "Joe the Boss" Masseria's forces had learned of Valachi's involvement in the murders of Mineo and Ferrigno and were looking for him.

After telling Valachi the backstory of the Castellammarese War and bringing him up to date on recent developments, Chic 99 left Valachi with friends Nick Paduano and Salvatore Shillitani in the Bronx and told him he would be brought out of the city in a couple of days.

At that time, Chic 99 drove Valachi, Paduano and Shillitani to a house about ninety miles north of New York and introduced them to Salvatore Maranzano, leader of the anti-Masseria forces in the New York area. Between thirty and forty mafiosi were present. One at a time, Valachi, Paduano and Shillitani went through the Mafia induction ceremony, becoming members of "cosa nostra."[62]

Francesco "Frank" Callace was born January 21, 1900, in Corleone, Sicily, to Filippo and Anna Maria DeLuca Callace. He later indicated on official records that his birth date was January 15.[63] While the "Chic" portion of his nickname apparently was a shortened form of "Francesco," no one has offered an explanation for the "99." His surname was sometimes written "Callace" and sometimes "Callaci."

Filippo exited Frank's life story at an early age, and is not mentioned in available records following Frank's baptism in Corleone. In December of 1913, thirteen-year-old Frank crossed the Atlantic with his mother Anna Maria and sister Giovanna to join an older brother Carlo, who had previously settled at 234 East 107th Street in East Harlem. For the passenger manifest of the *S.S. Canada*, Anna Maria reported that she was married but made no mention of a husband. She noted that she left behind in Corleone a brother Gaetano DeLuca. Sailing on the same ship were relatives, Angela Callaci Mione and daughter Maria Mione of Corleone, who were headed to the same East Harlem address to rejoin Maria's husband Angelo.[64]

When Frank Callace registered for the World War I draft in September 1918, he stated that he lived with his mother at 238 East 107th Street and worked as a maker of shirts for the Berlin Shirt Company at 404-412 East 104th Street. At that time, he was described as medium height, with a slender build, brown eyes and black hair.[65]

He continued to produce shirts for a number of years, but also began moonlighting as a burglar and gangster. Following an April 1924 in Manhattan for possession of blackjacks, Callace and William LaMoglia of 319 East 108th Street were identified as suspects in the recent burglary of a Brooklyn clothing store, 67 Myrtle Avenue. Store proprietor Max Larkin claimed that Callace and LaMoglia took $1,000 worth of clothing from his store. He said that suits valued at $575 had been recovered.[66]

Callace reported for the New York State Census of 1925 that he worked as chauffeur. He lived at that time in the apartment of his brother-in-law Gasper

Mione at 238 East 107th Street. The U.S. Census of 1930, showed a Frank Callace, thirty, living with widowed mother "Mary" within the home of Angelo Mione at 229 East 107th Street. Among the other residents were other units of the Callace-Mione clan, including the same brother-in-law Gasper Mione.[67]

Months after the end of the Castellammarese War, Callace joined Paduano, Shillitani and Eddie Coco in an ambush of young East Harlem gangsters who had been robbing a mafioso's saloon. The ambush went badly. On Thursday night, January 28, 1932, one of the targeted gangsters, Benedetto Bellini, was shot to death in front of Public School 89, Mace and Paulding avenues in the Bronx. The rest of the gang ran off. A police officer happened to be visiting with his father across the street and observed the mafiosi fleeing from the scene. He chased and exchanged fire with the gunmen. He fatally shot Paduano. Shillitani was arrested. Callace and Coco both escaped.[68]

In April, Callace and Joseph Magna were investigated for possession of counterfeit. They had given attendant John Papo a $10 bill for $1.70 of gasoline bought at Warner's service station, Main Street and Schenck Avenue in Beacon, New York. After they left in the direction of the Newburgh-Beacon Ferry, Papo grew concerned about the quality of the $10 bill and called police. State Police at Fishkill determined the bill was bogus and sent out a Teletype alarm describing the automobile used by Callace and Magna. Newburgh Police Officer William Dickinson spotted the car in his city and arrested both occupants. Callace told police he was thirty two and lived at 230 East 108th Street in East Harlem. Magna gave his age as forty two and provided two addresses, one was the Messina Farm in Wappingers Falls and the other was 375 Crosby Avenue in the Bronx. The men were booked on a preliminary charge of petit larceny while federal Secret Service agents were called in from New York City to investigate.[69]

It appears that Callace avoided a counterfeiting charge. But federal charges of a different sort were lodged against him in June 1937. A federal grand jury indicted him, along with codefendants Anthony Valenti and Rosario Cali, for possessing an unregistered still and illegally distilling alcohol. The still was seized by agents during a June 3 raid at 2726 Morgan Avenue in the Bronx. Callace reportedly served a year in prison for these offenses.[70]

Callace's home life in the period was untraditional. A son, named Philip Callace, was born in Poughkeepsie, New York, on November 23, 1932. It is uncertain that Frank Callace ever lived in Poughkeepsie. Census records from 1940, show Frank Callace, wife Catharine Callace, seven-year-old son Philip and five-year-old daughter Anne Marie living together at 236 East 107th Street. However, there is no marriage record for Frank and Catharine Summa Callace until two years after that.[71]

Callace was charged with narcotics violations in the early 1940s. He served a prison term of two and a half years following a 1943 conviction.[72] Charged with attempted extortion in Milford, Connecticut, in late 1947, Frank Callace posted bail and left the state. That brought about an additional federal charge of fleeing to avoid prosecution.[73]

For the 1950 U.S. Census, Callace reported that he was fifty and lived with his wife and two children at 144 East 107th Street. He did not indicate an occupation but claimed he had worked every week in 1949, earning a total of $2,800. Son Philip, then seventeen, was working in television repair. Later that year, Callace's mother passed away. Records indicated that she was eighty-eight at the time of death, but she may have been older.[74]

The following April, Frank Callace turned up in Rome, Italy. He was arrested there after transporting luggage containing a package of about three kilos of heroin from Milan to Rome. Callace claimed that he was given the package by some people in Milan and instructed to turn it over to a man in Palermo, Sicily. Giuseppe Pici, said to be Callace's uncle, got caught up in the matter as well, and both men were detained while police investigated. A press report stated that Pici had been deported from the U.S. to his native Italy after serving time in Sing Sing Prison. It was said that Callace secretly fled the U.S. just before an order came for his deportation. Pici eventually admitted that he previously shipped about 17 kilos of heroin into New York.[75]

Two months later, Italian authorities arrested former New York crime boss Salvatore "Charlie Luciano" Lucania. Deported from the U.S. in 1946 and from Cuba in 1947, Lucania was living in Rome at the time. Police believed he was connected to a narcotics smuggling ring that included Callace and Pici but apparently could not prove it. They released Lucania pending further investigation.[76] Police were able to link Italian military official, General Camillo Gastaldi, to the smuggling ring. Gastaldi was accused of selling forty pounds (18 kilos) of illegal narcotics through a Genoa drugstore he owned. As he faced criminal charges in spring of 1952, he was stripped of his military rank.[77]

Eugene Giannini, who had participated in a Mafia-linked narcotics smuggling ring, was murdered in New York City on September 20, 1952.[78] It was immediately reported that Giannini had been "'singing' to federal agents." While attributing the murder to Mafia discipline, the *New York Daily News* reported that Giannini had several discussions with U.S. narcotics agents:

> Giannini reportedly detailed meetings with Luciano, Joe Pici, Frank Callace, Dominick Petrelli and other crime syndicate chiefs who had been deported from the United States.[79]

Petrelli was shot to death in a Bronx bar and grill on December 9, 1953, when his underworld associates learned he was providing information to agents.[80]

In November 1954, it was Callace's turn. "Chic 99" had been quietly released by Italian authorities after serving time in prison and had made his way back to New York, where his wife and family resided in a top-floor apartment at 1241 Leland Avenue in the Bronx. He had been living with them and working at his son's donut shop since the summer of 1953. On Saturday night, November 13, he borrowed a dark green, 1951 Buick sedan registered to nephew Peter Mione of Flushing, Queens, and told his family he needed to go to a meeting.

The car was found at seven-thirty the next morning, with its headlights burning, parked in front of 1253 Crosby Avenue in the Bronx. Frank Callace's dead body was slumped over the steering wheel. He reportedly had one .38-caliber bullet wound behind his right ear and another at the base of his skull.[81]

Callace is found dead in his car. (NY Daily News)

Capobianco, Edward "Eddie Starr"

> *He started to say, "You know what happened to Eddie Starr?" I said, "No." He said, "Last night they cracked his head wide open."*[82]

A serious injury to "Eddie Starr" was the excuse used by Anthony "Tony Bender" Strollo and Girolamo "Bobby Doyle" Santuccio to send Joseph Valachi after the "Wackie Brothers." Valachi apparently knew the brothers by no other name but, in the late 1930s, he understood that the Wackies were numbers racketeers working with Vincent Rao and the 107th Street Gang. (107th Street Gang had become a synonym for the organization connected to Tommy "Brown" Lucchese.)[83]

Sometime after Ciro Terranova's death in February 1938,[84] Santuccio met with Valachi and told him the Wackie Brothers attacked Eddie Starr and left him near death. Santuccio passed along an order from Strollo that Valachi must find the Wackies and deliver a convincing beating. "Tony wants you to take personal charge and you must do it in twenty four hours," Santuccio said. "We don't want it to cool off."

Valachi was told to use Tommy "Ryan" Eboli and "Johnnie Dee" DeBellis for the assignment. He protested in vain that attacking the Wackies would damage his close friendship with Lucchese. While he did not say so, he also quietly resented having to work with DeBellis, who years ago abandoned Valachi in advance of a conflict with an East Harlem hoodlum known as Crazy Chuck. Valachi was also concerned that he would not be able to find the brothers in a day, but he considered that a potential excuse for not doing the job.[85]

The following morning, Valachi received a telephone call from "Fat Tony" Salerno, an aide to "Trigger Mike" Coppola. The call was a surprise, as Valachi knew he had never given Salerno his phone number. Salerno said he regularly did numbers business with the Wackie Brothers behind the back of

Vincent Rao and he was scheduled to meet with the brothers at Ninety-seventh Street and Third Avenue that afternoon. With Salerno providing the time and place for an attack on the brothers, Valachi concluded, "Now, I'm stuck."[86]

Valachi, Eboli and DeBellis drove over to Ninety-seventh Street that afternoon. On the way, Eboli told Valachi the story of the attack on Starr. The Wackie Brothers and "Joe Palisades" Rosato were out drinking together and sought female companionship. Starr was known to be popular with women, and they approached him to arrange some escorts. Starr made some calls, but none of his contacts were home. The Wackies and Rosato left and returned some hours later, making the same request. Again Starr was unable to arrange for dates. One of the brothers then picked up a heavy marble lamp and used it to open a gaping hole in Starr's forehead.[87]

At two o'clock that afternoon, one of the Wackie brothers came into view on Ninety-seventh Street, accompanied by a Vincent Rao nephew known as "Big Rocks." Valachi intercepted Big Rocks and pulled him aside, while Eboli and DeBellis beat the one Wackie brother. Valachi tried to explain the matter to Big Rocks before they sped away.[88]

Following the incident, great pressure fell on Strollo, and he deflected the blame to Valachi. Some in the Lucchese camp came to believe that Valachi acted on his own to avenge Eddie Starr. At the next encounter between Valachi and Lucchese, an annual Christmas party, it appeared that Lucchese understood Strollo's responsibility. He asked Valachi to tell him what happened. Valachi hinted that he did not act of his own volition, but he knew better than to outright betray his underworld superior.

After the holidays, the matter was brought to a regional council meeting. Valachi was let off the hook, "but all [Lucchese's] boys were very cold to me ever since."[89] Valachi provided no update on the status of "Eddie Starr" Capobianco.

Edward Capobianco was born in New York in April 1901. His parents were Italian immigrants Humbert (Albert), a tailor, and Olympia Capobianco. His early childhood home was 134 Sullivan Street, just south of Greenwich Village. Around 1915, the family lived in Union, New Jersey, before returning to New York.[90]

Capobianco was still in his teens when he first got into trouble with the law. He was sentenced to ninety days for larceny in 1919. In December of 1920, he was sent to Elmira Reformatory on a burglary conviction. The following December, he received a five year sentence for burglary.[91]

He was serving his sentence early in 1923, when his mother passed away. Authorities arranged to transport him from Elmira to New York City to attend her funeral.[92] He was freed from Elmira later in the year.

Near the end of November 1923, Capobianco was arrested with Nicholas "Cheeks" Luciano, Angelo Farino and others during a raid at 2712 Williamsbridge Road in the Bronx. The prisoners were held as material witnesses in a murder and robbery case against brothers Morris and Joe Diamond and their accomplices. Following the convictions of the defendants, Capobianco and the other material witnesses were released.[93]

Capobianco was arrested for attempted grand larceny in June 1925. He confessed to the crime four months later, and he was sentenced to a year and a day in Sing Sing Prison. As he entered the prison, he stated that he lived at 15 Waverly Place, in the eastern section of Greenwich Village, and that he worked as a chauffeur. He was released from the prison in July 1926.[94]

In the late 1920s and early 1930s, he was arrested and discharged for a variety of offenses, including rape, felonious assault, possession of burglar tools, assault and robbery.[95]

Following the $18,500 holdup of a bank in the Hamlet of Katona, New York, on March 12, 1937, witnesses identified a photo of Capobianco as possibly one of the bank robbers. Capobianco was taken into custody on the seventeenth. He was turned over to New York State Police and brought to Town of Bedford Police Headquarters in northern Westchester County. Bank President Edward Fielder looked him over and decided that he was not one of the robbers.[96]

If his bloody encounter with the Wackie Brothers occurred near the end of the 1930s, as suspected, the head wound did not lead to Capobianco's death.

Capobianco, then a resident of 172 Prince Street in Manhattan, was arrested January 10, 1940, on suspicion of involvement with the November 29, 1939, shooting death of Joseph Piscitello. Piscitello, a Brooklyn resident known to the authorities as a counterfeiter, was killed in a hallway at 181 Thompson Street in Manhattan.[97]

Apparently avoiding conviction in the Piscitello case, Capobianco continued to live in Manhattan for nearly six more years. His death was recorded on November 4, 1945, when he was just forty four. It was reported that he was married, residing at 205 Sullivan Street and working as a photographer at the time of his death.[98]

Caruso, Angelo

> He explained, "You see, Mr. Maranzano is nobody's fool. He
> put [Angelo Caruso] there so he can be his yes man."[99]

Following the April 1931 assassination of Giuseppe "Joe the Boss" Masseria and the end of the Castellammarese War, a victorious Salvatore Maranzano held a meeting of New York mafiosi at a hall near Washington Avenue in the Bronx. Crime family membership rolls had become muddled through the war, particularly among the anti-Masseria rebels led by Maranzano, and the meeting was held to reorganize the families and officially recognize family leaders.

Maranzano assigned to himself the supreme arbiter position of boss of bosses, previously held by Masseria. As his second-in-command, Maranzano appointed Angelo Caruso. (In his memoirs, Valachi wrote the surname "Cruiso" and "Crusio.")[100]

As the appointment was announced, a friend of Valachi commented that Caruso felt he did not earn the lofty role. Valachi, who did not recall any noticeable contribution from Caruso to the war effort, asked why Maranzano selected him. The friend offered the opinion that Maranzano merely wanted a "yes-man."[101]

Valachi apparently did not interact with Caruso and barely had reason to mention him. Months later, in a private September 9, 1931, conversation between Valachi and the boss of bosses, Maranzano explained that he had an important meeting at his Park Avenue offices the next day.

Valachi, already concerned that Maranzano had ordered his guards not to carry weapons into the office, was alarmed by the news of the meeting. "Why don't you let Angelo Caruso go in your place?" he protested. "Why must you take a chance going to the office?"[102]

Valachi was apparently correct to be concerned, as Maranzano was murdered at his office on September 10, 1931.[103]

Angelo Caruso was born January 7, 1895, to Luigi and Angelina Ilardo Caruso at Leonforte, a mountain community in central Sicily.[104] During Angelo Caruso's childhood, a number of family members relocated to New York City. His brother Gaetano Caruso, then seventeen, sailed from Palermo to New York in October 1909 to meet up with a maternal uncle, Domenico Ilardo, resident of 2220 Second Avenue in East Harlem.[105]

Angelo served in the Italian Army during the Great War. His military career ended the last day of October 1919. About a year later, Caruso, then twenty five, and his seventeen-year-old sister Mafalda crossed the Atlantic to join their brother Gaetano, who was living in Corona, Queens.[106]

At the time, Gaetano Caruso was working as both a barber and a tailor, but he found the time to engage in criminal activity as well. As Angelo and Mafalda joined him, operatives of the federal Department of Justice were tracking his movements.

Agents followed Gaetano Caruso to Waterbury, Connecticut, on September 22, 1920, and were present when he and five other men held up twenty two customers at an Italian restaurant, taking $4,000. Choosing not to reveal their identities, the agents made no move against the robbers at that time.[107]

A couple of weeks later, the federal investigators cooperated with police in the arrests of Caruso, Francesco Ferro and Vincenzo Abato. William J. Flynn, chief of the Justice Department's Bureau of Investigation, told the press that his men had been watching Caruso since May of 1919, believing him to be linked to a series of anarchist bombings, including the devastating Wall Street bombing of September 16, 1920. Federal authorities believed he was a disciple of anarchist-socialist activists Alexander Berkman, Emma Goldman and "Dynamite Louise" Berger. Gaetano Caruso admitted that he had met a number of radical leaders through editor Carlo Tresca during a barbers' strike years earlier, but he denied that he had any interest in the anarchist-socialist cause. Caruso's home was searched and it was found to contain radical political literature, much of it written in the Italian language.[108]

The BOI later established that its own surveillance proved that Gaetano Caruso was uninvolved in the Wall Street bombing.[109]

Angelo Caruso faced charges of his own in autumn 1925. According to shoe store proprietor Anthony Pomper, four men walked into his Union City, New Jersey, store on October 29, saying they wished to "talk business." When he said was too busy, one of the men struck him. All four then left.

Pomper telephoned police, who found three of the men at a nearby street corner waiting for the fourth to pick them up in a car. The police arrested Caruso, who hid his identity behind the name Angelo Ilanti,[110] with Anthony Sarosa, Ignatz Vaccaro and driver Anthony Colletti, charging the four with assault. Authorities theorized that the men had been planning a holdup of Pomper's shop or were setting the owner up for a sort of "fleecing game."

The suspects were arraigned before Recorder Alfred Modarelli in police court and released in $1,000 bail.[111] It appears that the charge against Caruso was later reduced to disorderly conduct and ultimately dismissed.[112]

In this period, Angelo Caruso married Maria Antonina Colletti. Their July 22, 1928, certificate of marriage described Caruso as a cafe proprietor living at 410 East 163rd Street in the Bronx. His bride was said to be a native of Sant'Anna, Italy, and a resident of 415 East Eighteenth Street in Manhattan.[116]

New England bootlegger(s)

Press reports indicate that one or more Angelo Carusos were arrested between 1926 and 1937 on liquor-related charges within New England. It is uncertain that any of the incidents relate to the Caruso who became Maranzano's underboss or to any of his relatives.

On April 12, 1926, local authorities were alerted to the delivery of twenty five gallons of alcohol to a store on Canal Street in Stamford, Connecticut. The Stamford police were tipped off by officials in Greenwich that an Angelo Caruso of Port Chester, New York, had passed through that community on his way to the delivery in Stamford.[113]

On December 7, 1928, federal Prohibition agents raided 247 Howe Street in Methuen, Massachusetts, about thirty miles north of Boston along the New Hampshire border. They discovered an illegal distillery. Angelo Caruso of 54 Sargent Street in Lawrence, Massachusetts, and Vincent Mattera, also of Lawrence, were arrested for operating the still. Landowner Joseph A. Morin was also arrested but was quickly discharged. Caruso and Mattera were brought before U.S. Commissioner Richard B. Walsh and charged with illegal manufacture and possession of intoxicating liquor. They were sent on to the Federal District Court in Boston.[114]

In spring of 1937, the Angelo Caruso of Lawrence, was arrested for violating Internal Revenue laws by running a still at a farm in Groveland, Massachusetts. When he and two accomplices were brought to trial in June, the federal prosecutor called Caruso an "old-time bootlegger." He was sentenced to four months in jail.[115]

When Maranzano officially became boss of a Brooklyn-based organization formerly led by Nicola Schiro, mafiosi from Maranzano's hometown of Castellammare del Golfo comprised the majority of that organization. Caruso was a member of the organization and a key figure in a non-Castellammarese faction. Future Mafia boss Joseph Bonanno, a member of the Castellammarese faction, felt that Maranzano appointed Caruso as underboss "in the interest of Family unity."[117]

Following the assassination of Maranzano in September 1931, Caruso momentarily became acting boss of the Castellammarese-dominated crime family. Once the dust settled, the organization selected Joseph Bonanno as its boss.[118]

Later in 1931, Angelo Caruso was implicated with other mafiosi in a kidnapping racket. Midwest police agencies investigated recent kidnappings of Chicago jeweler Meyer Gordon; Rockford, Illinois, gambler Ralph Pearce; and St. Louis furrier Alexander Berg. Officials said those were just a few of the dozens of abductions reported in Midwest cities in a period of just a few months. Pearce had been recently released. Gordon and Berg were still missing.

After a Berg family friend named Louis Spinelli offered to negotiate with kidnappers on the family's behalf, police arrested Spinelli and found him in a talkative mood. That led to the November 9 arrests of "Dago Lawrence" Mangano and four others – Sylvester Agoglia and Frank Chiavavolloti of Chicago, Paul Palmeri of Niagara Falls, New York, and Angelo Caruso – sitting in a parked automobile in Chicago.[119]

While Chicago investigators were questioning the suspects, Berg suddenly reappeared at his St. Louis home.[120]

By November 11, authorities acknowledged that evidence connecting the five Chicago suspects to the kidnappings was lacking. Caruso and the others were released.[121]

Angelo Caruso was again seen in company with underworld leaders when a flight from Aguascalientes Airport in Mexico landed at Lindbergh Field (more recently known as San Diego International Airport) in San Diego, California, on July 24, 1932. U.S. officials sought to detain nine passengers suspected of involvement in smuggling. The small passenger list included several well known underworld figures, including Los Angeles boss Jack Dragna, Cleveland boss Frank Milano and New Yorkers Vincent Mangano, Angelo Caruso and Philip Kovolick.

Caruso, who provided a home address of 297 Avenue B in New York, told authorities he would rather be returned to Mexico than be detained in the U.S. The designation "detained on board and deport" was added to his name on the passenger list.[122]

(The plane trip became a problem for Jack Dragna two decades later. Immigration officials sought to deport him because, at the time of his 1932 reentry into the country, he falsely claimed to be a U.S. native.[123])

During the 1940s and 1950s, Angelo Caruso largely avoided the notice of police and press. He held a number of occupations, working for a while as a plasterer, as a beer salesman, then as a bill collector and later as a roofer. Caruso's naturalization was approved in the summer of 1942. He and wife Maria raised five sons and a daughter at their home at 412 East Fifth Street in Manhattan.[124]

But Caruso became of interest to the FBI in 1963. Recently awakened to the reality of organized crime in the U.S., the Bureau was busily gathering all information it could find on the subject and researching every aspect of Joseph Valachi's story. Caruso was questioned by FBI agents on October 23, 1963. He provided basic information on his background and citizenship.[125]

The FBI found one detail of Caruso's personal history especially interesting. In 1942, when filing his draft registration, he said he worked for Sunland Beverage Corporation of 125 Lawrence Avenue in Brooklyn. That was two years after he claimed, for the 1940 U.S. Census, that he was employed as a salesman for the Stegmaier Beer brewery of Wilkes-Barre, Pennsylvania. Agents knew that a number of underworld figures had claimed to be employed by Sunland, a wholesale beer distribution company wholly owned in that period by Profaci Crime Family underboss Giuseppe Magliocco. Another Profaci member and Sunland employee, Salvatore Tornabe, served as witness for Caruso's 1942 naturalization petition.

Magliocco and Brooklyn undertaker Gaetano Mangano started Sunland in

1933. Magliocco bought out his partner's share in 1937 and held all the company stock until 1957, when his wife and his longtime office manager also became shareholders.[126]

Interest in Caruso intensified as the Bonanno Crime Family experienced internal conflict in the mid-1960s. Boss Joseph Bonanno disappeared and was presumed kidnapped on October 20, 1964. His son Salvatore "Bill" Bonanno attempted to take control of the organization but found much of the membership and the Mafia's Commission supported Gaspare DiGregorio as leader. In 1965, an informant told the FBI that Angelo Caruso was siding with the anti-Bonanno rebels.[127]

Joseph Bonanno resurfaced in May 1966, determined to restore order to his organization. DiGregorio's support diminished. Paul Sciacca emerged as Bonanno's top rival, but much of the crime family got in line behind Bonanno. The aging boss selected Angelo Caruso to deliver a message to the Commission, making it clear that Bonanno intended to retire from his organization once he had fully reunited it.[128]

In mid-1967, an informant told the FBI that Caruso had emerged as the leader of the Bonanno Crime Family, with Joe Zicarelli and Vito DeFilippo serving as underbosses in New Jersey and New York City, respectively.[129] This report may have been a misunderstanding. At about the same time, according to Bonanno's autobiography, a three-man panel was installed atop the organization to allow for Bonanno's retirement to Arizona:

> ...I appointed a three-man committee to fill the leadership vacuum temporarily until a new Father could be chosen. The committee included Angelo Caruso, a steady and peaceful man of the old Tradition. This was but a caretaker arrangement.[130]

By 1974, FBI learned that Caruso was no longer counted among the organization leaders. He was "considered a 'soldier' in the 'family' but because of his age and ill health, has not been active for years."[131]

Angelo Caruso passed away on November 13, 1991, in Flushing, Queens.[132]

Casertano, Stephen "Buck Jones"

> Buck was one of the boys that I grew up with, and this was
> nothing new to him. He kept saying he'll go anywhere with
> Joe at the wheel.[133]

Recently released from Sing Sing, Valachi learned in summer 1928 that members of his old burglary gang had graduated from street crime into racketeering.[134] "I didn't know just what it means," Valachi said, "but they were 'mobbed up' with Ciro [Terranova]."[135] Valachi assembled some neighborhood pals into a new burglary gang. Members included Stephen Casertano, Nick Paduano, John DeBellis, Peter Leone, Salvatore Shillitani and Johnny Gavellas. About once every three weeks, the group would target a New York area business and fence stolen items through a contact named Fat West.[136]

Casertano was known to the rest of the group as "Buck Jones," the result of his admiration for the popular star of numerous low-budget western movies.[137] (Proof of the actor's popularity, Casertano was one of two hoodlums Valachi knew by that nickname. He earlier worked with a "Buck Jones" who stole some of the loot from a burglary job and was cut across the face by Dominic "the Gap" Petrelli as a punishment.[138])

During one escape from a burglary job, a police car pursued, and Valachi accidentally drove the getaway car onto a dead-end street. Valachi made a U-turn, going up on sidewalks on both sides of the road to achieve it, and faced the police car. "I took a deep breath and I put it in first speed and then in second speed and I stepped on the gas, all she had," he later recalled. "...I aimed at the cops as though I was going to drive right into them with my bright lights on. Then when I got almost on top of them I swung right and left like a demon and I found myself in the clear." Valachi's companions laughed and cheered, and Casertano said he'd go anywhere with Valachi at the wheel.[139]

Valachi was inducted into the Mafia by Salvatore Maranzano late in 1930, at the peak of the Castellammarese War. Underworld superiors instructed him to give up burglaries, and he saw little of Buck for a time. When the war concluded with Maranzano's victory in spring 1931, Valachi introduced mafioso Girolamo "Bobby Doyle" Santuccio to his old buddies, including "Buck Jones." Santuccio recommended the group for Mafia membership.[140] As Maranzano was murdered in September, an attempt was made to kill Casertano, DeBellis and Leone, but a misfiring weapon allowed all three to escape. They later went to Valachi's apartment, where they all discovered their boss had been assassinated.[141]

In the post-Maranzano Mafia, Valachi was invited into two different crime families, one led by Tom Gagliano and Tommy Lucchese and one led by Salvatore "Charlie Luciano" Lucania and Vito Genovese.

The Gagliano group was uninterested in Casertano and the rest of the gang. So, Valachi, Casertano, Leone and DeBellis, went into the Lucania family. They were welcomed in a meeting with Genovese and Santuccio in the Cornish Arms Hotel at Twenty-third Street and Eighth Avenue in Manhattan.[142]

Stefano "Stephen" Casertano was born March 7, 1902, at San Prisco, north of Naples in Italy's Caserta Province. He was the second son of Lorenzo and Anna Zibella Casertano. Lorenzo settled with a brother-in-law in New York in autumn 1902. In January 1907, Anna and sons Andrea, ten, and Stefano, four, were reunited with Lorenzo at 2123 First Avenue near East 109th Street.[143] The Casertanos lived for a time at 330 East 109th Street. Lorenzo worked various jobs: pipe maker in a factory, peddler of skirts, traveling dry goods salesman. By 1920, the family had grown to include two more children.[144]

In 1928, while part of Valachi's burglary gang, Stephen Casertano filed his naturalization petition, indicating he was employed as a chauffeur and still living with his parents – their address recently changed to 333 East 109th Street. Two years later, he was missing from the family home in census records.[145] Casertano's mother died at age seventy one in July 1939. His father lived to be eighty three, passing away in June 1950. Stephen Casertano did not fare as well. He died in New York on June 14, 1954, a victim of cancer.[146]

Writer Peter Maas attributed to Valachi a story relating to Casertano's final days. In the 1950s, Casertano reportedly ran a modest loan sharking operation. "After Casertano got cancer," Maas wrote, "[boss Vito] Genovese generously assigned a man to collect his outstanding loans, amounting to about $20,000, with the explanation that he would turn the money over to Casertano's widow. When Casertano died, however, Genovese kept it all."[147]

Casertano was mentioned in a narcotics trial two years after his death. Brothers Benjamin and Joseph Licchi of New Jersey and codefendant Charles "the Mouse" Curcio were convicted of drug-related offenses. The Licchis testified at trial, asserting that drug processing equipment found in the cellar of Joseph Licchi's home had belonged to his boyhood friend Casertano. The brothers testified that Casertano asked to leave the equipment with them for a couple of weeks but never returned for it.[148]

Castaldo, Joseph "Muskie"

One of [Ciro Terranova's] agents was a guy named Muskie. He came from 106th Street, First Avenue. He used to run around with a 16-cylinder Cadillac, and he was sort of a nasty guy. You will hear remarks here and there: "If he wasn't with Ciro, I'd shoot him..."[149]

Joseph "Muskie" Castaldo was mentioned in Valachi's autobiography during an explanation of Ciro Terranova's domination in the New York artichoke market. Valachi said Terranova bought up every artichoke shipped to the city in order to control the retail price. According to Valachi's recollection, "Muskie" was one of the Terranova men who supported the racket.[150]

Born to Antonio and Eugenia Principale Castaldo at Brusciano near Naples, Italy,[151] Castaldo's birth date is in doubt. Castaldo may not have known it himself, as he often gave conflicting dates and ages for official documents.[152] Castaldo was brought to the U.S. as a boy, and he grew up in East Harlem. In 1903, young Castaldo was sent to the New York Catholic Protectory after being convicted of assault. He was in his early twenties when convicted in 1907 for receiving stolen property and sentenced to six months in county prison.[153]

Soon after his release, he married Giuseppa (Josephine) Salerno, daughter of Ferdinando and Eutilia Urzo Salerno, originally from Sarno, Italy. The wedding ceremony was performed by Father Philip Leone at St. Lucy's Catholic Church on 104th Street, with Giuseppe Urzo and Emilia Prisco as witnesses. For many years, Joseph Castaldo kept his family close to his Salerno in-laws.[154]

Castaldo returned to prison in May 1910, following a conviction for assault. The judge sentenced him to seven and a half years. After a couple of months at Sing Sing Prison, Castaldo served the bulk of his term at Auburn State Prison, before being released through Sing Sing late in 1914.[155]

He reported working as a stone cutter the following year, while he and wife lived alongside the Salerno family at 403 East 106th Street. His involvement in the sale of produce was first noted in his 1917 registration for the World War I draft, when he stated he ran his own fruit and produce business.[156]

Three sons were born to the Castaldo family between 1917 and the final days of 1919: Alfred "Fred," Anthony "Tony," and Generoso "James." The 1920 U.S. Census proves the family found room for these additions within the confines of 403 East 106th Street.[157] A daughter Eugenia was born in the early 1920s. Another daughter, Yolanda, followed nine years after that.[158]

In the later 1920s, Castaldo was deeply involved in the artichoke racket and other dealings. Late in 1930, he declared bankruptcy. A number of creditors initially filed suit but then dropped their cases. A federal grand jury in summer 1932 saw the bankruptcy as an effort to violate income tax laws and conceal assets, and indicted him for those offenses. Indicted on related conspiracy charges were Castaldo associates Columbus Christopher (James Cuneo) and Harry Bonsignore and Castaldo assistants Anthony Salerno, Thomas Salerno and Sebastiano Ciccone.

As the indictments were announced, U.S. Attorney George Z. Medalie told the press that Castaldo was the successor to Ciro "the Artichoke King" Terranova in the Harlem artichoke monopoly. Medalie said Castaldo controlled supply and wholesale pricing through the Union Pacific Produce Company of 230 West Street, formed in 1929. Medalie noted that Castaldo was also owner of two "taxi dance halls" on 125th Street.[159]

Castaldo's trial opened on February 1, 1933. On the third day of the proceedings, he pleaded guilty to six counts of tax evasion, related to income of $134,557 for the years 1929, 1930 and 1931; and two counts of concealment of assets totaling $20,000 in bankruptcy. He was sentenced to eleven months in the Federal House of Detention in Manhattan, with no possibility of early release (equivalent to a two-year sentence in federal prison).[160]

Soon after beginning his sentence, Castaldo was again indicted. This time the charge was violation of anti-trust laws. Union Pacific Produce partners Christopher (Cuneo) and Bonsignore, managers Ciccio Guira (Frank Romeo) and Joseph Migliaccia (Jack Romeo), and salesman Louis Prato were named as codefendants in the indictment returned on April 7, 1933.[161]

New York City's reform Mayor Fiorello La Guardia made an elaborate spectacle of halting the sale of artichokes in the city on December 21, 1935. The mayor announced that he was banning trade in the vegetable in order to prevent "racketeers, thugs or punks" from intimidating retailers – a situation that federal authorities already had been battling for several years. While the press and public still recalled Ciro Terranova as the leader of the artichoke racket, Terranova was not named in any indictment and claimed he had been uninvolved with artichoke sales for many years.[162]

La Guardia's dramatic action was still in recent memory when the anti-trust case against Castaldo and four codefendants (Guira remained at large) began late in January 1936. Federal Judge Julian W. Mack instructed jurors to disregard the mayor's edict relating to artichokes as they considered the evidence. That evidence included testimony relating to a pattern of violence and threats by Union Pacific Produce to compel produce shippers and retailers into purchase agreements.

Following twenty-four hours of deliberation, the trial jury on February 12 reported to Judge Mack that it was hopelessly deadlocked, with two of the twelve jurors voting for acquittal. Prosecutors planned to launch a new trial quickly. But Castaldo would not be part of it. On March 24, 1936, he pleaded guilty to anti-trust violation and received a sentence of one year on probation.[163]

The April 1940 U.S. Census found Castaldo, wife Josephine, son James and daughters Eugenia and Yolanda living at 401 East 106th Street, next door to their former residence. Castaldo reported working as proprietor of a restaurant. Son Antonio and his family lived in the same building. Son Alfred and his family lived nearby at 2058 First Avenue.[164]

Joseph Castaldo was retired at the time of the next federal census, in April 1950. The census recorded his age as sixty three. Josephine was working as a maker of artificial flowers. The one child still living with them was Yolanda, then eighteen. The family had recently moved to 3059 First Avenue, still in East Harlem.[165]

A little more than six weeks later, Castaldo passed away. A funeral Mass was celebrated at St. Lucy's Church, and he was buried at Calvary Cemetery. The official notice of his death stated his age as sixty two, suggesting that even in the closing moments of his life, Castaldo still had not settled on a birth date.[166]

Clementi, Carmine "Dolly Dimples"

> *Dolly and I used to walk around so much together that they started to call us the Dolly sisters.*[167]

Late in 1925, while serving time in Sing Sing Prison on a burglary sentence, Joseph Valachi met a new Sing Sing arrival he called, "Dolly Dimples."[168] Dolly was still in the segregated new-inmate area, known as the "ten-day house," when he asked to meet with Valachi. Their mutual friend "Joe," like Dolly, had recently arrived at the prison to begin a ten- to twenty-year sentence.

"So, I went and saw him," Valachi later wrote. In conversation, Dolly said he heard of the trouble Valachi had experienced with mob-linked gangsters in East Harlem. He said his own brother, known by the nickname "Coney Island," had been killed by mob gunmen years earlier.[169]

Valachi and Dolly decided to watch out for each other, and they became inseparable. Valachi joked that they were so often seen together that other inmates started calling them "the Dolly sisters."[170]

According to Valachi, Dolly's family was originally from the Naples area of Italy. An older inmate known to Valachi as "Alex" (Brooklyn Neapolitan gang boss Alessandro Vollero, who had warred against New York mafiosi) was aware of the family and recalled that Dolly's brother had been murdered by Sicilian-American gangsters.[171]

When Valachi was attacked by fellow inmate Pete LaTempa early in 1926, suffering a deep stab wound under his left arm, Dolly was first on the scene to assist Valachi and bring him to the prison hospital. To avoid retribution from Valachi's friends, LaTempa surrendered himself to prison officials and was transferred to Clinton State Prison at Dannemora.[172]

Valachi managed to talk Dolly out of a desperate prison escape plan. The plan, which included inmates known as "Tony" and "Pete the Greek," involved them setting up simultaneous visits from family and then forcing their way through guards in the visiting area and the front gate to a waiting car. Valachi convinced Dolly of the impossibility of success and the likelihood of their family members being harmed in the process.[173]

Valachi learned Dolly received his prison sentence after being convicted of a holdup at the Starlight Park swimming pool in the Bronx. "They were seven in all," he recalled of the robbery participants.[174] Valachi's pal, Dominick Petrelli arranged the holdup. "The job was his idea," Valachi wrote. "Only two of the guys got time for it – could have been three, I don't remember."[175]

"Dolly Dimples" had significant time left to serve in Sing Sing when Valachi was released. Valachi had conflicting memories about what happened to Dolly. In one story, he said "when [Dolly] was released from prison, he was out a week, and he went crazy and died in the crazy house at Dannemora State Prison."[176] The other account involved an inmate known as "Baldy," who once threatened Valachi with a knife only to be fought off by Dolly:

> ...I am about to go home. I told Dolly to behave and don't get into any trouble. I wasn't home a week when I heard on the outside that Dolly cut Baldy pretty bad and sent him to the hospital. And [Dolly] was shipped to Dannemora Prison, and he never was right ever since.[177]

Carmine "Dolly Dimples" Clementi was born in East Harlem near the end of 1904. He was the fourth son of Domenico and Filomena (Florence) Clementi. Domenico, who settled in the U.S. in the early 1890s, worked as a butcher. The family lived for many years in the same neighborhood near the intersection of East 114th Street and First Avenue.[178]

The oldest of the sons, Francesco "Coney Island" Clementi, in the 1910s involved himself in a Neapolitan-American criminal society known as the "Camorra." A branch of that organization, based at Brooklyn's Navy Street, was commanded by Alessandro Vollero. Clementi was a member when the Camorra went to war against the Terranova Mafia organization in East Harlem.

On September 7, 1916, Camorra leaders lured Nicholas "Coco" Terranova and his aide Eugene "Charles" Ubriaco to Brooklyn, where they were murdered.[179] Andrea Ricci, Camorra gunman and cousin of Vollero, was thought to be involved in the Terranova-Ubriaco murders, but evidence was insufficient to bring about his prosecution.[180] Lack of evidence did not prevent underworld retribution, however. Ricci was shot to death November 14, 1917, as he played cards in the back room of an Italian coffee house at 44 President Street in Brooklyn. The shot, which penetrated the left side of Ricci's head, apparently was fired through a window. The other card players bolted from the room, leaving behind their overcoats and a total of $34 in cash on the table.[181]

By that time, Camorra assassin Ralph "the Barber" Daniello was cooperating with investigators, as they assembled a murder case against Vollero and other gangland chiefs.[182] Prosecutors of Vollero in 1918 noted that a "Frank" Clementi, also known by the names "Rocco" and "Coney Island," insisted that Vollero guarantee the payment of funeral expenses for the murdered Ricci.[183]

Francesco Clementi also was murdered. He was shot to death on the night of February 25, 1918, on Philadelphia's Twelfth Street near Oxford Street. As Clementi neared Oxford Street, gunmen jumped out of an automobile behind him and shot him twice in the head. He died on the spot.

Reports indicated that police in several states had been looking for Clementi. They believed he and his Brooklyn-based gang were responsible for at least twenty five murders, with four of those killings occurring in Philadelphia. There were rumors that Clementi was killed by his own gangland buddies because they believed he had betrayed them.[184] But, in Sing Sing Prison, Vollero revealed that the rival Mafia organization was responsible.[185]

The holdup at the Starlight Amusement Park swimming pool occurred in the afternoon of August 12, 1925. Seven men bought pool tickets from a cashier at the 177th Street entrance and passed through a narrow, fifteen-foot-long corridor to the counter where valuables were checked by bathers. At that point, the men drew firearms on park employees and demanded that attendant May White turn over envelopes containing cash and other valuables from the check room. The value of the loot was estimated in thousands of dollars.

As they made their escape, they exchanged fire with off-duty police officer Sidney Rohn. Rohn was wounded in the shoulder. One of the robbers may have been wounded.[186]

Twenty-one-year-old Carmine Clementi was the first to be tried on charges of participating in the Starlight Park incident. He was convicted of first degree robbery, despite the absence of an important government witness – security guard William A. Peterson failed to appear in court. Bronx County Judge Albert Cohn sentenced Clementi to a minimum of ten years and a maximum of twenty years in prison. Cohn scheduled the Clementi sentencing to coincide with the September 30, 1925, sentencing of four other young thieves convicted in unrelated cases, in an effort to make an impression on young hoodlums.

"My duty here is a sad one," the judge said, "but a young highwayman is as great a menace as an older and, in fact, even greater since, in some cases, the younger may be more ready with his trigger finger."[187]

Clementi was delivered to Sing Sing on October 5. Two days later, prosecutors told Judge Cohn that the security guard did not appear at trial because Clementi had bribed him $1,000 to stay away. The judge found guard William Peterson in contempt and imposed a $250 fine and a thirty-day sentence.[188]

Clementi accomplices Joseph Pellegrino (possibly the "Joe" recalled by Valachi) and Basil Riccardi were brought to trial in the fall. Pellegrino was convicted and given a ten- to twenty-year sentence on October 13. On November 11, Riccardi was sentenced to twenty years.[189]

A possible fourth member of the seven-man robbery crew was arrested in early December. John Streppone was taken into custody on the complaint of an East Harlem tailor, who said Streppone robbed him of $132 in cash and a watch and chain. At the time of the arrest, authorities indicated that Streppone was a suspect in the Starlight Park robbery.[190]

At the time of the 1930 U.S. Census, Clementi was serving his sentence in Sing Sing, while Pellegrino and Riccardi were in Clinton State Prison at Dannemora. Clementi was transferred among state prisons in the early 1930s, apparently making stops at Clinton State Prison and Great Meadow State Prison in Comstock, New York.[191] Domenico Clementi passed away on September 28, 1935. His butcher shop was taken over by sons Ralph and Dominic Jr. By that time, Carmine Clementi was an inmate of the Dannemora State Hospital for the Criminally Insane. Filomena Clementi died eight years later. Carmine Clementi died at the Dannemora facility on June 29, 1950.[192]

Carmine Clementi enters Sing Sing in 1925.

Coco, Ettore "Eddie"

> *I asked was Eddie Coco there all afternoon. They said,*
> *"Yes," that he was asking all day, "Where is Joe?"*

After spending much of September 10, 1931, recreating with Dominick "the Gap" Petrelli and some women in Brooklyn, Valachi returned to East Harlem to find pals John DeBellis, Pete Leone and "Buck Jones" waiting for him. According to Valachi's autobiography, the three men had obvious powder burns to their faces and necks but no bullet wounds. They said they were attacked by a group of gangsters accompanied by Eddie Coco.

The group had been hanging around during the afternoon and, without warning, opened fire on them., They said their assailants included "Joe Swed, Micky Shapes, Danny Hogan and some other dog, and Eddie Coco was there." The mention of Coco interested Valachi, and he asked if Coco had been around all afternoon. "They said, 'Yes,' that he was asking all day, 'Where is Joe?'" They did not know why the attempt was made to shoot them, until they saw the newspaper and learned that their Mafia boss Salvatore Maranzano had been assassinated earlier in the day. They concluded that they were targeted because they were known to be Maranzano followers. Valachi decided that Petrelli had taken him to Brooklyn to keep him out of the way of the assassins.[193] Valachi's account does not make clear whether Coco was looking to kill Valachi or to warn him.

Valachi recalled Eddie Coco as one of the men he brought into the criminal society during the Castellammarese War of 1930-1931. Once the war ended – reigning Mafia boss of bosses Giuseppe Masseria was assassinated and Maranzano became the new boss of bosses in the spring of 1931 – New York's crime families reorganized. Valachi went into a Maranzano-run outfit, while Coco joined a crime family led by Tom Gagliano.[194]

While not discussed in his autobiography, Valachi revealed to the FBI that he heard Eddie Coco was involved in the December 1953 murder of Petrelli, who was believed to have become an informant for the Federal Bureau of Narcotics. According to Valachi, Coco was the driver of the three Mafia assassins who fatally shot "the Gap" in a Bronx saloon.[195]

Ettore "Eddie" Coco was born in Palermo, Sicily, on or about July 18, 1908.[196] His parents were Antonino and Felice Coco. He grew up in a household with two older brothers, Lodovico, born early in 1905, and Gaetano, born late in 1906. Felice died when Eddie was young. Antonino married again in the summer of 1912, taking Santina Sapienza, a native of Catania, as his bride.[197]

In the spring of 1921, Antonino Coco left his wife and sons in Sicily and sailed to the U.S. He reached New York on May 25 and joined an uncle in the Village of Lawrence in Nassau County. Santa and the three boys – all teenagers at the time – joined Antonino on Manhattan's Lower East Side near the end of July 1922.[198] By the time of the 1925 New York Census, the family was living at 167 East 110th Street in East Harlem. Antonino worked as a painter.[199]

Ettore married Louise Ippolito on November 19, 1927, at St. Ann's Roman Catholic Church on East 110th Street. He was twenty eight. According to the marriage certificate, his bride was just fifteen. The apartments of their two families sat across the street from each other. Ettore's big brother Lodovico was his best man.

During the 1930-1931 Castellammarese War, Ettore Coco became a "soldier" in a Bronx and East Harlem organization led by Tommaso Gagliano. He may have been introduced to that organization by Joseph Valachi. Gagliano's group was closely aligned with Salvatore Maranzano through the April 1931 conclusion of the conflict. However, in the late summer of 1931, as Maranzano plotting a new war against Salvatore "Charlie Luciano" Lucania, Vito Genovese and others, Gagliano lieutenant Gaetano Lucchese aided Lucania in setting up the September 10, 1931, assassination of Maranzano.[200] On the day that Maranzano was murdered, Ettore went looking for Valachi in East Harlem. His reason for doing so is unknown.

Valachi and Coco had roles in an early 1932 botched hit against a small gang known as the Shoemaker Brothers. The brothers and a friend from Yorkville, Manhattan, were to be murdered for the disrespect they showed by repeatedly robbing the saloon of a Gagliano member. Valachi had tried without luck to persuade the Shoemakers that they should leave the saloon alone. When the brothers later met with Valachi to discuss a suspicious invitation to work on a robbery with some members of the Gagliano Crime Family, Valachi told them it was safe. Coco, Frank "Chick 99" Callace, Salvatore "Sally Shields" Shillitani and Nick Paduano went to meet the Shoemaker Brothers in the Bronx on January 28, 1932, planning to eliminate all of them. The Gaglianos fatally shot the Shoemakers' friend from Yorkville, but the Shoemakers got away. An off-duty police officer emerged from a nearby residence and pursued the mafiosi, killing Paduano and arresting Shillitani. Coco and Callace escaped.[201]

Coco allegedly was involved in a curious autumn 1933 incident on the Upper West Side. Before dawn on October 30, two married couples were returning to their homes after a bridge party. As they passed a club at 244 West Seventy-first Street, five men on the sidewalk urged them to go inside. When they refused, the men became violent. The victims complained to the police, and Coco, Thomas Gonzo, Joseph Vannelli, Alfred Rinaldi and Frank Bruno were arrested for assault.[202]

A brush with the law on April 26, 1939, was more odd. A New York State trooper on motorcycle duty stopped a speeding car on the Bronx River Parkway Extension near Pinesbridge Road in Ossining. When the officer saw the four occupants of the vehicle, he became suspicious and brought them to the Hawthorne Barracks for questioning.

The four were identified as Charles "Charlie Bullets" Albero, thirty seven, who was the vehicle's driver despite having no license with him; Coco, thirty two; Carmine Paul Tramunti, twenty eight; and Frank Noto, thirty eight. The only occupant who did not have a criminal record was Noto.

The men were charged before a local justice of the peace with consorting with known criminals for an unlawful purpose. Surprisingly, all pleaded guilty. Noto received a suspended sentence. The others were sentenced to thirty days in the Westchester County Penitentiary. Albero was also fined $10 for speeding and another $5 for driving without a license.

An investigation revealed that Tramunti had recently been released from Sing Sing Prison on parole. The consorting case was deemed a violation of his parole terms, and he was returned to Sing Sing.[203]

Just a couple of days after beginning their sentences in Westchester, Coco and Albero filed appeals and were released on $250 bail each. They were brought before the Yorktown, New York, justice of the peace on August 3 for a hearing on their appeal. Early in the proceedings, Albero interrupted a prosecution witness with an announcement: "I want to plead guilty." Coco followed suit. They were then sentenced to the same thirty day sentences, and the justice of the peace added $50 fines and specified that they would serve an additional day in prison for each dollar of fine left unpaid. Both of the prisoners had about $100 on them at the time, but both refused to pay any portion of the fine at that time.[204]

Coco filed his military draft registration in October 1940. He indicated that he lived at 2043 Colonial Avenue in the Bronx and worked at Stillman's Gym, the historic training spot for New York boxers, on Manhattan's Eighth Avenue between Fifty-fourth and Fifty-fifth streets. As his closest relative, Coco listed his father, a resident of the same Colonial Avenue address. He did not mention his 1927 bride Louise.[205]

In the 1940s, Coco became part of the management of boxer Rocky Graziano. He also became a secret partner with other mafiosi in "The Combination," an undercover cartel of boxing managers. Graziano became Middleweight champion with a Chicago victory over Tony Zale in the summer of 1947. That occurred a year after Graziano was prohibited from fighting in his home state of New York because he failed to report to the New York State Athletic Commission about a bribe offer.[206]

Law enforcement became interested in Graziano. Early in 1948, Manhattan District Attorney Frank S. Hogan brought three of the boxer's managers before a grand jury. Each was asked to sign a waiver of immunity – giving up the right to remain silent – before they were questioned. Irving Cohen agreed to the waiver and testified. Coco and Jack Haley refused the waiver, and they were excused.[207]

Graziano postponed and then walked out on a scheduled bout in Oakland, California, in 1948. He stated, "I no longer have any desire to fight." That resulted in his suspension by the California Boxing Commission and by the National Boxing Association. Eddie Coco, the one Graziano manager who traveled with Graziano to California, was also suspended from activity in boxing. Manager Irving Cohen, who had remained in New York, was not named in the action.[208]

For the 1950 U.S. Census, Coco reported working as a freelance fight manager. He said he and a wife named Rosa, born in Missouri, were residents of 340 East Fifty-second Street in Manhattan.[209] A short time later in 1950, Coco acquired a boxing manager license from the Wisconsin State Athletic Commission. In his application, he pointed to the Colonial Avenue address in the Bronx as his home and indicated that his sole interest in boxing was representation of Rocky Graziano.[210]

In the New York underworld, Coco became a powerful member of the Bronx-based Mafia organization led by Gagliano until his death 1951 and then led by Tommy Lucchese. Coco was regarded as the proprietor of "one of the biggest floating crap games in town," which shifted locations between West Harlem and Westchester and catered to big-money gamblers. He also was suspected of involvement in large-scale narcotics trafficking rackets.[211]

Coco was described as "a former… fight manager" in February 1951, when he was charged in Florida with the murder of car washer Johnny Benjamin Smith. Smith washed the cars of residents at 6941 Bay Drive, Normandy Isle in the north of Miami Beach. Coco lived at that apartment building that winter. On Thursday morning, February 1, Coco drove up to the building with a young woman. Before they went inside, Smith approached Coco and mentioned some money Coco owed him. Coco took the woman inside, but soon returned. According to a witness, he drew a handgun and fired twice at Smith. When Smith staggered away, Coco fired again, sending him to the ground. Then the longtime New York mafioso stood over his fallen victim and put two more bullets into the man's body.[212]

Police arrived to find Coco asleep inside his apartment with a woman identified as his thirty-five-year-old common-law wife Rosalia Plas. He was taken into custody, charged with first-degree murder and held without bail in Dade County Jail. Rosalia Plas was held as a material witness.[213]

A jury convicted Coco of second-degree murder in June 1951. He was sentenced to life in prison but allowed to remain free on $25,000 bond during his lengthy legal appeals. On January 21, 1953, the Florida State Supreme Court found that the trial judge erred in not permitting cross-examination of an expert fingerprint witness and ordered a new trial for Coco.[214]

Coco was again convicted of second-degree murder on October 28, 1953. A six-man jury returned the verdict after five hours of deliberation. Once again on November 12, 1953, he was sentenced to life in prison, and once again he was permitted to remain free pending appeals. Shortly after receiving his sentence, the gangster attempted to avoid payment of $652 in court costs by arguing insolvency. He claimed that he was broke and being financially supported by friends in New Jersey. He later dropped this argument.[215]

While free awaiting his second appeal to the Florida Supreme Court, Coco reportedly served as driver for the assassins of Dominick "the Gap" Petrelli in New York City. The murder was committed December 9, 1953, at a bar run by Alfred Mauriello, brother of former boxer Tami Mauriello. Three gunmen entered the bar, pursued Petrelli to a bathroom and shot him to death.[216]

Early in May 1955, Florida's high court refused to hear Coco's appeal. He surrendered himself to Florida authorities, though he filed an appeal with the U.S. Supreme Court. On May 13, he was taken to the Florida State Penitentiary at Raiford to begin a life sentence for a murder committed more than four years earlier.[217]

Ettore Coco served just ten years of the sentence before he was paroled and quietly released from the state's Avon Park Correctional Institution on August 17, 1965. News of the parole did not reach the press until the following week.[218] Under the terms of his parole, Coco was not permitted to leave Florida for the remainder of his life.

Back in New York at this time, crime family boss Tommy Lucchese was hospitalized for a brain tumor. After surgery and a long stay at Columbia Presbyterian Medical Center, the sixty-seven-year-old Lucchese was sent to his home at Lido Beach, Long Island, in April 1967. He died there three months later.[219]

New York police believed Ettore Coco was a contender to succeed Lucchese as crime family boss. Sources within the FBI said Coco's parole restrictions prevented him from assuming the top spot but acknowledged that recent convictions had deprived the organization of other top men, such as John Dioguardi, James Plumeri, Vincent Rao and Carmine Tramunti. With limited options, it appears the organization had Coco operate remotely as "acting boss" for a time. Federal agents noted that crime family lieutenants Anthony "Tony Ducks" Corallo and Paul Vario made visits to Coco in Florida in 1967 and 1968.[220]

Near the end of 1967, an informant told the FBI that Tramunti was moving into the position of boss, with Corallo next in line.[221]

In March of 1972, Coco applied to the Florida Pardon Board for clemency, arguing that the parole restriction preventing travel was a hardship on his family. His timing was bad. In June, Ettore Coco and Fort Lauderdale resident Louis Nash were named in an eight-count federal indictment for loan sharking, conspiracy and extortion. They were arrested by agents of the Internal Revenue Service.[222]

At the conclusion of a three-day trial in Miami federal court, which included wiretap evidence of the use of threats to collect on usurious loans, Coco was convicted on six counts and Nash was convicted on five counts. Two weeks later, the Florida Parole Commission revoked Coco's parole and ordered him returned to state prison to resume his life sentence for murder.[223]

Federal Judge Peter Fay on October 17 sentenced Coco to fifteen years and a $60,000 fine in the loan-sharking case. Nash received ten years and a $5,000 fine. Coco appealed his conviction on the grounds that the wiretap evidence used against him was not legally obtained – an objection that famed underworld attorney Frank Ragano neglected to make during the trial. The Fifth Circuit Court of Appeals ruled against him in 1978.[224]

Ettore Coco's release from state prison was not noted. He was released from federal custody on October 25, 1984, when he was seventy six.[225] Coco apparently returned to New York City.

Late in October of 1990, when he was eighty two, he was named in a federal indictment for participating in a plot to launder mob money through a large-scale bingo parlor in Maryland. The racket involved underworld figures from Florida, Illinois and New York. According to prosecutors, the semi-retired Coco provided Lucchese Crime Family permission for the operation and arranged for an arsonist to damage a competing bingo hall.

Coco did not live long enough to stand trial. He passed away in New York City on the day after Christmas in 1991.[226]

D'Anna, Vincent "Doc"

> *Now as we walk in the house, Buster and the Doc came right*
> *over and shook hands with us, and Buster brought me to*
> *meet Salvatore Maranzano.*[227]

Valachi recalled first meeting "Doc," along with Nick Capuzzi, Joe Profaci and "Buster" in the autumn of 1930 at the Bronx apartment used to set up the murder of Giuseppe Masseria supporter Stefano Ferrigno. Following the November murders of Ferrigno and Manfredi "Al" Mineo, Valachi was brought to a location about ninety miles north of New York City, where he met Masseria's main Castellammarese War opponent Salvatore Maranzano. Both "Doc" and "Buster" were present for the meeting and for the ceremonial induction of Valachi into "Cosa Nostra," which followed.[228]

Apparently a top aide to Maranzano, "Doc" was next encountered when Valachi and a partner botched the responsibility of manning the former Maranzano residence in Brooklyn, jokingly referred to as "the haunted house." It appeared that both men had been frightened away from their task. Valachi was summoned to Maranzano headquarters near Yonkers, New York. When he arrived, "everyone was laughing... Joe Profaci and the Doc were kidding me and so was Bobby Doyle." Maranzano decided that Valachi was not at fault, and he had "Buster" and "Doc" drive him back to the Brooklyn house.[229]

A bit later, Maranzano sent "Doc" as an emissary to the home of Frank Scalise, a top man in an outfit aligned with Masseria. Scalise was preparing to switch sides in the war. As protection for "Doc," Maranzano also sent Valachi, "Buster" and "Solly Shields" Shillitani. Maranzano instructed the group: "You guys go, and Doc will do all the talking."[230]

Valachi, "Buster" and "Doc" became very close through the war. When it was over, "Buster" and Valachi had a quiet conversation about their commitment to each other's safety. They agreed that if the boss instructed either of them to kill the other, he would instead turn on the boss. Valachi asked if anyone else felt the same way about them, and "Buster" said, "Yes, the Doc."[231]

Vincent "Doc" D'Anna was born August 19, 1906, at Castellammare del Golfo, Sicily. He was not actually a doctor, but there were medical professionals in his family. His father Alessandro was a druggist, his brother Antonino became a physician in Canada, and his brother's wife Laura was a chemist. Vincent D'Anna appears to have settled in Brooklyn, in the late 1920s, as his brother was establishing himself in Montreal, Canada.[232]

Late in 1932, D'Anna, then working as a contractor, married Leonarda

"Nellie" Catanzaro. His bride was the New York-born daughter of Accursio "Gus" and Agostina DiMino Catanzaro. Sebastiano "Buster" Domingo was D'Anna's best man for the Manhattan civil ceremony. The other witness was Fay R. Maggio. D'Anna and his wife made a home at 183 Allen Street on Manhattan's Lower East Side, about a block from the Catanzaro home on Eldridge Street.[233] D'Anna and Domingo, closely associated during the Castellammarese War, remained emotionally and geographically close following the war. Domingo's residence in this period was 205 Allen Street.[234]

About half a year after the wedding, gunmen intruded on a late night card game in the Castle Cafe, 72 East First Street in Manhattan. One yelled out, "You bunch of rats!" as they opened fire. When police arrived at the scene near midnight on May 30, 1933, they found "Buster" Domingo dead on the sidewalk outside of the cafe. Inside the establishment, they found five wounded: Salvatore Ferraro, thirty two; Vito DiBenedetto, twenty; Ignacio Lobretto, twenty; Irving Mannes, sixteen; and Bernard Blaustein, fifteen.[235]

An autopsy determined that bullets had penetrated both of Domingo's lungs and his aorta, causing hemorrhage into his chest.[236]

Ferraro, a resident of 216 Eldridge Street, was taken to Bellevue Hospital with bullet wounds to his left chest, left arm, diaphragm and stomach. He succumbed to his wounds at six fifty the following evening. Like Domingo, Ferraro had a connection to Vincent D'Anna. The Italy-born son of Arcangelo and Rosa Curatolo Ferraro, Salvatore Ferraro was married to D'Anna's sister-in-law Carmela "Millie" Catanzaro.[237]

Funeral arrangements for Domingo and Ferraro were handled by undertakers Anello and Bonventre of Central Avenue in Brooklyn. Both men were buried June 3 at St. John Cemetery in Queens, New York.[238]

Whatever motivated the killings of Domingo and Ferraro, Vincent D'Anna appears to have been uninvolved. He continued to reside on Allen Street. He and his wife had two sons there: Alessandro, born in 1934, and Antonino, born in 1939. D'Anna worked for a time as partner to a retailer of ladies suits and coats. By the end of 1940, he also opened a florist shop on Driggs Avenue in Brooklyn.[239]

At the time of D'Anna's December 1945 naturalization petition, he and his family resided at 1343 Eighty-first Street in Brooklyn. The witnesses to that petition were Brooklynites Paul Sciacca of Barbey Street and Michael Biamonte of 265 Melrose Street. The petition was approved in March 1946.[240]

The D'Anna family resided at 1202 Tabor Court, between Tabor Street and Sixty-second Street in Brooklyn, when their third child, son Vincent Jr., was born in April 1950.[241]

Vincent D'Anna died three years later, on July 19, 1953, at the age of just forty six. Anello and Bonventre once again took charge of funeral arrangements. Following a Requiem High Mass at the Regina Pacis Roman Catholic Church in Brooklyn, D'Anna was interred at Calvary Cemetery.[242]

Vincent Danna (far right) at the Copacabana with (from left) Stefano Magaddino, Joseph Bonanno, Salvatore "Bill" Bonanno, Gaspare DiGregorio.
(A Man of Honor)

DeBellis, John "Johnny Dee"

> *I get at the wheel and Johnnie at my right... and someone comes up from the floor of the car in the back seat and he says, "Hello, Joe." I look around and I see Chuck. In the meantime Johnnie sees him and he gets out of the car and he says good night.*[243]

Valachi took great offense when "Johnny Dee" DeBellis, near the end of 1930, abandoned him to face East Harlem hoodlum "Crazy Chuck" alone. He avoided working with DeBellis for years after that, and only grudgingly did so around the late 1930s when instructed by Anthony Strollo to do so. In that assignment, Valachi supervised a beating administered by DeBellis and Tommy Eboli to one of the "Wackie brothers," linked with the crime family led by Tommaso Gagliano and Gaetano Lucchese. The assignment did not cause Valachi to feel any better about DeBellis, as Strollo made it appear that Valachi ordered the beating on his own.[244]

It appears that DeBellis was one of a number of men brought to Salvatore Maranzano during the 1930-31 Castellammarese War as prospective mafiosi. Shortly after the September 10, 1931, assassination of Maranzano, DeBellis and companions Stephen "Buck Jones" Casertano and Pete "Muggins" Leone were also attacked but escaped with just powder burns.[245]

A short time after the Maranzano assassination, Genovese called a handful of Maranzano's former aides to a meeting at the Cornish Arms Hotel on West Twenty-third Street. The meeting was attended by Valachi, DeBellis, Casertano, Leone and Girolamo "Bobby Doyle" Santuccio. Genovese explained to the group that he and his boss Salvatore "Charlie Luciano" Lucania had ordered the murder of Maranzano because Maranzano was plotting to kill them. All agreed to let bygones be bygones. The group was welcomed into the crime family of Lucania and Genovese and placed in the regime led by Anthony "Tony Bender" Strollo.[246]

Valachi worked with DeBellis and Leone on the assigned November 1932 murder of Michael "Little Apples" Reggione. Hearing that Genovese and Strollo wanted "Little Apples" dead, Valachi led Reggione to a building at 340 East 110th Street near First Avenue, where gambling was supposedly going on. DeBellis and Leone met Reggione in the building and shot him to death.[247]

Born April 10, 1891, in Corleone, Sicily, Giovanni DeBellis was the son of Giovanni Sr. and Antonia Cascio DeBellis. His father sailed to America around 1903 and settled in New York City. Antonia, Giovanni Jr. (Johnny Dee) and two other children crossed the Atlantic in June 1904 and joined Giovanni Sr. at 424 East 104th Street in East Harlem.[248]

Johnny Dee was eighteen and working as the wagon driver for his father's soda water business at the time of the 1910 U.S. Census. He resided with his parents and siblings at 323 East 106th Street.[249]

In spring of 1911, DeBellis and partner Barnett Shapiro were caught breaking into an East Harlem store owned by Isidore Cohen. They were convicted on May 11 of third degree burglary. DeBellis was sentenced to a year in prison and a $500 fine.[250]

At about the same time, he received a suspended sentence for carrying a concealed weapon. This made him a second-time offender when he was found to be illegally in possession of a revolver in December 1913. He was indicted in January 1914 for a second offense of criminally carrying a firearm. He was convicted February 11 and sentenced February 19 to a state prison term of seven years and nine months. He entered Sing Sing Prison near the end of the month.[251]

Legal appeals were filed, arguing that DeBellis was not yet an adult when first convicted on a weapons charge (his birth year was moved ahead a bit to support this position) and should have faced a less lengthy first-timer's penalty on the next possession conviction. The argument failed to persuade judges of the New York County General Sessions Court and the Appellate Division of the First Judicial Department.[252]

It did persuade Governor Charles Whitman. In February 1917, the governor commuted Johnny Dee's sentence to a minimum of three years and fifteen days from the time of his entry into Sing Sing. That minimum sentence expired in mid-March, and DeBellis returned to the family home at East 106th Street.[253]

DeBellis was inducted into the U.S. Army in May 1918. He served overseas as a private with the Quartermaster Corps through the final days of the Great War and for most of a year after that. He returned to the U.S. on August 17, 1919, and was honorably discharged on August 19.[254]

Johnny Dee went back to his parents' home and to his former job in his father's soda water company. During the 1920s, he likely began his association with Joe Valachi. DeBellis's mother died on October 31, 1929, following kidney failure.[255]

In May, 1943, John DeBellis was still residing with his widowed father, though their address had changed slightly to 309 East 106th Street, when Giovanni Sr. passed away at the age of ninety.[256]

Johnny Dee made a home for himself in the Amity Harbor section of Copiague hamlet in Suffolk County. That was his last recorded address at the time of his death on March 12, 1968.[257]

DeBellis gravesite. (Find A Grave)

DeQuarto, Dominick "Dom the Sailor"

> *...Dom the Sailor was kidding me, and there were most of the boys there, so I told Dom the Sailor, "Listen careful. I don't know you good enough, so I don't want you to kid me."*[258]

Valachi first encountered "Dom the Sailor," when he and Pete "Muggins" began hanging out at Valachi's Lido Restaurant. The two visitors annoyed Valachi by continually asking about a Valachi acquaintance named Vinnie, who was out of favor with their gangland boss Vito Genovese. Valachi suspected that Genovese had deliberately sent the two to pressure Valachi on his relationship with Vinnie, and that guess was later confirmed by Genovese.[259]

"Dom the Sailor" was merciless in his teasing of Valachi, even continuing it when both attended the wake of a fellow mafioso. Things changed at that wake, when Valachi confronted him and told him to stop.[260]

Genovese learned that Valachi was involving himself in narcotics trafficking despite a crime family rule against that racket. The boss summoned Valachi to a meeting about that at the home of "Dom the Sailor" in Yonkers, New York. Valachi brought his nephew and crime associate Fiore Siano with him to the meeting. After admitting to Genovese that he knowingly disobeyed the narcotics order, Valachi was given a simple scolding and told not to do it again. Valachi knew at the time that Genovese had received a large portion of the narcotics deal proceeds.[261]

After Genovese removed Anthony "Tony Bender" Strollo from his crime family's hierarchy, he inserted "Dom the Sailor" in Strollo's place.[262]

Dominick "Dom the Sailor" DiQuarto (whose surname has been written a variety of ways, including "DeQuarto," "DeQuatro" and "DiQuatro") was born in Manhattan on June 22, 1922, the third child and only son of Gioacchino "Jack" and Vincenzina "Jenny" Sicari DiQuarto. Jack DiQuarto, a native of Bagheria, Sicily, first arrived in New York as a toddler in the early 1900s, went back to Sicily with his family for a short time and then returned to New York in December 1909. At the time of Dominick's birth, Jack was working as a chauffeur.[263]

While born in Manhattan, Dominick spent much of his childhood in the boroughs of Queens and Brooklyn. He went back to live in Manhattan sometime after his World War II-era draft registration. The registration document, filed in Brooklyn on June 20, 1942, initially showed his home address as 250 Melrose Street, Brooklyn (where his parents lived at the time). That was crossed out, and 985 Flushing Avenue was written in, along with a date of December 16, 1942. That date also was crossed out and replaced with "67 Thompson Street, NYC."[264]

The Thompson Street address remained his home into the 1950s, as DiQuarto became a powerful member of the criminal organization run by Frank Costello. At the time of the 1950 U.S. Census, the twenty-seven-year-old DiQuarto was living at that address with his wife Lillian. He reported his occupation as "handyman."[265]

DiQuarto reportedly was handy with money and with gambling operations during the 1950s. He was thought to be overseeing financial arrangements for mob-run gambling enterprises in south Florida and the Bahamas. Travel documents from late July 1955, show him flying from New York City to Nassau, Bahamas, to Miami, Florida, and back to New York in a two-week period.[266]

About that time, he became a resident of Yonkers, New York. Police arrested him at his home, 42 Raybrook Road in the southeastern part of that city, on May 15, 1956, and turned him over to authorities in New York City, where he was wanted on fifteen counts of motor vehicle violations.[267]

In spring 1957, Vito Genovese planned to assassinate Frank Costello and assume command of his organization. Genovese initially met with crime family lieutenant Anthony "Tony Bender" Strollo and Vincent Mauro to set up the operation, and then assigned Joseph Valachi and another Mafia soldier to work with Mauro. (Valachi recalled that he was concerned by the fact that he was excluded from the planning session.) Mauro hesitated to do the job, and Genovese reportedly assigned a second team to carry out the assassination. The team went into action on May 2, but failed to eliminate Costello, delivering only superficial wound to Costello's scalp. The FBI, benefiting from Valachi's recollections, later identified Vincent Gigante, Dominick DiQuarto and Tommy Eboli as the members of the second team.[268] DiQuarto was suspected of being the driver of the getaway car.[269]

Though the assassination failed, Costello stepped aside, and Genovese became crime family boss. His direct control of family activities would last only a short time, as he was indicted on narcotics charges in the summer of 1958 and convicted the following spring.

Valachi recalled that Genovese shuffled leadership roles when he went to prison. He elevated Strollo to an underboss role and inserted Dominick the Sailor to command Strollo's former crew. While serving his sentence in Atlanta Federal Prison, Genovese had second thoughts about Strollo. From inside the prison walls, he ordered Strollo's elimination. On Sunday evening, April 8, 1962, Strollo told his wife he was going out for a few minutes. He left their Fort Lee, New Jersey, home and was never seen again.

At about the same time, Genovese demoted DiQuarto and put Pasquale "Patsy Ryan" Eboli in command of the former Strollo crew.[270]

DiQuarto, by then dividing his time between homes in Florida and New Jersey, was suspected of involvement in the apparent execution of Strollo. In September 1968, when summoned before a legislative committee in Florida, he was asked if he had been involved in the shooting of Frank Costello and in the elimination of Strollo. He refused to answer. He also refused to answer questions about his involvement in Florida and Bahamas gambling, about his reported roles in loan sharking and narcotics rackets, about his relationships to other Genovese Crime Family leaders. In fact, he refused to provide any information aside from his name.[271]

That Florida appearance led to a period of increased press and law enforcement attention for DiQuarto. He was called to testify before New Jersey's State Investigation Commission in April 1970.[272] A few months later, a New Jersey newspaper included him in a report about top mob figures who resided in the state:

> He has been identified by state investigators as a rising star in the Catena [part of the post-Genovese leadership] mob family... DeQuarto has business interests on the Brooklyn waterfront. In 1964, the Senate investigation identified him as a gambling figure

and loan shark. He has a long arrest record with the FBI and New York police.[273]

In 1973, a federal grand jury in Florida began investigating Dominick DiQuarto's lack of tax filings since 1939, despite an apparently luxurious lifestyle. Three grand jury witnesses were jailed for contempt in April. Despite being given immunity from prosecution, the witnesses refused to provide any information.

In December of that year, attorney Martin Blitstein, who represented those witnesses, was indicted for obstructing justice. Prosecutors charged that he had persuaded the witnesses not to cooperate in the grand jury probe.

One month later, in January 1974, DiQuarto was arrested in New York City on the same charge as Blitstein. Authorities also went in search of a DiQuarto aide Thomas Magana. Named in the same indictment, Magana had not been seen in two months. Months later, Frank Baffa, secretary-treasurer of an International Longshoremen's Association local in New York City, was indicted for making false statements about DiQuarto when brought before the grand jury in Florida.[274]

In spring 1975, another newspaper feature on mobsters in New Jersey listed DiQuarto among the underworld chiefs residing in Bergen County. The list included such names as Joe "Adonis" Doto, Albert Anastasia, Guarino "Willie Moore" Moretti, Tommy "Ryan" Eboli, Anthony Strollo and Eli "the Baker" Zeccardi.[275]

DiQuarto remained close to crime family leadership. He was characterized as a top aide to faction leader Eli Zeccardi. Acting as a screen for the real crime family leadership, Zeccardi was widely believed to be the top boss in April 1977, when he was reported abducted. There were stories of a ransom demand and a payment of $100,000, but Zeccardi did not return. Soon after Zeccardi disappeared, press reports said DiQuarto too was missing.[276]

But "Dom the Sailor" continued to reside in Bergen County, New Jersey, until his December 6, 1988, death at the age of sixty six.[277]

DiBenedetto, Michael

> *Valachi stated De Benedetta was killed because he was*
> *believed to be a "wrong guy," meaning police informer.*[278]

Michael DiBenedetto was not discussed in Joseph Valachi's biography, *The Valachi Papers*, or in his autobiography, *The Real Thing*, but Valachi provided some details about DiBenedetto's 1937 murder to FBI agents during an interview early in 1963.

Valachi indicated that DiBenedetto, who was known to him as "Mike the Crabber," was murdered on orders of "Trigger Mike" Coppola. According to Valachi, Coppola believed DiBenedetto was providing information to police. Valachi recalled that "the Crabber" was killed near his home on East 107th Street.[279]

DiBenedetto was born September 28, 1907, in East Harlem, to Michael Sr. and Grace DiBenedetto. His father worked as a stone cutter. Young Michael grew up at 400 East 107th Street, the sixth of seven children.[280]

He was in his teens when first arrested. A grand larceny charge was dropped. In the same year, he married Ernesta Lombardi in a Manhattan civil ceremony, and then faced a six-month prison term following a burglary conviction. After his release from prison, he and Ernesta were again married in a June 11, 1925, religious ceremony at St. Lucy's Church in East Harlem.[281]

"The Crabber" was sentenced in autumn 1925 to five years in state prison after confessing to a robbery. He served the sentence at the Sing Sing and Great Meadow facilities, and was identified as part of a prison gang fight at Great Meadow in 1928. He was paroled in April 1929, but was picked up for vagrancy that August. A five-day sentence at the workhouse became a return to Sing Sing for parole violation.[282] In 1930, DiBenedetto was living with wife Ernesta and their young son at the home of Ernesta's parents, 247 East 114th Street. He claimed employment as a theater usher.[283]

Police were drawn to a suspicious automobile parked in front of a cafe at 2311 Third Avenue on Thursday, February 12, 1931. As they approached, four men rushed out of the cafe to the car. Spotting the police, one of the men, later identified as Frank Viserto, twenty six, suddenly moved his hand to his back pocket. One of the officers shot Viserto in the arm. Michael DiBenedetto and

Richard Manfredoni dropped handguns to the sidewalk as they surrendered. The fourth man, identified as Stephen Niznick, was unarmed. A charge of illegal weapons possession against DiBenedetto was later dismissed.[284]

Harry Maranos and Samuel Drazen, proprietors of the Garfield Wet Wash Laundry on Third Street in Brooklyn, brought a complaint to police early in 1932. They said they had been robbed and kidnapped. Three men went to their business on January 18, they said, forced them into a car and drove them to 66 West Seventy-seventh Street on Manhattan's Upper West Side. The three took cash from Maranos and demanded a ransom of several hundred dollars. The laundrymen were released only after arranging to pay the ransom in a series of installments. After release, Maranos and Drazen faced additional demands for money and surrendered a total of $400 before going to the authorities.

On March 11, police arrested Frank Caiola and Joseph Morganelli of the Bronx for the kidnapping and robbery. Eleven days later, Michael DiBenedetto turned up in Yonkers, New York. Local police picked him up on a charge of illegal possession of a firearm, but dropped that as they turned him over to police in Brooklyn. He was charged as the third kidnapper.[285]

Real estate valued at $100,000 was pledged as security to win the April release of the three suspects. DiBenedetto couldn't escape law enforcement notice while awaiting trial. Late in 1932, he was convicted of disorderly conduct in Jersey City, New Jersey, and sentenced to ninety days behind bars.[286]

The kidnapping trial opened in Kings County Court in March 1933. The defendants had a team of lawyers, including disgraced former Magistrate Albert H. Vitale (removed from the bench after being shown to have had improper financial relationships with underworld figures). The defense also made use of the Berkshire Detective Agency led by Robert "Rocky" Lawrence.

According to the defense, no kidnapping occurred. There had been a conflict between Caiola and Drazen over a woman – a Manhattan nightclub entertainer named Marie Murdock – and the group went together to the Upper West Side to resolve it. In the prosecution's summation, Assistant District Attorney William W. Kleinman noted the curious involvement of the Berkshire Detective Agency in the case and commented, "There is something fishy here that we can't exactly put our finger on." Some portion of the jury apparently accepted the defense story. After five hours of deliberation, the panel reported on March 30 that it was hopelessly deadlocked.[287]

The kidnapping matter was discussed in separate legal proceedings in summer and autumn of 1933. Jacob "Red" Mellon went to trial in Brooklyn for overseeing a coercive monopoly of Brooklyn laundries. Mellon was found to have provided the bail for accused kidnappers DiBenedetto, Caiola and Morganelli, and the kidnappers were described by police as henchmen for racketeer Anthony "Little Augie Pisano" Carfano. At Mellon's trial, the alleged laundry czar claimed that he did not know the three men and only provided the bail when asked to do so by Kings County Sheriff James A. McQuade.[288]

In 1934, DiBenedetto was sentenced to an indefinite prison term for attempted extortion.[289]

He and seventeen others with criminal records were arrested in March 1936 in a raid at the American Confidential Bureau offices on Manhattan's Fifth Avenue. According to Charles W. Hansen, president of the private detective agency, DiBenedetto and other racketeers had taken over his business and were using it to supply thugs to combat a strike of city building service workers – generally furnace tenders and elevator operators. When police asked the expensively-dressed DiBenedetto his occupation, he responded that he had "several irons in the fire." One of the "irons" was reportedly welfare assistance from the Home Relief Bureau.[290]

Shots were fired outside of DiBenedetto's apartment building, 341 East 107th Street at the northwest corner with First Avenue, just before five in the morning of February 19, 1937. When police arrived, they found Michael DiBenedetto dead on the front steps. A post-mortem examination determined that he had suffered multiple bullet wounds to his "left back, right chest, abdomen, lumbar region, lung, liver, small and large intestines, left common iliac artery and vein." These caused a hemorrhage into his chest and abdominal cavity. It was surmised that a gunman opened fire on him as he entered the home he shared with his wife and child, as well as his mother and sister. The gunmen fired more shots when DiBenedetto turned and attempted to run.[291]

At the time of his death, DiBenedetto's police record included sixteen arrests for burglary, extortion, kidnapping, labor racketeering, robbery and vagrancy through a period of just thirteen years. He was not yet thirty years old. Newspaper reports linked him with East Harlem crime figure Joey Rao, but his killing remained unsolved.[292]

Elliott, Assoc. Warden Marion Jesse

> *Now Elliott calls me down and he tells me that he is going to burn me. I asked him is this what the mob wants and he said yes. Boy I thought that the underworld was bad this guy Ellicott is a monster.*[293]

In his autobiography, Valachi referred to the early-1960s associate warden at Atlanta Federal Prison as "Mr. Elliott" and "Mr. Ellicott."[294] In late spring of 1962, Valachi became convinced that Mafia boss Vito Genovese some other mafiosi, incarcerated with Valachi in Atlanta, were planning to kill him. He sought the protection of solitary confinement and sent a letter to his wife back in New York, which contained an appeal for help to friendly Mafia boss Tommy Lucchese.

These efforts were thwarted by "Ellicott." The associate warden removed him from solitary, though it clearly put Valachi's life in danger and, according to Valachi, was in violation of federal prison rules. He also refused to mail Valachi's letter to his wife. Ellicott tried to pressure Valachi to precisely state why he needed protection. Believing the associate warden was working with the mobsters who were planning to kill him, Valachi was deliberately vague.[295]

On June 22, 1962, Valachi assaulted a fellow prisoner with a length of pipe. He believed he was attacking a mobster called "Joe Beck" who had been sent to kill him, but he was actually striking lookalike inmate John Joseph Saupp, who had no link with the Mafia. Saupp was mortally wounded in the attack.[296]

Valachi again was brought before the associate warden and again felt that he was being manipulated. Ellicott created a sort of confession for Valachi, and had him sign it. The document stated that Saupp branded Valachi an informant when a recent escape attempt was discovered, and Valachi subsequently lashed out at Saupp.[297]

Saupp died of his wounds on June 24, and Ellicott confronted Valachi, saying he going to "burn" him.[298] The associate warden later tried to maneuver Valachi into making a tape-recorded confession.[299]

Eventually, attorneys and federal agents took charge of Valachi and removed him from Atlanta Federal Prison.[300]

Marion Jesse Elliott was born December 2, 1909, in Steubenville, Ohio, the first child of Jesse Edward and Daisy B. Elliott. His father worked for a time as a carpenter and as a foreman on railroad construction projects.[301]

The family moved west after 1920, and Jesse became a farmer at Rialto,

California. Marion Elliott attended school in San Bernardino. He enlisted as a private in the Marines in 1928.[302]

In the 1930s, Elliott graduated from the Indiana College of Embalming in Indianapolis. But he then joined the federal Bureau of Prisons and moved through different assignments and different states over the years. He was a junior officer at the U.S. penitentiary at Leavenworth, Kansas, in November 1937, when he married Edna Louise Woods.[303] Elliott and his wife were residents of Los Angeles, when their son Steve was born in 1939. The following year, Elliott was transferred to the Terre Haute federal prison at Vigo, Indiana. Son Michael was born in that state. Elliott became captain of guards at Terre Haute before being transferred to Atlanta and promoted to associate warden.[304]

In July of 1962, when FBI was investigating Valachi's murder of fellow prisoner John Saupp, Elliott may have confirmed one of Valachi's charges against him. An unnamed source, likely Elliott himself, provided the FBI a copy of a letter Valachi tried to send when he was desperate for help. The source "stated he refused to release this letter for mailing and instructed Valachi to rewrite the letter."[305] It is uncertain whether Elliott was ever investigated for his handling of the Valachi matter.

On March 15, 1964, Edna Elliott, fifty nine, passed away. Son Steve was grown and out on his own in Detroit, Michigan, but son Michael had only recently turned eighteen and continued living with his father.[306]

It is not entirely clear if Valachi's accusations against Elliott impacted the associate warden's career. (The charges were recorded in the autobiography Valachi penned for the Justice Department in 1964, and they were published in Peter Maas's *The Valachi Papers* a few years after that.) What is clear is that by the start of 1965, Elliott was looking to get out of the Bureau of Prisons.

In January 1965, he was named as one of five final candidates for the position of Louisiana State Penitentiary warden. He did not get the job. In that year, he retired as a federal prison administrator and moved to Gadsden, Alabama. He did part-time consulting work, assisting the prison systems in Missouri and Guam, and advising the American Correctional Association.[307]

Alabama State Prison Commissioner William M. Fondren announced in the summer of 1970 that Elliott had agreed to become warden of the recently opened Holman Correctional Facility at Atmore in the south of the state. Elliott remained in the job just fourteen months. He retired in October 1971 and returned to Gadsden. He died there on March 22, 1988.[308]

Franse, Stephen

> *Before I went to court, I... went and see Steve Francis from the 181 Club at 11th Street and First Ave., and he took care of everything.*[309]

Joseph Valachi knew "Steve Francis" in the 1930s and 1940s as a well connected member of the crime family led for a time by Frank Costello and later by Vito Genovese. Valachi was arrested in the late 1940s for running a numbers operation. When the case came to court, his lengthy record of arrests and convictions was missing from the proceedings, and Valachi received a suspended sentence. He said that was achieved by making just one pretrial visit to Francis.[310]

In his memoirs, during a tirade directed at crime boss Genovese, Valachi questioned a number of Genovese actions. He accused the boss of labeling as "rats" the men in his organization he wanted killed. That enabled Genovese to order their murders without bringing evidence of any wrongdoing to a hearing of a regional Mafia council. Valachi accused Genovese of having Francis killed for highly personal reasons:

> Tell us, who did Steve Francis rat on – the partner you had at the 181 Club. Tell us. You won't want to say the truth. You don't want to say that you blame him for your wife Ann's doings.[311]

Stephen Franse (whose surname was also spelled France and Francé) was a successful investor in underworld-linked gay nightclubs in Manhattan beginning in the 1930s. His 1953 murder, which occurred within Valachi's Lido restaurant, 1362 Castle Hill Avenue in the Bronx, was reportedly ordered by Vito Genovese. Genovese had blamed Franse for his wife Anna's involvement in homosexual nightlife and for the breakup of their marriage.[312]

Franse was born in New York City on November 28, 1894. His parents were Bernardo and Louise Sanguineti Franse, Italian immigrants. He grew up at 63 Sullivan Street, a block from Thompson Street, south of Greenwich Village in a Manhattan neighborhood today known as Soho. His father Bernardo was a laborer and later a driver. As he reached adulthood, Stephen worked as a tailor and as a driver.[313]

Franse married Emma Cerù (sometimes "Cern") in Manhattan on March 1, 1917. Cerù, daughter of Orlando and Rosa Prato Cerù, had been a resident of 148 Bleecker Street in Greenwich Village before the marriage. The ceremony was conducted at Our Lady of Pompeii Church, then at 210 Bleecker Street. Giorgio Farino and Franse's sister Paolina served as witnesses.[314]

A few months later, when Franse registered for the World War I draft, he was a resident of 23 Leroy Street in Greenwich Village and a teamster. He was described as short and slender, with brown eyes and brown hair. By 1920, the Franse home had moved a block north to Morton Street and the family had grown to include son Renard. In the later 1920s, the family appears to have lived in Yonkers and Franse was engaged in importing.[315]

The family, including second son Robert, was settled at 600 West 111th Street by the spring of 1930. At that time, Franse reported working as a real estate agent. Later in that year, Franse's father Bernardo died of heart and kidney ailments at his longtime home on Sullivan Street.[316]

Vito Genovese and recent widow Anna Petillo Vernotico were married on March 30, 1932. Within a half-dozen years, Vito Genovese left Anna in New York and fled to Italy to escape a murder prosecution. World War II, profitable relationships with Mussolini's Fascist government and the later American occupation, and the lingering murder charge kept him in Italy until 1945, when he was arrested by U.S. authorities and returned to New York.[317]

During Genovese's extended absence, Stephen Franse became owner of the Howdy Club at 47 West Third Street in Greenwich Village, which catered to gay and lesbian patrons and featured cross-dressing entertainers and staff.[318]

The club gained wider public attention on Tuesday, April 12, 1938. In the pre-dawn hours, a police officer and three bandits were wounded as an attempted holdup became a shootout. Officer Humbert Moruzzi was taken to Columbus Hospital in critical condition after suffering a head wound. Robbery suspects Chester Carson, John Kulka and Francis Dignam were arrested. Carson and Kulka were admitted to Bellevue Hospital with bullet wounds to the chest and side, respectively. Dignam was treated for a wound to his forearm and put into the lockup at the Mercer Street Police Station.[319]

In the investigation of the incident, police wondered if the robbery was an "inside job." Two club singers and a waiter were taken into custody as material witnesses.[320]

The matter grew more complex the next night, when a woman employee of the club, who had resisted the robbers and had been struck by a pistol butt, apparently jumped naked from a twelfth floor window to her death.

Twenty-two-year-old Norma DeMarco of the Bronx worked as a hat check girl. She had been heroic in her opposition to the robbers, grabbing a gun from one of them and kicking away a weapon dropped by another. These actions earned her the strike from the pistol butt and a bloody wound on her head.

She was questioned by detectives for much of day on Wednesday. DeMarco and friend Dorothy Lamar then went out drinking with two men and brought the men back to Lamar's apartment, 138 West Fifty-eighth Street. At the apartment, DeMarco reportedly "became wildly excited and threatened to jump out the window." The men decided to leave. Lamar tried to calm DeMarco by preparing her for a bath, but after DeMarco disrobed, she jumped out an open window. She fell dead in an alley behind the apartment building.

When questioned about the incident, Lamar told authorities that DeMarco had some emotional problems, had developed an addiction to marijuana cigarettes and had previously attempted to throw herself out a window.[321]

On Thursday, April 14, police officials identified the two men who were with DeMarco and Lamar just before DeMarco went out the window. They were Homicide Squad detectives Eugene Canaveri and James Hayden. The Detective Division and the Homicide Squad opened separate investigations into the circumstances leading to DeMarco's suicide.[322]

Officer Moruzzi died of his wounds on Sunday morning. The accused robbers became accused murderers the next day. Carson, Kulka and Dignam were formally charged with first degree murder. Following conviction, Carson and Kulka were sentenced to death in the electric chair. Dignam, for whom a jury recommended mercy, was sentenced to life in prison.[323]

Stephen Franse described himself as a manager of a restaurant for the 1940 U.S. Census. He and his family lived at 617 West 170th Street in the Washington Heights section of Manhattan. Two years later, when he registered for the World War II draft, he said he was self employed at 47 West Third Street, the address of the Howdy Club.[324]

A government crackdown on the Howdy Club and similar Greenwich Village establishments occurred in the 1940s. In December 1944, police forced Howdy Club and Tony Pastor's Downtown to suspend cabaret performances while morals charges were investigated. Franse, president of the Forty-Seven West Third Street Corporation which ran the Howdy Club, objected, stating that his club performances had not changed in ten years and had never previously received complaints.[325]

The Howdy Club soon ceased operation. But Stephen Franse moved on to other nightclub ventures. His best known spot was the Club 181 at 181 Second Avenue in the East Village, which had financial backing from Vito Genovese, whose murder charge was tossed out after the primary witness against him suddenly died in prison.[326]

On September 7, 1948, Franse's mother died at 54 Macdougal Street, where she had lived since the passing of her husband. Information for Louise Franse's death certificate was provided by Stephen Franse, then a resident of 1777 Grand Concourse in the Bronx.[327]

Franse called the police to his Club 181 in January 1949, when he found that three patrons were passing counterfeit money in the establishment. Brothers Douglas and Louis Walker and Douglas's wife Kathleen were arrested.[328]

Franse and wife Emma lived alone at 1777 Grand Concourse at the time of the 1950 Census. Franse described his occupation as restaurant proprietor. Just a year later, his "restaurant" was described in the press as "a hangout for perverts of both sexes."[329]

Following an undercover investigation of Club 181, the New York State Liquor Authority revoked the liquor license of the club in spring 1951, finding it in violation of the decency standards of the time:

> Performers of both sexes did strip-tease dances, punctuated with suggestive bumps and grinds and body contortions, used offensive language and sang degrading songs. In between shows the performance sat at tables with patrons and on occasion made dalliances with persons of their own sex.[330]

The State Liquor Authority investigation revealed that the club had been grossing nearly $500,000 a year.[331]

At the same time that Club 181 was being shuttered, Vito Genovese was being brought into court by his wife. Vito and Anna Genovese were living separately since spring 1950, when Anna moved out of their luxurious home in Atlantic Highlands, New Jersey. She filed for divorce in September 1950. She agreed to drop the divorce suit when Genovese began paying her $200 a week in support for her and son Phillip. She then sought a formal maintenance agreement amounting to $350 a week through a lawsuit filed in December 1952.[332] Early in 1953, Anna went into court in Freehold, New Jersey, and testified about her husband's role as a crime syndicate leader, about his massive financial investments and about his apparent infatuation with the wife of a henchman.[333]

Aside from filing his own divorce suit against her, Genovese took no known action against his wife for this exposure. Instead, he acted against Franse.

Joseph Valachi in late May 1953 received instructions from his crime family superior Anthony "Tony Bender" Strollo. He was to keep his Lido restaurant and bar open late each night until called by Strollo and told to close. Strollo told Valachi that Franse and his close ally Peter Petillo had been branded informants and condemned to death. Franse would go first, and the Lido was chosen as the site for his murder.

Night after night, Valachi kept the Lido open until Strollo's early morning call. The pattern continued until after midnight on June 19. Strollo then called and told Valachi to wait.

Just after 4 o'clock in the morning, Stephen Franse showed up at the Lido along with Pasquale "Pat" Pagano and Valachi's nephew Fiore Siano. Pagano and Siano said they wanted to show Franse around Valachi's place. They entered and went back to the kitchen.

Pagano and Siano then attacked Franse. They beat him, forced him to the floor and choked him into unconsciousness. Pagano then wrapped a chain around Franse's throat and pulled it tight while pressing his foot against the victim's neck. He held that position for about five minutes.

Franse's jewelry and wallet were taken from his lifeless body. Valachi took $90 from the wallet. Then the group waited. After about a half hour, Valachi went outside, got into Franse's automobile, started it and returned to the restaurant. Pagano and Siano emerged from the Lido carrying Franse between them, as if he was drunk. They put him in the back seat of the car and drove away.[334]

At close to ten o'clock that morning, Franse's body was found in the car parked outside 164 East Thirty-seventh Street near Third Avenue. Wife Emma and son Renard identified the remains. They noted that a diamond ring and a wristwatch he always wore were missing.[335]

His murder remained unsolved until Valachi provided details to the U.S. Department of Justice in July of 1963.

Stephen Franse stands at left in photo of the Franse family.

Gaffney, Narcotics Agent George H.

> Well, if there ever was a phony, this Gaffney is the king of all
> the phonies and the biggest frame artist in the whole wide
> world.[336]

Valachi blamed George Gaffney, New York district supervisor of the Federal Bureau of Narcotics, and his agent Frank Selvaggi (Valachi wrote it "Savaggie") for creating a phony narcotics case against him in the summer of 1961. Valachi had just started serving a fifteen-year sentence at Atlanta Federal Prison on a narcotics conviction, when he was pulled out of Atlanta and returned to New York on the new charges. Valachi was convicted of narcotics conspiracy and sentenced to twenty years.

Valachi always insisted that he was framed by the FBN agents with the aid of narcotics racketeer Salvatore "Solly" Rinaldo. Gaffney reportedly was disappointed that he could not convince Valachi to cooperate with FBN investigations. He had "offered me the armchair for the rest of my life if I join on his side." Valachi decided that the new charges were simply the result of his refusal to play ball with FBN. Whenever he came in contact with anyone from the FBN, Valachi remarked about the setup by Gaffney and Selvaggi.[337]

After being returned to Atlanta Prison, Valachi became convinced that his former underworld associates considered him an informant and were preparing to kill him. He had himself placed in solitary confinement and, recalling the promised "armchair," requested a meeting with Gaffney. Almost immediately, he concluded that his request for Gaffney would be considered proof that he was cooperating, and he feared that word of it would be circulated around the prison.[338]

When he finally decided to become an informant, he reluctantly dealt with Selvaggi and Gaffney for a time. Reflecting on this period in his memoirs, Valachi took issue with Gaffney claims that he got Valachi to talk and that he later turned Valachi over to the FBI.[339]

According to Valachi, Gaffney was having Selvaggi alter Valachi's information in order that it would agree with previous Gaffney statements. Valachi figured that out at about the same time that an FBI agent first visited him. Selvaggi advised Valachi to say little to the FBI agent "and get rid of him as fast as you can." Instead, Valachi began secret negotiations with the agent to become an FBI informant.[340]

George Henry Gaffney was born August 19, 1921, at Escanaba, Michigan. He graduated from Escanaba High School, in 1939, and from the U.S. Naval Academy at Annapolis, Maryland, and the submarine school at New London, Connecticut.[341]

In November 1944, he married Catherine "Kay" Barron of New York City. Together they would have a total of three daughters. A year after his marriage, Gaffney reportedly was serving in the Pacific aboard the U.S.S. Missouri when it became the site of the formal surrender of Japan, ending the Second World War.[342]

Gaffney left military service in 1948, After an unsuccessful effort to join the Central Intelligence Agency, he became an agent of the New York office of the Federal Bureau of Narcotics in 1949.[343] In spring 1955, He was appointed FBN acting supervisor in Atlanta, with a district that included the states of South Carolina, Georgia, Florida and Alabama.

He was assigned as New York district supervisor in 1957 and remained in that position until 1963, when he was moved to the post of deputy commissioner in Washington, D.C. Gaffney retired from the FBN in 1971. He and his wife moved to Missoula, Montana. During his retirement, the former FBN agent enjoyed hunting, fishing and carving decoys. He also did some law enforcement consulting work and delivered speeches about organized crime to police agencies.[344]

Gaffney passed away at the Riverside Health Center in Missoula on April 2, 2004. He was eighty two.[345]

Giannini, Eugene "Gene"

> Gene walked in the bar, and the first thing Gene told me was
> that he felt that he was going to die.[346]

Crime family lieutenant Anthony "Tony Bender" Strollo called Valachi downtown in the summer of 1952. They met at Rocco's Restaurant. While eating his dinner, Strollo told Valachi that Gene Giannini, a member of the Lucchese Crime Family, had been unmasked as an informant for the Federal Bureau of Narcotics.[347] Word of Giannini's betrayal had come from exiled New York crime boss Salvatore "Charlie Luciano" Lucania – known to Valachi as "Charlie Lucky" – in Italy.

According to the Lucania information, Giannini, who had recently returned to the U.S. from Italy, had been an FBN informant for about seventeen years. "Charlie Lucky said that Gene is the smartest stool pigeon that ever lived. Kill him and whoever comes and fronts for him." During his time in Italy, Giannini made an effort to get close to Lucania, so narcotics agents could begin to build a case against the deported Mafia leader. Reportedly tipped off by law enforcement connections, Lucania met with Giannini but did so very carefully.

Gunmen were already looking for Giannini when Valachi received this news. Strollo learned that Valachi earlier had loaned money to Giannini and cautioned him about that relationship. Valachi understood that, if Giannini escaped mob discipline, some would accuse Valachi of warning him in an effort to recover the loan. Valachi assured Strollo, "I'm going to forget all about the money."[348] In September, Strollo and Valachi met again to discuss the same subject. Strollo reported that gunmen were having a tough time locating Giannini. Valachi felt that "they are making some excuse to blame me if something goes wrong." He offered, "If they can't find him, I'll find him." Strollo obtained crime family leadership approval for Valachi to handle the Giannini matter.

Valachi had no trouble locating Giannini. They had been acquainted for a while.[349] Valachi called him at a known telephone number and asked him to come to a corner bar near Castle Hill and Westchester avenues in the Bronx. The location was close to Valachi's own Lido restaurant. Valachi waited at the bar with his associate Joey Pagano. When Giannini arrived, they could clearly see that Giannini's car was followed by a car of federal agents. In the bar, Valachi told Giannini that he spotted agents and they should postpone their meeting for a few days. When Giannini left, the agents' car again followed him.[350]

At their second meeting at a different bar, known as the Casa,[351] Valachi spotted the agents again, but this time did not mention it. Giannini immediately confided in Valachi that he was living in fear. "He felt that he was going to die." Valachi tried to calm him. They and Joey Pagano had some drinks together, and Valachi invited a bar waitress, who had previously worked for him at the Lido, to join them. Later, Valachi encouraged Giannini to take the waitress out on a date and provided him some cash to do so.[352]

Valachi soon learned that Giannini was working for a craps game in Harlem, checking out prospective players at a "drop" location on 112th Street and sending approved players on to the gambling site a short distance away. He obtained approval from higher-ups to execute Giannini at the drop spot.[353]

He had Joey Pagano obtain firearms from a downtown connection, and he assigned Joey's brother Pat Pagano to locate a nearby building that would allow gunmen to escape from 112th Street to a car waiting on 111th Street. Valachi assigned his nephew Fiore Siano to the team, and made Siano responsible for communicating with Valachi.

On the night scheduled for the murder, Pat Pagano admitted that he did not personally tour the selected escape building to ensure that no locked doors would interfere with passage to 111th Street. Valachi called off the hit until that could be done. The group assembled again the following night. Valachi waited at the Lido while Siano and the Paganos went to work.[354]

After about an hour's wait, "Siano calls me and tells me that 'He just got there.' By 'he,' Fiore meant Gene, as we did not want to mention his name on the phone. I tell Fiore to 'Go ahead and see him.' He knew what I meant." Half an hour later, Siano telephoned again. "He tells me that they saw him and that they are going away for a couple of days."[355]

Valachi later drove out to the drop location, saw no activity and went home. The next day, he heard on the radio that Giannini had been found murdered at East 107th Street between Second and Third avenues. The location, several blocks from where the hit was planned, was puzzling. Valachi learned his team discarded the firearms used in the job by dropping them into the water beneath the Third Avenue Bridge. He later pieced together that, after Giannini was shot, someone tried to move him to the closest hospital. When they decided that Giannini was beyond help, they left his body on East 107th Street.

Valachi was called to discuss the execution with Vito Genovese. Genovese said he received a complaint from a Lucchese Crime Family member known as "Paulie Ham." Ham ran the craps game that employed Giannini, and the mob hit so close to the game nearly put it out of business. Ham claimed that it cost him $10,000 in bribes to keep the game open.[356]

Valachi's role in planning the execution of Giannini reportedly cost him some friendships among Lucchese members. He later heard that the Luccheses were planning to eliminate Giannini on their own, and concluded that Genovese merely wanted to act first on the information provided by Lucania.[357]

Eugene Giannini was born April 17, 1910, to Joseph and Anna Simone Giannini in the town of Toritto, inland from the Adriatic seaport Bari in mainland Italy's southern region of Apulia (Puglia). The Giannini family left Italy in December 1920, traveling from Naples to New York aboard the *S.S. Re D'Italia* and meeting up with relatives in East Harlem.[358]

Eugene Giannini was ten when he reached the U.S. He was only seventeen at the time of his first arrest. He was reportedly picked up on May 31, 1927, in Newport, Rhode Island, on a concealed weapons charge.

Early the next year, he was convicted in New York City of armed robbery and sentenced to serve ten years in prison. That sentence introduced him to Sing Sing Prison in Ossining and to Clinton State Prison in Dannemora. It also removed him from the New York underworld violence of the 1930-1931 Castellammarese War.[359]

He hadn't been out of prison long when he married Amelia Pellegrino in Manhattan in November 1933. At that time, he reported living at 32 Thompson Street, south of Manhattan's Greenwich Village.[360]

Giannini was one of several men charged with participating in a May 1934 grocery store holdup at Cherry and Oliver streets that resulted in the shooting death of New York Police Officer Arthur P. Rasmussen. The gunfight between robbers and police also resulted in wounds to a sixteen-year-old girl, and seventeen-year-old and ten-year-old boys. In June, the homicide and robbery charges against Giannini were dismissed.

A Bronx robbery charge early in 1936 was also dismissed.[361]

In 1940, Giannini was living at 305 East 109th Street in East Harlem with his wife and their four-year-old son Joseph. Giannini reported that he worked as a chauffeur and was employed by Piccone & Company of East 108th Street.[362]

Convicted of narcotics peddling in 1942, Giannini was sentenced to fifteen months in prison for the first offense. His second offense, a conviction in

March of 1945, resulted in the same sentence. In that case, he was indicted with sixteen others of conspiring in a nationwide drug ring that imported narcotics from Mexico.[363]

In 1950, Giannini resided on West 234th Street in the Bronx. His family by then had grown to include daughter Ann. Giannini claimed to work as a general manager in the meat industry.[364] Giannini left the U.S. for Europe in that year. He reportedly planned to sell medical supplies and counterfeit American currency in then-rebuilding postwar Italy and to use the proceeds to purchase heroin he could smuggle back into the U.S.[365]

Just a short time later, he was an inmate in an Italian prison. About July 1951, he provided information to visiting U.S. narcotics agents (a relationship with the agents may have existed since earlier encounters). He revealed his meetings with organized crime figures, such as Lucania, Frank Callace, Dominick Petrelli and Joe Pici. After providing this information, he was given his release and a return trip to the U.S.[366]

A third U.S. narcotics charge was lodged against him on April 8, 1952. As he was released on bail, New York mafiosi learned that he was an informant and began plans to murder him.[367]

Valachi set up the successful hit. He used associates Joey and Pat Pagano and his nephew Fiore Siano as the gunmen. Giannini was murdered in the early morning hours of September 20, 1952, outside an East 112th Street crap game run by Paul "Paulie Ham" Correale, a Lucchese Crime Family member.[368]

Giannini was found dead of two gunshot wounds to the back of the head at six-twenty in the morning in the street in front of 221 East 107th Street. No witnesses to the shooting could be located. It became clear that Giannini had been shot at some other spot and moved to East 107th Street. Police learned that residents of Second Avenue between 111th and 112th streets had heard gunshots around five o'clock that morning. They discovered some blood stains on the sidewalk in front of 2173 Second Avenue between 111th and 112th streets.[369]

The press very quickly learned that Giannini's murder had been ordered by the Mafia because he had been "singing" to federal agents. One report indicated that he had been terrified that he would be discovered and asked agents to keep his role as informant a secret even from his own wife.[370]

Following the Giannini hit, Valachi was summoned to a meeting of New

York Mafia leaders. Though Correale complained through his lieutenant Joseph "Joe Palisades" Rosato about the negative impact of the Giannini murder on his craps game, leaders Tommy Lucchese and Vito Genovese were satisfied with the outcome and took no action against Valachi.[371]

Police investigate the Giannini murder. (NY Daily News)

Heslin, Peter "Thomas O'Neill"

At night we used to go to Joe's Restaurant at 116th St., and there all the window crashers came around... From the Irish mob there was the Dutchman, Pete Hestler, Steve Folley, Frank LaPuma, Nick the Burglar...[372]

Valachi met Peter Heslin in the mid-1920s. Heslin, whose name Valachi mangled into "Halssler," "Helssler" and "Hestler," was one of the few Irish-American gangsters in the organization Valachi knew as "the Irish mob." Valachi began socializing with the Irish mob when local gangsters congregated at Joe's Restaurant in East Harlem.[373]

Valachi was an inmate in Sing Sing Prison when he learned that Heslin had been convicted of killing a New York City police officer local gangsters derisively called "Monkey Riley." In his autobiography, Valachi recalled discussing the matter with Irish mob member Ludwig "Dutch" Augustine, when the two men met in Sing Sing: "I told him Pete Halssler is in the death house. He said he knew that."

Augustine told Valachi that Heslin fatally shot "Riley" over a personal grudge. The police officer reportedly hounded local gangsters, and during one confrontation he and Heslin threatened each other. During a tense moment, the officer referred to his pistol, then out of view in a raincoat pocket: "I got my hand on it." Heslin responded with his own warning: "You just pull that right arm out, and I'll leave you there." As he retreated, the police officer promised, "I'll get you." Heslin answered, "I'll be waiting for you."

When he heard the story, Valachi told Augustine, "So it came, the trouble, from that night."[374]

Peter Heslin, Jr., was born to Peter and Mary Dunn Heslin in New York City on November 15, 1898.[375]

Both of his parents were immigrants from Ireland. Peter Sr. was a thirty-two-year-old widower when he married Mary Dunn in 1895. Peter Jr. was the second child born to the couple. The family resided at 209 East Ninety-fifth Street in Manhattan's Yorkville section at the time, and Peter Sr. worked as a day laborer and a stableman.[376]

By 1910, the Heslin family included six children – five sons and one daughter. The family lived at 171 East Ninety-ninth Street at the time of that year's census. Young Peter Heslin was arrested late in 1914. He gave the false name of Ryan at the time of his arrest. He was convicted of juvenile delinquency and given a suspended sentence. Over the next few years, he added arrests for disorderly conduct, petit larceny and grand larceny. He managed to be discharged each time.[377]

On November 8, 1917, Heslin married Anna McAdams in a ceremony at Our Lady of Good Counsel Church on East Ninetieth Street in Manhattan. For the marriage certificate, Heslin claimed to be twenty one, though he was actually one week shy of his nineteenth birthday.[378]

Heslin reportedly was arrested for assault and rape about one month later. The charges were again dropped.[379]

When he filled out his registration for the military draft in September 1918, Heslin indicated his correct age of nineteen and a home address of 238 East Ninety-fourth Street. For employment, he stated he worked as a "file helper" for "Barnum." In the section of the form for the address of the business, he responded, "Unable to give it." Heslin was described as short, medium build, with brown eyes and hair.[380]

Heslin was arrested early in 1919 for felonious assault. He attempted without success to hide behind the alias of "Thomas O'Neill." He was convicted in Bronx Supreme Court. Judge McAvoy sentenced him on February 28 to serve a minimum of five years and a maximum of ten years and two months in prison. He entered Sing Sing Prison on March 4. He was transferred from Sing Sing to Auburn State Prison in June 1919 and then transferred to Clinton State Prison at Dannemora in June 1920. In October 1921, he was moved to Great Meadow Prison at Comstock.[381]

He was released in December 1922. His prison experience did little to change his habits. He was reportedly arrested for robbery, again giving the name O'Neill, in June 1924. He was paroled in December of the following year, just in time to meet up with Joseph Valachi and his pals in East Harlem.[382]

Heslin and New York City Police Officer Charles H. Reilly ran into each other in the early morning hours of April 5, 1926. Reilly reportedly intruded while Heslin was attempting to rob several people in front of Public School 168 on East 105th Street, between First and Second avenues. The officer succeeded in thwarting the robbery and in disarming Heslin of two pistols he was holding.

There was considerable confusion over what occurred next. Shots were fired, and police rushed to the scene. They found Officer Reilly dead on the sidewalk and Heslin gone. Reilly had multiple gunshot wounds to his neck, left shoulder, back and chest. A blood trail beginning in the hallway of 331 East 105th Street reportedly led investigators down the block, around a corner and across First Avenue to an apartment at 2042 First Avenue, where they found Heslin, with a gunshot wound to his leg. Heslin and another occupant of the apartment, Joseph Yannerelli, were arrested. On the way to the East 104th Street Police Station, Heslin protested that he had not shot Officer Reilly.

Police were able to locate the individuals Heslin had been trying to rob, and they identified him as the man disarmed by Officer Reilly. The witnesses apparently did not see what happened after Heslin was disarmed.[383]

Officer Reilly was given an "inspector's funeral" on Thursday, April 8. A funeral Mass was held at Our Lady of the Assumption Church in the Bronx, where Reilly lived with his wife and their children. A procession, including the police band, marched from the Reilly home on Crosby Avenue to the church and later from the church to Calvary Cemetery. On the way to the cemetery, the cortege passed the 105th Street location where Reilly was killed.[384]

Peter Heslin appeared on crutches before Judge Mancuso in General Sessions Court on April 28 to plead not guilty to a first-degree murder charge. He was tried and convicted in October 1926 before Judge Charles Nott. After deliberations of eleven hours, the jury returned its verdict at two-thirty Friday morning, October 22, 1926. Heslin was guilty of first-degree murder. While Judge Nott delayed sentencing until the following week, a sentence of death in the electric chair was mandated.[385]

On November 4, the judge formally sentenced Heslin to be electrocuted during the week of December 6. Heslin was returned to Sing Sing Prison that day, and became a resident of the prison's "Death House." Heslin continued to insist that he was innocent.[386] He denied any involvement in the shooting of Reilly and argued that he was wounded in the leg during a quarrel with another man, who shot him as he was fleeing.[387] Through legal appeals, he was able to postpone his date with the chair.

Heslin sparked some controversy in February 1927. New York City Police Commissioner George V. McLaughlin made public statements about the alleged coddling of prisoners at Sing Sing. As evidence, he read a portion of a letter supposedly written by Heslin to his friend "Bum" Rodgers: "I've got a big cell and plenty of service and I can't kick."

Sing Sing Warden Lewis Lawes took issue with the remarks:

> Peter Heslin did not write a letter to Bum Rodgers as stated. Every piece of mail entering or leaving Sing Sing is censored by an official and a record made of it. It would have been possible, of course, for Rodgers to have come in possession of a letter written by Heslin to some one else.
>
> It is obvious that Heslin's statement, as given out, about having a "big cell and plenty of service" was made in a facetious vein. Heslin has been isolated in the death house since he was received on November 4, 1926, where he is kept in solitary confinement for twenty-three and a half hours a day and his thirty minutes of recreation are spent in the custody of guards.
>
> No sane person envies Heslin this "service" or would call this coddling.[388]

New York's Court of Appeals affirmed Heslin's conviction on May 31, 1927. Warden Lawes set the time of the execution for the night of July 21.[389]

As dusk fell on that date, it was clear that there would be no reprieve. Heslin spent several hours with Father John P. McCaffrey, the prison's Catholic chaplain, and then met with Warden Lawes. At about eleven o'clock, Heslin was led to the electric chair. As he entered the death chamber, he stated, "I was planted on circumstantial evidence. You are watching an innocent man die." He was strapped into the chair at one minute past eleven. He was pronounced dead several minutes later.[390]

Leone, Peter "Muggin"

...I hear a rustle of feet come up the stairs, and I have a gun in my hand, and I asked, "Who is it?" And they said Buck, Johnnie D and Pete Muggin, his right name is Leno... So I opened the door and I saw the impossible: all three of them had powder marks on their necks and faces and none of them were hurt.[391]

"Pete Muggin" was a member of Valachi's burglary gang in the late 1920s. In 1930, when the combined Gagliano-Maranzano Mafia organization was looking for new recruits to fight against the powerful Giuseppe "Joe the Boss" Masseria in the Mafia's Castellammarese War, Muggin was one of the new members proposed by recently inducted Valachi.[392]

The anti-Masseria rebellion was successful, and Maranzano became U.S. Mafia boss of bosses in the spring of 1931. But Maranzano was assassinated on September 10 of that year. Valachi did not learn of his boss's death until after Muggin, "Johnnie D" DeBellis and "Buck Jones" Casertano showed up at his apartment in the early morning hours of September 11.

The three visitors had powder burns on their faces but no gunshot wounds. According to Valachi's autobiography, they reported that they had been confronted by "Joe Swed, Micky Shapes, Danny Hogan and some other dog, and Eddie Coco was there."[393] In Valachi's 1963 Senate testimony, he stated that "Joe Sweet" and "a guy named Yap" took a shot at Muggin and friends, known Maranzano loyalists, at close range but missed.[394]

When underworld order was restored following Maranzano's assassination, Valachi, Muggin, Johnnie D, Buck Jones and Girolamo Santuccio joined a crime family led by Salvatore "Charlie Luciano" Lucania and Vito Genovese.[395]

Muggin became very close to Genovese. He once admitted to Valachi that he helped murder the husband of Anna Petillo Vernotico. The man was strangled on the roof of a downtown building. Very soon after the killing, Genovese and the widow were married.[396]

When Valachi invested in racehorses, he spent considerable time with a gambler named Vinnie. He later provided Vinnie with some cash to start up a dice game. Vito Genovese apparently had some concerns about Vinnie, and he sent Muggin and "Dom the Sailor" DiQuarto to Valachi's Lido restaurant to spy on him. Much later, Valachi learned that Vinnie was trafficking narcotics.[397]

Peter Angelo Leone was born in New York City on Christmas Day in 1899. His parents were Pietro and Rosina DeCesare Leone, both natives of Sorrento, Italy, near Naples, who had lived for a time close to Manhattan's Hudson River docks before moving to Borough of Brooklyn.[398]

Peter left little evidence of the activities of his younger years. A Peter Leone turned up in the 1910 U.S. Census as an inmate of St. Joseph's Home, an orphanage in Peekskill, Westchester County, New York. The next document mentioning him was a prison record from 1919.[399]

In Queens County Court on May 12, 1919, Leone was convicted of second-degree grand larceny and was sentenced to a minimum of two and a half years and a maximum of five years in prison. He served that sentence in Sing Sing Prison and in Auburn Prison.[400]

He had not been out of prison long when he was picked up by police in April 1922 as a suspect in an East Harlem payroll theft. A gold watch and $1,450 in cash was stolen from Frank Rodonfo, part owner of the North American Shirt Company, 2082 First Avenue. Rodonfo had just returned to the business with payroll cash withdrawn from a nearby bank when he was held up by two bandits. Leone, then twenty two and a resident of 244 East 110th Street, matched Rodonfo's description of one of the robbers. He was charged with robbery and assault. It appears he was not convicted of either offense.[401]

On January 19, 1923, he was convicted of criminally carrying a concealed weapon. He was sentenced to four years and three months in prison. He arrived at Sing Sing on January 23. For the prison's admission register, he stated that his parents were both deceased, he had been living with a brother and sister at 255 East 110th Street and he worked as a clerk. In addition to Sing Sing, he served portions of this sentence at Auburn Prison and Great Meadow Prison. He was released in the fall of 1925.[402]

In 1928, Valachi emerged from his own prison sentence to find that many of his former pals had become associates of a Mafia organization run by Ciro Terranova. Valachi assembled a new crew of burglars, which included Leone. Valachi later joined a Mafia faction led by Tommaso Gagliano and became a soldier in the gangland war against Masseria and allies, including Terranova. Valachi introduced Leone and others to mafioso Girolamo Santuccio, who endorsed them for membership in the combined Gagliano-Maranzano organization. After the war and the assassination of Maranzano, Valachi, Leone and others moved with Santuccio into the Lucania-Genovese organization.[403]

The strangled bodies of Gerard Vernotico and Luigi Lanza, minor hood-lums, were discovered March 16, 1932, on the roof of 191 Prince Street, south of Greenwich Village. The murders were unsolved until Valachi became an informant in the 1960s and revealed that Leone admitted that he and Mike Barrese were responsible.[404]

Valachi also accused Leone and John DeBellis with committing the Genovese-ordered murder of Michael "Little Apples" Reggione, who was found shot to death in an East Harlem hallway on November 25, 1932.[405]

Leone married Belle Innenberg on September 12, 1933. For the marriage certificate, he stated he worked as a clerk. At the time of the 1940 U.S. Census, the couple resided at 250 East 110th Street in East Harlem. While Leone stated for the record that he worked thirty five hours the previous week, he apparently did not mention his line of work.[406]

He said he was employed by the Triboro Pastry store on East 110th Street when he registered for the World War II draft a couple of years later. He and Belle continued to live at 250 East 110th.[407]

Leone, fifty, divorced, and working as a building handyman, was still a resident of the same East 110th Street address at the time of the 1950 U.S. Census. His date of death is uncertain.[408]

Livorsi, Frank "Cheech"

> *They are thinking about asking you about Frank... He is with the people we intend to have trouble with... I think they want you to take care of him.*[409]

Joseph Valachi held Frank in high esteem. He never forgot that Frank interceded on Valachi's behalf with Mafia leader Ciro Terranova. Terranova had ordered the death of Valachi and a pal named LaPuma after they sided with a rival gang in East Harlem. Valachi's life may have been saved by an April 1925 prison sentence. Two months later, LaPuma was shot to death by a gunman paid by Terranova.[410] When Valachi emerged from prison in 1928, Frank, a top aide to Terranova, convinced the boss to rescind the death sentence against Valachi. He tried, though without success, to convince Terranova to invite Valachi into their organization.[411]

Valachi and Frank socialized, going out on double-dates with girlfriends May and Helen. Frank regularly spent nights at Valachi's apartment in Van Nest, Bronx. Valachi gave him a key to the place.[412]

The two men had candid discussions about Mafia membership and committed to watching out for each other. Valachi admitted that he was being courted for membership by a rival organization. Frank said he was still trying to convince Terranova to extend a welcome. (Valachi felt he was being blocked by Terranova lieutenant "Big Dick" Amato.) Because they knew that membership in rival crime families could bring them into violent conflict, they arranged an unspoken signal. If Valachi was inducted into a rival organization, he would quietly empty his Van Nest apartment and move away.[413]

As Valachi was pulled into the rival organization, established members asked him about his relationship with Frank. The conversations made Valachi uncomfortable. Dominick "the Gap" Petrelli, already a member, explained to him, "They are thinking about asking you about Frank... the one who comes and sleeps over at your house... Don't get excited... he is with the people we intend to have trouble with... I think they want you to take care of him."

Valachi exploded, "What are they crazy?" He told Petrelli he wanted no part of an organization that called on him to harm someone who had saved his life. "How would you like for someone to ask me to take you?" he asked Petrelli. Gap said he would explain the situation to higher-ups and ensure that Valachi was not asked to take any action against Frank. Petrelli told Valachi that he must not warn Frank.[414]

Frank Livorsi, whose family surname was also written LiVolsi and Livolsi, was born November 10, 1903, to Bartolomeo and Rosaria Beritelli Livorsi. His parents were both Italian immigrants living in East Harlem – Bartolomeo, a stone cutter, was a native of Nicosia in central Sicily – but Frank claimed that Chicago was his birthplace.[415]

The third child and first son in a large family, Frank Livorsi grew up along East 107th Street near Second Avenue. Family home addresses included 316, 232 and 235 on East 107th.[416]

Livorsi had his first known trouble with the law in spring of 1924. Just after midnight on Wednesday, May 7, police spotted Livorsi and nine companions crammed into a single automobile driving down Amsterdam Avenue on Manhattan's West Side. A short time earlier, the proprietor of a drugstore on Amsterdam Avenue near West 112th Street reported being robbed by several bandits. Police decided to check the automobile. When they began following it, the car accelerated. It was finally brought to a stop after police fired several warning shots.

Inside, were Livorsi, then reporting an address of 229 East 107th Street; Otto Romano, twenty four, of East 117th Street; Frank Dallavella, twenty seven, of Crescent Avenue in the Bronx; Joseph Cioffi, twenty one, of Pleasant Avenue; Frank Mega, twenty five, of East 114th Street, Joseph Shallace, twenty three, of 317 East 107th Street; and four other young men. Police arrested the group as suspects in the drugstore robbery.[417] Store owner Max Rosen did not recognize any of them as the bandits.

On Monday, May 12, the ten men were brought into West Side Court and formally discharged. They were all quickly rearrested in connection with two other matters. Four of them were charged with theft of silk fabrics. Livorsi, Romano, Dallavella, Cioffi, Mega and Shallace were hauled to the West 123rd Street Police Station as suspects in the $100,000 robbery of the Metropolitan

Jewelry Credit Company back on April 13. The *New York Post* reported, "Livolsi is said by the police to have been the 'find man' and to have entered the store the day before the robbery on the pretext of buying a ring, to get 'the lay of the land.'"[418]

In 1925, the entire Livorsi family – Bartolomeo and Rosaria and their nine children, aged four through twenty four – relocated from East Harlem to 615 Crescent Street in Long Island City, Queens.[419]

Frank "Cheech" Livorsi was considered a trusted driver and bodyguard of Ciro Terranova by 1928, when he tried to repair the relationship between Terranova and Valachi.

Gunmen smashed through the steel door of a Ravenswood, Queens, apartment at 611 Boulevard, in the early morning of March 30, 1929, and shot to death the two occupants. Samuel Joseph Sacco, thirty six, and his wife Rose, thirty, were found dead. Samuel apparently jumped out of bed in response to the break-in and managed to reach a handgun he stored in a bedroom bureau. But he was killed before he could fire the weapon. Rose was murdered in her bed.

A medical examiner found that Samuel died following gunshot wounds to his right eye, skull and brain; left chest and lung; and upper left arm. Rose had bullet wounds to the left chest, lungs and spinal cord. Authorities surmised that Samuel, recently released from Sing Sing Prison, was killed because he had squealed on fellow inmates plotting an escape from the institution. Rose reportedly was killed merely because she was present.[420]

The killers did not leave many hints to their identities. When tenant Rose Lagonia moved her belongings out of the building at 611 Boulevard on the day after the double murder, police interpreted it as a clue. They took Rose into custody as a material witness and arrested her brother-in-law Pasquale Rosetti, an East Harlem resident, for suspicion of homicide. He was soon released for lack of evidence.

On April 22, police arrested Frank Livorsi, then living at 101 Thirty-first Street in Astoria, Queens. They claimed to have discovered his hat in the Sacco apartment, and they suggested that Livorsi had been absent from his usual hangouts since the day of the Sacco double-murder.[421]

Livorsi was held without bail for a time, while detectives tried to assemble a murder case against him. On May 8, they were forced to admit that evidence was lacking, and Livorsi was released.[422]

Despite the relationship with "Helen" that was reported by Valachi, when Frank Livorsi married on August 29, 1930, his bride was Dorina Gazzola. Dorina was twenty one, about five years younger than Livorsi, and she resided in East Harlem.[423]

Though the leadership of the Mafia organization that Valachi joined in 1930 was clearly gunning for Livorsi, "Cheech" managed to survive the 1930-1931 Castellammarese War. He may have played a significant role in bringing that war – a rebellion of mafiosi against the forces of boss of bosses Giuseppe Masseria – to a close.

Livorsi and other members of Masseria's organization reportedly plotted with their opponents and against their own chief as they arranged his assassination in a Coney Island restaurant on April 15. Valachi spoke about the plot when he testified before a U.S. Senate subcommittee in fall of 1963. According to Valachi, Masseria's own top men, including Salvatore "Charlie Luciano" Lucania, Vito Genovese and Ciro Terranova lured him out to what was supposed to be a victory celebration.

Valachi said he heard that Masseria was killed by Joseph "Stretch" Stracci and Valachi's old friend Frank "Cheech" Livorsi: "They were sitting down. They talked awhile. In the course of, you know, of having conversation in between maybe a half hour or an hour, I don't know how long it lasted, they shot him in this time."[424]

Livorsi's immediate superior in the underworld, Ciro Terranova, lost his fearsome reputation on the same day. When the plotters were fleeing from the site of Masseria's murder, according to Valachi, Terranova was shaking so badly that he was unable to put the key into his car's ignition. He was pushed aside to get the car started, and he was subsequently pushed aside in the underworld rackets as well. Valachi stated that Terranova's position as underworld authority in East Harlem was handed to Michael "Trigger Mike" Coppola.[425]

During Terranova's decline, the police also took advantage of his diminished underworld clout and hounded him at every opportunity. On one occasion, they arrested him, along with Frank Livorsi, Charles Donato of Manhattan and Rocco Delarmi of the Bronx after they completed a round of golf at the Pelham Bay Golf Course. Following the May 23, 1934, arrest, the four men were charged with consorting with known criminals – all four of the men had criminal records – and they were locked into jail cells overnight.

The next day they were brought to police headquarters and put into a lineup of criminals. They were then brought to West Farms Court in the Bronx, where Magistrate George V. DeLuca dismissed the charge and released the men.[426]

In summer of 1936, travel documents show that Frank Livorsi sailed back to New York City after a trip to Italy. On the same ship were Michael Coppola, thirty six, a resident of Corona, Queens, and his father Joseph.[427]

Livorsi's reentry into the U.S. was noted after another trip early in 1940. Livorsi, then a resident of 5178 Seventy-second Place in Maspeth, Queens, and Charles Albero, thirty eight, of Mount Vernon, New York, were recorded on the passenger list of a seaplane traveling from Havana, Cuba, to Miami, Florida, on February 19.[428] The nature of their business was not noted, but it may have been related to narcotics charges that were filed against both men two years later.

Federal prosecutors announced on April 8, 1942, that the work of narcotics agents had resulted in indictments against a ring believed to have smuggled $1 million worth of heroin across the U.S.-Mexico border through a period of eighteen months. Seventeen suspected members of the ring in New York and Arizona were indicted. The New Yorkers, described as members of East Harlem's "107th Street Mob," included Livorsi, Albero, Phillip Lombardo, Salvatore Santora, Joseph Spitaleri, Joseph Gagliano and Mariano Mersalisi. Valachi friend Dominick "the Gap" Petrelli also became a defendant in the case.[429]

Over time, many of the case defendants admitted their roles in the smuggling operation. Between May 18 and May 26, Livorsi, Albero, Petrelli and Spitaleri changed their pleas from not guilty to guilty. On July 28, Livorsi and Albero were sentenced to two years in prison, Santoro and Petrelli were sentenced to five years, and Spitaleri was sentenced to a year and a day. Each was also fined $1,000 and sentenced to serve a year of probation following their prison releases.[430]

Following prison, Livorsi appears to have returned to his rackets. But he moved his home from Long Island City, Queens, to further out on Long Island. He, wife Dorina and their four daughters resided near Ocean Boulevard in Atlantic Beach, Nassau County, at the time of the 1950 U.S. Census. For the census, he reported working as an "agent." Next to that position, the term "race horses" was written in and then scratched out.[431]

Livorsi was again arrested later that year. Federal authorities on September 25 filed income tax evasion charges against Livorsi, accountant Louis J. Roth of New York City, William J. Giglio of Port-au-Peck, New Jersey, and former federal prosecutor Howard M. Lawn of Long Branch, New Jersey. The four men reportedly avoided paying income taxes on the large profits of a postwar black-market sugar racket.

The racket included setting up a number of companies used to acquire then-rationed sugar in large quantities from mysterious sources and sell it illegally. The government initially stated that it was owed $135,000 in taxes for the year 1946. It later estimated that the evaded taxes totaled $855,000. Prosecutors claimed that each of the participants in the racket had accumulated $100,000 through the enterprise by 1947, when its main company, American Brands Corporation, was permitted to go bankrupt.[432]

Federal indictments were returned against the four men in October 1952. However those indictments were later thrown out on a legal technicality. Additional indictments were returned in January 1954. By then, the estimate of the evaded taxes had risen to $1 million.[433]

Prosecutor J. Edward Lumbard told the press that the sugar racket was born following Livorsi's release from his narcotics sentence. Lumbard said Howard Lawn resigned from the U.S. attorney's office in Newark, New Jersey, to take part in the scheme.[434]

Louis Roth pleaded guilty to conspiracy and concealment of assets, and he agreed to testify as a government witness in the case. His three codefendants went to trial. All were convicted in February 1955. The following month, Judge Lawrence E. Walsh sentenced Livorsi and Giglio to fifteen years in prison. He delayed sentencing for Lawn. Late in 1955, Lawn was sentenced to serve a year and a day in federal prison.[435]

A dispute over the validity of the 1954 tax evasion indictments arose in spring of 1958. Attorneys for Livorsi and Giglio attempted to have their convictions reversed. Judge Gregory F. Noonan rejected that appeal as well as a request for a reduction in the fifteen-year sentences.[436]

An FBI report written in November 1963, after Valachi testified before the Senate subcommittee, indicated that Livorsi was then still serving his sentence in federal prison. Livorsi was apparently released soon after that. His death in Atlantic Beach on September 22, 1967, is reported in New York State records.[437]

Medaglia, Samuel "Sam Medal"

Medaglia (left), Kreisberger (right).

> *Sam Medole killed her boyfriend. His name was Otto. He came from 116th Street and First Avenue.[438]*

Valachi knew "Sam Medole" as a love interest of a female gangster he knew as "Lottie." According to Valachi, Sam was not Lottie's only love interest.

Around 1924-1925, when Valachi was accused of helping an "Irish Mob" in an attack against Joey Rao and a Mafia-affiliated "Italian Mob" based at East 116th Street and First Avenue, Lottie was with the Italian gangsters.[439]

"I'm not sure I knew her when she hung around 116th Street and First Avenue," Valachi later wrote of that period. "She was very pretty... She was about five feet ten inches in height, and she had a fine shape, and everyone used to admire her."[440]

Lottie was linked with an Italian gangster Valachi knew as "Otto." The relationship came to a sudden end in the summer of 1927. According to Valachi, Otto was murdered by Sam Medole. Lottie apparently had a relationship with Sam, but then moved on to Vincent "Mad Dog" Coll. "Vince took Lottie for his girl, and then I think he married her," Valachi wrote.[441]

Valachi inaccurately recalled that Vincent Coll was responsible for the later murder of Sam Medole: "Vincent Coll killed Sammy Medole because of Lottie."[442] (Coll actually died seven months before Sam disappeared. Coll was shot to death in a Manhattan drugstore phone booth on February 8, 1932.)

Samuel "Sam Medal" Medaglia[443] was born about 1902 in New York City. His parents were Italian immigrants Francesco and Teresa DeRosa Medaglia. Francesco left Teresa and their two oldest sons in Italy, when he settled in the

U.S. He found work as a day laborer in East Harlem. Teresa and sons Antonio and Stefano joined him a short time later, crossing the Atlantic in the summer of 1895. The "Miraglia" family showed up in the 1900 U.S. Census as residents of 318 East 115th Street in East Harlem. The family had increased by two additional children by then.[444]

Documentation of Samuel's birth has not yet been located. He first appears in the 1915 New York State Census as a thirteen-year-old, the youngest of five children in the Medaglia family, 318 East 115th Street. The census recorded Francesco's 1915 occupation as street sweeper. His two oldest sons were then working as electricians.[445]

Francesco Medaglia died on March 19, 1917. He was about fifty seven. Samuel was about fourteen when his father passed away.[446]

Charlotte Dora "Lottie" Denninger was a few years older than Samuel Medaglia. She was born to Ignatz and Lizzie Wittleder Denninger on March 2, 1899, at 161 West Thirty-second Street in Midtown Manhattan, close to Pennsylvania Station. Her father, an immigrant from Bavaria and proprietor of a saloon, died at a Bronx hospital in December 1901 while being treated for tuberculosis.[447] Lottie added a few years to her age and claimed she was twenty two when she married salesman Sam Kreisberg in June 1917. The couple reportedly went their separate ways two years later, following the birth of a daughter.[448] Though parted from Sam Kreisberg and later divorced from him, she adopted a version of his surname as her own and was subsequently known as Lottie Kreisberger. Lottie probably began associating with Adolfo "Otto" Romano by 1921. By that time, she had already been arrested twice (and discharged twice) on burglary charges.[449]

Romano, roughly the same age as Lottie, had some early entries on his arrest record as well. In the summer of 1917, while a resident of 405 East 117th Street in East Harlem, he was charged with being a pickpocket. In the spring of 1920, he and two companions were arrested for participating in the February robbery of two Manhattan women.[450]

Valachi first became aware of Lottie around the time that her boyfriend "Otto" and Valachi's close acquaintance Frank Livorsi were charged in connection with a drugstore stickup and later with a jewelry robbery.[451]

Sam Kreisberg formally divorced Lottie in April 1925. Taking their daughter with him, he moved back into the home of his parents, then at 700 East 158th Street in the Bronx.[452]

A couple of miles away in the same borough, "Sam Medal" was living with his sister and brother-in-law on Elder Avenue as he finished up a law degree at Columbia University Law School. While he is not known to have met fellow Bronxite Sam Kreisberg, he did somehow come into contact with Kreisberg's ex-wife, Lottie, and with her current boyfriend Adolfo "Otto" Romano.

Romano had become part owner of a speakeasy on East 117th Street in East Harlem and may have engaged in other bootlegging-related rackets, lucrative but dangerous lines of work. Romano and Medaglia reportedly quarreled early in 1927. Lottie was believed to be the cause of their disagreement.[453]

In the early evening of July 7, 1927, Romano was driving his automobile slowly, through a heavy rain, northward on Morris Avenue in the Bronx. According to published accounts, gunmen jumped to the running board of his vehicle as he neared 140th Street and opened fire on him. A slug pierced his chest and tore through his aorta, causing him to quickly bleed to death. As Romano's life poured out, his car continued to move along Morris Avenue until it crashed into a fence about a block later.

Romano was dead when police arrived at the scene. In the car, they found his identification and some labels for bootleg whiskey bottles. They had him taken to the morgue in Fordham and brought his sister Rose there to officially identify the body.[454]

Learning of Romano's recent quarrel, detectives went looking for Medaglia but could not locate him. After a period of months, one detective happened to notice him on a New York City subway and placed him under arrest. Medaglia was tried in 1928 for the murder of Romano, but he was acquitted.[455]

Rather than pursue a career in law, Sam Medal reportedly became a bookmaker. He also briefly held the role of Lottie Kreisberger's boyfriend. But, by about 1929, he was replaced in that role by Irish-American gangster Vincent Coll. Once allies of Dutch Schultz, brothers Vincent and Peter Coll broke away from Schultz and gathered a gang around them that opposed the allied organizations of Schultz and Mafia leader Ciro Terranova.[456]

The Coll mob was believed responsible for the May 28, 1931, killings of Terranova aide Frank "Big Dick" Amato and Dominick "Louis Slats" Bologna on East 116th Street.[457] In an apparent retaliatory strike, Vincent Coll's brother Peter was fatally shot while driving on St. Nicholas Avenue near 111th Street just two days later.[458] Following the loss of his brother, Vincent Coll became reckless, expanding his war and even turning on some of his Irish-American underworld sympathizers.[459]

Police repeatedly raided the Cornish Arms Hotel at West Twenty-third Street and Eighth Avenue, which was used as a Coll headquarters. They arrested Vincent Coll there in July of 1931 and charged him with murder. In an October roundup of Coll gang members at the hotel, Lottie Kreisberger was arrested for illegal possession of a firearm and a blackjack.[460]

Coll was acquitted of murder charges in December. A week later, he and Lottie obtained a marriage license. Lottie gave her name as Charlotte Van Kressberger. Both gave fictitious addresses. They appear not to have gone through the formality of a wedding ceremony, but Lottie regarded herself as Mrs. Vincent Coll. Of her "husband," she once remarked, "I'd rather live on bread and water with him than in luxury with any other man."[461]

Coll walked into an ambush at about one o'clock in the morning of February 8, 1932. He entered a drug store at 314 West Twenty-third Street, near the Cornish Arms, and went into a phone booth. Gunmen appeared and shot him to death. The death certificate reported bullet wounds to his "head and brain, right chest, right lung and heart."[462] He was the second of Lottie's lovers to meet a violent end.

"Sam Medal" Medaglia had become the successful proprietor of Conte's restaurant, 147 West Forty-seventh Street, a short distance from Times Square. He was reported to be friendly with Coll's enemy Dutch Schultz and other underworld figures, who were observed dining at his establishment. Following the murder of Coll, Medaglia restarted his relationship with Lottie Kreisberger-Coll and supported her during her brief and unsuccessful legal battle against the weapons possession charge.[463]

Wearing a black dress and veil for her February 26 court appearance, Lottie was convicted of violating the Sullivan gun control law. Sentencing was scheduled for Friday, March 11, but Lottie did not show up for court that day. Instead, the court received a doctor's note that reported she was too ill to leave her bed. A bench warrant was issued for her. Authorities located her at Fordham Hospital on Monday, the fourteenth. She reportedly entered the hospital on the twelfth. A police guard was placed outside her door, and Lottie remained in the facility for several months. The cause of her hospitalization was not disclosed, but one report indicated that she required minor surgery.[464]

Lottie and Medaglia saw each other for the final time in June 1932. On the seventeenth of that month, she was removed from the hospital and began a six-month sentence in the workhouse. A defense motion to have the time of her hospital confinement subtracted from her sentence was unsuccessful.[465]

On the night of September 6, 1932, Sam Medal disappeared. At about eleven o'clock that night, he telephoned his sister Catherine Gerviano, with whom he lived at 1442 Harrod Avenue in the Bronx, and told her he would be home later than usual, as he had a business appointment. Employees saw him walk out of his restaurant near midnight with two men they did not recognize. He got into their car and rode away.[466]

Medaglia's sister telephoned police when she learned that he did not make it home. His disappearance was kept out of the news until police announced it on September 18. Detectives questioned Lottie, then held at a women's detention center at Tenth Street and Greenwich Avenue. She said she knew nothing of Medaglia's whereabouts and last saw him at the time of her sentencing. Restaurant employees told investigators of the strangers they saw with Medaglia as he left the restaurant on the sixth, and they noted that he was carrying about $4,000 when he got in their car.

The media explored a number of theories: Sam Medal was kidnapped and held for enormous ransom, he was killed because of his connection to Coll's widow, he was a casualty of a war between rival gangs, he was the third victim of Lottie's "curse," he was again in hiding as he had been following the murder of Romano.[467]

About a month later and about a hundred miles from the spot where he was last seen, authorities believed they recovered the body of Samuel Medaglia. At Swan Lake, four miles southwest of the Town of Liberty in New York's Sullivan County, a hunter found the body of a dead man hidden in a thicket. It took some time for investigators to link the remote October 16 discovery to the September disappearance in New York City.

Early in November, police announced that the body from Swan Lake – an obvious murder victim, with .38-caliber bullet wounds in the left side and the left temple – had been identified as Sam Medal.[468]

The identification was not entirely certain. Two of Medaglia's brothers, brought to the morgue to view the body on November 2, were divided in their opinions. While body measurements were a match for Medaglia, police admitted that fingerprints obtained from the remains were different than those recorded on a Medaglia pistol permit application. They concluded that Medaglia had someone else provide the fingerprints on that application.[469]

On November 3, New York City dentist A.T. Goldwater provided charts of Medaglia dental work that seemed to prove that the body found at Swan Lake was not Medaglia. By that time, media interest in the subject had waned.[470]

Paduano, Nick

> *...They sent us, that is Nickie and I, to what we called the "haunted house"... Mr. Maranzano was living there, and he moved from there to Yonkers... If one of the guys that had that phone number on his person is caught by the opposite mob, God knows how many will come to this house... thinking that the boss is still there.[471]*

Nick "Padovana" was a friend of Valachi and a member of his small burglary gang.[472] He was inducted into the Mafia organization of Salvatore Maranzano near the end of 1930, during Maranzano's war against reigning U.S. Mafia boss of bosses Giuseppe Masseria.[473]

During that "Castellammarese War," Valachi and Nick were assigned to a number of tasks that did not go as planned. They were sent out with Salvatore Shillitani to "hit" an enemy gunman on St. Ann's Avenue between East 138th and East 139th streets in the South Bronx. Valachi was the driver. They quickly spotted their target. "Now, before I came to a stop, Nickie and Solly started to shoot from in the car. The first thing you know, that... guy ran in a hallway and got away."[474]

Though Valachi protested that he didn't want any more assignments with Nick, they were sent together to keep an eye on Maranzano's former residence in Brooklyn. Maranzano had quietly relocated to Yonkers, but enemies might go gunning for him at that address and allies might try to reach him there. Valachi and Nick agreed that they would alternate nights at the house while the one off-duty could go out with his girlfriend. One night when Valachi was with his girlfriend May, he learned that Nick became frightened and abandoned the house. Maranzano heard of this and called Valachi to Yonkers to answer for it.

Maranzano decided to remove Nick from the house, and sent "Joe Palisades" Rosato with Valachi back to Brooklyn.[475]

After the war, Valachi recalled that Nick was killed by a police officer in the same incident that resulted in Shillitani getting sent to prison for twenty years.[476]

Nicholas Paduano was born about 1907 in East Harlem. His parents were Sabato "Sam," a baker, and Maria, both natives of Italy. The family name was sometimes written "Padovano," "Padvano" or "Padowani."[477]

The New York State Census of 1915 appears to hold two entries for Nick Paduano. One was in the family residence, 2038 First Avenue in East Harlem. The other was in the New York Catholic Protectory in the Bronx, where a young Paduano was committed on September 18, 1914. Joseph Valachi served several years in the protectory in the same period.[478]

He became Valachi's friend and criminal colleague during the 1920s. Together they did some "work" for East Harlem mafioso Tom Gagliano: they "roughed up some guys in building unions who were causing trouble."[479]

Paduano married Louise Esposito in March 1930. In November, Paduano helped to hide Valachi after he assisted a combined Gagliano-Maranzano team in the murders of Masseria allies Manfredi "Al" Mineo and Stefano Ferrigno. After that, Paduano, Valachi and Salvatore Shillitani were formally inducted into the Maranzano Mafia organization.[480]

Months after the end of the Castellammarese War, an older Gagliano group member had some trouble with a group of street toughs. "Don Abate" complained to crime family higher-ups that the young gangsters had robbed his saloon. "Joe Palisades" Rosato, of the Gaglianos, shared the information with Valachi. Valachi was then a soldier in the crime family led by Salvatore "Charlie Luciano" Lucania, but Rosato was friendly with him and knew him to be well connected to the neighborhood. Valachi was sure that the robbery had been done by the "Shoemaker brothers." The brothers generally worked with a friend Valachi believed to be an Irish-American teen from Yorkville on Manhattan's Upper East Side. (The friend was an Italian American from the southern section of Yorkville.)

Valachi met with the gang and explained that they had made a mistake and should return what they took. The Shoemakers said they could not return the cash, as they had already spent it. Valachi sent word of the meeting back to the Gaglianos and believed the young gangsters had been forgiven for their transgression. But, about a week later, the gang robbed "Don Abate's" saloon a second time. Another meeting was arranged. The Shoemakers and their "Irish" friend showed up armed. They told Valachi they intended to continue robbing as it pleased them. They didn't care whose toes they stepped on. They expressed respect only for Valachi and local mafioso Dominick Petrelli.

Mafia leaders decided that the Shoemakers needed to be killed. Orders came down from Lucania that Valachi should help set up the boys for a hit by gunmen working with Rosato. Valachi was uncomfortable about betraying the boys who trusted him. New arrangements were made in which Petrelli and Nick Paduano would set up the hit.

Soon after that, the Shoemakers went to Valachi and said they had been offered a chance to rob a slot machine site alongside Paduano, Shillitani, Frank "Chic 99" Callace and Eddie Coco. They wanted to know if Valachi felt it would be safe to accept the job. Certain it was a trap, but unable to warn them without offending his bosses, Valachi assured the boys it was OK. He made an effort to convince the "Irish" kid to do a job with him instead but was unable to prevent him from going with his friends on the night of January 28, 1932.[481]

That night, Thomas Quales Jr., police officer and chauffeur for Second Deputy Police Commissioner Felix Muldoon, was visiting his father, a clerk in the Bronx County Court, at his home, 939 Mace Avenue at the corner with Paulding Avenue in the Bronx. The house sat across the street from Public School 89. The sound of gunshots attracted the Quales's attention to the area in front of the school. They saw a man fall to the sidewalk and other men run off. They went in pursuit. The younger Quales exchanged shots with the fleeing gunmen as they ran north on Paulding, cut westward through a vacant lot to Colden Avenue and entered an apartment building.[482] Quales followed them inside, used a phone to summon assistance and then went back out to see if the gunmen were trying to escape the building. He saw a man scramble down a rear fire escape into a small back yard and scale a fence in the direction of 2553 Williamsbridge Road. Quales fired several shots.

Nicholas Paduano, then just twenty four, dropped to the ground, dead with a bullet in his brain. A quick investigation showed that Paduano was a resident of 2550 Colden Avenue, very close to the spot where he died.[483] Salvatore Shillitani arrived in the back yard by the same fire escape, but was halted there by the elder Quales. When police arrived at Public School 89, they found Benedetto Bellini, nineteen, a resident of 348 East Seventy-seventh Street, dead of gunshot wounds to the brain and left lung. Bellini was the young man Valachi knew as the Shoemakers' "Irish" friend.

Years later, Valachi explained to federal agents that the Shoemakers and Bellini met with Callace, Coco, Paduano and Shillitani in front of the school. When they got there, the Shoemakers became nervous and decided to leave. The brothers ran off, but Bellini was shot down. Callace and Coco separated from Paduano and Shillitani during the Quales' pursuit and eluded police.[484]

Reggione, Michael "Little Apples"

> *Vito Genovese and Anthony Strollo… feared that Little*
> *Apples would attempt to revenge the deaths of his brothers.*

Valachi reportedly told a federal investigator that crime family underboss Vito Genovese and his aide Anthony "Tony Bender" Strollo ordered Peter "Muggins" Leone and "Johnny Dee" DeBellis to murder Michael "Little Apples" Reggione. He said Genovese and Strollo were concerned that Reggione would try to avenge the murders of several brothers, who were killed by mafiosi was Reggione was a child.

Leone, DeBellis and Reggione met Valachi at a diner on East 109th Street and Lexington Avenue on November 25, 1932. Leone pulled Valachi aside and explained that Reggione was about to be killed. At Leone's request, Valachi acted friendly toward Reggione and offered to take him to a gambling spot a few blocks away in a building on East 110th Street near First Avenue.

Leone and DeBellis left Reggione with Valachi, and Valachi and Reggione soon went out to the gambling site. Valachi led "Little Apples" to the front hallway of the building and left him. As he walked away, he heard gunshots.[485]

The basic premise of the Reggione murder story provided by Valachi was flawed. Michael Reggione was not the last of a group of brothers to be killed by the Mafia. While he was one of the younger siblings in his family, he appears to have been the first to be murdered. The motivation for the hit against "Little Apples" could not have been fear of a vendetta arising from his brothers' murders, as those killings had not yet occurred.

Born in 1920, the same year that his father John passed away, Michael "Little Apples" Reggione had six brothers and two sisters.[486]

The Reggiones appear to have organized their own gang in Lower Manhattan. They engaged in robberies, burglaries, gambling and counterfeiting.

Pasquale "Patsy" Reggione was arrested in Stamford, Connecticut, in 1928 – the year that mother Filomena Reggione passed away in a diabetic coma. Patsy was convicted of possession of burglar's tools, carrying concealed weapons and possession of explosives. He was sentenced to fifteen to twenty years in Connecticut State Prison at Wethersfield.[487]

Tommy Reggione was convicted of first-degree armed robbery two years later. He robbed a number of restaurant patrons at gunpoint. He was sentenced to twenty to forty years in Sing Sing.[488]

Early in 1932, Louis Reggione was arrested in a Secret Service raid at Queens, New York. He was charged with conspiring with a currency counterfeiting operation. Six accomplices all pleaded guilty, but Louis maintained his innocence. When brought to trial, Louis managed to disappear. A jury found him guilty on April 11, 1932. Authorities later caught up with him and he began a long sentence in prison.[489]

Those three brothers had experienced some trouble, but were still alive when Michael was found shot to death – bullet wounds in his left cheek, left side of neck, lower jaw and throat – in the front hallway of 340 East 110th Street on November 25, 1932. His death certificate noted that the funeral director for Michael was hired by another brother, Joseph.[490]

In reporting the news of Michael's murder, the press stated that he had been convicted of third-degree burglary and served a recent sentence at Elmira Prison. His record included arrests on suspicion of counterfeiting, criminal assault and automobile theft. At the time of his death, he was wanted by police for violating the terms of his parole. Michael was just twenty two. He was said to be married. Sources differed on his home address. While a newspaper report said he lived at 126 Thompson Street on Manhattan's Lower West Side, the death certificate put his residence at 449 East 183rd Street in the Belmont section of the Bronx.[491]

James Reggione, thirty eight, was taking a walk with a twelve-year-old niece on West Broadway near Houston Street on the evening of May 23, 1935, when he was shot down. A gunman came up behind him and fired five slugs into his back. An autopsy found that bullets had torn through his neck, spine, heart, lungs, liver and intestines. A resident of 2467 Belmont Avenue in the Bronx, James was apparently downtown visiting relatives on Prince Street. The press reported that he had been arrested eleven times since childhood and had served several prison sentences. To brother Joseph once again fell the duty of hiring the funeral director.[492]

Louis "Fat Elevator" Reggione finished his counterfeiting sentence and was released from Lewisburg, Pennsylvania, federal prison in spring 1940. By midsummer he was dead. The forty-seven-year-old apparently was entering his residence, 282 Mulberry Street in Manhattan, early Monday morning, August 26, when he was shot by two gunmen. Slugs entered his left side, piercing his kidney, duodenum and liver. He died of hemorrhage and shock. Brother Joseph, who was standing beside Louis at the moment of the shooting but escaped unharmed, performed his usual funeral responsibility.[493]

Following the killing of Louis, his sister Nancy Sandino told the press, "It's a vendetta. Somebody has sworn to kill us all. Oh, God, who's going to be next?"[494]

Joseph was the sole Reggione brother alive and on the streets for a time. Patsy and Tommy were still in prison. One other brother, Johnny, was reportedly a resident patient at a veterans' hospital.

Patsy, then forty-five, was released from prison in February 1943. Just a few months later, he was arrested in Brooklyn on a charge of illegal possession of a firearm.[495]

He was back in the news again early in 1950. Responding to an afternoon robbery at a Manhattan pastry shop, 374 Second Avenue, Police Officer Reuben Flier pursued a suspect and cornered him in a fifth floor hallway at 235 East Twentieth Street. The suspect raised a handgun toward the officer, but Flier quickly fired four shots. One penetrated the chest of the suspect, later identified as Patsy Reggione. Reggione, then fifty one, was taken to Bellevue Hospital. He died there.

Police stated that Patsy's criminal record included seventeen arrests, dating back to 1912. The *New York Daily News*, perhaps forgetting the fate of the other Reggione brothers (or perhaps by this time tired of repeating the story), did not note in its reporting of the incident that Patsy was the fourth of the brother-criminals to come to a violent end.[496]

Murder scenes of Michael (left) and Pasquale (right) Reggione. (NY Daily News)

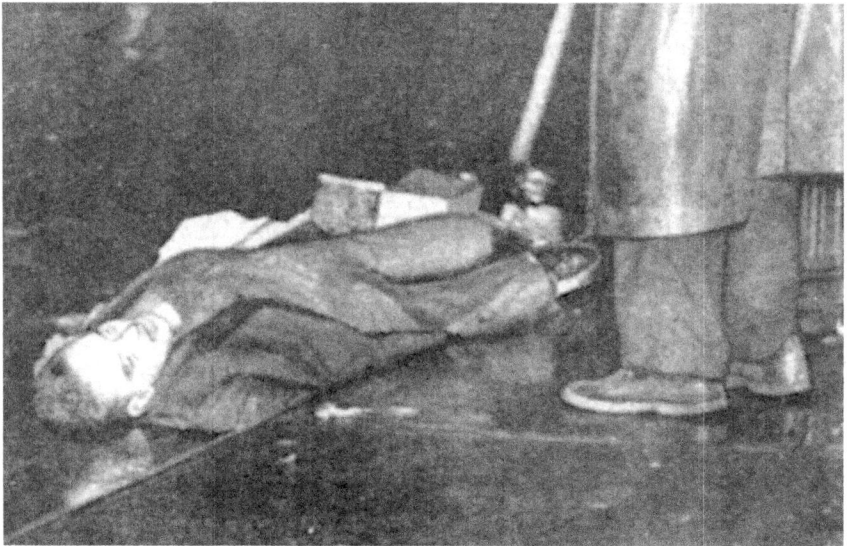

Murder scene of Louis Reggione. (NY Daily News)

Rodgers, John "Bum"

> *He went on to say the Bum got Frank. He did it for Ciro Terranova and Ciro gave the Bum a hundred dollars.*[497]

Joseph Valachi did not say a great deal about "Bum." According to his autobiography, Valachi knew "Bum" as a member of an early Prohibition Era East Harlem gang he called the "Irish Mob." Despite that name, the gang had few Irish-American members at the time and was led by an Italian-American gangster named Nick Caputo.

Though Valachi had a number of old friends in the local "Italian Mob," a group which had become closely linked to regional Mafia chief Ciro Terranova, he sided with the nominal Irish when a mid-1920s conflict erupted between the two gangs. Just as the conflict was resolved, Valachi was taken off the streets to begin serving a sentence in Sing Sing Prison.

A top member of the Irish Mob, "Dutch" Augustine, soon began a sentence of his own at Sing Sing. Valachi and Augustine met inside the prison early in 1926 and discussed recent events in the East Harlem underworld.

Augustine revealed that the Terranova-aligned Italian gang put a condition into the peace treaty with the Irish: Valachi and Frank LaPuma, associates of the Irish group, were both to be murdered. According to Augustine, Irish gang leader Caputo agreed to the condition.

"In other words, Nick Caputo sold Frank and I out?" Valachi asked.

"That's right," answered Augustine, who explained that Terranova convinced "Bum" to murder fellow Irish gang member LaPuma and paid "Bum" $100 for the June 9, 1925, killing.

Valachi also referred to "Bum" when considering the extraordinary crime figures he met during his lifetime:

> I met lots of men that were very impressive. For instance Bum Rogers, who later on was wanted for every crime that was committed. He finally was arrested a few years later. I don't remember how much time he got, but he hung himself in Dannamora State Prison.[498]

John Joseph "Bum" Rodgers, Jr., was born February 8, 1892, to John Sr. and Ellen "Nellie" Rodgers. His place of birth remains uncertain. He repeatedly stated he was born in Brooklyn, but newspapers insisted instead on locations in Harlem – either on East 100th Street near the base of Duffy's Hill or on East 113th Street between Lexington and Third avenues.[499]

In early childhood, his home was was an East Harlem apartment at 1986 Second Avenue near the intersection with East 102nd Street. He grew up there as the second-youngest of five children – three boys and two girls. While still young, he exhibited two tendencies for which he would be known the rest of his life: He had a "slovenly manner and careless appearance," which led to his "Bum" nickname, and he felt a strong attraction toward criminal activity.[500]

Rodgers was only about ten years old when he was sentenced to the New York Catholic Protectory for juvenile delinquency. Additional juvenile criminal activity – picking pockets, petit larceny, disorderly conduct, etc. – caused him to be branded "incorrigible," and he was repeatedly sent to the House of Refuge reformatory on Randalls Island.[501]

As a teenager, he joined the violent Car Barn Gang led by Daniel "Bosco" Lynch, who was just about one year older. That gang, which numbered about fifty, was known to be active in the area of Second Avenue and Ninetieth Street beginning around 1909. At one point, the gang reportedly posted a "deadline" notice, warning police that they would be attacked if they "trespassed" in the neighborhood.[502]

Rodgers' first prison sentence was a 1909 stay in the New York County Penitentiary earned for petit larceny. Upon his release, he immediately returned to the gang and to his criminal life.[503]

In Car Barn Gang territory, there were frequent assaults directed against police officers, as the gang's young members threw bricks and other projectiles from tenement rooftops. In 1911, member Joseph Murphy was captured after firing a handgun at patrol officer William Porter. Murphy was sentenced to nine and a half years in prison. The Car Barn Gang promised retribution against Officer Porter. On Sunday night, May 21, 1911, Porter spotted Bosco Lynch at First Avenue and Ninety-sixth Street and confronted him. Lynch commented, "We'll fix you for getting Murphy," and Porter arrested him for threatening a police officer.[504]

While Bosco Lynch was being held on that charge, a rival named John McNally reportedly attempted to take control of the gang. Lynch soon returned to the streets. That meant trouble for McNally. Late on Saturday night, September 16, John McNally and his brother Frank were in the apartment building where Lynch lived, 195 East 100th Street. Frank McNally later reported that they were visiting merely to retrieve some clothing John McNally had left in his former rooms in the building. Alerted by allies to the presence of John McNally, Lynch grabbed a handgun and went after his rival. As the McNallys fled down the building stairs, Lynch planted two bullets in John McNally's back.

Police patrolling nearby heard the shots and rushed into the building. John Lynch was unconscious and dying. The gangster passed away before an ambulance arrived. Frank McNally told the officers that Lynch had shot him and had then gone upstairs toward the roof. The police found Lynch on the roof and arrested him.[505]

Daniel "Bosco" Lynch was charged with first-degree murder. He went to trial in New York General Sessions Court in December. The jury convicted him of second-degree murder, and Judge Edward Swann sentenced him to twenty years to life in prison. That concluded a criminal career in which Lynch reportedly accumulated twenty two arrests by the age of just twenty one.[506]

Following Lynch's conviction (and with the ambitious John McNally no longer a concern), Bum Rodgers became the leader of the Car Barn Gang. He too soon ran into trouble with the law. On January 25, 1912, a man named Frank Heisch was fatally stabbed at a dance hall on Lexington Avenue. Before Heisch died, he told police that Rodgers stabbed him. Rodgers was arrested and held at the Tombs jail.

He was still held there when, in early March, the gang held a fundraising dance for him at Corey's Hall on Fulton Street in Astoria, Queens. Couples were charged twenty five cents for admission, just ten cents for an unaccompanied woman. The dance was interrupted by a police raid, which resulted in several arrests for possession of weapons such as revolvers, knives and slungshots.[507]

While Rodgers avoided conviction for the stabbing of Heisch, he was arrested in April for carrying a billy club. He was convicted of illegal weapons possession and, on June 17, was sentenced to prison for a minimum of three years and four months and a maximum of seven years. He was received at Sing Sing Prison on June 28, 1912, and was moved to Clinton State Prison at Dannemora the following year.[508]

He was released after serving about the minimum sentence, but he may still have been in prison when his father passed away in autumn 1915.[509]

In summer of 1916, he began adding more entries to his criminal résumé. He was then arrested for assault and robbery, but was acquitted at trial in autumn. Early in 1917, he was arrested for another assault and robbery – the stickup of a Second Avenue grocery store which involved the shooting of one proprietor and the clubbing of another. A Rodgers accomplice, Mickey Herlihy, was quickly convicted. Rodgers was tried on the charge several times during the year before being convicted by a jury in December. At that time, the *New York Tribune* reported that Rodgers was "the only leader of the notorious Car Barn gangsters alive and not doing time in prison."[510]

Judge William Goff sentenced Rodgers on February 15, 1918, to fourteen years in prison. He was received at Sing Sing three days later and then moved on for a time to Auburn State Prison.[511]

Bum Rodgers served only a small portion of his sentence. In early August 1920, New York Governor Alfred E. Smith commuted his sentence to a minimum of two years, seven months and two days from his arrival at Sing Sing, so he would be eligible for parole the following month. The commutation was conditional on reform. If Rodgers was convicted of a felony again, "he shall be deemed an escaped convict with respect to the said commuted term..." and returned to prison for the remainder of his original fourteen-year sentence (about eleven and a half years) in addition to any new sentence.[512]

Immediately following his release, Rodgers took a bride. He married Catherine "Kitty" O'Brien in Manhattan on September 26, 1920.[513]

But the "Bum" didn't stay out of trouble for long. Late in April 1921, Charles "Pelly" Pelletier was about to join his brother John in a restaurant at 208 West Ninety-sixth Street when he fell to the sidewalk with a bullet wound through his body. After the gunshot, witnesses reported seeing several men flee from the dark doorway of the neighboring building. John Pelletier told police he was certain he knew who shot his brother. The police vaguely announced that they were looking for an ex-convict.[514]

Charles Pelletier was rushed to Bellevue Hospital. Though initially said to be near death, he made a surprising recovery. Newspapers reported that he had been a criminal of some note in earlier years and had recently been released from Sing Sing after serving a burglary sentence.[515]

Pelletier, also known as Charles Devere, had been associated with a gang on the Upper West Side in 1912, when he was wounded in a central Harlem pistol battle with two police officers and arrested on felonious assault charges. He was then seventeen and a resident of 124 West 101st Street.[516] In March of 1917, he was sentenced to five years in prison following a second-degree assault conviction. As he entered Sing Sing, he reported that he was the son of immigrants from Potenza, Italy.[517]

Police eventually found the ex-convict they were looking for, though they appear to have arrested him on a burglary charge before realizing he was wanted for shooting Pelletier. John "Bum" Rodgers was brought into West Side Court on a felonious assault charge on May 11, 1921. In the courtroom, Rodgers was recognized by a police detective, who informed the judge of previous encounters with Rodgers – by then also known as John Hughes and John O'Brien – and his old Car Barn Gang. The detective recalled that the gang had been broken up after a month of street fighting that sent eight police officers to the hospital.[518]

The burglary charge was dropped, and the attack against Pelletier resulted in an October conviction for carrying a concealed weapon. Rodgers reportedly remained unsentenced on the weapons charge for almost three years.

In the interim, Rodgers kept busy. In January 1922, he was arrested in connection with the December 15 holdup of bank messengers in Greenpoint, Brooklyn. The messengers were robbed of more than $17,000. Rodgers was discharged by a Brooklyn magistrate, but the arrest was enough to have him returned to prison as a parole violator.[519]

He was shuffled around among Sing Sing, Clinton and Auburn prisons. In spring of 1924, he returned to New York City and was given a suspended sentence for his earlier weapons possession charge. Another weapons charge in the summer resulted in an indeterminate sentence at the county penitentiary on Welfare Island.[520]

Welfare Island was not the most secure location. The home of several city hospitals, it was exposed to a great deal of unmonitored traffic. Rodgers took advantage. On January 19, 1925, he and two other inmates, Vincent McCormick and James "Killer" Cunniffe, went out a window of the penitentiary's second floor medical ward, slid down a short rope and dropped to the ground outside the building. From there, they simply walked away.[521]

Rodgers and Irish Mob gangsters Ludwig "Dutch" Augustine, Frank LaPuma and Raymond Fallon were believed responsible for the March 7, 1925 robbery of payroll cash from two employees of H. and D.R. Wadsworth of Valley Stream, New York. Three months later, LaPuma was found dead on the front steps of a tenement building at 327 East 105th Street. He had been shot through the head and abdomen.[522]

Weeks later, a police officer spotted Rodgers as he attempted to extort money from a store owner on Lexington Avenue near 118th Street. As the officer approached, Rodgers saw him and fired a handgun in his direction. Another officer was drawn to the scene, and a chase ensued. Anticipating his escape route, the officers apprehended Rodgers as he descended a fire escape behind 161 East 118th Street.[523]

On July 1, Rodgers was indicted for first-degree assault, extortion and a Sullivan's Law weapons offense. At that time, it was calculated that he already owed fourteen years in state prison for parole violation and three years in county penitentiary. On the fourteenth, he was sentenced to another five years for his more recent offenses. He reentered Sing Sing Prison the next day.[524]

Rodgers was transported to Mineola, Long Island, in December to face trial for the March payroll robbery of the Wadsworth Company. Trial became unnecessary, when he confessed to participating in the crime. Judge Lewis A. Smith of the Nassau County Court sentenced him to another fifteen years in prison.[525]

Auburn Prison Deputy Warden Edward Beckwith went to Mineola to retrieve Rodgers. Nassau County Detective Julian Heberer drove them to Grand Central Terminal on December 14. Beckwith and Rodgers, handcuffed together, boarded a New York Central Railroad train at two o'clock that afternoon. About ten minutes later, as the train approached the West 125th Street Station, Beckwith was knocked unconscious by a blow from behind. Rodgers and two other men jumped off the train at the station, ran down a flight of stairs and hopped into a waiting taxi.[526]

A manhunt was launched, but Rodgers remained out of sight for months. While he was a fugitive, a variety of robberies and a car theft were blamed on him. Some concern was raised when "Killer" Cunniffe, one of his partners in the Welfare Island escape, was found shot to death in Detroit at the end of October 1926.[527]

In an effort to discover Rodgers's location, detectives began following his wife, Catherine "Kitty." In the early morning hours of Thanksgiving Day, November 25, 1926, detectives spotted Kitty in a taxicab with another woman and a man, who appeared to be West Side gang leader Martin Aloysius "Marty" Madden, brother of the better known Owen "Owney" Madden. Marty Madden was thought to be an underworld enemy of Rodgers.

The detectives forced the taxi to halt. (According to some reports, they fired a shot that wounded the driver in order to accomplish that.) Then they took the taxi occupants to a police station for questioning. At about seven that morning, uniformed and plain clothes police surrounded an apartment building at 4274 Third Avenue in the Bronx, and officers battered down the door of apartment 30 on the top floor. Tenants James Pacificio and Helen Gershowitz were arrested for harboring a criminal. Rodgers was found asleep in a bedroom, with a .38-caliber pistol nearby. He had a new mustache and several days of beard growth. In his pockets were a single penny and a button.

He admitted ownership of the firearm, disputed the various accounts of his criminal activity since his escape and refused to identify those who helped him off the train. He vehemently denied reports that he was a user of narcotics, and stripped off his clothes, challenging detectives to find needle marks. He claimed he had not committed any crimes since his escape and had lived in several locations, including rooming houses at 705 East Sixth Street, 156 Goerck Street, 407 East Nineteenth Street and an unnumbered building on East Seventeenth Street. He had been at the Bronx address for several months, he said.[528]

Two competing explanations were offered for the police swarming the Bronx building. In one, the address was divulged during the question of Kitty Rodgers and Marty Madden. In the other, police observed the pair sending a messenger to warn Rodgers and followed the messenger to the Bronx address.[529]

Rodgers was charged with illegal possession of a firearm. If convicted, he would be sentenced under the Baumes Law to a mandatory life prison sentence as a four-time offender. Following an initial arraignment, Rodgers revealed that he was more concerned about issues relating to his wife. He released a statement to the press, in which he insisted that Marty Madden was a "personal friend of mine." He said that he knew Kitty was with him, as they were attending a christening event together, and that he had the "utmost confidence" in his wife.[530]

Rodgers pleaded guilty December 3 to violating the Sullivan Law. On the seventh, he was formally sentenced, and he reached Sing Sing the same day. He was subsequently transferred to Clinton State Prison at Dannemora.[531]

In July 1929, he was believed to be partly responsible for initiating a prison riot. According to one report, he arranged to smuggle enough dynamite into the prison to blow up the entire facility. After the riot was suppressed, Rodgers was moved into solitary confinement. He had no personal interaction except for the glances from a guard who passed his cell at fifteen-minute intervals.[532]

During one of those intervals on January 13, 1931, Rodgers fashioned a rope out of the fabric of his shirt and used it to hang himself from the ceiling of his cell. Technically, he was still serving terms for burglary and prison escape. His life sentence as a four-time Sullivan Law violator was not to begin until August 1935.[533]

A brother claimed Rodgers' remains. A steady stream of visitors, including a few friends and relatives, filed through the Quinn Funeral Home, 460 Broadway, in Astoria, on January 18 to view the body in its plain coffin. No explanation was given for the selection of an Astoria for the wake. A funeral Mass was celebrated for Rodgers at St. Joseph's Church in Astoria the next day. Only a small group attended. Two carload of flowers and four cars of relatives followed the hearse to Long Island City's Calvary Cemetery, where he was interred.[534]

Newspaper obituaries listed his mother, two brothers and one sister as his survivors. Wife Kitty was not mentioned.[535]

THUG FLEES TRAIN ON WAY TO PRISON

"Bum" Rogers, Notorious Gangster, Escapes in Harlem After Confederate Fells Guard.

OUTWITTED HIS KEEPER

NY Times, December 1925.

Russomano, John "Curley"

> *This place where the boys hung around was a very large pool room and cafe... It was owned by an old timer of the old days... He was the nephew of one of the old timers [who] was a big boss of the Naples gang. His name was Curley.*[536]

Joseph Valachi said very little about "Curley" and probably knew little about him. Curley ran the mid-1920s East Harlem cafe and poolroom at 116th Street and First Avenue that, while Valachi was serving a prison sentence in Sing Sing, drew in all of Valachi's old East 107th Street friends.

Some weeks after returning home, Valachi went to the establishment. "It was so big that it could hold about seventy five men."

Valachi identified Curley as "an old timer," less an indicator of the man's age than of the period of East Harlem history when he was an active gangster. "As I said, there were very few that survived from the old days," Valachi recalled about the earlier underworld era, "and this was one of them. He was the nephew of one of the old timers [who] was a big boss of the Naples gang."[537]

John "Curley" Russomano was nephew to Giosue Gallucci, remembered as the most influential East Harlem Neapolitan gang boss of the 1910s.[538]

Named "Gennaro" upon his birth in Naples, Italy, on January 27, 1889, Russomano's parents were Raffaele and Barbara Gallucci Russomano. Raffaele, born about 1858, and Barbara, about three years younger, were married in Italy in 1884. Gennaro/John was their first son. They had another boy in 1890 and named him Nicola. The family sailed together from Naples to New

York in June 1894, settling in the Little Italy community on Manhattan's Lower East Side.[539]

Nicola did not fare well in his new home. He died in late spring 1897, just as a little sister, Antoinette, was born. Raffaele and Barbara gave his name new life, when another son was born to them in February 1900 and christened Nicola.[540]

The family home was at 109 Mulberry Street in 1900. But the Russomanos soon relocated to East Harlem, near Barbara's brother Giosue Gallucci, and could be found at 347 East 109th Street in 1905 and at 337 East 109th Street in 1910. Raffaele earned a living through a variety of jobs, including day laborer, peddler and plasterer.[541]

John Russomano was in his early twenties when he became an aide to his uncle Giosue Gallucci. Gallucci ran a bake shop and cafe at 318 East 109th Street. He was regarded as leader of a politically connected gang involved in gambling and other early rackets.

In 1912, Gallucci was reportedly targeted for extortion by Aniello "*Zoppo*" (Lame) Prisco, another Neapolitan gang boss who was considered the "terror" of East Harlem. Prisco arranged to meet Gallucci on the night of December 15, 1912. Gallucci sent word that he was sick and could not make it to the meeting. Prisco showed up near midnight at 318 East 109th Street and found Gallucci in the cafe's kitchen. He reportedly demanded $100 and threatened to shoot Gallucci if he did not receive it. Russomano was nearby and put two bullets in Prisco's head before the intruder could fire a shot.[542]

Russomano subsequently surrendered himself to the coroner and confessed to killing Prisco. He told the story of Prisco's threats to an assistant district attorney. A coroner's jury found that the fatal shooting of Prisco was justifiable, and Russomano was released after a few days.[543]

Russomano found himself targeted by the remaining members of Prisco's gang. He quickly hired gunman Tony Capilongo, also known as Tony Vivola, to be his bodyguard. In this period, Russomano was proprietor of a saloon at 116th Street and First Avenue, possibly the same establishment that Valachi recalled from about a decade later. Russomano made his way between the saloon and his residence, 329 East 109th Street (diagonally across the street from his uncle's cafe), by walking or riding a streetcar. Capilongo accompanied him on those daily journeys.

On the morning of February 18, 1913, Russomano and Capilongo approached the entrance of Russomano's apartment building, when Capilongo suddenly shouted and collapsed. Russomano then felt a sharp sting in his arm. As he looked around, there were additional stings. He understood he was being shot, though he heard no gunshots. He cried out for help.

Giosue Gallucci rushed over from across the street. Police officers on nearby patrol duty quickly arrived – they later indicated that they heard gunshots from the area.

Capilongo was dead, killed by bullet wounds to his back. Russomano was taken to Bellevue Hospital with wounds to both arms and his right side.[544]

Ignoring the police statement that shots were heard, a report published in the *Washington Post* emphasized that Russomano heard nothing: "The missiles of death came true and silently. Nobody knew that a shooting had occurred until the cry of Russomano startled the neighborhood." The newspaper concluded that a rifle fitted with a Maxim Silencer – a fairly recent invention[545] – was used in the attack.[546]

Other news reports tried to merge the conflicting statements. The *New York Evening World* noted that five bullets struck the victims but only two gunshots were heard by police. The newspaper offered the possible explanation that a silencer was attached to just one of two different weapons used.[547]

Russomano may have suffered long-term ill effects from this shooting. He was exempted from U.S. military service in the Great War because of a broken arm.[548]

He was well enough to be back on the street and carrying a revolver in late July 1913 when police arrested him, Giosue Gallucci and Gallucci aide Joe "Chuck" Nazzaro together at 115th Street and First Avenue. All three men were charged with illegal possession of firearms. While Gallucci avoided a conviction on the charge, Nazzaro was given a year in prison, and Russomano in March 1914 was sentenced to a minimum of three years and three months and a maximum of six years and six months.

Russomano entered Sing Sing Prison on April 1, 1914. The admission register noted that he was five feet and one inch tall, 135 pounds and a resident of his parents' home at 310 East 109th Street.[549] In summer, he was transferred to Auburn State Prison. He was discharged from Auburn on June 18, 1915, and showed up in the Russomano family entry in the 1915 New York State Census.[550]

John Russomano was home about two months before his father Raffaele passed away.[551]

Russomano, twenty eight, was working as an automobile mechanic for Packet Transportation Company of West Forty-first Street in Manhattan at the time of his draft registration in June 1917, though he was said to have one non-functioning arm. He was described at the time as short, stout and balding.[552]

New York Governor Nathan L. Miller issued a pardon for Russomano in the summer of 1922, erasing the weapons charge for which he had been imprisoned.[553]

Russomano led a quiet life from that point on. He was a resident of 200 East 109th Street in 1924. In 1930, at forty one and unmarried, he lived with an uncle and aunt, Pasquale and Mary Criscuolo, at 2199 First Avenue. He reported employment as a helper in the trucking industry. He reporting living at the same address when he filed his registration for the World War II draft in spring 1942. He said he was employed at that time by New York City's Market Department at the Bronx Terminal Market. Russomano moved to 2414 Belmont Avenue in the Bronx by spring of 1950, when he reported working as a porter at a bar and grill.[554]

He passed away six years later. He was buried at Calvary Cemetery in Woodside, Queens.[555]

"Sadie"

> *Of course she was paying protection, and so we felt safe.*[556]

As Joseph Valachi was growing up in East Harlem, he steered away from relationships for a combination of reasons. He was embarrassed of how he was living, both of the poor conditions and of the criminal activity he felt was necessary to remedy them. His attitude was interpreted by interested young women as conceit, but "I was ashamed, not stuck up."[557] In addition to embarrassment, Valachi was aware that his priorities at the time were immature and incompatible with a serious relationship. "I never used to go out with any of the girls around the block," he recalled. "I didn't intend to get married, so why bother. If I wanted to play, I knew where to go without getting married."[558]

Around 1923, Valachi and his friends made regular visits to a brothel he referred to, probably without recognizing the ethnic slur, as "Sadie Chink's":

> About once a week we would visit a Sadie Chink's. She had a few girls there all the time. She was well-known and still is talked about today. Of course, she was paying protection and so we felt safe. Now I was starting to get over my shyness and starting to feel like a real knock around guy.[559]

When "Big Jack" Zelig was murdered in October 1912, he was found to be carrying a slip of paper. On one side was written, "Dr. Morris J. Klein, 307 East Sixth Street, near Second Avenue." On the other side appeared, "Ed. Hess, Sadie Chink, Seventeenth Street and Third Avenue, Twenty-first Street and Third Avenue." Authorities were unable to settle on the reason Zelig was carrying that paper.

Sadie, also identified as Sadie Rothenberg, was mentioned a few years later as one of a prostitution ring's links between New York City and Boston. Following a police raid at a brothel at 32 Dwight Street in Boston, police noted that the woman who managed the house, Mrs. Morris Bernstein, had previously been convicted of prostitution in New York. Police officers interviewed three of the women who worked at the house. They were Sadie, Dora Block and Jennie "the Factory" Fischer. All three told police that they had been taken to Boston from New York. They all said they were willing to return to New York to testify against prostitution racketeers and the New York police officers who were taking large sums of money in exchange for protection.[560]

Sadie did make her way back to New York. It is uncertain if she ever provided evidence against anyone in the prostitution racket. She opened her own establishment, and reportedly paid handsomely to keep police from shutting it down.

In August 1930, Judge Samuel Seabury was appointed to head an investigation into corruption at New York City magistrates' courts.[561] One of Seabury's earlier discoveries was the protection paid to police and prosecutors by the houses of prostitution. In December 1930, John C. Weston, who served as an assistant district attorney between 1921 and 1927, testified that he received about $20,000 in bribes during those years. The money was paid to him by lawyers, bondsmen and police officers, as he aided in discharging about 900 defendants in about 600 vice cases. Weston's testimony included mention of Sadie, Jenny Fischer, Polly Adler and other well known New York madams.[562]

Police raided a number of "disorderly houses" across the city on September 28, 1931. In the raids, they arrested sixty-year-old Rebecca "Blind Becky" Leibstone of Eldridge Street in Manhattan, who was called the "queen of the white slave ring." Leibstone was found in possession of a card index containing names of 5,000 women connected to 200 brothels.[563]

She confessed to using her connections to set women up in various houses of prostitution, including those run by Sadie, Jenny "the Factory," Polly Adler and "Gertie the Garter." She said she received $5 for each woman she delivered to the brothels, plus 10 percent of the woman's earnings.[564]

Despite the early 1930s revelations of corruption and human trafficking, the prostitution business went on as usual. On February 1, 1936, Special Prosecutor Thomas E. Dewey, a former assistant U.S. attorney who had experienced some success against city racketeers, launched simultaneous police raids against eighty brothels. Dewey later recalled the results:

> Somehow, for reasons we decided not to investigate, the raids on forty of [the brothels] were failures. But we had a hundred prostitutes and madams jammed into our offices, including some of the best-known women in the business.[565]

Sadie was one of the madams arrested. Others included Jenny "the Factory," "Silver-tongued Elsie" and "Cockeyed (Cokey) Florence." Those women and others taken into custody later were held as material witnesses for the compulsory prostitution trial of Salvatore "Charlie Luciano" Lucania in May and June of 1936. Sadie appears not to have been called as a witness in that case, but she was mentioned by witness Helen Hayes, who discussed the monopolistic nature of the prostitution business in New York. Hayes had worked in a Sadie-run brothel for a couple of years before attempting to open her own establishment. She found it impossible to operate without paying for permission from a regional vice organization.

Lucania and eight codefendants were convicted on June 7, 1936. Following conviction, the 120 material witnesses could be turned loose. A news article mentioned the eagerness of Jenny "the Factory," Cokey Flo Brown and Sadie for their freedom.[566]

Siano, Fiore "Fury"

Now Pat, Fiore and Joey are coming to the Lido Restaurant more often and the [narcotics] agents are coming to the Lido. I know Pat ain't fooling around with any "junk," but Joey and Fiore are partners and they are very hot, and they are bringing more guys at the Lido that are in the "junk" business.

Valachi's nephew Fiore Siano was drawn into criminal activity – initially burglaries and later narcotics trafficking and gambling rackets – in East Harlem and the Bronx. He closely associated with brothers Joe and Pat Pagano.

An incident, probably in the 1950s, caused Valachi to involve himself in Siano's relationship with underworld figures. A racketeer known as "Joe Stutz" struck Siano following an argument. Stutz was known to be close to a mobster named Lanza and to Mike Coppola. Valachi learned of the incident and went looking for Stutz, with Siano and the Paganos following him. He found Stutz at the "Lizzy Bar," East 116th Street and Second Avenue, and marched toward him: "...The first thing he said as we walked in the bar, 'Gee, Joe, I'm sorry; I did not know that he is your nephew." At Valachi's insistence, Stutz apologized to Siano. They shook hands, and Stutz treated the group to some drinks.[567]

Fiore Siano and Joe Pagano persuaded Valachi to invest in a craps game. After about six weeks, he was disappointed to find that those young men were participating in and losing money in their own game. Siano admitted that he had squandered Valachi's investment. He suggested that he could recover the money if Valachi would connect him with a supply of narcotics.[568]

In his autobiography, Valachi suggested that Siano may have set up a burglary of his own father's business, taking $12,000 from a safe.[569]

Siano and the Paganos participated in the murder of informant Eugene Giannini in September 1952. They were assigned to that task by Valachi.[570] The following June, Siano and Pat Pagano murdered Stephen Franse in the kitchen of Valachi's Lido restaurant. While Franse had also been branded an informant, Valachi believed Franse was killed because crime family leader Vito Genovese blamed Franse for problems between Genovese and his wife.[571]

During the 1950s, Siano and his friends became more and more involved with narcotics trafficking. Valachi felt that their visits to his Lido restaurant caused narcotics agents to assume that Lido was a center for narcotics distribution. Valachi admitted that he did help Siano arrange narcotics purchases.[572] Eventually, Valachi began feeling that Siano's activities and irresponsibility were damaging Valachi's reputation with gangland figures as well as with law enforcement agents.[573]

Late in 1954, Siano was charged with violating federal narcotics laws. He pleaded guilty and was sentenced to eight years in prison.[574] He was finishing up his prison term in Lewisburg, Pennsylvania, when he happened to meet up with his uncle again.

Valachi had been convicted in his own narcotics trial and spent a few days in Lewisburg on the way to Atlanta Federal Prison. During their meeting, Valachi entrusted Siano with his jukebox business, telling Siano he could expect to earn $600 to $700 a week with it and asking him to share the proceeds with Valachi's wife and son.[575] Valachi later learned that his wife was receiving only token sums from Siano.[576]

Fiore Siano was born in New York City on June 22, 1927. He was the second child, first son, born to Michael Siano, a mechanic, and Joseph Valachi's sister Filomena. The Siano family resided in East Harlem. They lived at 2014 Second Avenue in 1930 and at 327 East 113th Street in 1940.[577]

The East 113th Street address was reported by eighteen-year-old Fiore Siano when he registered for the World War II draft in June 1945. At that time, he claimed to be an employee of an iron works at East Harlem's Second Avenue. His first arrest, for burglary, occurred in 1948.[578] Twenty-two-year-old Fiore Siano was still living with his parents at East 113th Street at the time of the 1950 U.S. Census. His father was then the proprietor of a candy store (likely the business that Valachi suggested Fiore Siano robbed of $12,000).[579]

Siano's involvement in the early 1950s Giannini and Franse murders remained unknown to authorities until Valachi revealed it in the 1960s. Federal narcotics agents, however, were well aware of Siano's involvement in narcotics trafficking. Undercover agents were able to purchase $10,000 worth of cocaine from him. Siano was sentenced November 27, 1954, to eight years in prison following a conviction for violating federal narcotics laws. Several codefendants were also convicted and sentenced to federal prison.[580]

Soon after Valachi turned informant, revealing his nephew's involvement in rackets and gangland murders, Fiore Siano disappeared. Author Peter Maas reported that three men escorted Siano out of an East Harlem restaurant, 2287 First Avenue, in April or May and he was never seen again. The FBI reported that Siano disappeared from his East Harlem home on April 26, 1964.[581]

Stoppelli, Innocenzio "John the Bug"

*As I will talk about the boys down[town], you will see that
they all have the same ways. By the boys, I mean Vito
Genovese, Tony Bender, Bobby Doyle, Tommy Rye, Joe
Conti, Pete Herman, not too much Sandie, Johnnie the Bug.
All treacherous. That's why I never went down there.*[582]

Valachi knew "Johnnie the Bug" as a member of Vito Genovese's inner circle, which gathered around Thompson Street, south of Manhattan's Greenwich Village. Over time, according to his autobiography, Valachi learned not to trust any of that group or anyone connected with it.

During early interactions with Eugene Giannini, Valachi learned that Giannini was a business partner with Johnnie the Bug.

A bit later, he found that a pal named Vinnie started "hanging out with John the Bug, so I don't bother with him... I figured anyone that hangs out downtown I don't want any part of it."[583]

Innocenzio Stoppelli was born in Manhattan on April 10, 1907. His Italian given name translated to "innocent." It was discarded in favor of "John" by the time he was three.[584] Through the rest of his long life, Stoppelli was seldom known to be innocent.

His parents were Rocco and Carmela Miraglia Stoppelli, Italian immigrants who settled on Mulberry Street in Lower Manhattan in the 1890s. Carmela was Rocco's second wife, following the death of his first. After their April 1900 marriage, Rocco and Carmela lived for a time with other Stoppellis at

339 East Thirty-fourth Street. Rocco initially worked as a bartender but became a cigar maker. By 1905, the family, including three young children, lived at 238 Mott Street.[585]

When Innocenzio/John was born, the Stoppellis resided at 143 Thompson Street. The Thompson Street neighborhood would be a source of underworld strength for John "the Bug" Stoppelli for many years. The family home was reported at 145 Thompson Street for Rocco Stoppelli's 1918 military draft registration and for the 1920 U.S. Census.[586]

John's first known trouble with the law occurred just before his fifteenth birthday. He and four friends were arrested for stealing pigeons in Queens. Elizabeth Desthers of Long Island City accused the boys of breaking into her pigeon coop and taking four carrier pigeons she was raising for the use of the military at Camp Upton on Long Island. Frank Clark of Astoria filed a complaint stating that two of those boys, Stoppelli and Joseph Alvino, had stolen fifteen pigeons from his coop. The case was heard in Children's Court at Jamaica, Queens.[587]

On June 7, 1924, four young men broke into the New Star Theatre on Lexington Avenue in East Harlem. They attempted to force open the theater's safe. When night watchmen Julius Katz and John Seligman interfered, the watchmen were beaten and robbed. Nearly a month later, police arrested four young men at a nearby coffeehouse. They charged John Stoppelli, James Santuccio, Michael Purazzo and Joseph Bruno with the attempted burglary of the theater and with the assault and robbery of Katz and Seligman. When processed, Stoppelli gave his home address as 926 East 216th Street in the Bronx.[588] That Bronx location had become the residence of his parents and siblings.

Stoppelli was charged with violating federal drug laws later in the summer of 1924. Convicted of that offense, he was fined $200.[589]

He did not get off so lightly when brought into federal court on a similar charge early in 1925. Stoppelli, James Liggiardo, Joseph Mecca and Patrick Giacomo were arrested in Greenwich Village for selling narcotics. Stoppelli and Liggiardo pleaded guilty. In March, they were sentenced to a year and a day in Atlanta Federal Prison. Mecca and Giacomo pleaded not guilty. After being convicted at trial, they were sentenced to three years in Atlanta.[590]

Stoppelli must have served only a portion of that sentence. He and Peter Cinnamo were believed responsible for an October 2, 1925, robbery that became a homicide. Louis Bernardi was working in his pool hall business in the basement of 106 Thompson Street, when Stoppelli and Cinnamo stopped their game and attempted to rob the place. Bernardi attempted to fight off the robbers. They pulled firearms and began shooting. Bernardi suffered bullet wounds to his back, neck and mouth. The robbers fled.

Bernardi lost consciousness shortly after police arrived. His wife Josephine reported seeing Stoppelli and Cinnamo in the business just before the shooting, when she went next door to prepare Bernardi's lunch. Bernardi was taken to St. Vincent's Hospital. He remained there for several weeks before he succumbed on October 29 to an infection resulting from the gunshots.[591]

Stoppelli and Cinnamo were not apprehended until March of 1926. Cinnamo quickly claimed responsibility for the shooting of Bernardi. He claimed that Bernardi was first to pull out a firearm and that he knocked it from the pool hall owner's hand. He said he only fired at Bernardi when he was about to turn two vicious guard dogs loose.

Cinnamo was booked on charges of homicide and robbery. Stoppelli faced only a robbery charge. When questioned, the pair said they had been living off the proceeds of their recent robberies.[592]

Stoppelli and pals Armond Castellano, Joseph Greco and Basil Andreacchi were arrested in early September 1926 while sitting in a parked car on East Lincoln Avenue in Mount Vernon. A local judge assured them they were not wanted in Mount Vernon. He instructed them to leave the community and not return.[593]

In March of 1927, Stoppelli was convicted of illegal possession of a firearm. He was sentenced to serve a minimum of two and a half years and a maximum of five years in state prison. After a brief stay at Sing Sing Prison, he was moved on to Clinton State Prison in Dannemora. For prison documents, he attributed his criminal acts to "evil associates." John the Bug noted that he was a user of both tobacco and drugs and had been unemployed for a year before his arrest. He gave 926 East 216th Street as his address.

He spent close to the minimum term in prison. He was back out on the New York City streets by fall 1929. At that time, he was married. A deputy city clerk presided over a ceremony at the Manhattan Municipal Building, as Stoppelli was wed to Mary Groger.[594]

The following summer, Stoppelli and four friends were arrested for acting suspiciously in front of Brooklyn's Raymond Street Jail. When questioned,

Stoppelli and Brooklyn resident Anthony DiLaura were found to fit the descriptions of two men wanted in connection with the June 13 payroll robbery of the S.W. Farber Tin Works at 141 South Fifth Street in that borough.[595]

It appears the robbery charge did not stick. "John the Bug" reportedly had similar good luck when arrested for a safe burglary in November 1935.[596]

In April of 1938, Stoppelli was questioned in connection with the apparent suicide of an adult entertainer, Vera "Thelma Thais" Giroux.

Giroux, twenty five, was a Greenwich Village club performer whose specialties were feather and bubble dances performed while nude. About two-fifteen on Tuesday morning, April 19, she apparently jumped naked from a fifth floor window of the Hotel Lincoln, Forty-fourth Street and Eighth Avenue, and suffered fatal multiple fractures and shock on the sidewalk below. She died about two hours later at Bellevue Hospital.

The press noted that just six days earlier, twenty-two-year-old Norma DeMarco, an employee of Stephen Franse's Howdy Club in Greenwich Village, had killed herself in a similar jump from a twelfth floor window.

Stoppelli admitted to investigators that he spent much of the night with Giroux. They previously had a relationship, he said, though they parted after a quarrel early in 1938. Giroux went to Chicago for a time, performing there under the name May Daniels, he said. She had recently returned to New York. He spotted her and a companion at a Greenwich Village nightclub the evening before her death. Later, Stoppelli walked her to her hotel room, and she began making desperate remarks.

According to Stoppelli, she said, "I'm sick and tired of it all. Goodbye. So long. It's all over." He left her at that point. Returning later to check on Giroux, he found her gone and the room window left open. When police arrived, they found Stoppelli in the hotel room. His account of Giroux's depression satisfied investigators, and he was let go.[597]

A Stoppelli draft registration in October 1940 indicated a home address of 40 Monroe Street in Manhattan for Stoppelli and his wife. It cited the family residence, 926 East 216th Street in the Bronx, as Stoppelli's work address. Curiously, the registration appeared to be initially filed from Lufkin, Texas, and later stamped by Local Board No. 1 of New York City.

One month later, "the Bug" was picked up by federal agents on a charge of violating narcotics laws. Almost immediately, another charge of attempting to bribe a government officer was added. Stoppelli was convicted of the bribery offense in June 1941 and sentenced to a six-month stay at the Federal Correctional Institution at Danbury, Connecticut. He returned to New York from Danbury in November. Noting his return, police arrested him for vagrancy in early December.[598]

Agents of the Federal Bureau of Narcotics watched Stoppelli and his associates closely through the early 1940s.

A New York federal grand jury on March 26, 1945, indicted Stoppelli and sixteen others, including Joseph Marone, Charles Albero and Eugene Giannini, for conspiring in the illegal import of opium from Mexico. Defendants in the case included residents of New York, California, Massachusetts and Florida. Two of those indicted – Charles LaGaipa and Joseph Dentico – were missing and thought to be dead.[599]

In early November, the narcotics bureau revealed charges against a narcotics distribution ring that included more than a hundred people. Stoppelli also was charged in that case.[600]

Near the end of the month, Stoppelli was sought by police as a possible accomplice in the Greenwich Village shooting death of Rocco Loscalzo. Loscalzo had been drinking at DeMartino's Bar, 171 Bleecker Street in Manhattan. After he left the bar, he was shot down around the corner on Sullivan Street. A short time later, gangster Vincent Mauro was stopped in his automobile as he drove along Sixty-fifth Street just west of Central Park. Police noticed blood stains on his hat, pants and shoes. While he denied involvement in the shooting of Loscalzo, Mauro could not explain the blood on his clothes and had no alibi.

Thomas Annichiarico, manager of DeMartino's Bar, was taken into custody as a material witness in the case. (Annichiarico and Stoppelli later were business partners in Tommy's Bar, which occupied the same address as DeMartino's in 1945.)[601]

Detectives learned that Loscalzo recently had been charged with grand larceny of $20,000 worth of liquor from a warehouse. He was released on bail. While drinking in DeMartino's, he reportedly spoke about "what he would do if the gang did not obtain a lawyer for him."[602] It is uncertain that Stoppelli was ever questioned about the Loscalzo killing.

On April 9, 1946, "John the Bug" was convicted of illegal sale of opium. He was sentenced on May 6 to a federal prison term of three years. He entered the Federal Correctional Institution at Milan, Michigan, two days later. A writ of habeas corpus removed him from the facility in spring 1947. While records are lacking, it appears Stoppelli won an appeal of the conviction and was released in early May.[603]

Federal efforts to put "the Bug" behind bars for drug trafficking continued. As several narcotics traffickers were arrested in Oakland, California, in October 1948, packages of heroin were seized. A fingerprint found on a package of heroin was identified as John Stoppelli's left ring finger. The single print triggered his arrest on December 23 and a San Francisco federal grand jury indictment on January 12, 1949.[604] At trial in June, a government finger-print expert testified not only that the fingerprint discovered on the package belonged to Stoppelli but also that the shape of the print indicated a concavity in the packaging at the time it was contacted by the finger. This, the witness stated, indicated that a soft powdery substance was contained in the package at that moment.

Stoppelli's codefendants insisted that they were unacquainted with him. Stoppelli presented an alibi: He was meeting with a probation officer in New York City at the time of the narcotics raid in Oakland. These defenses were insufficient. On June 13, Stoppelli and his codefendants were convicted fol-lowing less than two hours of jury deliberation. Stoppelli was sentenced to a $100 fine and concurrent prison sentences of six years for concealment of nar-cotics and five years for sale of narcotics.[605] Stoppelli remained free on bail during his legal appeals. The Ninth Circuit Court of Appeals affirmed his con-victions and two concurrent sentences on June 26, 1950. Near the end of October, the U.S. Supreme Court refused to review the case. In December, Stoppelli was ordered to report to prison to begin his sentence.[606]

His return to Milan, Michigan, was delayed. "John the Bug" was relaxing in Milady's Cafe, a saloon at 162 Prince Street, in the early morning hours of December 29, when Thompson Street resident Samuel Urchioli entered and made some antagonistic remarks. Stoppelli told Urchioli to leave, and he did, but he soon returned with a .32-caliber pistol and put a bullet in Stoppelli's back. Urchioli ran from the place, pursued by angry patrons. They caught up with him at 171 Thompson Street, beat him and struck him over the head with an ashcan. Stoppelli and Urchioli were brought to St. Vincent's Hospital. Stop-pelli recovered there for six weeks before entering Milan in February.[607]

Stoppelli's attorney filed new appeals to the convictions in spring 1952. These were based on a finding by the FBI Laboratory that the fingerprint on the heroin package was not a convincing match for Stoppelli. Federal Judge Dal M. Lemmon denied a motion for a new trial. An appeal was brought to the Ninth Circuit, but it was withdrawn when it appeared that President Harry Truman would consider executive clemency for Stoppelli. Given the new evidence, a clemency application was supported by the FBI, as well as the head of the Federal Bureau of Narcotics, the Department of Justice's Board of Pardons and Paroles and Colonel George White, the former FBN district supervisor responsible for Stoppelli's arrest.

On August 20, 1952, the President commuted the remainder of Stoppelli's prison sentence and removed the $100 fine, ordering that Stoppelli be released. FBN Commissioner Harry Anslinger explained his position to the press: "Johnny Stoppelli is no good. He's a bum, a crook and a notorious racketeer. But he was innocent of the charges in this case. I am completely convinced of his innocence and that's why I recommended his release."[608]

"John the Bug" did not face another serious charge until January 1977, when a long-term New York Police undercover operation resulted in the indictment of twelve people for conducting a numbers gambling racket. The accused leaders of the racket, which was said to have grossed between $35 million and $50 million a year, were James "Jimmy Nap" Napoli, Sr., of Manhattan; his son James Jr. of North Bellmore on Long Island; and Stoppelli, then nearly seventy and said to be a resident of Brooklyn. "Jimmy Nap" was reputed to be a major organized crime figure in the New York area.[609]

Stoppelli passed away in New York on January 10, 1993. He was eighty five. He was buried at Woodlawn Cemetery in the Bronx.[610]

Urchioli beating. (NY Daily News)

Viserti, Giuseppe "Diamond Joe Pep"

> *...One night he asked me to go down the cellar with him and there he had a guy hanging. He pulled out a knife and he cut one finger off and put it in his pocket and said to me, "See this fellow? Well, he was no good. You look like a nice kid. That's why I want to teach you. Now if you tell my cousin or anyone else, I'll put you up there." Well, you can rest assured that I never told anyone until he was long dead.*[611]

Joseph Valachi was about seventeen when he got to know "Diamond Joe Pep." Pep was a Harlem underworld leader and the cousin of a Valachi friend known as "Tonno." Valachi and Tonno regularly visited Pep's cabaret, The Zoo on Fordham Road in the Bronx, and borrowed one of his cars "to go joy riding."

On one occasion, Valachi visited The Zoo alone and Pep brought him down into the cellar to "teach him" about the underworld. A man's body was hanging in the basement, and Pep cut a finger from the body and pocketed it for some reason. Pep threatened to hang Valachi in a similar fashion if he told anyone about what he saw.[612]

Valachi learned that Pep held a secret grudge against some of his "old friends," the result of a lengthy imprisonment in Sing Sing, and opened his cabaret to lure them into his control. "When he saw fit, he would kill them and then hang them down the cellar," recalled Valachi.[613]

Soon after Valachi's horrifying visit, Pep was murdered. In his autobiography, Valachi said he later found out who was responsible, but he did not state the name.[614]

Valachi remembered that The Zoo cabaret changed hands and became known as the "Garden Inn." By the 1950s and 1960s, it became the site of a used car dealer, "Bel Monte Motors." Valachi stopped in at the business in the 1950s. "I noticed the dance floor was still there. So, I asked the fellow to take me down [into the cellar]. He said, 'What are you, crazy?' ... He said, "I don't go down there if you pay me."

Valachi convinced the proprietor to allow him into the cellar. There were no bodies, but "to my amazement," he said, "the rope was still on the beam."[615]

Giuseppe Viserti was born March 11, 1891, to Aniello and Anna Robustelli Viserti in Sarno, Italy, east of Naples. When he was eleven, he traveled to the United States with his mother and an older sister, Colomba. Father Aniello had crossed the Atlantic earlier and was already a resident of 2213 First Avenue in East Harlem.[616] Giuseppe's older brother Giovanni "John" was likely already a resident of East Harlem.[617]

The Viserti family, except for Colomba (by then married), lived together at 333 East 112th Street at the time of the 1905 New York State Census. Aniello and Giovanni, then seventeen, worked as rag dealers. Giuseppe Viserti, thirteen, was reported to be "at home," neither working nor in school.[618]

Giuseppe used the anglicized form of his name, Joseph Viserti, in the spring of 1910 as he filed his Declaration of Intention to become a U.S. citizen. He was nineteen, a resident of 335 East 108th Street and working as a driver. In the summer of 1911, he married seventeen-year-old Maria "Mamie" Santora, born in New York City and a resident of 318 East 113th Street. They soon had a daughter, they named Anna.[619]

In that period, competing factions emerged in the Neapolitan-American underworld of East Harlem. Between late 1911 and early 1913, the conflict took the lives of Frank "Chick" Monaco, Pasquarella Musone Spinelli, Tony Zaccaro, Giuseppe Jacko, Aniello "Zoppo" Prisco and Tony Capilongo.

Following the December 1912, killing of Prisco by John Russomano, who was a nephew and aide to East Harlem rackets leader Giosue Gallucci, Amedeo Buonomo emerged as top man in the Prisco faction. Buonomo took a number of precautions against an unpleasant end, including the purchase of a chain mail shirt in Chinatown. When he went out into the East Harlem community, he generally wore the heavy mail shirt and had bodyguards close by.

But, on Saturday morning, April 5, 1913, Buonomo decided to take a quick walk without guards or armor. He left his home, 1758 Madison Avenue, and walked about half a mile southeast to Thomas Jefferson Park, near the Harlem

River. At the park, he was greeted by several men. One reached out cordially and shook Buonomo's hand, as the others put revolvers against Buonomo's body and fired. The twenty-seven-year-old Buonomo was rushed to Harlem Hospital. Despite a severe gunshot wound to the neck, he reportedly communicated to police: "I knew they would get me, but my friends will get them, and this feud will go on until all of them are wiped out of existence." Buonomo passed away the next day, suffocated by the swelling in his throat.[620]

Among the suspects questioned in connection with the murder of Buonomo was Joseph Viserti, already known around East Harlem's "Little Italy" as "Joe Pep" or "Joe Peppe."[621]

Viserti was arrested for another homicide near the end of the month. He was one of six men taken into custody after the early morning April 29 shooting death of Jerry "the Lunchman" Maida on West Forty-first Street. Press accounts described Viserti as a "junk dealer," living at 338 East 107th Street. The other suspects were James Gesto, Frank Tedesco, Santo Barbara, James Nolan and Eugene Donnelly. Donnelly was freed after questioning.

Authorities believed that Maida was a former member of the Paul Kelly gang of Manhattan's Lower East Side and noted that he was killed near an automobile business run by Kelly. They surmised that he was murdered for providing information on criminal activity to the district attorney's office.[622]

Viserti and Barbara were indicted for the murder. In June, they were locked up in the Tombs jail to await trial. It appears they remained there for half a year. During their January 1914 trial, testimony suggested that Maida was killed as the result of a gangland quarrel over prostitution territories.[623]

Both defendants were convicted of manslaughter. Judge Otto Rosalsky sentenced them to long prison terms, remarking, "Gangs of young hoodlums such as these infest our city, quarreling among themselves and shooting promiscuously, with the result that innocent persons are often killed or badly injured. It is time to call a halt." Barbara was sentenced to a serve a minimum of eight years and three months and a maximum of nineteen years and six months. Viserti received a minimum sentence of seven years and nine months and a maximum sentence of eighteen years and six months.[624]

Viserti entered Sing Sing Prison on January 16, 1914. The prison register noted that he was twenty two, five feet and five and a quarter inches tall, and 145 pounds. He was said to have worked as a junk dealer and expressman.

Though his home address at the time of his arrest was said to be on East 107th Street, his wife's address was recorded as 335 East 108th Street.[625]

While he was in prison, his brother John was arrested as a suspect in the October 1915 killing of "Murder Stable" owner Ippolito Greco. John Viserti, resident of 335 East 108th Street, was one of four men, including the victim's brother Vincenzo Greco, believed present when Ippolito Greco was shotgunned to death at the stable, which ran between East 107th and East 108th streets. It appears John Viserti was not prosecuted. He registered for the U.S. military draft in June 1917, reporting self-employment as a driver and previous military experience in Italy. He claimed an exemption from further service, as he was the source of support of his parents, a wife and a child.[626]

"Joe Pep" Viserti was still a Sing Sing inmate when he filed his military draft registration in June 1917. Like his older brother, he too stated that he supported both his parents, a wife and a child. He indicated a home address of 320 East 113th Street.[627]

According to Valachi, this Sing Sing sentence caused Joseph Viserti to plan the demise of those he felt had wronged him. New York Governor Charles S. Whitman unwittingly aided Viserti's quest for revenge by granting him a sentence commutation in August 1918. Under the conditional commutation, "Joe Pep" was eligible for release on September 20 but needed to avoid any additional felony convictions to keep from being returned to prison for the remainder of his original maximum sentence – nearly fourteen years.[628] During 1919, he reportedly twice escaped being convicted on grand larceny charges.[629]

Antonio "Little Cooch" Deluca received some bad news in the afternoon of September 23, 1919. According to friends, he was informed that "the time had come for the score to be settled." The score apparently related to an incident two summers earlier: Deluca had shot to death gangster Joseph Sacco, following an attack on the Deluca family saloon, on the southeast corner of 110th Street and Second Avenue. Deluca was acquitted of any wrongdoing, but Sacco's friends saw things differently. "Little Cooch" brought the news of his impending death to the police officer on patrol in the neighborhood at about seven o'clock that evening: "I'm going to be croaked tonight." The officer laughed. Deluca said, "Just wait and see."

At about nine o'clock, the officer heard four gunshots and ran toward them. He found Antonio Deluca dead in the street in front of the Sydenham Hospital on 116th Street. Deluca had a gunshot wound through the heart, one in his hip and another through his left eye.[630]

Enrico Esposito, a recent parolee from Sing Sing, was arrested four days later and charged with the killing. Police spotted him fleeing the scene of the murder. Esposito reportedly confessed shooting Deluca. According to his story, he was waiting for a girlfriend at 116th Street when he got into an argument with Deluca and Deluca drew a revolver. Esposito claimed he wrested the gun away from Deluca and fired it at him three times in self-defense.[631]

Esposito's story was less than satisfying for law enforcement. Near the end of November, Viserti was connected with the Deluca killing. He was arrested but later discharged for lack of evidence.[632] Esposito went to trial for the murder in April 1920. His defense counsel Charles E. LeBarbier argued that two police officers had beaten the confession out of Esposito. A jury acquitted Esposito on April 23.[633]

In the summer of 1920, "Joe Pep" Viserti was suddenly wealthy, having benefited from some early Prohibition Era opportunities. He was known as the owner of a large cabaret/casino at 681 East Fordham Road in the Bronx. The establishment was called "The Zoo," drawing its name from the Bronx Zoo, which had an entrance just a few blocks away. Viserti also owned several expensive automobiles, which were of special interest to Joseph Valachi. Viserti got himself into a bit of trouble with his cars, as he became notorious for ignoring speed limits. After receiving fines of $50 and $75, he was sentenced in July to a $100 fine plus five days in jail. The sentencing magistrate ordered that non-payment of the fine would result in another fifty days behind bars. The specific offense was driving 32 miles per hour at the intersection of Hillside Avenue and Queens Boulevard in Jamaica, Queens.[634]

Police in the Bronx were convinced that The Zoo was the location of a shooting in September, but they could not confirm it. A patrol officer nearby heard several shots from there at twenty minutes after two in the morning of September 6. When he investigated, patrons denied any shooting had taken place. An hour later, William Daly of East Harlem appeared at Lebanon Hospital in the Bronx with several bullet wounds to his right arm and shoulder.[635]

The press soon reported on another shooting that left a man dead in an East Harlem business that seemed to be linked with Viserti. Joseph Fasanello, twenty seven, was fatally shot on the night of March 29, 1921, in a poolroom, 315 East 115th Street, that he co-owned with a "Joe Peppe." When questioned by police, the business partner said he had been in the poolroom earlier and saw Fasanello playing cards with several men in a back room. He left for awhile and returned to find the business empty except for Fasanello, dead with two bullet wounds in his head. Despite the similar name, the partner was not Viserti. This Joe Peppe was born in Caggiano, Italy, on November 9, 1886, and had some trouble with the law after settling in New York – he was convicted of highway robbery, possession of narcotics and illegal weapons possession. He served as a sergeant in the U.S. Army during the Great War in Europe, losing his left arm to a bullet wound and a surgical amputation. After returning to civilian life, he became co-owner of the East 115th Street poolroom.[636]

Valachi's tour of the Bronx cabaret cellar likely occurred in this period. Viserti's Zoo soon announced that it had new management and was reopening as the Park View Inn (Valachi recalled the name as "Garden Inn").[637]

The name of Joseph Lagumina first appeared in the New York newspapers in connection with the 1914 murder of poultry businessman Barnet Baff. That murder was reportedly set up by industry racketeers and executed by East Harlem mafiosi. Several suspects in the case reportedly implicated Lagumina, and he was arrested in connection with the murder in June of 1916. The arrest occurred on the eve of Lagumina's scheduled wedding. He was picked up as he brought a rose bouquet to the home of his prospective bride.[638] Lagumina was eventually discharged and married. In following years, he opened an olive oil and cheese importing company and then became part owner of an ice cream company at 233 East 107th Street. He and his wife Bessie lived a short distance from the business at 251 East 109th Street.

About noon on May 17, 1921, Lagumina stepped outside of his business and walked westward along East 107th Street toward Third Avenue. He did not make it to the corner. As he passed 207 East 107th Street, shots were fired. Lagumina collapsed with two bullet wounds in his chest, one in his stomach and one in his back. He died instantly.

Police found that Lagumina was carrying a fully loaded revolver and a pistol permit issued by a justice of the peace in Mineola, Long Island. Witnesses reported seeing several men running from the scene. Detectives heard reports that Lagumina had been targeted by Black Hand extortionists and had received death threats. Lagumina's business partner Giuseppe Mastruzzi was arrested and accused of hiring the gunmen.[639]

Viserti was appearing in traffic court for yet another speeding ticket on October 3, 1921, when a detective noticed that he matched the description of one of the gunmen involved in the Lagumina killing. The traffic proceeding was suspended, and Viserti was arrested for homicide. One newspaper report on the matter commented on "Joe Pep's" wealth. It said he wore a $10,000 diamond ring and a three-carat diamond scarf pin into court and had investments that included a row of tenement houses in the Bronx.[640] Following arraignment, Viserti was released in bail.[641] He had just ten days more to live.

At about four-thirty in the afternoon of October 13, he burst through the doors of the Caffe Croce di Savoia coffeehouse at 365 Broome Street in Manhattan. He rushed to hide himself behind a pillar in the establishment and fired a handgun toward a gunmen who followed him to the doorway. A bystander, Louis Rango, was killed by a stray bullet. "Joe Pep" was probably already dying when he entered the coffee house. Bullets fired into his back had torn through his lungs. He soon collapsed and was dead when police arrived.[642]

Acting Captain Michael Fiaschetti, leader of the New York Police Department's Italian Squad, took charge of the investigation at the coffee house. Some time after the murders, the telephone at the coffee house rang, and Fiaschetti answered it. The caller thought Fiaschetti was someone named Tony, and Fiaschetti played along.

"Is that you, Tony?" the caller asked. "Yes," said Fiaschetti. The caller wanted to know, "Is that guy dead?" Fiaschetti replied, "Yes, he's dead."

The caller wanted to meet with Tony immediately at the corner of Court and Degraw streets in the section known as South Brooklyn. Fiaschetti said he'd be right there, and went to Brooklyn with a group of detectives. Annibale Stilo, an immigrant from the Calabria region of Italy, was found waiting at the intersection. Police arrested him. He had a pistol in his pocket, along with a pistol permit and a key to a safe deposit box.

Further investigation showed that the safe deposit box contained official authorizations for withdrawing alcohol from government warehouses. Stilo claimed he used the alcohol to make perfume, but the police were sure he was a bootlegger. Despite their certainty that Stilo was involved in wrongdoing, lacking specific evidence authorities were forced to release him.[643]

About a month after the murder of "Joe Pep," his brother John Viserti was involved in a shooting incident. Police picked him up at his home, 312 East 108th Street, on November 24. They noted he had a fresh bullet wound in his right leg. The wound reportedly was received when John Viserti got into an argument with an armed watchman, Fiore Chicone, who fired a shot at him. A newspaper headline referred to Viserti as "Joe Pep's brother."[644]

Annabile Stilo relocated to the Boston area a short time later. On December 14, 1922, he was fatally shot at Hanover and Union streets following a brief quarrel with Albert J. Bruno, resident of Randolph, Massachusetts. Bruno was arrested for the killing, but it took more than a dozen years to bring him to trial. Following his arrest, he was turned over to Chicago authorities to respond to murder allegations in that city, and he promptly disappeared. He was picked up in Connecticut in May 1934 for being idle and disorderly. Police learned he was a fugitive from Massachusetts and returned him there.[645]

Bruno went to trial for murder and unlawful weapon possession in February 1935. Boston police had lost track of two handguns involved in the case, the murder weapon and a firearm carried by Stilo. But several witnesses to the shooting testified that Bruno fired into Stilo from behind while Stilo was holding no weapon. The medical examiner testified that death was caused by a bullet, which entered the back of Stilo's neck and exited from his left cheek. Bruno testified that the shooting was self-defense. He said the two men knew each other from years earlier in Brooklyn. On the day of the shooting, he claimed, Stilo threatened to kill him and grabbed him by the throat. Bruno said he only fired his weapon when he saw Stilo moving to draw his own pistol.

After ten hours of deliberations, the jury convicted Bruno of second-degree murder. He was sentenced to life in state prison.[646]

John Viserti in the 1930s worked as a "junkman." He became ill with tuberculosis and was moved from his 312 East 108th Street home into the Metropolitan Hospital on Welfare Island. He died there on February 3, 1937.[647]

Zaccaro, Tony "Sharkey"

...We got so used to hearing someone getting killed that us kids would try and guess who was next. Every kid had a favorite. So did I. My favorite had died already. He happened to be Sharky.[648]

An East Harlem gangster known as "Sharkey" or "Young Sharkey"[649] was a childhood hero for Joseph Valachi. Young neighborhood boys all had their favorite gangland figures and shared their opinions of which was next to be murdered. Initially shocking to Valachi, the killings quickly became run-of-the-mill.

Valachi was a fan of Sharkey though he knew, from the time of his early school days, that Sharkey and his gang were extorting payments from Valachi's father and other pushcart peddlers in the area. "My father used to pay a dollar a week," Valachi recalled for his autobiography. "He used to tell me that he was broke because of Sharkey."[650] Valachi may once have served as a human shield during a Sharkey shootout with a rival:

> When I was a kid, I was standing next to the counter of a lemonade stand which was in front of the cafe [likely 336 East 109th Street]. All of a sudden the tough guy of this block, his name was Sharkey, threw me on the floor in back of the counter and all I heard was bang, bang. The fellow across the street didn't fire a shot. All he did was hold his gun in his hand. Later I found out why he didn't fire a shot, It was for fear that he might hit some of the kids or women that was in front of the building which was in the same building of the cafe.

According to Valachi, Sharkey always carried a handgun "and you could always see the gun when he sat on a chair in front of the cafe."[651]

Valachi lived in the same apartment building as Sharkey for about half a year in 1912. The building had a street-level coffee house and saloon where

Sharkey and his gang gathered. Sharkey was murdered in the establishment. Valachi – not yet ten – spied on the bloody scene through a door keyhole.[652]

Speaking with former crime boss Frank Costello in Atlanta Federal Prison in 1960, Valachi had occasion to reminisce about the violent days of his childhood in East Harlem:

> ...I lived in the same building where Sharky got killed in the cafe and, until this day. I remember how I was peeping in the cafe through the keyhole and saw Sharky laying with his head on the card table and his face on the table in a pool of blood. How can a kid forget such a thing. And, to tell the truth, I was always afraid to go home at night ever since it happened.

Valachi's parents decided to move after confronting him about his failure to come home. "They would ask me where I have been all night," Valachi recalled. "I would say that I was afraid to come home because of Sharky."[653]

Tony "Sharkey" Zaccaro was born in New York City in 1892. His parents were Italian immigrants Bonifacio and Luigia Zaccaro. They settled in New York with their infant son, Tony's older brother Giuseppe, in 1890.[654]

The family lived upstairs at 336 East 109th Street in April 1910. Bonifacio was then employed as a street laborer. Giuseppe, twenty, worked as a truck driver. Seventeen-year-old Tony was not employed. But, at this point, it appears he was already associated with the street gang that shook down push-cart peddlers for regular payments.[655]

In the early 1910s, Tony reportedly served time at Elmira State Prison for robbery. The institution at about the same time held someone who went by the name Giuseppe Jacko and was also associated with the 336 East 109th Street address.[656] Given the later closeness noted between this Jacko and Sharkey, as well as their similar paths, it is possible that Jacko was Sharkey's older brother, Giuseppe Zaccaro.[657]

Italian-American gangs in East Harlem feuded during the period. On October 29, 1911, gangster Frank "Tough Chick" Monaco was stabbed to death in the home of Pasquarella Musone Spinelli. Spinelli's daughter claimed responsibility for the killing, insisting that Monaco was about to rob the family home when she got a kitchen carving knife and used it on him.[658] Spinelli, who ran a profitable but underworld-linked livery stable, was murdered in the stable on March 20, 1912.[659] Aniello "*Zoppo*" (meaning lame) Prisco, who had been Monaco's superior, was suspected of killing Spinelli out of revenge. He was arrested on suspicion of murder in June, but freed for lack of evidence.[660]

It is uncertain whether Tony Zaccaro was a member of the Prisco gang or of a rival organization. There is some reason to believe Zaccaro served as a bodyguard for East Harlem underworld and political boss Giosue Gallucci.[661]

Sometime in the late summer of 1912, Zaccaro and fellow gang members performed a burglary and quarreled over division of the loot. They resolved the matter through the use of playing cards, with the lowest drawn card designating the winner. Zaccaro pulled a four of hearts out of the deck and got the preferred portion. Zaccaro had a reputation as a card player, and his fellow gang members believed he cheated them. A rumor went around that Zaccaro had bragged about doing so, using the street slang, "skinning the boobs," to refer to his swindle of his comrades.

Zaccaro received a promise of retribution in the mail. It was reportedly written across the face of a four of hearts playing card. The note may have specifically referred to the street-level cafe in the building where Zaccaro lived. After receiving it, Zaccaro reportedly avoided the business, referred to in the press as "Caffe Degli,"[662] for several days.[663]

On Monday night, September 2, 1912, Zaccaro cautiously returned to the hangout. As he entered, he spoke with cafe proprietor Giuseppe Jacko, described as Zaccaro's "close companion and adviser."[664] Jacko's advice on that night was simple: "Beat it; it's a trap."[665]

But Sharkey stayed. He sat at a table in the back of the establishment's front room and played cards with Jacko. Sharkey's attention seemed directed toward the other customers in Caffe Degli and at the cafe's entrance. He stepped away from the card table briefly at one point and returned to find a face-up four of hearts playing card deposited there.[666]

There were gunshots. Zaccaro rose and reached for his pistol. However, the assassin was much closer than he imagined. Two .44-caliber slugs hit him behind his right ear and tore through his brain. He dropped onto the card table. Another slug struck Jacko in the left temple.[667]

Police arrived to find cafe patrons fleeing the scene, Zaccaro dead on the card table and Jacko unconscious and mortally wounded in a chair beside the table. According to one report, another man known as "Coney Island Joe" was also wounded in the incident.[668]

Police later suspected "Coney Island Joe," also referred to as "Coney Island the Wop," of being involved in the killings of Zaccaro and Jacko, but they were unable to locate him.[669] (The nickname possibly referred to Francesco "Coney Island" Clementi, older brother of later Valachi associate

Carmine "Dolly Dimples" Clementi. Francesco Clementi, a traveling assassin for a Neapolitan criminal organization known as the Navy Street Gang, was murdered in Philadelphia early in 1918.[670])

"Zoppo" Prisco was arrested in connection with these murders as well. He was taken into custody on October 2. But he was again let go when no witnesses came forward to testify against him.[671]

Prisco was shot to death two months later, reportedly during an attempt to extort money from wealthy and influential Giosue Gallucci. Gallucci's nephew and bodyguard John Russomano put bullets through Prisco's head when he came to a Gallucci-run cafe, 318 East 109th Street (on the same block as the Caffe Degli), pulled a handgun and made a threat to use it.[672]

Gallucci purchased the former Caffe Degli in spring 1915 and set it up as a business for his nineteen-year-old son Luca to run. On May 18, 1915, both Giosue and Luca Gallucci were fatally shot at that cafe.[673]

Brief Bios Notes

Newspaper abbreviations: *BC – Brooklyn Citizen; BDE – Brooklyn Daily Eagle; BDT – Brooklyn Daily Times; BSU – Brooklyn Standard Union; BODG – Boston Daily Globe; BOEG – Boston Evening Globe; NYA – New York American; NYDN – New York Daily News; NYEJ – New York Evening Journal; NYEP – New York Evening Post; NYET – New York Evening Telegram; NYEW – New York Evening World; NYH – New York Herald; NYHT – New York Herald Tribune; NYP – New York Post; NYPR – New York Press; NYS – New York Sun; NYT – New York Times; NYTR – New York Tribune.*

1 We have added punctuation and corrected some misspellings in order to improve the readability of quotations from Valachi's autobiography, *The Real Thing.*

2 A number of these articles appeared in *Informer's* five-part "Gunmen of the Castellammarese War" series written by David Critchley, Lennert van't Riet and Steve Turner. Domingo was discussed in a biographical article in January 2012, Rannelli in April 2012 (an issue which focused on Salvatore "Charlie Luciano" Lucania), Santuccio in July 2012, Petrelli in October 2012 and Shillitani in April 2013. The entire August 2019 issue was focused on Maranzano. A biography of Vito Genovese was published in the January 2014 issue.

3 Valachi, Joseph, *The Real Thing: Second Government - The Expose and Inside Doings of Cosa Nostra*, unpublished manuscript, John F. Kennedy Presidential Library and Museum, 1964, p. 978.

4 Valachi, *The Real Thing*, p. 400.

5 Maas, Peter, *The Valachi Papers*, New York: G.P. Putnam's Sons, 1968, p. 255-260; Andrews, Leon F. Jr., "La Causa Nostra, Buffalo Division," FBI report of Buffalo Office, file no. 92-6054-296, NARA no. 124-10200-10453, June 14, 1963; Joseph Valachi Classification Study, register no. 82811-A, U.S. Department of Justice Bureau of Prisons, 1960, p. 4.

6 Joseph Valachi Presentence Report, Judge Matthew T. Abruzzo, United States District Court for the Eastern District of New York, indictment no. 45869, sentence date Feb. 19, 1960.

7 Testimony of Joseph Valachi, *Organized Crime and Illicit Traffic in Narcotics*, Part 1, Hearings before the Permanent Subcommittee on Investigations of the Committee on Government Operations (McClellan Hearings), U.S. Senate, 88th Congress, 1st Session, Washington D.C.: U.S. Government Printing Office, 1968, p. 78; SA, "Joseph Valachi, aka Anthony Sorge...," FBI report from Atlanta Office, file no. 70-35395-5, June 28, 1962.

8 Matthew Thomas Abruzzo, 107-36-2304, Social Security Applications and Claims Index; "Judge Matthew T. Abruzzo, 82, of federal district court, dies," NYT, May 30, 1971, p. 41; Matthew T. Abruzzo World War I Draft Registration Card, no. 79, Precinct 152, Kings County, NY, June 5, 1917.

9 "Screen depiction of gangsters as Italians assailed," *BDE*, April 19, 1931, p. 3; "Resents depicting Italians as gunmen," *Helena MT Independent*, April 26, 1931, p. 11.

10 "Judge Matthew T. Abruzzo, 82, of federal district court, dies"; "Mathew T. Abruzzo," *NYDN*, May 31, 1971, p. 16.

11 "Judge Matthew T. Abruzzo, 82, of federal district court, dies."

12 "Judge Matthew T. Abruzzo, 82, of federal district court, dies"; "Mathew T. Abruzzo."

13 Valachi, *The Real Thing*, p. 351.

14 Valachi, *The Real Thing*, p. 308, 351; Maas, *The Valachi Papers*, p. 98.

15 Valachi, *The Real Thing*, p. 308-309; Maas, *The Valachi Papers*, p. 99.

16 Valachi, *The Real Thing*, p. 351.

17 Frank Amato Certificate and Record of Birth, Borough of Manhattan, certificate no. 45213, Nov. 6, 1902, reported Nov. 13, 1902, received Nov. 14, 1902; Passenger manifest of the *S.S. Italia*, departed Palermo, arrived New Orleans on Nov. 9, 1891.

18 *Los Angeles California City Directory 1906*, p. 857; "Bullets kill and wound," *Los Angeles Times*, April 18, 1906, p. 16.

19 "Bullets kill and wound"; "Shot from ambush," *Los Angeles Record*, April 18, 1906, p. 12; "Men may belong to 'black hand,'" *Los Angeles Herald*, April 19, 1906, p. 10; Faro Amato Duplicate Certificate of Death, registered no. 1307, County of Los Angeles, City of Los Angeles, California State Board of Health Bureau of Vital Statistics, April 19, 1906, filed April 22, 1906. The death certificate reports a date of April 19 for Faro Amato's death. However, multiple newspapers reported death followed the shooting by two hours, at about 1 a.m. on April 18.

20 "Italian shot by negroes," *Stockton CA Evening Mail*, April 18, 1906, p. 2; "Two Italians shot by negroes,"

San Francisco Chronicle, April 18, 1906, p. 2; "Bullets kill and wound"; "Mafia is seen in a shooting," *Los Angeles Express*, April 18, 1906, p. 8; "Men may belong to 'black hand.'"

21 New York State Census of 1925, New York County, Assembly District 18, Election District 23; United States Census of 1930, New York State, New York County, Assembly District 18, Enumeration District 31-820.

22 United States Census of 1930, New York State, New York County, Assembly District 18, Enumeration District 31-820.

23 Maas, *The Valachi Papers*, p. 98-99.

24 Kivel, George, "Machine gun kills 2 in Harlem beer war," *NYDN*, May 29, 1931, p. 3; "2 slain in Harlem in beer price war," *NYT*, May 29, 1931, p. 2; "Dutch brews Harlem beer war reprisal," *NYDN*, May 30, 1931, p. 4; "Two more slain in Harlem beer racketeers' war," *BDE*, May 29, 1931, p. 4; "Machine gun kills two on Harlem street," *BSU*, May 29, 1943, p. 42; Downey, Patrick, *On the Spot: Gangland Murders in Prohibition New York City 1930-1933*, 2016.

25 Domenick Bologna World War I Draft Registration Card, New York City, NY, June 1917; Dominick Bologno Passport Application, certificate no. 150192, Dec. 17, 1919; Dominick Bologno and Grace Gasparino Certificate and Record of Marriage, Bronx Borough, certificate no. 4832, City of New York Department of Health Bureau of Records, June 4, 1923; New York State Census of 1925, Bronx County, Assembly District 6, Election District 33; United States Census of 1930, New York State, Bronx Borough, Assembly District 6, Enumeration District 3-486; Dominick Bologna Certificate of Death, Borough of Manhattan, registered no. 14649, Department of Health of the City of New York Bureau of Records, May 28, 1931.

26 "Gangsters use machine gun in Harlem killings," *Binghamton NY Press*, May 29, 1931, p. 11.

27 Kivel, "Machine gun kills 2 in Harlem beer war"; "2 slain in Harlem in beer price war"; "Dutch brews Harlem beer war reprisal"; "Two more slain in Harlem beer racketeers' war"; "Machine gun kills two on Harlem street"; Downey, *On the Spot*.

28 Frank Amato Certificate of Death, Borough of Manhattan, registered no. 14650, Department of Health of the City of New York Bureau of Records, May 28, 1931.

29 Dominick Bologna Certificate of Death, Borough of Manhattan, registered no. 14649, Department of Health of the City of New York Bureau of Records, May 28, 1931; "2 slain in Harlem in beer price war."

30 "2 slain in Harlem in beer price war"; "Machine gun kills two on Harlem street"; Kivel, "Machine gun kills 2 in Harlem beer war."

31 "Dutch brews Harlem beer war reprisal"; Kivel, "Machine gun kills 2 in Harlem beer war."

32 Peter Coll Certificate of Death, Borough of Manhattan, registered no. 14761, Department of Health of the City of New York Bureau of Records, May 30, 1931; "Trio in car riddle brother of man slain by gunmen," *BDE*, May 30, 1931, p. 7.

33 "Exit Big Dick. Beer and blood was his racket," *NYDN*, June 3, 1931, p. 27; Frank Amato Certificate of Death.

34 Valachi, *The Real Thing*, p. 114.

35 Valachi, *The Real Thing*, p. 112-114.

36 Valachi, *The Real Thing*, p. 118-119.

37 Valachi, *The Real Thing*, p. 140-142; Maas, *The Valachi Papers*, p. 74-78; "Taking no chances," *NYDN*, Feb. 8, 1926, p. 30. Without explanation, Maas referred to this "Dutchman" as "Dutch Hogey."

38 Ludwig Augenstein Certificate and Record of Birth, Borough of Manhattan Bureau of Records, certificate no. 4466, Jan. 18, 1899, record date Jan. 31, 1899; Ludwig Augustine, 104-14-4687, Social Security Death Index, September 1972; Ludwig Augustine World War II Draft Registration Card, serial no. T460, Order no. T11753, Local Board no. 79, Bronx, NY, Feb. 15, 1942. Mary Weidner Augenstein was a native of Endingen, Germany. In Ludwig Augustine's World War II draft registration, he provided a birth date of February 18, 1899.

39 "New York orphan/juvenile asylums," Records of New York Juvenile Asylums, Oct. 29, 2022, newyorkjuvenileasylum.com; "History," The Children's Village, July 5, 2017, childrensvillage.org.

40 United States Census of 1910, New York State, Westchester County, Town of Greenburgh, New York Juvenile Asylum, Enumeration District 193; United States Census of 1910, New York State, New York County, Ward 12, Enumeration District 351.

41 Names of Convicts Received at Auburn Prison during month of July 1921; New York State Census of 1915, Bronx County, Department of Correction Harts Island, Assembly District 32, Election District 73.

42 "Shot by assassins with silent revolver," *BSU*, Feb. 13, 1916, p. 5.

43 Names of Convicts Received at Auburn Prison during month of July 1921; Names of Convicts Discharged from Auburn Prison during the month of October 1921.

44 United States Census of 1920, New York State, Clinton County, Village of Dannemora, Clinton Prison, Enumeration District 16; Names of Convicts Received at Auburn Prison during month of July 1921; Names of Convicts Discharged from Auburn Prison during the month of October 1921,

45 "Bum Rogers's pal gets double dose for crime," *NYDN*, Dec. 25, 1925, p. 24; "Pal of 'Bum' Rogers found guilty as robber," *BSU*, Dec. 23, 1925, p. 2.

46 "Wounded suspect arrested," *BDE*, April 7, 1925, p. 2.

47 "Nassau holdup suspect caught in Manhattan," *BDT*, Oct. 11, 1925, p. 9; "'Dutch' Augustine held in robbery," *BDE*, Oct. 10, 1925, p. 2.

48 "Pal of 'Bum' Rogers found guilty as robber"; "30 years for Rogers aid," *NYH*, Dec. 25, 1925, p. 9.

49 Ludwig Augustine, no. 77952, Sing Sing Prison Receiving Blotter, Dec. 30, 1925; Valachi, *The Real Thing*, p. 141-142. Valachi recalled that Augustine was in the prison hospital because of his wounded leg. Augustine told Valachi that he would ensure he was soon transferred from Sing Sing to Dannemora by striking someone on the head with his crutches.

50 "Taking no chances," *NYDN*, Feb. 8, 1926, p. 30; Names of Convicts Received at Auburn Prison during the month of December 1928; United States Census of 1930, New York State, Cayuga County, Auburn City, Auburn State Prison, Enumeration District 6-8; Names of Convicts Discharged from Auburn Prison during the month of March 1931; Ludwig Augustine, no. 77952, Sing Sing Prison Receiving Blotter, Dec. 30, 1925; United States Census of 1940, New York State, Washington County, Great Meadow Prison, Enumeration District 58-13.

51 Ludwig Augustine World War II Draft Registration Card, serial no. T460, Order no. T11753, Local Board no. 79, Bronx, NY, Feb. 15, 1942; United States Census of 1950, New York State, Bronx County, Enumeration District 3-564.

52 Ludwig Augustine, 104-14-4687, Social Security Death Index, September 1972; XCHIEF, "Ludwig Augustine," memorial no. 219497341, Find a Grave, findagrave.com, Dec. 7, 2020.

53 Valachi, *The Real Thing*, p. 6e. Valachi misspelled Brother Abel's name as "Alble."

54 Valachi, *The Real Thing*, p. 6, 6d.

55 Valachi, *The Real Thing*, p. 6e.

56 "Brother Abel is dead; teacher at protectory," *BSU*, Jan. 21, 1917, p. 14; "Four choral hosts to sing in new year," *NYT*, Dec. 29, 1912, p. 13; "The band contest," *Yonkers NY Herald*, Aug. 18, 1899, p. 4; "Catholic Protectory band," *New Haven CT Morning Journal and Courier*, Feb. 20, 1905, p. 8.

57 "Died," *NYT*, Jan. 20, 1917, p. 11; "Brother Abel is dead; teacher at protectory;" Valachi, *The Real Thing*, p. 6e.

58 "Died," *NYT*, Jan. 20, 1917, p. 11; "Deaths," *NYTR*, Jan. 21, 1917, p. 13; "Brother Abel is dead; teacher at protectory."

59 Valachi, *The Real Thing*, p. 168.

60 Valachi, *The Real Thing*, p. 17, 146, 168, 298. Valachi also used the derogatory term, "greaseball" (23 times) to refer in a far less flattering way to Italian-born men he did not like.

61 Valachi, *The Real Thing*, p. 168.

62 Valachi, *The Real Thing*, p. 297-307; Testimony of Joseph Valachi, Oct. 1, 1963, McClellan Hearings, p. 180-185.

63 Franciscus Callace baptism record, Corleone, Monreale Diocese, Sicily, no. 42, Jan. 23, 1900; Frank Callace World War I Draft Registration Card, serial no. 453, order no. A845, Local board no. 160, New York, NY, Sept. 12, 1918.

64 Passenger manifest of *S.S. Canada*, departed Palermo on Dec. 18, 1913, arrived New York on Dec. 30, 1913.

65 Frank Callace World War I Draft Registration Card.

66 "Two suspects taken on burglary charge," *BDT*, April 10, 1924, p. 4; "Cleared of burglary; rearrested and held," *BSU*, April 24, 1924, p. 2.

67 New York State Census of 1925, New York County, Assembly District 18, Election District 23; United States Census of 1930, New York State, New York County, Assembly District 18, Enumeration District 31-820.

68 Evans, C.A., FBI Memorandum to Mr. Belmont, accompanied by Joseph Valachi debriefings collected by Assistant Attorney General Herbert Miller, file no. 92-6054-406, NARA Record no. 124-10220-10111, Aug. 13, 1963, enclosure p. 19-20.

69 "Two held here for passing counterfeit," *Beacon NY News*, April 5, 1932, p. 1; "Arrest 2 at Newburgh in bogus bill case," *Peekskill NY Evening Star*, April 5, 1932, p. 1; "The Newburgh-Beacon Bridge: History," New York State Bridge Authority, nysba.ny.gov, Nov. 7, 2014, accessed May 15, 2024. The New-

burgh-Beacon Bridge, which now carries Interstate-84 over the Hudson River at this point, was not opened until November 1963. A ferry still takes vehicles between Newburgh and Beacon each day.

70 "Three Bronx men held as distillers," *Mount Vernon NY Daily Argus*, July 1, 1937, p. 8; Marino, Anthony, and Henry Lee, "Ex-Luciano henchman taken for the ride he long feared," *NYDN*, Nov. 15, 1954, p. 26.

71 Philip Callace, New York State Birth Index, Poughkeepsie, NY, certificate no. 75573, Nov. 23, 1932; Philip Callace, 075-26-6832, Social Security Death Index, Dec. 6, 2001; United States Census of 1940, New York State, New York County, Assembly District 18, Enumeration District 31-1604-B; Frank Callace and Catherine Summa, New York City Index to Marriage Licenses, Borough of Manhattan, certificate no. 2119, Feb. 9, 1942.

72 "Ex-Luciano henchman taken for the ride he long feared."

73 "Frank Callace," Identification Order no. 2185, Federal Bureau of Investigation, FBI no. 206,139, June 12, 1948; Fulbright, Newton H., "Found slain at wheel of car in Bronx," *NYHT*, Nov. 15, 1954, p. 1. The *Herald Tribune* article, written seven years after the incident, states that he was charged in Milford, CT, with "idleness."

74 United States Census of 1950, New York State, New York County, Enumeration District 31-2433; Maria Collace, Deaths reported in the City of New York - 1950, Borough of Manhattan, certificate no. 19818, Sept. 17, 1950. The age of Anne Marie DeLuca Callace was inconsistently reported. She was said to be 57 at the time of her immigration (possibly a stated age of 47 was incorrectly recorded), placing her birth about 1856 and making her 94 at the time of her death. The 1930 U.S. Census said she was 65 at that time, placing her birth about 1865 and making her 85 when she died. The stated death age of 88 would make her year of birth 1862.

75 "Seize 100G dope in Rome," *NYDN*, April 8, 1951, p. 36; Packard, Reynolds, "Lucky Luciano tagged in Italy as a smuggler," *NYDN*, June 10, 1951, p. C3; "Deported ex-convict freed in Milan case," *Knickerbocker News*, April 9, 1952, p. 23; Marino, Anthony, and Henry Lee, "Ex-Luciano henchman taken for the ride he long feared," *NYDN*, Nov. 15, 1954, p. 26

76 "Lucky Luciano tagged in Italy as a smuggler."

77 "Italian general stripped of rank," *Albany NY Times Union*, May 15, 1952, p. 16; "Italian general stripped of rank," *Troy NY Record*, May 15, 1952, p. 34.

78 Evans, C.A., FBI Memorandum to Mr. Belmont, accompanied by Joseph Valachi debriefings collected by Assistant Attorney General Herbert Miller, file no. 92-6054-406, NARA Record no. 124-10220-10111, Aug. 13, 1963, enclosure p. 17.

79 "Hear Mafia had hand in Giannini's slaying," *NYDN*, Sept. 22, 1952, p. 15.

80 SAC New York, "La Causa Nostra, AR - Conspiracy," FBI Memorandum to Director, file no. 92-6054-249, NARA no. 124-10284-10259, May 26, 1963; Maas, *The Valachi Papers*, p. 220-230.

81 Deaths reported in the City of New York - 1954, Borough of Bronx, M.E. case no. 2741, certificate no. 10608, Nov. 14, 1954; "Ex-Luciano henchman found shot to death in car," *Newsday* (Nassau Edition), Nov. 15, 1924, p. 5; "Ex-Luciano henchman taken for the ride he long feared"; Fulbright, Newton H., "Found slain at wheel of car in Bronx"; "Gun picked up in park may be clue in killing of ex-Luciano aide," *NYP*, Nov. 15, 1954, p. 4.

82 Valachi, *The Real Thing*, p. 454.

83 Valachi, *The Real Thing*, p. 454; Maas, *The Valachi Papers*, p. 155.

84 Valachi did not state the date but suggested that the early 1938 death of Terranova and the 1935 murder of Dutch Schultz were fairly recent developments.

85 Valachi, *The Real Thing*, p. 455.

86 Valachi, *The Real Thing*, p. 456; Maas, *The Valachi Papers*, p. 156.

87 Valachi, *The Real Thing*, p. 459.

88 Valachi, *The Real Thing*, p. 460.

89 Valachi, *The Real Thing*, p. 462-463; Maas, *The Valachi Papers*, p. 157-158.

90 United States Census of 1910, New York State, New York County, Ward 8, Enumeration District 116; New Jersey State Census of 1915, Bergen County, Union Township, Enumeration District 1.

91 Eddie Capobianco Identification Record, FBI no. 176 797, in Carr, Charlie, *New York Police Files on the Mafia*, Hosehead Productions, 2012, p. 541-542.

92 "Inmate attends funeral," *Elmira NY Star-Gazette*, Feb. 12, 1923, p. 5.

93 Harpman, Julia, "Diamond's story jails 5 more," *NYDN*, Nov. 29, 1923, p. 3; "Big celebration marks release of Diamond witness," *Olean NY Evening Herald*, March 1, 1924, p. 1.

94 Edward Capobianco, no. 77650, Sing Sing Prison Receiving Blotter, received Oct. 22, 1925; Eddie Capobianco Identification Record.

95 Eddie Capobianco Identification Record.

96 Martin, John, "Ex-convict talks himself into jail as bank holdup," *NYDN*, March 18, 1927, p. 3; "Bankers fail to identify newest suspect as robber," *New Rochelle NY Standard-Star*, March 18, 1937, p. 1; "Bank holdup victims fail to identify gang suspect," *Mount Vernon Argus*, March 18, 1937, p. 1.

97 "Denied bail in fatal ambush of ex-convict," *NYDN*, Jan. 12, 1940, p. 26B; Eddie Capobianco Identification Record.

98 Edward Capobianco, New York City Extracted Death Index, certificate no. 23613, Nov. 4, 1945; Edward Capobianco, New York City Municipal Deaths, certificate no. 23613, Nov. 4, 1945, FamilySearch, familysearch.org.

99 Valachi, *The Real Thing*, p. 344.

100 Valachi, *The Real Thing*, p. 343.

101 Valachi, *The Real Thing*, p. 344.

102 Valachi, *The Real Thing*, p. 362.

103 Salvatore Maranzano Certificate of Death, Borough of Manhattan, certificate no. 22124, Department of Health of the City of New York Bureau of Records, Sept. 10, 1931; "Gang kills suspect in alien smuggling," *NYT*, Sept. 11, 1931, p. 1; "Salvatore Maranzano slashed and shot in Park Avenue," *Poughkeepsie Eagle-News*, Sept. 11, 1931, p. 1

104 Leonforte was once part of the Province of Catania. In 1927, long after the Caruso family emigrated, it became part of the Province of Enna.

105 Passenger manifest of *S.S. Regina D'Italia*, departed Palermo, arrived New York on Oct. 19, 1909.

106 "Angelo Caruso, Anti-Racketeering," FBI report of New York Office, file no. 92-6856-42, Oct. 21, 1974, p. 1-3, 5; Passenger manifest of *S.S. Belvedere*, departed from Palermo, Sicily, on Oct. 20, 1920, arrived New York on Sept. 6, 1920; Angelo Caruso Petition for Naturalization, U.S. District Court for the Southern District of New York, no. 433112, filed Sept. 6, 1920; Angelo Caruso Certificate of Arrival, no. 2 448146, Immigration and Naturalization Service, issued July 6, 1936.

107 "Federal agents furnish alibi for a bomb suspect," *NYDN*, Oct. 8, 1920, p. 3.

108 "Hold Queens barber for possible part in bomb explosions," *BDE*, Oct. 7, 1920, p. 3; "Questioned in bomb investigation," *NYDN*, Oct. 8, 1920, p. 16; "Federal agents furnish alibi for a bomb suspect," *NYDN*, Oct. 8, 1920, p. 3; "Weapons confiscated in home of bomb suspect," *NYDN*, Oct. 9, 1920, p. 1.

109 "Federal agents furnish alibi for a bomb suspect."

110 The alias appears to have been adapted from his mother's maiden name.

111 "Hold four for assault," *Jersey Journal*, Oct. 30, 1925, p. 20; "Heavy bail is asked for 4 in assault case," *Jersey Journal*, Oct. 31, 1925, p. 8.

112 "Angelo Caruso, Anti-Racketeering," FBI report of New York Office, file no. 92-6856-42, Oct. 21, 1974, p. 3.

113 "Greenwich 'tip' causes arrest of Port Chester man," *Stamford Advocate*, April 13, 1926, p. 1.

114 "Three held in $2000 bonds each," *Lowell MA Sun*, Dec. 8, 1928, p. 3; "Two Lawrence men held in $2000 each," *Lowell MA Sun*, Dec. 17, 1928, p. 10; "Greater Lawrence trio face U.S. commissioner," *Boston Globe*, Dec. 18, 1929, p. 4.

115 "Two arrested, still seized in Groveland raid," *Springfield MA Daily News*, March 15, 1937, p. 10; "Tatel again faces still indictment," *Boston Globe*, April 23, 1937, p. 36; "Two jailed for still, one given probation," *Boston Globe*, June 5, 1937, p. 2; "Two sent to jail," *Lynn MA Daily Evening Item*, June 5, 1937, p. 2.

116 Angelo Caruso and Maria Antonina Colletti Certificate and Record of Marriage, Borough of Manhattan, certificate no. 17926, City of New York Department of Health Bureau of Records, July 22, 1928; Angelo Caruso Petition for Naturalization, U.S. District Court for the Southern District of New York, no. 433112, filed Nov. 30, 1942, admitted Aug. 31, 1944. The mention of Sant'Anna is a bit vague, but it seems it likely refers to Sant'Anna, Enna province, which sat about eight miles to the east of Caruso's birthplace in Leonforte.

117 Bonanno, Joseph, with Sergio Lalli, *A Man of Honor: The Autobiography of Joseph Bonanno*, New York: Simon and Schuster, 1983, p. 124.

118 "Angelo Caruso, Anti-Racketeering," p. 1.

119 "Hunt jeweler believed held by kidnap gang," *Chicago Daily Tribune*, Nov. 10, 1931, p. 4; "Seize Mangano as kidnaper of Rockford gambler," *Chicago Daily Times*, Nov. 10, 1931, p. 2; "End of the 'ring' believed near," *NYT*, Nov. 11, 1931, p. 32; "Nab Capone aid as head of kidnap ring," *NYDN*, Nov. 11, 1931, p. 18.

120 "Police nab kidnap gang," *Chicago Daily Times*, Nov. 11, 1931, p. 37; "Kidnap victim freed as police hold Mangano," *Chicago Daily Tribune*, Nov. 11, 1931, p. 6.

121 "Angelo Caruso, Anti-Racketeering," p. 3; "Free Mangano and gang, held as kidnapers," *Chicago Daily Tribune*, Nov. 12, 1931, p. 7.

122 Passenger master list, Aircraft no. 388, from Agua Caliente, Mexico, to Lindbergh Field, San Diego, CA., July 24, 1932; "Angelo Caruso, Anti-Racketeering," p. 3.

123 "Dragna arrested for deportation by U.S.," *Hollywood CA Citizen-News*, Dec. 8, 1952, p. 1; "U.S. nabs Jack Dragna on illegal entry charge," *Los Angeles Times*, Dec. 9, 1952, p. 2.

124 Angelo Caruso Declaration of Intention, U.S. District Court for the Southern District of New York, no. 451235, Jan. 18, 1940; United States Census of 1940, New York State, New York County, Assembly District 8, Enumeration District 674; Angelo Caruso World War II Draft Registration Card, serial no. U2319, local board no. 10, New York County NY, April 25, 1942; Angelo Caruso Petition for Naturalization, U.S. District Court for the Southern District of New York, no. 433112, filed Nov. 30, 1942, admitted Aug. 31, 1944; "Angelo Caruso, Anti-Racketeering," p. 3; United States Census of 1950, New York State, New York County, Enumeration District 31-547.

125 "Angelo Caruso, Anti-Racketeering," p. 2.

126 Angelo Caruso World War II Draft Registration Card; Angelo Caruso Petition for Naturalization; "Giuseppe Ambroagio Magliocco," FBI memo of New York Office, file no. 92-4224-14, June 8, 1959; Giuseppe Ambroagio Magliocco summary by New York office, June 28, 1960, contained in Director FBI, "Information concerning alleged racketeering figures," memorandum to Assistant Attorney General Malcolm R. Wilkey, file no. CR 62-9-408, NARA no. 124-10347-10001, July 12, 1960, p. 4; "John Michael Balsamo," FBI Memo of New York Office, file no. 92-422502, NARA no. 124-10221-10177, June 27, 1959.

127 Bonanno, *A Man of Honor*, p. 259; "Angelo Caruso; Anti-Racketeering."

128 Bonanno, *A Man of Honor*, p. 283, 286.

129 Newark, "La Cosa Nostra, Anti Racketeering - Conspiracy," FBI to Director, Teletype, file no. 92-6054-2031, June 8, 1967.

130 Bonanno, *A Man of Honor*, p. 291.

131 "Angelo Caruso, Anti-Racketeering," p. 1.

132 Angelo Caruso, Social Security Death Index, 052-14-5948, Nov. 13, 1991.

133 Valachi, *The Real Thing*, p. 255.

134 Valachi, *The Real Thing*, p. 164.

135 Testimony of Joseph Valachi, Oct. 1, 1963, McClellan Hearings, p. 152.

136 Testimony of Joseph Valachi, Oct. 1, 1963, McClellan Hearings, p. 151-154.

137 Valachi, *The Real Thing*, p. 253; "Buck Jones (1891-1942)," Internet Movie Database, imdb.com.

138 Valachi, *The Real Thing*, p. 92-94.

139 Valachi, *The Real Thing*, p. 254-255.

140 Valachi, *The Real Thing*, p. 305-307, 337, 341; Testimony of Joseph Valachi, Oct. 2, 1963, McClellan Hearings, p. 225.

141 Valachi, *The Real Thing*, p. 365; Testimony of Joseph Valachi, Oct. 1, 1963, McClellan Hearings, p. 223.

142 Valachi, *The Real Thing*, p. 367-370; Testimony of Joseph Valachi, Oct. 2, 1963, McClellan Hearings, p. 226-227; Maas, *The Valachi Papers*, p. 115, 117.

143 Stefano Casertano *Atti di Nascita*, no. 30, San Prisco, Italy; Lorenzo Casertano and Anna Zibella *Atti di Matrimonio*, no. 38, San Prisco, Italy; Lorenzo Casertano Declaration of Intention, no. 361376, U.S. District Court for the Southern District of New York, Feb. 28, 1935; Passenger manifest of the *S.S. Citta di Napoli*, departed Naples on Oct. 4, 1902, arrived New York on Oct. 20, 1902; Passenger manifest of *S.S. Moltke*, departed Naples on Jan. 5, 1907, arrived New York on Jan. 18, 1907; Stefano Casertano Certificate of Arrival, no. 569114, U.S. Department of Labor Bureau of Naturalization, issued July 7, 1928. Slightly different birthdays – between March 6 and March 8 – were given for Stephen Casertano in some official records.

144 United States Census of 1910, New York State, New York County, Ward 12, Enumeration District 337; New York State Census of 1915, New York County, Assembly District 28, Election District 3; United States Census of 1920, New York State, New York County, Assembly District 18, Enumeration District 1270.

145 Stephen Casertano Declaration of Intention, no. 178250, U.S. District Court for the Southern District of New York, July 13, 1925; Stephen Casertano Petition for Naturalization, no. 139926, U.S. District Court for the Southern District of New York, Aug. 10, 1928; United States Census of 1930, New York State, New York County, Assembly District 18, Enumeration District 31-835.

146 Anna Casertano Certificate of Death, Borough of Manhattan, certificate no. 14734, Bureau of Records

Department of Health, July 4, 1939; Lorenzo Casertano, Deaths reported in the City of New York, certificate no. 17849, June 19, 1950; Stephen Casertano, Deaths Reported in the City of New York, certificate no. 12764, June 14, 1954.

147 Maas, Peter, "Mafia: The inside story," *Saturday Evening Post*, Aug. 10-17, 1963, p. 19. No Stefano Casertano marriage is mentioned in any of available documents.

148 "Jury finds three guilty in 13-day narcotics trial," *Bergen NJ Evening Record*, May 3, 1956, p. 1.

149 Valachi, *The Real Thing*, p. 241.

150 Valachi, *The Real Thing*, p. 241.

151 Joseph Castaldo World War II Draft Registration, serial no. U00 586, Local Board no 47, New York, NY, April 21, 1942.

152 When married in October 1908, Castaldo reported he was 22, placing his birth in 1886. When sentenced for assault a year and a half later, he claimed he was just 21 (born 1888-1889). He reported being 25 at the time of the June 1915 New York State Census (born 1889-1890). For his 1917 draft registration, he indicated a specific birth date of Oct. 26, 1887. But when he registered for the draft in 1942, he moved the date to May 26, 1888.

153 Auburn Prison Register of Foreign Born Inmates, 1910; Names of Convicts Received at Auburn Prison During the Month of July 1910. The Auburn Prison register stated that Castaldo arrived in New York aboard the S.S. California in July of 1899.

154 Giuseppe Castaldo and Giuseppa Salerno Certificate and Record of Marriage, Borough of Manhattan, certificate no. 19273, Oct. 14, 1908.

155 Sing Sing Prison Admission Register, No. 60263, May 7, 1910; Names of Convicts Received at Auburn Prison During the Month of July 1910.

156 New York State Census of 1915, New York County, Assembly District 28, Election District 3; Joseph Castaldo World War I Draft Registration, no. 502, Precinct 39, New York, NY, June 5, 1917.

157 United States Census of 1920, New York State, New York County, Enumeration District 1229.

158 United States Census of 1940, New York State, New York County, Enumeration District 31-1592.

159 "Five more indicted in racket clean-up," *NYT*, July 16, 1932, p. 26; "True bills name 'Artichoke King' and four in fraud," *BDE*, July 16, 1932, p. 16

160 "Lists huge profits of 'Artichoke King,'" *NYT*, Feb. 3, 1933, p. 8; "'Artichoke King' gets prison term," *NYT*, Feb. 4, 1933, p. 6; "'Artichoke King' gets 11 months for tax evasion," *BDE*, Feb. 3, 1933, p. 15.

161 "Six are indicted as artichoke trust," *NYT*, April 8, 1933, p. 3; "Jury is locked up in Castaldo trial," *NYT*, Feb. 12, 1936, p. 44. Bonsignore eventually pleaded guilty and was sentenced to six months in prison. He later turned up as chief lieutenant for Joseph "Socks" Lanza, rackets boss at the Fulton Fish Market.

162 "Mayor puts a ban on artichoke sale to curb rackets," *NYT*, Dec. 22, 1935, p. 1.

163 "Bars mayor's edict in artichoke trial," *NYT*, Jan. 22, 1936, p. 20; Siler, Leon, "Artichoke jury hears details of racket's origin," *NYP*, Jan. 23, 1936, p. 7; "4 'abducted,' court told," *NYT*, Jan. 24, 1936, p. 40; "Jury is locked up in Castaldo trial"; "Artichoke trial ends in deadlock," *NYT*, Feb. 13, 1936, p. 40; "Guilty in artichoke case," *NYT*, March 25, 1936, p. 17.

164 United States Census of 1940, New York State, New York County, Enumeration Districts 31-1592 and 31-1597.

165 United States Census of 1950, New York State, New York County, Enumeration District 31-2435.

166 "Death notices," *NYDN*, June 7, 1950, p. 22; Joseph Castaldo, New York City Death Index, certificate no. 12708, June 4, 1950.

167 Valachi, *The Real Thing*, p. 150.

168 "Dolly Dimples" was the name of a popular comic character created by Grace Drayton. The character became the focus of a syndicated newspaper comic strip in the 1920s. (Terry, Hazel, "Grace Drayton," *Little Red Riding Hood and Other Wolfish Things*, hazelterry.blogspot.com, Dec. 30, 2014.) The name "Dolly Dimple" was used in children's books in the 1860s. (Sketches of authors – 'Sophie May,'" *Evansville IN Daily Journal*, Aug. 5, 1867, p. 4.

169 Valachi, *The Real Thing*, p. 145.

170 Valachi, *The Real Thing*, p. 150.

171 Valachi, *The Real Thing*, p. 147.

172 Valachi, *The Real Thing*, p. 148-149; Maas, *The Valachi Papers*, p. 75-76.

173 Valachi, *The Real Thing*, p. 152-153.

174 Valachi, *The Real Thing*, p. 153-154.

175 Valachi, *The Real Thing*, p. 192.

176 Valachi, *The Real Thing*, p. 154.

177 Valachi, *The Real Thing*, p. 161.

178 New York State Census of 1905, New York County, Assembly District 33, Election District 11; United States Census of 1910, New York State, New York County, Ward 12, Enumeration District 343; United States Census of 1920, New York State, New York County, Ward 18, Enumeration District 1293.

179 "Warbasse grills Vollero on stand," *BDE*, March 11, 1918; "Jury finds gunman guilty of murder," *NYTR*, March 15, 1918, p. 8; "Brooklyn slayer to die," *NYEW*, April 1, 1918, p. 4.

180 "Italian shot dead in feud," *BDT*, Nov. 14, 1917, p. 1.

181 Andrew Ricci Certificate of Death, Borough of Brooklyn, registered no. 22069, Department of Health of the City of New York Bureau of Records, Nov. 14, 1917; "Mystery in murder," *BDE*, Nov. 14, 1917, p. 3; "Italian shot dead in feud."

182 "Says gambling ring killed 23," *NYS*, Nov. 28, 1917, p. 1.

183 People of the State of New York v. Alessandro Vollero, Case on Appeal Vol. I, Court of Appeals of the State of New York, 226 New York 587 Pt 1, New York: Stillman Appellate Printing Co, 1918. They did not explain why it was necessary for Clementi to insist on this.

184 Francis Clementi Certificate of Death, registered no. 4553, County of Philadelphia, Feb. 5, 1918; "Gunmen slay victim in revenge; other murders baffle police," *Evening Public Ledger*, Feb. 6, 1918, p. 3; "Italian is murdered by gunmen, who leap from passing motor," *Philadelphia Inquirer*, Feb. 6, 1918, p. 8; "Gangster is slain after he squeals upon former pals," *Philadelphia Inquirer*, Feb. 7, 1918, p. 1; "One man arrested in gunman murder," *Philadelphia Inquirer*, Feb. 8, 1918, p. 7.

185 Valachi, *The Real Thing*, p. 147.

186 "Four bathing suit robbers loot pool, wound policeman," *NYDN*, Aug. 13, 1925, p. 4; "8 rob Bronx bathhouse; shoot guard," *NYHT*, Aug. 13, 1925, p. 1; "2 shot in hold-up; 200 bathers robbed," *NYT*, Aug. 13, 1925, p. 1.

187 "Five Bronx youths get terms totaling 77 years," *NYHT*, Oct. 1, 1925, p. 15; "Long terms for robbers," *NYT*, Oct. 1, 1925, p. 16; "Convicts Subject Jurisdiction Board of Parole," Report from Great Meadow Prison, Comstock, NY, Jan. 20, 1933.

188 Carmine Clementi, no. 77579, Sing Sing Prison Receiving Blotter, received Oct. 5, 1925; "Convicts Subject Jurisdiction Board of Parole," Report from Great Meadow Prison, Comstock, NY, Jan. 20, 1933; Great Meadow Prison Record, 1930; "Failed to show up in court, guard jailed," *NYEJ*, Oct. 7, 1925, p. 3.

189 "Two young gun bandits get heavy sentences," *New York Journal*, Oct. 13, 1925, p. 1; "15 gunmen jailed in fight on crime," *NYT*, Oct. 14, 1925, p. 27; "Ricciardi gets 20 years for park holdup," *NYEJ*, Nov. 12, 1925, p. 1; Basil Ricciardi, inmate no. 77748, Sing Sing Prison Admission Register, Nov. 11, 1925.

190 "Bandit held as aid in park holdup," *NYEJ*, Dec. 2, 1925, p. 26.

191 United States Census of 1930, New York State, Westchester County, Ossining Township, Sing Sing State Prison, Enumeration District 60-294; United States Census of 1930, New York State, Clinton County, Dannemora Village, Clinton State Prison, Enumeration District 10-16; Great Meadow Prison Record, 1930; "Convicts Subject Jurisdiction Board of Parole," Report from Great Meadow Prison, Comstock, NY, Jan. 20, 1933.

192 Domenico Clementi Certificate of Death, Borough of Manhattan, registered no. 20670, Department of Health of the City of New York Bureau of Records, Sept. 28, 1935; United States Census of 1940, New York State, New York County, Assembly District 18, Enumeration District 31-1579; United States Census of 1940, New York State, Clinton County, Dannemora Village, Dannemora State Hospital for the Criminally Insane, Enumeration District 10-19; Filomena Clementi, certificate no. 7930, New York City Index to Death Certificates, April 1, 1943; Filomena Clementi Certificate of Death, Borough of Manhattan, certificate no. 7930, April 1, 1943; United States Census of 1950, New York State, Clinton County, Dannemora, Dannemora State Hospital form the Criminally Insane, Enumeration District 10-23; New York State Death Index, 1950. The 1940 Census, placing Carmine Clementi in the Dannemora Hospital, indicated that he was in the same facility on April 1, 1935.

193 Valachi, *The Real Thing*, p. 365.

194 Valachi, *The Real Thing*, p. 366.

195 Evans, C.A., FBI Memorandum to Mr. Belmont, accompanied by Joseph Valachi debriefings collected by Assistant Attorney General Herbert Miller, file no. 92-6054-406, NARA Record no. 124-10220-10111, Aug. 13, 1963, enclosure p. 17. Valachi reported that he was told Anthony "T.Balls" LoPinto was one of the gunmen. While never told the identities of the other two, he believed they were Joseph "Joe Babes" Bendinelli and Anthony "Tony Higgins" Castaldi.

196 The dates July 12 and July 13 appear in some records, but July 18 is most frequently used as his date of birth.

197 Antonino Coco Declaration of Intention, no. 129344, Bronx County Supreme Court, March 26, 1937; Antonino Coco Petition for Naturalization, no. 433527, U.S. District Court for the Southern District of New York; Edward Coco, 267-96-9219, Social Security Death Index, death date Dec. 26, 1991; Ettore Coco Declaration of Intention, no. 355255, U.S. District Court for the Southern District of New York, July 9, 1934; Lodovico Coco, Palermo Italy Births, Vol. 494, No. 535, Feb. 25, 1905.

198 Passenger manifest of S.S. San Rossore, departed Naples on May 9, 1921, arrived New York on May 25, 1921; Passenger manifest of S.S. Providence, departed Palermo on July 16, 1922, arrived New York on July 28, 1922; Ettore Coco Declaration of Intention.

199 New York State Census of 1925, New York County, Assembly District 18, Election District 24.

200 Valachi, The Real Thing, p. 366; Bonanno, A Man of Honor, p. 106, 118, 124, 139.

201 Evans, C.A., FBI Memorandum to Mr. Belmont, accompanied by Joseph Valachi debriefings collected by Assistant Attorney General Herbert Miller, file no. 92-6054-406, NARA Record no. 124-10220-10111, Aug. 13, 1963, enclosure p. 19-20.

202 "Refusing to enter resort, 4 beaten," NYEP, Oct. 30, 1933, p. 5; "5 men are held in street attack," NYS, Oct. 30, 1933, p. 3; "5 held in beating of two couples in 71st Street," NYDN, Oct. 31, 1933, p. 16.

203 "Troopers nab four speeders," Ossining NY Citizen-Register, April 27, 1939, p. 16; "Troopers nab four speeders," NYDN, April 27, 1939, p. 4; "Nab gang in speeding car along parkway," Peekskill NY Evening Star, April 27, 1939, p. 1; "Man arrested by troopers returned to Sing Sing," NYDN, June 15, 1939, p. 8; "Jail trio seized in speeding car," Peekskill NY Evening Star, June 15, 1939, p. 1.

204 "Pair re-jailed on charge of plotting," Peekskill NY Evening Star, Aug. 4, 1939, p. 1.

205 Ettore Coco World War II Draft Registration Card, serial no. 2451, order no. 11, Local Board no. 98, Bronx, New York, Oct. 16, 1940.

206 United States Treasury Department Bureau of Narcotics, Mafia: The Government's Secret File on Organized Crime, New York: Collins, 2007, p. 399; Smith, Wilfrid, "Graziano stops Zale in 6th; champion!" Chicago Daily Tribune, July 17, 1947, p. 25.

207 "D.A. questions Rocky's pals," NYDN, Feb. 6, 1948, p. 18.

208 Mozley, Dana, "NBA suspends Graziano for Apostoli 'walkout,'" NYDN, Nov. 27, 1948, p. 24.

209 United States Census of 1950, New York State, New York County, Enumeration District 31-1244.

210 Eddie Coco Application for Manager's License, no. 314, State Athletic Commission of Wisconsin, May 9, 1950.

211 "The biggest floating crap game...," NYDN, Jan. 14, 1955, p. 28; Bureau of Narcotics, Mafia, p. 399.

212 "Johnny Smith slain by Beach gunman," Miami Times, Feb. 3, 1951, p. 1.

213 "Death hearing fixed Monday," Miami Herald, Feb. 3, 1951, p. 23; "Coco held for grand jury," Miami News, Feb. 5, 1951, p. 22.

214 McLemore, Morris, "Heard in court," Miami News, June 16, 1951, p. 7; Bohne, Robert F., "Murderer still out on bail long past Dade conviction," Miami News, Aug. 5, 1952, p. 22; "High court orders new trial for Dade man who slew Negro," Tampa Tribune, Jan. 22, 1953, p. 24.

215 "Eddie Coco found guilty of murder," Miami Herald, Oct. 30, 1953, p. 10; "Eddie Coco given life in slaying," Miami News, Nov. 12, 1953, p. 1; "Eddie Coco gets life," NYHT, Nov. 13, 1953, p. 7; "Ring figure gets life term," NYT, Nov. 13, 1953, p. 19; "Coco loses plea," Miami Times, Nov. 21, 1953, p. 2.

216 Evans, C.A., FBI Memorandum to Mr. Belmont, accompanied by Joseph Valachi debriefings collected by Assistant Attorney General Herbert Miller, file no. 92-6054-406, NARA Record no. 124-10220-10111, Aug. 13, 1963, enclosure p. 17.

217 "Jeer Coco, Tongay to prison," NYDN, May 14, 1955, p. 12

218 "Hoodlum paroled to Dade," Miami Herald, Aug. 24, 1965, p. 20; Krunholz, June, "Coco loses parole on life sentence," Miami Herald, Sept. 12, 1972, p. 25. Coco was transferred from Raiford to Avon Park in May 1961.

219 "Luchese leaves hospital," NYT, April 12, 1967, p. 35; "Thomas Luchese, rackets boss called 3-Finger Brown, is dead," NYT, July 14, 1967; Lee, Henry, "3-finger Brown, Cosa big, dies," NYDN, July 14, 1967, p. 4C.

220 Carroll, Margaret, "Coco, Nash found guilty of extortion," Miami Herald, Aug. 27, 1972, p. 37; Grutzner, Charles, "Cat-and-mouse game: U.S. and Luchese mafia gang's leaders," NYT, Dec. 23, 1967, p. 11; Trankley, Allan M., "La Cosa Nostra Miami Division," FBI report, file no. 92-6054-2391, NARA Record No. 124-10297-10125, Aug. 22, 1968.

221 O'Neil, Robert G., "La Cosa Nostra," FBI report of New York Office, file no. 92-6054-2175, NARA no. 124-10277-10308, Oct. 20, 1967, p. 56.

222 Carroll, Margaret, "2 arrested on loan-sharking charge," *Miami Herald*, June 15, 1972, p. 41; "Loan shark suspects get bail reduced," *Miami Herald*, June 19, 1972, p. 37.

223 Carroll, "Coco, Nash found guilty of extortion"; "Coco and Nash await sentencing," *Miami News*, Aug. 28, 1972, p. 2; "Jail-time for Eddie Coco," *Miami Herald*, Sept. 8, 1972, p. 6; Krunholz, June, "Coco loses parole on life sentence," *Miami Herald*, Sept. 12, 1972, p. 25.

224 Ettore Coco, petitioner-appellant, v United States of America, respondent-appellee, 569 F.2d 367 (5th Cir. 1978). Ragano appeared more interested in keeping secret the basis used by the government to obtain its wiretapping warrant. This case was ignored in Ragano's autobiography, *Mob Lawyer*. The longtime legal counsel for Tampa Mafia boss Santo Trafficante, Ragano noted that he was facing financial ruin and his own tax charges at the time. See Ragano, Frank, and Selwyn Raab, *Mob Lawyer*, New York: Charles Scribner's Sons, 1994, p. 295.

225 Ettore Coco, register no. 01595-004, "Find an inmate," Board of Prisons, bop.gov.

226 "Hollywood man one of 6 charged with laundering money via bingo," *Miami Herald*, Oct. 28, 1990, Broward section, p. 2; McCord, Joel, "Chicago man admits scheme at Bingo World," *Baltimore Sun*, April 8, 1992, p. 2; "Reputed mobster gets conspiracy sentence," *Baltimore Sun*, June 9, 1993, p. 2; Edward Coco, 267-96-9219, Social Security Death Index, death date Dec. 26, 1991.

227 Valachi, *The Real Thing*, p. 304.

228 Valachi, *The Real Thing*, p. 285, 304-305.

229 Valachi, *The Real Thing*, p. 314-315.

230 Valachi, *The Real Thing*, p. 322.

231 Valachi, *The Real Thing*, p. 356.

232 Vincent D'Anna Petition for Naturalization, no. 439811, U.S. District Court for the Eastern District of New York, Dec. 12, 1945, Certificate 6616557 issued March 26, 1946; Vincenzo D'Anna World War II Draft Registration Card, serial no. 2394, order no. 3928, New York NY, Oct. 16, 1940; Passenger manifest of *S.S. Roma*, departed Genoa on Oct. 29, 1929, arrived New York on Nov. 8, 1929; Passenger manifest of *S.S. Roma*, Canadian Immigration Service, departed Genoa on Oct. 29, 1929, arrived New York on Nov. 8, 1929.

233 Vincenzo D'Anna and Leonarda Catanzaro Certificate and Record of Marriage, Borough of Manhattan, certificate no. 23308, City of New York Department of Health Bureau of Records, Nov. 5, 1932; United States Census of 1930, New York State, New York County, Assembly District 2, Enumeration District 31-116.

234 Sebastiano Domingo Certificate of Death, Borough of Manhattan, registered no. 13044, Department of Health of the City of New York Bureau of Records, May 30, 1933.

235 "Youth slain, 5 shot in raid by gunmen," *NYT*, May 31, 1933, p. 13.

236 Sebastiano Domingo Certificate of Death, Borough of Manhattan, registered no. 13044, Department of Health of the City of New York Bureau of Records, May 30, 1933.

237 Salvatore Ferraro and Carmela Catanzaro Certificate and Record of Marriage, Borough of Manhattan, certificate no. 22840, City of New York Department of Health, June 26, 1923; Salvatore Ferraro Certificate of Death, Borough of Manhattan, registered no. 13045, Department of Health of the City of New York Bureau of Records, May 31, 1933.

238 Sebastiano Domingo Certificate of Death, Borough of Manhattan, registered no. 13044, Department of Health of the City of New York Bureau of Records, May 30, 1933; Salvatore Ferraro Certificate of Death, Borough of Manhattan, registered no. 13045, Department of Health of the City of New York Bureau of Records, May 31, 1933.

239 Vincent D'Anna Petition for Naturalization, no. 439811, U.S. District Court for the Eastern District of New York, Dec. 12, 1945, Certificate 6616557 issued March 26, 1946; United States Census of 1940, New York State, New York County, Enumeration District 31-114; Vincenzo D'Anna World War II Draft Registration Card, serial no. 2394, order no. 3928, New York NY, Oct. 16, 1940.

240 Vincent D'Anna Petition for Naturalization, no. 439811, U.S. District Court for the Eastern District of New York, Dec. 12, 1945, Certificate 6616557 issued March 26, 1946.

241 United States Census of 1950, New York State, Kings County, Enumeration District 24-986.

242 "D'Anna," *BDE*, July 22, 1953, p. 11.

243 Valachi, *The Real Thing*, p. 344.

244 Valachi, *The Real Thing*, p. 455, 458-463.

245 Valachi, *The Real Thing*, p. 363; Maas, Peter, *The Valachi Papers*, New York: G.P. Putnam's Sons, 1968, p. 111.

246 Valachi, *The Real Thing*, p. 370; Maas, *The Valachi Papers*, p. 115, 117.

247 Miller, Assistant Attorney General Herbert, Department of Justice Memorandum forwarded to New York

County District Attorney on July 22, 1963, p. 17, enclosed within Evans, C.A., "La Cosa Nostra," FBI memorandum to Mr. Belmont, file no. 92-6054-406, NARA no. 124-10220-10111, Aug. 13, 1964; Maas, *The Valachi Papers*, p. 126-127.

248 Baptism record of Joannes Di Bellis, p. 252. no. 221, April 21, 1891, FamilySearch, familysearch.org; Passenger manifest of *S.S. Nord America*, departed Palermo, Sicily, on June 9, 1904, arrived New York on June 23, 1904; John Debellis, U.S. Veterans Administration Master Index, death date March 12, 1968; People v. John DeBellis, New York District Attorney file no. 97359, 1914, New York City Municipal Archives. U.S. military records show a birth date of Aug. 22, 1895.

249 United States Census of 1910, New York State, New York County, Ward 12, Enumeration District 340.

250 Giovanni DeBelis, B 26060, Prisoner's Criminal Record, Police Department, City of New York, within People v. John DeBellis, New York District Attorney file no. 97359, 1914, New York City Municipal Archives.

251 People v. John DeBellis, New York District Attorney file no. 97359, 1914, New York City Municipal Archives; People vs John DeBellis, New York County Court of General Sessions, file no. 97359, 1914, New York City Municipal Archives; John De Bellis, no. 64285, Sing Sing Prison Admission Register, received Feb. 27, 1914; New York State Census of 1915, Westchester County, Ossining Town, Sing Sing Prison, Assembly District 3, Election District 1.

252 People v. John DeBellis, New York District Attorney file no. 97359, 1914, New York City Municipal Archives; People vs John DeBellis, New York County Court of General Sessions, file no. 97359, 1914, New York City Municipal Archives.

253 People v. John DeBellis, New York District Attorney file no. 97359, 1914, New York City Municipal Archives; People vs John DeBellis, New York County Court of General Sessions, file no. 97359, 1914, New York City Municipal Archives; New York Executive Order for Commutation, Feb. 21, 1917; "Twenty-three set free by Whitman," *Knickerbocker Press*, Feb. 22, 1917, p. 14; "Whitman pardons 23 now in prison," *NYT*, Feb. 22, 1917, p. 13.

254 John DeBellis, serial no. 789967, Abstract of World War I Military Service; Passenger list of S.S. Maunganui, U.S. Army Transport Service, departed from New York on Oct. 27, 1918; Passenger list of *U.S.S. Antrim*, U.S. Army Transport Service, departed from New York on Nov. 11, 1918; John Debellis, U.S. Veterans Administration Master Index, death date March 12, 1968.

255 United States Census of 1920, New York State, New York County, Assembly District 18, Enumeration District 1264; Antonietta De Bellis Standard Certificate of Death, Borough of Manhattan, registered no. 26175, Department of Health of the City of New York Bureau of Records, Oct. 31, 1929.

256 United States Census of 1930, New York State, New York County, Assembly District 18, Enumeration District 31-818; John DiBellis World War II Draft Registration Card, Local Board no. 47, New York, NY, April 27, 1942; Giovanni De Bellis Certificate of Death, Borough of Manhattan, certificate no. 10773, Bureau of Records Department of Health, May 4, 1943.

257 John Debellis, certificate no. 25131, New York State Death Index, March 12, 1968; John Debellis, U.S. Veterans Administration Master Index, death date March 12, 1968.

258 Valachi, *The Real Thing*, p. 743.

259 Valachi, *The Real Thing*, p. 742-743, 1015.

260 Valachi, *The Real Thing*, p. 743.

261 Valachi, *The Real Thing*, p. 837; Testimony of Joseph Valachi, Oct. 9, 1963, McClellan Hearings, p. 638.

262 Valachi, *The Real Thing*, p. 1015.

263 Passenger manifest of *S.S. Carmania*, departed Naples on Nov. 27, 1909, arrived New York on Dec. 9, 1909; Gioacchino Di Quarto and Vincenzina Sicari Certificate and Record of Marriage, Borough of Manhattan, certificate no. 31470, City of New York Department of Health, Nov. 19, 1917; Births reported in 1922 - Borough of Manhattan, p. 131; Domenick DiQuarto World War II Draft Registration Card, serial no. N140, order no. V12,090, Local Board no. 191, Kings County, NY, June 20, 1942.

264 United States Census of 1930, New York State, Queens County, Assembly District 2, Enumeration District 41-134; United States Census of 1940, New York State, Kings County, Assembly District 19, Enumeration District 24-2308; Domenick DiQuarto World War II Draft Registration Card, serial no. N140, order no. V12,090, Local Board no. 191, Kings County, NY, June 20, 1942.

265 United States Census of 1950, New York State, New York County, Enumeration District 31-195.

266 Collins, Maureen, "Four held in contempt," *Fort Lauderdale FL News*, Sept. 19, 1968, p. 11; "Mob bodyguard sought in jury probe of boss," *Newsday* (Nassau Edition), Jan. 9, 1974, p. 20; Passenger manifest of Flight no. 649/088, British Overseas Airways Corporation, departed New York International Airport, arrived Oakes Field, Nassau, Bahamas, July 13, 1955; Passenger manifest of Flight no. 408, Aircraft N-6107C, Pan American World Airways, departed Nassau, Bahamas, arrived Miami, FL, July

20, 1955; Passenger manifest of Flight no. BA650-090, British Overseas Airways Corporation, departed Nassau, Bahamas, arrived New York International Airport, July 28, 1955.

267 "Yonkers man held on 15 auto counts," *Yonkers NY Herald Statesman*, May 15, 1956, p. 6.

268 Miller, Assistant Attorney General Herbert, Department of Justice Memorandum forwarded to New York County District Attorney on July 22, 1963, p. 17, enclosed within Evans, C.A., "La Cosa Nostra," FBI memorandum to Mr. Belmont, file no. 92-6054-406, NARA no. 124-10220-10111, Aug. 13, 1964; Federici, William, and Henry Lee, "How Genovese took over mob," *NYDN*, Sept. 30, 1963, p. 3.

269 "Mob bodyguard sought in jury probe of boss," *Newsday* (Nassau Edition), Jan. 9, 1974, p. 20.

270 "F.B.I.-taped conversation sheds light on 1962 gangland slaying of Strollo," *NYT*, Jan. 8, 1970, p. 33; Valachi, The Real Thing, p. 470; Durkin, Paul G., "Harold Konigsberg," FBI Report of New York Office, file no. 92-5177-161, NARA no. 124-10348-10067, Aug. 16, 1965, p. 135.

271 Collins, Maureen, "Four held in contempt," *Fort Lauderdale FL News*, Sept. 19, 1968, p. 11.

272 "SIC postpones mob testimony by La Placa," *Hackensack NJ Record*, April 9, 1970, p. 27.

273 "Neighborly - when they're home," *Hackensack NJ Record*, Aug. 13, 1970, p. 1.

274 "Union official indicted," *Miami Herald*, Sept. 19, 1974, p. 43.

275 "Men jailed in tax quiz," *Miami Herald*, April 12, 1973, p. 48; "Three jailed for silence in probe of crime figure," *Miami Herald*, April 12, 1973, p. 55; "Indicted lawyer pleads not guilty," *Miami News*, Dec. 10, 1973, p. 7; "Mafia figure is arrested." *Miami News*, Jan. 8, 1974, p. 5; "Mob bodyguard sought in jury probe of boss," *Newsday* (Nassau Edition), Jan. 9, 1974, p. 20; Stuart, Mark, "Bergen: mob's bedroom," *Hackensack NJ Record*, May 11, 1975, p. 5.

276 Federici, William, and Paul Meskil, "Cops sift mystery of the missing mobsters," *NYDN*, May 17, 1977, p. 5; Breslin, Jimmy, "When Mafia elects, there are no recounts," *NYDN*, May 19, 1977, p. C5

277 Dominick DiQuarto, New Jersey Death Index, Dec. 6, 1988.

278 Miller, Assistant Attorney General Herbert, Department of Justice Memorandum forwarded to New York County District Attorney on July 22, 1963, p. 17, enclosed within Evans, C.A., "La Cosa Nostra," FBI memorandum to Mr. Belmont, file no. 92-6054-406, NARA no. 124-10220-10111, Aug. 13, 1964.

279 Miller, Assistant Attorney General Herbert, Department of Justice Memorandum forwarded to New York County District Attorney on July 22, 1963, p. 17, enclosed within Evans, C.A., "La Cosa Nostra," FBI memorandum to Mr. Belmont, file no. 92-6054-406, NARA no. 124-10220-10111, Aug. 13, 1964; "Mob scene's shooting cast," *NYDN*, Aug. 12, 1963, p. 6.

280 Michael Benedetto Jr. Certificate and Record of Birth, Borough of Manhattan, certificate no. 49708, Sept. 28, 1907; United States Census of 1910, New York State, New York County, Ward 12, Enumeration District 286; New York State Census of 1915, New York County, Assembly District 28, Election District 3.

281 "Man slain on porch: shot to death as he is about to enter his home," *NYS*, Feb. 18 1937, p. 3; "Gangland shots kill ex-convict," *BDE*, Feb. 18, 1937, p. 3; Michele Di Benedetto and Ernesta Lombardi Certificate and Record of Marriage, Borough of Manhattan, certificate no. 13385, City of New York Department of Health, May 5, 1924; Michael DiBenedetto and Ernesta Lombardo Certificate and Record of Marriage, Borough of Manhattan, certificate no. 18513, June 11, 1925.

282 Definite Sentences, Department of Correction - Office of Great Meadow Prison, Feb. 1, 1929; Michael DiBenedetto, register no. 8602, Great Meadow Prison Record; "Criminal courts: New York County," *NYDN*, Feb. 27, 1926, p. 4; Michael Di Benedetto, no. 78190, Sing Sing Prison Receiving Blotter, received March 1, 1926; "Man slain on porch: shot to death as he is about to enter his home," *NYS*, Feb. 18 1937, p. 3; "Gangland shots kill ex-convict," *BDE*, Feb. 18, 1937, p. 3.

283 United States Census of 1930, New York State, New York County, Assembly District 18, Enumeration District 31-1248.

284 "Robbers let man keep his pay," *NYS*, Feb. 12, 1931, p. 6; "Man slain on porch: shot to death as he is about to enter his home," *NYS*, Feb. 18 1937, p. 3; "Gangland shots kill ex-convict," *BDE*, Feb. 18, 1937, p. 3.

285 "Beset to buy books, kidnaped pair rebel," *BSU*, March 10, 1932; "2 held in $100,000 on kidnap charges," *NYDN*, March 12, 1932, p. 4; "Man slain on porch: shot to death as he is about to enter his home," *NYS*, Feb. 18 1937, p. 3; "Gangland shots kill ex-convict," *BDE*, Feb. 18, 1937, p. 3; "3d suspect held in kidnapping of two laundrymen," *BDE*, March 31, 1923, p. 6; "$50,000 bail holds kidnaping suspect," *NYDN*, April 1, 1932, p. 14; "$50,000 bail set for 3d suspect in kidnap case," *BDE*, April 1, 1932, p. 12.

286 "Kidnap suspects get $100,000 bail in instalment ransom racket," *NYDN*, April 3, 1932, p. 2B; "Man slain on porch: shot to death as he is about to enter his home," *NYS*, Feb. 18 1937, p. 3.

287 "Trio on trial in laundry kidnapping," *NYEJ*, Feb. 27, 1933, p. 2B; "Three put on trial in double kidnapping," *NYA*, March 25, 1933, p. 17; "Say 'kidnapping' was tiff over girl," *BDE*, March 25, 1933, p. 1;

"Deadlocked jury in kidnap case forces retrial," *BDE*, March 30, 1933, p. 15; "Jurors disagree in kidnap trial," *Brooklyn Times Union*, March 30, 1933, p. 10.

288 Emery, Frank, "Says Mellon bailed thugs," *BDE*, Aug. 14, 1933, p. 1; "M'Quade asked bail -- Mellon," *NYEJ*, Oct. 16, 1933, p. 3; "Racket trial of 3 goes to jury today," *NYEJ*, Oct. 17, 1933, p. 1.

289 "Man slain on porch: shot to death as he is about to enter his home," *NYS*, Feb. 18 1937, p. 3; "Gangland shots kill ex-convict," *BDE*, Feb. 18, 1937, p. 3.

290 "Thugs muscle in on soft thing in strike breaking," *NYP*, March 12, 1936, p. 7.

291 Michele DiBenedetto Certificate of Death, Borough of Manhattan, certificate no. 4865, Feb. 18, 1937; "Gang foes slays racketeer on his Harlem doorstep," *NYP*, Feb. 18, 1937, p. 13; "Man slain on porch: shot to death as he is about to enter his home," *NYS*, Feb. 18 1937, p. 3; "'Bad man' slain at his door," *NYA*, Feb. 19, 1937, p. 6; "Gangland shots kill ex-convict," *BDE*, Feb. 18, 1937, p. 3; "Harlem 'bad man' slain at his door," *NYEJ*, Feb. 19, 1937, p. 2.

292 "Gang foes slays racketeer on his Harlem doorstep," *NYP*, Feb. 18, 1937, p. 13. According to other newspaper reports, his 13-year arrest total was either 13 or 14.

293 Valachi, *The Real Thing*, p. 1134.

294 Valachi, *The Real Thing*, p. 1134. He used both spellings in a single paragraph.

295 Valachi, *The Real Thing*, p. 1104-1105, 1108; Maas, *The Valachi Papers*, p. 29-30.

296 Valachi, *The Real Thing*, p. 1121-1122.

297 Valachi, *The Real Thing*, p. 1130-1131.

298 Valachi, *The Real Thing*, p. 1134.

299 Valachi, *The Real Thing*, p. 1141.

300 Valachi, *The Real Thing*, p. 1142.

301 Marion Jesse Elliott World War II Draft Registration Card, serial no. 002021, order no. 2187, Local Board no. 2, Vigo County IN, Oct. 16, 1940; United States Census of 1910, Ohio, Jefferson County, Steubenville, Enumeration District 135; United States Census of 1920, Indiana, Jefferson County, Steubenville, Enumeration District 231.

302 "Marion Jesse Elliott weds Kansas girl," *San Bernardino County CA Sun*, Dec. 5, 1937, p. 9; U.S. Marine Corps Muster Rolls, Naval Station, Guam, June 1930; United States Census of 1930, Island of Guam, Naval-Military, Naval Reservations and Ships; United States Census of 1930, California, San Bernardino, Rialto, Enumeration District 36-71.

303 "Marion Jesse Elliott weds Kansas girl," *San Bernardino County CA Sun*, Dec. 5, 1937, p. 9

304 United States Census of 1940, California, Los Angeles County, Enumeration District 60-1252; Marion Jesse Elliott World War II Draft Registration Card, serial no. 002021, order no. 2187, Local Board no. 2, Vigo County IN, Oct. 16, 1940; United States Census of 1950, Indiana, Vigo County, Honey Creek, U.S. Penitentiary, Enumeration District 84-34; "Mrs. M.J. Elliott," *Atlanta Constitution*, March 16, 1964, p. 10.

305 SAC Atlanta, "Joseph Valachi, aka; John Joseph Saupp, aka - victim," FBI Report to Director, file no. 70-35395-9, July 23, 1962, p. 74.

306 "Mrs. Marion Elliott," *Atlanta Journal*, March 16, 1964, p. 32.

307 "Committee picks warden for Angola," *Lake Charles LA American-Press*, Jan. 9, 1965, p. 1; "Holman to get new warden," *Selma AL Times-Journal*, Aug. 5, 1970, p. 10. Elliott had been stationed at Guam while with the Marines.

308 "Holman to get new warden," *Selma AL Times-Journal*, Aug. 5, 1970, p. 10; "Elliott new prison chief," *Columbus GA Enquirer*, Aug. 5, 1970, p. 13; "Warden retires," *Montgomery AL Advertiser*, Oct. 9, 1971, p. 5; M.J. Elliott, 309-22-1938, Social Security Death Index, March 22, 1988.

309 Valachi, *The Real Thing*, p. 427.

310 Valachi, *The Real Thing*, p. 427.

311 Valachi, *The Real Thing*, p. 479.

312 Hortis, C. Alexander, *The Mob and the City: The Hidden History of How the Mafia Captured New York*, Amherst NY: Prometheus Books, 2014, p. 168; Evans, C.A., FBI Memorandum to Mr. Belmont, accompanied by Joseph Valachi debriefings collected by Assistant Attorney General Herbert Miller, file no. 92-6054-406, NARA Record no. 124-10220-10111, Aug. 13, 1963. The Lido restaurant sat near the southeastern corner of the property formerly occupied by the New York Catholic Protectory, where Valachi spent years of his childhood.

313 Stefano France Certificate and Record of Birth, County of New York, certificate no. 51998, Nov. 28, 1894, reported Dec. 6, 1894; Stephen Franse World War I Draft Registration Card, no. 393, New York City, June 5, 1917; Stephen Franse World War II Draft Registration Card, serial no. U3493, Local

Board no. 3, New York City, April 27, 1942; New York State Census of 1915, New York County, Assembly District 1, Election District 12; New York City Directory 1916, p. 641.

314 Stefano Franse and Emma Cerù Certificate and Record of Marriage, Borough of Manhattan, certificate no. 7726, City of New York Department of Health, March 1, 1917. A decade later, a new Our Lady of Pompeii Church was built at Carmine and Bleecker streets.

315 Stephen Franse World War I Draft Registration Card; United States Census of 1920, New York State, New York County, Ward 2, Enumeration District 211; R.L. Polk & Co.'s Yonkers NY City Directory 1928, p. 310.

316 United States Census of 1930, New York State, New York County, Assembly District 11, Enumeration District 31-507; Bernardo Franse Standard Certificate of Death, Borough of Manhattan, registered no. 26999, Department of Health of the City of New York Bureau of Records, Nov. 28, 1930.

317 Vito Genovese and Anna Vernotico Certificate and Record of Marriage, Manhattan, certificate no. 7209, City of New York, March 30, 1932; Girard Vernotico Certificate of Death, Borough of Manhattan, registered no. 6707, Department of Health of the City of New York Bureau of Records, March 16, 1932, filed March 17, 1932; "Vito Genovese," FBI report, file no. 92-2938-5, Jan. 31, 1958, p. 3; "King of the underworld: Vito Genovese," NYT, Sept. 28, 1963, p. 6; Murphy, J.J., "Vito Genovese (From files of N.Y. Police Department)," Memorandum for File, Senate Committee to Investigate Organized Crime in Interstate Commerce, Nov. 9, 1950. Anna Petillo Vernotico may have been a relative of Genovese. Her mother's maiden name was Concetta Genovese, and later in life Anna lived with a cousin named Sabato Genovese.

318 Hortis, The Mob and the City, p. 168.

319 "3 bandits shot with patrolman at Howdy Club," NYHT, April 13, 1938, p. 5; "Hold waiter, 2 singers in club stickup," NYDN, April 13, 1938, p. 4; "Night-club bandits shoot a policeman," NYT, April 13, 1938, p. 3.

320 "Hold waiter, 2 singers in club stickup."

321 "Heroine of cafe holdup killed in 12-floor plunge," NYDN, April 14, 1938, p. 3; "12-story plunge kills heroine of Howdy Club," NYHT, April 14, 1938, p. 1; "Witness in killing plunges to death," NYT, April 14, 1938, p. 12.

322 "2 cops visited girl in holdup before death," NYDN, April 15, 1938, p. 2; "Witness's suicide starts 2 inquiries," NYT, April 16, 1938, p. 28.

323 "Policeman dies of hold-up wound," NYT, April 17, 1918, p. 12; Taylor, Sloan, "3 cafe gunmen face chair as hero cop dies," NYDN, April 18, 1938, p. 2; "3 bandits indicted in police killing," NYT, April 19, 1938, p. 16; "2 cop killers doomed – grin and chew gum," NYDN, May 27, 1939, p. B25.

324 United States Census of 1940, New York State, New York County, Assembly District 23, Enumeration District 31-2120; Stephen Franse World War II Draft Registration Card.

325 "Queer doings net suspension for Vill. clubs," Billboard, Dec. 2, 1944, p. 24.

326 "Vito Genovese," FBI report, file no. 92-2938-5, Jan. 31, 1958, p. 3; Karsten, Thomas L., "Vito Genovese," Memorandum, Senate Committee to Investigate Organized Crime in Interstate Commerce, Nov. 3, 1950; Hortis, The Mob and the City, p. 169-170.

327 Louise Franse Certificate of Death, Borough of Manhattan, certificate no. 20164, Bureau of Records Department of Health, Sept. 7, 1948.

328 Mahler, Julius, and James Desmond, "$19 tip the tipoff, bogus dough jails 3." NYDN, Jan. 9, 1949, p. 3; "3 held for passing counterfeit bills: big top to a hat-check girl in night club in 2nd Ave. leads to arrests," NYT, Jan. 9, 1944, p. 53.

329 United States Census of 1950, New York State, Bronx County, Enumeration District 3-159; "Which-Sex-Is-Which Club loses license," NYDN, April 28, 1951, p. 21.

330 "Which-Sex-Is-Which Club loses license."

331 "'Club' loses liquor license," NYHT, April 28, 1951, p. 7.

332 "Wife suing Genovese," NYT, Dec. 10, 1952, p. 55.

333 "Mrs. Genovese bares racket rule of mate," NYDN, March 3, 1953, p. 3; "Racket guys cosy up," NYDN, March 3, 1953, p. 8.

334 Evans, C.A., FBI Memorandum to Mr. Belmont, accompanied by Joseph Valachi debriefings collected by Assistant Attorney General Herbert Miller, file no. 92-6054-406, NARA Record no. 124-10220-10111, Aug. 13, 1963; Maas, The Valachi Papers, p. 226-227.

335 Dwyer, Robert, and Leeds Moberley, "Village nitery boss found slain in auto," NYDN, June 20, 1953, p. 28; "Village night club manager slain," NYHT, June 20, 1953, p. 11; "Brutal mugging fatal," NYT, June 20, 1953, p. 32; United States Congressional Record, 1970, p. 42.

336 Valachi, The Real Thing, p. 1146.

337 Valachi, *The Real Thing*, p. 1064, 1104.

338 Valachi, *The Real Thing*, p. 1102, 1104, 1112.

339 Valachi, *The Real Thing*, p. 1064, 1146, 1148.

340 Valachi, *The Real Thing*, p. 1157-1158, 1172-1174, 1179.

341 "George Henry Gaffney," *Missoula MT Missoulian*, April 4, 2004, p. 15; "George Gaffney supervisor for Narcotics Bureau," *Escanaba MI Daily Press*, April 23, 1955, p. 2.

342 "George Henry Gaffney"; "George Gaffney supervisor for Narcotics Bureau."

343 Valentine, Douglas, "Sal Vizzini & George H. Gaffney," Internet Archive, archive.org.

344 "George Henry Gaffney"; "George Gaffney supervisor for Narcotics Bureau."

345 "George Henry Gaffney."

346 Valachi, *The Real Thing*, p. 802.

347 Valachi, *The Real Thing*, p. 798.

348 Valachi, *The Real Thing*, p. 799-800.

349 Valachi, *The Real Thing*, p. 469-475. Valachi's earlier encounters with Giannini suggested that he was a false friend.

350 Valachi, *The Real Thing*, p. 802.

351 The Casa was reportedly located on the east side of Castle Hill Avenue at Westchester Avenue. This was close to Valachi's Lido restaurant and to the bar that was earlier used as a meeting spot for Valachi and Giannini.

352 Valachi, *The Real Thing*, p. 802-803.

353 Valachi, *The Real Thing*, p. 804.

354 Valachi, *The Real Thing*, p. 801, 804-805.

355 Valachi, *The Real Thing*, p. 805-806.

356 Valachi, *The Real Thing*, p. 807.

357 Valachi, *The Real Thing*, p. 808.

358 Eugene Patrick Giannini World War II Draft Registration Card, serial no. 3293, order no. 729, Local Board no. 50, New York City, Oct. 16, 1940; Passenger manifest of *S.S. Re D'Italia*, departed Naples on Dec. 2, 1920, arrived New York on Dec. 19, 1920.

359 Marino, Anthony, and Henry Lee, "Ex-Luciano aid slain, hurled in Harlem gutter," *NYDN*, Sept. 21, 1952, p. 3; "Gang bullet kills narcotics suspect," *NYT*, Sept. 21, 1952, p. 35.

360 Eugene Giannini and Amelia Pellegrino Certificate and Record of Marriage, Borough of Manhattan, no. 24023, Department of Health Bureau of Records, Nov. 10, 1933.

361 Marino and Lee, "Ex-Luciano aid slain, hurled in Harlem gutter"; "Gang bullet kills narcotics suspect."

362 United States Census of 1940, New York State, New York County, Assembly District 18, Enumeration District 31-1589; Eugene Patrick Giannini World War II Draft Registration Card.

363 Marino and Lee, "Ex-Luciano aid slain, hurled in Harlem gutter"; "Gang bullet kills narcotics suspect."

364 United States Census of 1950, New York State, Bronx County, Enumeration District 3-1925; Eugene Giannini, Index to Petitions for Naturalization, U.S. District Court for Southern District of New York, June 19, 1950.

365 Maas, *The Valachi Papers*, p. 214-216.

366 "Slain racketeer called informer," *NYT*, Sept. 22, 1952, p. 20

367 "Gang bullet kills narcotics suspect"; Marino and Lee, "Ex-Luciano aid slain, hurled in Harlem gutter."

368 Maas, *The Valachi Papers*, p. 221-222; Evans, C.A., FBI Memorandum to Mr. Belmont, accompanied by Joseph Valachi debriefings collected by Assistant Attorney General Herbert Miller, file no. 92-6054-406, NARA Record no. 124-10220-10111, Aug. 13, 1963.

369 Marino and Lee, "Ex-Luciano aid slain, hurled in Harlem gutter"; "Bronx dope peddler taken for gang ride," *NYP*, Sept. 21, 1952, p. 3; "Gang bullet kills narcotics suspect"; Evans, C.A., FBI Memorandum to Mr. Belmont, accompanied by Joseph Valachi debriefings collected by Assistant Attorney General Herbert Miller, file no. 92-6054-406, NARA Record no. 124-10220-10111, Aug. 13, 1963; Eugene Giannini, New York City Death Index, certificate no. 20247, Sept. 20, 1952

370 "Hear Mafia had hand in Giannini's slaying," *NYDN*, Sept. 22, 1952, p. 15; "Slain racketeer called informer."

371 Evans, C.A., FBI Memorandum to Mr. Belmont, accompanied by Joseph Valachi debriefings collected by Assistant Attorney General Herbert Miller, file no. 92-6054-406, NARA Record no. 124-10220-10111, Aug. 13, 1963.

372 Valachi, *The Real Thing*, p. 81.

373 Valachi, *The Real Thing*, p. 81.

374 Valachi, *The Real Thing*, p. 140-143.

375 Peter Heslin Certificate and Record of Birth, Borough of Manhattan, certificate no. 7579, Bureau of Records, Nov. 15, 1898, reported Feb. 21, 1899; Peter Heslin World War I Draft Registration Card, serial no. 3058, order no. 2460, Local Board no. 150, New York, NY, Sept. 12, 1918.

376 Peter Heslin and Mary Dunn Certificate of Marriage, County of New York, City of New York, certificate no. 14704, Sept. 15, 1895; United States Census of 1900, New York State, New York County, Borough of Manhattan, Enumeration District 881.

377 "Cop is riddled with bullets by holdup man," *NYS*, April 5, 1926, p. 6.

378 Peter Heslin and Anna McAdams Certificate and Record of Marriage, Borough of Manhattan, certificate no. 29359, City of New York Department of Health, Nov. 8, 1917.

379 "Cop is riddled with bullets by holdup man."

380 Peter Heslin World War I Draft Registration Card, serial no. 3058, order no. 2460, Local Board no. 150, New York, NY, Sept. 12, 1918.

381 "Cop is riddled with bullets by holdup man"; Peter Heslin, no. 69853, Sing Sing Prison Receiving Blotter, received March 4, 1919; Names of convicts received at Auburn Prison during the month of June 1919; United States Census of 1920, New York State, Cayuga County, Auburn City, New York State Prison for Men, Ward 4, Enumeration District 8; Names of convicts discharged from Auburn Prison during the month of June 1920; Records of Great Meadow Correctional Facility.

382 "Cop is riddled with bullets by holdup man."

383 Johnson, John, "Policeman shot dead," *NYDN*, April 5, 1926, p. 2; O'Brien, Jack, "Trail of blood the downfall of policeman killer suspect," *NYDN*, April 6, 1926, p. 10; "Cop is riddled with bullets by holdup man."

384 "Police to honor slain comrade in rites tomorrow," *NYDN*, April 7, 1926, p. 7; "Crowds pay tribute to slain policeman," *NYDN*, April 9, 1926, p. 3; "Patrolman Charles Henry Reilly," Officer Down Memorial Page, odmp.org.

385 "Cripple held as killer," *NYDN*, April 29, 1926, p. 1; "Cripple limps into court as holdup slayer," *NYDN*, April 29, 1926, p. 3; "Three deny killings," *NYT*, April 30, 1926, p. 8; "Convicted of murder of a policeman," *NYS*, Oct. 22, 1926, p. 7.

386 "Increases guard for doomed man," *NYS*, Nov. 4, 1926, p. 3; Peter Heslin, no. 79141, Sing Sing Prison Receiving Blotter, received Nov. 4, 1926.

387 "Slayer's conviction is upheld in decision by court of appeals," *Knickerbocker Press*, June 1, 1927, p. 6

388 "Denies coddling at Sing Sing," *NYS*, Feb. 23, 1927, p. 3.

389 "Slayer's conviction is upheld in decision by court of appeals"; "Judd glad to miss 'good-by' to slayer," *NYDN*, July 19, 1927, p. 6.

390 Peter Heslin, New York State Death Index, certificate no. 41989, July 21, 1927; "Heslin dies in chair protesting his innocence," *NYHT*, July 22, 1927, p. 8; "Policeman's slayer pays death penalty," *NYT*, July 22, 1927, p. 2; "Ruth and Judd sees lights dim as Heslin dies," *NYDN*, July 22, 1927;

391 Valachi, *The Real Thing*, p. 365.

392 Valachi, *The Real Thing*, p. 255-256.

393 Valachi, *The Real Thing*, p. 365-366, 373.

394 Testimony of Joseph Valachi, Oct. 2, 1963, *Organized Crime and Illicit Traffic in Narcotics*, Part 1 (McClellan Hearings), Hearings before the Permanent Subcommittee on Investigations of the Committee on Government Operations, U.S. Senate, 88th Congress, 1st Session, Washington D.C.: U.S. Government Printing Office, 1968, p. 225

395 Valachi, *The Real Thing*, p. 368, 370.

396 Valachi, *The Real Thing*, p. 418.

397 Valachi, *The Real Thing*, p. 739, 742-743, 755.

398 Peter Angelo Leone World War II Draft Registration Card, serial no. T615, order no. T10937, Local Board no. 60, New York City, Feb. 15, 1942; Giovanni Lione Birth Return, County of New York, certificate no. 377985, Sept. 27, 1883; Maria Grazia Liono Certificate of Birth, Brooklyn, certificate no. 9184, May 29, 1894; Pasquale Renna and Lucian Leone Certificate and Record of Marriage, Borough of Manhattan, certificate no. 17888, City of New York Department of Health, July 23, 1911.

399 United States Census of 1910, New York State, Westchester County, Enumeration District 12; Names of Convicts Received During Month of June 1919, Auburn Prison.

400 Names of Convicts Received During Month of June 1919, Auburn Prison; United States Census of 1920, New York State, Westchester County, Ossining, Enumeration District 159.

401 "Held in payroll robbery," *NYT*, April 12, 1922, p. 3; "Other crimes of last 24 hours," *BDE*, April 12, 1922, p. 2; "Two murders committed," *NYHT*, April 12, 1922.

402 Peter Leone, inmate 74584, Sing Sing Prison Receiving Blotter, received Jan. 22, 1923; Names of Convicts Received During Month of February 1923, Auburn Prison; Great Meadow Prison Record, Admission Register, 1924; Great Meadow Prison Discharge Register, Sept. 5, 1925.

403 Testimony of Joseph Valachi, Oct. 1, 1963, McClellan Hearings, p. 151-154; Testimony of Joseph Valachi, Oct. 2, 1963, McClellan Hearings, p. 222-225; Maas, *The Valachi Papers*, p. 111, 115, 117.

404 Girard Vernotico Certificate of Death, Borough of Manhattan, registered no. 6707, Department of Health of the City of New York Bureau of Records, March 16, 1932; Luigi Lanza Certificate of Death, Boroough of Manhattan, registered no. 6676, Department of Health of the City of New York Bureau of Records, March 16, 1932; "2 men found strangled on tenement house roof," *NYHT*, March 17, 1932, p. 3; "2 strangled, left on roof in gang war," *NYDN*, March 17, 1932, p. 2; Maas, *The Valachi Papers*, p. 149.

405 Evans, C.A., FBI Memorandum to Mr. Belmont, accompanied by Joseph Valachi debriefings collected by Assistant Attorney General Herbert Miller, file no. 92-6054-406, NARA Record no. 124-10220-10111, Aug. 13, 1963, enclosure p. 17; Michael Reggione Certificate of Death, Borough of Manhattan, certificate no. 25436, Department of Health of the City of New York Bureau of Records, Nov. 25, 1932, filed Nov. 29, 1932.

406 Peter Leone and Bella Innenberg Certificate and Record of Marriage, Borough of Brooklyn, certificate no. 13083, Department of Health Bureau of Records, Sept. 12, 1933; United States Census of 1940, New York State, New York County, Assembly District 18, Enumeration District 31-1587.

407 Peter Angelo Leone World War II Draft Registration Card, serial no. T615, order no. T10937, Local Board no. 60, New York City, Feb. 15, 1942.

408 United States Census of 1950, New York State, New York County, Enumeration District 31-2422.

409 Valachi, *The Real Thing*, p. 266.

410 Valachi, *The Real Thing*, p. 112-117, 136, 141.

411 Valachi, *The Real Thing*, p. 228, 230, 266; Maas, *The Valachi Papers*, p. 78.

412 Valachi, *The Real Thing*, p. 229-230, 257, 496.

413 Valachi, *The Real Thing*, p. 229-230, 252, 496.

414 Valachi, *The Real Thing*, p. 266-267.

415 Frank Livorsi World War II Draft Registration Card, serial no. T454, order no. T12428, Maspeth, Queens, NY, Feb. 16, 1942; Bureau of Narcotics, Mafia, p. 500; Bartolomeo Livarsi Declaration of Intention, no. 171331, U.S. District Court for the Southern District of New York, April 30, 1925; Passenger manifest of *S.S. Burgundia*, departed Naples on July 23, 1898, arrived New York on Aug. 12, 1898; Bartolomeo Livorse and Rosario Beritelli Certificate of Marriage, Borough of Manhattan, certificate no. 13165, Sept. 2, 1899.

416 New York State Census of 1905, New York County, Assembly District 32, Election District 21; United States Census of 1910, New York State, New York County, Ward 12, Enumeration District 341; New York State Census of 1915, New York County, Assembly District 28, Election District 2.

417 "Shots halt ten in auto after hold-up," *NYET*, May 7, 1924, p. 3; "Ten arrested for West Side holdup," *NYS*, May 7, 1924, p. 13.

418 "$100,000 gem theft suspects arrested," *NYP*, May 12, 1924, p. 8.

419 Bartolomeo Livarsi Declaration of Intention; New York State Census of 1925, Queens County, Long Island City, Assembly District 1, Election District 33.

420 Samuel Joseph Sacco Certificate of Death, Borough of Queens, registered no. 2273, Department of Health of the City of New York Bureau of Records, March 20, 1929; Rose Sacco Certificate of Death, Borough of Queens, registered no. 2274, Department of Health of the City of New York Bureau of Records, March 20, 1929; "Murder of Sacco and wife nets 2," *NYDN*, April 24, 1929, Bklyn Sec. p. 7.

421 "Murder of Sacco and wife nets 2"; "Nab new suspect in Ravenswood double murder," *Brooklyn Daily Star*, April 23, 1929, p. 1; "Sacco murder hearing goes over to May 3," *Brooklyn Daily Star*, April 27, 1929, p. 3.

422 "Court frees man in Sacco killing," *NYDN*, May 9, 1929, p. 56.

423 Frank Livorsi and Dorina Gazzola, Borough of Manhattan, certificate no. 21633, City of New York Department of Health, Aug. 29, 1930.

424 Molloy, James T., "Crime conditions in the New York Division," FBI Report of New York Office, file no. CR 62-9-34-811, NARA no. 124-10348-10069, Nov. 27, 1963, p. 22; Testimony of Joseph Valachi, Oct. 2, 1963, McClellan Hearings, p. 211-212.

425 Testimony of Joseph Valachi, Oct. 2, 1963, McClellan Hearings, p. 211.

426 "Seize 4 in links as public enemies," *BDT*, May 24, 1934, p. 1; "Terranova takes 19th hole," *NYA*, May 25, 1934, p. 5; "Ciro Terranova freed by court," *Mount Vernon NY Daily Argus*, May 24, 1934, p. 1; Conway, Robert, "4 Terranovas just golfers, rule a court," *NYDN*, May 25, 1934, p. 2; "Terranova is line-up's guest," *NYS*, May 24, 1934, p. 11; "Artichoke King on display for 200 detectives," *NYHT*, May 25, 1934, p. 36; "Artichoke King irked by his latest arrest," *NYT*, May 25, 1934, p. 17.

427 Passenger manifest of *S.S. Rex*, departed Genoa on June 18, 1936, arrived New York on June 25, 1936.

428 Master list of passengers carried aboard American Seaplane NC 822-M from Habana, Cuba, to Miami, Florida, on Feb. 19, 1940.

429 "Dope ring smashed as 8 are arrested," *NYDN*, April 9, 1942, p. 18; "Dope imports trial pending," *Arizona Daily Star*, April 18, 1942, p. 5; "Four members of dope ring change pleas," *Tucson Daily Citizen*, May 26, 1942, p. 1.

430 "Four members of dope ring change pleas," *Tucson Daily Citizen*, May 26, 1942, p. 1; "Narcotics gang given sentence," *Arizona Daily Star*, July 29, 1942, p. 5; "Opium ring jailed," *Poughkeepsie NY Eagle-News*, July 29, 1942, p. 5; "Narcotics plot 'mob' jailed," *Albany NY Knickerbocker News*, July 29, 1942, p. 1.

431 United States Census of 1950, New York State, Nassau County, Hempstead, Enumeration District 30456.

432 Abrams, Norma, "Tax rap nips 4 sugar black mart suspects," *NYDN*, Sept. 26, 1950, p. 6; "U.S. indicts four in sale of sugar," *NYT*, Oct. 21, 1952, p. 34.

433 "LI man indicted in $855,000 tax dodge," *Newsday* (Nassau Edition), Oct. 21, 1952, p. 14; "U.S. indicts four in sale of sugar," *NYT*, Oct. 21, 1952, p. 34; "LI ex-con, 3 others in sugar ring held as $ million tax dodgers," *Newsday*, Jan. 27, 1954, p. 18; "Freed 4 face new tax trial," *NYDN*, Jan. 27, 1954, p. 10; "4 accused in sugar case," *NYT*, Jan. 27, 1954, p. 10.

434 "LI ex-con, 3 others in sugar ring held as $ million tax dodgers."

435 Davis, James, "Two sugar racketeers get 15 years for cheating U.S.," *NYDN*, March 12, 1955, p. 5; "Ex-U.S. att'y gets 1 year in tax fraud," *Newsday* (Suffolk Edition), Dec. 15, 1955, p. 17.

436 "Former prosecutor hits U.S. evidence in Livorsi tax case," *Newsday*, May 10, 1958, p. 7; "Williams assails ex-U.S. attorney," *NYT*, May 10, 1958, p. 14; "Racketeer loses appeal of income tax conviction," *Newsday*, May 16, 1958, p. 26; "Judge heaves out testimony of ex-U.S. aid," *NYDN*, May 16, 1958, p. 29; "Tainted evidence plea fails in $850,000 tax case," *NYHT*, May 16, 1958, p. 10.

437 Molloy, James T., "Crime conditions in the New York Division," FBI Report of New York Office, file no. CR 62-9-34-811, NARA no. 124-10348-10069, Nov. 27, 1963, p. 22; Frank Livorsi, New York State Death Index, certificate no. 68682, Sept. 22, 1967; "Death notices," *NYDN*, Sept. 23, 1967, p. 21.

438 Valachi, *The Real Thing*, p. 351.

439 Valachi, *The Real Thing*, p. 112-113, 351.

440 Valachi, *The Real Thing*, p. 351.

441 Valachi, *The Real Thing*, p. 351.

442 Valachi, *The Real Thing*, p. 351.

443 The family name was written a variety of ways, including "Madaglia" and "Miraglia."

444 Passenger manifest of *S.S. Kaiser Wilhelm II*, departed Genoa, Italy, arrived New York on Aug. 20, 1895; United States Census of 1900, New York State, New York County, Ward 12, Enumeration District 928.

445 New York State Census of 1915, New York City, New York County, Assembly District 28, Election District 12.

446 Francesco Medaglia, New York City Extracted Death Index, Manhattan, certificate no. 9839, March 19, 1917; JFonseca, "Francesco Medaglia," memorial ID 240892554, Find A Grave, findagrave.com, June 23, 2022.

447 Charlotte Dora Denninger Certificate and Record of Birth, Borough of Manhattan, certificate no. 9282, City of New York Bureau of Records, March 2, 1899; Ignatz Denninger Certificate and Record of Death, Borough of Bronx, certificate no. 4431, Ignatz Denninger, New York City Index to Death Certificates, Borough of Bronx, certificate no. 4431, Dec. 3, 1901.

448 Sam Kreisberg and Lottie Denninger Certificate and Record of Marriage, Borough of Manhattan, certificate no. 1663, Office of the Assistant Registrar, June 19, 1917; New York City Birth Index, 1910-1965; Delap, Breandan, and Rich Gold, *Mad Dog Coll: An Irish Gangster*, Las Vegas: Huntington Press, 2016, p. 73.

449 Delap and Gold, *Mad Dog Coll*, p. 73.

450 "Alleged pickpocket," *BDE*, July 14, 1917, p. 3; "Woman's memory causes arrest of pair as robbers,"

NYDN, April 6, 1920, p. 9; "Actresses in thief chase," *NYEP*, April 5, 1920, p. 2; "Woman's memory causes arrest of pair as robbers," *NYDN*, April 6, 1920, p. 9.

451 "Shots halt ten in auto after hold-up," *NYET*, May 7, 1924, p. 3; "Ten arrested for West Side holdup," *NYS*, May 7, 1924, p. 13; "$100,000 gem theft suspects arrested," *NYP*, May 12, 1924, p. 8; "Fail to catch East Side bandits," *NYT*, May 13, 1924, p. 23.

452 Samuel Kreisberg v. Lottie Kreisberg, Bronx County Divorce and Civil Case Records, Vol. 3, p. 21, file no. 2241, April 18, 1925; New York State Census of 1925, Bronx County, Assembly District 3, Election District 11.

453 "Saloonkeeper killed while driving his car," *BDE*, July 8, 1927, p. 14; "Believe Medal slain up state," *NYS*, Nov. 2, 1932, p. 8.

454 Adolph Romano Certificate of Death, Borough of Bronx, registered no. 4867, Department of Health of the City of New York Bureau of Records, July 7, 1927; "Autoist shot dead driving in Bronx," *NYDN*, July 8, 1927, p. 12; "Shot dead at wheel, his car runs a block," *NYT*, July 8, 1927, p. 2; "Saloon owner murdered," *NYEP*, July 8, 1927; "Saloonkeeper killed while driving his car."

455 "Believe Medal slain up state"; "Left cafe with $4,000, missing since Sept. 6," *NYT*, Sept. 19, 1932, p. 36; Delap and Gold, *Mad Dog Coll*, p. 75.

456 "Young arsenal and eight men nabbed in raid," *BSU*, Dec. 13, 1928, p. 1; "Suspect in crime here again held," *Yonkers Statesman*, March 5, 1930, p. 1; Valachi, *The Real Thing*, p. 348-349, 351-352. Valachi reported his belief that the toughest member of the Coll gang was neither of the Coll brothers but one Edward "Fats McCarthy" Popke.

457 Valachi, *The Real Thing*, p. 350-351; Frank Amato Certificate of Death, Borough of Manhattan, registered no. 14650, Department of Health of the City of New York Bureau of Records, May 28, 1931; Dominick Bologna Certificate of Death, Borough of Manhattan, registered no. 14649, Department of Health of the City of New York Bureau of Records, May 28, 1931.

458 "Trio in car riddle brother of man slain by gunmen," *BDE*, May 30, 1931, p. 7.

459 Valachi, *The Real Thing*, p. 352-353; Davidson, Louis, "Indict Coll, 4 gunmen held as baby killers," *NYDN*, Oct. 6, 1931, p. 3.

460 "Coll gets license to marry Lottie," *NYDN*, Jan. 5, 1932, p. 9; "Mrs. Coll given 6-month term on gun charge," *NYDN*, June 18, 1932, p. 17.

461 "Coll gets license to marry Lottie." *BSU*, Jan. 5, 1932, p. 4; "Coll gets license to marry Lottie," *NYDN*; Vincent Coll, New York Marriage License Index, Vol. 1, p. 161, January 1932; Valachi, *The Real Thing*, p. 351; Delap and Gold, *Mad Dog Coll*, p. 202; "Cops hunt Mrs. Coll for questioning as sweetie disappears," *NYDN*, Sept. 19, 1932, p. 2.

462 Vincent Coll Certificate of Death, Borough of Manhattan, registered no. 3110, Department of Health of the City of New York Bureau of Records, Feb. 8, 1932.

463 Delap and Gold, *Mad Dog Coll*, p. 248; "Cops hunt Mrs. Coll for questioning as sweetie disappears," *NYDN*, Sept. 19, 1932, p. 2; "Left cafe with $4,000, missing since Sept. 6."

464 "Coll's window found guilty of possessing gun," *NYDN*, Feb. 27, 1932, p. 8; "Coll's widow to hear fate as gun-toter," *NYDN*, March 6, 1932, p. 4; "Call Coll widow on gun charges," *NYDN*, March 12, 1932, p. 10; "Vincent Coll's widow gets warrant in bed," *Buffalo News*, March 15, 1932, p. 27; "Mrs. Lottie Coll held as gun-toter," *Rutland VT Daily Herald*, March 15, 1932, p. 2; Delap and Gold, *Mad Dog Coll*, p. 245. Delap and Gold concluded that Kreisberger was being treated for addiction to sedatives.

465 "Mrs. Coll given 6-month term on gun charge," *NYDN*, June 18, 1932, p. 17.

466 "Cops hunt Mrs. Coll for questioning as sweetie disappears"; "Left cafe with $4,000, missing since Sept. 6"; "Widow Coll's friend missing," *NYS*, Sept. 19, 1932, p. 2.

467 "Cops hunt Mrs. Coll for questioning as sweetie disappears"; "Left cafe with $4,000, missing since Sept. 6"; "Widow Coll's friend missing."

468 "Gunman's victim is identified as Lottie Coll suitor," *BDE*, Nov. 2, 1932, p. 2; "Coll aide's slaying approaches solution," *Yonkers Herald Statesman*, Nov. 2, 1932, p. 3; "Believe Medal slain up state," *NYS*, Nov. 2, 1932, p. 8; "Identified as Sam Medal," *NYT*, Nov. 3, 1932, p. 22.

469 "Believe Medal slain up state"; Cassidy, Tom, "Ride victim's body Medal's, brother says," *NYDN*, Nov. 3, 1932, p. 2.

470 "Dentist's chart refutes Medal identification," *NYDN*, Nov. 4, 1932, p. 6.

471 Valachi, *The Real Thing*, p. 309-310.

472 Valachi, *The Real Thing*, p. 178, 231, 305.

473 Valachi, *The Real Thing*, p. 303-307.

474 Valachi, *The Real Thing*, p. 309.

475 Valachi, *The Real Thing*, p. 309-315.

476 Valachi, *The Real Thing*, p. 778.

477 New York State Census of 1905, New York County, Assembly District 33, Election District 5; New York City Directory of 1916, p. 1294.

478 New York State Census of 1915, New York County, Assembly District 24, Election District 17; New York State Census of 1915, Bronx County, Assembly District 32, Election District 56; Valachi, The Real Thing, p. 4.

479 Maas, *The Valachi Papers*, p. 82.

480 Testimony of Joseph Valachi, Oct. 1, 1963, *Organized Crime and Illicit Traffic in Narcotics*, Part 1, Hearings before the Permanent Subcommittee on Investigations of the Committee on Government Operations, U.S. Senate, 88th Congress, 1st Session, Washington D.C.: U.S. Government Printing Office, 1963, p. 180-185; Maas, *The Valachi Papers*, p. 93-97.

481 Evans, C.A., FBI Memorandum to Mr. Belmont, accompanied by Joseph Valachi debriefings collected by Assistant Attorney General Herbert Miller, file no. 92-6054-406, NARA Record no. 124-10220-10111, Aug. 13, 1963, enclosure p. 19-20.

482 According to press accounts, the building was 2550 Colden Avenue. However, this address may have been confused with the home address of Nicholas Paduano. It seems unlikely that Paduano would have led a pursuing police officer to his home. A more likely location is the large apartment building next door, at 2556 Colden Avenue, which sits directly behind the yard of 2553 Williamsbridge Road, where Paduano was fatally shot.

483 "Cop kills 1, nabs 1 in spot death chase," *NYDN*, Jan. 29, 1932, p. 7; "Policeman kills gunman fleeing slaying scene," *NYHT*, Jan. 29, 1932, p. 32; "Thug slain by youth as dad nabs another," *BC*, Jan. 29, 1932, p. 1; "Policeman kills murder suspect," *NYT*, Jan. 29, 1932, p. 11; "3 racketeers are slain, one by policeman," *BDE*, Jan. 29, 1932, p. 25; "Cop kills gunman while his father captures fugitive," *BDT*, Jan. 29, 1932, p. 4; "Gunman slain after killing," *BSU*, Jan. 29, 1932, p. 3; Nicholas Paduano Certificate of Death, Bronx Borough, registered no. 1002, Department of Health of the City of New York Bureau of Records, Jan. 28, 1932.

484 "Cop kills 1, nabs 1 in spot death chase"; "Policeman kills gunman fleeing slaying scene"; "Thug slain by youth as dad nabs another"; "Policeman kills murder suspect"; "3 racketeers are slain, one by policeman"; "Cop kills gunman while his father captures fugitive"; "Gunman slain after killing"; Benedetto Bellini Certificate of Death, Bronx Borough, registered no. 934, Department of Health of the City of New York Bureau of Records, Jan. 28, 1932. Evans, C.A., FBI Memorandum to Mr. Belmont, accompanied by Joseph Valachi debriefings collected by Assistant Attorney General Herbert Miller, file no. 92-6054-406, NARA Record no. 124-10220-10111, Aug. 13, 1963, enclosure p. 19-20. According to Valachi, the Shoemakers confronted him after the incident. He convinced them they were lucky to still be alive and they should leave the area. Shillitani was convicted April 28, 1932, of first-degree manslaughter. See "Found guilty of killing," *NYT*, April 28, 1932, p. 22.

485 FBI Memorandum to Mr. Belmont, accompanied by Joseph Valachi debriefings collected by Assistant Attorney General Herbert Miller, file no. 92-6054-406, NARA Record no. 124-10220-10111, Aug. 13, 1963, enclosure p. 17.

486 Thomas Regione, no. 83521, Sing Sing Prison Admission Register, received Oct. 10, 1930; "One Regione saved by rain, brother slain," *NYDN*, Aug. 27, 1940, p. 41.

487 Filomena M. Reggione Standard Certificate of Death, Borough of Manhattan, certificate no. 29646, Nov. 30, 1928; "Prisoner's kin slain by gangdom," *New London CT Evening Day*, Aug. 27, 1940, p. 12.

488 Thomas Regione, no. 83521, Sing Sing Prison Admission Register, received Oct. 10, 1930.

489 "Arrest 5 men, women in bogus money plot," *Press of Atlantic City NJ*, Feb. 6, 1932, p. 1; "Capture $24,000 synthetic cash and 6 persons," *NYDN*, Feb. 6, 1932, p. 7; "Missing counterfeit suspect convicted in his absence," *BDE*, April 12, 1932, p. 17.

490 Michael Reggione Certificate of Death, Borough of Manhattan, certificate no. 25436, Department of Health of the City of New York Bureau of Records, Nov. 25, 1932, filed Nov. 29, 1932.

491 "Young ex-convict is shot to death," *NYS*, Nov. 26, 1932, p. 3; "Village tough is put on spot in Harlem hall," *NYDN*, Nov. 26, 1932; "Ex-convict is slain," *NYT*, Nov. 26, 1932, p. 9; Michael Reggione Certificate of Death.

492 James Reggione Certificate of Death, Borough of Manhattan, certificate no. 12312, Department of Health of the City of New York Bureau of Records, May 23, 1935, filed May 27, 1935; "Man slain on walk," *BDE*, May 24, 1935, p. 15; "Reggiones' Pasquale seized in holdup trail," *NYDN*, May 3, 1943, p. 31B.

493 Louis Reggione Certificate of Death, certificate no. 18020, Bureau of Records, Department of Health, Borough of Manhattan, Aug. 26, 1940; "Reggiones' Pasquale seized in holdup trail"; "One Reggione saved by rain, brother slain"; "Mystery shots kill leader of New York counterfeiters," *Buffalo Evening News*, Financial Edition, Aug. 26, 1940, p. 1; "Mystery shots kill leader of New York counterfeiters,"

Buffalo Evening News, Home Edition, Aug. 26, 1940, p. 1; "Prisoner's kin slain by gangdom," *New London CT Evening Day*, Aug. 27, 1940, p. 12.

494 "One Reggione saved by rain, brother slain."

495 "Reggiones' Pasquale seized in holdup trail."

496 Patterson, James, "Cops corner bandit in hall, kills him," *NYDN*, Feb. 23, 1950, p. 3.

497 Valachi, *The Real Thing*, p. 141.

498 Valachi, *The Real Thing*, p. 76.

499 John Jos. Rodgers World War I Draft Registration Card, no. 207, New York County, NY, June 4, 1917; John J. Rodgers, no. 68930, Sing Sing Prison Receiving Blotter, received Feb. 18, 1918; United States Census of 1900, New York State, New York County, Enumeration District 894; "'Bum' Rodgers, on life term, hangs self in Clinton cell," *BSU*, Jan. 15, 1931, p. 2; "Car Barn Gang Rodgers' crime training school," *NYHT*, Nov. 26, 1926, p. 5; "Gangster Rodgers always foe of society," *NYA*, Nov. 26, 1926, p. 4. A birth certificate for John Joseph Rodgers could not be located by presstime.

500 United States Census of 1900, New York State, New York County, Enumeration District 894; New York State Census of 1905, New York County, Borough of Manhattan, Assembly District 32, Election District 12; "Gangster Rodgers always foe of society."

501 "'Bum' Rodgers' record of 24 years' crime," *BDE*, Nov. 27, 1926, p. 3; "'Bum' Rogers' charm ends with years in pen," *NYHT*, Dec. 12, 1925, p. 13; "Bum Rogers gets 15 year sentence," *NYS*, Dec. 11, 1925, p. 3; "One gunman's record," *NYA*, Nov. 26, 1926, p. 4; Names of convicts received at Auburn Prison during the month of February 1918; "Car Barn Gang Rodgers' crime training school."

502 "'Bum' Rodgers, on life term, hangs self in Clinton cell," *BSU*, Jan. 15, 1931, p. 2; "Bum Rodgers, lifer, hangs self in cell," *NYDN*, Jan. 15, 1931, p. 3; "Old gang leader arrested again," *NYH*, May 12, 1921, p. 9; Cassidy, L.G., "Pardoned," *NYET*, letter to the editor, May 13, 1921, p. 6; "Car Barn Gang Rodgers' crime training school." Earlier, in 1903-1904, a small group of young toughs known as the "Car Barn Bandits" or the "Car Barn Gang" operated in Chicago. (The term "car barn" refers to a structure where railroad cars are stored.) The earliest known use of the name in association with Harlem gangsters occurred in summer of 1907.

503 Names of convicts received at Auburn Prison during the month of February 1918; "'Bum' Rodgers' record of 24 years' crime"; "One gunman's record."

504 "Arrests gang leader," *NYT*, May 22, 1911, p. 3.

505 "Slayer kills one more," *NYS*, Sept. 17, 1911, p. 2; John McNally, Borough of Manhattan, certificate no. 28557, New York City Extracted Death Index, Sept. 16, 1911.

506 "Head of Car Barn Gang held for murder," *NYS*, Oct. 3, 1911, p. 2; "Gang leader convicted," *NYT*, Dec. 24, 1911, p. 20.

507 "Car Barn Gang dance painfully interrupted," *NYS*, March 3, 1912, p. 2.

508 "Car Barn Gang Rodgers' crime training school"; "One gunman's record"; "'Bum' Rodgers' record of 24 years' crime"; John J. Rogers, no. 62407, Sing Sing Prison Admission Register, received June 28, 1912; Names of convicts received at Auburn Prison during the month of February 1918. The Auburn State Prison register contained notations relating to Rodgers' earlier incarcerations.

509 John J. Rodgers, Borough of Manhattan, certificate no. 29184, New York City Extracted Death Index, Oct. 10, 1915. Prison registers indicate that his father was alive in summer of 1912 and dead by spring of 1917.

510 "Gang leader convicted," *NYTR*, Dec. 14, 1917, p. 16.

511 "One gunman's record"; "'Bum' Rogers' charm ends with years in pen"; John J. Rodgers, no. 68930, Sing Sing Prison Receiving Blotter, received Feb. 18, 1918; Names of convicts received at Auburn Prison during the month of February 1918.

512 United States Census of 1920, New York State, Westchester County, Ossining, Sing Sing Prison, Enumeration District 159; Smith, Governor Alfred E., Executive Order for Commutation for John J. Rodgers, New York State Executive Chamber, Aug. 6, 1920.

513 John J. Rodgers and Catherine O'Brien, Borough of Manhattan, certificate 30946, New York City Extracted Marriage Index, Sept. 26, 1920.

514 "Man is shot from ambush," *NYS*, April 28, 1921, p. 4; "Ex-convict shoots man," *NYEW*, April 28, 1921, p. 12; "Gunmen shoot former pal in feud," *NYEJ*, April 28, 1931, p. 3; "Fatal street shots are feud result, police say," *NYDN*, April 29, 1921, p. 10; "Shooting in Broadway," *NYEP*, April 28, 1921, p. 1.

515 "Ex-convict shoots man."

516 "2 policemen wound man in pistol battle," *NYEJ*, Feb. 13, 1912, p. 6; "Two patrolmen are shot at," *NYPR*, Feb. 14, 1912, p. 2; "Boy shot in a running pistol fight," *Albany Times-Union*, Feb. 13, 1912, p. 1; "Charles Pelletier....," *NYH*, Feb. 14, 1912, p. 1.

517 Charles Devere, no. 68024, Sing Sing Prison Receiving Blotter, received March 21, 1917.

518 "Old gang leader arrested again"; Cassidy, "Pardoned."

519 "Pardoned life convict faces holdup charge," *BSU*, Jan. 3, 1922, p. 12; "One gunman's record"; "'Bum' Rodgers' record of 24 years' crime."

520 Names of convicts received at Auburn Prison during the month of February 1918; "One gunman's record"; "'Bum' Rodgers' record of 24 years' crime"; "Three flee prison on Welfare Island," *NYT*, Jan. 20, 1925, p. 48.

521 "Three flee prison on Welfare Island"; "3 prisoners flee Welfare Island," *NYDN*, Jan. 20, 1925, p. 3; "3 gunmen stroll to freedom at Welfare Island," *NYHT*, Jan. 20, 1925, p. 6.

522 "Bum Rogers's pal gets double dose for crime," *NYDN*, Dec. 25, 1925, p. 24; "Pal of 'Bum' Rogers found guilty as robber," *BSU*, Dec. 23, 1925, p. 2; Frank LaPuma Certificate of Death, Borough of Manhattan, registered no. 15989, Department of Health of the City of New York Bureau of Records, June 9, 1925.

523 "Escaped convict shot and seized after hold-up," *NYHT*, July 1, 1925, p. 5; "Escaped gang head caught in gun duel," *NYDN*, July 1, 1925, p. 3.

524 "Gun charge bail fixed at $50,000," *NYDN*, July 2, 1925, p. 24; "Escaped convict held on double indict-ment," *NYHT*, July 2, 1925, p. 30; "Provide speedy trial for notorious thug," *NYT*, July 2, 1925, p. 8; "Owes 17 years, gets 5 more," *NYEJ*, July 14, 1925, p. 3; "Rodgers gets 5 years but must serve 22," *NYEJ*, July 15, 1925, p. 1; "Gun toter has 5 years added to 17 years 'owed,'" *NYHT*, July 15, 1925, p. 14; "5 years for gun carrier," *NYT*, July 15, 1925, p. 21; John J. Rodgers, no. 77430, Sing Sing Prison Receiving Blotter, received July 15, 1925.

525 "Bum Rogers gets 15 year sentence," *NYS*, Dec. 11, 1925, p. 3; "'Bum' Rogers' charm ends with years in pen"; "'Bum' Rodgers' record of 24 years' crime."

526 "Fell jail guard in train, free 'Bum' Rogers," *NYHT*, Dec. 15, 1925, p. 21; "Thug flees train on way to prison," *NYT*, Dec. 15, 1925, p. 3; "Bum Rogers escape under Mineola quiz," *NYDN*, Dec. 16, 1925, p. 33.

527 "Car Barn Gang Rodgers' crime training school."

528 "'Bum' Rodgers captured asleep in hall bedroom," *NYA*, Nov. 26, 1926, p. 4; "'Bum' Rodgers caught like rat while sleeping," *BDT*, Nov. 26, 1926, p. 1; "'Bum' Rodgers is captured in bed, 'broke,'" *NYHT*, Nov. 26, 1926, p. 1; "Bum Rodgers trapped in sleep by surprise raid on Bronx flat," *NYDN*, Nov. 26, 1926, p. 3; "Seize Bum Rodgers asleep in his flat near police station," *NYT*, Nov. 26, 1926, p. 1. The New York American newspaper reported hideout locations on East Third Street and East Fifth Street.

529 "'Bum' Rodgers captured asleep in hall bedroom"; "Seize Bum Rodgers asleep in his flat near police station."

530 "Bum Rodgers seems eager for life term," *NYT*, Nov. 27, 1926, p. 9; "'Bum' Rodgers denied bail; may get life term," *NYHT*, Nov. 27, 1926, p. 5.

531 "'Bum' Rogers' plea of guilty entails sentence for life," *Ithaca NY Journal*, Dec. 3, 1926, p. 2; John J. Rodgers, no. 79269, Sing Sing Prison Receiving Blotter, received Dec. 7, 1926; "Bum Rogers begins term on Sing Sing coal pile," *Buffalo Evening News*, Dec. 9, 1926, p. 21; United States Census of 1930, New York State, Clinton County, Dannemora, Clinton State Prison, Enumeration District 10-16.

532 "Bum Rodgers kills himself in prison," *BDT*, Jan. 15, 1931, p. 1; "'Bum' Rodgers hangs himself at Dan-nemora," *NYHT*, Jan. 15, 1931, p. 7.

533 John J. Rodgers, certificate no. 4162, Dannemora, New York State Death Index 1931, Jan. 13, 1931; "'Bum' Rodgers hangs himself in Clinton cell' was in 'solitary' for part in July, 1929, riot," *NYT*, Jan. 15, 1931, p. 1; "'Bum' Rodgers, on life term, hangs self in Clinton cell," *BSU*, Jan. 15, 1931, p. 2; "Bum Rodgers kills himself in prison"; "Suicide closes Bum Rodgers' crime record," *BDE*, Jan. 15, 1931, p. 19; "Bum Rodgers, lifer, hangs self in cell," *NYDN*, Jan. 15, 1931, p. 3; "'Bum' Rodgers hangs himself at Dannemora."

534 "No one wants body of 'Bum' Rodgers," *BDT*, Jan. 16, 1931, p. 3; "One-time underworld hero has no one to claim his body," *BC*, Jan. 16, 1931, p. 1; "Bum Rodgers' body claimed by his brother," *NYDN*, Jan. 16, 1931, p. 4; "Crowds in Astoria view body of 'Bum' Rodgers," *NYHT*, Jan. 19, 1931, p. 16; "'Bum' Rodgers rites held in Queens," *BDE*, Jan. 19, 1931, p. 3; "'Bum' Rodgers buried," *BDT*, Jan. 19, 1931, p. 1; "'Bum' Rodgers buried as cops guard funeral," *BC*, Jan. 19, 1931, p. 3; "Floral gifts, gangland's tribute to 'Bum' Rodgers," *BSU*, Jan. 19, 1931, p. 1

535 "Floral gifts, gangland's tribute to 'Bum' Rodgers"; "'Bum' Rodgers' funeral rites held in Astoria," *Long Island Daily Star*, Jan. 19, 1931, p. 1

536 Valachi, *The Real Thing*, p. 81.

537 Valachi, *The Real Thing*, p. 81.

538 Russomano may have been awarded nickname "Curley" because of a lack of hair. He was already

balding at the time of his 1917 registration for the military draft. He was 28 at that time. Much later in his autobiography, Valachi referred to a bookmaker and loan shark customer who was widely known as "Curly Top" because "he had no hair." See: Valachi, *The Real Thing*, p. 475-476.

539 John Russomano, 082-12-0114, Social Security Applications and Claims Index; John Russomano World War I Draft Registration Card, no. 157, Precinct 38, New York, NY, June 5, 1917; Raphael Russomano, New York City Extracted Death Index, Borough of Manhattan, certificate no. 25204, Aug. 25, 1915; Passenger manifest of *S.S. Scotia*, departed Naples, arrived New York on June 15, 1894; United States Census of 1900, New York State, New York County, Borough of Manhattan, Enumeration District 117.

540 Nicola Russomano, New York City Death Index, certificate no. 17450, June 8, 1897; United States Census of 1900, New York State, New York County, Borough of Manhattan, Enumeration District 117; Nicola Russomano Certificate and Record of Birth, Borough of Manhattan, certificate no. 7245, Feb. 10, 1900, reported Feb. 19, 1900.

541 United States Census of 1900, New York State, New York County, Borough of Manhattan, Enumeration District 117; New York State Census of 1905, New York County, Assembly District 33, Election District 6; United States Census of 1910, New York State, New York County, Ward 12, Enumeration District 335.

542 Aniello Prisco, New York City Extracted Death Index, Borough of Manhattan, certificate no. 35154, Dec. 15, 1912; "'Zopo the Terror' dies as he draws weapon to kill," *NYEW*, Dec. 16, 1912, p. 6; "Noted blackmailer is shot demanding cash," *NYA*, Dec. 16, 1912, p. 13; "Blackmailer killed as he made threat," *BDE*, Dec. 16, 1912, p. 4; "Bold blackmailer slain," *NYEP*, Dec. 16, 1912, p. 16; "'Zopo the Gimp,' king of the Black Hand, slain," *NYTR*, Dec. 17, 1912, p. 16; "Prisco, lame gunman, meets death at last," *NYS*, Dec. 17, 1912, p. 16.

543 "Kills a gangster to save his uncle," *NYT*, Dec. 17, 1912, p. 12; "Confesses killing blackmail chief," *NYA*, Dec. 17, 1912, p. 10; "Slayer of 'Zopo' freed," *NYEW*, Dec. 20, 1912, p. 9; "Prisco's slayer released," *NYH*, Dec. 20, 1912, p. 8.

544 Tony Vivola, New York City Extracted Death Index, Borough of Manhattan, certificate no. 5559, Feb. 18, 1913; "Killed by gang to get square," *BC*, Feb. 18, 1913, p. 1; "First actual use of rifle silencer," *Niagara Falls Gazette*, Feb. 19, 1913, p. 9; "Man shot, bodyguard slain, by Black Hand," *NYPR*, Feb. 19, 1913, p. 4; "Shot down from doorway," *NYTR*, Feb. 19, 1913, p. 16;

545 "Maxim Silencer," Forgotten Weapons, forgottenweapons.com; Rupertus, Emily, "Suppressors: the history," NRA Blog, nrablog.com, Oct. 5, 2016. The Maxim Silencer sound and recoil suppressor device was invented by Hiram Stevens Maxim in 1902. It was patented in 1909. It could easily be fitted to a rifle, but was not made for pistols.

546 "Death shots silent," *Washington Post*, Feb. 19, 1913, p. 1.

547 "Silencer is used on rifle to kill Harlem gunman," *NYEW*, Feb. 18, 1913, p. 9.

548 John Russomano World War I Draft Registration Card, no. 157, Precinct 38, New York, NY, June 5, 1917.

549 "35 are caught in Black Hand bomb round-up," *NYET*, July 26, 1913, p. 3; Thomas, Rowland, "The rise and fall of Little Italy's king," *Pittsburgh Press*, Dec. 12, 1915, Sunday Magazine p. 4; John Russomano, no. 64408, Sing Sing Prison Admission Register, April 1, 1914.

550 Names of Convicted Received at Auburn Prison during the Month of August 1914; Names of Convicts Discharged from Auburn Prison during the Month of June 1915; New York State Census of 1915, New York County, Assembly District 28, Election District 3. The date preprinted onto the New York census forms was June 1, 1915, which was actually weeks before Russomano's release from Auburn. If Russomano was held in custody from the time of his arrest, he would have served about one month less than two years of his sentence.

551 Raphael Russomano, New York City Extracted Death Index, Borough of Manhattan, certificate no. 25204, Aug. 25, 1915.

552 John Russomano World War I Draft Registration Card, no. 157, Precinct 38, New York, NY, June 5, 1917.

553 John Russomano, New York Executive Orders for Commutations, Pardons, Restorations, Clemency and Respites, July 1, 1922.

554 John Russomano, New York City Voter List, 1924, p. 11; United States Census of 1930, New York State, New York County, Assembly District 18, Enumeration District 31-839; John Russomano World War II Draft Registration Card, serial no. U1618, Local board no. 50, New York, NY, April 25, 1942; United States Census of 1950, New York State, Bronx County, Enumeration District 3-1879.

555 Gennaro Russomano, New York City Death Index, Bronx County, certificate no. 3780, April 13, 1956; Gennaro Russomano, memorial ID no. 204023033, Find A Grave, findagrave.com, Oct. 20, 2019.

556 Valachi, *The Real Thing*, p. 58.

557 Valachi, *The Real Thing*, p. 6k, 24.

558 Valachi, *The Real Thing*, p. 6k.

559 Valachi, *The Real Thing*, p. 58.

560 "'Big Jack' Zelig, state's witness, slain on eve of the Becker trial," *NYT*, Oct. 6, 1912, p. 1; "Secure six vice witnesses here," *Boston Globe*, Sept. 1, 1916, p. 1; "Assert police protected the white slavers," *Pittsburgh Press*, Sept. 1, 1916, p. 5

561 Burstein, Devin J., "Samuel Seabury," Historical Society of the New York Courts, history.nycourts.gov, March 28, 2019, accessed May 11, 2024.

562 Jones, Howard J., "New Yorkers stunned by vice revelations; police jail innocent," *Paterson NJ Morning Call*, Dec. 16, 1930, p. 9.

563 "Girl slave ring queen arrested; 28 vice raids," *NYDN*, Sept. 29, 1931, p. 4; "Unsegregated vice indicated rampant here," *BDE*, Sept. 29, 1931, p. 13.

564 "N.Y. vice queen bares secrets of slave ring," *NYDN*, Oct. 4, 1931, p. 3.

565 Greene, Roger D., "Grand jurors' demand starts rackets probe," *Boston Globe*, July 27, 1937, p. 4; Dewey, Thomas E., *Twenty Against the Underworld*, Garden City NY: Doubleday & Company, 1974, p. 192-193.

566 Pevear, Barton, "Ex-booker due to clinch case against Lucania," *BDE*, May 20, 1936, p. 1; Symontowne, Russ, "Luciano and eight guilty, face life as vice lords," *NYDN*, June 8, 1936, p. 3.

567 Valachi, *The Real Thing*, p. 761-763.

568 Valachi, *The Real Thing*, p. 774-776.

569 Valachi, *The Real Thing*, p. 787.

570 Valachi, *The Real Thing*, p. 798-808, 837.

571 Evans, C.A., FBI Memorandum to Mr. Belmont, accompanied by Joseph Valachi debriefings collected by Assistant Attorney General Herbert Miller, file no. 92-6054-406, NARA Record no. 124-10220-10111, Aug. 13, 1963, enclosure p. 17; Valachi, *The Real Thing*, p. 479.

572 Valachi, *The Real Thing*, p. 763-764, 768-769. 836.

573 Valachi, *The Real Thing*, p. 868.

574 Valachi, *The Real Thing*, p. 871.

575 Valachi, *The Real Thing*, p. 982-983.

576 Valachi, *The Real Thing*, p. 1023-1025.

577 Fiore F. Siano, certificate no. 21593, Births Reported in 1927 - Borough of Manhattan, June 22, 1927; Fiore Ernest Siano World War II Draft Registration Card, serial no. W487, order no. W13068, New York City, June 25, 1945; United States Census of 1930, New York State, New York County, Assembly District 18, Enumeration District 31-1247; United States Census of 1940, New York State, New York County, Assembly District 18, Enumeration District 1577.

578 Fiore Ernest Siano World War II Draft Registration Card; Bureau of Narcotics, *Mafia*, p. 635.

579 United States Census of 1950, New York State, New York County, Enumeration District 31-2410.

580 "500G dope seized with 3 suspects," *NYDN*, Aug. 4, 1954, p. 7; "U.S. to rush dope trials," *NYDN*, Nov. 30, 1954, p. 15; "5 get long terms in narcotic cases," *NYT*, Nov 30, 1954, p. 30; Bureau of Narcotics, *Mafia*, p. 635.

581 Federici, William, and Henry Lee, "How Genovese took over mob," *NYDN*, Sept. 30, 1963, p. 3; Healy, Paul, and Frank Holeman, "Death of a squealer – play by play," *NYDN*, Oct. 10, 1963, p. 3; Abrams, Norma, and Henry Machirella, "Bender & Squillante too?" *NYDN*, March 25, 1967, p. 3; Maas, Peter, "Anatomy of a Cosa Nostra contract," *New York Magazine*, Jan. 13, 1969, p. 31; Maas, *The Valachi Papers*, p. 224; McCoy, Leonard H., "Cosa Nostra aka," FBI report of New York Office, file no. 92-6054-740, NARA no. 124-10205-10471, Aug. 21, 1964, p. 127.

582 Valachi, *The Real Thing*, p. 465.

583 Valachi, *The Real Thing*, p. 475, 543.

584 Innocenzio Stopelli Certificate and Record of Birth, Borough of Manhattan, certificate no. 19843, City of New York Bureau of Records, April 10, 1907, reported April 18, 1907; John Stoppelli, 131-03-2116, Social Security Applications and Claims Index, Jan. 10, 1993; United States Census of 1910, New York State, New York County, Enumeration District 117.

585 Rocco Stoppelli and Carmela Miraglia Certificate of Marriage, Borough of Manhattan, certificate no. 7114, City of New York Bureau of Records, April 22, 1900; United States Census of 1900, New York State, New York County, Ward 21, Enumeration District 506; New York State Census of 1905, New York County, Assembly District 6, Election District 11.

586 Rocco Stoppelli World War I Draft Registration Card, New York City NY, Sept. 8, 1918; United States Census of 1920, New York State, New York County, Enumeration District 201.

587 "The Children's Court," *Daily Long Island Farmer*, March 1918.

588 "4 seized as theatre yeggs," *NYEP*, July 2, 1924, p. 3; "Brooklyn police praised to Enright for daring acts," *BDE*, Sept. 24, 1924, p. 20.

589 John Stoppelli FBI record no. 67-640, in Carr, Charlie, *New York Police Files on the Mafia*, Hosehead Productions, 2012, p. 566.

590 "Slip on bills he raised hurls him into a U.S. prison," *NYDN*, March 20, 1926, p. 26; "Four drug sellers sentenced to terms in federal prison," *NYHT*, March 20, 1925, p. 8; "Dope peddlers get year in Atlanta," *Schenectady NY Gazette*, March 20, 1925, p. 1; John Stoppelli FBI record no. 67-640, p. 563.

591 "Bandits shoot man and flee," *BDE*, Oct. 2, 1925, p. 13; "Poolroom keeper shot by 2 holdup men, dying," *BSU*, Oct. 3, 1925, p. 11; "Pool room man shot; affray mysterious," *NYT*, Oct. 3, 1925, p. 17; "Father of four shot 3 times in supposed holdup," *NYDN*, Oct. 3, 1925, p. 2; Louis Bernardi Certificate of Death, Borough of Manhattan, registered no. 26121, Department of Health of the City of New York Bureau of Records, Oct. 29, 1925.

592 John Stoppelli FBI record no. 67-640, p. 566; "Two men held as robbers," *NYT*, March 22, 1926, p. 3.

593 "Forbidden to return here," *Mount Vernon Daily Argus*, Sept. 9, 1926, p. 1.

594 John Stoppelli and Mary Groger Certificate and Record of Marriage, Borough of Manhattan, certificate no. 31379, City of New York Department of Health, Nov. 18, 1929.

595 John Stoppelli FBI record no. 67-640, p. 563; "Five nabbed in suspected jail delivery," *BSU*, July 15, 1930, p. 1. The S.W. Farber Tin Works company later became known as Farberware.

596 John Stoppelli FBI record no. 67-640, p. 563.

597 Vera Giroux Certificate of Death, Borough of Manhattan, certificate no. 8798, New York City Department of Health Bureau of Records, April 19, 1938; "Bubble dancer dives to death," *Buffalo Evening News*, April 19, 1938, p. 1; "Dancer leaps to death," *NYT*, April 20, 1938, p. 9; "Dancer's leap to death is held suicide," *NYDN*, April 20, 1938, p. 4; "Bubble dancer, 'tired of it all,' leaps to death," *NYHT*, April 20, 1938, p. 13.

598 John Stoppelli World War II Draft Registration Card, serial no. 6951, order no. 1176, Precinct 1, Lufkin, Texas, Oct. 16, 1940 (later stamped by Local Board No. 1, New York City); John Stoppelli FBI record no. 67-640, p. 563, 566.

599 "17 indicted in dope ring," *NYS*, March 27, 1945, p. 10. While Charles LaGaipa probably was dead at this time, Joseph Dentico was alive. Dentico remained a fugitive until July 1951, when he surfaced in the Bronx. He was sentenced to 10 years in prison for narcotics violations. LaGaipa reportedly left his Santa Cruz, California, home in June 1944 to meet a friend in San Jose. He was never seen again. His automobile, with particles of human brain tissue on its instrument panel, was found abandoned in Oakland. Agents concluded that LaGaipa had been shortchanging underworld business partners on narcotics shipments.

600 "Dope raiders seize 137 in NY, capital," *NYEP*, Nov. 3, 1945, p. 5.

601 Luce, Betsy, "2 a.m. curfew tested; suspect in slaying seized," *NYEP*, Nov. 24, 1945, p. 4; Feinberg, Alexander, "71 in police line-up; Wallander hails inroads on crime," *NYT*, Nov. 25, 1945, p. 1; "Police gather in 71 suspects as crime slackens," *NYHT*, Nov. 25, 1945, p. 1; Bureau of Narcotics, *Mafia*, p. 644.

602 "50 seized in crime roundup," *NYS*, Nov. 24, 1945, p. 16.

603 John Stoppelli FBI record no. 67-640, p. 564-565.

604 Sherrer, Hans, "John Stoppelli," Wrongly Convicted Database, forejustice.org; John Stoppelli FBI record no. 67-640, p. 565; "Indicted on dope charge," *Santa Rosa CA Press Democrat*, Jan. 13, 1949, p. 11; "Pleads not guilty," *Salinas CA Californian*, Feb. 24, 1949, p. 1; "Not guilty plea to dope charge," *Contra Costa Gazette*, Feb. 25, 1949, p. 5; Johnson, Edd, "Johnny (the Bug) goes free," *San Francisco Chronicle*, Sept. 5, 1952, p. 1;

605 Sherrer, "John Stoppelli"; Stoppelli v. United States, 183 F.2d 391, Ninth Circuit Court, 1950; "Five found guilty in dope case," *San Francisco Chronicle*, June 14, 1949, p. 17; John Stoppelli FBI record no. 67-640, p. 565.

606 Stoppelli v. United States, 183 F.2d 391, Ninth Circuit Court, 1950; Sherrer, "John Stoppelli"; "Dope peddler starts term," *Oakland Tribune*, Dec. 14, 1950, p. 56.

607 "Dope peddler shot in tavern brawl," *BDE*, Dec. 29, 1950, p. 1; "Narcotics suspect shot in Village bar," *NYHT*, Dec. 30, 1950, p. 11; Mahler, Julius, "Both suspect, victim held in cafe shooting," *NYDN*, Dec. 30, 1950, p. 9; "Judge takes assault jury to visit scene," *NYDN*, Sept. 11, 1951, p. 11; John Stoppelli FBI record no. 67-640, p. 565.

608 "Retrial move fails in dope conspiracy," *Long Beach CA Press Telegram*, April 9, 1952, p. 24; "Stoppelli refused new narcotic trial," *San Diego Union*, April 9, 1952, p. 14; "John the bug's attorneys withdraw his appeal," *San Francisco Chronicle*, June 5, 1952, p. 2; Johnson, "Johnny (the Bug) goes free"; Sherrer, "John Stoppelli."

609 Ain, Stewart, "Indict Napoli, his son & 10 in bet ring," *NYDN*, Jan. 13, 1977, p. KL7; Siegel, Max H., "James Napoli Sr. held in gambling count," *NYT*, Jan. 13, 1977, p. 32; Seigel, Max H., "James Napoli Sr. held on gambling count," *NYT*, Jan. 13, 1977, p. 32.

610 John Stoppelli, 131-03-2116, Social Security Applications and Claims Index, Jan. 10, 1993; John Stoppelli, 131-03-2116, Social Security Death Index, Jan. 10, 1993; "John Stoppelli," memorial ID 255968482, Find A Grave, findagrave.com.

611 Valachi, *The Real Thing*, p. 11-12.

612 Valachi, *The Real Thing*, p. 11-12.

613 Valachi, *The Real Thing*, p. 13.

614 Valachi, *The Real Thing*, p. 12.

615 Valachi, *The Real Thing*, p. 13-14.

616 Joseph Viserti World War I Draft Registration Card, no. 597, Sing Sing Prison, Westchester County, NY, June 5, 1917; Passenger manifest of *S.S. Trojan Prince*, departed Naples on Sept. 10, 1902, arrived New York on Sept. 26, 1902.

617 New York State Census of 1905, New York County, Borough of Manhattan, Assembly District 33, Election District 10; John Viserto, Borough of Manhattan, certificate no. 3681, New York City Index to Death Certificates, Feb. 3, 1937. The timing of John's first arrival in the U.S. is uncertain. The census indicates that John had been in the U.S. for four years (placing his arrival at about the same time as his mother and siblings in 1901), but the death record indicates that John was in the U.S. for 32 years (approximately from 1905).

618 New York State Census of 1905, New York County, Borough of Manhattan, Assembly District 33, Election District 10.

619 Joseph Viserta Declaration of Intention, no. 35586, U.S. Circuit Court for the Southern District of New York, March 29, 1910; New York City Marriage License Index, vol. 6, no. 20088, July 20, 1911; Giuseppe Viserta and Maria Santora, Borough of Manhattan, certificate no. 21340, New York City Extracted Marriage Index, Sept. 10, 1911; Giuseppe Viserta and Maria Santora, Borough of Manhattan, certificate no. 21340, City of New York Department of Health, Sept. 10, 1911; New York State Census of 1925, New York County, Assembly District 18, Election District 30. The existence of two marriage license entries spaced more than seven weeks apart suggests that the couple was married in an earlier civil ceremony before the church wedding occurred in September.

620 "Black Hand slays victim who doffs his Chinese armor," *NYH*, April 10, 1913, p. 1; Amadeo Buonomo Certificate of Death, registered no. 11224, Department of Health of the City of New York, date of death April 6, 1913.

621 "Mystery in murder of Jerry Maida," *NYS*, April 30, 1913, p. 5; "East Side gunmen take second victim," *NYTR*, April 30, 1913, p. 5.

622 "Kelly gang kills man who 'squealed,'" *BDT*, April 29, 1913, p. 13; "Police aid shot to death from street ambush," *BC*, April 29, 1913, p. 1; "Alleged informer is riddled with bullets," *BSU*, April 29, 1913, p. 3; "Gunmen slay 'squealer' just as a warning," *NYEW*, April 29, 1913, p. 2; "East Side gunmen take second victim," *NYTR*, April 30, 1913, p. 5.

623 "Held for informer's death," *NYTR*, May 2, 1913, p. 4; "Four suspects held for inquest," *NYEW*, May 1, 1913, p. 3; "Slayers of spy not named," *NYH*, June 7, 1913, p. 6; "Judges blamed for conditions in Tombs," *NYS*, Sept. 18, 1913, p. 4; "Long terms for gangmen," *NYT*, Jan. 13, 1914, p. 18.

624 "Police doing well, declares Mitchell; told to use clubs," *NYEW*, Jan. 12, 1914, p. 1; "'Be sure of your man, then get him,' new police order," *NYH*, Jan. 13, 1914, p. 4; "Long terms for gangmen."

625 Joseph Viserti, no. 64101, Sing Sing Admission Register, received Jan. 16, 1914.

626 "Murder barn fatal again," *NYTR*, Oct. 8, 1915, p. 16; "Harlem's 'Little Italy' has killing," *NYPR*, Oct. 8, 1915, p. 5; "Four held in Greco case," *NYT*, Oct. 9, 1915, p. 5; Giovanni Viserta World War I Draft Registration Card, no. 605, Precinct 39, New York County, New York, June 5, 1917.

627 Joseph Viserti World War I Draft Registration Card, no. 597, Sing Sing Prison, Westchester County, NY, June 5, 1917.

628 Joseph Viserti Executive Order for Commutation, Governor Charles S. Whitman, Aug. 20, 1918, passed Secretary of State Office on Aug. 23, 1918; "Two slain, one a bystander, in new bootleg war," *NYDN*, Oct. 14, 1921, p. 2.

629 "Bootleggers' chief killed as he shoots an innocent victim," *NYH*, Oct. 14, 1921, p. 1; "Court of General Sessions," *NYS*, Dec. 17, 1919, p. 14; "Court of General Sessions," *NYS*, Dec. 22, 1919, p. 14.

630 "One man killed, three wounded in saloon hold-up," *NYH*, Aug. 21, 1917, p. 3; "7 Italians shoot up saloon; 1 dead," *NYS*, Aug. 21, 1917, p. 5; "N.Y. police seek six gunmen," *Corning NY Evening Leader*, Aug. 21, 1917, p. 1; Anthony Deluca, Borough of Manhattan, certificate no. 26474, New York City Municipal Deaths, Sept. 23, 1919; "Knew of his doom and warned police," *NYS*, Sept. 25, 1919, p. 7; "Knew of his doom warned police," *Auburn Citizen*, Oct. 3, 1919, p. 7.

631 "Out of Sing Sing 7 months, again taken as slayer," *NYET*, Sept. 27, 1919, p. 4.

632 "Bootlegger killed, bystander slain, in coffee house duel," *NYT*, Oct. 14, 1921, p. 1; "'J. Pep' held for murder," *NYDN*, Dec. 1, 1919, p. 18; "Two slain, one a bystander, in new bootleg war," *NYDN*, Oct. 14, 1921, p. 2; "Bootleggers' chief killed as he shoots an innocent victim," *NYH*, Oct. 14, 1921, p. 1.

633 "Signed 'confession' but freed by jury," *BDE*, April 23, 1920, p. 2; "Forced confession rejected by jury," *BSU*, April 23, 1920, p. 1; "Murder confession signed from fear wins man freedom," *NYDN*, April 24, 1920, p. 8.

634 "Speeder gets stiff fine for 3d offense," *Long Island City Daily Star*, July 17, 1920, p. 1; "Speeders go to jail," *BDT*, July 7, 1920, p. 6; "Other violations dealt with," *Long Island Daily Farmer*, July 19, 1920.

635 "Mystery in shooting," *NYTR*, Sept. 7, 1920, p. 8.

636 "Poolroom owner shot dead after card game in place," *NYTR*, March 30, 1921, p. 6; Giuseppe Peppe World War I Draft Registration Card, no. 315, Bronx, NY, June 4, 1917; General Register of Patients, *U.S.S. Comfort*, 1918-1921; "Joe Peppe…," *NYH*, Oct. 10, 1919, p. 10; "Joseph Peppe…," *NYTR*, Oct. 10, 1919, p. 24; Joseph Peppe World War II Draft Registration Card, serial no. U458, Local Board no. 81, Bronx, NY, April 27, 1942.

637 "Park View Inn," *NYET*, advertisement, June 11, 1921, p. 8.

638 "Seized on eve of wedding as slayer of Baff," *NYH*, June 4, 1916, p. 11; "Baff suspect arrested," *NYS*, June 4, 1916, p. 2.

639 Joseph Lagumina Certificate of Death, Borough of Manhattan, Registered no. 13023, Department of Health of the City of New York Bureau of Records, May 17, 1921; "Ice cream man slain on street by gunmen," *NYT*, May 18, 1921, p. 17; "Joseph Lagumina…," *NYTR*, May 18, 1921, p. 1; "Ice cream man slain; partner is arrested," *NYH*, May 18, 1924, p. 4; "Shot dead on way to his luncheon," *NYEW*, May 17, 1921, p. 20; "Man is killed by black handers," *NYET*, May 17, 1921, p. 2; "Police net fails to trap slayers of rich Italian," *NYDN*, May 18, 1921, p. 6.

640 "Speeder held for shooting," *BDE*, Oct. 3, 1921, p. 18; "Gem-bedecked speeder seized in court in hunt for assassin," *NYTR*, Oct. 4, 1921, p. 1; "Alleged thief held for death," *BDT*, Oct. 3, 1921, p. 3; "At bar as speeder; accused of murder," *BSU*, Oct. 3, 1921, p. 1; "Auto speeder seized in court held as slayer," *NYDN*, Oct. 4, 1921, p. 5; "Arraigned as speeder, seized on murder charge," *NYEW*, Oct. 3, 1921, p. 10. The interrupted speeding case against Viserti came up again in traffic court on October 21, 1921, one week after Viserti was murdered.

641 "Alleged thief held for death," *BDT*, Oct. 3, 1921, p. 3; "At bar as speeder; accused of murder," *BSU*, Oct. 3, 1921, p. 1; "Auto speeder seized in court held as slayer," *NYDN*, Oct. 4, 1921, p. 5; "Arraigned as speeder, seized on murder charge," *NYEW*, Oct. 3, 1921, p. 10.

642 Joseph Viserti Certificate of Death, Borough of Manhattan, registered no. 23533, Department of Health of the City of New York Bureau of Records, Oct. 13, 1921; Luigi Rango Certificate of Death, Borough of Manhattan, registered no. 23546, Department of Health of the City of New York Bureau of Records, Oct. 13, 1921; "Two slain, one a bystander, in new bootleg war"; "Bootleggers' chief killed as he shoots an innocent victim."

643 "Bootlegger killed, bystander slain, in coffee house duel"; "'Joe Pep,' ruler of Little Italy in Harlem, slain," *NYTR*, Oct. 14, 1921, p. 1; "Bootleg roundup follows slaying; suspect trapped," *NYDN*, Oct. 15, 1921, p. 3; "Held in murder in East Side cafe," *NYEP*, Oct. 14, 1921, p. 2; "Admits phone call to learn of killing," *NYT*, Oct. 15, 1921, p. 6; "Slayer of 'Pep' sought in raid on bootleggers," *NYHT*, Oct. 15, 1921, p. 10; "Brooklynite held in rum feud slaying," *BSU*, Oct. 14, 1921, p. 1; "Man held in dual bootleg killing," *NYET*, Oct. 14, 1921, p. 1; Warner, Richard, Angelo Santino and Lennert van't Riet, "The New York Mafia: An Alternative Theory," *Informer: The History of American Crime and Law Enforcement*, May 2014

644 "Joe Pep's brother shot in argument," *NYEW*, Nov. 25, 1921, p. 8.

645 "Man shot to death on Union St," *BOEG*, Dec. 14, 1922, p. 1; "Unidentified man murdered," *BODG*, Dec. 15, 1922, p. 1; "Annibale Stilo, North End murder victim," *BOEG*, Dec. 15, 1922, p. 24; "Bruno held in Stilo murder," *BOEG*, Dec. 19, 1922, p. 8; "Bruno held for murder of Stilo," *BODG*, Dec. 20, 1922, p. 7; "Bruno is charged with two murders," *BOEG*, March 29, 1923, p. 4; "Bailed in murder case, Bruno is rearrested," *BODG*, March 29, 1923, p. 19; "Revolver missing, prosecutor hears," *BOEG*, Feb. 18, 1935, p. 4.

646 "Confining jury at Bruno trial," *BOEG*, Feb. 19, 1935, p. 7; "'Lock up' jury in murder case," *BODG*, Feb. 20, 1935, p. 5; "How Stilo died told at court," *BOEG*, Feb. 20, 1935, p. 10; "Bruno claims self-

defense," *BODG*, Feb. 21, 1935, p. 13; "Jurors retire in Bruno case," *BOEG*, Feb. 21, 1935, p. 17; "Murder verdict ordered sealed," *BODG*, Feb. 22, 1935, p. 5; "Jury convicts Albert Bruno," *BOEG*, Feb. 25, 1935, p. 13; "Bruno gets life term for murdering Stilo," *BODG*, Feb. 26, 1935, p. 28.

647 John Viserto, Borough of Manhattan, certificate no. 3681, New York City Index to Death Certificates, Feb. 3, 1937.

648 Valachi, *The Real Thing*, p. 17.

649 The nickname "Sharkey" was often awarded to men proficient with their fists. It is a reference to Irish-American prizefighter "Sailor Tom" Sharkey, a punishing Heavyweight who knocked out 37 of his 52 opponents between 1896 and 1904. Boxer Jack Sharkey, who fought in the Prohibition Era, took his name from "Sailor Tom."

650 Valachi, *The Real Thing*, p. 6L.

651 Valachi, *The Real Thing*, p. 15.

652 Valachi, *The Real Thing*, p. 15-16.

653 Valachi, *The Real Thing*, p. 998-999.

654 Tony Zacaro, New York City Death Index, certificate no. 25840, Sept. 2, 1912; United States Census of 1910, New York State, New York County, Ward 12, Enumeration District 337. The press used various spellings of his surname, including "Zacaro," "Zaraco" and "Zaraca."

655 United States Census of 1910, New York State, New York County, Ward 12, Enumeration District 337. The scribbled Zaccaro surname looks very much like "Jaccan" in the census entry.

656 "Two gang members shot by gunmen," *New York Call*, Sept. 3, 1912, p. 1; "'Young Sharkey' killed," *NYTR*, Sept. 3, 1912, p. 2; "Kills a gangster to save his uncle," *NYT*, Dec. 17, 1912, p. 12.

657 "Kills a gangster to save his uncle." Documents that could prove or disprove this relationship were not available by presstime.

658 "Murdered in vendetta," *NYTR*, March 21, 1912, p. 2; "'Zopo the Terror' dies as he draws weapon to kill," *NYEW*, Dec. 16, 1912, p. 6; "Prisco, lame gunman, meets death at last," *NYS*, Dec. 17, 1912, p. 16; "Cycle of murders," *BDE*, Feb. 20, 1914, p. 3.

659 Pasqua Musoni Lener Certificate of Death, Borough of Manhattan, certificate no. 9128, Department of Health of the City of New York, March 20, 1912, corrected copy filed March 3, 1915.

660 "Kills a gangster to save his uncle."

661 Critchley, David, *The Origin of Organized Crime in America: The New York City Mafia, 1891-1931*, New York: Routledge, 2009, p. 109.

662 The name of the establishment, translated as "Cafe of the...," appears to be missing its final element.

663 "Four of Hearts Tony's death card in gang shooting," *NYEW*, Sept. 3, 1912, p. 6; "Pistol man slain by his own gang," *Virginia Enterprise*, Oct. 11, 1912, p. 11.

664 "Harlem's 'Murder Stable Feud' counts 21st victim," *NYH*, Jan. 7, 1917, p. Mag-2.

665 "Four of Hearts Tony's death card in gang shooting"; "Pistol man slain by his own gang"; "Two gang members shot by gunmen."

666 "Gang man shot dead after card warning," *Springfield MA Evening Union*, Sept. 3, 1912, p. 2; "Four of Hearts Tony's death card in gang shooting"; "Pistol man slain by his own gang"; "'Young Sharkey' killed," *NYTR*, Sept. 3, 1912, p. 2.

667 "Two gang members shot by gunmen"; "Two shot at cards," *NYT*, Sept. 3, 1912, p. 6.

668 "'Young Sharkey' killed"; "Gang man shot dead after card warning."

669 "Four of Hearts Tony's death card in gang shooting"; "Pistol man slain by his own gang."

670 Francis Clementi Certificate of Death, registered no. 4553, County of Philadelphia, Feb. 5, 1918; "Gunmen slay victim in revenge; other murders baffle police," *Evening Public Ledger*, Feb. 6, 1918, p. 3; People of the State of New York v. Alessandro Vollero, Case on Appeal Vol. I, Court of Appeals of the State of New York, 226 New York 587 Pt 1, New York: Stillman Appellate Printing Co, 1918.

671 "Notorious gunman arrested," *New York Call*, Oct. 4, 1912, p. 3; "'Zopo the Terror' dies as he draws weapon to kill," *NYEW*, Dec. 16, 1912, p. 6; "Blackmailer killed as he made threat," *BDE*, Dec. 16, 1912, p. 4.

672 "'Zopo the Terror' dies as he draws weapon to kill."

673 "Italian boss of New York and his son shot," *Passaic NJ Daily News*, May 18, 1915, p. 11.

JUST ONE MORE THING

Elusive crime figures

*Identities of some Valachi underworld
associates remain frustratingly uncertain*

By Thomas Hunt and Steve Turner

Our plan to define the vaguely described characters in Joseph Valachi's life story encountered a few significant obstacles. While we were able to establish the identities and outline the activities of many of the individuals Valachi referred to in his autobiography[1] and other statements, a number of individuals continue to be frustratingly unknown.

Some have managed to remain entirely mysterious. "The Wackie Brothers," brutal racketeers featured in a fairly detailed Valachi account and mentioned on eight different pages in Valachi's autobiography, and a supposed one-time crime boss with a name something like *"Mastromeine"* could not be matched up with any known crime figures.

In our pursuit of the crime figure referred to by Valachi as "Crazy Chuck," we turned up some hopeful leads but then found that those insisted on pointing to more than one person. So, Valachi's often-mentioned East Harlem neighbor-hood archfoe remains a puzzle.

A single person was identified as a likely candidate for the Valachi Castel-lammarese War-Era associate he called Nick Capuzzi. However, we could not decisively establish the person's relationship with Valachi or even his presence in the New York City-area during the war years.

In addition to being enormously frustrating, it is shocking that so much of Valachi's story, carefully studied for decades, is still so lacking in definition. Valachi's cryptic references to his associates have been on the record in one form or another since 1962-1963. We have frequently wondered how so many – the Federal Bureau of Narcotics agents and FBI agents interrogating him as an informant, the Department of Justice staff reviewing his memoirs, the Senate Investigations Subcommittee members and staff hearing his testimony and the journalist-author researching and writing his biography – all managed to avoid pinning Valachi down on these individuals. None is known to have asked, "Who was this 'Crazy Chuck'?" or "What can you tell us about the 'Wackie Brothers'?"

More than sixty years later, the identities of these gangsters still must be categorized as unknown, but we are not yet convinced that they are unknow-able. While we continue on their trails, we hope that some readers of this column will be inspired to launch their own investigations.

Nick Capuzzi

Valachi reported very little about Nick Capuzzi in his autobiography. He said he first met Capuzzi around early November 1930 at a Bronx apartment the Salvatore Maranzano-led rebel Mafia faction planned to use to ambush Steve Ferrigno, a lieutenant of Mafia boss of bosses Giuseppe Masseria. At the same time and place, he recalled meeting Maranzano's Castellammarese War allies Joseph Profaci, "Doc," and "Buster." Valachi liked all four but seemed to have the least interaction with Capuzzi.[2]

Soon after that ambush resulted in the deaths of Ferrigno and Al Mineo, Valachi was formally inducted into Maranzano's Mafia organization. Capuzzi was one of the mafiosi present for the ceremony.[3]

A few months later, Capuzzi was placed in charge of an effort by the Maranzano group to assassinate another Masseria lieutenant, Joe "Baker" Catania. Valachi, who was assigned to drive the getaway car for the operation, noted that Capuzzi was one of the shooters who murdered Catania on February 3, 1931.[4]

There seemed to be no other interactions between Valachi and this Capuzzi, whose sudden appearance in the story late in 1930 was followed by a sudden disappearance early in 1931. When Valachi spoke of Capuzzi in his fall 1963 McClellan Committee testimony, he noted that Capuzzi had been a member of the rebel Mafia faction (generally immigrant mafiosi from the Castellammare del Golfo area of Sicily) and that he was dead by 1963.[5]

The Valachi-described Nick Capuzzi did not match up with any known crime figure in the New York City area. One Dominick Capozzi, age thirty and a U.S. resident since arriving from Italy as an infant, showed up in the 1920 U.S. Census as an inmate at the city's Hart Island Prison.[6] But we could find no reason to connect this Capozzi to Valachi or to the Castellammarese War.

Another interesting possibility turned up about two hundred and fifty miles away from the city.

Nicola "Nick" Capozzi, born in 1887 in Gioia Del Colle, within the Bari province of Italy's Apulia region, became involved in the underworld of Syracuse, New York, by around 1912.[7] He worked with a Black Hand gang in that upstate community and reportedly succeeded as its leader following the 1919 murder of boss Donato Scarafino.[8] He also quickly succeeded Donato Scarafino as husband of Crescenza Posato Scarafino.[9]

Capozzi and several alleged accomplices – Tony Mauriello, Saverio DiBenedetto, Saverio DeSimone and Carlo Mancini – were arrested in 1920 and charged with extortion. Capozzi was convicted and sentenced to four years in prison.[10]

Information on Capozzi is lacking for the critical period of 1930-1931. A press report from September 1931, indicated that his wife Crescenza was startled awake by the attempted burglary of the Capozzis' home at 614 Salina Street. (Her scream reportedly caused the burglar to flee.) But the report does not mention Capozzi himself.[11] His absence from the report suggests that he may have been away from home during this period.

In 1934, Capozzi filed for bankruptcy protection from business creditors in Syracuse. He had amassed $9,000 in debts through his fish market enterprise.[12] He was refused U.S. citizenship in 1936 because of his earlier felony conviction.[13]

Capozzi died May 21, 1959, following a short illness. His wife Crescenza had passed away about two and a half years earlier.[14]

Capozzi's leadership role in the underworld of Syracuse, which sat within the western New York region dominated by Castellammarese Mafia boss Stefano Magaddino, and Capozzi's apparent absence from the area during the rebellion of the Castellammaresi leave open the possibility that he spent time in New York City fighting alongside Maranzano. Magaddino's organization was known to be a source of manpower, armament and financial support for the Maranzano war effort.[15] Capozzi would not have been the only underworld figure from outside New York to relocate to assist the rebellion. Others were Calogero "Charley Buffalo" DiBenedetto of Magaddino's crime family,[16] Sebastiano "Buster" Domingo of the Chicago area[17] and perhaps Salvatore Sabella of Philadelphia.[18]

If Nicola Capozzi was sent by Magaddino to assist the Maranzano rebellion, it would explain Capozzi's absence from Syracuse during the period, as well as Capozzi's sudden appearance and disappearance from Valachi's account of the Castellammarese War. At this time, it seems to us likely that Nicola Capozzi was Valachi's Nick Capuzzi.

Crazy Chuck

One of the more intriguing characters in the Valachi story, "Crazy Chuck" was older than Valachi and terrorized a young Valachi and his friends while they were growing up in East Harlem. When young robbers like Valachi stole items from wagons and trucks around East 108th Street and First Avenue, Chuck insisted that they could sell the stolen goods only to him.

"He was the most feared guy on the block," Valachi recalled.[19]

Later in his autobiography, Valachi reported that Chuck had attempted to organize young hoodlums under his leadership: "Believe it or not, he used to march the boys [of] 108th Street up and down the block. He will tell them that he was going to make them soldiers…"[20]

According to Valachi, Crazy Chuck once palled around with Valachi's older brother Anthony, who went by the alias of Frank Rocco.[21]

Valachi blamed his 1921 weapons possession arrest on Crazy Chuck.[22] When Valachi first discussed that arrest in his autobiography, he did not specifically mention Chuck:

> I got arrested in Jersey City. I went there with four more guys, and we were supposed to rob a fur store. But we got a flat tire and, while fixing the flat, the cops came along. While the cops were questioning the driver, one of the guys dropped a gun on the floor. And the gun came right near my foot, so I kicked it away. The other guy kicked it back to me. Well, anyway, we all got arrested. Believe me, none of us knew that this guy had a gun when we started from New York. We were all young, and this fellow was the oldest. When we went to the police station, we found out why he was carrying a gun. He had escaped from the New York Penitentiary. We didn't even know that he was wanted.[23]

Much later in the manuscript, as he described a bad-tempered conversation he had with Chuck, Valachi connected Chuck to the gun-kicking incident: "I said to him, 'You got me pinched in Jersey in 1920 for having a gun in the car...'"[24]

When Anthony Valachi / Frank Rocco began serving a life prison sentence in 1929, Chuck approached Joseph Valachi with the idea of working together on burglaries. Valachi dreaded the idea but agreed to give it a chance. When he told his burglary partner Nickie about the arrangement, it caused Nickie to mention giving up his life of crime. "Joe, I think that I will quit for a while," Nickie kidded Valachi.

Nickie mentioned his concern over stories of Chuck's murder of a man known as "Canarsi" (likely a nickname indicating some connection with the Canarsie neighborhood of Brooklyn). Chuck supposedly put six bullets in Canarsi's head early one morning. Though later arrested for the killing, no witnesses would testify against Crazy Chuck and he beat the charge.[25]

The planned burglary of a clothing store on Long Island went smoothly until the group was driving away from the scene. Then Crazy Chuck suddenly drew a handgun and began firing through a closed car window. Chuck later claimed he was firing at someone who was trying to take down the getaway car's license plate (not possible, as Valachi always made it a point to fold the plates on cars used in crimes so they could not be seen).[26]

Chuck tried to pressure Valachi to work with him again, but Valachi refused. The disagreement became physical. Chuck punched Valachi on the jaw. The impact made Valachi momentarily dizzy, but he remained conscious and kept his cool. When he recovered, he delivered a blow that knocked Chuck off his feet, and then he pounced on Chuck and grappled with him. A crowd gathered, and Valachi felt sure that a friend of Chuck had run off to retrieve a handgun. Valachi got up and ran off.[27]

Certain that Crazy Chuck was gunning for him, Valachi stayed away from his old East 108th Street neighborhood for a time.[28]

Following the conclusion of the Mafia's Castellammarese War in spring 1931, Valachi began hanging out in the old neighborhood again. One night, as he and friend John DeBellis climbed into Valachi's car, Chuck sprang up in the rear seat. DeBellis quickly said goodnight and left the two men to settle things (an offense that Valachi never forgave).

Chuck adopted a friendly tone, though he asserted he was carrying two handguns. Valachi looked him over and decided that he was unarmed at the moment. They talked for a while. After a short drive, they got out of the car and walked. At one point, Chuck made an excuse to go into a building, and Valachi figured it was there that Chuck was going to retrieve his weapons. When Chuck went inside, Valachi bolted.

Crazy Chuck showed up later at the apartment Valachi shared with his mother and siblings. Valachi's sister Lena confronted Chuck: "So, you're Chuck that is looking to shoot my brother." Chuck denied it, showed that he was unarmed and promised he would do nothing to harm Valachi.[29]

During what seemed to be a temporary truce, Valachi and Chuck spent some time in the apartment, talking over coffee. When they parted, Valachi, now a respected member of the Maranzano Mafia organization, warned Chuck to stay away. Valachi later told Maranzano about the interaction with Chuck.

Valachi's last comments about Crazy Chuck related to news that he was sent to a prison out of town and was killed by a fellow inmate in the prison: "I was told that the punk killed him in defending his honor."[30]

Despite numerous clues, we have been unable to establish the identity of Valachi's Crazy Chuck. Periodicals of the period make no mention of any such person. ("Crazy chuck" does turn up in a number of newspaper reports, as it was a common slang term for an errant throw by a baseball fielder.)

The mention of Chuck being charged with the killing of "Canarsi" seemed a hopeful lead, but no press reports could be found that matched the names and descriptions provided by Valachi. The description of an East 108th Street hoodlum terrorizing younger criminals also proved to be untraceable. We located no press reports of gunshots following a clothing store robbery in

1929. And there was insufficient detail to the story of Chuck being killed in an out-of-town prison for us to have any hope of following that lead.

The most useful details related to Valachi's 1921 weapons possession arrest. In his autobiography, Valachi revealed that he gave police a false name, Anthony Sorge, when arrested on that charge. The arrest under the assumed name showed up on Valachi's criminal record,[31] and it was documented in reports in a New Jersey newspaper.

Immediately after the incident, the *Hudson Observer* reported that five men were arrested in an automobile on Central Avenue in Jersey City. The five included four New York City residents – Anthony Sorge (Valachi) of 312 East 106th Street, "Dominick Pucselli" of 2076 First Avenue, "Joseph Tilligrino of 400 East 106th Street and "Charles Chisingo" of 405 East 106th Street – along with New Jersey resident "Fred Russo" of 561 Palisade Avenue. All were charged with possession of a concealed weapon. Russo, apparently the owner and the driver of the car, was charged also with driving without a license.[32]

As this matched the incident details provided by Valachi, it appeared that Crazy Chuck must have been one of the five men arrested. "Chuck" is a common nickname for the given name "Charles," so the "Charles Chisingo" mentioned in the *Observer* emerged as the best candidate for Crazy Chuck.

But that didn't resolve the matter. A check of the U.S. Census for 1920 showed no "Chisingo" family at the 405 East 106th Street address or anywhere else in East Harlem.[33] (The census did show Joseph Pellegrino, not "Tilligrino," living at 400 East 106th Street, and a 1925 prison admission record confirmed that that data.[34] No "Dominick Pucselli" or anything like that name could be found in the 1920 Census as a resident of 2076 First Avenue. However, a Domenick Puciarelli was noted as a resident of East Harlem in the 1925 New York State Census.[35])

Things became more complicated when New Jersey newspapers covered the weapon possession trial in May, 1922. At that time, the four New York men were brought before a jury. And the names of some of those men had changed since the earlier report. They were said to be Anthony Sorge (Valachi); "Dominick Piccarelli" (formerly Pucselli); "Joseph Pellegrini" (formerly Tilligrino) and "Charles Crescenzo" (formerly Chisingo), who was also known as "Albers." The trial jury could not reach a verdict.[36] (The four men later pleaded non vult contendere. They were fined and given probation by the court.[37])

The fifth defendant, the New Jersey resident previously said to be "Fred Russo," was referred to in the trial reporting as "Frank Russo." The press reported that Russo did not stand trial with the others because he earlier pleaded guilty to the charges against him. He was sent to a New Jersey county prison and then transferred to a prison in New York, where he owed time on a sentence interrupted by his escape.[38]

Returning to the census records, we noted that there was no "Crescenzo" or "Albers" living at the 405 East 106th Street address. Some close matches – Crescenzi, Creszenzo, Crecenzi, Albero, Alberti, etc. – were located in area homes, but none looked to be a match for the Charles Crescenzo of the news report.

At the same time, Frank Russo suddenly became an excellent fit for Valachi's statement that the gun-carrying member of the 1921 burglary team, who he appeared to identify as Chuck, was carrying his firearm and dropped it when police approached because he had previously escaped from a New York prison. The press clearly reported that Frank Russo had escaped from prison. The name "Frank" could be made to fit the story if Russo adopted an atypical nickname or if Valachi had originally written (or intended to write) "Crazy Chick" instead of "Crazy Chuck," as "Chick" was often used as a nickname for Italian males named "Francesco."

But we failed to find a strong connection between Frank Russo and East Harlem. If he was the one carrying the firearm in 1921, we cannot explain why Valachi later blamed East Harlem gangster Crazy Chuck for that.

It is conceivable that the backgrounds of two different people became merged in Valachi's memory of this early event, but this seems unlikely. Valachi's experiences with Crazy Chuck were so numerous and so intimate that he should not have been confused at all about Chuck's identity. Possibly Valachi was awkwardly relating a story involving both a gun-carrying Chuck (perhaps Chisingo/Crescenzo) and a different gun-carrying prison escapee (Frank Russo). The records are not specific enough to rule this out. And, apparently, no one attempted to clarify these issues while Valachi was alive.

Mastromeine

Valachi had very little to say about a crime figure who may have been an an early Italian-American underworld boss in East Harlem. Probably in 1924, while Valachi was serving time in Sing Sing Prison, a friend named Dom introduced him to an older inmate. When he wrote about the introduction for his autobiography, Valachi struggled with the older man's name:

> This fellow had a very hard name – it was an Italian name. I can't remember. I'll try to write it the best way I can. It was a long name, and it went something like this, "Mastromeine."

Valachi learned that Mastromeine was "some kind of a don in the old days," based at East Harlem's 116th Street. Mastromeine was the partner of a "real tough guy" known as "Little Eddie" and reportedly lost much of his power following Eddie's death.

Valachi recalled that Mastromeine was released from prison soon after their introduction and then was killed after he returned home. Valachi's friend Dom "felt bad" when he heard the news, not out of sympathy for Mastromeine but because Dom had wanted to kill Mastromeine himself. Dom, too, was murdered soon after his release from the prison. According to Valachi, the murders of Mastromeine and Dom occurred before the murder of Frank LaPuma on June 9, 1925.[39]

As interested as we were in Valachi's mention of this early Harlem underworld leader, we were entirely unable to find a suitable match for Mastromeine.

Wackie Brothers

Sometime in the very late 1930s or early 1940s,[40] Valachi was ordered to oversee an act of gangland retributive justice against the "Wackie Brothers." The order reportedly originated with Valachi's superior Anthony "Tony Bender" Strollo and was transmitted to Valachi through Girolamo "Bobby Doyle" Santuccio.

> [Santuccio] started to say, "You know what happened to Eddie Star?" I said, "No." He said, "Last night, they cracked his head wide open." And I said, "Who did it?" And he asked me, "Do you know the Wackie Brothers?" I said, "Yes, they are with Vince Rao, 107th Street. They are in the numbers business, and they turn all their work to Vincent Rao…"[41]

The Wackie Brothers reportedly worked in the numbers racket in association with the crime family led by Tommaso Gagliano and Gaetano Lucchese.

Valachi was a member of the organization led by Salvatore "Charlie Luciano" Lucania (then in prison) and Vito Genovese (then in Italy), but he was a long-time friend of Lucchese and wanted no part of an attack against the Wackies.

Santuccio told him there was no choice and Valachi needed to act within twenty four hours: "We don't want it to cool off." Santuccio explained that the Wackies were to be beaten but not killed for what they did to "Eddie Starr" Capobianco, and Valachi was to supervise "Tommy Rye and Johnnie D." in the job. "Tommy Rye" was Valachi's nickname for Tommy Eboli (also known as "Tommy Ryan"). "Johnnie D." was the nickname of John DeBellis.[42]

While setting up the attack, Valachi learned from Eboli about the Wackies' attack against Capobianco. The Wackie Brothers and Joe "Palisades" Rosato were out drinking on a Saturday night. They visited Capobianco, known to have a number of women friends, and asked him to arrange some escorts for them that night. Capobianco called around but found none of his friends available. One of the Wackie Brothers was angered, picked up a stone table lamp and cracked open Capobianco's head with it.

Working from a tip, Valachi, Eboli and DeBellis spotted one of the Wackies with a Vincent Rao nephew, known as "Big Rocks," on Third Avenue near Ninety-seventh Street. Valachi pulled Big Rocks aside, and tried to explain to him what was going on, as Eboli and DeBellis went to work, beating the lone Wackie with baseball bats.[43]

When Valachi and Lucchese met at a holiday party, they privately discussed the beating. Valachi wanted to reveal that the attack had been ordered by Strollo and Santuccio. But he knew that would expose those crime family leaders to retribution and would cause them to lash out at him.

Lucchese seemed to understand the situation, and gave Valachi an opportunity to confirm his suspicions. Valachi reportedly made no statement to clear himself of responsibility. The matter was brought before a regional underworld council. Lucchese did not push for disciplinary action against Valachi, "but all [Lucchese's] boys were very cold to me ever since," Valachi recalled.[44]

Though the series of Wackie Brothers-related incidents recounted by Valachi involved very well known underworld figures, the Wackie Brothers themselves have remained unknown, except by their Valachi nickname.

Just One More Thing Notes

1 When quoting from Valachi's autobiography, we have made minor modifications to punctuation, language and spelling in order to improve readability.

2 Valachi, Joseph, *The Real Thing: Second Government - The Expose and Inside Doings of Cosa Nostra*, unpublished manuscript, John F. Kennedy Presidential Library and Museum, 1964, p. 285.

3 Valachi, *The Real Thing*, p. 305.

4 Valachi, *The Real Thing*, p. 323-325; Testimony of Joseph Valachi, Oct. 1, 1963, *Organized Crime and Illicit Traffic in Narcotics*, Part 1, Hearings before the Permanent Subcommittee on Investigations of the Committee on Government Operations (McClellan Committee), U.S. Senate, 88th Congress, 1st Session, Washington D.C.: U.S. Government Printing Office, 1963, p. 168, 172, 178, 190, 192.

5 Valachi testimony, McClellan Committee, p. 178.

6 United States Census of 1920, New York State, Bronx County, Harts Island Reformatory Prison, Assembly District 5, Enumeration District 369.

7 Nicola Capozzi Declaration of Intention, no. 14265, Supreme Court of Onondaga County, NY, June 26, 1928; Nicola Capozzi Petition for Citizenship, no. 11943, Supreme Court of Onondaga County, NY, at Syracuse, June 21, 1935; "Stabbed seven times in fight," *Syracuse Journal*, July 5, 1912, p. 6; "Italians fight with stilettos," *Syracuse Herald*, July 5, 1912, p. 3; "News of Syracuse," *Auburn Citizen*, July 6, 1912, p. 11. The declaration of intention stated a birthdate of July 4, 1886. The naturalization petition stated a birthdate of July 5, 1887.

8 "Gangster murders North Side food dealer," *Syracuse Journal*, June 21, 1919, p. 2; "Slayer says victim led holdup gang," *Syracuse Herald*, June 22, 1919, p. 16; North Side dealer slain in brawl," *Syracuse Post-Standard*, June 22, 1919, p. 1; "Statements given on Saturday murder," *Syracuse Herald*, June 23, 1919, p. 6; "Gallo pleads not guilty to murder charge," *Syracuse Herald*, June 24, 1919, p. 6.

9 "Widow to wed man who saw her husband slain," *Syracuse Post-Standard*, Aug. 25, 1919, p. 6; Nicola Capozzi and Crescenza Scarafino, New York State Marriage Index, certificate no. 46290, June 28, 1920.

10 "Seven Italians, alleged members of secret band, face charge of extortion," *Syracuse Journal*, Jan. 26, 1920, p. 2; "Zello brands Nick Capozzi Black Hander," *Syracuse Journal*, Feb. 17, 1920, p. 2; "Capozzi held in great fear, Zello testifies," *Syracuse Herald*, Feb. 17, 1920, p. 15; "Capozzi, found guilty, faces term in prison," *Syracuse Herald*, Feb. 19, 1920, p. 18; Nicola Capozzi, no. 37734, Auburn Prison Records, admitted July 14, 1920.

11 "Busy burglars get little," *Syracuse Journal*, Sept. 5, 1931, p. 11.

12 "Varied petitions in bankruptcy filed," *Syracuse Journal*, April 15, 1934, p. 16

13 "Citizenship is denied Capozi," *Syracuse Journal*, June 21, 1936, p. 14.

14 Crescenza Capozzi, New York State Death Index, 1956; Nicola Capozzi, New York State Death Index, 1959.

15 Bonanno, Joseph, with Sergio Lalli, *A Man of Honor: The Autobiography of Joseph Bonanno*, New York: Simon & Schuster, 1983, p. 96-97.

16 Hunt, Thomas, and Michael A. Tona, *DiCarlo: Buffalo's First Family of Crime, Vol. 1, to 1937*, Lulu Press, 2013, p. 255.

17 Critchley, David, "Gunmen of the Castellammarese War: 'Buster from Chicago' revealed to be Sebastiano Domingo," *Informer: The History of American Crime and Law Enforcement*, January 2012, p. 36-44.

18 Morello, Celeste, *Before Bruno: The History of the Philadelphia Mafia, Book 1, 1880-1931*, Morello, 1999, p. 94. With interviews of Harry Riccobene cited as her source, Morello stated that Sabella and "a crew of about nine" moved to New York City to aid Maranzano.

19 Valachi, *The Real Thing*, p. 6f-6f1.

20 Valachi, *The Real Thing*, p. 234.

21 Valachi, *The Real Thing*, p. 234; Frank Rocco, Sing Sing Prison Receiving Blotter, inmate no. 81933, received April 23, 1929.

22 Valachi, *The Real Thing*, p. 345.

23 Valachi, *The Real Thing*, p. 19.

24 Valachi, *The Real Thing*, p. 345.

25 Valachi, *The Real Thing*, p. 235.

26 Valachi, *The Real Thing*, p. 236-237.

27 Valachi, *The Real Thing*, p. 244.

28 Valachi, *The Real Thing*, p. 251.

29 Valachi, *The Real Thing*, p. 344-346.

30 Valachi, *The Real Thing*, p. 347-348.

31 Joseph Valachi Classification Study, register no. 82811-A, U.S. Department of Justice Bureau of Prisons, 1960.

32 "Take five armed men in an auto," *Hudson NJ Observer*, Nov. 10, 1921, p. 1.

33 United States Census of 1920, New York State, New York County, Manhattan Borough, Assembly District 18, Enumeration District 1229.

34 United States Census of 1920, New York State, New York County, Manhattan Borough, Assembly District 18, Enumeration District 1228; Joseph Pellegrino, no. 77626, Sing Sing Prison Receiving Blotter, received Oct. 16, 1925. Pellegrino was sentenced to prison in October 1925 after being convicted of a first degree robbery in the Bronx.

35 New York State Census of 1925, New York County, Assembly District 18, Election District 34.

36 "In the Hudson County courts," *Hudson NJ Observer*, May 11, 1922, p. 13; "No agreement in revolver case," *Jersey Journal*, May 11, 1922, p. 7.

37 "Admit they had gun in auto," *Jersey Journal*, Oct. 17, 1922, p. 9; "Court acquits woman in embezzlement case," *Hudson NJ Observer*, Oct. 18, 1922, p. 3; "Two years and fine are given Di Faro," *Hudson NJ Observer*, Oct. 20, 1922, p. 14.

38 "In the Hudson County courts"; "No agreement in revolver case."

39 Valachi, *The Real Thing*, p. 140.

40 A timeframe of the very late 1930s or early 1940s was indicated by Valachi (*The Real Thing*, p. 454) noting that both Dutch Schultz and Ciro Terranova were dead and Thomas Dewey was a threat to numbers racketeers. Schultz was murdered in 1935. Terranova passed away in 1938. While Valachi referred to Dewey as "Gov. Dewey," it seems likely he was referring to the period (1938 to 1941) when Dewey was Manhattan district attorney rather than the period (1943 to 1954) when he was governor. Earlier (*The Real Thing*, p. 453), Valachi stated that neither Vito Genovese nor Salvatore "Charlie Luciano" Lucania were in New York. Genovese was out of the U.S. between 1939 and 1945. Lucania was imprisoned in 1936. Put together, the comments suggest the period between 1939 and 1941.

41 Valachi, *The Real Thing*, p. 454.

42 Valachi, *The Real Thing*, p. 455.

43 Valachi, *The Real Thing*, p. 456, 459-460.

44 Valachi, *The Real Thing*, p. 462-463.

FEATURE 15

Getting the story printed

Deemed dangerous, Valachi's autobiography was suppressed by the White House

Though the Lyndon Johnson Administration initially endorsed a plan to publish Joseph Valachi's autobiography, political pressures caused the administration to quickly reverse course and block publication. When journalist Peter Maas attempted to publicize the details of Valachi's life story, the government sued to stop him.

Soon after Joseph Valachi began telling the secrets of "Cosa Nostra" to agents of the Federal Bureau of Narcotics (FBN) in the summer of 1962, officials of the John F. Kennedy Administration became excited about getting word out about Valachi's defection. As control of the informant passed from the Treasury Department's FBN to the Justice Department's FBI, officials mulled the options for disseminating the Valachi story.[1]

Valachi himself sought publicity, believing that exposure was the best way to damage the organized crime leaders, such as Vito Genovese, who Valachi felt had betrayed him and condemned him to death.[2]

Late that summer, Valachi was transferred from the FBN-preferred Westchester County Jail in New York to the Fort Monmouth military base in New Jersey. He was frequently visited at the base by FBI Special Agent James P. Flynn. William G. Hundley, chief of the Justice Department's Organized Crime and Racketeering Section, also visited the underworld turncoat.[3]

At one of their meetings, Hundley promised Valachi that his story would be widely released through public testimony and through a series of articles.[4] The DOJ, led by Attorney General Robert F. Kennedy, made Valachi information available to trusted writers, Peter Maas and Miriam Ottenberg.[5]

Articles by Maas and Ottenberg and others appeared in print in late summer 1963, while the U.S. Senate's Permanent Subcommittee on Investigations prepared to feature Joseph Valachi in televised hearings into organized crime. Part of that preparation was setting up a Valachi residence in the former "death house" on the top floor of the District of Columbia Jail.[6]

The hearings took place in late September and early October.[7] The following month, President John F. Kennedy was assassinated, and Lyndon B. Johnson was sworn in as the thirty-sixth President of the United States. President Johnson retained the late President's brother Robert Kennedy as DOJ head for a time, and DOJ continued to seek publicity for Valachi information.

Peter Maas

Peter Maas was born in New York City on June 27, 1929. He graduated from Duke University in 1949. About 1952, he was a journalist for the *New York Herald Tribune's* overseas office in Paris. He returned to New York several years later to become an entertainment writer for *Collier's* magazine.[35]

He began working for the *Saturday Evening Post* in 1963. The U.S. Department of Justice gave him access to Joseph Valachi files for an article he wrote on the U.S. Mafia in that year. Maas's reporting on Valachi's testimony before a U.S. Senate subcommittee was run in various newspapers.[36]

Maas worked with Joseph Valachi on the Valachi autobiography for several months in 1965-1966. The Department of Justice prevented publication of the autobiography, but Maas released *The Valachi Papers* late in 1968.[37]

In that year, Maas went to work for *New York Magazine*, as *The Valachi*

Papers became a best seller and had its movie rights purchased by Italian producer Dino De Laurentiis.

Maas went on to write additional popular books about crime and law enforcement, including *Serpico: The Cop Who Defied the System* (1973) and *Underboss: Sammy the Bull Gravano's Story of Life in the Mafia* (1997). He became a contributing editor of *Parade Magazine* in 1983.[38]

He died at Mount Sinai Hospital in Manhattan on August 23, 2001. The cause of death was complications following surgery for an ulcer. He was seventy two. He was survived by a his wife and their son and an ex-wife. A memorial service was held in his honor on November 12, 2001, with Frank Serpico, newsman Peter Jennings, Senator Fred Thompson and former New York Governor Hugh Carey among the speakers.[39]

Around June of 1964, Robert Kennedy's Justice Department officials urged Valachi to write a history of his underworld career. The officials told Valachi that the government would support publication of his memoirs.[8] However, Kennedy would not remain in the administration long enough to see the project completed. He resigned his position in September. Deputy Attorney General Nicholas deBelleville Katzenbach filled in as acting attorney general. Early in 1965, President Johnson named Katzenbach to fill the vacant attorney general post.[9]

Valachi had little formal education and was a clumsy writer, but he was highly motivated to tell his story in his own words. Over the course of thirteen months, he filled many hundreds of notepad pages with his often-rambling memories. He completed his manuscript around July 1965. His handwritten memoirs were typed up by Justice Department staff, producing about 1,200 typed pages.[10]

The plan to have the memoirs published faced some obstacles. Since June 1956, the DOJ and its Bureau of Prisons had a regulation prohibiting the publication of inmate autobiographical works. And, even if that regulation was waived, Valachi's work was an unwieldy length and largely unreadable.[11]

Apparently intending to suspend its regulation, DOJ permitted Valachi to begin working with Maas on the editing of his massive manuscript late in December 1965. DOJ Director of Public Information Jack Rosenthal communicated the news to Maas, and revealed several reasons the department was prepared to view a Valachi autobiography as an exception to the rule against inmate publication: Valachi wrote his life story at the specific request of the government, interest in the story had been sparked by Valachi's public testimony, publication of the book could serve the interests of law enforcement.

As it turned over typed copies of the manuscript, the DOJ had Peter Maas and Valachi's attorney sign a "Memorandum of Understanding," guaranteeing the department the right to approve the edited manuscript before it could be released:

> The Department retains the complete and absolute right to approve the final edited manuscript prior to publication or dissemination thereof in any form.[12]

In January of 1966, Maas sat down with Valachi for the first time. They met in Valachi's quarters in the District of Columbia Jail, and visits continued on a regular basis. Through a series of interviews, Maas hoped to be able to clarify vague portions of the manuscript, enhance discussions of greater interest to readers and provide the book with organization and more readable language. According to Maas, the two men met twenty-two times over the course of seventy-two days, talking for four or five hours each time.[13]

Less than a month into the process, word of the plan to publish Valachi's manuscript leaked. Many were critical of the project, feeling a Cosa Nostra tell-all would harm the reputations of the vast majority of Italian Americans, who were law-abiding citizens, and they brought their objections to their elected officials. Jack Valenti, a special assistant to President Johnson, handled the protests when they reached the White House.

Early in February, four members of Congress accompanied by a number of Italian-American civic leaders met with Katzenbach and DOJ officials William Hundley and Fred M. Vinson, Jr., to express their disapproval of the Maas project.

The administration considered the matter, and, despite the objections of Hundley and Vinson, decided that the Valachi manuscript must not be published.[14] One day after Maas signed an agreement with a literary agent to handle the marketing of the manuscript, Jack Rosenthal telephoned Maas with the bad news: "There was a substantial likelihood that publication would not be allowed and that further efforts toward publication might prove useless."[15]

The White House tried to reach some deal with Maas, but the writer would not bargain. Maas hired an attorney and, with the assistance of Hundley, he continued his visits with Valachi.[16] Understanding that the government had every right, under its existing regulations and the Memorandum of Understanding, to pull back the Valachi memoirs before publication, Maas became determined to use the remaining interviews to acquire much of the same information direct from Valachi. The government would have no legal right to the independently gathered data preserved in Maas's interview notes:

> ...During these sessions I had got Valachi to repeat all the key sections of his manuscript I intended to include in the book.[17]

Maas also moved ahead with plans to find a publisher for a completed book on Valachi. He created an outline of Valachi's life story. On March 14, 1966, without consulting the Justice Department, he sent the outline to his agent for use in communications with prospective publishers. On the fifteenth, he sent copies of the outline to be registered with the U.S. Copyright Office.[18]

On Thursday, March 16, the Department of Justice took action to halt publication. The attorney general filed an affidavit asserting that publication would be "detrimental to law enforcement" and a violation of Bureau of Prisons policy. The attorney general noted that Maas's dissemination of the unapproved outline made immediate action necessary.[19]

Notes to Maas

Several notes Valachi sent to Peter Maas are preserved with the Valachi manuscript at the Kennedy Presidential Library in Boston.

On February 16, 1969, Valachi acknowledged receipt of a copy of *The Valachi Papers*: "I received your book and I thank you very much. I like what Mr. Hundley and Bob Kennedy had to say. I am a Kennedy man and as you know if it were not from my experience in the underworld knowing who was who, meaning that I knew the honesty of the Kennedys, I would have not done what I done. Every man that I met in the Kennedy Adminstration was 100% honest..."

Valachi wrote about Robert Kennedy's campaign for President, which ended with his June 1968 assassination. Valachi said he was "100% for Bob Kennedy" and, likely referring to penpal Marie Jackson, he added, "I had Marie working hard for him." Regarding the death of crime boss Vito Genovese, just two days before the note was written, Valachi suggested it was more than merely coincident with the release of *The Valachi Papers*: "As soon as I heard that the book was to be published, I said to myself it will kill the old man. Sure enough."[40]

Around April of that year, Valachi sent an Easter card to Maas, in which he discussed plans to make a movie from *The Valachi Papers*. "Who is going to portray me in the movies?" he asked. He then made a suggestion for a star to play a former Valachi girlfriend: "N. Wood is a dead ringer of May."[41]

Early in May, Valachi penned an apology to Maas. He wasn't clear about the nature of his offense, only that he had been talked into signing some papers: "Mr. Hundley will explain to you how I came to sign those papers. The first thing that came out of my mouth was that I'm not going to hurt Peter. You can ask Mr. Hundley. ...Duffy assured me that it was your wish and Mr. Hundley's. You can believe me, I won't dare do anything like that otherwise. I'm sorry, Peter. Please forgive me."[42]

Valachi suddenly was removed from his comfortable suite atop the District of Columbia Jail the following Tuesday. He was taken more than five hundred miles away to the frigid federal prison at Milan, Michigan. Maas interpreted the move as retribution:

> It would be discovered that I was still meeting with Valachi, and the Government, unable to stop me, took it out on him instead; officials whisked him away from the relative comfort of the District of Columbia jail to a prison in Michigan...[20]

On April 6, the Mafia turncoat received official word that the planned publication of his memoirs had been called off. Three days later, a desperate Valachi attempted to use an electrical cord to hang himself in his prison shower. When the cord broke, Valachi suffered a number of bruises and a loss of consciousness but survived.[21]

As Valachi recovered from the suicide attempt, Maas was permitted to visit him in Milan:

> When I saw him, he still had a deep, ugly red line running three-quarters of the way around his neck where the cord had left its mark. His left ankle was still quite swollen after catching the force of his fall. Both knees and his left shoulder were black and blue from slamming to the sides and floor of the [shower] stall.[22]

Maas brazenly sent word to the Justice Department on May 4, 1966, that he would begin sending book outlines to prospective publishers in one week's time. The department responded in court, seeking an injunction to prevent the circulation of the outlines and demanding the return of the Valachi manuscript.[23]

During a hearing, the Justice Department's counsel was questioned about the extent of the government's concern. The attorney's response suggested that the DOJ was interested far more in separating itself from the book project than it was in seeing that the book not be published at all:

> We certainly concede that [Maas] can write a book. And if there are any publishers listening, he can write a biography of Valachi... The injunction just relates to this book... it just relates to this manuscript, nothing beyond.[24]

Maas later revealed that the attorney's concession on that point was made to satisfy a judge who was troubled by the idea of government action to prevent publication of a book.

A preliminary injunction was granted. The court found that the government was "threatened with immediate and irreparable harm for which it had no adequate remedy at law." It stated that publication of the memoirs could cause damage to the government and the public interest which "far outweighed any possible injury" to Maas.[25]

While apparently cleared to author his own work based on his interviews with Valachi, Maas appealed the injunction. He did not explain his reason for doing so, but possibly he felt a book authored by Valachi with Maas as editor would be more of a sensation than a book authored by Maas.

The writer set to work on his own manuscript, incorporating material from Valachi interviews with material from other sources, including crime reports from police, FBN and FBI, as well as an account of the struggles with fickle government officials.[26]

On November 25, 1966, The U.S. Court of Appeals for the District of Columbia backed the government injunction, requiring that Maas comply with the Memorandum of Understanding and publish no part of the Valachi memoirs without DOJ approval.[27]

Through much of 1967 and into 1968, Maas learned that book publishers were not eager to associate themselves with the story of Valachi's life and criminal career. There was no data on the marketability of a Mafia tell-all – it had never been done in the U.S. before. "Twenty two publishers turned down the book," Maas recalled. "The message at the time was that the Mafia didn't sell. Even G.P. Putnam's Sons, the house that finally bought it, did so only because of the insistence of one iconoclastic editor there, Arthur C. Fields."[28]

The publisher released *The Valachi Papers* in the days after Christmas, 1968, considered a "dead" period for retail. Sales of the book were surprising. According to Maas, "the book was an instant critical and commercial success." A *New York Times* review by Emanuel Perlmutter praised Maas's efforts:

> He has produced a narrative that is exciting as well as informative, as fascinating as fiction, a bloody history of the Mafia as lived by one of its members for three decades.[29]

Eventually, the book became an international best-seller and was used as the foundation for a financially successful motion picture. Joseph Valachi received a prison allowance generated from a share of book and movie proceeds, though the Internal Revenue Service siphoned off more than $10,000 of that for back taxes owed by Valachi.[30]

The location of Valachi's original manuscript – the document that supposedly could have caused "immediate and irreparable harm" to the government – was uncertain for some time. When Valachi passed away in 1971, it was speculated that the manuscript would become the property of Marie Jackson of Niagara Falls, New York, named as beneficiary in Valachi's will.[31]

Almost a decade later, the lengthy manuscript turned up in the possession of Peter Maas. He apparently had not surrendered it at the time of the court actions in 1966. On December 24, 1980, Maas donated one copy of Valachi's handwritten manuscript (1,075 pages) and one copy of the typed manuscript (1,180 pages), along with some handwritten pages of communication received from Valachi, to the John F. Kennedy Presidential Library in Boston.

In his "Deed of Gift" to the Kennedy Library, Maas expressed his desire "that the materials be made available for research as soon as possible, and to the fullest extent possible…"[32]

On December 30, Henry Gwiazda of the National Archives wrote a memorandum further explaining Maas's gift:

Maas is donating to the National Archives various papers he acquired while writing *The Valachi Papers*... Joseph Valachi wrote the holograph manuscript entitled *The Real Thing: The Expose and Inside Doings of Cosa Nostra* and entered into an agreement with Maas to edit and publish the manuscript. Valachi ultimately received $75,000.00 as his share of the royalties from *The Valachi Papers*.

Valachi died in 1971. He had a will, and his estate went through the normal probate procedures. According to Maas' attorney, no question from Valachi's heirs about the rights to the manuscript or copyright arose during the settlement of the estate. Maas, therefore, has had the manuscript and accompanying transcript since 1965 without anyone questioning his right to the material.[33]

The Valachi memoirs remain available to researchers at the John F. Kennedy Presidential Library and Museum. A portion of the typed pages can be viewed online at the JFK Museum's website. The full text of the document has been available on The American Mafia (*mafiahistory.us*) website since November 2020.[34]

Valachi writes in his cell. (Thibaut Maïquès collection)

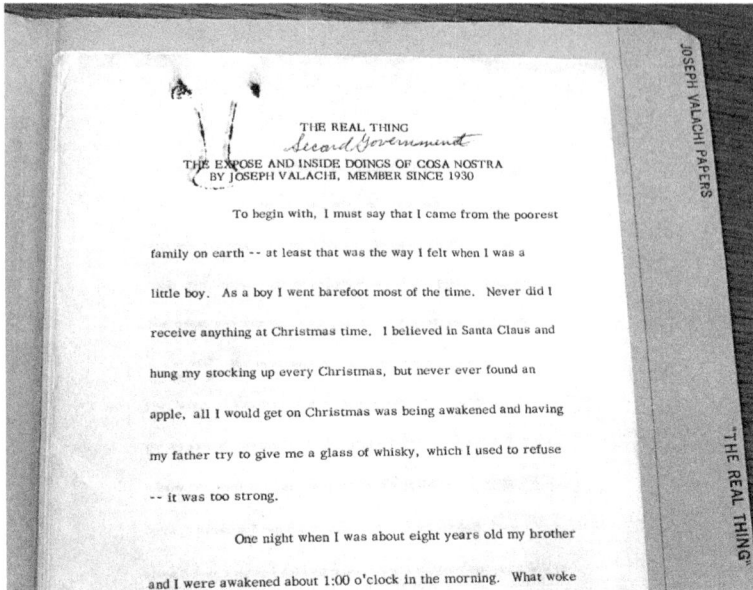

Typed page from Valachi memoirs. (JFK Library)

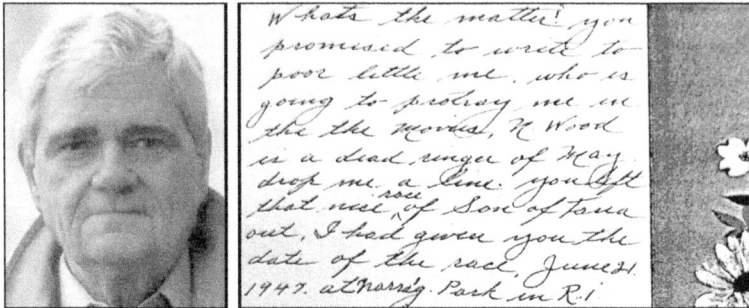

Peter Maas (left). Easter card sent to Maas by Valachi. (JFK Library)

Feature 15 Notes

1 William G. Hundley, recorded interview by James A. Oesterle, Feb. 22, 1971, Robert F. Kennedy Library Oral History Project of the John F. Kennedy Library, p. 49; Edwin O. Guthman Oral History Interview - JFK #1, Feb. 21, 1968, John F. Kennedy Presidential Library and Museum, jfklibrary.org, p. 18.

2 Maas, Peter, *The Valachi Papers*, New York: G.P. Putnam's Sons, 1968, p. 45; DeLoach, Cartha D., *Hoover's FBI: The Inside Story by Hoover's Trusted Lieutenant*, Washington, D. C. : Regnery Publishing, 1995, p. 313.

3 DeLoach, *Hoover's FBI*, p. 310, 313; Hundley recorded interview, p. 49-50; Maas, *The Valachi Papers*, p. 44-45.

4 Evans, C.A., "La Causa Nostra, Criminal Intelligence Matters," FBI Memorandum to Mr. Belmont, file no. 92-6054-227, NARA no. 124-10284-10232, May 1, 1963.

5 DeLoach, C.D., "The *Washington Star* feature article dealing with La Cosa Nostra by Miriam Ottenberg," FBI Memorandum to Mr. Mohr, file no. 82-6-54-375, 376, NARA no. 124-10220-10072, July 31, 1963.

6 Maas, *The Valachi Papers*, p. 46.

7 Testimony of Joseph Valachi, *Organized Crime and Illicit Traffic in Narcotics*, Part 1, Hearings before the Permanent Subcommittee on Investigations of the Committee on Government Operations, U.S. Senate, 88th Congress, 1st Session, Washington, D.C.: U.S. Government Printing Office, 1963.

8 Maas, *The Valachi Papers*, p. 9-10.

9 "Letter accepting resignation of Robert F. Kennedy as attorney general," The American Presidency Project: Lyndon B. Johnson, presidency.ucsb.edu; "Historical biography: Attorney General: Nicholas deBelleville Katzenbach," Department of Justice, justice.gov, Oct. 24, 2022.

10 Maas, *The Valachi Papers*, p. 9-10.

11 Maas v. United States, U.S. Court of Appeals, District of Columbia Circuit, 371 F.2d 348 (D.C. Cir. 1966), decided Nov. 25, 1966; Maas, The Valachi Papers, p. 11.

12 Maas v. United States; Maas, *The Valachi Papers*, p. 11.

13 Maas, *The Valachi Papers*, p. 49.

14 Maas, *The Valachi Papers*, p. 16-17.

15 Maas v. United States.

16 Maas, *The Valachi Papers*, p. 17.

17 Maas, Peter, "The White House, the Mob and the book biz: Footnotes to *The Valachi Papers*," *New York Times*, Oct. 12, 1986, Section 7 (Book Review), p. 3.

18 Maas v. United States.

19 Maas v. United States.

20 Maas, "The White House, the Mob and the book biz."

21 Hayes, Loy S., "Memo of phone call from Warden Sartwell, Milan," Federal Bureau of Prisons, April 11, 1966, in Carr, Charlie, *New York Police Files on the Mafia*, Hosehead Productions, 2012, p. 570; Walsh, Robert, and Henry Lee, "Valachi testifies about 3 hijack suspects," *New York Daily News*, April 24, 1968, p. 3; Maas, *The Valachi Papers*, p. 54-55.

22 Maas, *The Valachi Papers*, p. 55.

23 Maas v. United States.

24 Maas v. United States.

25 Maas v. United States.

26 Perlmutter, Emanuel, "*The Valachi Papers*," *New York Times Book Review*, Jan. 12, 1969, p. 41; Maas, *The Valachi Papers*, p. 20.

27 Maas v. United States.

28 Maas, "The White House, the Mob and the book biz."

29 Perlmutter, "*The Valachi Papers*."

30 "Tax lien placed on Valachi share of book on Mafia," *New York Times*, Jan. 18, 1969, p. 22; Gage, Nicholas, "Will of Valachi is filed upstate," *New York Times*, Aug. 25, 1971, p. 24.

31 Gage, "Will of Valachi is filed upstate."

32 Maas, Peter, "Gifts of papers and other historical materials," Deed of Gift to the John F. Kennedy Library, Dec. 24, 1980.

33 Gwiazda, Henry, "Gift of papers of Peter Maas," Memorandum to Robert Warner and Maygene Daniels,

General Services Administration, John F. Kennedy Library, National Archives and Records Service, Dec. 30, 1980.

34 Joseph Valachi Personal Papers, John F. Kennedy Presidential Library and Museum, jfklibrary.org; "Valachi's *The Real Thing*," The American Mafia, mafiahistory.us/a023/therealthing.htm.

35 Barron, James, "Peter Maas, writer who chronicled the Mafia, dies at 72," *New York Times*, Aug. 24, 2001, p. 17.

36 Maas, Peter, "Mafia: The inside story," *Saturday Evening Post*, Aug. 10-17, Issue no. 28, 1963; "Still to be told by Valachi: early fights for Mafia power," *Buffalo Evening News*, Sept. 30, 1963, p. 8.

37 Maas, "The White House, the Mob and the book biz."

38 Weiler, A.H., "DeLaurentiis buys 'Valachi' film rights," *New York Times*, Feb. 27, 1969, p. 34; Barron, "Peter Maas, writer who chronicled the Mafia, dies at 72."

39 Barron, "Peter Maas, writer who chronicled the Mafia, dies at 72; "Memorial for Peter Maas," *New York Times*, Nov. 11, 2001, p. 1.

40 Valachi, Joseph, Letter to Peter Maas, Feb. 16, 1969, Joseph Valachi Personal Papers, John F. Kennedy Presidential Library and Museum.

41 Valachi, Joseph, Easter card to Peter Maas, undated, Joseph Valachi Personal Papers, John F. Kennedy Presidential Library and Museum. The date of the card is assumed to be spring 1969, as it mentions the recent release of The Valachi Papers and Peter Maas's promotional appearance on television.

42 Valachi, Joseph, Letter to Peter Maas, May 1, 1969, Joseph Valachi Personal Papers, John F. Kennedy Presidential Library and Museum.

MOB CORNER

End of Days

By Thom L. Jones

This is how it might have been...

It's hard work being Joe Valachi.

Sitting in his prison cell, just this side of the Texas border from Ciudad Juarez, he spends his days in reflection. A lot.

La Tuna is a federal penitentiary, medium security. It's on Doniphan Road, near the small town of Anthony, in El Paso County, Texas.[1] The Bureau of Prisons moved him here in September 1968. It was his third move after his time in Washington, DC, and 1963's great Mafia bean fest that grabbed America by the throat for days and reintroduced millions of Americans to the strange, mystical world of the Mafia.

The word earlier became common knowledge across the country in 1950 and 1951 when the Kefauver Hearings, a senate special senate investigation into interstate crime, revealed a world of gangsters and hoodlums that apparently existed as almost a second government.[2]

The star witness in the 1963 hearings is Joe, giving his version of an organization he calls Cosa Nostra, the way the mob refers to itself. He claims. He's been a member, part of it since 1930, so knows a great deal. "Our thing," or "this thing of ours," is perhaps the way Joe and his peers spoke of each other, but across America, the Mafia as a noun seemed to mean different things, depending where you found yourself.[3]

However this thing of ours is interpreted, it's amounting to the same thing. A bunch of crooks doing what crooks do best, except the Mafia is a lot more than the sum of its parts. Law enforcement, at most levels, including the FBI, struggle to understand it. Until Joe Valachi rolls and becomes a government informant. He reveals a lot of secrets, exposing a collection of hidden information. It is *Aufklärung*, squared. The German word for enlightenment does not do it justice.

Guarded by US Marshals, Joe gives testimony over four days and becomes the first person in the United States to be offered government protection for testimony. He did not disappoint.[4]

He remembers how warmly Senator McClellan, the chairman of the senate hearing, had greeted him and counselled him during his thirty-one hours of testimony.[5]

And then it was all over.

Following his evidence, he knows he must continue to serve a life sentence for a murder he had committed while in prison at Atlanta Penitentiary, in June 1962.[6] Six years later, he arrives at his final destination, a prison closer to Mexico than to what he knows as "America."

Back in his past, there is a woman who lives closer to Canada than "America," and she is not his wife.

Prediction is a vexing game. Tring to figure a future based on a past that really never had a present makes forecasting more a thing of chance that a science. Did he really meet Marie at that party in Niagara Falls in 1958, or was it some kind of dream? Did they connect in New York and enjoy the delights of America's biggest city as he wines and dines her, buying her presents? She is twenty years younger, and not the first woman he's dallied with, and his marriage to Mildred is long gone.

Such an old-fashioned English name, Mildred. Christened Carmela after her birth in 1906, her father, Gaetano Reina, is the boss of one of the early New York Mafia clans, based in The Bronx. She is the eldest child, and she falls for Joe, who is then a foot-soldier in her father's mob. They marry two years after her father is murdered, maybe by a man called Vito Genovese, who will come to play such a significant part in future events, waiting to fill Joe's life with endless misery.

In 1932, later in the year of his marriage, he receives his first hit as part of the Luciano mob, the third and final Mafia family he transferred into in 1931.

He chooses two men who had been inducted with him, Peter Mione, aka Petey Muggins, and John Di Bellis, known as Johnny D, as the actual shooters and he arranges a meet with the target, he knew only as "Little Apples," one Michael Reggione. They agree to connect at a coffee shop on 110th Street in Harlem, and just before the meeting, the killers shoot the target, whose body is discovered on November 25th.[7] Like all the men he kills for his boss, whoever that was at the time, the dead are an inevitable by-product of the life they live.

He's spent his whole being living dangerously. A man of quiet desperation. From a miserable childhood in the slums of East Harlem, where he is born in 1904, he comes from what he recalls as "the poorest family on earth," through a life of juvenile crime, into the maelstrom of the Mafia underworld that sucks him into not one or even two but three Mafia families before he's thirty.[8]

Stealing, hi-jacking, extortion and murder. Lots of murder. *Dies Irae*, days of wrath and terror looming, the Latin hymn on The Last Judgement could be a battle cry for people like Joe, living their days of uncertainty, fraught with frustrations, terrors and complexities.

It's all leading, inevitably, to somewhere bad. Mark Twain once said, "Everyone is a moon, and has a dark side which they never show to anybody." Joe knows men like him are on the dark side their whole lives.

It's hard work being Joe Valachi.

He remembers trying to kill himself back in 1966 in the prison in Milan, in Michigan. He's been there briefly, in solitary. Attempts to hang himself. Feeling depressed, sick of the cold draughts in his cell. Enough, already.[9]

Sixty-six might also have been the year Marie Jackson contacts him and starts her correspondence campaign. By then, he had written his long, rambling story following a request in 1964 by the Department of Justice. They wanted him to get it down on paper. His life. He calls it *"The Real Thing."* Over a thousand pages. He hopes it's all worthwhile. It is.[10]

Joe meets Peter Maas, the writer from New York, who visits him while he's still held in Washington. That was early in the year, before the move to Michigan. He writes this book about Valachi and his life in the mob, which is a really big seller, and Joe gets a lot of money as his part of the deal. Most of it, of course, goes to the government, as Joe was never big on paying taxes.[11]

Whatever is left goes to this woman, Marie, who continues to communicate with him at La Tuna prison.

By early 1970, Joe is beginning his twelfth year behind bars. Although he has a two-room suite, with air conditioning and couches and a television and cooking facilities, it's still a prison cell.

At least Vito Genovese is gone. The previous year, on the day when lovers around the world unite, he dies of a heart attack in a federal prison hospital in Springfield, Missouri.[12]

Joe's nemesis for almost his entire mob-life, Genovese, a man of Byzantine bent, raises treachery, guile and deceit to a mind-numbing height as he fights his way up the ladder, striving to become the boss of bosses of all America's Cosa Nostra. Although he and his wife Anna were the signed witnesses to the wedding of Joe and Mildred, showing how close were the links, he was always a dark shadow, and Joe would learn to his cost that the most dangerous of enemies was the one that walked beside him as a friend.[13]

Genovese triggers the events that force Joe into making a wrong decision, killing a man he thought was his enemy in the prison yard at Atlanta Penitentiary. From that point, destiny takes over and, like Ogden Nash, Joe has a bone to pick with fate.[14]

The day Joe mistakenly kills John Joseph Saupp, beating him around the head seven times with a lead pipe and gets arrested for his murder, may well be the day the music dies for Cosa Nostra. It is all downhill from that point on. In the social clubs of New York where mobsters congregate, the word everywhere is "*sta rompendo*," our thing is broken.

For Joe, it is a case of acute embarrassment. On the murder, Valachi, a long-time mob hit man, remembers saying, "You can imagine my embarrassment when I killed the wrong guy."[15]

He recalls killing a lot of the right ones, though. He knows the government claims the number is thirty-three and maybe they are right. Then again.

Sometimes, especially towards the end, as his sentence segues into 1971, he will sit on the prison patio, reserved for trustees and inmates of good conduct, catching the sun, watching the hawks circling in the endless sky. *The Big Sky*, as Bud Guthrie called it.[16]

Maybe he wonders if all those years and all his undertakings are simply a punctuation mark in a life's story which, in the greater picture, is just a microscopic interlude in the march of mankind.

This late in his life he's suffering from various ailments – arthritis, high blood pressure – the worst, prostate cancer. He remembers writing the last words of his biography, "I am alone in the world. I write to no one in my family. As the world knows, they disown me and I don't blame them."[17]

Vinnie Teresa, a mob boss from New England, is another government informant lodged in La Tuna, although he is in C Block, along with other inmates. He spends time with Joe, helping him through the bad days, listening to Joe's ramblings, how much he enjoys hearing from Marie, how much she has supported him through all these years.[18]

It's hard work being Joe Valachi.

And then it's not.

On Saturday, April 3rd, 1971, he suffers gall bladder pain. The prison doctor sedates him with a shot of morphine, and he dies late in the afternoon. His official cause of death is listed as myocardial infarction, colloquially known as a heart attack.[19]

It's now the strange story of Marie Jackson unravels.

She is born in 1926 and, as Marie K. Murray, grows up in Niagara Falls. After completing high school, she works as office manager at Amberg's, the menswear store on Falls Street in the major business and entertainment district in the city. She marries a man who works at the shop, but after three years, they call it quits.

According to her, she meets Joe at a party in The Falls, and they spend time together. Then he leaves, and that is that. Like millions of Americans, the television coverage of the McClellan Hearings fascinates her, along with Joe's testimony about his life in the mob, and it is this that spurs her to write to him.

Antonio Ruedas Fields of the Texas State Department of Health signs the death certificate on Joe.

Mildred, the ex-wife, and his son Donald want nothing to do with the burial arrangements.

Marie contacts the authorities and arranges for Joe's body to be shipped to her three days after his death and Fields also signs off the transit permit to ship the body to Niagara Falls.[20]

Marie arranges a simple ceremony at Our Lady of Carmel Church in Niagara Falls, and she buries Joe on a grassy knoll, in plot 64, a mile from the river, in The Gate of Heaven Cemetery in Lewiston. Marie pays $254 for Joe's plot, but hers, beside him, only costs her $115. Even in death, there seems to be deals to be done.

In the only interview she ever gives to a reporter from *The Buffalo News*, she claims, "After Joe died, I cried for a long time."

Marie is well known to the local police as someone who frequently contacts them with the skinny on mob activities in Niagara Falls. She works in a porn shop as duty manager, so maybe crosses paths with all the wrong people. The police know she is often seen in bars and lounges frequented by gangsters, but they write her off as some kind of nut or mob groupie.

Ironically, perhaps, she buries Joe in a cemetery that is just a few hundred yards from the home, at 5118 Dana Drive, of Stefano Maggadino, the longest serving Mafia boss in America who will die in 1974 and be waked from his own funeral chapel.[21]

Marie's daughter, Karen Carlino, of Youngstown, Ohio, confirms with the reporter that her mother and Valachi maintained a long relationship through correspondence, and claims to have the letters in her possession.[22]

Marie Jackson dies May 28, 1999 in Niagara Falls Memorial Hospital, after a long illness.[23]

Whatever else Joe will carry in his haversack of life, there must be room, perhaps a lot, for guilt.

About the failure of his marriage and the break-up of his family. The business ventures that flounder. The laws he breaks, the people he kills, and the collateral damage to their families. Above all, guilt surrounds him like a London Fog, for the brutal murder of an innocent man in a prison yard in Georgia.

His existence has been a complicated journey for a man who rose from almost complete obscurity to a level of fame and notoriety, for all the wrong reasons. All the difficulty and trauma and loss Joe has experienced throughout his life is perhaps always edging him to look back into the past to help him find the links that will make him feel more secure with the future.

As Gillian Reynolds observed, "The arithmetic of ordinary life becomes the algebra of universal human experience."[24]

La Tuna Prison

VALACHI LEAVES ESTATE TO PEN PAL

Property Valued at Between $5,000 and $10,000

Joseph Valachi, the Mafioso turned government informant, left an estate estimated between $5,000 and $10,000 in a will probated Thursday in Niagara County Court at Lockport, N. Y.

NY Times, Aug. 28, 1971.

"The tragedy of life is not death, but what we let die inside of us while we live."

- Norman Cousins.

Mob Corner Notes

1 "FCI La Tuna," Federal Bureau of Prisons, bop.gov.

2 "Special Committee on Organized Crime in Interstate Commerce, (The Kefauver Committee)," United States Senate, senate.gov.

3 Finkenauer, James O., "United Nations Activities: La Cosa Nostra in the United States," U.S. Department of Justice, Office of Justice Programs, December 2007, ojp.gov.

4 "Portraits in oversight: Congress investigates the Mafia," Levin Center Home, June 1, 2023, levin-center.org.

5 "Investigations: Killer in prison," *Time*, Oct. 4, 1963.

6 *New York Daily News*. April 24, 1968.

7 Mass, Peter, *The Valachi Papers*, New York: G.P. Putnam's Sons, 1968.

8 *The Valachi Papers*.

9 *New York Daily News*. April 24, 1968.

10 The JFK Presidential Library in Boston, Massachusetts, holds the document, which runs to over 1,000 pages.

11 *The Valachi Papers*.

12 *New York Times*, Feb. 15, 1969.

13 Certificate and Record of Marriage, No 15917, City of New York, June 24, 1932.

14 Nash, Ogden, "Lines on Facing Forty."

15 "John Joseph Saupp," *Mafia Stories*, February 2017, mafiasome.blogspot.com.

16 Guthrie, A.B. Jr., *The Big Sky*, New York: William Sloane Associates, 1947.

17 Valachi, Joseph, "Valachi's The Real Thing – Part 4 of 4," The American Mafia, mafiahistory.us.

18 Teresa, Vincent, and Thomas C. Renner, *My Life in The Mafia*, New York: Doubleday & Co, 1973.

19 Jones, Thom L., "Catching the Bounce: The Story of Joseph Valachi," Gangsters Inc., May 18, 2017, gangstersinc.org.

20 *Naples Daily News*, April 5, 1973.

21 *Naples Daily News*.

22 *Buffalo News*, Dec. 6, 2020.

23 *Buffalo News*, June 5, 1999.

24 Coldstream, John, *Dirk Bogarde: The Authorised Biography*, Phoenix, 2005.

FEATURE 16

Valachi's exit

Much was omitted from official reports

The New York newspapers of April 4, 1971, reported that Joseph Valachi had died of a "heart attack" the previous day. The *New York Daily News* suggested, "It was an incongruously peaceful end for a professional killer who had run with the mobs since he was 15…"[1] While the final narcotic-dulled seconds of Valachi's troubled life must have been tranquil, his last moments of full consciousness were tortured.

Officials of La Tuna Federal Correctional Institution announced that Valachi passed away at ten minutes before noon on Saturday, April 3. Valachi had been an inmate of the facility in El Paso County, Texas, since the summer of 1968, living apart from other prisoners, taking meals separately and exercising separately. Aside from two hours of outdoor recreation daily, he spent his time reading, watching television and exercising.

When the local newspaper, the *El Paso Times*, reported on Valachi's death, it stated the cause as "heart failure." That apparently was the wording used by La Tuna Warden William E. Zachem.[2] The difference between "heart attack" and "heart failure," while medically significant, was not explored by the press.[3]

After conducting an autopsy, medical authorities used neither term on Valachi's certificate of death. The certificate stated that death was caused by "severe atherosclerotic cardiovascular disease."[4] The notation fills the form line reserved for "Cause." No entries were made in three remaining sections reserved for related factors and contributing conditions.

The result of plaque accumulation in arteries, atherosclerosis reduces blood flow and may lead to heart attack and/or heart failure. It may also lead to stroke.[5] The terse reporting of the medical authorities may give an accurate picture of the clinical condition that led to Valachi's death, but it did not specifically indicate the event that took his life.

Compared to the sparse information in the form's cause of death section, its signature area was overly congested. Several names and signatures were crammed in there, including E.M. Donowho Jr., Dr. Lee Morton and Albert A. Mestan.[6]

Mestan was the El Paso County registrar and judicial officer who noted receipt of the certificate in May 1971. A former Army officer, who first settled in El Paso in 1949, Mestan won election as an El Paso justice of the peace in 1970.[7]

Morton was a medical doctor, perhaps responsible for the Valachi autopsy. His typed name lines up with the address of Anthony, Texas, and the date of April 5, 1971. In addition to being the location of La Tuna prison, the town of Anthony was the longtime home of Dr. Morton's medical practice.[8]

Donowho's name aligns with the notation, "MAJ, M.C. William Beamont Gen Hosp, El Paso, Tex." The abbreviations suggest that Donowho was an officer in the U.S. Army Medical Corps, assigned with the hospital at Fort Bliss, about twenty five miles from the prison. Donowho also was a medical doctor. He is recalled as one of the coauthors of a 1970 *New England Journal of Medicine* article describing "Sudden death in sickle-cell trait."[9]

Witness

Vincent Charles Teresa, a former New England mobster who became a government informant, was also held at the La Tuna prison beginning in the spring of 1970 and became close to Valachi. He wrote about that in a 1973 autobiography, *My Life in the Mafia*.

According to Teresa, Valachi was suffering in those days with a variety of ailments:

> He had cancer, high blood pressure, gall bladder trouble, and prostate gland trouble. He was in pain all the time with arthritis, and he was always cold. It could be 110 degrees outside, but inside his room it would be 130 because he had all the electric heaters turned on…[10]

Teresa reported that he saw Valachi on the morning of April 3. Valachi was violently ill with vomiting and diarrhea. He asked to see Teresa, and the guards brought Teresa to his room. Teresa helped clean and settle the famous prisoner:

> There I was, cleaning him up, wiping the dirt off him, washing him, putting clean pajamas on him. Then he'd do it all over again and I'd change him again as well as the sheets to his bed.[11]

Valachi was vomiting a greenish bile, Teresa stated. Panicked by his affliction, Valachi became certain that he was dying. There was no doctor at the facility on Saturdays. Guards rushed in "some sort of medic," who assisted Teresa in getting Valachi cleaned up and as comfortable as possible. Seeing Valachi's condition, the medic concluded that he was experiencing a gall bladder attack, Teresa recalled.

The medic gave Valachi "a shot of morphine and something else," and Valachi went to sleep. Teresa was called away. He later learned that Valachi died moments after he left the room.[12]

Unexplained

Strangely, the official certificate of death made no mention of the violent illness or the medic-administered injections which immediately preceded Valachi's death. There appears to be good reason to question whether the several individuals – Donowho, Morton and Mestan - who signed off on the certificate were fully informed of the situation witnessed by Teresa. None of the signers appears to qualify as the medic remembered by Teresa.

The Valachi symptoms reported by Teresa could have been triggered by the atherosclerosis reported on the certificate. Diminished blood flow could have resulted in severe damage to his digestive organs. In the form of peripheral artery disease, this affliction also may have contributed to Valachi's inability to get warm.[13]

Attempts were made in March 2024 to resolve the differences in the accounts of Valachi's last moments.

The La Tuna Federal Correctional Institution advised that it maintains no historical records related to Joseph Valachi and recommended that a Freedom of Information request be sent to the archives of the Federal Bureau of Prisons.[14]

A request was made to the Bureau of Prisons on March 18. It was given a reference number and assigned to the central office. Communication was sent to the office on April 4 to focus the request on the final twenty four hours of Valachi's life in the prison. Government Information Specialist Sandy Raymond responded two weeks later, stating that records relating to Valachi probably no longer exist:

> Please be advised federal inmate records have a retention period of ten (10) years after expiration of sentence, and are thereafter scheduled for disposal. Since the records you are requesting appear to be older than ten years, it is likely they have been destroyed. However, a search will still be conducted to confirm whether or not there are any records responsive to your request.

The specialist explained that archives in a field office would need to be examined to determine if the records still exist. The search was completed by July 29, at which time the Bureau of Prisons stated that no records relating to Valachi's time at La Tuna could be located: "The information you request no longer exists as the retention period has passed."[15]

STATE OF TEXAS 071-09-2 3120-00 CERTIFICATE OF DEATH 412.4 3 STATE FILE NO. **32917**

1. PLACE OF DEATH			2. USUAL RESIDENCE (Where deceased lived. If institution; residence before admission)		
a. COUNTY	El Paso		a. STATE New York	b. COUNTY New York	
b. CITY OR TOWN (If outside city limits, give precinct no.) La Tuna, Tex. USPHSH, FCI	c. LENGTH OF STAY in 1 b. 2 years		c. CITY OR TOWN (If outside city limits, give precinct no.) Bronx		
d. NAME OF (If not in hospital, give street address) HOSPITAL OR INSTITUTION FCI, La Tuna, Texas, USPHSH			d. STREET ADDRESS (If rural, give location) 45 Shawnee Avenue		
e. IS PLACE OF DEATH INSIDE CITY LIMITS? YES☐ NO☒			e. IS RESIDENCE INSIDE CITY LIMITS? YES☒ NO☐	f. IS RESIDENCE ON A FARM? YES☐ NO☒	

3. NAME OF DECEASED (Type or print)	(a) First JOSEPH	(b) Middle M.	(c) Last VALACHI	4. DATE OF DEATH April 3, 1971		
5. SEX Male	6. COLOR OR RACE White	7. Married☒ Never Married☐ Widowed☐ Divorced☐	8. DATE OF BIRTH 9-22-04	9. AGE (in years last birthday) 66	IF UNDER 1 YEAR Months Days	IF UNDER 24 HRS. Hours Minutes
10a. USUAL OCCUPATION (Give kind of work done during most of working life, even if retired) Management	10b. KIND OF BUSINESS OR INDUSTRY Dress Company		11. BIRTHPLACE (State or foreign country) Manhattan, New York		12. CITIZEN OF WHAT COUNTRY? United States	
13. FATHER'S NAME Dominick Valachi (Deceased)			14. MOTHER'S MAIDEN NAME Mary Casali Valachi (Deceased)			
15. WAS DECEASED EVER IN U.S. ARMED FORCES? (Yes, no, or unknown) No	16. SOCIAL SECURITY NO. None Listed	(If yes, give war or dates of service)	17. INFORMANT Institution Record Files			

18. CAUSE OF DEATH (Enter only one cause per line for (a), (b), and (c).)		INTERVAL BETWEEN ONSET AND DEATH
PART I. DEATH WAS CAUSED BY:		
IMMEDIATE CAUSE (a) SEVERE ATHEROSCLEROTIC CARDIOVASCULAR DISEASE		
Conditions, if any, which gave rise to above cause (a) stating the under- lying cause last. DUE TO (b)		
DUE TO (c)		
PART II. OTHER SIGNIFICANT CONDITIONS CONTRIBUTING TO DEATH BUT NOT RELATED TO THE TERMINAL DISEASE CONDITION GIVEN IN PART I(a)	19. WAS AUTOPSY PERFORMED? YES☒ NO☐	

TEXAS DEPARTMENT OF HEALTH
REC'D MAY 25 1971
BUREAU OF VITAL STATISTICS

20a.	ACCIDENT☐	SUICIDE☐	HOMICIDE☐	20b. DESCRIBE HOW INJURY OCCURRED. (Enter nature of injury in Part I or Part II of item 18.)		
20c. TIME OF INJURY	Hour a.m. p.m.	Month	Day	Year		
20d. INJURY OCCURRED WHILE AT WORK☐ NOT WHILE AT WORK☐	20e. PLACE OF INJURY (e.g., in or about home, farm, factory, street, office building, etc.)		20f. CITY, TOWN, OR LOCATION		COUNTY	STATE

21. I hereby certify that I attended the deceased from April 3, 19 71 to April 3, 19 71 and last saw the deceased alive on April 3, 19 71 . Death occurred at 11:50 A.m. on the date stated above, and to the best of my knowledge, from the causes stated.

22a. SIGNATURE E.M. Donowho Jr. CMAJ, M.C. Dr. Lee Morton M.D.	22b. ADDRESS William Beaumont Gen Hosp, El Paso, Tex Anthony, Texas	22c. DATE SIGNED 4-5-71
23a. BURIAL, CREMATION, REMOVAL (specify) REMOVAL	23b. DATE -APRIL 6, 1971	23c. NAME OF CEMETERY OR CREMATORY 614 WELLINGTON ROAD, EL PASO, TEXAS
23d. LOCATION (City, town, or county) NIAGARA FALLS, NEW YORK	(State)	24. FUNERAL DIRECTOR'S SIGNATURE Salazar Funeral Home
25a. REGISTRAR'S FILE NO. M-3	25b. DATE REC'D BY LOCAL REGISTRAR 20 May 1971	25c. REGISTRAR'S SIGNATURE

Joseph Valachi death certificate.

Vincent Teresa.

Feature 16 Notes

1 "Valachi dies in jail; bared mob secrets," *New York Daily News*, April 4, 1971, p. 3; "Joseph M. Valachi, informer, dies at 67," *New York Times*, April 4, 1971, p. 69.

2 "Joseph Valachi, informer, dies in La Tuna," *El Paso TX Times*, April 4, 1971, p. 1; "Officials seek kin to claim Valachi," *Passaic NJ Herald-News*, April 5, 1971, p. 4. A former deputy associate commissioner of Federal Prison Industries, Zachem was named warden of La Tuna Prison in 1970, replacing Lox S. Hayes. The appointment was announced early in July, and Zachem's arrival was noted in two months later. Zachem retired from the post in June 1973 and was replaced by James Riggsby.

3 Rees, Mathiew, "Heart attack vs. heart failure: What to know," *MedicalNewsToday*, medicalnewstoday.com, reviewed by Payal Kohli, M.D., April 20, 2021.

4 Joseph M. Valachi Certificate of Death, State file no. 32817, El Paso County, Texas Department of Health Bureau of Vital Statistics, April 3, 1971, received May 25, 1971.

5 "What is atherosclerosis?" National Heart, Lung and Blood Institute, National Institutes of Health, nhlbi.nih.gov, "Atherosclerosis," Cleveland Clinic, clevelandclinic.org, last reviewed Feb. 15, 2024.

6 Joseph M. Valachi Certificate of Death.

7 "GOP, Dems tell stands," *El Paso TX Herald-Post*, Oct. 27, 1970, p. 11; "Split decision given in EP election case," *El Paso TX Times*, Dec. 5, 1970, p. B1.

8 "Gigantic estate sale of Dr. Lee Morton...," *El Paso TX Times*, classified advertisement, April 18, 2004, p. 50.

9 Jones, Stephen R. M.D., Richard A. Binder M.D. and Everett M. Donowho Jr. M.D., "Sudden death in sickle-cell trait," *New England Journal of Medicine*, Vol. 282, No. 6, Feb. 5, 1970, nejm.org.

10 Teresa, Vincent, with Thomas Renner, *My Life in the Mafia*, Garden City NY: Doubleday & Company, 1973, p. 322.

11 Teresa, *My Life in the Mafia*, p. 325-326.

12 Teresa, *My Life in the Mafia*, p. 326-327.

13 "Intestinal ischemic syndrome," UC Davis Health Vascular Center, health.ucdavis.edu, Dec. 14, 2018; "Gallbladder gallstone disease is associated with newly diagnosed coronary artery atherosclerotic disease: A cross-sectional study," PloS One, National Library for Medicine, National Institutes for Health, Sept. 18, 2013, ncbi/nlm.nih.gov; "Peripheral artery disease," Mayo Clinic, mayoclinic.org, June 21, 2022. Atherosclerosis has been linked with serious gall bladder and intestinal problems. There seems to be both an indirect link, as these ailments may all spring from accumulation of cholesterol, and a more direct link in which atherosclerosis cuts off blood supply to digestive organs. If blood flow is impeded, the resulting intestinal ischemic syndrome can cause pain, frequent vomiting, urgent diarrhea and other dire symptoms.

14 LAT-ExecAssistant-S (BOP), La Tuna FCI email to Thomas Hunt, March 18, 2024.

15 Raymond, Sandy, Board of Prisons email to Thomas Hunt, April 18, 2024; Lilly, S., "Request Number: 2024-02711," U.S. Department of Justice Federal Bureau of Prisons, July 29, 2024.

FEATURE 17

Last will and testament of Joseph Valachi

Joseph Valachi composed his last will and testament in the spring of 1967, while he was in the Federal Correctional Institution at Milan, Michigan. In contrast with the extraordinarily lengthy autobiography he wrote in 1964-1965, the will was just a page and a half. It was penned about a year after Valachi – desperately unhappy over his transfer to Milan and the government's withdrawal of permission to publish his book – tried to take his own life. The bruises he suffered in the attempted hanging had healed, and author Peter Maas was moving ahead with plans to publish Valachi's story, but the famous informant still had death on his mind.

The document, signed by Valachi on May 23, 1967, named "Marie Katherine Ann Jackson" of 2433 Willow Avenue in Niagara Falls, New York, as Valachi's executor and primary beneficiary. The will merely identified Miss Jackson. It did not describe her connection to Valachi.

It also did not list much in the way of the assets to be left to her. At that moment, Valachi possessed very little, but he was entitled to a share of income generated by Maas's planned book.

On the same date, Valachi signed a publishing contract related to the book and created an *inter vivos* trust to handle the expected proceeds. He noted in the will that upon his death all his assets would be given to Miss Jackson. If she was not still alive, the assets would go to her mother Grace Murray Allen of the same address.

The will was witnessed by three prison employees, John Kuslak, Gene Freeman and Robert L. Hendricks.[1]

About a year after making out his will, Valachi was transferred from the chilly and drafty Milan facility he hated to the more agreeable (for him) desert climate of La Tuna Federal Correctional Institution in the town of Anthony, Texas.[2] *The Valachi Papers* was published a few months later and became a best-seller in 1969.

Before his death, Valachi knew of plans to turn the Maas book into a movie, which also would add significantly to the assets he was leaving to Marie Jackson. He died about a year before production of the movie started. He passed away at the La Tuna prison on April 3, 1971.

While Valachi's remains were transported to Jackson in Niagara Falls a few days later, his last will and testament was not filed with Niagara County Surrogate's Court until midday on July 12, more than three months later. The filing was handled by attorney Bernard Sax of the Niagara Falls firm of Sbarbati and Sax. He had been in possession of the will for several years after its delivery to him by an attorney who had represented Valachi in Washington, D.C.[3]

Noting that the witnesses to the will were not New York residents and would not be available to testify, Sax provided a letter from Milan Warden James D. Henderson, stating the assigned locations and duties of those prison employees.

Freeman was the only witness remaining at the Milan prison. He served as "chief of classification" there. John Kuslak had been given a new assignment at the Medical Center for Federal Prisoners in Springfield, Missouri. Hendricks was moved to a Bureau of Prisons office on Indiana Avenue N.W., in Washington, D.C.[4]

An affidavit from witness Gene Freeman was completed on August 9. He noted that he was present when Valachi signed the will and knew Kuslak and Hendricks were there also.[5]

Late in August, Sax filed with the court an affidavit describing difficulties related to officially notifying Valachi's legal wife Carmela "Mildred" Reina Valachi and their grown son Donald of the probating of Valachi's will:

> I spoke several times on the telephone to Assistant Attorney General Cripe and Kischbaum, the Bureau of Prisons, Washington, D.C., concerning the problem of probating this will as it pertained to decedent's widow and son. Finally on April 30, 1971, I wrote a letter enclosing a Waiver of Citation to Mr. Cripe who had assured me that after consultation with the FBI they would present it to these two distributees and have the waiver executed. The FBI, I had learned previously from Mr. Cripe, were adamant in not disclosing the address of the widow or son for obvious security reasons.

Sax submitted to the court the completed and notarized waiver of citation dated May 18, 1971, and bearing the signatures of Mildred and Donald Valachi.[6]

Surrogate's Court Judge John V. Hagan deemed Valachi's will valid and approved Marie Jackson as Valachi's executor in the afternoon of August 26.[7]

Some additional documents were added to the probate file in October. At that time, the Buffalo law firm of Barth, Sullivan and Lancaster submitted "notices for enforcement of judgment," requiring Jackson to pay a total of $7,087 plus interest on an old debt to Amberg & Company, Inc., of Falls Street in Niagara Falls. The debt related to a legal judgment from May 9, 1967, two weeks before Valachi created his will.[8]

The reason for the debt is not noted. Amberg & Company was the name of a longtime menswear store in the Niagara Falls business district. Sources suggest that Jackson was once an employee of the Amberg store.[9]

LAST WILL AND TESTAMENT
OF
JOSEPH VALACHI

I, JOSEPH VALACHI, being of sound and disposing mind, memory and understanding, and domiciled and intending to reside in the State of New York, do hereby make, publish and declare this as and for my last Will and Testament, hereby revoking any and all wills or other writings of a testamentary nature by me at any time heretofore made.

FIRST: I leave my bodily remains for burial to, and in a manner in the discretion of my Executrix, hereinafter named, and direct my Executrix, or anyone duly appointed in her stead, to pay all my just debts, expenses of my last illness and expenses of my funeral and burial, including an appropriate marker, as soon after my death as may be convenient and practical. I further direct that all succession, legacy, inheritance, transfer and estate taxes levied or assessed by any jurisdiction upon or with respect to any property which is included as part of my gross estate for the purpose of any such tax shall be paid by my Executrix out of my estate in the same manner as an expense of administration and shall not be prorated

or apportioned among or charged against the respective devisees, legatees

or beneficiaries, nor charged against any property passing to them; and my Executrix shall not be entitled to reimbursement from any person for any portion of any such tax.

SECOND: All the rest, residue and remainder of my estate, consisting

of all property of every nature owned by me at my death or acquired by my estate and not effectively disposed of at my death or by the preceding articles of this Will, including but not limited to any trust funds subject to the power of appointment under the inter vivos trust I have this day created, and any proceeds of the publishing contract I have this day executed, I give, devise and bequeath, absolutely and in fee simple, as follows:

(A) To MARIE KATHERINE ANN JACKSON, of 2433 Willow Avenue, Niagara Falls, providing she survives me.

(B) If the said MARIE KATHERINE ANN JACKSON, of 2433 Willow Avenue, Niagara Falls does not survive me, then to her mother, MRS. GRACE MURRAY ALLEN, of the same address.

(C) If neither the said MARIE KATHERINE ANN JACKSON nor the said MRS. GRACE MURRAY ALLEN survives me, then to whomsoever the said MARIE KATHERINE ANN JACKSON may appoint either by will or other writing duly acknowledged during her lifetime.

THIRD: I nominate, constitute and appoint MARIE KATHERINE ANN JACKSON as Executrix of this Will. I give to my Executrix, during the administration of my estate, without license or approval of any court, full power and authority to sell, convey, lease, mortgage or otherwise encumber or dispose of any real property or other asset of my estate upon any terms whatsoever;

Joseph Valachi May 23. 1967

First page of Joseph Valachi's will.

Feature 17 Notes

1 Valachi, Joseph, Last will and testament, May 23, 1967, Joseph Valachi Probate File, no. 37509, Niagara County NY Surrogate's Court.

2 "Valachi dies in jail; bared mob secrets," *New York Daily News*, April 4, 1971, p. 3; "Joseph Valachi, informer, dies in La Tuna," *El Paso TX Times*, April 4, 1971, p. 1; "Joseph M. Valachi, informer, dies at 67," *New York Times*, April 4, 1971, p. 69.

3 Sax, Bernard, "In the matter of proving the last will and testament of Joseph M. Valachi," affidavit, Aug. 26, 1971, Joseph Valachi Probate File. Bernard J. Sax was born June 18, 1906, in Jersey City, NJ. He settled in Niagara Falls in 1932, two years after graduating from Columbia University Law School. Sax served as an Army investigator in the Philippines during World War II. He was a partner in Sbarbati & Sax from the 1950s until retirement in 1984. He died Jan. 29, 1987, at the age of 80 in Buffalo's Veterans Hospital. See: "Bernard J. Sax, Falls attorney, is dead at 80," *Buffalo News*, Jan. 30, 1987, p. 8; Index of Births in New Jersey, Jersey City, 1902-06; Bernard Julius Sax World War II Draft Registration Card, serial no. 149, order no. 840, Local Board no. 583, Niagara Falls, NY, Oct. 16, 1940.

4 Henderson, James D., Letter to Sbarbati & Sax Law Offices, May 25, 1971, Joseph Valachi Probate File.

5 Freeman, Gene, "In the matter of proving the last will and testament of Joseph M. Valachi," affidavit, Aug. 9, 1971, Joseph Valachi Probate File.

6 Sax, "In the matter of proving the last will and testament of Joseph M. Valachi."

7 Hagan, Judge John V., "In the matter of proving the last wil and testament of Joseph M. Valachi," Decree of Probate, Aug. 26, 1971, Joseph Valachi Probate File.

8 Barth, Philip C., "Estate of Joseph M. Valachi #37509," Letter to Surrogate;s Court of the County of Niagara, Oct. 19, 1971, Joseph Valachi Probate File; Amberg & Company, Inc., against Marie Jackson, Restraining notice to judgment debtor, Supreme Court, County of Niagara, Sept. 24, 1971, Joseph Valachi Probate File. The amount of $7,087 in May 1967 is equivalent to about $67,000 in current U.S. dollars.

9 Farrell, Cecil, "'Mystery woman' arranged for burial of Joe Valachi," *Naples FL Daily News*, April 1, 1973, p. 9; Michel, Lou, "Falls woman tells of love affair with hit man," *Buffalo News*, June 25, 1995; Hudson, Mike, "Mystery woman took secrets to grave," *Niagara Falls Reporter*, Jan. 20, 2009. Amberg's store was located on Falls Street between First and Second streets. A popular pool hall, "Empire Billiards," occupied the floor above it for many years. Much of the traditional downtown business district was replaced in the 1970s by construction related to the Niagara Falls Convention and Civic Center. The area was again altered around 2000 by the Seneca Niagara Casino & Hotel and related construction and by the new Niagara Falls Convention Center, which sits on the block formerly occupied by Amberg's.

FEATURE 18

Marie Jackson
mysteries remain

Much about the relationship between Joseph Valachi and Marie Katherine Jackson still remains a mystery more than five decades after it concluded with Valachi's passing.

Some details have been established. Valachi is known to have corresponded with Jackson, a resident of Niagara Falls, New York, while he was held in federal custody as a convicted murderer and narcotics trafficker during the final years of his life. He named Jackson in his will as the executor and beneficiary of his estate. Following his death, Jackson took charge of Valachi's remains and had the famous Mafia turncoat transported from Texas to western New York and quietly buried at Gate of Heaven Cemetery in Lewiston, New York, near Jackson's home.[1]

However, we do not know for certain if Valachi and Jackson ever met before Valachi became an incarcerated informant or if they ever met at all or if there was any plan to move their relationship beyond that of pen pals.

The details of Jackson's life story suggest that she grew up largely without a father figure, exhibited a long-term fascination with organized crime and had only brief personal experience with married life. These factors may have caused her to admire Valachi and to engage in a mutually supportive but safely distanced relationship through the mail.

Before Valachi

Jackson was born Marie Murray in Niagara Falls, New York, on December 18, 1926, to Eugene F. and Grace Reid Murray.[2]

Eugene Murray was originally from the town of Le Roy in New York's Genessee County. He grew up there in a large farming family. He was inducted into the U.S. Army in March 1918, received some mechanical training at the Aviation School of Kelly Field outside of San Antonio, Texas, and served overseas from the summer of 1918 through the end of the war and into spring of 1919. Following his honorable discharge in June 1919, he began work as an auto mechanic in Niagara Falls.[3]

Grace Reid's birthplace was the village of Alexandria Bay along the St. Lawrence Seaway in New York's Jefferson County. Her father, Canadian citizen Charles Vought Reid, appears to have been a fluid engineer. At an early age, the Reid household relocated to Lancaster, an eastern suburb of the city of Buffalo, where Charles Reid was contracted to work on sewer projects. Upon U.S. entry into the First World War, the Reids were residents of Niagara Falls, and Charles Reid was employed as a foreman at the Reid and Coddington Engineering Company.[4]

On November 29, 1922, Eugene Murray and Grace Reid were joined in marriage in a civil ceremony before Niagara Falls Justice of the Peace George E. Carrie. The newlyweds set up their first home at 1511 Whitney Avenue in Niagara Falls. Marie was the third of four children born to Eugene and Grace Murray, and may have lived the earliest years of her life at the Whitney Avenue address.[5]

If so, and if that fact was later explained to her, that could help explain some of her later interest in organized crime figures. Whitney Avenue was in that period the home address of a number of important western New York mafiosi originally from Castellammare del Golfo, Sicily.

Regional Mafia boss Stefano Magaddino purchased property on the next block to the east in 1922 and had his family home built at 1653 Whitney Avenue. Early Mafia leader "Don Simone" Borruso and Magaddino in-law Gaspare DiGregorio lived on the same street during the 1920s. Paul Palmeri's address in that decade was 1525 Whitney Street, just a few doors from the Murray home.

Eugene Murray died of pneumonia at Mount St. Mary's Hospital on January 16, 1929. He was just thirty three. The Murray family resided at 341 Eighth Street in Niagara Falls at the time of Eugene's death.[6]

Grace Reid Murray remarried within the year. On September 28, 1929, she and Thomas Edward Allen, a motorman originally from Garbutt, Monroe County, were married by Le Roy Justice of the Peace Francis Matthews. Thomas Allen joined the former Murray family in its Eighth Street home in Niagara Falls. But he would not be there very long.[7]

The 1930 United States Census found him living there with Grace and his four stepchildren. Marie was three years old then. By the time of the 1940 Census, he was gone, but Grace and the four children, including thirteen-year-old Marie, remained at 341 Eighth Street. An item in the New York State Death Index for 1930 stated that a Thomas E. Allen of Niagara Falls died in mid-May of 1930, about a month after the taking of that year's census.[8]

This evidence suggests that, by the age of three, Marie had lost both her father and her stepfather. Grace apparently did not make another attempt at marriage.

Six days after her nineteenth birthday, Marie Murray exchanged vows with Alfred Jackson at Niagara Falls. A daughter Karen Jackson was born to the couple in the following year, 1946. Soon after that, the marriage dissolved. Sources indicate that the difficult union between Marie and Alfred Jackson was annulled for religious reasons.[9]

Continuing to use her married surname of Jackson, Marie was noted in the 1950 U.S. Census as a resident of 408 Elmwood Avenue in Niagara Falls. Her daughter Karen was with her. The head of that household was Marie's mother Grace. Also residing there were Marie's twenty-six-year-old brother and a lodger. Within a couple of years, the family relocated to 3026 Panama Street. That remained the home of Grace Allen and Marie Jackson at least through 1955.[10]

What Marie did for a living in the period is uncertain. One report suggested she worked as a clothing store salesperson. Another said she was a department store bookkeeper. She later worked as a sales clerk in an adult bookstore.[11]

Pen pals

Marie Jackson reportedly began writing to the imprisoned Valachi well after his autumn 1963 televised testimony before the McClellan Committee. Their correspondence and their growing affection for each other were not known to the press or the public.

Looking back after Valachi's 1971 death, Jackson's attorney Bernard Sax estimated that the pen pal relationship began in 1966, after Valachi was transferred from the Washington D.C. Jail to a federal prison at Milan, Michigan.

Valachi biographer Peter Maas later revealed that many people wrote to the former mafioso following the McClellan hearings. "Most of them were women," Maas said. "Miss Jackson was the most constant, writing as often as twice a week at times."[12]

Maas also pointed to 1966 as the moment the exchange of letters between the two began. He noted that Valachi was dangerously depressed following arrival at the Milan facility. He reportedly attempted suicide in April 1966, shortly after the move.

"Miss Jackson's letters lifted his spirits," recalled Maas, who was also communicating with Valachi by mail at the time. "When she would not write for a while, he would go back into depression and accuse the Justice Department of holding her letters."[13]

In addition to her letters, Jackson also sent Valachi some money and gifts, according to a source within the Justice Department. That source specifically stated that Jackson and Valachi never met.[14]

Valachi wrote out his will in spring 1967, while held at Milan. At that time, he had no communication with his wife Mildred or their grown son Donald. He decided to leave whatever he had to his faithful pen pal Marie Jackson. She was named the primary beneficiary, and her mother Grace was named as secondary beneficiary. No assets were enumerated in the document. At that moment, Valachi had very little of any worth, aside from a rambling autobiography he was legally prevented from publishing and a hope that a book produced in cooperation with Peter Maas would find an audience.[15]

In spring of 1968, Valachi served as a prosecution witness in the Brooklyn hijacking trial of Carmine "the Snake" Persico, Jr., and four others. His testimony included mentions of a "girlfriend" named Marie, but it did not provide any detailed information.[16] By the end of that summer, the Bureau of Prisons acceded to Valachi's request for a warmer climate than Milan, Michigan, and he was moved to La Tuna Federal Correctional Institution north of El Paso.[17] Though the distance between them increased by to nearly two thousand miles, their postal romance endured. The relationship appears to have grown to include occasional telephone calls.

The Valachi Papers by Peter Maas was officially released by publisher G.P. Putnam's Sons late in December of 1968 and reached bookstore shelves early in January, 1969. It quickly became a best seller. Maas and Valachi shared in the royalties. Though the IRS staked a claim to a good portion of Valachi's money and Valachi reportedly sent some to his estranged family, thousands of dollars went into a Valachi account. Prison rules prevented him from spending more than $15 a month at the commissary, so much remained untouched.[18]

A copy of the 1967 will was sent to Jackson in 1969.[19]

Mystery woman

Valachi, age sixty six, died at La Tuna on April 3, 1971. Prison officials notified his apparently disinterested wife and son. Valachi's body remained unclaimed for days.[20]

On April 6, authorities revealed that the body had been claimed, but they refused to provide any details. Warden William E. Zachem told the press, "Joseph Valachi's wishes were that his burial was to be handled as inconspicuously as possible" The warden said the body was being shipped to an undisclosed location.[21]

It took journalists about a month to learn that Valachi had been transported on an American Airlines plane from Texas to Niagara Falls, New York, and that he had been buried without ceremony in an unmarked grave at Gate of Heaven Cemetery, in Lewiston, New York.

Pressured for confirmation, the federal Bureau of Prisons acknowledged the body was "claimed by a Niagara Falls woman who requested anonymity." A spokesman for Gate of Heaven confirmed that Valachi was buried somewhere in its cemetery on April 7.[22]

Noting an area of disturbed ground with no grave marker, investigative reporters were able to identify Valachi's final resting place as Plot 64 of the St. Matthew Section:

There is no tombstone, no temporary marker, not even grass on the freshly-turned earth. There was one overturned, green, plastic pot of wilted geraniums carrying a $2.69 price tag, and some hay strewn over the dirt.[23]

Very quickly, reporters discovered that the transportation and burial arrangements had been overseen by Marie Jackson of Niagara Falls. At that time, they knew nothing about her. They succeeded in finding Jackson's home, 2433 Willow Avenue, about four miles from the Lewiston gravesite, but found that she was not there. She was said to be staying in Buffalo and using an assumed identity there to avoid the hounding of the media.[24]

Pieces of the puzzle began to fall in place, even as reporters encountered lingering information roadblocks at the Bureau of Prisons, the Catholic Diocese of Buffalo, American Airlines and the Rhoney Funeral Home of Niagara Falls, New York.[25] Late in August, *New York Times* crime reporter Nicholas Gage wrote of the filing of the Valachi will for probate at Niagara County Surrogate's Court in Lockport, New York. In his article, Gage included comments from Peter Maas and attorney Bernard Sax about the length of the pen pal relationship between Jackson and Valachi. Sax explained that the U.S. government paid for the basic funeral expenses.[26]

There were no quotes in the story from Marie Jackson. Her attorney said she was out of town and could not be reached. A few days later, the New York Times reported that Jackson was vacationing in the Canary Islands.[27]

In that article, the *Times* revealed that Valachi's estate was then valued at between $5,000 and $10,000 (roughly $38,000 to $76,000 in 2024 dollars).[28] According to the newspaper, the IRS already had taken the taxes owed by Valachi, and Valachi earlier had sent about $10,000 to his wife Mildred. The estate also was in line to benefit from a movie deal arranged by Maas.[29]

More about Marie

While Marie Jackson protected her privacy for years, stories about her began to surface in the local and national press.

According to one report, Jackson had made herself familiar to Niagara Falls police. Jackson "on many occasions called them and told them she had information on certain mob operations in Niagara Falls but was always written off as 'some kind of a nut.'"

Police reportedly observed her at various bars accompanied by suspected underworld figures. "...They always felt she cultivated them out of perverse desires."

A journalist with the *Niagara Falls Gazette* recalled receiving a telephone tip from a local woman who was planning that day to fly to Texas to marry Valachi. She said federal officials were prepared to release the couple into protective custody at a remote army compound where they could set up housekeeping. That call was received the morning of Valachi's death.[30]

Grace Allen passed away on September 20, 1981. For a time into the early 1990s, Marie Jackson resided at 638 Twenty-first Street in the Little Italy section of Niagara Falls.[31] By the early summer of 1995, the sixty-eight-year-old Jackson was a resident at a nursing home. At that time, she became interested in telling her story to the press.[32]

The story she told did not fit very well with the authoritative accounts released earlier, but in many ways it was a better explanation for the strong and mutually beneficial connection between her and Valachi. Jackson claimed that she first met Valachi many years earlier at the home of a mutual friend in Niagara Falls. She said their relationship grew from that moment. "Joe was always good to me. He gave me gifts and money, and we took a lot of trips. When he went to prison, I wrote to him every day."[33]

Her mention of trips and gifts signaled a pre-prison romance. Except for transportation between federal lockups, Valachi had not made any trips since 1962. (Even before that, his travels were generally confined to the Northeast U.S. and nearby Canada.) While he was known to give money and presents to women friends before his incarceration, the $15 a month federal inmate allowance prevented him from any lavish gift-giving in more recent times.

Jackson said she was visited by gangsters following Valachi's televised testimony in 1963. She described the visit as a sort of threat concealed within a promise of security: "They said to me, 'We'll take care of things.' That was their way of speaking, but the mob left me alone."[34]

That encounter suggested that gangsters connected her to Valachi three years before prison officials, Maas and Sax said the Valachi-Jackson correspondence began, five years before she was referred to – but not fully identified – in the Persico trial testimony and eight years before she was outed as Valachi's executor and beneficiary. This, too, suggested that a relationship existed between the two before the letters, before the testimony, even before Valachi went to prison.

The death of Valachi was devastating for Jackson. "After Joe died, I cried for a long time. I didn't bother with anyone or anything. When I die, I will be buried beside him." Jackson told her interviewer that she purchased a burial plot for herself beside Valachi's at Gate of Heaven and invested $254 for two, small, stone grave markers.

In a futile effort to confirm the surprising details of Jackson's story, the reporter reached out for comment to Jackson's daughter Karen. Her only statement was unhelpful: "It was something that happened. It's in the past, and we're trying to forget about it." Jackson said her collection of letters from Valachi had been entrusted to Karen. Unfortunately, Karen was determined not to release them to the press.[35] Viewing the earliest of the letters might have helped to confirm or to disprove Jackson's tale of an in-person relationship. Without access to the correspondence and lacking the statement of anyone who witnessed a relationship, the story has been accepted as fact by some and dismissed as fantasy by others.

Marie K. Jackson passed away on May 28, 1999. Her grave marker shows through the cemetery grass next to Joseph M. Valachi's.[36]

'It was something that happened'

We are prevented from knowing which parts of Marie Jackson's story and the stories told about her were true and which were fabricated. We can only speculate on the reasons she was drawn to underworld characters and entered into a long-distance romance with a career criminal and convicted killer. We may imagine various reasons that Valachi entrusted Jackson with his final arrangements and awarded her everything he possessed of value at the time of his death.

The reader is free to decide whether the Valachi-Jackson drama deserves to be labeled a classic tragedy. The participants probably did not consider it one. Valachi may have felt it was a personal triumph. Deprived late in life of his freedom, his friendships and his family, as well as his riches and his reputation, Valachi was able to establish a remote link with someone who saw in him both virtue and value.

Jackson, who had ample cause to view the masculine figures in her life as merely temporary and untrustworthy, in her final moments may have viewed the affair as a victory for the strength and permanence of love.

Jackson's home in 1971. (Newsday)

Feature 18 Notes

1 "Valachi leaves estate to pen pal," *New York Times*, Aug. 28, 1971, p. 29.

2 Marie K. Murray, New York State Birth Index, Niagara Falls, certificate no. 95258, Dec. 18, 1926; Marie K. Jackson, 071-20-1617, Social Security Death Index, May 28, 1999.

3 Eugene Francis Murray World War I Draft Registration Card, no. 119, Precinct 3, Le Roy, NY, June 5, 1917; New York State Census of 1905, Genessee County, Le Roy, Election District 1; Eugene F. Murray, serial no. 1058427, Abstracts of World War I Military Service; Eugene Murray and Grace Reid Marriage License, Niagara Falls, Niagara County, registered no. 491, Nov. 29, 1922.

4 Grace Allen, 071-14-3944, Social Security Death Index, Sept. 1981; Thomas E. Allen and Grace Mae Murray Marriage License, Town of Le Roy, Genessee County, registered no. 95, New York State Department of Health, Sept. 28, 1929; United States Census of 1910, New York State, Erie County, Town of Lancaster, Village of Lancaster, Enumeration District 286; Charles Vought Reid World War I Draft Registration Card, serial no. 6390, order no. A5596, Niagara Falls, NY, Sept. 12, 1918.

5 Eugene Murray and Grace Reid Marriage License, Niagara Falls, Niagara County, registered no. 491, Nov. 29, 1922; United States Census of 1930, New York State, Niagara County, Niagara Falls, Ward 2, Enumeration District 32-39.

6 "Niagara Falls, Eugene Murray," *Buffalo Times*, Jan. 18, 1929, p. 1.

7 Thomas E. Allen and Grace Mae Murray Marriage License, Town of Le Roy, Genessee County, registered no. 95, New York State Department of Health, Sept. 28, 1929; Thomas Edward Allen World War I Draft Registration Card, serial no. 814, order no. N753, Monroe County, NY, Sept. 12, 1918.

8 United States Census of 1930, New York State, Niagara County, Niagara Falls, Ward 2, Enumeration District 32-39; United States Census of 1940, New York State, Niagara County, Niagara Falls, Ward 2, Enumeration District 32-54; New York State Death Index 1930, certificate no. 29313, May 13, 1930.

9 Alfred Jackson and Marie Murray, New York State Marriage Index, Niagara Falls, certificate no. 44141, Dec. 24, 1945; Karen J. Carlino, 072-38-8667, Social Security Death Index, Sept. 13, 2011; Karen J. Carlino, U.S. Obituary Collection, 1930-Current, Ancestry.com; Michel, Lou, "Falls woman tells of love affair with hit man," *Buffalo News*, June 25, 1995; Hudson, Mike, "Mystery woman took secrets to grave," *Niagara Falls Reporter*, Jan. 20, 2009.

10 United States Census of 1950, New York State, Niagara County, Niagara Falls, Enumeration District 68-59; *Polk's Niagara Falls City Directory 1952*, Buffalo: R.L. Polk & Co., 1953, p. 6, 206; *Polk's Niagara Falls City Directory 1955*, Buffalo: R.L. Polk & Co., 1955, p. 7, 255.

11 "Falls woman tells of love affair with hit man"; Farrell, Cecil, "'Mystery woman' arranged for burial of Joe Valachi," *Naples FL Daily News*, April 1, 1973, p. 9.

12 Gage, Nicholas, "Will of Valachi is filed upstate," *New York Times*, Aug. 25, 1971, p. 24.

13 "Valachi leaves estate to pen pal," *New York Times*, Aug. 28, 1971, p. 29.

14 "Valachi leaves estate to pen pal."

15 Valachi leaves estate to pen pal"; "Falls woman tells of love affair with hit man"; Demma, Joseph, and Tom Renner (of *Newsday*), "Lone mourner buries Valachi," *Boston Globe*, May 6, 1971, p. 1; "Mysterious Marie buries a mobster," *Rochester Democrat and Chronicle*, May 7, 1971, p. 6A; Demma, Joe, and Tom Renner, "Valachi grave located upstate," *Newsday* (Nassau), May 8, 1971, p. 3; Gage, Nicholas, "Will of Valachi is filed upstate," *New York Times*, Aug. 25, 1971, p. 24.

16 "Lone mourner buries Valachi."

17 Maas, Peter, *The Valachi Papers*, New York: G.P. Putnam's Sons, 1968, p. 53; "Officials seek kin to claim Valachi," *Passaic NJ Herald-News*, April 5, 1971, p. 4; "Joseph Valachi, informer, dies in La Tuna," *El Paso TX Times*, April 4, 1971, p. 1; "Valachi dies in jail; bared mob secrets," *New York Daily News*, April 4, 1971, p. 3.

18 "Tax lien placed on Valachi share of book on Mafia," *New York Times*, Jan. 18, 1969, p. 22; Maas, *The Valachi Papers*, p. 54.

19 "Will of Valachi is filed upstate."

20 "Joseph Valachi, informer, dies in La Tuna"; "Valachi dies in jail; bared mob secrets"; "Lone mourner buries Valachi"; "Officials seek kin to claim Valachi," *Passaic NJ Herald-News*, April 5, 1971, p. 4.

21 "Valachi body gets claimed," *New York Daily News*, April 7, 1971, p. 89; "Valachi body claimed in secret move," *Arizona Daily Star*, April 7, 1971, p. 10; "Claimant gets Valachi's body, details secret," *Fort Worth TX Star-Telegram*, April 7, 1971, p. 9.

22 "Lone mourner buries Valachi"; "Valachi burial upstate bared," *New York Daily News*, May 7, 1971, p. 74.

23 Demma, Joe, and Tom Renner, "Valachi grave located upstate," *Newsday* (Nassau), May 8, 1971, p. 3.

24 "Lone mourner buries Valachi"; "Mysterious Marie buries a mobster," *Rochester Democrat and Chronicle*, May 7, 1971, p. 6A

25 "Lone mourner buries Valachi"; "Mysterious Marie buries a mobster"; "Valachi burial upstate bared."

26 Gage, Nicholas, "Will of Valachi is filed upstate," *New York Times*, Aug. 25, 1971, p. 24. Bernard Sax gave a different timeline for the burial, indicating that the remains were flown in from Texas on May 6 rather than April 6, and buried on May 7 rather than April 7.

27 "Valachi leaves estate to pen pal," *New York Times*, Aug. 28, 1971, p. 29.

28 CPI Inflation Calculator, bls.gov.

29 "Valachi leaves estate to pen pal."

30 Farrell, Cecil, "'Mystery woman' arranged for burial of Joe Valachi," *Naples FL Daily News*, April 1, 1973, p. 9.

31 Grace Allen, 071-14-3944, Social Security Death Index, Sept. 1981; Marie K. Jackson, U.S. Public Records Index, 1950-1993, Vol. I, Ancestry.com.

32 "Falls woman tells of love affair with hit man."

33 "Falls woman tells of love affair with hit man."

34 "Falls woman tells of love affair with hit man."

35 "Falls woman tells of love affair with hit man." Karen passed away in September 2011.

36 Marie K. Jackson, 071-20-1617, Social Security Death Index, May 28, 1999; Marie Catherine Murray, 071-20-1617, Social Security Applications and Claims Index, May 28, 1999; Lander, Erik, "Joseph Valachi," memorial ID 17075812, Find A Grave, findagrave.com, Dec. 18, 2006.

FEATURE 19

Valachi's life:
the motion picture

Benefited from Godfather movie coattails
but suffered in comparison with it

The movie, *The Valachi Papers*, was a financially successful business venture, earning substantial sums for its investors, for Valachi biographer Peter Maas and for the estate of Joseph Valachi, as it brought Valachi's story to millions around the world. However, it is generally regarded as an entertainment failure and as a missed opportunity to present factual organized crime history in a movie format.

Joseph Valachi's televised Senate testimony was still very recent history when U.S. movie producers first considered how best to adapt the Valachi life story to the big screen.[1] They considered it, but they did not act on it. Through more than five years – between the testimony of autumn 1963 and the release of Peter Maas's book, *The Valachi Papers*, just after Christmas 1968[2] – no action was taken. As Maas's book was released, the author was assured that there would be immediate interest in purchasing its movie rights: "I was advised that I could bet the farm on a film sale."[3] Still, the major Hollywood studios took no action.

"Studio after studio 'passed' on the project, as they like to say in Hollywood," Maas recalled in a 1986 article. There were some hazards associated with bringing a factual history of the secretive Mafia criminal society to movie theaters. One of the hazards was obvious. "The head of one studio explained to my agent that it was quite simple: he did not wish to spend the rest of his life worrying about starting his car in the morning," wrote Maas.[4]

While the major studios rejected the project, Maas actually did not wait very long for the sale of his Valachi biography movie rights. Italian producer Dino De Laurentiis arranged to purchase the rights near the end of February 1969.

De Laurentiis committed to making an English-language feature for an American audience. It was to be filmed on location in New York City and in De Laurentiis's studios in Italy. The purchase price reportedly was set at $200,000 (equivalent to $1.7 million in 2024 dollars) plus 5 percent of movie profits, with a percentage of the sale amount going to Valachi. Maas was named as technical consultant for the film project.[5]

Valachi was aware of the sale of movie rights and had some discussions with Maas about casting. In an Easter card to Maas, Valachi expressed interest in "who is going to play me in the movies." He also mentioned, "N. Wood is a dead ringer of May," apparently suggesting actress Natalie Wood to play Valachi's first serious love interest.[6]

De Laurentiis convinced actor Charles Bronson to play Valachi and used Bronson's notoriety in Europe to persuade investors to help finance the modest $5 million (about $43 million in 2024 dollars) project. Bronson's recent bride, actress Jill Ireland, joined the cast in the role of Valachi's wife.[7]

Production on *The Valachi Papers* motion picture began near the first day of spring in 1972, about one year after Joseph Valachi passed away in La Tuna Federal Correctional Institution in Texas.

Terence Young, who had overseen several successful James Bond (featuring Sean Connery) spy thrillers, served as director of the film. Writer Stephen Geller developed the screenplay based – somewhat loosely in parts – on Maas's bestselling book.[8]

De Laurentiis told the press that he worked on six different versions of a script before finally approving Geller's screenplay.[9] The cast included Lino Ventura as New York crime boss Vito Genovese, Walter Chiari as Dominic "the Gap" Petrelli, Guido Leontini as Anthony "Tony Bender" Strollo, Joseph Wiseman as boss of bosses Salvatore Maranzano, Gerald S. O'Loughlin as "Agent Ryan" (a composite character representing agents of the Federal Bureau of Narcotics and the Federal Bureau of Investigation), Amedeo Nazzari as Gaetano Reina, Angelo Infanti as Salvatore "Charlie Luciano" Lucania, Franco Borelli as "Buster," Alessandro Sperli as Giuseppe "Joe the Boss" Masseria and Mario Pilar as "Salerto" (or "Salierno," depending on your source, a composite of several mafiosi).[10]

Godfather-envy

The start of production roughly coincided with the 1972 release of the Paramount blockbuster film *The Godfather*, directed by Francis Ford Coppola and based on a work of Mafia fiction written by Mario Puzo.[11] Critics were instantly awed by *Godfather's* gripping story and its visual depth and artistry; Coppola's skilled directing; and the masterful performances by Marlon Brando, Al Pacino, James Caan, Diane Keaton, Richard Castellano and others.[12]

Enormous crowds were drawn to theaters to view the underworld epic, despite escalating ticket prices.[13] Movie houses in New York City quickly increased their showings of the film to seven a day, beginning at nine in the morning and permitting only a few minutes between showings to clear out one audience and pack in the next. The movie earned an estimated $454,000 during its first week at five New York City theaters and ultimately earned a quarter of a billion dollars return on an initial $6 million investment.[14] From the first moment, De Laurentiis tried to ride *The Godfather's* coattails, though he must have suspected his film ultimately would suffer in comparison to Coppola's masterpiece. Two days after *The Godfather's* March 14 premiere, De Laurentiis held a party at New York's 21 Club to announce his planned Valachi movie. The press reported that it would be distributed by Paramount.[15]

Observing the great early success of *The Godfather* and desiring to capitalize on a Mafia craze, De Laurentiis worked to accelerate production of *The Valachi Papers*. Within a month, however, he complained that his on-location filming in New York had been halted due to protests by the Italian-American Civil Rights League.[16]

The same organization, which at the time was under the influence of Mafia boss Joseph Colombo, had forced *The Godfather* producers to remove from their script any mention of the term "Mafia," as well as the synonym "Cosa Nostra" (popularized through Valachi's 1963 testimony). Crime journalist Nicholas Gage noted that there were plenty of ethnic slurs against Italian Americans in *The Godfather*, "but there was not a single offending five-letter word beginning with 'M.'"[17]

While "Cosa Nostra" was spoken in *The Valachi Papers* movie, no character enounced the term "Mafia." (The term is voiced once in the movie, however, in a radio broadcast overheard by Valachi while he is a fugitive from the law facing narcotics charges.[18])

Despite the protests, De Laurentiis pledged that "Nothing will stop my project."[19]

The Valachi Papers was originally scheduled for a February 1973 release. But De Laurentiis urged that it open earlier. He could not come to terms with Paramount. In September 1972, Columbia Pictures agreed to be distributor for the movie.

The Valachi Papers opened in select locations near the end of October. It was widely released the first weekend of November.[20]

Advertisements promoted *The Valachi Papers* as a true-to-life alternative to *The Godfather*. Some promotions directly compared the two movies and stated that *The Valachi Papers* was the better of the two films. Ads generally featured a tag line: "Fact not fiction."[21]

The timing of its release, just half a year after the spectacle of *The Godfather*, helped make the movie a box office success. Through its first eight months, it reportedly earned $9.4 million. The figure eventually rose to $20.3 million.[22]

Panned

Critics generally gave the movie poor reviews. As entertainment, it was simply not in the same league as the more polished, visually powerful and emotionally gripping *The Godfather*.

New York Times reviewer Roger Greenspun stated, "Often ludicrous and often just dull, Terence Young's '*The Valachi Papers*' has the look of a movie project that ran short of ideas before it was finished, and ran short of class almost before it was begun." The reviewer expressed surprise at how bad the film turned out, noting the previous successes of those involved. "But in '*The Valachi Papers.*'" he wrote, "everyone undoes himself."[23]

Peter Maas, whose "technical consultant" impact on film was likely minimal, judged that "it was one of the worst movies ever made."[24]

The Valachi Papers did not merely fail on an entertainment level. The movie, promoted for its historical accuracy, also turned out to be riddled with factual errors and anachronisms, apparently the results of inattentive writing and careless production. These mistakes were not at all difficult to detect. In the Greenspun review, published as the movie was released, the reviewer noted that a scene showing the murder of a gangster in 1929 had its victim slumped over the steering wheel of a 1960s-era automobile. He suggested that releasing the film with such blatant inconsistencies was "like laziness raised to the level of willful contempt."[25]

Maas pointed out another similar problem: "My favorite scene was a 1930s gang confrontation against a backdrop of the twin towers of Manhattan's World Trade Center, which was built 40 years later."

On the bright side, Maas wrote in 1986, "It turned out to be quite profitable, and can still be seen on late-night television."[26]

Rewriting history

The De Laurentiis film ignored much of Valachi's documented history and much of the Maas book it claimed as its foundation. The opening moments of the movie are described below:

Valachi returns to Atlanta Federal Prison in 1962 after a New York trial that added to his prison term for narcotics conspiracy. He finds former friends in the prison yard have grown hostile toward him. Not understanding the reason for their attitude, he says he will "talk to Don Vito" Genovese, who is also serving a narcotics sentence in the prison. "What makes you think he'll talk to you?" an inmate says to him. (In reality, Genovese requested that Valachi be assigned to the Genovese cell.) Valachi responds with a gesture. He walks away, as all gathered in the yard make banging noises to indicate their solidarity against him. (While such a scene may never have occurred, it accurately portrays Valachi's feeling, soon after his return, that Cosa Nostra had turned against him.)

The movie's Valachi is then attacked by a knife-wielding assassin in an entirely fabricated shower scene. (The real Valachi avoided the showers after he began to feel threatened.) He survives the fictional murder attempt, and asks for the protection of solitary confinement. (Valachi actually sought solitary after a confrontation with Genovese.)

While in solitary, he exhibits concern that his food may be poisoned, and he tries in vain to arrange a meeting with Genovese. Without explanation, the movie immediately returns Valachi from solitary to the general population prison yard. He sees men approaching and decides they are a threat. He moves to an out of the way spot, grabs a length of pipe and uses it to beat to death the first man who walks in his direction. As guards rush over, he says, "At least I got Salerto." (The invented character Salerto, sometimes referred to as "Salierno," stands in for various historical figures during the film. In this instance, he stands in for "Joe Beck" DiPalermo, the mobster Valachi thought he killed in the prison yard on June 22, 1962.)

Valachi learns in the warden's office that he has killed Joseph Saupp (John Joseph Saupp), a lookalike for Salerto (DiPalermo). Saupp was not a mobster and not a threat to Valachi. Immediately, "Agent Ryan" appears, antagonizes Valachi with a largely fictional description of the mental health and criminal challenges of largely fictional Valachi family members, and introduces himself as "Ryan, Federal Board." (Viewers are not told what the "Federal Board" is, but for the remainder of the movie, the Ryan character is presented as an agent of both the FBI and the Federal Bureau of Narcotics.) Ryan uses news of the disappearance of Anthony "Tony Bender" Strollo and a surveillance tape recording of Vito Genovese calling Bender and Valachi "rats" in an effort to convince Valachi to become an informant against Genovese.

When Valachi refuses, Ryan (apparently also some sort of prison official) instructs guards that Valachi should no longer be afforded the protection of solitary (though he clearly had been out of solitary a scene earlier). Valachi learns Genovese is willing to give him an audience, and he is taken to a large group cell where Genovese is having a haircut. They exchange warm greetings. For some reason, they both need to lie down next to each other in a bunk in order to have a quiet conversation.

Genovese confides that he distrusted Anthony "Tony Bender" Strollo, who had been Valachi's immediate superior in the Genovese Crime Family. Genovese confirms the Ryan news that Bender has disappeared. Valachi reveals that he feels he was betrayed by Bender in the narcotics deal that caused his imprisonment, and he recounts the (fictional) attempt on his life that occurred when he entered Atlanta Prison's general population after completing a thirty-day quarantine. (Valachi did not go through the quarantine upon his return to Atlanta.)

Genovese discusses the "bad apple" principle, suggesting that Valachi needs to be eliminated to preserve the rest of the organization. Genovese then plants a kiss on Valachi. Salerto (now standing in for Genovese buddy and cellmate Ralph Wagner) remarks that it was the kiss of death. When Valachi realizes that he has just received an underworld farewell, he gives Genovese an aggressive kiss in return. As Valachi is taken out of the cell by guards, he and Genovese further threaten each other by asking about their families.

Valachi next appears in the custody of Agent Ryan, as he is transported to a secure location under U.S. Military Police escort (Ryan may have some role in the armed forces, as well). In Valachi's new quarters, he is interviewed by Ryan and recalls various events of his many years in Cosa Nostra. The film then bounces back and forth between Valachi flashbacks and developments in the 1962-1963 period.[27]

Some other inaccuracies

The film specifies that Valachi was initiated into the Mafia on the night of November 5, 1930. The event occurred at least several days later. By moving the induction ceremony earlier, it omitted Valachi's last known trip to visit his brother at Dannemora.

At least a couple of inaccuracies appeared to be an effort to avoid naming living people. Gaetano Reina could not have been Valachi's sponsor at the induction ceremony, as he had been dead for more than eight months. Valachi recalled that his sponsor was Joseph Bonanno. Bonanno was still alive when the movie was made. A similar reason may be behind the misnaming of Valachi's still-living wife, Carmela "Mildred" Reina as "Maria Reina."

The moviemakers entirely invented the castration punishment inflicted on Dominick "the Gap" Petrelli.

Valachi's suicide attempt is incorrectly placed at the conclusion of his 1963 Senate testimony. In fact, it occurred years later in April 1966.[28]

NBC-TV in Chicago says this about
The Valachi Papers:

"Is it as good as 'The Godfather'? The answer is ...no, it is better."
—NBC-TV (Chicago)

"Is it as good as The Godfather? The answer is no. It is better.

The two films, however, do not compete. The Godfather was a romantic movie made from a romantic novel. THE VALACHI PAPERS is a cold, hard reenactment of the confessions of an underworld soldier.

THE VALACHI PAPERS lacks the polish of The Godfather. It is even awkward at times as it shifts between prison confession scenes and Valachi's recreated memories. But Charles Bronson and a cast of lesser known actors give you reality. There is no cheering for good killers, no laughter at clever butchery.

The audience is simply garrotted by these men who calmly murder and maim and shrug their shoulders.

THE VALACHI PAPERS is a history lesson. It is a nearly half century of ugly Americana with Genovese, Maranzano, Luciano, Anastasia and the others. You may even recognize some scenes because many of the killings mimic old newspaper photographs.

Producer Dino de Laurentiis and Director Terence Young manage to handle globs of violence without close-ups of exploding flesh.

The emphasis is on the story and the story is powerful enough to start a swing to non-fiction films.

If you have seen The Godfather, see THE VALACHI PAPERS.

If you have not seen The Godfather, see THE VALACHI PAPERS."

—PHILLIP WALTERS, WMAQ-TV(NBC), CHICAGO

DINO DE LAURENTIIS presents
CHARLES BRONSON
LINO VENTURA
in A TERENCE YOUNG Film
"THE VALACHI PAPERS"
JOSEPH WISEMAN JILL IRELAND
WALTER CHIARI GERALD S. O'LOUGHLIN
AMEDEO NAZZARI
Screenplay by STEPHEN GELLER
Based on the book "The Valachi Papers"
by PETER MAAS Music by RIZ ORTOLANI
From Columbia Pictures [R]

Valachi Papers advertisement explicitly compares the movie to The Godfather.

Dino De Laurentiis (left), Charles Bronson (center), Jill Ireland.

Feature 19 Notes

1 "*The Valachi Papers* (1972)," AFI Catalog of Feature Films, catalog.afi.com.

2 "Tax lien placed on Valachi share of book on Mafia," *New York Times*, Jan. 18, 1969, p. 22; Maas, Peter, "The White House, the Mob and the book biz: Footnotes to The Valachi Papers," *New York Times*, Oct. 12, 1986, Section 7 (Book Review), p. 3. The official release was in the final days of 1968, though Maas noted the book began appearing in bookstores in the opening days of 1969.

3 "The White House, the Mob and the book biz..."

4 "The White House, the Mob and the book biz..."

5 "*The Valachi Papers* (1972)," AFI Catalog; "The White House, the Mob and the book biz..."; CPI Inflation Calculator, U.S. Bureau of Labor Statistics, bls.gov. There was speculation that Valachi was to receive 50 percent of the movie rights sale.

6 The Easter card to Peter Maas is part of the Valachi documents retained by the John F. Kennedy Presidential Library and Museum in Boston. Natalie Wood, whose film *Bob & Carol & Ted & Alice* was released in 1969, took the next few years off, before making a brief appearance (as herself) in 1972's *The Candidate* with Robert Redford. ("Natalie Wood (1938-1981)," Internet Movie Database, imdb.com.)

7 "The White House, the Mob and the book biz..."; "*The Valachi Papers*," Internet Movie Database, imdb.com; CPI Inflation Calculator.

8 "The Valachi Papers," "Terence Young (1915-1994)" and "Stephen Geller (L)," Internet Movie Database, imdb.com. Geller is better known for his *Slaughterhouse-Five* screenplay, which won 1973's Hugo (Science Fiction writing) Award. Sources point to March 20 or March 22 of 1972 as the date of the start of production.

9 "DeLaurentiis starts 'Valachi Papers,'" *Variety*, March 22, 1972, p. 5.

10 DeLaurentiis, Dino (Producer), Terence Young (Director) and Stephen Geller (Screenplay), *The Valachi Papers*, 1972.

11 Canby, Vincent, "Moving and brutal '*Godfather*' bows," *New York Times*, March 16, 1972, p. 56; "*The Godfather*," Internet Movie Database, imdb.com. *The Godfather* premiered on March 14, 1972, opened in five New York theaters on March 15, 1972. It was widely released nine days later, March 24.

12 Canby, "Moving and brutal '*Godfather*' bows"; Kelly, Kevin, "'*Godfather*' epic gangster film," *Boston Globe*, March 23, 1972, p. 40; Huddy, John, "Splendid '*Godfather*' enriched by meticulous detail, filming," *Miami Herald*, March 24, 1972, p. 2-D; Masaro, John J., "'*Godfather*': sickening masterpiece," *Hartford Courant*, March 25, 1972, p. 17; White, Ron, "'*Godfather*' best gangster film ever," *San Antonio Express*, March 28, 1972, p. 13.

13 The movie ticket price was first set at $3.50, half a dollar over normal rates, and then jumped to $4.

14 "Mob handle hard on mgrs, stores," *Variety*, March 22, 1972, p. 5; "Paramount's 350 kickoff deals," *Variety*, March 22, 1972, p. 5; "*The Godfather*," Internet Movie Database, imdb.com.

15 "Mob handle hard on mgrs, stores."

16 "*The Valachi Papers* (1972)," AFI Catalog.

17 Maeder, Jay, "No such thing as the Mob: The end of Joe Colombo, June-July 1971," *New York Daily News*, June 28, 2001, p. 63; Gage, Nicholas, "*The Godfather*: A few family murders, but that's show biz," *New York Times*, March 19, 1972, p. E6.

18 DeLaurentiis, Dino (Producer), Terence Young (Director) and Stephen Geller (Screenplay), *The Valachi Papers*, 1972.

19 "DeLaurentiis starts '*Valachi Papers*.'"

20 "*The Valachi Papers* (1972)," AFI Catalog; "*The Valachi Papers*," Internet Movie Database; Greenspun, Roger, "The Screen: '*Valachi Papers*' arrives," *New York Times*, Nov. 4, 1972, p. 21; "The White House, the Mob and the book biz..."

21 "*The Valachi Papers*," Columbia Pictures Pressbook, 1972, scanned by Wisconsin Center for Film and Theater Research, Media History Digital Library, mediahist.org.

22 "*The Valachi Papers* (1972)," AFI Catalog; "*The Valachi Papers*," Internet Movie Database.

23 "The Screen: '*Valachi Papers*' arrives."

24 "The White House, the Mob and the book biz..."

25 "The Screen: '*Valachi Papers*' arrives."

26 "The White House, the Mob and the book biz..."
27 DeLaurentiis, Dino (Producer), Terence Young (Director) and Stephen Geller (Screenplay), *The Valachi Papers*, 1972.
28 DeLaurentiis, Dino (Producer), Terence Young (Director) and Stephen Geller (Screenplay), *The Valachi Papers*, 1972.

OPINION

Historians review 'Valachi Papers' movie

Informer asked a number of crime historians a set of questions about the popular 1972 movie, *The Valachi Papers*. Here are their responses:

1. Describe your overall impression of *The Valachi Papers* movie.

Justin Cascio: It is the kind of movie that would have played on broadcast television on a Saturday afternoon in my childhood. After a few hours of cartoons and cold cereal, my father would take over the big color console in the living room and watch crime thrillers, kung fu, war or western dramas, and sword and sandals extravaganzas, until the evening sports programming began... Macho melodramas like those Charles Bronson was famous for had no draw for me..., until college, when I got into Quentin Tarantino and Oliver Stone movies... I watched *The Valachi Papers* for the first time recently, having already read Peter Maas' book and the unpublished memoir Joseph Valachi wrote in prison. I hoped to learn more about the personalities of Valachi and his contemporaries, and get a light refresher on the Mafia history he testified about. Overall, the general story is more or less correct. I'm most familiar with the Corleonesi participants in the Castellammarese War, so I perked up when I heard Gaetano Reina's name. But I also know that Reina's wife was named Angela Oliveri, not Letizia Profaci, and their daughter, whom Valachi married, was named Carmela and called Mildred or Millie, not Maria. More importantly, Angela Reina was of no relation to the Olive Oil King. Her father was Andrea Oliveri, an East Harlem mafioso from Corleone, and contemporary of Giuseppe Morello. Most people haven't heard of Oliveri, but Profaci rings a bell. *The Valachi Papers* was created for entertainment purposes only; it is not a documentary.

Scott Deitche: While *The Valachi Papers* was released eight months after *The Godfather*, in December 1972, it's certainly not the same kind of movie. Comparisons were made at the time, and they were, as expected, very lopsided in favor of Francis Ford Coppola's film. *The Valachi Papers*, produced by Dino De Laurentiis, was essentially a lower budget B-movie trying to be a big budget epic. It didn't quite live up to its aspirations. The overall feel of the movie was a bit stilted, and it could have used a heavier hand editing. But for what it was, it was enjoyable.

Thibaut Maïquès: The movie might be interesting for fans of gangster films, but less so for those who are familiar with the history of organized crime in the United States. For example, the depiction of the Castellammarese War period is filled with inaccuracies, which is quite disturbing from a historian's perspective.

Ellen Poulsen: I liked the movie. The low-key flavor lent this film a grey-toned ambiance that worked for the story. As far as facts, it started realistically enough with the etched-in-prison-stone tales of deceit and betrayal culminating in the kiss of death between Don Vito and Joe.

Fabien Rossat: I remember first seeing the film about fifteen years ago during a cable TV airing, at the time I was starting to be interested in the history of the mafia. I couldn't missed a film where Vito Genovese was played by Lino Ventura, who although Italian spent the majority of his career in France and is considered a legend here. Besides, like any self-respecting action cinema fan, I really like Charles Bronson. But I must admit that he is quite bland as Joseph Valachi, and Ventura steals the show. Although the film is far from being a masterpiece (and anything but accurate), it is quite well made.

Thomas Hunt: I know some people enjoy really bad movies, and I suppose there may some people who enjoy really bad history. This film's best audience will be found where those two groups intersect.

2. What scene of the movie was most memorable for you (and was that scene historically accurate)?

Cascio: My favorite scene is the end of Albert Anastasia. It's very funny, and the best choreographed death in the film. His last movements as he lunges toward his attackers are almost balletic. My least favorite scene comes a few minutes earlier, with the end of The Gap ("The gun, Joey, the gun!") I don't have room here to explain why the scenes involving Donna and the Gap are misogynist and transphobic, but they are.

Deitche: The most memorable scene was one that did not happen in real life. It was the emasculation, and subsequent murder, of Dominick "The Gap" Petrilli. I was not familiar with this hit and after seeing the scene, I had to look it up and see if indeed Petrilli had his manhood removed by his assailants, while he was still alive. It turns out that the scene was not accurate. Petrilli was murdered in a Bronx tavern, but he was shot multiple times while running away from his three assailants. They quickly fled the scene, leaving the dead Petrilli, wholly intact.

Maïquès: The scene that struck me the most was Salvatore Maranzano's speech after the murder of Joe Masseria. It's a visually appealing scene with good cinematography, although there are many historically inaccurate points. The film suggests that Maranzano created the Mafia hierarchy (capo, soldier, consigliere, etc.) and also the five families, whereas they already had distinct foundations before Maranzano. It also states that there should be only one family per city, which is completely false as several families had already operated in the same city. Maranzano also names Anthony Strollo as one of his lieutenants, although he was not close to Maranzano. The film heavily emphasizes Strollo on acts he did not commit, such as the assassination of Manfredi Mineo and the betrayal of Maranzano.

Poulsen: Best part of the film: The sets with their tiny houses whose wallpaper did nothing to open up the functional rooms. The living room where Joe proposes to his future wife, with the scary Mrs. Reina and her living-room ghosts watching from the mantel. Very good representation of life in the Bronx in the olden days when a nice house still had three bedrooms, one bath and a front room. Outside these enclaves, the private restaurant tables flush with wine and men again added to the idea that families were large and rooms were small.

Rossat: I really like the scene in prison where Genovese (Ventura) explains to Valachi (Bronson) that in a basket of apples, it sometimes happens that an apple is rotten. To preserve the basket, you have to remove the rotten apple to avoid contaminating the others. Once again Ventura shines with his class. The murders of Masseria, Maranzano and Anastasia are also well done, in my opinion

Hunt: I do enjoy the few moments following soggy Joseph Valachi sloshing through a restaurant, where Salvatore Maranzano is sitting with Gaetano Reina (incorrectly presented as a Maranzano lieutenant), Anthony "Tony Bender" Strollo and Dominick "the Gap" Petrelli. While nothing like it ever happened, the scene does reinforce (comically and with great exaggeration) the idea of a Mafia / Cosa Nostra hierarchy. Each person at the table only asks questions to and receives answers from the (alleged) subordinate immediately to his right. Maranzano's question about Valachi: "Why he's wet?" slowly makes its way down the table - Maranzano to Reina to Strollo to Petrelli - and the answer eventually returns by the reverse route: "We don't know why he's wet."

3. What were The Valachi Papers' greatest strengths (if any)?

Cascio: It doesn't seem fair to judge a fifty-two-year old movie for being cliched. There are scenes in *The Valachi Papers* that I can imagine other directors being inspired by. In *Blade Runner*, when Decker interviews a snake dancer in her dressing room, it looks exactly like the future Mrs. Genovese meeting her new bodyguard.

Deitche: The period sets looked good overall, despite a few anachronisms. While there were some liberties taken with historical accuracy, the movie generally followed the rise of the mob in America from the 1920s through Valachi's appearance at the McClellan hearings in 1963. Some of the actors were well-cast. One that immediately comes to mind is Lino Ventura, who played Vito Genovese. I think he did a good job in the role and even looked like Vito Genovese.

Maïquès: The greatest strengths of the film are the actors who play their roles perfectly, the screenplay, although historically inaccurate, and it highlights Joe Valachi's testimony and his courage to expose the Mafia.

Poulsen: The quirky actors cast to play these iconic mob stars lent that elusive touch of class quite lacking in the earthen character of Bronson. Luciano looking like he just left Saville Row (and maybe he did). Maranzano with his busts and books, sounding for all time in the classic tradition -- just like we pictured him. My holdout on casting is Bronson's beautiful wife, actor Jill Ireland, not looking much like Valachi's real-life wife.

Rossat: The main attraction of the film for me is its casting. In addition to Ventura, I think Fausto Tozzi, who plays Albert Anastasia is very good (although I admit he is a little hysterical at times). Angelo Infanti who plays Lucky Luciano is also very good and the resemblance is striking.

Hunt: I suppose the single greatest "strength" would be its groundbreaking use of time travel. About thirty minutes in, we are shown the date "November 5th, 1930," and we see Valachi inducted into Cosa Nostra. Maranzano selects Reina as Valachi's superior, introduces the two men and assigns Valachi to be Reina's personal driver. About five minutes of movie later, without fanfare or flashing lights (or even a flux capacitor-powered DeLorean), Valachi drives Reina more than eight months into the past. The screen then shows a date of "February 26th, 1930." Creating an interesting time-travel paradox, Reina is shot to death as he gets out of the car. While the movie does not explore this paradox, the death of Reina logically (and historically, by the way) results in Reina not being present for Valachi's induction in November or for the assignment of Valachi as his personal driver. That, of course, becomes grounds to assert that Valachi wasn't in a position to drive Reina into the past where he was killed. So Reina could have been alive in November, after all…

4. What were the movie's greatest weaknesses (if any)?

Cascio: Weaknesses: The direction, writing, wigs, acting and casting, in that order.

Deitche: Well, the one thing that stands out, somewhat negatively, is that Charles Bronson is basically playing Charles Bronson. He doesn't try to fake an accent, sticking to his normal voice and cadence, which make sit difficult to believe he is an Italian gangster. Bronson has a strong screen presence, but he is not the most well-rounded actor. Of note though, this role came right at the start of Bronson's "apex mountain" era. Within the next two years, he makes *Mr. Majestyk*, *The Mechanic*, and *Death Wish*, three of his most popular movies.

Maïquès: The weakness of the film is that it is based on Joe Valachi's story and testimony, but many of the facts he recounted have been altered. Therefore, the film is not truly based on the true history of the Mafia. There are scenes that are chronologically inaccurate, such as Joe Valachi's ceremony appearing in the film after the assassination of Manfredi Mineo. In the scene, Gaetano Reina becomes his mentor, whereas historically, Reina died months before Mineo's assassination. It is also said that the Castellammarese War is Neapolitan (Joe Masseria) against Sicilians (Maranzano), which is completely false. It is also said that Reina's wife is Joe Profaci's sister, or that Dominick Petrilli was the lover of Vito Genovese's wife. The film also states that Albert Anastasia was the boss of the Genovese family. In short, there are many inconsistencies and false information, making it a fictional rather than historical film.

Poulsen: Bronson/Valachi's associates The Gap and Tony Bender were less defined and left me struggling with what I should be feeling about them. The fabricated castration scene was an unnecessary step into torture and gore, which the film didn't need. This film reeked with a violence living inside the heads of the characters, which went deeper than the actual depictions. Bronson brought a mid-Euro tint to the role which was characteristic of his body of work but out of place as a Bronx Joe. Bronson overcame any ethnic missteps with his deep sense of defeat mixed with flashes of hubris. He had to work with the image of the real Valachi, whose face was a gargoyle of impassivity. Valachi left Bronson a blank slate in that sense, and Bronson picked it up and put his anti-social arsenal to work. The result was a subtle, sublime performance. Who else but Bronson? Ernest Borgnine, who was the Bronx butcher of the 1955 Paddy Chayefsky classic *Marty* and sadistic Fatso Judson of *From Here to Eternity*. Borgnine would have brought to the role of Valachi a depth of underworld pathos mixed with the sadism that Bronson seemed unable to attach to his performance.

Rossat: The main weakness of the film is, in my opinion, its storyline. Unlike other films of the genre, we never really empathize with Bronson, who also seems to be royally bored during the two hours of the film. Moreover, the length of the film is also a flaw, an hour and forty five minutes would have been sufficient. Some notes of humor are also quite unwelcome. The scene where Genovese arranges with Mrs. Reina to have Valachi date Mildred Reina is quite atrocious.

Hunt: Sadly, there is no shortage of weaknesses, and many of them qualify as "great" weaknesses (the only way that the word "great" could be used honestly in connection with this film). As most viewers likely did not detect all the many historical inaccuracies, the most glaring weakness would be the movie's overall sloppiness. The terribly screwed up chronology relating to Reina (which I assume resulted from an extraordinary effort to avoid mentioning Valachi's first actual superior, Joseph Bonanno, who was still living when the movie came out), is just one example. The presence of 1970-era automotive traffic in 1930-era scenes and of the 1972 New York skyline in a scene that took place a decade earlier have been noted by others. Accompanying Valachi narration with the use of some real-life crime scene photos taken from other eras and incidents was terribly sloppy. The movie also seems not to notice that it bestowed upon fabricated "Agent Ryan" awesome simultaneous authority with the Bureau of Prisons, the Bureau of Narcotics, the FBI and the Army. The list goes on and on…

5. What grade would you give *The Valachi Papers* for its historical accuracy (and why)?

Cascio: I'd give the movie a "D" for historical accuracy: not so much for the Mafia history, which deserves a "C-minus," but for its depictions of Italian American gangsters from New York City. Not only don't I believe Bronson is holding a gun in the scene where he shoots his friend, he doesn't look Sicilian or sound like a New Yorker. None of them do. Bender sounds like he's from Philly, or had his jaw wired shut. Maybe both. When I think of the wedding scene that opens *The Godfather*, I feel the warm flush of nostalgia. I grew up in a big Sicilian family that gathered on Sundays for dinner, and Coppola got a lot of the details right, from the proper ways to show respect and defiance in a traditional, hierarchical Italian family, to interior design tastes and the sound and gestures of the language. Nothing rings so true in *The Valachi Papers*: not the Lithuanian-American Bronson as Valachi, not even Guido Leontini, mooking around like Steven Van Zandt as Silvio Dante in *The Sopranos*. *The Valachi Papers* is unintentional camp that shows us more about the biases of the filmmakers than their putative subjects and as such, it has to be treated like the relic that it is. Watch it to learn about the era's ethnic hostility toward Italian Americans, or attitudes about gender and sexuality. But don't watch

The Valachi Papers to understand the Mafia or even what Joe Valachi knew about Cosa Nostra. There are better ways to fill a Saturday afternoon.

Deitche: I'd give it a B- for historical accuracy. In some ways the movie is very accurate in terms of specific dates for certain events, like the killing of Albert Anastasia. But other events fall short of sticking to the historical narrative. One example: the death of Gaetano Reina in the movie differed significantly from what happened in real life. Most notably Joe Valachi was not with Reina when he was killed.

Maïquès: I give it a rating of four out of ten for its historical accuracy. Most of the scenes did indeed take place in Joe Valachi's life, but they were almost all modified in the film. So, these are events that mostly took place (not Petrilli's affair with Genovese's wife, for example, or the peace meeting at Reina's funeral), but Petrilli's assassination did happen, as did Anastasia's, even though he wasn't the boss of the Genovese family, the same goes for Mineo and Ferrigno, and the film even used the exact location if I remember correctly. In conclusion, it's an enjoyable film to watch, but there are many inconsistencies compared to the real life of Valachi and even the book *The Valachi Papers*.

Poulsen: I would say 80 percent. The filmmakers explored the character of Maranzano, of which there is a lack of photographic evidence. I would say "A" for effort, because they tried hard to present a gritty, realistic mob movie with human emotions attached.

Rossat: So as for the accuracy of the film, we are something like 1.5 out of 5. This can be explained very simply: it is an adaptation of the complex book *The Valachi Papers*. The screenwriters were obliged to adapt so as not to make a film that was indigestible and too long. This explains certain aberrations like Tony Bender as member of the Maranzano borgata or Dominick Petrilli as lover of Genovese's wife who ends up in bad shape (without giving any spoilers, let's just say that it would be quite painful for any male). On the other hand, I completely understand that inaccuracies can annoy historians. If we remain objective, the film is nevertheless quite faithful to the spirit of the book. Note that just after this film, in 1974, Dino De Laurentiis produced another gangster biopic, *Crazy Joe*, about Joe Gallo. This film is more accurate, and the cast is huge. (You don't want to miss a film with Peter Boyle, Rip Torn, Eli Wallach, Henry Winkler Fred Williamson and … Hervé Villechaize?)

Hunt: The makers of this movie deserve an "F" in history (and those responsible really should have been forced to apologize).

Petrelli, Bender, Reina and Maranzano (left to right) in The Valachi Papers.

Autos from very different eras.

Bronson as Valachi.

Reviewers

Justin Cascio grew up on Long Island, sitting too close to the TV and riding his bike without a helmet. He is a regular contributor to Informer. His first book, *In Our Blood: The Mafia Families of Corleone*, is about his family's ancestral hometown of Corleone, Sicily, and its contributions to Mafia history. Read more of his work at mafiagenealogy.com.

Scott M. Deitche is an author specializing in organized crime. His books include *Cigar City Mafia: A Complete History of the Tampa Underworld*, *Garden State Gangland: The Rise of the Mob in New Jersey*, and *Hitmen: The Mafia Drugs, and The East Harlem Purple Gang*. He has been featured on The Discovery Channel, The History Channel, NatGeo, and various other news shows, documentaries, and podcasts. He is a member of The Mob Museum's Advisory Council. He also runs the Tampa Mafia Tours at tampamafia.com.

Thibaut Maïquès, known also by the social media pseudonym "Harry Horowitz," became interested in Mafia history after viewing documentaries on Frank Sinatra's organized crime links. His focus is early Mafia history (1800-1930), but he also studies the economic and social factors contributing to the emergence of the Mafia in Sicily. He is active on Pinterest and on Instagram (@capodetutticapi and @storyofoldmafia) and has started a blog called, *La Fratellanza*.

Ellen Poulsen is the author of *The Case Against Lucky Luciano: New York's Most Sensational Vice Trial*. She has also written two non-fiction books on John Dillinger. She was last seen lecturing on the mob at the East Bronx Historical Society.

Fabien Rossat, passionate about the history of organized crime and the Mafia, is primarily interested in vendettas and drug trafficking activities in France, Canada, Australia, Italy and U.S. He shares his stories and connections among different underworld groups in a blog, *Une Histoire de Crime Organisé* (A Story of Organized Crime) at unehistoiredecrimeorganise.blogspot.com. He also moderates "The Early History of the American Mafia" and "The Canadian Mafia Archives" groups on Facebook.

Thomas Hunt is the editor and publisher of *Informer*. He has written or co-written several books on U.S. Mafia history and maintains organized crime history websites.

CRIME HISTORY BOOKSHELF

New books

In Our Blood
The Mafia Families of Corleone

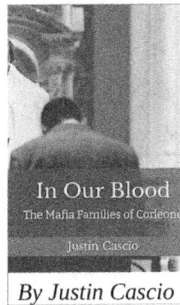

By Justin Cascio

While the Mafia criminal society is traditionally viewed as a hierarchical organization, *In Our Blood* author Justin Cascio argues that Mafia networks are largely based on kinship ties.

The publisher of the Mafia Genealogy website and a frequent contributor to *Informer,* Cascio has channeled years of research into his first book-length project. He notes that pivotal figures in Mafia history, including present-day mafiosi, have direct genealogical ties to one another and to the earliest recorded gangs in Corleone, Sicily. In addition to bloodline and marriage connections, some mafiosi also linked through the significant religious/family role of godparent.

Cascio discusses dozens of gangland figures in the United States and Sicily as he analyzes family-based networks that include thousands of individuals. Along the way, he tackles some of the lingering questions about the Mafia: How old is the criminal society? Where was it formed? How did it spread from Sicily to the U.S.?

For the benefit of researchers, Cascio has provided references supporting his assertions. The hardcover and paperback editions of *In Our Blood* weigh in at 390 pages. The Kindle ebook is rated by Amazon at a print length of 532 pages. They can be ordered now through Amazon.com.

The Bulldog Detective
William J. Flynn and America's First War Against the Mafia, Spies, and Terrorists

By Jeffrey D. Simon

America in the early twentieth century was rife with threats. Organized crime groups like the Mafia, German spies embedded behind enemy lines ahead of World War I, package bombs sent throughout the country and the 1920 Wall Street bombing dominated headlines. Yet the story of the one man tasked with combating these threats has yet to be told.

The Bulldog Detective: William J. Flynn and America's First War Against the Mafia, Spies, and Terrorists tells the story of Flynn, the first government official to bring down the powerful Mafia, uncover a sophisticated German spy ring in the United States and launch a formal war on terrorism on his way to becoming one of the most respected and effective law enforcement officials in American history.

Decades before the *"Untouchables"* battled Al Capone's Outfit in Chicago, Flynn dismantled an early Mafia organization based in New York City. Next stop for the indefatigable crime fighter would be Chief of the Secret Service where he would set his crosshairs on the country's most notorious currency counterfeiters.

Known as "the Bulldog" for his tenacity, Flynn's fame soared as he exposed a sophisticated German spy and sabotage ring on the cusp of America's entry into World War I. As the director of the Bureau of Investigation (the forerunner of the FBI), the Bulldog would devise the first counterterrorist strategy in U.S. history.

In this riveting biography, author Jeffrey D. Simon brings to life the forgotten saga of one of America's greatest crime and terrorist fighters.

The Witch of New York
The Trials of Polly Bodine and the Cursed Birth of Tabloid Justice

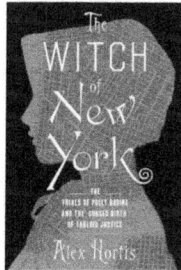

By Alex Hortis

On Christmas night in 1843, shocked residents of a serene Staten Island village discovered the burnt remains of Emeline Houseman and her infant daughter, Ann Eliza. Someone had bludgeoned to death a mother and child in their home and then attempted to cover up that crime through arson.

An ambitious district attorney charged Emeline's sister-in-law Polly Bodine with the double homicide, and the new "penny press" exploded in sensational reports. Polly was a perfect media villain: a separated wife who drank gin, committed adultery and had multiple abortions. Between June 1844 and April 1846, the nation was enthralled by her three trials for the "Christmas murders."

Edgar Allen Poe and Walt Whitman covered her case as young newsmen. P. T. Barnum made a circus of it. James Fenimore Cooper's last novel was inspired by her trials.

The Witch of New York is the first narrative history about the dueling trial lawyers, ruthless newsmen and shameless hucksters who turned the Polly Bodine case into America's formative tabloid trial. An origin story of how America became addicted to sensationalized reporting of criminal trials, *The Witch of New York* vividly reconstructs an epic mystery from old New York and uses the Bodine case to challenge today's tabloid justice.

Gangster Hunters
How Hoover's G-Men Vanquished America's Deadliest Public Enemies

By John Oller

John Dillinger, Bonnie and Clyde, Baby Face Nelson and Pretty Boy Floyd – these infamous Depression-era criminals have been immortalized as some of the most vicious felons in our history, but they share another commonality: every single one was brought down by the Federal Bureau of Investigation during a chaotic war on crime, which started in 1933 and thrust the FBI into the national spotlight for the first time.

Surprisingly little has been written about field-level agents responsible for hunting down the most dangerous criminals and bringing them to justice... until now. In his meticulously researched new book, *Gangster Hunters* (Dutton, November 26, 2024), critically acclaimed author John Oller brings to light the true stories of FBI's unsung heroes. He gives play-by-play accounts of the G-men's blood-soaked shootouts and reckless car chases but also explores their methodical detective work.

It might come as a surprise that most young FBI agents in the 1930s weren't prepared for the wild lifestyle their careers would require. The Bureau had no jurisdiction over murders, bank robberies and kidnappings for decades. But with Hoover at its helm, FBI quickly gained power and its fresh-faced agents found themselves in high-speed car chases wearing bullet-proof vests. Some agents sacrificed everything in the pursuit of justice, some were unceremoniously blacklisted by Hoover, and others simply never received the attention they deserved.

Gangster Hunters is full of exciting brand-new primary research and dozens of never-before-seen photos. Oller interviewed thirty descendants of the early FBI agents he profiles. Weaving together their accounts, his book is able to correct historical accounts and myths about gangsters and manhunts that have long been considered fact.

ACKNOWLEDGMENTS

Our thanks

This *Informer* special issue owes its existence to the generous contributions of crime historians around the globe. It was our great pleasure to team once more with United Kingdom-based researcher Steve Turner. He earned our special thanks for his tireless and enormously productive labors, as well as for his keen insight and supportive manner. We enjoyed the privilege of working again with some of our old friends and past contributors (from the United States) Patrick Downey, J. Michael Niotta, Ellen Poulsen, Justin Cascio and Scott Deitche, (from the United Kingdom) Jon Black and (from New Zealand) Thom L. Jones. We were delighted to work alongside new friends (from France) Fabien Rossat and Thibaut Maïquès. And we were aided in this project by the advice and encouragement of our longtime friend and colleague David Critchley.

We also benefited from the assistance of Bronx Historian Thomas Vasti, Archivist Brian Ferree of the New York City Municipal Archives, Reference Archivist Frances Lyons of the General Commission on Archives and History, Niagara County Surrogate's Court Assistant Sandra Shufelt, Government Information Specialist Sandy Raymond of the Federal Bureau of Prisons, the John F. Kennedy Presidential Library in Boston and the U.S. National Archives and Records Administration. Finally, we acknowledge the immense utility of many online historical databases including the New York City Historical Vital Records Project, the Mary Ferrell Foundation, The *New York Times* Archives, Ancestry.com, FamilySearch.org, Newspapers.com and FultonHistory.com.

Thank you all.

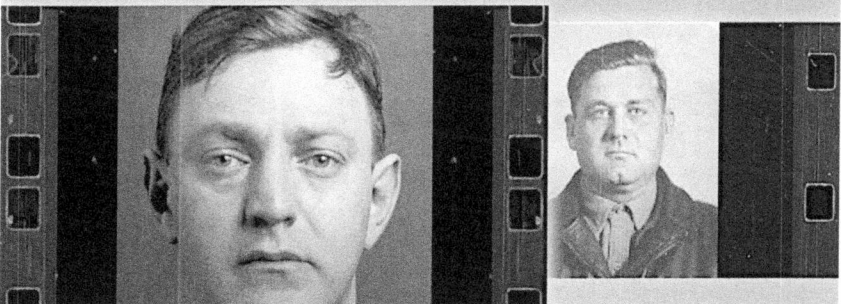

RAT TRAP

Combing through declassified government documents, Edmond Valin detects subtle clues that point to the identities of secret underworld informants

Visit mafiahistory.us/rattrap

MEET ME AT THE CORNER

Mob Corner

A growing collection of underworld history articles and crime-related short stories

By Thom L. Jones
Hosted by GangstersInc.Org

Joseph P. Macheca served as a street warrior for the
intensely corrupt New Orleans Democratic machine,
as a pioneer of the Crescent City's fruit trade,
as a Confederate privateer in the Gulf and,
according to legend, as the 'godfather' of
the first Mafia organization on American soil.

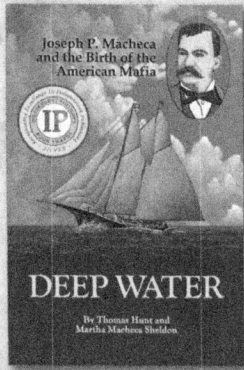

Joseph P. Macheca
and the Birth of the
American Mafia

IP

DEEP WATER

By Thomas Hunt and
Martha Macheca Sheldon

Second edition available as
trade paperback and Kindle ebook

Deep Water is the historical biography of Joseph P. Macheca,
a victim of the 1891 'Mafia' lynchings in the Crescent City.
It establishes the factual details of Macheca's epic life story
and sets them against the vivid backdrop
of Gilded Age New Orleans.

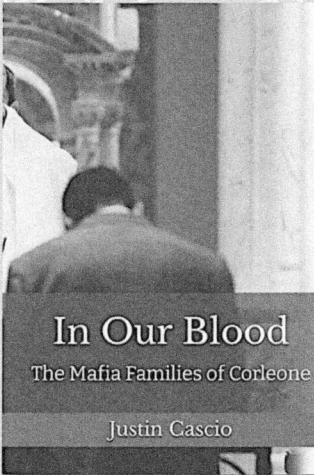

His father was a fugitive anarchist-terrorist.
His in-laws were notorious Mafia bosses.
Was a fair trial for Charles Sberna even possible?

WRONGLY EXECUTED?
The Long-Forgotten Context of Charles Sberna's 1939 Electrocution

Articles presented in French and English
(translator available on the site)

Une Histoire de Crime Organisé

unehistoiredecrimeorganise.blogspot.com

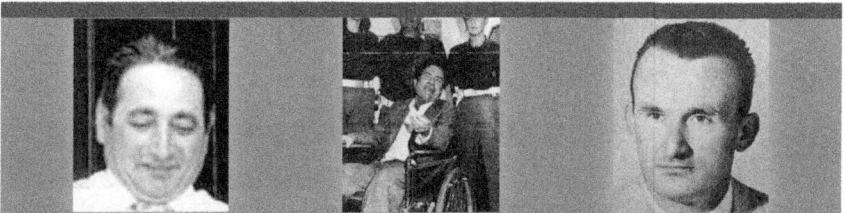

A blog dedicated to the little stories that make up the history of organized crime in France, Canada, Australia, Italy & USA.
By Fabien Rossat

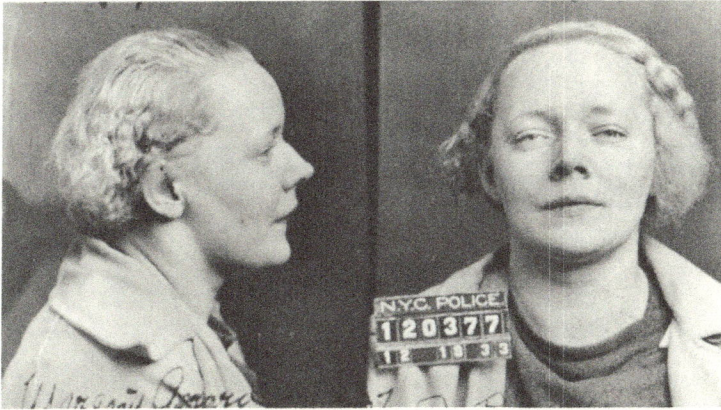

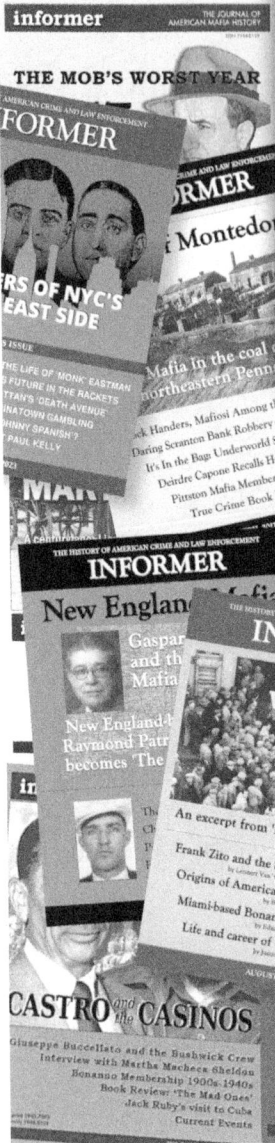

INFORMER BACK ISSUES
2008-2024

All issues of Informer remain available in print and electronic magazine formats. The special issues released in print book and ebook formats remain available in those formats as well. Browse all the past issues and link to preview and purchase sites through this website:

mafiahistory.us/informer/

INDEX

Alphabetical index

B

C

D

F

G

H

M

N

O

Q

R

S

T

Made in the USA
Las Vegas, NV
01 February 2025